U0897526

书籍点燃希望
智慧创造财富
学习改变人生
献给永远追求卓越的朋友

英汉双语

精华版

心灵鸡汤全集

主 编 青 闰

副主编 王艳玲 辛 倩

中国城市出版社

·北 京·

图书在版编目（CIP）数据

心灵鸡汤全集：英汉双语精华版／青闰主编．—北京：中国城市出版社，2011.1（2013.8 重印）
ISBN 978－7－5074－2372－3

Ⅰ．①心… Ⅱ．①青… Ⅲ．①英语—汉语—对照读物②人生哲学—通俗读物 Ⅳ．①H319.4：B

中国版本图书馆 CIP 数据核字(2010)第 216270 号

选题策划 徐昌强(greatbook@sina.com)
责任编辑 华 风
装帧设计 美信书籍设计工作室
责任技术编辑 张建军
出版发行 中国城市出版社
地 址 北京市西城区广安门南街甲 30 号（邮编 100053）
网 址 www.citypress.cn
发行部电话 (010) 63454857 63289949
发行部传真 (010) 63421417 63400635
总编室电话 (010) 68171928
总编室信箱 citypress@sina.com
经 销 新华书店
印 刷 北京集惠印刷有限责任公司
字 数 740 千字 印张 30
开 本 787×1092(毫米) 1/16
版 次 2011 年 1 月第 1 版
印 次 2013 年 8 月第 4 次印刷
定 价 45.00 元

目
contents
录

第一卷　奏响人生的交响乐

第二卷　感谢生命的恩赐

第三卷　幸福点亮人生

第四卷　每个人都会成功

第五卷　心态改变命运

第六卷　真诚赞美的力量

第七卷　予人玫瑰,手留余香

第八卷　最伟大的亲情

第九卷　有爱就有奇迹

奏响人生的交响乐

The Coordinates of Life

In India, a computer software company was on the verge of bankruptcy because of intense market competition and inefficiency.

At this time, a computer programmer of the company developed a new software operating system. When it was put into the market, it was well sold and revived the company. To commend this programmer's major contribution for the company, the general manager recommended that he be promoted to the branch manager.

Unexpectedly, the programmer rebuffed, "I'm good at the program design, but unversed in personnel management. If you raise me, I will be wasting everybody's time and accomplish nothing. Oh, I have a program to be done. May I go?" Then he hurried away.

Later, this computer programmer created his own software kingdom, and he is Darberz, now the president of Chesney, one of the world's leading software companies.

If a person is in the wrong place, he or she will be garbage. So we should first determine the coordinates of our life.

人生的坐标

印度一家电脑软件公司因为市场竞争激烈、效益不好而濒临破产的境地。

正在这时,公司的一名电脑程序员开发出一个新软件操作系统,投入市场后大受欢迎,销售火爆,使公司起死回生。为了嘉奖这名程序员为公司做出的重大贡献,总经理建议晋升他为部门经理。

没想到,这位程序员一口回绝:"我学的是程序设计,不谙人事管理。如果您提升我的话,我只会浪费大家的时间而一事无成。噢,我手头还有一个程序要做,我可以走了吗?"说完匆匆而去。

这位电脑程序员后来缔造了自己的软件王国,他就是当今世界著名软件公司——切斯尼公司的总裁达伯兹。

人摆错了地方,就是垃圾。所以,要首先确定好自己的人生坐标。

The Patch of Life

Not long ago, my daughter's frosting shoes were scratched by someone's knife. She burst into tears. I took the shoes to the shoemaker to get them repaired.

The young apprentice glanced at the opening and said, "there is nothing I can do but to replace the upper."

His master looked at them and said to me, "If you trust me, I will add more scratches on both of the shoes."

I was confused and asked why.

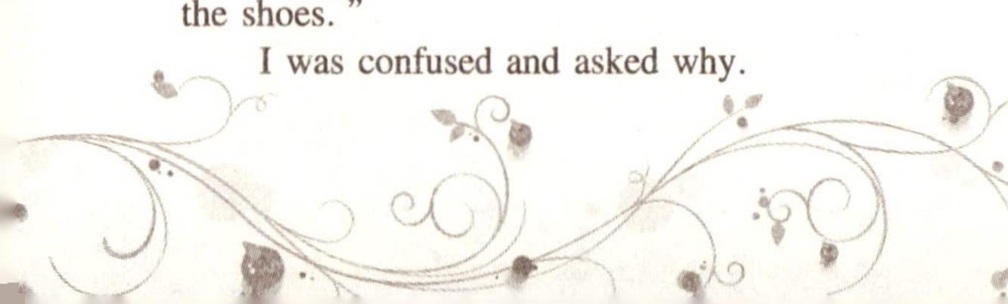

He explained, "As if the openings were made on purpose for the sake of special style and reuse."

I didn't fully understand him, but I decided to leave the shoes.

Two days later I dropped by from work to fetch the shoes. At the first sight I found they were indeed five or six more scratches on each shoe, but all the openings were patched by soft leather in rust red with edges sewed by thick hemp thread; the stitches were twisted with the appearance of roughness and plainness which was in accordance with the quality of frosting leather, more unique and interesting than ever. I couldn't help making compliments on the master's craftsmanship.

Another time, my wife's sister's white blouse was torn a large opening on the back. My wife took it over and checked carefully, and then said, "Let me take it home and mend it."

Three days later, seeing the blouse again, I was shocked: all the cracks and openings were sewed up by thin and white thread and they took on a look of branches, like the ice crystal on winter's branches in the north. In order to intensify the effect, she attached a fatty snowman and a cabin made of flowery cotton rags on the shirt. I sighed with praise, "It's just as beautiful as a piece of art!"

"I was inspired by that craftsman. Patches are supposed to be a regret, but a skillful craftsman can make it take on a kind of perfection," replied my wife.

Her words inspired me even more: perfection is impossible to achieve in everything; patches are unavoidable, so is human's life, which will appear in the form of injury, disability or disease. Since you can't change the existence of wound, you should not expect people's sympathy by exposing the wound, which reveals nothing meaningful. All you can do and have to do is to suture the wound by patches and try your best to bloom a most beautiful flower on the wound, and that is the significance of life.

人生的补丁

不久前,女儿的磨砂鞋被人用刀子划了几道。她失声痛哭。我把鞋子拿到补鞋店去修。

年轻的学徒看了一眼上面划的口子,说:"除了换鞋帮,我无能为力。"

他的师傅看了看鞋子,对我说:"你要是相信我,我就在两只鞋上再划几道口子。"

我百思不解,问为什么。

他解释说:"这样看起来那些口子仿佛是刻意而为,会显得别具一格,还能再穿。"

我还是不完全理解他的意思,但还是决定把鞋子留下。

两天后,我下班顺便去取鞋。我一眼就发现那双鞋上果然又划了五六道口子,但所有的口子都用铁锈红软皮补缀,四周用粗麻线缝合,针脚歪歪扭扭,显得朴素粗犷,和磨砂皮的品质协调一致,比先前更独特、更有趣。我禁不住称赞师傅妙手回春。

还有一次,妻妹的白衬衣后背上被挂了一个大口子。妻子接过来,仔细看了看,说:"我拿回去给你补补吧。"

3 天后,再见到那件衬衣时,我大吃了一惊,只见所有的裂痕和口子都用细白线缝合,看上去如同树枝,仿佛北方冬天树枝上的冰花。为了增强这种效果,她还用花棉布片拼了一个胖乎乎的雪人和一座小木屋。我连声赞叹道:"这就像艺术品一样漂亮!"

"我是受了那个补鞋师傅的启发。尽管补丁原本是一种遗憾,但能工巧匠却能让它们呈现出一种完美。"妻子回答说。

她的话给了我更大的启发:世间万物不可能十全十美。补丁无法避免,人的生命也一样,会出现伤害、残疾和疾病。既然你无法改变伤口的存在,就不要指望暴露伤口让人同情，那没有任何意义。你能做的和必须做的就是用补丁缝合伤口，尽力在伤口上开出最美丽的花朵，而这正是人生的意义。

The Rainy Season of Your Life

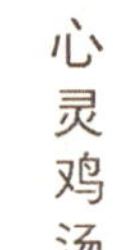

My life suffered a lot in a summer five years ago. My father died of an accident resulted from drinking, leaving my emaciated mother and two younger brothers alone. At that time, I was in a senior high school. After my father's funeral, the whole family was in a worse condition than ever. As the eldest son, I had no choice but to quit school and work in a factory.

Life went on without any wonder. I dare not to ask for more, just hoping to bring up two younger brothers. However, that's not an easy thing, for I can't afford their tuition even if I work from day to night without stopping, and much worse, I must take my sick mother into account... The present misery made me want to have another try, but it seems impractical, for I can't lose this job any more.

A thread of hope sparkled in those gloomy days suddenly.

It was a rainy dusk when I put myself in the rain and walked in the street.

Suddenly the rain stopped! To my bewilderment, I raised my head, and found that "the sky" was in fact a dark blue umbrella. Then I heard a deep voice.

"Why not running without an umbrella?" a middle-aged man with one leg on crutch said to me, "If you run, you would get less drenched."

I shook my head, but after a second I thought: Right, why not running without an umbrella?

His words shocked me deeply. Without my father's protection, could I only be a slave to the fate, and my dream in childhood only an illusion?

While walking together in the rain, I knew that he was a promoter from the city, and he received an order and paid much time on it. Facing this guy, I had no sympathy but admiration.

I took the umbrella from his right hand and he told me that he once had dreamed of being a policeman, but an accident ruined his dream. Though his present work was demanding and did not suit for his leg, every outing was a wonderful start to him. He was glad that he didn't lose heart and still "ran" on the road of life...

It seems that everything is destined but not always. Enlightened by the man's remarks, I went to a city in the south and became an assurance representative. After two years' "running", I got somewhere and my family turned better gradually. I came back to my senior high school for the dream in my childhood. The year before last summer, I eventually succeeded in my entrance to university.

Life is like this: when you are in rainy days in your life, if you couldn't find a way to prevent you from being drenched earlier, you would have been overwhelmed by it, but if you decide to get rid of it, you'll discover that the rainy days last not so long as you imagined.

Everything is so simple: to run without an umbrella!

When you run out of the rainy season of your life, there will be bright sky ahead of you.

人生的雨季

5年前的夏天，我的人生痛苦不堪。父亲因酗酒死于一场事故，撇下了我瘦弱的母亲和两个弟弟。当时，我正上高中。父亲葬礼后，全家人比以前的状态更加糟糕。作为长子，我别无选择，只好退学，到一家工厂打工。

日子就这样平淡无奇地过着。我不敢再有更多的奢求，只希望把两个弟弟抚养成人。然而，那不是轻而易举的事儿，因为即使我每天从早到晚不停工作，也难以支付他们的学费，更何况我必须考虑多病的母亲……眼前的困境使我想再努力一次，但又好像不切实际，因为我不能再丢掉这份工作。

一线希望突然照亮了那些阴暗的日子。

那是一个雨天的黄昏，我置身雨中，走在街上。

雨突然停了！我感到迷惑，就抬起头，发现“天空”其实是一顶深蓝色的伞。随后，我听到一个深沉的声音。

“没有伞，为什么不跑?”一位拄着拐杖的独腿中年人对我说。“如果跑，你就不会这么淋湿了。”

我摇了摇头，却转念又一想：没有伞，为什么不跑呢？

他的话深深地震撼了我。没有了父亲的保护，我就只能做命运的奴隶，童年的梦想就只能是幻想吗？

雨中同行时，我知道了他是城里来的推销员。他接到了一份订单，为此花费了很多时间。面对这个人，我没有怜悯，只有钦佩。

我默默地从他的右手里接过了伞。他告诉我说，他曾想做一名警察，但一次意外事故毁灭了他的梦想。尽管现在的工作非常苛刻，不适合他这腿，但每次出门对他来说都是一个奇妙的开始。他很高兴自己没有丧失勇气，仍然“跑”在人生的道路上……

一切都似乎是命中注定，但又不总是那样。那个人的话让我深受启发，我去了南方的一个城市，成了一名保险代理人。通过两年的“奔跑”，我取得了一些业绩，家境也渐渐好转了。因为童年的梦想，我又回到了高中。前年夏天，我终于考上了大学。

生活就是这样：当你处在人生的雨季时，如果你无法尽快找到防止雨淋的方法，就要被雨水淋透，但如果你决定摆脱，你就会发现，雨季并不像你原来想的那样长。

一切都是那么简单：没有伞，就跑！

跑出人生的雨季，你前面就会是一片晴朗的天空。

The Lubricating Oil of Life

There was an old man, who would carry a small pot of oil wherever he went.

If he went through a door, which made a creaky noise, he would pour some oil on the hinge. If he faced a door hard to open, he would smear some oil on the hinges. The old man was called an eccentric, but he still did his work of lubricating.

There are many people, whose daily life is in discord, often making harsh creaky noises. They need joy to warm the lubricating oil that softens the joints.

Do you have the "oil" on yourself? Distribute it to others from dawn to dusk, starting from the person closest to you. How significant to distribute the oil of joy to the depressed or speak an encouraging word to the desperate!

On the road of life, there are many people, who we may meet only once in our lifetime, and never

will again ever since. Soften the rigid life with the loving oil and life will be brighter.

人生的润滑油

有一位老人，无论走到什么地方，身边总带一小罐油。

如果他走过一扇门，门上发出嘎吱的响声，他就会在铰链上倒一点油。如果遇到一扇难开的门，他就会在门轴上涂一点油。人称他怪人，但这位老人依旧做他的润滑工作。

有许多人，他们每天的生活很不和谐，常常发出刺耳的嘎吱声。他们需要喜乐，温暖柔和关节的润滑油。

你身上有这种“油”吗？从早到晚地分给别人，从你最近的人分起。把喜乐的油分给沮丧的人，对绝望者说一句鼓励的话，这是何等有意义的事情！

在人生的道路上，有许多人，我们也许一生只会遇到一次，以后永远不会再相逢。用慈爱的油使僵硬的生命变得柔软吧，人生会因此而更加灿烂。

Life Is a Process of Making Honey

In a harvest season, a beekeeper tried making honey. He had no knowledge of the skills, so he consulted his father. The retired, old beekeeper told his son, "It's okay to make it with the common method. However, on the point of completing it, remember to drop a little bitter medicine into the honey."

On hearing this, he objected, "Why to do so? It is simply to ruin the precious honey." His father just smiled without reply.

Upon this, he made honey as he liked. Until the honey was done, he took a bit to taste. But his honey was not as sweet as his father's.

He was so confused that he had to ask his father. "Excuse me, why did you ask me to add bitter medicine to the done honey? Won't it ruin the taste of the honey?"

"It is the little bitterness in the honey that excites your tongue and makes the honey sweet."

Yes. Actually, the process of making honey is like that of going from youth to old age. A little tear in life can make the reminiscences sweeter and more beautiful.

人生是酿蜜

在一次收获季节里，养蜂人想要尝试酿蜜。他并不懂得其中的技巧，便请教他的父亲。这位已经年老退休的养蜂人告诉儿子说：“你照着一般的方法做就行了。不过，在即将完成时，记住要在蜂蜜里滴一点苦药。”

他听了不以为然：“为什么要这么做呢？这样简直是糟蹋宝贵的蜂蜜。”他的父亲只是笑了笑，并不回答。于是，他按照自己的意思来酿蜜。等做成蜂蜜后，他取出一点尝了尝,可他做的蜂蜜没有父亲做的甜。

他百思不解,最后只好问父亲:“请问,为什么您告诉我要在酿好的蜂蜜里加苦药呢? 这样不会破坏蜂蜜的味道吗?”

“正是因为里边有点苦味,刺激人的舌头,才能显出蜂蜜的香甜。”

是啊,其实酿蜜的过程就像是由青春到老年的过程。人生里的一点泪水可以使回忆变得更加甜美。

Life Is a Handful of Candy

One sunny morning, when Einstein was about to go out of his office, the assistant came to tell him, "Someone wants to invite you to make a speech on the weekend, whose reward is 10,000 dollars."

Einstein didn't hesitate at all and refused, "I have arranged this weekend, so I have no time."

"Can't you cut down tutoring Sophie once?" The assistant knew he would go to tutor math to Sophie who studied in a junior high school.

"No, I'm still thinking of her candy," Einstein said with a smile.

"Is her candy so sweet?" the assistant didn't understand why he was at pains for the young girl he happened to know. You know, Sophie paid the old man who was expert in math only half of her candy.

That day, seeing Einstein come back from Sophie cheerfully, the assistant couldn't help asking him why he was so pleased.

Einstein told him, "Today, Sophie's teacher praised her progress, saying that she had an excellent teacher. The young girl was also so pleased that she awarded me a handful of candy, which makes me particularly happy."

Later, in Einstein's diary, people once again read he thought much of such a trifle. He said Sophie's candy that day made him so sweet in his heart as long as he saw it, bringing him great joy and precious treasure.

It turned out that in the world famous scientist's eyes, the young girl's sunny smile and a handful of common candy were the sweetest spring that nourished his life.

Many years have passed, and many earthshaking events have been forgotten. But that handful of aged candy passes through the vicissitudes of years and keeps wafting wisps of fragrance that still nourishes our hearts.

人生是一把糖果

一个阳光明媚的上午,爱因斯坦刚要走出办公室,助手过来告诉他说:“有人想请你周末去作一次演讲,报酬是一万美元。”

爱因斯坦毫不犹豫,便一口回绝:“我周末有安排,没时间。”

“难道您不能少给苏菲补一次课吗?”助手知道他每个周末都去给读初中的苏菲辅导数学。

“不能,我还想着她的糖果呢。”爱因斯坦笑道。

“她的糖果就那么甜吗?”助手不明白他对那个偶然认识的小女孩为何那样用心。要知道,苏菲付给这位“数学特棒的老头”的报酬就是她的一半糖果。

这一天,看到爱因斯坦满面春风地从苏菲那里回来,助手忍不住好奇地问他为什么那样高兴。

爱因斯坦告诉他说:“今天,苏菲的老师夸奖了她的进步,说她找了一个优秀的家庭教师。小姑娘也特别高兴,奖励了我一把糖果,这让我特别愉快。”

后来,在爱因斯坦的日记中,人们又看到了他对这件小事的重视。他说苏菲那天的一把糖果,只要看着,心里就有特别的甜味儿,它带给了他无比的快乐和珍贵的财富。

原来,在这位闻名遐迩的大科学家眼里,小女孩灿烂的笑容和一把普通的糖果,就是滋润生命的最好甘泉。

多少年过去了,许多惊天动地的大事已被人们淡忘了,但那把陈年糖果却穿过沧桑岁月,向我们传来依然滋润心灵的缕缕芬芳。

The Tent of Life

One day, the famous detective Sherlock Holmes went camping with his fellow, Dr. Watson. After a nice meal and a bottle of good wine, these two men got into their tent and soon slept on both ears.

Several hours later, Holmes woke up and pushed his friend. He said, “Watson, open your eyes! Say what you see?”

Watson said, “I see beautiful stars all over the sky.”

“Can you tell me the reason?” Holmes continued.

Watson hesitated for several minutes and said, “Astronomically, this beautiful scene is due to thousands of galaxies and innumerable planets. Look, there is the Leo; and there is the Saturn. Pragmatically, I presume it's three o'clock in the morning. Technologically, I think the universe is so marvelous, and that compared with him we are so insignificant. And meteorologically, the weather of tomorrow must be wonderful. Well then, Holmes, what are you feeling?”

Holmes said slowly, “Watson, you are so dull. Someone has stolen our tent.”

Even Holmes's tent could be stolen, and then how can the common avoid the awkward situation of losing their tent? It is obvious that tents cannot prevent from thieves, even from wolves. They are only used to shelter from night winds, starlight and dewdrops. Many people spend their whole life looking for a tent for themselves; many other people wake up overnight to find his tent lost. The changes of life are unfathomable forever.

Overnight, the tent of life is lost suddenly. Some people would get out of their wits, some would feel like the world falls down and some would think a disaster would loom soon. We get used to the life with a tent overhead. Virtually, the true beauty is often detected by accident.

It is our habitual thought that we would feel safe with a tent. The tent of life may be wealth, profession, steady income, sociality or human relations, which are regarded as a shelter in the daily life. It is seemingly important, but only when we lose it, can we find the more beautiful things are kept off. For instance, losing the tent, we have stars twinkling all over the sky.

人生的帐篷

有一天，著名侦探福尔摩斯和好友华生医生一起去露营。美酒佳肴之后，两人钻进了帐篷，很快就进入了梦乡。

几小时后，福尔摩斯醒来，推了推朋友，说："华生，睁开眼！说说你看见了什么？"

华生说："我看见满天美丽的繁星。"

"你能告诉我原因吗？"福尔摩斯接着问。

华生迟疑了几分钟，说："从天文学来说，这美景是由于成千上万的星系和无计其数的行星。瞧，那里是狮子座，那个是土星。从实用主义来说，我认为现在是凌晨3点。从技术上来说，我认为宇宙真奇妙，和他相比，我们真是微不足道。从气象学看来，明天的天气肯定很棒。那么，福尔摩斯，你有何感想啊？"

福尔摩斯慢慢地说："华生，你太笨了。有人偷走了我们的帐篷。"

就连福尔摩斯的帐篷都会被盗，平凡人又怎能避免丢失帐篷的尴尬呢？帐篷显然不能防盗，也防不了狼。它们仅仅是用来遮挡夜风、星光和露珠。许多人用一生时间，来为自己寻找一顶帐篷；又有许多人一夜醒来，却发现自己的帐篷丢失了。生活中的变化永远捉摸不定。

一夜间，人生的帐篷突然丢了，有人惊慌失措，有人以为天塌地陷，有人以为大难将至。人们习惯了头顶有帐篷的生活。其实，真正的美好往往是在意外中发现的。

有一顶帐篷，才有安全感，这是人们惯常的思维。人生的那顶"帐篷"，可能是财富、职业、固定的收入、社交或人际关系，在日常生活中被当作庇护，貌似重要无比，丢了才会发现，其实更美好的事物被它挡在外面。比如，丢了帐篷，却拥有了满天的星星。

Life Is Not About Keeping Score

Life is not about keeping score.

It is not about how many friends you have or how accepted you are.

It is not about if you have plans this weekend or if you're alone.

It is not about who you're dating, who you used to date, how many people you've dated, or if you haven't been with anyone at all.

It isn't about who you have kissed.

It isn't about sex.

It isn't about who your family is or how much money they have.

Or what kind of car you drive.

Or where you are sent to school.

It isn't about how beautiful or ugly you are.

Or what clothes you wear, what shoes have on, or what kind of music you listen to.

It isn't about if your hair is blonde, red, black, or brown or if your skin is too light or too dark.

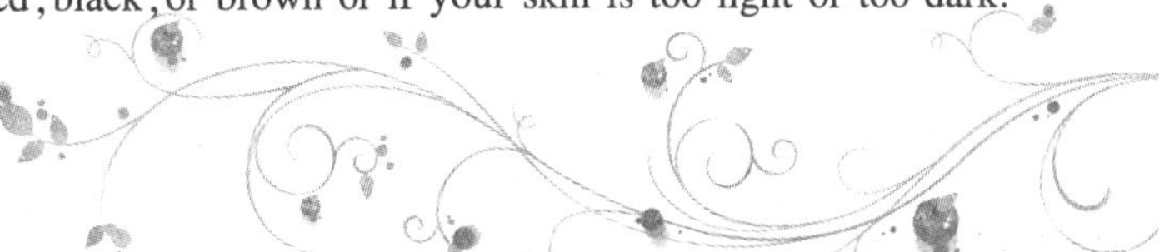

Not about what grades you get, how smart you are, how smart everybody else thinks you are, or how smart standardized tests say you are.

It isn't about representing your whole being on a piece of paper and seeing who will accept the written you. Life just isn't.

But life is about who you love and who you hurt.

It's about who you make happy or unhappy purposefully.

It's about keeping promises or breaking faith.

It's about friendship, used as a sanctity or a weapon.

It's about what you say and what you mean, maybe hurtful, maybe heartening.

It's about starting rumors and contributing to petty gossip.

It's about what judgements you make and why. And who your judgements are spread to.

It's about who you've ignored.

It's about jealousy, fear, ignorance and revenge.

It's about carrying inner hate and love.

But most of all, it's about using your life to touch other people's hearts.

Only you choose the way those hearts are affected, and those choices are what life's all about.

人生不是在积分

人生不是在积分。

人生不是你有多少朋友或你如何被人接受。

人生不是这个周末你是有安排还是独自度过。

人生不是你要和谁约会、曾和谁约会、曾约会了多少人，也不是你有没有和谁约会。

人生不是你曾吻过什么人。

人生不是性。

人生不是你的家人是谁，也不是他们有多少钱。

不是你开哪种车。

不是送你去哪里上学。

人生不是你有多美或多丑。

不是你穿什么衣服、穿什么鞋子、听哪种音乐。

人生不是你的头发是金色、红色、黑色还是棕色，也不是你的肤色太浅还是太深。

不是你得了多少分，你有多聪明，别人认为你有多聪明，也不是标准化测试说你有多聪明。

人生不是把你所有的情况写在一张纸上，看谁会接受纸上的你。人生不仅仅是这样。

但是，人生是你爱谁和伤害了谁。

人生是你故意让谁开心还是惹谁生气。

人生是遵守诺言还是背信弃义。

人生是把友谊作为一种圣洁还是一种武器。

人生是你说的话和你的用意，也许使人痛苦，也许振奋人心。

人生是飞短流长。

人生是你做出的判断和理由,以及你对谁做出的判断。

人生是你对谁忽视。

人生是嫉妒、恐惧、无知和报复。

人生是内心深处的恨与爱。

而最重要的是,人生是用你的生命触动他人的心灵。

只有你选择触动他人心灵,那些选择才是人生的全部。

Life Is a Full-Time School

You are enrolled in a full-time school called "life." Each day in this school you will have the opportunity to learn lessons. Whether you like the lessons or not, they are all your required courses.

Why are you here? What is your purpose? Humans have sought to discover the meaning of life for a very long time. What we and our ancestors have overlooked, however, is that there is no one answer. The meaning of life is different for every individual.

Each person has his or her own purpose and distinct path. As you travel your life path, you will be presented with numerous lessons that you will need learn in order to fulfill that purpose. The lessons you are presented with are specific to you; learning these lessons is the key to discovering the meaning of life and fulfilling your own goal.

As you travel through your lifetime, you may encounter challenges that others don't have to face while others spend years struggling with challenges that you don't need to deal with. You may never know why you are blessed with a wonderful marriage, while your friends suffer through bitter arguments and divorces, just as you cannot be sure why you struggle financially while your peers enjoy abundance. The only thing you can count on for certain is that you will be presented with all the lessons that you are capable of you specifically need to learn; whether you choose to learn them or not is entirely up to you.

The challenge here, therefore, is to align yourself with your own unique path by learning individual lessons. This is one of the most difficult challenges you will be faced with in your lifetime as sometimes your path will be radically different from others. But remember, don't compare yourself to the people around you. You need to remember that you will only be faced with the lessons specific to your own growth.

Our sense of fairness is the expectation of equity. Life is not, in fact, fair. Maybe fate shouldn't arrange in this way. But you may indeed have a more difficult life path than others around you. Everyone's circumstances are unique, and everyone needs to handle his or her own circumstances differently. If you want to move toward serenity, you will be required to move out of the complaining phase of "it's not fair." Focusing on the unfairness of circumstances keeps you comparing yourself with others rather than appreciating your own special uniqueness. You miss out on learning your individual lessons by distracting yourself with feelings of bitterness and resentment.

人生是一所全日制学校

你是被称为"人生"这所全日制学校的学生。你在这所学校里每天都会有机会学习各门功课。无论你喜不喜欢这些功课,它们都是你的必修课。

为什么你在这里？你的目的是什么？人们已经寻找人生的意义很长时间。然而，我们和我们的先人都没有注意到没有一个答案。人生的意义对每个人都不一样。

每个人都有各自的目的和截然不同的道路。在人生道路上，你要学习许多功课，来实现人生的目标。提供给你的功课对你非常明确；学习这些功课是发现人生意义、实现人生目标的关键。

在人生旅途中，你也许要面对别人不必面对的挑战，而别人与之奋斗多年的挑战，你也许不必应对。你也许永远都无法明白你为什么拥有幸福的婚姻，你的朋友却要忍受痛苦的争吵和离婚，就像你无法明白自己为钱疲于奔命，你的同龄人却安逸富有一样。你唯一可以毫无疑问依靠的就是所有提供给你、你有必要、也有能力去学的那些功课，你是否愿意学则完全取决于自己。

所以，这里的挑战就是你要学会各种不同的功课，走出一条独特的人生道路。这是你一生都要面对的最艰难的一次挑战，因为你的道路有时和别人截然不同。但要记住，不要把自己和周围的人相比。你需要记住你只有面对特意为你的成长量身定制的那些功课。

我们的公平感就是期望公正。其实，生活并不公平。也许命运不应该这样安排。但你确实可能会比别人的人生道路艰难。每个人的情况都非常独特，所以每个人都需要用不同的方法对待自己的境遇。如果想趋向平静，就要走出“这不公平”的抱怨状态。如果把心思都用在境遇的不公上，就会使你把自己和别人比较，而不是去欣赏自己的独特之处。如果一味感到痛苦怨恨，你就会使自己分心，错过要学的各门功课。

Life Lies in Persistence

There was a young hunter, who was a marksman, but couldn't catch wild geese.

So he went to an old man to ask for advice.

The old man took him to the reed habitat of wild geese, pointed at a wild goose standing at the highest point and said, "That wild goose is a sentry, which we call it wild goose slave. As long as it finds something unusual, it will give an alarm to the wild geese. So it is very hard to approach the wild geese. But I have a method: Now you deliberately start the slave and then lurk there motionless."

The young man did as he was told. Having found the young man, the slave immediately gave an alarm to its companions. After hearing the news, the wild geese roosting there fled, but they flew back in situ when they found nothing happened.

The old man let the young man followed suit for a few times. Finally, a few wild geese thinking they were fooled started attacking the slave. Repeatedly, almost all the wild geese thought the slave gave false military intelligence and vented all their discontent on the slave. The poor slave was pecked all over with cuts and bruises.

"Now, you can approach the geese," reminded the old man.

So the young man strutted into the reeds.

The slave saw the young man, but it was tired of caring.

The young man raised his gun...

The tragedy often occurs in this way: the loyal are misunderstood while the misunderstood cannot stick it out.

人生在于坚持

有一位年轻的猎手，枪法极准，但总捕不到大雁。

于是，他去向一位长者求教。

长者把他领到一片大雁栖息的芦苇地，指着站得最高的一只大雁说："那只大雁是放哨的，我们管它叫雁奴。它只要一发现异常情况就会向雁群报警，所以接近雁群往往是很难的。但我有办法，你现在故意惊动雁奴，再潜伏不动。"

年轻人照着做了。雁奴发现年轻人后，立即向同伴发出警告。正在栖息的雁群闻讯后纷纷出逃，但没发现什么，便又飞回原地。

长者让年轻人如法炮制了好几回。终于，有几只以为受骗的大雁向雁奴发动攻击。如此再三，几乎所有的大雁都以为雁奴谎报军情，纷纷把不满发泄在雁奴身上。可怜的雁奴被啄得伤痕累累。

"现在，你可以逼近雁群了，"长者提醒道。

于是，年轻人大摇大摆地走进了芦苇地。

雁奴虽瞧在眼里，但也懒得再管。

年轻人举起了枪……

悲剧往往就是这样发生的：忠诚的人被误解，被误解的人不能坚持到底。

Life Is an Opportunity

Life is an opportunity. A chance to influence someone else's life by your daily example.

I have experienced loss, gain, hope and sorrow. My experiences have made me into the person I am today. Yes, I could wallow in the despair that comes with the loss of a loved one or the failure of a venture, but why choose sorrow when you can choose joy?

When my dear friend and mentor Debbie passed away, my family and I took it very hard. She was a wonderful person. An inspiration to everyone she met. I was devastated when I found out that she had cancer. I prayed, cried, and was very angry for a long time. She did not deserve this! When I went to visit her she looked wan. I did everything I could to hold back my tears. There before me was a beautiful woman who did so much for so many, as a teacher and a friend. She was obviously in a great deal of pain, but she smiled. I'll never forget it. In her weakness she reached out to me. She chose to have a good outlook on her life.

She chose to be strong. She chose to live, and so do I.

人生是一次机遇

人生是一次机遇。是一次用你的日常典范去影响他人生命的机会。

我曾经历过失败、收获、希望和悲伤。我这些经历使我成了今天这样的人。是的，我可以沉迷在痛失我爱的绝望中或沉迷在冒险的失败中，但在你可以选择快乐时，为什么要去选择悲伤？

我的良师益友黛比去世时，我和家人都很难接受。黛比是一个了不起的人，她对遇到的每个人都是一种鼓舞的力量。发现她患癌症时，我不知所措。我祈祷过，哭泣过，而且愤怒了很长时间。她不该得到这种结局！我去看望她时，她面无血色。我竭尽全力忍住眼泪。我面前的是一位美丽大方的女人，她既是老师又是朋友，为这么多人做了这么多事。显然她剧痛难忍，但她面带微笑。这情景我永远难忘。她虚弱地向我伸出手。她选择快乐地面对生活。

她选择坚强。她选择活下去，我也要这样。

The Three Boxes of Life

A rich man lives in his enormous villa, enjoying the extremely luxurious life.

Every day there are some strangers who take away a couple of boxes from his home. The rich man decided to follow them and came to a mysterious valley. Seeing they were about to throw the three boxes in the abyss, he demanded with surprise, "Please tell me what's in them."

The strangers answered indifferently, "They are the feelings that you have abandoned."

"No, it's impossible!" The rich man disbelieved them and opened them.

In the first box there was his beloved one walking alone slowly along the beach at night.

His close friend was in the second box. After bankruptcy, he was longing for help and consolation from the rich man.

His parents were seen in the third box. They have prepared a table of delicious food for dinner, waiting for him to reunion.

Seeing them, he felt that his heart was lashed by a burning whip full of misery and guilt. He begged the strangers, "Please give them back to me. I have a lot of money. You can take as much as you want!"

However, the strangers told him with a serious look, "It's too late to take them back. The woman you loved never showed up again at charming night; your friend, having endured the long daytime, finally made out the stars with different distance; your parent bought a dog and found love and warmness from it."

After finishing their words, they threw the three boxes down to the abyss and disappeared.

With a lonely look, the rich man stood there still, gazing at the hollow of the valley in front of them...

人生的三只箱子

富翁住在巨大的别墅里，享受着非常豪华的生活。

每天都有几个陌生人从他家里搬走几只箱子。富翁决定跟踪他们，随后来到了一个神秘的山谷。他看到这些人正准备把三只箱子扔进深渊，便吃惊地问道："请告诉我，这些箱子里装的是什么。”

陌生人冷冷地回答说:“它们是你抛弃的那些感情。”

“不,这不可能!”富翁不相信他们的话,就打开了那三只箱子。

第一只箱子里装的是他心爱的人夜晚独自在海滩慢慢地走着。

第二只箱子里装的是他的密友。公司破产后,他渴望富翁的帮助和安慰。

第三只箱子里装的是他的父母亲。他们做了一桌美餐等待他回家团聚。

看完后,他感到心像被火辣辣的鞭子抽打了一般,充满了痛苦和愧疚。他哀求陌生人说:“请把它们还给我吧。我有的是钱。你们要多少都可以拿去!”

然而,陌生人一脸严肃地告诉他说:“太晚了,无法收回了。你爱的女人在迷人的夜晚再也没有出现。你的朋友熬过长长的白天后,终于看清了那些远近不一的星星。你的父母买了一条狗,从它身上找到了爱和温暖。”

说完,陌生人把三只箱子扔下了山谷,就消失了。

富翁神情孤独,站在那里一动不动,凝望着眼前空荡荡的山谷……

The Orientation of Life

In 1957, in an Arkansas primary school, there were two good friends: one was named Bill, the other John. Once, they lay basking on the lawn. After drinking a coke, John said to Bill as if he suddenly discovered the New World, "Originally, Roosevelt who led the Americans to win World War II was handicapped!"

"Yes, he is my idol!" Bill said. "His spirit of perseverance is worth studying for us."

"He is my idol, too!" John said. "I think the most important point of his success is his adversity!"

Later, John stubbornly amputated his legs because he wanted to create the same adversity for himself as Roosevelt and became a great man like Roosevelt. However, he did not become the President of the United States, but only won a medal in the Games for the Disabled.

Bill learned Roosevelt's industrious character and indomitable spirit. Finally, he became master of the White House. His name was Bill Clinton.

人生的定位

1957年,在美国阿肯色州一所小学里有一对好朋友,一个叫比尔,一个叫约翰。一次,两人躺在草坪上晒太阳。约翰喝了一口可乐后,突然像发现新大陆似的对比尔说:“原来带领美国人赢得二战胜利的罗斯福是一个残疾人呀!”

“是的,他是我的偶像!”比尔说。“他做事执著的精神值得我们学习。”

“他也是我的偶像!”约翰说。“我认为他成功的最重要一点是他的不幸!”

后来,约翰固执地锯掉了双腿,因为他想给自己创造一个和罗斯福一样的逆境,成为像罗斯福一样的伟人。不过,他并没有成为总统,只是在一届残疾人运动会上拿到了一枚奖牌。

比尔则学习罗斯福刻苦勤奋的品格和不屈不挠的精神。最后，他成了美国白宫的主人。他的名字叫比尔·克林顿。

The Draft of Life

A man who suffered repeated defeats was playing the lute and singing under the tree.

He sang so happily, as if another failure he had just experienced hadn't happened at all.

The passer-by was puzzled. "How are you in the mood to play and sing?"

"Why shouldn't I?"

"Because you have failed again."

"I haven't because it is not the end now. I just made another draft for my life."

人生的草稿

一个屡战屡败者在树下弹琴唱歌。

他唱得那样开心，仿佛刚刚经历的又一次失败全然没有发生过一样。

过路人非常不解："你怎么还有心思弹琴唱歌？"

"我为什么要没心思弹琴唱歌呢？"

"因为你又失败了。"

"我并没有失败，现在还不是结局，我只不过是为人生又打了一遍草稿。"

Look at Life from the Snow

At the equator, a primary school teacher was trying to explain the forms of "snow" to the children, but no matter how he said, the children couldn't understand.

The teacher said that snow was lily-white.

The children guessed that snow was like salt.

The teacher said that snow was.

The children guessed that snow was like ice cream.

The teacher said that snow was rough.

The children guessed that snow was like sand.

The teacher could never tell the children what snow was. Finally, he entitled "snow" as the subject of the examination. As a result, some of the children replied, "Snow is sand in light yellow, with its taste cold and salty."

This story tells us that the truth of some things can't be expressed with a language. For the people who have never seen snow, we're hard to make him know what snow is. The snow visible and tangible can't be understood, so how can the unfathomable state of mind without sound, color or image be clearly expressed?

If we want to know snow, we have to reach the country of snow in person.

If we want to listen to the song of an oriole, we have to sit under the tree with an oriole.

If we want to smell the fragrance of the evening primrose, we have to go into the courtyard with the evening primroses.

The most beautiful things in the world are hard to be expressed and represented in words.

As we stand in the snow, we will know what snow is, with no need to say anything.

雪中看人生

在赤道,一位小学老师努力地给孩子们说明“雪”的形态,但无论他怎么说,孩子们也不能明白。

老师说:雪是纯白的东西。

孩子们就猜测:雪像盐一样。

老师说:雪是冷的东西。

孩子们就猜测:雪像冰淇淋一样。

老师说:雪是粗粗的东西。

孩子们就猜测:雪像沙子一样。

老师始终不能告诉孩子雪是什么。最后,他考试时,出了“雪”的题目,结果有几个孩子这样回答:“雪是淡黄色,味道又冷又咸的砂。”

这个故事使我们知道,有一些事物的真相,用言语是无法表白的。对于没有看过雪的人,我们很难让他知道雪。像雪这种可看、有形的事物都无法明明白白,那么,对于无声无色、没有形象、不可捕捉的心念,如何能清楚表达呢?

我们要知道雪,只有自己到有雪的国度。

我们要听黄莺的歌声,就要坐到有黄莺的树下。

我们要闻夜来香的清香,只有夜晚走到有花的庭院去。

这个世界最美好的事物都是语言文字难以形容与表现的。

就像我们站在雪中,什么也不必说,就知道雪了。

The Life in a Child's Eyes

When the cloud hovered overhead, we all looked up.

"Look, it's just like my 'snowflake'," said my wife. 'snowflake' was her pet.

"Hmm. It's a lot like it," I agreed.

Just then, a hungry man took a look and said, "It's like a piece of bread."

A tired traveler said, "It's like a cozy couch."

A politician said, "It's like countless votes, on each of which my name is written."

A businessman said, "It's like my goods shipped from the sky."

Only one child took a look and said, "It's like my grandma's hoary hair."

All the eyes drew back and focused on the child.

Sometimes we really need the child to show us the way. Our world will always need the children's eyes and heart unmasked.

孩子眼里的人生

当那片云停在头顶时，我们一起抬头仰望。

"看，它多像我的'雪花'。"太太说。雪花是她的宠物。

"嗯，是挺像的。"我应和着太太。

这时，一个饥饿的人望了望说："像一块面包。"

一个疲惫的旅人说："像一张舒适的沙发床。"

一个政客说："像数不清的选票，每张都写着我的名字。"

一个商人说："像我的货物从天上运来。"

只有一个孩子看了看说："像奶奶的白头发。"

所有的目光都收回来，聚拢到孩子身上。

有时，我们真的需要孩子指路，我们的世界永远需要孩子的眼睛，需要孩子毫无遮拦的心。

The Philosophy of a Mirror

"Dr. Papaderos, what is the meaning of life?" I asked.

Papaderos looked at me for a long time, and taking his wallet out of his hip pocket, he fished into a leather billfold and brought out a very small round mirror, about the size of a quarter.

And what he said went like this, "When I was a small child, during the war, we were very poor living in a remote village. One day, on the road, I found the broken pieces of a mirror. A German motorcycle had been wrecked in that place.

"I tried to find all the pieces and put them together, but it was not possible, so I kept only the largest piece. By polishing it on a stone, I made it round. I began to play with it as a toy and became fascinated by the fact that I could reflect light into dark places where the sun would never shine—in deep holes and crevices and dark closets. It became a game for me to get light into the most inaccessible places I could find.

"As I became a man, I grew to understand that this was not just a child's game but a metaphor for what I might do with my life. I came to understand that I am not the light or the source of light. But light—truth, understanding, knowledge—is there, and it will shine in many dark places as long as I reflect it.

"I am a fragment of a mirror whose whole design and shape I do not know. Nevertheless, with what I have I can reflect light into the dark places of this world—into the black places in the hearts of men—and change some things in some people. Perhaps others may see and do likewise. This is what I am about. This is the meaning of life."

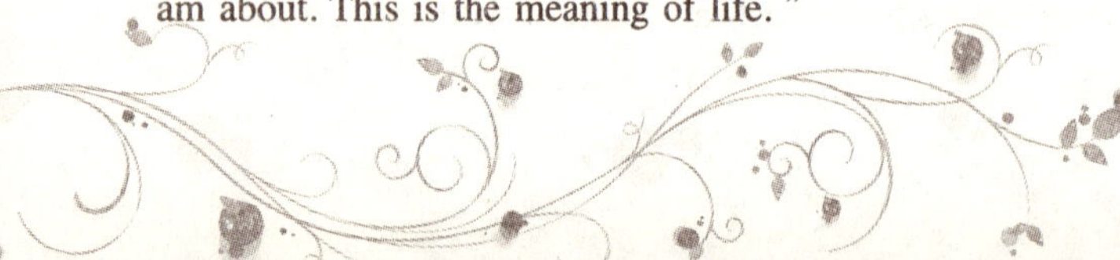

一面镜子的人生哲理

“帕帕德罗斯博士，人生的意义是什么？”我问。

帕帕德罗斯看了我好一阵子，然后从裤子后面的口袋里掏出一只皮夹，拿出了一块非常小的圆镜，大概有25分硬币大小。

随后，他这样说道：“战争期间，我还很小的时候，我们很穷，住在一个偏僻的村里。有一天，我在路上发现了一只镜子的那些碎片。是一辆德国摩托车在那个地方发生了事故。

“我设法找到所有的碎片，把它们拼在一起，但那不可能做到，所以我只保留了最大的那块碎片。我在一块石头上打磨，使它变圆。我开始把它当玩具玩，渐渐着迷，发现自己可以用它把光线反射到太阳永远照不到的暗处：深洞、裂缝和黑暗的壁橱。这渐渐成了我的一种游戏，把光线照到我能找到的那些最难接近的地方。

“随着我渐渐长大，我慢慢明白了这不只是一个孩子的游戏，而且对我的人生是一种象征。我最终明白自己既不是光，也不是光源，但真理、理解和知识这些光就在那里，只要我反射，它就会照亮许多黑暗的地方。

“我是镜子的一个碎片，我并不知道整个镜子的图案和形状。不过，我尽力把光照射到世界上那些黑暗的地方，照射到人们心灵的黑暗处，让一些人有所改变。说不定其他人看到，也会这样做。这就是我的看法。这就是人生的意义。”

Look at the Life from a Different Angle

One teacher entered the classroom and dotted a black spot on the whiteboard.

He asked the students in the class, “What's this?”

Everyone said in unison, “A black spot.”

The teacher said in pretended surprise, “Only one black spot? Can't you see such a big whiteboard?”

What do you see? Each one has some shortcomings, but which do you see? Do you only see the others' black spots and ignore their large whiteboard (merits)? In fact, every person must have a lot of advantages. So look at them from a different point of view! You'll have more new discoveries.

换个角度看人生

有位老师进了教室，在白板上点了一个黑点。

他问班上的学生：“这是什么？”

大家都异口同声说：“一个黑点。”

老师故作惊讶地说:"只有一个黑点吗？这么大的白板大家都没有看见?"

你看到的是什么？每个人身上都有一些缺点,但你看到的是哪些呢？是否只看到别人身上的黑点,却忽略了他拥有了一大片的白板(优点)？其实,每个人必定有很多优点,换一个角度去看吧！你会有更多新的发现。

The Art of How to Hold Life

The art of living is to know when to hold fast and when to let go. For life is paradox: it gives us many gifts, but eventually it will take them back. Someone said in this way, "A man comes to this world with his fists clenched, but when he dies, his hands are open."

Surely we ought to hold fast to life, for it is wondrous, and full of beauty on God's earth. We know that this is so, but all too often we recognize this truth only in our backward glance and then suddenly realize that it is no more.

A recent experience re-taught me this truth. Due to a severe heart attack I was hospitalized for several days.

One morning I had to have some additional tests, so I had to be wheeled across the courtyard. As we emerged from our ward, the sunlight hit me. I looked to see whether anyone else relished the sun's golden glow, but everyone was hurrying to and fro, most with eyes fixed on the ground. Then I remembered how often I, too, had been indifferent to the grandeur of each day.

So we should be reverent before each dawning day. Embrace each hour. Seize each minute.

Hold fast to life, but not so fast that you cannot let go. This is the second side of life's coin, the opposite pole of its paradox: we must accept our losses, and learn how to let go.

At every stage of life we sustain losses and grow in the process.

把握人生的艺术

生活的艺术是知道何时抓紧、何时放手,因为生活自相矛盾:它赐给我们很多礼物,但最终会一一收回。有人这样说道:"人紧握拳头来到世间,离世时却两手张开。"

的确,我们应该紧紧抓住生活,因为生活非常精彩,上帝的土地上充满了美。尽管我们知道如此,但我们常常是在回首的那一刻才认识到这个真理,随后突然明白一切都不复存在。

最近的一次经历又教给了我这个真理。由于严重心脏病,我住院治疗了好几天。

一天早上,我必须做一些额外的体检,所以必须坐轮椅穿过院子。我们刚一出病房,阳光就照在了我身上。我看了看周围,看其他人不是也喜欢太阳的金色光芒,但每个人都来去匆匆,大部分人眼睛盯着地面。随后,我想起了自己平时对每天的壮观景象也是无动于衷。

所以,我们要虔诚地对待每个黎明,拥抱每个小时,抓住每一分钟。

紧紧抓住生命,但不能抓得太紧而无法放手。这就是生活的另一面,也是生活矛盾体的另一面:我们必须接受失去、学会放手。

在生命的每个阶段，我们既忍受失去，又在这个过程中成长。

The Law of Life Grandma Taught Me

Two years ago my grandma left this earth. It wasn't until she died that I truly recognized how much she meant to me. She was my friend, my teacher and my inspiration. She taught me things that became my own personal laws of life, which have helped me get through each day with a smile, have made me aware of my strong points as well as my weaknesses, and helped me overcome those weaknesses. They are true lessons to live by, and I hope I will never forget them.

One day, my grandma told me something I will always remember. She said, "Your talent is God's gift to you. What you do with it is your gift to God."

Those words have become a part of me over the years. Each day I thank God for the many talents He has given me, and I try to use those talents. I believe that we were all born to reveal the glory of God that is within us. As we each let our own light shine, through our talents and ideas, we unconsciously give others permission to do the same. Just think about what our world could be like if each and every one of us let our own light shine through. I think it would be a better place.

One more lesson my grandma taught me was to always go for my dreams and never give up. She once told me, "Shoot for the moon because even if you fall, you'll land among the stars."

I have never heard anything truer in all my life. I have tried to live by these words, and have figured out that it is very important to go for your dreams and never let anything get in your way. Even if you have had a bitter experience in the past, never limit your view of life by that experience. I believe that life is constantly testing our commitment, and I am convinced life's greatest rewards are reserved for those who show a never-ending commitment to act until they achieve. This kind of determination can accomplish miracles, but it must be continual and consistent. Simple as this may sound, it is still the common denominator separating those who live their dreams from those that live in regret.

Another great lesson my grandma taught me was, "Never let anyone come to you without coming away better and happier." Everyone should see goodness in your face, in your eyes, in your smile. Too often we underestimate the power of such things: a touch, a smile, a kind word, a listening ear, an honest compliment, or even the smallest act of caring. All have the potential to turn a life around.

My grandma is no longer present here on earth, but she will always remain present in my heart. Her words and personality have affected my life. Her lessons on life have become a part of me, and have made me a better person. I will never forget the great love my grandma shared with everyone. She is my idol. My grandma's laws of life will live in me forever.

奶奶教给我的人生准则

两年前，奶奶离开了这个世界。她去世后，我才真正认识到，她对我有多么重要。她是我的朋友、我的老师和我的灵感。她教给我的东西渐渐成了我个人生活的准则。这些准则帮助我微笑度过每一天，使我认识到自己的优点与缺点，并帮助我克服那些弱点。它们是我赖以为生的真正训诫，我希望自己永远不要忘记它们。

有一天，奶奶告诉了我一件我终生难忘的事情。她说："你的才能是上帝赐给你的礼物。利用它是你给上帝的礼物。"

这些年来，那些话已经成为我生活的一部分。每天我都感谢上帝赐给我的许多才能，而且尽力利用那些才能。我相信我们生来就是为了展现上帝赐予我们的光荣。当我们各自通过自己的才能和思想让自己发光时，我们无意中就同意别人也这样做。试想一下，如果每个人都让自己的光照亮别人，我们的世界会是什么景象。我想那会是一个更加美好的地方。

奶奶教给我的另一训诫是，要永远追逐自己的梦想、绝不放弃。她曾告诉我说："争取摘到月亮，因为即使你坠落，也会落在群星间。"

我一生从来没有听过比这更真实的事情。我努力按照这些话去生活，而且明白这对追逐梦想非常重要，永远不要让任何事情阻挡你的道路。即使过去曾有过惨痛经历，也永远不要让那种经历限制自己的人生观。我相信，生活总在考验我们的责任感，而且我确信，生活最大的奖赏就是为那些不懈奋斗、直至成功的人而准备。这种决心可以成就奇迹，但必须始终如一。尽管这听起来可能简单，但仍是区分追逐梦想者和懊悔过去者的共同点。

奶奶教给我的又一大训诫是："离开时不能给人留下更幸福、更美好的印象，千万不要让任何人到你身边来。"每个人都应该从你的脸上、你的眼里和你的微笑中看到善意。我们常常会低估一次抚摸、一个微笑、一句善言、一只倾听的耳朵、一声真诚的赞美甚或最小的一个关爱之举这些东西的力量。所有这些都有转变人生的可能。

尽管奶奶已不在人世，但她会永远活在我的心里。她的话语和人格魅力已经影响了我的人生。她对人生的训诫已经成为我的一部分，使我更加出色。我永远不会忘记奶奶和每个人分享的大爱。她是我的偶像。奶奶的人生准则将永远活在我的心里。

The Best Time of My Life

It was June 15, and in two days I would be turning thirty. I was insecure about entering a new decade of my life and feared that my best years were now behind me.

My daily routine included going to the gym for a workout before going to work. Every morning I would see my friend Nicholas at the gym. He was seventy-nine years old and in terrific shape. As I greeted Nicholas on this particular day, he noticed I wasn't full of my usual vitality and asked if there was anything wrong. I told him I was feeling anxious about turning thirty. I wondered how I would look back on my life once I reached Nicholas's age, so I asked him, "What was the best time of your life?"

Without hesitation, Nicholas replied, "Well, Joe, this is my philosophical answer to your philosophical question.

"When I was a child in Austria and everything was taken care of for me and I was nurtured by my parents, that was the best time of my life.

"When I was going to school and learning the things I know today, that was the best time of my life.

"When I got my first job and had responsibilities and got paid for my efforts, that was the best time of my life.

"When I met my wife and fell in love, that was the best time of my life.

"The Second World War came, and my wife and I had to flee Austria to save our lives. When we

were together and safe on a ship bound for North America, it was the best time of my life.

"When we came to Canada and started a family, that was the best time of my life.

"When I was a young father, watching my children grow up, that was the best time of my life.

"And now, Joe, I am seventy-nine years old. I have my health, I feel good and I am in love with my wife just as I was when we first met. This is the best time of my life."

我一生中最好的时光

那天是6月15日,再过两天我就要30岁了。我对要进入生命中又一个新的十年没有把握,害怕自己最好的时光现在远去。

我每天上班前都要去体育馆锻炼一会儿。每天早上,我都会在体育馆见到我的朋友尼古拉斯。他79岁了,身材特棒。那天我跟他打招呼时,他注意到我不像往常那样充满活力,便问我是不是有什么毛病。我对他说我对自己快要30岁感到担忧。我不知道自己到了尼古拉斯的岁数会怎么回顾一生,就问他:"你一生中最好的时光是什么时候?"

尼古拉斯毫不犹豫地回答说:"噢,乔,这是我对你的哲理问题做出的哲理回答。

"小时候我在奥地利时,一切都被照顾很好,我被父母抚养成人,那是我一生中最好的时光。

"我上学时学会了我现在熟悉的那些事情,那是我一生中最好的时光。

"我找到第一份工作,承担职责并因努力而拿到报酬时,那是我一生中最好的时光。

"当我遇到妻子并坠入爱河时,那是我一生中最好的时光。

"二次大战来临,我和妻子为了活命,不得不逃离奥地利。当我们一起平安坐上驶向北美洲的一艘轮船时,那是我一生中最好的时光。

"当我们来到加拿大建立家庭时,那是一生中最好的时光。

"当我成了一位年轻的父亲,看着自己的孩子长大时,那是我一生中最好的时光。

"而现在,乔,我都79岁了。我身体健康,感觉良好,和我们初次相遇时一样爱我的妻子。这是我一生中最好的时光。"

A Miracle Changes Life

A little girl sat alone in the park. Everyone passed by her, never stopping to care why she looked so sad. Dressed in a worn pink dress, barefoot and dirty, the girl just sat there watching the people come and go. She never tried to speak. She never said a word.

The next day I decided to go back to the park out of curiosity to see if the little girl would be still there. Yes, she was there, right on the very spot where she was yesterday, and still with the same sad look in her eyes. Today I decided to try to approach her, for as we all know a park full of strange people is not a place fit for children to play alone.

As I got closer, I could see the back of the little girl's dress was grotesquely shaped. I figured that

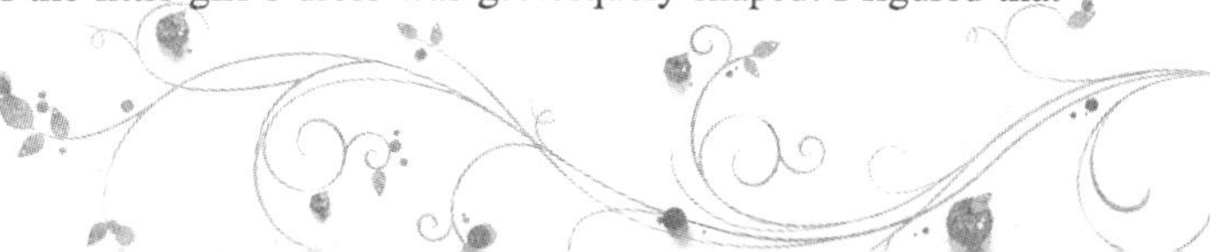

was why people just passed by and never wanted to speak to her. As I got closer and closer, the little girl lowered her eyes slightly to avoid my stare. When I approached her, I could see the shape of her back more clearly. Her back was deformed with a hump. I smiled to let her know it was OK; I came here to help and talk with her. I sat down beside her and said with a smile, "Hi!"

She was startled, and stammered a "hi" after she had been staring at my eyes for a long while.

I smiled at her and she shyly smiled back. We talked until the night fell and the park was completely empty. I asked why she was so sad. The little girl said to me with a worried look, "Because I'm different from others."

I immediately said, "That's no other than you!" The little girl said more sadly, "I know."

"Little girl," I said, "you remind me of an angel, who is sweet and innocent." She looked at me and smiled. Then, slowly, she got to her feet and said, "Really?"

"Yes, you're like a little guardian angel sent to watch over all those passersby."

She nodded with a smile. With that, she opened the back of her pink dress, spread her wings and said, "Yes, I'm your guardian angel." There was a twinkle in her eyes.

I was stunned: yes, I was watching a miracle going on.

The little girl said, "This time you thought of others, not yourself. My task here is done."

I stood up and asked, "Wait. Why does no one stop to help an angel?"

She looked at me and said with a smile, "You're the only one who can see me." Then she was gone.

Since then, my life was changed dramatically. So when you think you're the most important, please remember, your angel is always watching over you.

奇迹改变人生

一个小女孩独自坐在公园里。人们从她身边经过，但没有人停下来去关心她为什么面带悲伤。小女孩身穿一件破旧的粉红裙子，光着脚，浑身脏兮兮的。她只是坐在那里看着身旁人来人往。她根本不愿说什么，从没说过一个字。

第二天，我怀着好奇心决定去公园看看她是否还在那里。是的，她在那里，就在昨天她坐的地方，眼睛里依然流露出那种悲伤的神情。今天我决定要试试走近她。因为众所周知，一个到处都是陌生人的公园并不适合小孩子们单独玩耍。

当我走得离她稍微近些时，我看到她穿着裙子的后背形状古怪，我想那就是为什么人们只是从她身旁经过而从不想要和她搭腔了。当我走得更近时，小女孩微微垂下眼睛，避开我注视她的眼神。我靠近她时，我可以更清楚地看到她后背的形状了。她后背畸形，有一块隆起的肉峰。我笑了笑想让她明白那没什么，我来这里愿意帮助她，和她聊天。我挨着她坐下，面带微笑说："你好！"

她受到了惊动，盯着我的眼睛看了好大一会儿，才结结巴巴地说："嗨！"

我朝她笑了笑，她对我也报以羞怯一笑。我们一直聊到夜幕降临，聊到公园里空无一人。我问她为什么如此悲伤，小女孩满脸愁容地看着我说："因为我和别人不同。"

我马上说："那才是你啊！"小女孩更加悲伤地说："我明白。"

"孩子，"我说。"你让我想起一位天使，她既可爱又天真。"她看着我笑了笑，然后慢慢站起来说："真的吗？"

"真的，你就像一个小守护神，被派来守卫那些过往的行人。"

她微笑着点头称是。说着，她张开粉红裙的后摆，展开了双翅，然后说："我是，我就

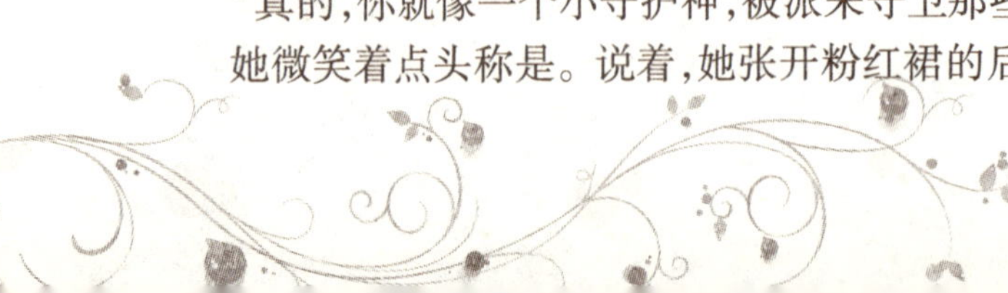

是你们的守护神。”她的眼睛闪过一道光。

我惊呆了：是的，我正在看着奇迹发生。

小女孩说：“这次你想到了别人而不是自己，我在这里的任务完成了。”

我站起来问：“等一等，为什么没有人愿意停下来帮助一个天使呢？”

她看着我笑着说：“你是唯一能看见我的人。”说完就消失了。

从那以后，我的生活发生了翻天覆地的变化。因此，当你认为自己最重要时，请记住，你的天使总是在守护着你。

The Inquiry of Life

During my junior year in high school, Mr. Reynolds, my English teacher, handed each student a list of thoughts or statements written by other students, then gave us a creative writing assignment based on one of those thoughts.

At 17, I was beginning to wonder about many things, so I chose the statement, "I wonder why things are the way they are?" That night, I wrote down in the form of a story all the questions that puzzled me about life. I realized that many of them were hard to answer, and perhaps others could not be answered at all.

When I turned in my paper, I was afraid that I might fail the assignment because I had not answered the question, "I wonder why things are the way they are?" I had no answers. I had only written questions.

The next day Mr. Reynolds called me to the front of the class and asked me to read my story for the other students. He handed me my paper and sat down in the back of the room. The class became quiet as I began to read my story:

Mommy, Daddy... Why?

Mommy, why are the roses red?
Mommy, why is the grass green and the sky blue?
Why does a spider have a web and not a house?
Daddy, why can't I play in your toolbox?
Teacher, why do I have to read?
Mother, why can't I wear lipstick to the dance?
Daddy, why can't I stay out until 12:00? The other kids can.
Mother, why do you hate me?
Daddy, why don't the boys like me?
Why do I have to be so skinny?
Why do I have braces and wear glasses?
Why do I have to be 16?
Mom, why do I have to graduate?
Dad, why do I have to grow up?
Mom, Dad, why do I have to leave?
Mom, why don't you write more often?
Dad, why do I miss my old friends?
Dad, why do you love me so much?
Dad, why do you spoil me?
Your little girl is growing up.

Mom, why don't you visit?
Mom, why is it hard to make new friends?
Dad, why do I miss being at home?
Dad, why does my heart skip a beat when he looks in my eyes?
Mom, why do my legs tremble when I hear his voice?
Mother, why is being "in love" the greatest feeling in the world?
Daddy, why don't you like to be called "Gramps"?
Mother, why do my baby's tiny fingers cling so tightly to mine?
Mother, why do they have to grow up?
Daddy, why do they have to leave?
Why do I have to be called "Grannie"?
Mommy, Daddy, why did you have to leave me? I need you.
Why did my youth slip past me?
Why does my face show every smile that I have ever given to a friend or a stranger?
Why does my hair glisten shiny silver?
Why do my hands quiver when I bend to pick a flower?
Why, God, are the roses red?

At the conclusion of my story, my eyes locked with Mr. Reynolds' eyes, and I saw a tear slowly sliding down his cheek. It was then that I realized that life is not always based on the answers we receive, but also on the questions that we ask.

问人生

我上初中时，英语老师雷诺先生给每位同学发了一个其他同学写的各种想法或说法的清单。随后，他要我们据此写一篇有创意的作文。

17 岁的我对很多事都想知道，所以就选了"我想知道为什么事情是这样?"这个题目。那天晚上，我以故事形式写下了我对人生的所有困惑。我知道很多问题很难回答，也许有些问题根本无法回答。

交过作文后，我担心作业可能过不了关，因为我没有回答"我想知道为什么事情是这样?"这个问题。我找不到答案，只写出了问题。

第二天，雷诺先生让我到堂前，让我把自己的作文念给其他同学听。他把我的作业递给我，在教室后面坐下来。我开始念自己的故事时，全班鸦雀无声：

妈妈、爸爸……为什么?

妈妈，为什么玫瑰是红的?
妈妈，为什么草是绿的、天是蓝的?
为什么蜘蛛有网、没有房?
爸爸，为什么我不能在你的工具箱里玩耍?
老师，为什么我得读书?
妈妈，为什么我不能抹口红参加舞会?
爸爸，为什么我不能在外面待到 12 点? 别的小孩都可以。
妈妈，为什么你讨厌我?
爸爸，为什么男生不喜欢我?

为什么我得那样骨感？
为什么我要系背带、戴眼镜？
为什么我得过16岁？
妈，为什么我得毕业？
爸，为什么我得长大？
妈，爸，为什么我得离开家？
妈，为什么您不常写信来？
爸，为什么我想老朋友？
爸，为什么您这样爱我？
爸，为什么您这样宠我？
您的小女儿渐渐长大。
妈，为什么您不来看我？
妈，为什么交新朋友这样难？
爸，为什么我想在家的日子？
爸，为什么每次他看着我的眼睛时我就怦然心动？
妈，为什么听到他的声音我就双腿打颤？
妈妈，为什么"堕入爱河"是世界上最美妙的感觉？
爸爸，为什么您不喜欢有人叫您"外公"？
妈妈，为什么我宝宝的小手指那样紧地抓住我的手？
妈妈，为什么他们得长大？
爸爸，为什么他们得离开家？
为什么要有人叫我"奶奶"？
妈妈、爸爸，为什么你们要离我而去？我需要你们呀！
为什么我的青春悄悄从我的身边溜走？
为什么我对朋友和陌生人面带微笑？
为什么我的头发银光闪闪？
为什么我弯腰摘花时双手颤抖？
上帝，为什么玫瑰是红的？

我念完故事，望着雷诺先生，雷诺先生也望着我。我看到一颗泪珠正慢慢地滑过他的脸颊。就在那时，我意识到，生活并不总是以我们得到的答案为基础，而且也以我们提出的问题为基础。

First Change Yourself

A man hired a taxi outside the airfield. The cab had a woolen carpet with brilliant laces. On the

grass partition that shielded the driver's seat was a replica of a famous painting. Its windows were all clean.

The passenger was very much surprised and said to the driver, "I've never seen a nicer cab."

"Thank you for your praise," the driver answered smilingly.

"How did it occur to you to decorate your car?" asked the passenger.

"The car isn't mine," said the driver. "It belongs to the company. I used to be a cleaner of cabs. When they returned, all of them were as dirty as garbage cans with cigarette butts and rubbish scattered here and there. On the seats and door-handles could be found something sticky like peanut sauce or chewing gum. Why so? I thought if the car itself were very clean, the passengers would mostly likely be considerate and refrain from littering.

"So when I got a license to be a taxi-driver, I began to put my idea into practice-to tidy and decorate the car. Now before a new passenger gets on my car, I'd make a check and be sure it is in good order. When my car returns after a day's work, it always remains spotless."

When doing a thing, one makes efforts and wants to see the result. To change others, one has to make twice the effort but get half the result. To change oneself is the other way round. One had better ask oneself why one makes demands on others much more than on oneself. If you take enough care to do as best you can for other people's sake, your efforts will yield results. If you look into the inner world of your own, examine yourself and wipe out the dust and dirt, instead of fixing your eyes on other people, you will find a cheerful mood for yourself and create a pleasant environment for others.

改变人生从自己做起

一个人在机场租了一辆出租车。出租车铺着绣有鲜艳花边的羊毛地毯，保护司机座的玻璃隔板上是一幅名画的复制品，车窗都非常干净。

乘客非常惊讶，对司机说："我从未见过这样漂亮的出租车。"

"谢谢你的赞扬，"司机笑着回答说。

"你为什么要装饰你的车呢？"乘客问道。

"车不是我的，"他说。"车是公司的。我以前是出租公司的清洁工。每当出租车回来时，都像垃圾桶一样脏，地板上到处都是烟蒂和垃圾，座位上或车门把手上还有花生酱、口香糖之类的粘东西。为什么会这样？我当时想，如果车本身很干净，乘客们十有八九都会体谅我们，不乱扔东西。

"所以，我取得出租车驾驶执照后，就开始把自己的想法付诸行动——收拾并装饰车子。现在每位乘客上车前，我都要检查，确保车子井然有序。经过一天工作，我的车子回公司时仍然一尘不染。"

有人做一件事付出努力，就想看到结果。改变别人是事倍功半，改变自己则事半功倍。一个人最好扪心自问，为什么要求别人的多，要求自己的少。如果你尽最大可能去关心别人的利益，你的努力就会产生效果。如果你审视自己的内心世界，检查自我，打扫干净其中的尘埃，而不是眼睛盯着别人，你会发现，在自己愉快的同时，也为别人创造了舒适的环境。

The Dignity of Life

Once I sent off a friend to the railway station. We called a taxi and put several heavy suitcases in the trunk. Getting off, a middle-aged man leaning on a crutch opened the door for us. After that, he stretched out a small dirty pot to us. On the pot were stacked with coins and banknotes of one or two jiao.

I asked the friend if she had some changes. She shook her head. I had to give two yuan used for buying the platform ticket to the middle-aged man. Shocked, he kept jerking the small pot, as if he received so much money for the first time.

Not caring, we went straight to the trunk to fetch the suitcases. My friend took out one suitcase with all her might. Just as she was about to pick up another, a dark stout large hand stretched in. "Let me do it!" He picked up the suitcase and insisted on carrying it for us to the station entrance. "No, thank you. You're also inconvenient!" My friend and I didn't give the heart. "No, I must send you off!" He limped towards the station, his left hand leaning on a crutch and his right hand carrying the large suitcase.

Compassion and dignity have sublimated love.

人生的尊严

有一次，我去火车站送朋友。我们叫了辆出租车，把重重的几个箱子放在车后面。下车时，一个拄着拐杖的中年人帮我们开了车门。接着，他又向我们伸出一只肮脏的小盆。盆上堆满了一毛两毛的硬币和纸币。

我问朋友，有没有零钱。朋友摇了摇头。我只好把准备用来买站台票的两元钱都给了那个中年人。中年人大吃了一惊，手不停地抖动着小盆子，好像他第一次收到这么多钱。

我们没在意，径直往后车厢去拿箱子。朋友费了很大力气，才提出了一只。刚要提起另一只时，一只粗壮黝黑的大手伸了进来。"我来!"他一把拿起那只箱子，坚持要帮我们把箱子提到车站门口。"不用了，谢谢。你也不方便啊!"我和朋友都不忍心。"不行，一定要送!"他左手拄着拐杖，右手提着大箱子，一瘸一拐地往车站方向走去。

怜悯与尊严使爱心得到了升华。

Life Has the Time to Bloom

My friend went afar to work, so he asked me to take care of the courtyard in the mountains. The place adjacent to the wall in the courtyard was built with a fence to plant green vegetables. Every morning or evening, I would take a chair to sit in the courtyard sipping tea or reading. I felt it so charming.

My friend was an assiduous man, so he often kept the courtyard clean and tidy without any weed.

And I was so lazy, apart from occasionally sweeping some fallen leaves in the courtyard, that I never plucked grass shoots breaking through the earth, letting them grow secretly. In the early spring, by the stone bench on the left side of the courtyard, sprouted several clusters of green buds, whose leaves were tender and flimsy. Over 20 days later, when their leaves unfurled richly, I discovered they were like wild orchids in the woods beyond the courtyard—if they were really the lingering wild orchids, it would be poetic with the quiet orchids wafting their fragrance gently.

In the late summer, the grass really bloomed. The little five-petal flowers steamed wisps of delicate fragrance. They shaped like those forest orchids, but they were wax yellow, unlike those forest wild orchids, whose flowers were purple or brown red. I picked one flower and some blades of grass, then came down the mountains to find a friend who botanized. On seeing them, my friend immediately asked me where I picked them. After that, he congratulated on me, "You get rich!" I looked at my friend in puzzlement. He excitedly explained, "This is a strain of rare orchid, for many people are hard to find it even in their lifetime. At the city flower market, this strain of orchid is worth at least 10, 000 dollars each."

I called to tell the good new to the friend who had gone to work in the south. At this, my friend was stunned. After a while, he said gently, in fact, the orchid broke through the earth each year, but he thought it was an ordinary weed, so he often uprooted it each spring it just sprouted. My friend couldn't help sighing, "I have almost destroyed a kind of rare flower; if I could wait for it to blossom with patience, it would have been discovered a few years before."

Yes, who will never miss some rare orchids in their own lives? We always pluck those wild weeds that haven't yet bloomed in time and don't give them the time to flower and bear fruit to prove their value.

Give each grass the time to flower and give everyone a chance to prove his or her value. Don't blindly pull out a blade of grass or negate a person curtly and how many "rare orchids" we will get in our lives!

人生都有开花的时间

朋友去远方做事，把他在山中的庭院交给我看守。院里邻墙的地方扎了一道篱笆，种一些青菜。清晨或黄昏，我搬一把小椅，坐在院里品茶读书，挺有韵味。

朋友是一个勤快人，院里常常收拾得干干净净寸草不生。而我很懒，除了偶尔扫扫院里被风吹进的一些落叶，从不去薅那些破土而出的草芽，任它们滋长。初春时，院子左侧的石凳旁冒出了几簇绿绿的芽尖，叶子嫩嫩的、薄薄的。20多天后，它们的叶子蓬蓬勃勃伸展开来，我才发觉它们像是院外林间幽幽的野兰——如果真是野兰，家有幽兰徐徐绽香，那该多富有诗意啊！

晚夏时，那草果然开花了。五瓣小花氤氲着一缕缕幽香，花形如林地里那些兰花一样，只可惜它是蜡黄的，不像林地里的那些野兰，花朵是紫色或褐红的。我采撷了其中的一朵花和几片叶子，下山去找一位研究植物的朋友。朋友一看，忙问我这花在哪里采到的。之后，他恭贺我说："你发财了！"我不解地望着朋友，他兴奋地解释说："这是兰花的一个稀有品种，许多人穷尽了一生都很难找到它。如在城市的花市上，这种腊兰一株至少价值万余元。"

我打电话把喜讯告诉了远在南方的朋友。朋友一听，也愣了。过了一会儿，他轻轻地说，其实，那株腊兰每年都要破土而出，只是他以为它不过是一株普通的野草，每年春天芽儿刚冒头就被他拔掉了。朋友不禁叹道："我几乎毁掉了一种奇花啊，如果我能耐心地等它开花,几年前就能发现的。”

是的,我们谁又不曾错过自己人生中的几株腊兰呢?我们总是盲目地拔掉那些还没有来得及开花的野草,没有给它们开花结果证明自己价值的时间。

给每棵草开花的时间,给每个人以证明价值的机会,不要盲目地拔掉一棵草,不要草率地否定一个人,那我们将会得到多少人生的“腊兰”啊!

The Ebb and Flow of Life

During my first year in Japan I took a hitchhiking trip and went to numerous fishing villages on the west coast of Japan.

In one village I had the privilege of meeting a very special man. He was in his sixties and walked with a noticeable limp. He told me that as a youth he was very involved in karate, but at the age of twenty-five he was injured while working on his father's fishing boat, and he had been limping ever since.

We sat out on a small wooden dock one night as he told me about his life. He said once he realized he would no longer be able to actively take part in karate, he made up his mind to use his life as a fisherman to further his martial arts studies. He read various martial arts books and then applied what he read to his work life.

"One of the most important things I have learned," he said. "is to create a rhythm with your presence, movements, and breathing, which matches the rhythm of nature. This is a phrase numerous martial arts masters wrote about in the books I have read."

As we sat by the water, he asked me to notice the ebb and flow of the ocean and the sounds of the tide lapping against the pillings of the pier. "As you notice your movements and breathing, you can sense the movement and sounds of the ocean, and realize how you go with the rhythm of this flow."

I began to do as he suggested, and I quickly felt I was being drawn into a parallel world, that I was somehow usually ignoring, or simply not noticing.

"Feel the life force of the ocean," he said. "And breathe with the ocean. Feel the life force of the ocean, and without doing anything, allow yourself to move with the ocean... Breathe, move, and feel your heartbeat... Invite your heartbeat to synchronize with the heartbeat of the ocean."

Now you are becoming one with the water, and the fluid inside your body begins to become a tiny powerful ocean that ebbs and flows throughout your system.

Now, like the ocean, you can begin to feel the power of flowing without resisting. Flowing without fighting against.

The water surrounds and moves past all obstacles. There is no forcing, and no need for strength. Only flow... The power is IN the flow, and each drop of water is pliant and soft. No one drop of water is powerful on its own.

We sat there together for a while. The man, myself, and the ocean. I felt the power and presence of the ocean, myself, and the fisherman. Not separate, but together. And I knew very clearly that all this power was really One.

The one tiny drop of water that you are.

The ebb and flow of your life mirrors the ebb and flow of all life. When you calm yourself, slow down, and become one with your surroundings, you realize that nature offers you a parallel understanding of life. The tiny drop of water known as "me" is an integral part of the ocean of life, and your power manifests most gracefully when you join your individual spirit with the spirit of all creation.

Breathe deeply, calm yourself, and begin to notice and appreciate the ebb and flow of the world

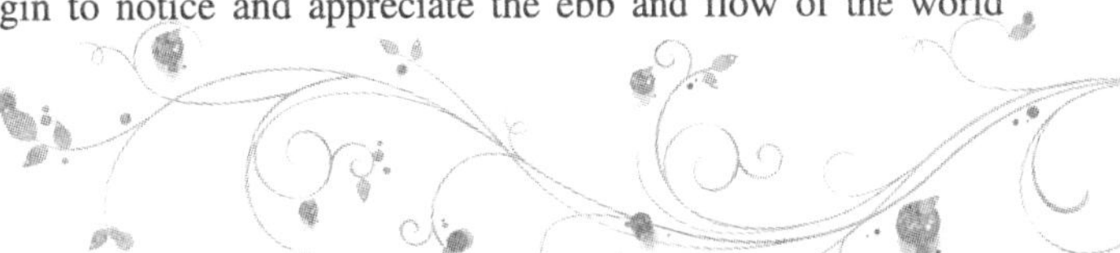

人生的涨落

在日本的第一年，我搭便车旅行，到过日本西海岸的无数渔村。

我在一个村里有幸遇到了一个非常特别的人。他年过花甲，走路明显一瘸一拐。他告诉我说，他年轻时热衷空手道，但他25岁在父亲的渔船上干活时受伤，从那以后就一直一瘸一拐。

一天夜里，我们坐在外面的一个木制小码头上，他对我说起了自己的人生。他说，一旦意识到自己再也不能积极参加空手道，他就下定决心这辈子做个渔民，进一步研究武术。他阅读了各种武术书籍，然后把看到的知识运用到了工作生活中去。

"我学到的最重要的一件东西，"他说。"就是创造一种与自然韵律协调一致的自身、运动和呼吸的节奏。这是我看过的书里许多武术大师都写到的一个用语。"

我们坐在水边，他让我注意大海的涨落和潮水拍打码头木桩的声音。"就像你注意自己的运动和呼吸一样，你可以感受到大海的运动和声音，然后领悟到你怎样和这流水的节奏保持一致。"

我开始像他建议的那样去做，很快就感到自己正被引入一个常常忽视或根本没有注意过的相似世界。

"感受大海的生命力，"他说。"和大海一起呼吸。感受大海的生命力，什么也不做，让自己和大海一起运动……呼吸，运动，感受自己的心跳……让自己的心跳和大海的心跳保持同步。"

现在你渐渐和海水融为一体，体内的液体开始变成在你全身涨落、威力无穷的小小海洋。

现在，像大海一样，你能渐渐感受到没有阻挡的流动力量，没有对抗的流动力量。

海水包围并流过了一切障碍。没有强迫，无需用力。只是流动……力量就在流动中，每一滴水都顺从温柔。哪一滴水本身都不强大。

我们一起坐了一会儿。老人、我自己和大海。我感受到了大海、我自己和渔民的力量与存在。不是各自孤立，而是合为一体。而且我非常清楚所有这力量其实都是一体的。

你就是那小小的一滴水。

你的生命涨落反映了所有生命的涨落。当你平静下来，放慢速度，与周围环境融为一体时，就会认识到大自然为你提供了对生命的相似理解。被称为"我"的小小水滴是生命海洋的一个完整部分。当你自己的精神和天地万物的精神合在一起时，你的力量才会最优美地呈现出来。

深呼吸，保持平静，开始注意和欣赏你周围世界的涨落……你会发现宇宙的力量正是滋养你生命的力量。

The Journey of Life Starts from the Set Goal

Bissel is a small village of the West Sahara. It lies next to a patch of 1. 5-square-kilometer oasis, from where three days and nights are generally required to go out of the desert. However, before Ken Levin discovered it in 1926, none of the people had walked out of the desert. Reportedly, they were not reluctant to leave this barren land, but had no way to walk out of it after they had tried many times.

As an academician of the British Royal College of Sciences, Ken Levin, of course, did not believe this viewpoint. He asked the reason of the people here. As a result, the answer of each was the same: To whichever direction they went from here, they would eventually return to this place. To prove this parlance, he did an experiment. He went north from Bissel Village and finally walked out from it in three and a half days.

Why couldn't the Bissel villagers walk out of it? Ken Levin was very puzzled. In the end, he had to employ a Bissel villager to lead the way and wanted to find out the reason. They prepared the water that could be used for half a month and two camels while only leaning on a stick, Ken Levin put away the compass and other facilities, following the man.

Ten days later, they walked for about 800 miles. On the 11th morning, an oasis came into their view. They really came back again to Bissel. This time, Ken Levin came to understand: the Bissel people couldn't walk out of the desert because they had no knowledge of the North Star.

In the boundless desert, if a person goes forward relying on his or her sense, he or she will make lots and lots of circles of different sizes, and the final footprints will be most likely the shape of a tape. Bissel Village was in the middle of the immense desert with more than one thousand square kilometers, so without a compass, it was indeed impossible to walk out of the desert.

Leaving Bissel Village, Ken Levin brought a young man called Argutel, who was the man who had cooperated with him last time. He told the young man, "As long as you rest in the daytime and walk towards the brightest star at night, would be able to walk out of the desert." Argutel did as he was told. Three days later, he, sure enough, came to the edge of the desert.

Now in the West Sahara Bissel has been a bright pearl, where tens of thousands of tourists come here. As the pioneer of Bissel, Argutel's bronze statue stands in the center of the town. On the base of the bronze statue the following line were engraved, "A new life starts from the fixed direction."

人生之旅从选定目标开始

比塞尔是西撒哈拉沙漠中的一个小村庄,它靠在一块1.5平方公里的绿洲旁,从这里走出沙漠一般需要3昼夜。可是,在肯·莱文1926年发现它之前,这里的人没有一个走出过大沙漠。据说,他们不是不愿意离开这块贫瘠的地方,而是尝试过很多次都没有走出来。

作为英国皇家学院的院士,肯·莱文当然不相信这种说法。他用手语向这里的人问其原因,结果每个人的回答都是一样的:从这里无论向哪个方向走,最后都还要转回到这个地方。为了证实这种说法,他做了一次试验。从比塞尔村向北走,结果3天半就走了出来。

比塞尔人为什么走不出来呢?肯·莱文非常纳闷。最后,他只得雇一个比塞尔人,让他带路,看看到底是怎么回事。他们准备了能用半个月的水,牵上两匹骆驼,肯·莱文收起指南针等设备,只拄了一根木棍,跟在后面。

10天过去了，他们走了大约800英里的路程，第11天早晨，一块绿洲出现在眼前，他们果然又回到了比塞尔。这一次肯·莱文终于明白了，比塞尔人之所以走不出大沙漠，是因为他们根本就不认识北极星。

在一望无际的沙漠里，一个人如果凭感觉往前走，会走出许许多多、大小不一的圆圈，最后的足迹十有八九是一把卷尺的形状，比塞尔村处在浩瀚的沙漠中间，方圆上千公里，没有指南针，想走出沙漠，确实是不可能的。

离开比塞尔村时，肯·莱文带了一个叫阿古特尔的青年，这个青年就是上次和他合作的人。他告诉这个青年说："只要你白天休息，夜晚朝着北面那颗最亮的星星走，就能走出沙漠。"阿古特尔照着去做，3天后果然来到了大漠边缘。

现在比塞尔已是西撒哈拉沙漠中的一颗明珠，每年有数以万计的旅游者来到这里。阿古特尔作为比塞尔的开拓者，他的铜像竖立在小城中央，铜像底座上刻着一行字："新生活从选定方向开始。"

Lower Your Height

There was a famous singer who recalled her own growth, saying that when she was young, she often encountered such a problem: when she sang trebly, she could get them done without any letup, but sometimes she was hard to sing trebly, so she was very distressed over this. Later, she consulted a renowned teacher. The teacher let her audition, suggesting that she not be eager to sing trebly, but practise the ordinary vocalization every day.

Then the war broke out, and she had no chance to sing. After the war ended, she went to visit her teacher again and found she sang trebly very easily.

I remember a friend said to me, "The moon is high, but if your goal is an apple, you won't have to fly so high. If your goal is an apple, when you fly to the altitude of 10, 000 meters, you will neither get the moon nor see the apple. For the moon, there is no difference between the 10, 000 meters and starting from scratch, and for the apple, you fly too high."

Reconsider your determined goal and remeasure your height and arm length, are you required to reduce your flying altitude? Sometimes, as long as you lower a little bit, your life will be much better.

降低人生高度

曾有一位著名歌唱家，回忆自己的成长道路时说，她年轻时经常遇到这样的问题，高音唱得很圆润，一气呵成，但有时却很难唱上去，为此她非常苦恼。后来，她去请教一位名师。那位老师让她试唱，建议她不要急着去唱高音，每天做普通的发声练习。

后来，战争爆发了，她没有机会唱歌。战争结束后，她再去见她的老师时，发现自己居然非常轻松地就唱出了高音。

记得一个朋友跟我说过："高处有月亮，假如你的目标是苹果，就不必飞得那么高。如果你的目标是苹果，而你飞到一万米高空，那你既得不到月亮，也看不见苹果。对月亮来说，一万米和从零开始没有什么区别，而对苹果来说，你又飞得太高了。”

重新考虑一下你给自己定的目标，再重新丈量一下自己的身高和臂长，你是不是需要降低自己的飞行高度？有时，只需要降低一点点，生活就会好很多。

The Addition, Subtraction, Multiplication and Division of Life

One writer once said, "Life is a process of self-operation, and to operate is to calculate. So, life cannot separate itself from the addition, subtraction, multiplication and division. Whether a person lives joyfully and happily, it depends on his or her arithmetic level.

Life needs addition. A person who lives in the world will always be in pursuit of something significant; the addition of life makes the life richer and more colorful. A progressive society should encourage individuals with their own hands to increase the value and meaning of life so that the material world and the spiritual world are richer and more substantial. The principle of addition of life is to advocate the fair competition, in which whether in the material wealth or in the spiritual wealth, the winners should be encouraged. The additive life is a positive one.

Life needs subtraction. Life is the opposed unity. A sage said that life is like a wagon, its carrying capacity limited and the overload making life go to its opposite. Human life is limited, but the desire is unlimited. We have to learn to look at life and on gains and losses dialectically, and detract the heavy burden of life with subtraction. Otherwise, the burden is so heavy that life will be overwhelmed and things often go contrary to our wishes.

Life needs multiplication. The success or failure in life relates with the personal efforts, more relevant to the opportunities. A sage said that the road of life is long, but there are only a few steps at the junction. For life, struggle is, of course, important but it is also very crucial whether you can seize the opportunities. In this sense, at the critical moment, you will achieve the multiplication of life if you get hold of it.

Life needs division. Someone has written a well-known formula for happiness: degree of happiness = achieved goal value ÷ expected goal value, i. e., on the premise of the target fixed value, the higher the expected goal value, the lower the degree of happiness, and vice versa. "Contentment is happiness" that we usually talk about also includes such a meaning. As far as a lofty goal in life is concerned, to set up a recent small target is of actual significance and scientific factors, and this is the revelation that the division of life shows us.

人生的加减乘除

有一位作家曾这样说过：人生是一种自我经营的过程，要经营就要讲运算。所以，人生离不开加减乘除。一个人生活得是否快乐、幸福，取决于其算术水平的高低。

人生需要加法。人生在世，总要追求一些东西。人生的加法，使人生更加丰富多彩。一个进步的社会应该鼓励个人用自己的双手增加人生的价值和内涵，使人生物质世界和精神世界都更加富有和充实。加法人生的原则是提倡公平竞争，无论在物质财富上还是在精神财富上胜出者，都应给予鼓励。加法人生是一种积极的人生。

人生需要减法。人生是对立统一体。哲人说，人生如车，其载重量有限，超负荷运行促使人生走向其反面。人的生命有限，而欲望无限。我们要学会辩证地看待人生，看待得失，用减法减去人生过重的负担。否则，负担太重，人生不堪重负，往往事与愿违。

人生需要乘法。人生的成功与否，与个人努力有关，更与机遇有关。哲人说，人生的道路尽管漫长，但要紧处就那么几步。对人生来说，奋斗固然重要，但能否抓住机遇也十分关键。从这一意义上说，在关键时刻把握住人生，就实现了人生的乘法。

人生需要除法。曾有人写下一个著名的幸福公式：幸福程度 = 目标实现值 ÷ 目标期望值。也就是说，在目标实现值固定的前提下，目标期望值越高，幸福程度越低，反之亦然。我们平时所说的"知足者常乐"也包含这种意思。与树立人生远大目标来说，人生树立"近小"目标也有现实意义和科学因素，这就是人生除法对我们的启示。

The Jigsaw Puzzle of Life

When I was once asked the question like, "How do you rank love, cause, family and friends? Which one is the most important in your heart?" I would think of it very seriously, what would I give the first rank? Now, when I hear this kind of question, I will only feel it meaningless. No need to arrange the order of priority.

Some people put love in the first rank; when he lost his love, he found that love was not so important, but the cause was more important instead.

Some people put the cause in the first rank and the family in the last. But when he was at the peak of his career, he felt so lonely that he would rather use everything to exchange the time with their families.

For love, career, family, friends, ideal, aspiration, principle and dignity, each one is important, impossibly existing independently, so it is just self-deceptive to arrange them according to their order of importance.

Life is a jigsaw puzzle, so which one can you tell is the most important? Each one is important and none of them can lack. When you set up a 2,000-piece jigsaw puzzle, you found the last one was missing, and was that one the most important? No. That one was merely the biggest regret.

Does life have some regrets? As the time passes, it cannot make up. All of us have an incomplete jigsaw puzzle, but we can only try our best to put together a seemingly perfect jigsaw puzzle. Don't ask which one is the most important and the most important is to put together the jigsaw puzzle.

人生的拼图

以前有人问道："爱情、事业、家庭、朋友，你会怎样排列？哪一样在你心中最重要？"这一类问题时，我会很认真地想，我会把什么排在第一位。现在，再听到这一类问题，只觉得没意思，根本没必要去排列先后次序。

有人把爱情排在第一位。当他没有爱情时，他才发觉，原来爱情不是那么重要，事业更重要。

有人把事业排在第一位，把家庭排在最后。可是，当他在事业高峰时，他却觉得孤独，宁愿用一切换回与家人相处的时光。

爱情、事业、家庭、朋友、理想、抱负、原则、尊严，每一样都重要，不可能独立存在，把它们按重要程度排列起来，只是自欺欺人。

生命是一张拼图，你能说哪一块最重要吗？每一块都重要，都不能缺少。你砌好一张两千块的拼图，最后竟然发现缺了一块，那一块是最重要的吗？也不是。那一块只是最大的遗憾。

人生总有些遗憾吧？时日过去，也就无法弥补。我们都有一张不完整的拼图，但我们也只能尽量拼出一张看似完美的拼图。不要再问哪一块最重要，最重要的是你把图拼出来。

Life Also Has the Crossroad

In 1899, when Einstein studied at the Swiss Federal University of Technology in Zurich, his tutor was Minkevsky, a mathematician.

Once Einstein asked Minkevsky, "How can a person, like me, leave his distinct footprints on the road of life and make an outstanding contribution in the scientific field?" It was a "sophisticated" problem. Minkevsky said that he had to think about it better and then gave him an answer.

Three days later, Minkevsky told Einstein that the answer was coming! He pulled Einstein to walk towards a building site and straight set foot on the cement ground that the construction workers had just paved.

In the workers'scolding, Einstein was confused to ask Minkevsky, "Sir, don't you lead me astray?"

"Right, exactly!" Minkevsky said. "Have you seen it? Only the cement road surface can leave deep footprints. On those old road surfaces that have long solidified and on those places that have been passed by countless steps, you cannot tread out your footprints..."

Hearing this, Einstein thought long and nodded significantly.

Since then, a very strong sense of innovation and pioneering consciousness began dominating Einstein's thinking and action. He said, "I never memorize and reflect what dictionaries and manuals carry, for my brain only memorize and reflect those things that are not included in books." It was such a reason that Einstein left his deep sparkling footprints in the history of science.

人生也有歧路

1899 年，爱因斯坦在瑞士苏黎世联邦理工大学就读时，他的导师是数学家明可夫斯基。

有一次，爱因斯坦问明可夫斯基："一个人，比如我吧，究竟怎样才能在科学领域、在人生道路上，留下自己的闪光足迹、做出自己的杰出贡献呢？"这是一个"尖端"的问题，明可夫斯基说他要好好想一想再予以解答。

3 天后，明可夫斯基告诉爱因斯坦说答案来了！他拉起爱因斯坦就朝一处建筑工地走去，而且径直踏上了建筑工人们刚刚铺平的水泥地面。

在建筑工人们的呵斥声中，爱因斯坦被弄得一头雾水，不解地问明可夫斯基："老师，您这不是领我误入歧途吗？"

"对，正是这样！"明可夫斯基说。"看到了吧？只有尚未凝固的水泥路面，才能留下深深的脚印。那些凝固很久的老路面，那些被无数脚步走过的地方，你别想再踩出脚印来……"

听到这里，爱因斯坦沉思良久，意味深长地点了点头。

从此，一种非常强烈的创新和开拓意识，开始主导着爱因斯坦的思维和行动。他说："我从来不记忆和思考词典、手册里的东西，我的脑袋只用来记忆和思考那些还没载入书本的东西。"正因为此，爱因斯坦才在科学史册上留下了深深的、闪光的足迹。

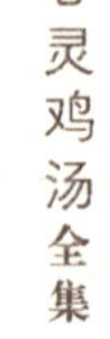

Position Your Life

Everyone has two natures. One wants us to advance and the other wants to pulls us back. The one that we cultivate and concentrate on decides what we are at the end. Both natures are trying to gain control. The will alone decides the issue. A man by one supreme effort of the will may change his whole career and even create miracles. You may be that man if you will, for will can find a way or make one.

You alone can decide when the turning point will come. He is the director of his life if he wills to be. What we are to do is the result of our training. We can be completely controlled by our will power.

Habit is a matter of acquirement. You hear people say, "He comes by this or that naturally, a chip off the old block," meaning that he is only doing what his parents did. This is quite often the case, but there's no reason for it, for a person can break a habit just the moment he masters the "I will." A man may have been a "good-for-nothing" all his life up to this very minute, but from this time on he begins to amount to something. Even old men have suddenly changed and accomplished wonders.

"I lost my opportunity," says one. That may be true, but by sheer force of will, we can find a way to bring us another opportunity. There is no truth saying that opportunity knocks at our door but once in a lifetime. The fact is, opportunity never seeks us; we must seek it. What usually turns out to be one man's opportunity was another man's loss. In this day one man's brain is matched against another's. It is often the quickness of brain action that determines the result.

Many people read good books, but say they do not get much good out of them. They don't realize that the knowledge of books can awaken their potentials; to stimulate them to use their will power. A sage said, "You can lead him to the fountain, but you can't make him drink."

定位你的人生

每个人都有两种天性。一种想让我们前进，另一种想拉我们后退。我们培养并聚精会神的那种天性常常决定我们最终会成为什么样的人。这两种天性都在设法得到控制权。只有意志决定这个问题。一个意志坚强、竭诚努力的人可以改变整个事业，甚至可以创造奇迹。只要你愿意，就可能成为那种人，因为意志能找到方法或创造方法。

只有你能决定转折点何时会来。只要愿意，他就可以成为生活的主人。我们要做什么,是看我们训练的结果,完全是由自己的意志力控制。

习惯是慢慢养成的一种东西。你常常听人们说:“他生来就是这样,活像他的父母。”这意味着他父母亲做什么他也会做什么。事情常常就是这样,但绝不是原因,因为一个人只要把握“我一定会行”,就能打破一种习惯。一个人也许一直到此刻都一无是处,但从这一刻起,他会开始有所作为。就是老年人也会突然发生改变,创造奇迹。

有人常常说:“我错失了良机。”那也许没错,但凭借绝对的毅力,我们可以找到给我们带来另一次机遇的方法。说机遇一辈子只敲我们的门一次,根本没有事实依据。其实,机遇根本不会寻找我们,我们必须寻找机遇。通常的结果是,一个人得到的机遇正是另一个人错失的良机。当今时代,一个人的大脑与另一个人的大脑不相上下,常常是反应迅速的大脑决定最后的结果。

尽管许多人曾看过好书,但又说自己并没有从中获得多少好处。他们没有意识到书里的知识能唤醒自己的潜能,激励他们运用自己的毅力。一位智者说过:“你可以把他领到泉水边,但你不能强迫他喝。”

The Punctuation of Life

I hope my life is a full stop, satisfactory and substantial.

Mother told me, "My child, life should be a comma, which always has the unfinished continual sound, so that it won't end and be full of hope." So when I failed, I was no longer willing to let the withered grass appease my wounds and refused to let the breeze soothe my memory. I will stand up on my own, yes, on my own; I will finish the text after the comma. Gradually, I know the true meaning of "comma".

Father told me, "My son, life should be a colon, which always enlightens us and makes us ponder." So I try to discover and innovate in life. I remember it is the soft light of the sun and the dancing of the fallen leaves that make me really feel the autumn succeeding the spring, so I have written down the most precious feelings with my heart behind the colon of life.

Grandpa told me, "My child, life should be a quotation mark, which quotes the fragment of the most heartfelt experience to hide it in the bottom of your heart and makes it the treasure of your memory and the encouragement of your progress." I can't help thinking of my first teacher: it was her who led me to the door of life and taught me how to behave myself. It was her who gave me spiritual comfort when I was sad and revived my courage when I failed. I quote this memory in the quotation mark and make it the jewel in the depths of my soul.

Grandma told me, "My child, life should be a string of long ellipsis. Faced with your honor and flowers, omit some. In this way, you can be indifferent to all fickleness and seek a more permanent sureness than life. Faced with the others' faults, omit some. In this way, you can smilingly accept the whole world with your mind." So I learn what composure is and what tolerance is.

Finally one day, my mother said to me, "My son, in fact, no one's life can be a perfect full stop. It is that 'gold can't be pure and man can't be perfect.' But it is admirable that you have been pursuing the full stop. This is not an aim but a process. However, what is important is this process."

I suddenly find I have grown up in seeking the "full stop". I have known life is a process. So I have come to learn how to cherish all I have experienced. What I have experienced is like an ebbed sea. Though no longer surging, it has still left the shell to the beach.

Though I don't get the full stop of life, I have had the most treasured experiences. After all, as

long as I have tried to pursue, I won't regret.

I'm sure I will become an erect exclamation point someday!

人生的标点

我希望我的人生是一个句号，圆满而充实。

母亲告诉我："我的孩子，人生应是一个逗号，总有未完的续音，这样才不会终结，才会充满希望。"于是，我失败时，再也不愿让衰草抚慰伤痕，拒绝让微风抚平记忆。我要自己站起来，是的，要靠自己，我要去写完逗号后面的文章。渐渐地，我明白懂得了"逗号"的真正含义。

父亲告诉我："我的儿子，人生应是一个冒号，总是给人启迪，让人深思。"于是，我在生活中尽力发现、创新。我记得那是太阳的柔光、落叶的飞舞，让我真切感受到春去秋来，因此我便用心灵在人生的冒号后面写下了最珍贵的感受。

爷爷告诉我："我的孩子，人生应是一个引号，把经历中最刻骨铭心的片断引起来，藏在心底，让它成为记忆的珍宝和进步的鼓励。"我不禁想起了自己的启蒙老师：是她引导我走向了人生之门，教会了我怎样做人。是她在我悲伤时给了我心灵的安慰，在我失败时让我恢复了勇气。我把这段记忆放在了引号里，使它成为我心灵深处的宝石。

奶奶告诉我："我的孩子，人生应是一串长长的省略号。面对荣誉和鲜花，省略一些。这样，你才能淡泊一切浮躁，寻找比生命更持久的一种信心。面对别人的过错，省略一些。这样，你才能面带微笑以自己的心胸去接纳整个世界。"于是，我学会了什么是沉着、什么是宽容。

终于，有一天，母亲对我说："我的儿子，其实，谁的人生也不能成为一个完美的句号。正是'金无足赤，人无完人'。但值得称赞的是，你一直都在追求句号。这不是目的，而是过程。然而，重要的就是这个过程。"

我突然发现，我在寻求"句号"时已经长大了。我明白了人生就是一个过程。所以，我已经学会了如何去珍爱我曾经历过的一切。我曾经历的一切就像退潮的大海。尽管不再汹涌澎湃，但它仍然给海滩留下了贝壳。

尽管没有得到人生的句号，但我已经拥有了最珍贵的经历。毕竟，只要我曾努力追求过，就不会后悔。

我相信我终有一天会成为一个挺立的感叹号！

Life Is a Symphony

The symphony is a symbol for life, especially in a community. The blend of each instrument gives the symphony its unique sound. This is also true in life and the world we live. Individuals bring in their own influence. A symphony orchestra is composed of a variety of brass, woodwind, percussion and

stringed instruments. Each of these instruments has its own unique sound but when played together they complement each other. Like a symphony and its instruments, the world is composed of many races and cultures. They are uniquely different but can have an influence on each other even if it is not intentional.

Individuality is an important part of the symphony. Each player has his or her own part to perform. These parts can be played on their own but do not have the same effect as when they are combined with the other parts of the orchestra. They blend into a harmonious piece of music. In other words, you can hear what each person has to contribute and how each performer works together. In life, each person has a talent that they are particularly good at. When they work together, it accentuates their talent.

Carnegie said that individuality was important, but should not be taken so far that it separates everyone from each other. Each person should contribute their own ideas that better help the community as a whole.

Another similarity between life and the symphony is that a performer may not have the melody but will accompany someone who does. In life, everybody has their moments of glory although they may go unnoticed like the accompanist. This does not mean, however, that they are any less important than anyone else. The melody doesn't stay with one instrument for the whole song but moves throughout the orchestra. As in life, everyone eventually has their moment to shine and their chance to be in the spotlight.

When preparing for a concert, the musicians are reminded by their conductor to stagger their breathing. They can, of course, breathe when they need to but they have to try not to breathe at the same time as the person sitting next to them. If everyone breathed at the same time, there would be a noticeable moment of silence in the song. This is yet another example that can be applied to life.

The orchestra continues to play. It moves together as a group yet separately. Each musician is an active member of the symphony. In life, we contribute what we have to offer from day to day as active members in our community. The orchestra plays their last note and the song is over. There is a moment of silence that is broken by the thunderous applause of the audience.

人生是一曲交响乐

交响乐是生命的象征，尤其是在团队中。各种乐器交织在一起，使交响乐发出独一无二的声音。我们的人生和居住的世界也是这样。每个人都会带来各自的影响。交响乐队由多种不同的铜乐器、木管乐器、打击乐器和弦乐器组成。每种乐器都有其独特的声音，但一起演奏时，它们总是互补。像交响乐和它的乐器一样，世界也是由许多种族和文化组成。尽管它们各不相同，但能在不经意间相互影响。

每个人都是交响乐中重要的一部分。每个演奏者都有其演奏的片段。尽管这些片段都可以独自演奏，但和交响乐团中的其他部分合奏时，它们会产生不同的效果，合成为一首和谐曲。换句话说，你可以听到每个人都得独奏，也可以听到每个演奏者怎样一起合奏。在生活中，每个人都拥有各自的特长。他们一起合作时，各自的天赋就会更加突出。

卡耐基认为个性非常重要，但不应该和他人偏离太远。每个人都应该贡献自己的观点，这更有助于整个社会。

生活和交响乐的另一个相似点是，演奏者不可能总是演奏出优美的旋律，但可以为演奏出优美旋律的人伴奏。在人生中，每个人都有其辉煌的时刻，尽管他们也许会像伴奏者那样不引人注目。然而，这并不意味着他们没有别人重要。整首歌曲的优美旋律不会停留在一种乐器上，而是要通过整个乐队演奏。人生也是这样，每个人最终都会有发光的时刻，也会有聚焦的机会。

准备一场音乐会时，乐队指挥会提醒音乐家们交错呼吸。需要呼吸时，他们当然可以呼吸，但必须尽量不要和邻座的人同时呼吸。如果大家同时呼吸，音乐中就会出现明显寂静的时刻。这是实用于人生的另一个例子。

乐队继续演奏。他们既是一个团体，又是分离的个体。每个音乐家都是交响乐中发挥作用的一名成员。在生活中，作为社会中发挥作用的成员，我们每天都贡献自己的一切。乐队演奏完最后的音符，乐曲结束，观众们雷鸣般的掌声便会打破片刻的宁静。

Sense Life

I've learned that sometimes all a person needs a hand to hold and a heart to understand.

I've learned that the Lord didn't do it all in one day. What makes me think I can?

I've learned that love, not time, heals all wounds.

I've learned that everyone you meet deserves to be greeted with a smile.

I've learned that there's nothing sweeter than sleeping with your babies and feeling their breath on you cheeks.

I've learned that no one is perfect until you fall in love with them.

I've learned that opportunities are never lost; someone will take the ones you miss.

I've learned that when you harbor bitterness, happiness will dock elsewhere.

I've learned that I wish I could have told my mom that I love her one more time before she passed away.

I've learned that one should keep his words both soft and tender because tomorrow he may have to eat them.

I've learned that a smile is an inexpensive way to improve your looks.

I've learned that I can't choose how I feel, but I can choose what I do about it.

I've learned that everyone wants to stand on top of the mountain, but all the happiness and growth occurs while you're climbing it.

I've learned that it is best to give advice in only two circumstances: when it is requested and when it is a life-threatening situation.

I've learned that the less time I have to work with, the more things I get done.

感悟人生

我已经明白了，有时一个人想要的只是一只可握的手和一颗明白的心。

我已经明白了，上帝一天做不完所有的事情。我又怎么可能做到呢？

我已经明白了，治愈一切创伤的是爱，而不是时间。

我已经明白了，你相遇的每一个人都值得你笑脸相迎。

我已经明白了，没有比和宝宝睡在一起并感受到他们的呼吸吹在你脸上更甜蜜的事情。

我已经明白了,只有爱一个人时才会认为他/她十全十美。

我已经明白了,机会从来不会失去,有人会抓住你错过的机会。

我已经明白了,当你心怀痛苦时,幸福就会停靠到别的地方。

我已经明白了,我本应在妈妈去世前再对她说一次我爱她。

我已经明白了,一个人应该信守诺言,因为明天他可能必须自食其言。

我已经明白了,微笑是改善容貌的一种便宜的方式。

我已经明白了,我无法选择自己的感觉,但我可以选择做事的方式。

我已经明白了,每个人都想站在山顶,但所有的幸福和成长都发生在爬山的过程中。

我已经明白了,最好只在两种情况下提出忠告:别人要求时和生命攸关时。

我已经明白了,工作时间越少,工作效率越高。

The Splashes of Life

My grandfather took me to a fish pound on the farm when I was about seven, and he told me to throw a stone into the water and watch the circles created by the stone. Then he asked me to think of myself as that stone.

"You may create lots of splashes in your life, but the waves that come from those splashes will disturb the peace of all your fellow creatures," he said.

"Remember that you are responsible for what you put in your circle and that circle will also touch many other circles.

"You will need to live in a way that allows the good that comes from your circle to send the peace of that goodness to others. The splash that comes from anger or jealousy will send those feelings to other circles. You are responsible for both."

That was the first time I realized that each person creates the inner peace or discord that flows out into the world. We can't create world peace if we are riddled with inner conflict, hatred, doubt, or anger.

We radiate the feelings and thoughts that we hold inside, whether we speak them or not. Whatever is splashing around inside of us is spilling out into the world, creating beauty or discord with all other circles of life.

人生的波纹

我大约7岁那年,祖父带我来到农场的一个鱼塘边。他让我把一个石子扔进水里,吩咐我观察石子激起的一圈圈波纹,然后让我把自己当成那个石子。

他说:"你在人生中也许能激起许多波纹,但你激起的波纹会打破别人的平静。

"记住,你要对自己激起的波纹负责,你的波纹会触及其他许多的波纹。

"你需要让自己波纹中善的一面把平和传给他人。来自愤怒或嫉妒的波纹会把这些情绪传给其他的波纹,你要对双方负责。"

这是我第一次认识到,每个人内心的平静或不和,都会流向世界。如果我们内心充

满了冲突、仇恨、疑虑或愤怒,就无法创造世界和平。

无论说不说,我们都会传播内心的感觉和想法。无论我们内心激起的是什么波纹,它们都会流向世界,创造美或与人生的其他所有波纹产生不和。

Life Is Like a Bird

Goethe said,"As long as you trust yourself,you will know how to live."I talk with many people who don't trust one thing or another in life. Ultimately,what they don't trust is themselves and their ability to make right choices. The result is dissatisfaction and a feeling of restriction with jobs,relationships or life. As birds are locked into their cages,we cage ourselves.

When we start our journey of life,people who care for us and have our total trust repeat their limiting beliefs as facts. There comes a time for many of us,when we realize we were told beliefs,not truths. That's the moment we can either get struck in the past or choose to rewrite our life scripts. It's the moment we can decide to take total possession of our lives.

Our limiting beliefs are our self-imposed cages. Once we decide to trust ourselves,we do know how to live because we learn to ask ourselves the right questions. We also begin to trust right timing rather than attempt to force it. We try to go beyond our limiting beliefs, whatever they are and however long it takes,so we can expand into who we came here to be.

If there's anything about your life you desire to experience differently,first look at your level of self-trust to make the best choices on your behalf. Self-trust is where true security lives. Decide to possess your life. You just might find out that not only can you fly,but you can soar.

人生如飞鸟

歌德说过:“只要相信自己,你就会懂得如何生活。”

我和许多在生活中这也不信那也不信的人聊天。从根本上说,他们不相信的是自己和自己做出正确选择的能力。其结果是不满和对工作、人际关系或生活的束缚感。就像小鸟被锁进笼子里那样,我们把自己关进了笼子里。

我们开始人生之旅时,关心我们并得到我们完全信任的人们,反复把他们限制性的信条当成了事实。我们中的许多人终有一天会意识到,他们告诉我们的是信条,而不是真理。那是我们要么陷入过去的泥沼,要么选择重写人生篇章的时刻。那是我们能决定去完全拥有自己生命的时刻。

我们限制性的信条就像我们自愿接受的笼子。一旦决心相信自己,我们就知道该如何生活,因为我们学会了亲自问正确的问题。我们也开始相信正确的时机,而不是设法强求。我们努力超越自己限制性的信条,无论它们是什么信条,无论要花多长时间,这样我们才能发展成原来的自己。

如果你想以不同方式去体验生活中的一切,首先要看看你自信的水平,然后再做出对你最好的选择。自信是真正的安全所在。决定拥有自己的生活。你也许会发现自己不仅能飞,而且能高高飞翔。

感谢生命的恩赐

Survive as Camels

Camels certainly like eating green grass, not dry grass. But strangely camels always keep looking for dry grass until their stomachs are filled up.

A classmate of mine whose home is on the edge of Turpan Basin in Xinjiang told me his home has two camels; he said you couldn't imagine a camel's appetite, for it can slowly swallow dozens of kilograms of hay.

I asked the classmate why camels eat grass, not hay. He said the camel is a kind of animal with a very strong sense of suffering, fearing its master letting it travel through the desert the next day, and the hay in its stomach is more hunger-resistant than green grass.

The camel has the best endurance whereas the southerners can only see a camel's outstanding performance, but few understand its preparation for this.

My classmate said the camel has the human conscience while an old camel would be aware of its master's mind. Before the journey, it would chew the hay all the night, drink enough water and wait for the first light of morning.

Life, like a camel traveling through the desert, needs the adequate accumulation, but not everyone can understand it.

像骆驼那样生存

骆驼肯定喜欢吃青草,而不是枯涩的干草。但令人奇怪的是,骆驼总是不断寻找干草,直到把它的胃装满。

家住新疆吐鲁番盆地边缘的一位同学就告诉我,他家有两头骆驼。他说你根本无法想象骆驼的胃口,它可以慢慢咽下几十公斤干草。

我问同学为什么骆驼不吃青草而吃干草。他说骆驼是一种忧患心理很强的动物,它害怕主人第二天就让它穿过沙漠,而胃中的干草要比青草更耐饥。

骆驼的耐力是一流的,南方人只看到骆驼的出色表现,却很少了解骆驼为此所做的准备。

同学说,骆驼是通人性的,老骆驼会觉察到主人的意思。在跋涉前,它一夜都会咀嚼干草,饮足水,然后等着晨光出现。

人生像骆驼穿越沙漠那样,需要足够的积累,但并不是每个人都能领会。

The Clock of Life

I often don't know what to do. The childhood dream was moving farther and farther from me, the more hardships and burdens always made me at a loss.

The story of three clocks always enlightened me at this moment.

A newly-assembled small clock was put between the two old clocks, which were ticking every minute and second.

One of the old clocks said to the small clock, "Come, you should also work. But I'm a bit worried you won't stand anymore after you go for 32 million times."

"Gosh! 32 million times!" The small clock was surprised. "Do I have to do such a big thing? Impossible. Impossible."

Another old clock said, "Don't listen to his nonsense. Don't be afraid as long as you tick every second."

"How can there be such a simple thing in the world," the small clock half believed. "If so, I'll try it."

The small clock ticked easily every second. Unconsciously, when one year passed, it had ticked for 32 million times.

Everybody hope his or her wishes to come true, but success seems remote in the horizon. So languidness and lack of self-confidence make us doubt our ability and abandon our efforts. In fact, we don't have to think of things to come. As long as we think what we should do today or tomorrow and then try our best to finish it, just as the clock ticks every second, the joy of success will slowly permeate our lives.

生命的时钟

我常常不知道自己该做些什么。幼时的梦想越走越远，风霜的磨砺和肩上的重担时时让我不知所措。

有一个3只钟的故事总在此时给我启迪。

一只新组装好的小钟放在了两只旧钟当中。两只旧钟"滴答"、"滴答"一分一秒地走着。

其中一只旧钟对小钟说："来吧，你也该工作了。可我有点担心，你走完3200万次后，恐怕就吃不消了。"

"天哪！3200万次！"小钟吃惊不已。"要我做这么大的事儿？办不到，办不到！"

另一只旧钟说："别听他胡说八道。不用害怕，你只要每秒'滴答'摆一下就行了。"

"天下哪有这样简单的事儿。"小钟将信将疑。"如果这样，那我就试试吧。"

小钟很轻松地每秒钟"滴答"摆一下。不知不觉中，一年过去了，它摆了3200万次。

每个人都希望梦想成真，成功却似乎远在天边、遥不可及，倦怠和不自信让我们怀疑自己的能力，放弃努力。其实，我们不必想以后的事情，只要想着今天要做些什么，明天该做些什么，然后努力去完成，就像那只钟一样，每秒"滴答"摆一下，成功的喜悦就会慢慢地浸润我们的生命。

You Have Only One Life

The best kind of friend is the kind you can sit on a porch swing with, never say a word, and then walk away feeling like it was the best conversation you've ever had.

Don't go for looks; they can deceive. Don't go for wealth; even that fades away. Go for someone

who makes you smile because it takes only a smile to make a dark day seem bright.

Dream what you want to dream; go where you want to go; be what you want to be, because you have only one life and one chance to do all the things you want to do.

A careless word may kindle strife; a cruel word may wreck a life; a timely word may level stress; a loving word may heal and bless.

A sad thing in life is when you meet someone who means a lot to you, only to find out in the end that it was never meant to be and you just have to let go.

Always put yourself in the other's shoes. If you feel that it hurts you, it probably hurts the person, too.

The happiest of people don't necessarily have the best of everything they just make the most of everything that comes along their way.

When you were born, you were crying and everyone around you was smiling. Live your life so that when you die, you're the one smiling and everyone around you is crying.

To see a world in a grain of sand.
And a heaven in a wild flower.
Hold infinity in the palm of your hand.
And eternity in an hour.
Let's write that letter we thought of writing "one of these days".
Don't cry because it is over;
Smile, because it happened.
And forever has no end.

你只有一次生命

最好的朋友就是那种你可以促膝而坐，默默无语，分别时却感到这是你曾有过的最好的交谈。

不要追求容貌，它们可能蒙骗人。不要追求财富，那会渐渐消散。追求能让你微笑的人吧，因为仅仅一个微笑就能使黑天变得光明。

做你想做的梦，到你想去的地方，做你想做的人吧，因为你只有一次生命、一个机会去做你想做的一切。

一句粗心的话可能引发冲突，一句无情的话可能毁灭生命，一句适时的话可能消除压力，一句关爱的话可能愈合伤口、带来祝福。

生命中的一件伤心事是你遇到了一个对你至关重要的人，最终却发现有缘无份，你不得不放手。

总是要设身处地为别人着想。如果你感到伤害了你，也可能会伤害别人。

最幸福的人不见得胜过一切，他们只是充分利用顺其自然的一切。

你出生时，哇哇大哭，你身边的每个人都在微笑。好好生活吧，这样你去世时，你就能一人含笑，身边的每个人都号啕大哭。

一沙一世界，
一花一天堂。
把握掌中无限。
把握瞬间永恒。
我们原想着"有一天"去写的那封信，现在就写。

不要因为结束而哭泣。
要因为发生而微笑。
而且永无止境。

A Promise of Flowers

Early in the spring, about a month before my grandpa's stroke, I began walking for an hour every afternoon. Some days I would walk four blocks south to see Grandma and Grandpa. At eighty-six, Grandpa was still quite a gardener, so I always watched for his earliest blooms and each new wave of spring flowers.

I was especially interested in flowers that year because I was planning to landscape my own yard and I was eager to get Grandpa's advice. I thought I knew pretty much what I wanted—a yard full of bushes and plants that would bloom from May till November.

It was right after the first rush of purple violets in the lawns and the sudden blaze of forsythia that spring that Grandpa had a stroke. It left him without speech and with no movement on his left side. The whole family gathered around Grandpa. We all spent many hours by his side. Some days his eyes were eloquent—laughing at our reported mishaps, listening alertly, revealing painful awareness of his inability to care for himself. There were days, too, when he slept most of the time, overcome with the weight of his approaching death.

As the months passed, I watched the growing earth with Grandpa's eyes. Each time I was with him, I gave him a garden report. He listened, gripping my hand. But he could not answer my questions. The new flowers would blaze, peak, fade, and die before I knew their names.

Grandpa's illness held him through the spring and on, week by week, through summer. I began spending hours at the local nursery, studying and choosing seeds and plants. It gave me special joy to buy plants I had seen in Grandpa's garden and give them humble starts in my own garden. I discovered Sweet William, which I had admired for years in Grandpa's garden without knowing its name. And I planted it in his honor.

As I waited and watched in the garden and by Grandpa's side, some quiet truths emerged. I realized that Grandpa loved flowers that were always in bloom; he kept a full bed of roses in his garden. But I noticed that Grandpa left plenty of room for the brief highlights. Not every nook of his garden was constantly in bloom. There was always a treasured surprise tucked somewhere.

I came to see, too, that Grandpa's garden mirrored his life. He was a hard worker who understood the law of the harvest. But along with his hard work, Grandpa knew how to enjoy each season, each change.

In July, Grandpa worsened. One hot afternoon arrived when no one else was at his bedside. He was glad to have me there, and reached out his hand to pull me close.

I told Grandpa what I had learned—that few flowers last from April to November. Some of the most beautiful bloom for only a month at most. To really enjoy a garden, you have to plant corners and drifts and rows of flowers that will bloom and grace the garden, each in its own season.

His eyes listened to every word: "If I want a garden like yours, Grandpa, I'm going to have to work." His grin laughed at me.

"Grandpa, in your life right now the chrysanthemums are in bloom. Chrysanthemums and roses." Tears clouded both our eyes. Neither of us feared this last flower of fall, but the wait for spring seems longest in November. We knew how much we would miss each other.

Sitting there, I suddenly felt that the best gift I could give Grandpa would be to give voice to the testimony inside both of us. He had never spoken of his testimony to me, but it was such a part of his

life that I had never questioned.

"Grandpa," I began, and his grip tightened as if he knew what I was going to say, "I want you to know that I have a testimony. I know the Savior lives. I know our Father in Heaven loves you."

Grandpa and I wept together.

It was the end of August when Grandpa died, the end of summer. As we were choosing flowers from the florist for Grandpa's funeral, I slipped away to Grandpa's garden and walked with my memories of columbine and Sweet William. Only the tall lavender and white phlox were in bloom now, and some baby's breath in another corner.

On impulse, I cut the prettiest strands of phlox and baby's breath and made one more arrangement for the funeral. When they saw it, friends and family all smiled to see Grandpa's flowers there. We all felt how much Grandpa would have liked that.

The October after Grandpa's death, I planted tulip and daffodil bulbs, snowdrops, crocuses, and bluebells. Each bulb was a comfort to me, a love sent to Grandpa, a promise of spring.

鲜花的承诺

初春时节，大约在爷爷中风前的一个月，我开始每天下午散步一小时。有一段日子，我常常向南步行4个街区，去看望爷爷奶奶。86岁的爷爷仍是个了不起的花匠，所以我总是留意他那些最早盛开的鲜花和春天新开的每一片花海。

因为那年我打算美化自己的院子，所以对花特别感兴趣，渴望听到爷爷的建议。我以为自己非常清楚需要什么——满院子花草树丛，从5月一直开到11月。

爷爷就是那年春天在草坪里第一丛紫罗兰出现和连翘突然盛开后中风的。他无法言语，身体左半侧也无法动弹。家里所有人都聚到了爷爷身边。我们都花了很多时间守在他身边。有几天，他的眼睛炯炯有神——他一边笑我们报告的不幸，一边留意倾听，露出了他生活不能自理的痛苦。有一段日子，他大多数时间都处于睡眠状态，死亡随时都会向他逼近。

几个月过去了，我像爷爷一样望着地上的东西渐渐长大。我每次和他在一起，都要向他汇报花园的情况。他一边听，一边紧握着我的手。可是，他无法回答我的问题。很多新的花朵常常绽放、憔悴、枯萎，还没等我知道它们的名字就死去了。

从春天开始，爷爷周复一周疾病缠身，一直持续到夏天。我开始泡在当地的苗圃，研究、选种和栽培。我买了一些曾在爷爷的花园里见过的幼苗，恭恭敬敬种在自己的花园里，这让我感到特别开心。我在爷爷的花园里发现了自己喜欢多年的美洲石竹，以前一直不知道它的名字。而且我以爷爷的名义栽下了它。

我待在花园、守在爷爷身边时，一些真理悄悄涌现出来。我知道爷爷爱那些怒放的鲜花；他在花园里种了满满一苗圃的玫瑰。可是，我注意到爷爷留了很多空当，让光线暂时照进来。他的花园并不是每个角落都经常鲜花怒放。总有某个珍藏的惊喜躲在某个地方。

我最终也明白爷爷的花园是他一生的写照。他是一个勤劳的人，明白收获的规律。但说起辛勤劳动，爷爷知道如何享受每一个季节、每一种变化。

7月，爷爷病情恶化。一个炎热的下午，其他人都不在他身边。有我在那里，他很高兴，就伸出一只手将我拉近。

我把自己学到的告诉了爷爷：能从4月开到11月的花寥寥无几。大部分花最多只开一个月。为了真正欣赏花园，你必须在各个角落都种上花，美化花园，一丛丛一行行，鲜花开放，四季如春。

他用目光听着我的每一个字："爷爷，如果想要一个像你的一样的花园，我必须得去工作。"他咧开嘴对我笑了笑。

"爷爷，在您的人生中，现在菊花正在开放。菊花和玫瑰花。"泪水模糊了我们的眼睛。我们俩都不害怕秋天的最后一朵花，但在11月等待春天似乎太长，我们都知道我们会多么想念对方。

我坐在那里，突然感到我能给爷爷的最好礼物就是说出我们内心的箴言。他从来没有对我说过他的箴言，但我从来没有怀疑过的就是他人生中的这一部分。

"爷爷，"我开口说道，他嘴唇紧闭，好像知道我要说什么，"我想要你知道我有一条箴言。我知道救世主存在。我知道我们的天父爱你。"

我和爷爷都泪流满面。

8月底、夏末之际，爷爷撒手而去。当大家都在花店为爷爷的葬礼选花时，我悄然离去，来到爷爷的花园。我一边走，一边回忆着那些耧斗菜和美洲石竹。现在只有高高的熏衣草和白色夹竹桃在开花，另一个角落还有一些水香花菜。

我一时冲动，剪下了最漂亮的几束夹竹桃和水香花菜，又给爷爷的葬礼装点了一番。看到这些花，亲友们都露出了微笑。我们都知道爷爷一定会多么喜欢。

爷爷去世后的10月，我种了一些郁金香、水仙花、雪花莲、藏红花和蓝铃花。对我来说，每一棵花根都是一种安慰，都是送给爷爷的一份爱，都是春天的一份承诺。

The Tree of Life Also Has Fallen Leaves

One day in October, some friends went to get together in a small bar. After they drank some beer, a friend's face turned red. Looking at the bleak autumn scenery out of the window, he couldn't help sighing, "Every year today, I always mark it because 10 years ago today was the day the tree of my life began to have fallen leaves."

Ten years before, he had just graduated from college and stepped into the society. He was ambitious to go into business, expecting to become a rich man overnight. However, against all his expectations, he not only became a rich man, but also fell into debt and his girlfriend who had made an oath of eternal love parted with him.

He felt the autumn bone-chilling, the tree of life having no green leaves. He lay prone on the track, wanted to turn into the white cloud flying in the sky and would be carefree since then. However, when the distant rumble of the train came with the rolling rhythm of life, he suddenly heard a fervent call of life—the tree of life also had fallen leaves and would regerminate. Life shouldn't be too fragile to stand the frost. He rapidly got to his feet, again got into business, finally made it and became a well-known man in the whole city.

Life should go through the seasons of being. When the tree of a person's life has fallen leaves, he has to admonish himself: what he lost is yesterday while it will be soon green. It is good at bearing the heaviness as it is good at accepting the success.

生命之树也有落叶

10月里的一个日子，几个朋友到一家小酒吧聚会。几杯啤酒下肚，一个人的脸开始泛红。望着窗外秋日萧萧的景色，他不禁感慨："每年的今天，我都要纪念一下，因为10年前的今天也是我的生命之树开始有落叶的日子。"

10年前，他刚走出大学校门，迈进了社会。他雄心勃勃，匆匆下海，希望自己在一夜之间成为富翁。然而，事与愿违，他不但"富翁"没做成，反而欠了一身债，与他海誓山盟的女友也和他分道扬镳。

他感到秋凉刺骨，生命之树已经没有了绿叶。他趴到铁轨上，想化作天上飘浮的白云，从此无忧无虑。然而，当远处传来火车隆隆滚动的生命节奏时，他突然听到了生命热切的呼唤——生命之树也有了落叶，还会重新萌发。人生本不该这样脆弱，不该这样经不起霜打。他迅速爬起来，重又下海，终于获得了成功，成了全城闻名的人物。

人生是要走过生命四季的。当一个人的生命之树有了落叶时，要告诫自己：失去的只是昨天，绿意不再遥远。如此善于承受沉重，就像善于接受成功一样。

The Addition and Subtraction of Life

A new year begins. Some people say, "We've lost one year." Some people say, "We've gained one year." This is the addition and subtraction of life.

Some people use the thinking of subtraction, so it will be less when he subtract, making life crisis-ridden and filled with stress:

The 20-year-old people lost childhood;
The 30-year-old people lost romance;
The 40-year-old people lost youth;
The 50-year-old people lost illusion;
The 60-year-old people lost health.

Some people use the thinking of addition, making life full of vitality and joy:

The 20-year-old people are young;
The 30-year-old people are talented;
The 40-year-old people are mature;
The 50-year-old people are experienced;
The 60-year-old people are relaxed.

In the course of life, we have to use "subtraction." Man has only one life, so at the end and the beginning of a year, we have to challenge ourselves to count what we have lost and what we have gained, and to count "harvest" more than "payout" or vice versa.

In the course of life, we have to use "addition." Because life can't be presumed, we have known the innocence in childhood and the recklessness in youth, accumulated the experience of life and come to see how to be master of our own destiny.

"Subtraction" brings us the pressure, making us understand the fleeting of life and the mercilessness of years. We look around ourselves and find how many outstanding people have gone ahead, so can't we catch up with them?

"Addition" brings us hope, making us add the experience and accumulate the wealth. The Sage of Time is fair to everyone, even if you went through countless difficulties and setbacks, which were the accumulation of experience. This accumulation will make us more intelligent and more sensible. With this accumulation, in the New Year, we will be more vigorous, steadier and more self-confident.

生命的加减法

新的一年开始了。有人说:"我们又少了一年。"有人说:"我们又多了一年。"这就是生命的加减法。

有人用的是减法思维,所以越减越少,使人生充满危机,充满压力:

20 岁的人失去童年;

30 岁的人失去浪漫;

40 岁的人失去青春;

50 岁的人失去幻想;

60 岁的人失去健康。

有人用的是加法思维,使人生充满生机,充满快乐:

20 岁的人拥有青春;

30 岁的人拥有才干;

40 岁的人拥有成熟;

50 岁的人拥有经验;

60 岁的人拥有轻松。

在生命的进程中,我们不能不用"减法"。人的生命只有一次,我们在岁末年初时,不能不鞭策自己,算一算自己失去了什么,得到了什么,是"收获"大于"支出",还是"支出"大于"收获"。

在生命的进程中,我们不能不用"加法"。因为人生不能假设,我们知道了儿时的天真,知道了年轻时的莽撞,积累了人生经验,知道了如何把握自己。

"减法"给我们带来了压力,使我们明白了人生的苦短、岁月的无情。我们看看周围,有多少佼佼者已经走到了前面,我们能不奋起直追?

"加法"给我们带来了希望,使我们增添了阅历,积累了财富。时光老人对每个人都是公平的,哪怕你历尽坎坷,遭遇挫折,也都是一种经历的积累。这种积累使我们更加聪明、更加理智。有了这种积累,新的一年里,我们的步伐就会更矫健,更加沉稳,更加自信。

Life Is the Cookie

One of my patients, a successful businessman, tells me that before his cancer he would become depressed unless things went a certain way. For him, happiness was "having the cookie." If you had the cookie, things were good. If you didn't have the cookie, life wasn't worth a damn. Unluckily, the cookie kept changing. Sometimes it was money, sometimes power, sometimes sex. At other times, it was the new car, the biggest contract, the most prestigious address. A year and a half after his diagnosis of prostate cancer he sits shaking his head ruefully. "It's like I stopped learning how to live after I was a kid. When I give my son a cookie, he is happy. If I take the cookie away or it breaks, he is unhappy. But he is two and a half and I am forty-three. It's taken me this long to understand that the cookie will never make me happy for long. The minute you have the cookie it starts to crumble or you start to worry about it crumbling or about someone trying to take it away from you. You know, you have to give up a lot of things to take care of the cookie, to keep it from crumbling and be sure that no one takes it away from you. You may not even get a chance to eat it because you are so busy just trying not to lose it. Having the cookie is not what life is about."

My patient laughs and says cancer has changed him. For the first time he is happy whether his business is doing well or not, whether he wins or loses at golf. "Two years ago, cancer asked me, 'What is important? What is really important?' Well, life is important. Life. Life any way you can have it, life with the cookie, life without the cookie. Happiness does not have anything to do with the cookie; it has to do with being alive. But who can make the time go back?" He pauses thoughtfully. "I guess life is the cookie."

生命就是小甜饼

我的一个病人是一名成功商人，他告诉我说，他患癌症前，如果事情没有按照某种方式发展，他就会情绪低落。对他来说，幸福就是“拥有小甜饼”。如果你拥有小甜饼，事情就一帆风顺。如果你没有小甜饼，生活就一文不值。不幸的是，小甜饼总是不断变化，有时是金钱，有时是权力，有时是性。在其他时候，它则是新车、数额最大的合同、享有声望的演讲。诊断出患有前列腺癌一年半后，他坐在那里，悲伤地摇了摇头。“长大后，我好像不去学如何生活了。当我送给儿子一块小甜饼时，他就开心。如果我拿走小甜饼或小甜饼破碎，他就不开心。但他才两岁半，我已经43岁了。我花了这么长时间才明白，小甜饼并不能使我长久幸福。你一拥有小甜饼，它就开始破碎，或者你就开始担心它会破碎，要么担心别人会从你手里拿走。你知道，你不得不放弃很多东西为我的是看护好小甜饼，防止它破碎，并确保别人不会从你手里拿走。因为你忙着尽力不让失去它，所以说不定没有机会去吃它。拥有小甜饼并不是生活的全部。”

我的病人笑着说癌症已经改变了他。无论他的生意是否一帆风顺，无论他在打高尔夫时是输是赢，他第一次感到幸福。“两年前，癌症问我：‘什么重要？什么才真正重要？’对，生命重要。生命。生命，无论你拥有什么样的生命，无论有没有小甜饼，幸福和小甜饼没有任何关系，而是和活着有关。可谁又能让时间倒回去呢？”他若有所思地停顿了一下，“我想生命就是小甜饼。”

The Best Nourishment of Life

A little boy almost thought of himself as most unfortunate child in the world because poliomyelitis made his leg lame and his teeth uneven and protrudent. He seldom played with his classmates; and when the teacher asked him to answer questions, he always lowered his head without a word.

One spring, the boy's father asked for some saplings from the neighbor. He wanted to plant them in front of the house. He told his children to plant one sapling each person. The father said the children, "Whose seedling grows best, I'll buy him or her a favorite gift." The boy's also wanted to get his father's gift. But seeing his brothers and sisters carry water to water the trees bouncily, anyhow, I hit upon an idea: he hoped the tree he planted would die soon. So after watering it once or twice, I never attended to it.

A few days later, when the little boy went to see his tree again, he was surprised to find it not only didn't wilt, but also grew some fresh leaves, and compared with the tree of his brothers and sisters, his appeared greener and more vital. His father kept his promise, bought the little boy one of his favorite gifts and said from the tree he planted, he would surely become an outstanding botanist when he grew up.

Since then, the little boy slowly became optimistic. One night, the little boy lay on the bed but couldn't sleep. Looking at the bright moonlight outside the window, he suddenly recalled what the biology teacher once said, plants generally grow at night. Why not go to see his tree? When he came to the courtyard on tiptoe, he found his father was splashing something under his tree with a ladle. All of a sudden, he understood: his father had been secretly fertilizing his small tree! He returned to his room, tears running without restraint...

Decades passed. The little boy didn't become a botanist, but he was elected President of the United States. His name was Franklin Roosevelt.

Love is the best nourishment of life; even if it is just one ladleful of clear water, it can make the tree of life thrive.

生命中最好的养料

一个小男孩几乎认为自己是世界上最不幸的孩子，因为患脊髓灰质炎而留下了瘸腿和参差突出的牙齿。他很少跟同学们玩耍；老师叫他回答问题时，他也总是低着头一言不发。

一年春天，小男孩的父亲从邻居家讨了些树苗，他想把它们栽在房前。他叫他的孩子们每人栽一棵。父亲对孩子们说："谁栽的树苗长得最好，我就给谁买一件最喜欢的礼物。"小男孩也想得到父亲的礼物。但看到兄妹那蹦蹦跳跳提水浇树的身影，不知怎么的，他萌生出一种想法：希望自己栽的那棵树早日死去。因此，浇过一两次水后，他再也没去管它。

几天后，小男孩再去看他种的那棵树时，惊奇地发现它不仅没有枯萎，而且还长出了几片新叶子，与兄妹们种的树相比，显得更嫩绿、更有生气。父亲兑现了他的诺言，为小男孩买了一件他最喜爱的礼物，并对他说，从他栽的树来看，他长大后一定能成为一个出色的植物学家。

从那以后，小男孩慢慢地变得乐观起来。一天晚上，小男孩躺在床上睡不着，看着窗外皎洁的月光，突然想起生物老师曾说过的话：植物一般都在晚上生长。何不去看看自己种的那棵小树？当他轻手轻脚来到院子里时，却看见父亲用勺子在向自己栽种的那棵树下泼洒着什么。顿时，一切他都明白了，原来父亲一直在偷偷地为自己栽种的那棵小树施肥！他返回房间，任凭泪水肆流……

几十年过去了。尽管那个瘸腿小男孩没有成为植物学家，他却成了美国总统，他叫富兰克林·罗斯福。

爱是生命中最好的养料，哪怕只是一勺清水，它都能使生命之树茁壮成长。

The Worth of Life

A well-known speaker started his speech by holding up a $20 bill. In the room of 200, he asked, "Who would like this $20 bill?"

Hands started going up. He said, "I am going to give this $20 to one of you—but first, let me do this."

He proceeded to crumple the 20-dollar note up. He then asked, "Who still wants it?" Still the hands were up in the air.

"Well," he replied, "what if I do this?" He dropped it on the ground and started to grind it into the floor with his shoe. He picked it up, now crumpled and dirty. "Now, who still wants it?"

Still the hands went into the air.

"My friends, you have all learned a very valuable lesson. No matter what I did to the money, you still wanted it because it did not decrease in value. It was still worth $20.

"Many times in our lives, we are dropped, crumpled, and ground into the dirt by the decisions we make and the circumstances that come our way. We feel as though we are worthless; but no matter what happened or what will happen, you will never lose your value. Dirty or clean, crumpled or finely creased, you are still priceless to those who love you.

"The worth of our lives comes, not in what we do or who we know, but by WHO YOU ARE.

"You are special—don't ever forget it."

生命的价值

一位著名的演说家举起一张20美元的钞票开始了演讲。他在一个200人的房间里问道："谁想要这20美元的钞票？"

人们的手都举了起来。他说："我准备把这张钞票给你们其中一个人，但首先让我这样做。"

他接着把20美元的钞票揉了揉，举了起来，然后问道："谁还想要？"那些手仍然举向了空中。

"好，"他回答说。"如果我这样做会怎么样？"他把钞票扔在地上，开始用鞋使劲在地板上踩。随后，他拾起钞票，现在钞票又皱又脏。"现在，谁还想要？"

那些手仍然举向空中。

"我的朋友们，你们都已经学到了非常宝贵的一课。无论我对这钱做了什么，你们都仍然想要它，因为它没有降低价值。它仍然是20美元。

"我们生命中会多次遇到挫折、坎坷，并让我们做出的决定和周围的环境逼到卑微的境地。我们感到自己似乎毫无价值。但无论发生什么和将会发生什么，你都永远不会

失去自己的价值:无论是肮脏还是干净,无论是被揉成一团还是整齐折叠,对爱你的人看来,你都极其珍贵。

“我们的价值不在于我们做什么、知道是谁,而在于你是谁。

“你与众不同——永远别忘记这一点。”

The Moral of Life

If life is a flower, it is good when it is in bloom, so is it when it fades. I'll scatter the petals of life on the road to life.

If life is grass, I'll never be inferior! I'll unite all the same species and offer the faint greenness to the world without grudge. The earth will be filled with youthful vitality for it.

If life is a tree, I'll dedicate myself to taking root in the earth. Even it is a rock ground, I'll get in the crevice with perseverance to draw the source of life.

If life is a ship, don't berth or follow the winds and waves! I'll raise the sails high and steer towards the sea no one has ever reached.

If life is water, I'll be surging! Even a clear spring or a stream, I'll keep running day and night.

If life is cloud, I'll never show off my charm, but turn into the rain and sprinkle into the sea.

If life is a log, I'll be a simple bridge!

If life is a piece of deadwood, I'll be a torch...

生命的寓意

假如生命是花,花开时是美好的,花落时也是美好的,我要把生命的花瓣,一瓣一瓣撒在人生的路上。

假如生命是草,绝不能因此自卑!要联合起来所有的同类,毫不吝惜地向世界奉献出自己的一星浅绿。大地将因此充满青春的活力。

假如生命是树,要一心一意把根扎向大地。哪怕脚下是一片坚硬的岩石,我也要锲而不舍地将根须钻进石缝,汲取生命的源泉。

假如生命是船,不要停泊,也不要随波漂流!我将高高地升起风帆,驶向无人到达的海域。

假如生命是水,要成为一股奔腾的活水!哪怕是一眼清泉,哪怕是一条小溪,也要日夜不停地奔流。

假如生命是云,绝不在天空里炫耀自己的姿色,而要化成雨,无声地洒向大海。

假如生命是一段原木,我就做一座朴实无华的桥!

假如生命只是一根枯枝,那我就变成一支火炬……

Feathers in the Wind

A good woman one day said something that hurt her best friend of many years. She regretted it immediately and would have done anything to take the words back. But they were said in a moment of thoughtlessness, and as close as she and her friend were, she didn't consider the effects of her words beforehand.

What she said hurt her friend so much that this good woman was herself hurt for the pain she caused. In an effort to undo what she had done, she went to an older, wiser woman, explained her situation, and asked for advice.

The older woman listened patiently in an effort to determine just how sincere the younger woman was, how far she was willing to go to correct the situation. She explained that sometimes, in order to put things back in order, great efforts must be made.

She then asked, "Just what would you be willing to do to repair the harm done?"

The answer was heartfelt, "Anything!"

Listening to her, the older woman sensed the younger woman's distress and knew she must help her. She also knew she could never lessen her pain, but she could teach, if the younger woman would first listen and then learn.

She knew the outcome would depend solely on the character of the younger woman. She said, "There are two things you need to do to make amends. The first of the two is extremely difficult.

"Tonight, take your best feather pillows and open a small hole in each one. Then, before the sun rises, you must put a single feather on the doorstep of each house in town.

"When you are through, come back to me. If you've done the first thing completely, I'll tell you the second."

The younger woman hurried home to prepare for her chore, even though the pillows were very dear and very expensive.

All night long, she labored alone in the wind. She went from doorstep to doorstep, taking care not to overlook a single house. Her fingers were frozen, the wind was so sharp it caused her eyes to water, but she ran on through the darkened street, thankful there was something she could do to put things back the way they once were.

Finally as the sky was getting light, she placed the last feather on the steps of the last house. Just as the sun rose, she returned to the older woman.

She was exhausted but relieved that her efforts would be rewarded.

"My pillows are empty. I placed a feather on the doorstep of each home."

"Now," said the wise woman, "Go back and refill your pillows. Then everything will be as it was before."

The young woman was stunned. "You know that's impossible! The wind blew away each feather as fast as I placed them on the doorsteps! You didn't say I had to get them back! If this is the second requirement, then things will never be the same."

"That's true," said the older woman. "Never forget. Each of your words is like a feather in the wind. Once spoken, no amount of effort, regardless of how heartfelt or sincere, can never return them to your mouth. Choose your words well and guard them most of all in the presence of those you love."

风中的羽毛

有一天，一个好女人无意间说了几句话，伤害了她交往多年的一位好友。她马上就感到后悔，愿意不惜一切收回自己说过的那些话。这些话都是她未经思索脱口说出的，而且她跟这位朋友情同姐妹，因此她事先根本就想不到自己说的话会有什么样的后果。

她的话深深地伤害了她的朋友，所以她自己也因为造成这样的伤害而备受折磨，心神不安。她想尽力与朋友重修旧好，就去找了一位长者，向长者解释了她目前的处境，并想虚心求教。

长者耐心地听着，以确定这个年轻女士的心有多诚，要弥补过失的愿望有多强。听完之后，长者解释说，有时为了恢复原状，需要付出巨大努力。

接下来，长者问："请问，为了重修旧好，你愿意做什么？"

年轻女士的回答发自肺腑："什么都愿意做。"

听着年轻女士的回答，长者知道年轻女士心里有多么痛苦，知道自己必须帮助她，同时也知道自己永远也无法减轻她的痛苦，但只要年轻女士愿意先听后学，她可以言传身教。

她知道结果如何完全取决于这个年轻女士的性格。她说："要重修旧好，有两件事情你需要去做。其中第一件非常难做。

"今晚，带上你最好的羽毛枕头，每个枕头上都打开一个小孔。然后，在太阳出来之前，你必须在镇上每一家房前的台阶上放上一根羽毛。

"你做完后，再回到我这里。如果你善始善终做完了第一件事，我会告诉你第二件事怎么做。"

年轻女士匆忙回到家里准备起来，纵使那些枕头非常昂贵，而且她爱不释手。

整整一夜，她独自一人在寒风中忙活着。她在一家一家房前的台阶上放着羽毛，小心翼翼惟恐漏掉一家。天寒地冻，她的手指冻僵了；寒风呼号，她眼睛不停地流着泪，但她仍然坚持穿过黑黝黝的街道，谢天谢地，不管怎样，她可以做一些力所能及的事情来将功补过了。

最后，天渐渐放亮，她终于在最后一家的门阶上放上了最后一根羽毛。这个时候，太阳刚好升起。她又回到了那位长者的身边。

尽管筋疲力尽，但她如释重负，心里想着自己的努力终会有所回报。

"我那些枕头都空了。我在每一家门阶上都放上了一根羽毛。"

长者说："现在，回去把那些羽毛再填进枕头里去，然后一切都会回到原状。"

年轻女士一下子目瞪口呆："你知道那是不可能的事儿！我一把羽毛放在台阶上，风就飞快地把它们吹跑了！你没有说过我必须得把它们装回去呀！如果这就是第二个要求，那事情再也无法回到原状了。"

"你说的没错，"长者说，"切勿忘记。你说过的每一句话就像风中的羽毛一样。话一出口，任何的努力——无论这种努力是多么发自肺腑、真心实意——都不能再将这些话收回去了。在你所爱的人面前，说话要注意分寸，才能有备无患。"

The River and the Rock

A river was running towards the valley and the plain, but when it came to a rock, it was afraid

and started trembling.

The rock said, "Hi, where are you going?"

The river said timidly, "I'm going to the valley and the plain. They are waiting for me."

The rock made fun of the river and said, "You are still very young. Go back to the hill immediately, and don't come back here again!"

Startled, the river said, "I can only go forwards. There is no river that goes backwards!"

The rock became angry and said, "Speak no more! If you don't go back, you will have to change your direction."

The river helplessly asked, "Where should I go?"

"You go anywhere you like, just don't come close to me!"

More and more water gathered as the river hesitated. Then it began to get out of control. The river surged over the rock. When it saw the rock being tossed about pitifully, it said, "Only a weak person will make a detour. A person who is strong will only go ahead, and nothing will stop him!"

河与岩石

一条河流向山谷和平原,但当流到一块岩石边时,它因害怕而开始颤抖。

岩石说:"嗨,你要去哪里?"

河羞怯地说:"我要去山谷和平原。它们在等着我呢。"

岩石戏弄河说:"你还很小。马上回到山里,别再回到这里来!"

河感到吃惊,说:"我只能往前流。河绝不会倒流!"

岩石发起了火,说:"别再说了! 你要不倒流,那就必须改变流向。"

河无奈地说:"我该怎么流呢?"

"你爱怎么就怎么流,只是别靠近我!"

在河犹豫的当儿,水越聚越多,随后就开始失控了。河汹涌着漫过岩石。看到岩石被可怜地冲来冲去,河说:"只有弱者才会绕道。强者只会勇往直前,任何东西都无法阻挡他!"

When the Wind Blows

Years ago a farmer owned a land along the Atlantic seacoast. He constantly advertised for hired hands. Most people were reluctant to work on farms along the Atlantic. They dreaded the awful storms that raged across the Atlantic, wreaking havoc on the buildings and crops. As the farmer interviewed applicants for the job, he received a steady stream of refusals.

Finally, a short, thin man, well past middle age, approached the farmer. "Are you a good farmhand?" the farmer asked him.

"Well, I can sleep when the wind blows," answered the little man.

Although puzzled by this answer, the farmer, desperate for help, hired him. The little man worked well around the farm, busy from dawn to dusk, and the farmer felt satisfied with the man's work.

Then one night the wind howled loudly in from offshore. Jumping out of bed, the farmer grabbed a lantern and rushed next door to the hired hand's sleeping quarters. He shook the little man and yelled,"Get up! A storm is coming! Tie things down before they blow away!"

The little man rolled over in bed and said firmly,"No sir. I told you,I can sleep when the wind blows."

Enraged by the response, the farmer was tempted to fire him on the spot. Instead, he hurried outside to prepare for the storm. To his amazement, he discovered that all of the haystacks had been covered with tarpaulins. The cows were in the barn, the chickens were in the coops, and the doors were barred. The shutters were tightly secured. Everything was tied down. Nothing could blow away.

The farmer then understood what his hired hand meant, so he returned to his bed to also sleep while the wind blew.

When you're prepared spiritually and physically, you have nothing to fear.

当风起时

几年前,一个农场主在大西洋沿岸拥有一块土地,他经常打广告雇人。多数人都不愿在大西洋岸边的农场上干活,他们害怕横扫大西洋严重破坏建筑和庄稼的可怕风暴。这个农场主招工面试时,收到的是一连串坚定的拒绝。

最后,一名个子矮瘦、已过中年的男人走近农场主。"你是个干农活的能手吗?"农场主问他。

"是的,起风时我可以睡觉。"矮个子回答说。

尽管对这个回答感到迷惑,但农场主急需帮手,就雇佣了他。这个矮个子在农场干活很卖劲,从早忙到晚。所以,农场主对他的工作非常满意。

后来,有一天夜里,从海面上呼呼刮来了大风。农场主从床上一跃而起,飞快提起灯笼,向隔壁雇工睡的地方跑去。他晃着那个矮个子大声喊道:"起来!风暴来了!趁还没刮跑,快把东西捆好!"

矮个子在床上翻了个身,口气坚定地说道:"不,先生。以前我告诉过你,刮风时我可以睡觉。"

听到这个回答,农场主勃然大怒,禁不住想把他当场解雇。不过,他没有这样做,而是赶紧跑出去应对暴风雨。让他惊愕的是,他发现所有的干草垛都已经盖上了防水油布,牛都在牲口棚里,小鸡待在鸡笼里,而且门闩也好了,百叶窗关得严严实实的,一切都拴牢了,什么东西都无法刮走。

农场主这才明白了雇工的话意。于是,当风刮起时,他也回自己的床上睡觉去了。

当你身心都做好准备时,就会无所畏惧。

Talking with a Flower

I stood in front of a flower growing alone in a deserted garden, located in a courtyard on the desert. The flower felt isolated, or it was what I imagined it like that. There was nothing but her in this place. I had thought she must be longing to have a green friend to comfort her solitude in the endless space.

I said to her, "Good morning! You are the beautiful flower in here!"

She said, "What's the meaning of 'the most beautiful'?"

I knew that she was so modest that she didn't know she herself was beautiful. The law of the Creator that the flowers all followed surprised me. I asked her again, "When you open up the path in the dark and heavy earth, what are you thinking about? Do you feel painful?"

The flower asked, "What is 'the pain'?"

I came to see that the pain only existed in the human life, so she didn't understand what pure beauty was.

I asked her again, "I'm so sorry. What are you thinking about now?"

She said, "I'm thinking about sending the fragrant moment to the air."

I asked her, "Do you like the air to such a degree?"

She said, "The sun is the reason."

I asked, "Have you fallen in love with the sun?"

The flower answered, "The sun gives me the energy and the heaven permits the sun to give me the energy that makes me full of fragrance, which will stay in my heart all the time. So I think, when the fragrance flows from me and into the air around me. And it is what is happening."

I asked, "O Flower, what will you get from your devotion?"

The flower answered, "I don't think it over. Nor do I care about what I will get but give."

I told her, "I expect you to answer my question. Think it over again, what kind of compensation and repayment from your giving?"

The flower said, "What is the repayment?"

I told her, "I appear to be talking with you in another language. I'm so sorry. What is your dream now?"

The flower answered, "Wither and fall and then go to the tranquil of old age. How wonderful the creation falls down the earth! It gives fragrance, leaving wisdom."

与花儿私语

我站在一株花面前。它孤零零地生长在一座荒弃的花园里。花园坐落在沙漠中的一个庭院里。花儿感到孤寂,或者我是这样想象的。在这个地方没有任何别的东西,只有她。我以为她一定渴望着一个绿色伙伴,来慰藉她那无边空旷中的孤独。

我对她说:"早上好! 你是这里最美丽的花朵!"

她说:"'最美丽'是什么意思?"

我明白了,她太谦虚了,谦虚到这种程度——不知道自己是美丽的。造物主的法则——花儿们都顺从这法则——使我感到惊奇。我又问她:"你在泥土的黑暗和沉重中开辟道路时,想着什么? 你感到很痛苦吗?"

花儿说:"什么叫'痛苦'?"

我明白了,痛苦只存在于人类的生活中,而纯美也是她所不了解的。

我又问她:"我很遗憾,你现在想些什么?"

她说:"我在想给空气送去芬芳的时刻。"

我问她:"你喜欢空气到这种程度吗?"

她说:"太阳是原因。"

我说:"你陷入对太阳的爱了吗?"

花儿说:"太阳给我能量,上天恩准太阳给我能量,使我充满了馨香。这馨香将一直

留在我的内心。所以，我想，何时芳香将从我溢出，散发在我周围的空气中。而这就是正在发生的事情。”

我问：“花儿哟，对你的奉献，你将得到什么？”

花儿说：“我不考虑这些。我不问将获得什么，我只给予。”

我对她说：“我希望你回答我的问题。再想一想，对你的给予你将得到何种补偿、何种回报？”

花儿说：“什么叫‘回报’？”

我对她说：“我似乎在和你用另一种语言说话。我很遗憾。你现在的梦想是什么？”

花儿说：“凋谢，走向老年的平静。创造物落于大地，这多么美妙啊！它给予馨香，留下智慧。”

A Maple

My neighbor Mrs. Gargan first told me about it. "Have you seen the tree?" she asked as I was sitting in the back yard enjoying the October twilight.

"The one down at the corner," she explained. "It's a beautiful tree—all kinds of colors. Cars are stopping to look. You ought to see it."

I told her I would, but I soon forgot about the tree. Three days later, I was jogging down the street, my mind swimming with petty worries, when a splash of bright orange caught my eye. For an instant, I thought someone's house had caught fire. Then I remembered the tree.

As I approached it, I slowed to a walk. There was nothing remarkable about the shape of the tree, a medium-sized maple. But Mrs. Gargan had been right about its colors. Like the messy whirl of an artist's palette, the tree blazed a bright crimson on its lower branches, burned with vivid yellows and oranges in its center, and simmered to deep burgundy at its top. Through these fiery colors cascaded thin rivulets of pale-green leaves and blotches of deep-green leaves, as yet untouched by autumn.

Edging closer—like a pilgrim approaching a shrine—I noticed several bare branches near the top, their black twigs scratching the air like claws. The leaves they had shed lay like a scarlet carpet around the trunk.

With its varied nations of color, this tree seemed to become a globe, embracing in its broad branches all seasons and continents; the spring and summer of the Southern Hemisphere in the light and dark greens, the autumn and winter of the Northern in the blazing yellows and bare branches. The whole planet seemed poised on the pivot of this pastiche.

As I marveled at this all-encompassing beauty, I thought of Ralph Waldo Emerson's comments about the stars. If the constellations appeared only once in a thousand years, he observed in "Nature," imagine what an exciting event it would be. But because they're up there every night, we barely give them a look.

I felt the same way about the tree. Because its majesty will last only a week, it should be especially precious to us. And I had almost missed it.

Once when Emily Dickinson's father noticed a brilliant display of northern lights in the sky over Massachusetts, he tolled a church bell to alert townspeople. That's what I felt like doing about the tree. I wanted to become a Paul Revere of autumn, awakening the countryside to its wonder.

I didn't have a church bell or a horse, but as I walked home, I did ask each neighbor I passed the same simple but momentous question Mrs. Gargan had asked me: "Have you seen the tree?"

一棵枫树

起初,这件事是我的邻居贾根太太告诉我的。“你看到那棵树了吗?”当我坐在后院观赏10月的黄昏景色时,她问。

“街角那棵,”她解释道,“那是一棵美丽的树——五颜六色的。好多车子都停下来看呢。你应该去看一下才是。”

我告诉她说我会去看的,但很快我便将那棵树给忘到了脑后。3天后,我因一些鸡毛蒜皮的烦心事而心神不定,正懵懵懂懂地沿着大街慢跑。突然,一道鲜橙色彩映入了我的眼帘。一瞬间,我还以为是谁家的房子着火了呢。随后,我才想起了那棵树。

我走近那棵树时,放慢了脚步。那是一棵不高不低的枫树,外形毫无突出显眼之处。但是,贾根太太所说的颜色倒是不错。那棵枫树像画家的颜色斑斓的调色板一般,下枝鲜亮粉红,中部鲜黄与橙黄交相辉映,顶端渐至深红。通过这些火焰般的色泽,只见深深浅浅斑斑点点、尚未被秋天触摸的绿叶小溪般涓涓流下。

我慢慢地向前移动脚步,像朝圣者走近圣殿一般。这时,我注意到在接近树顶的地方有几根秃枝,黑黢黢的枝条虬曲着指向天空,枝条上掉落的树叶如鲜红的毯子一般聚拢在树干四周。

这棵树色彩斑斓,变化多端,仿佛成了我们的地球,以其博大的枝蔓拥抱五洲和四季:那深深浅浅的绿色代表南半球的春夏季节,那耀眼夺目的黄色和秃枝则象征北半球的秋冬风光。整个地球似乎都落在了这只五光十色的制品的主轴上。

我惊叹其包罗万象的美的同时,想起了拉尔夫·瓦尔多·爱默生对星辰的有关论述。他在《自然》一书中说道,倘若星辰一千年仅出现一次,试想一下那该是何等激动人心的情景。但因为它们每天晚上都在夜空中出现,所以我们几乎对它们不屑一顾。

由此,我想到了那棵树。由于它的辉煌仅持续一周,因此它对我们应该是极其珍贵的。而我差点儿错失良机。

有一次,艾米丽·狄金森的父亲注意到马萨诸塞州上空北极光辉煌展现,便敲响教堂的钟声以警示市民。我想对那棵树也应该那样做。我想成为秋天的保罗·里维尔,去唤醒世人对美的发现。

我既没有教堂的钟,也没有保罗的马。但当我步行回家时,还是将贾根太太问我的那个简单而又重要的问题向遇到的每个邻居提了出来:“你看到那棵树了吗?”

The Catch of Lifetime

He was eleven years old and went fishing every chance he got from the dock as his family's cabin on an island in the middle of a New Hampshire's lake.

On the day before the bass season opened, he and his father were fishing early in the evening, catching sunfish and perch with worms. He tied on a small silver lure and practiced casting. The lure struck the water and caused golden ripples in the sunset, then silver ripples as the moon rose over the lake.

When his pole doubled over, he knew something huge was on the other end. His father watched with admiration as the boy skillfully worked the fish alongside the dock.

Finally, he very gingerly lifted the exhausted fish from the water. It was the largest one he had ever seen, but it was a bass.

The boy and his father looked at the handsome fish, gills playing back and forth in the moonlight. The father lit a match and looked at his watch. It was 10 p. m. two hours before the season opened. He looked at the fish, then at the bay.

"You'll have to put it back, son," he said.

"Dad!" cried the boy.

"There will be other fish," said the father.

"Not as big as this one," cried the boy.

He looked around the lake. No other fishermen or boats were nowhere around in the moonlight. He looked again at his father. Even though no one had seen them, nor could anyone ever know what time he caught the fish, the boy could tell by the clarity of his father's voice that the decision was not negotiable. He slowly worked the hook out of the lip of the huge bass and lowered it into the black water.

The creature swished its powerful body and disappeared. The boy suspected that he would never again see such a great fish.

That was 34 years ago. Today, the boy is a successful architect in New York City. His father's cabin is still there on the island in the middle of the lake. He takes his own son and daughters fishing from the same dock.

And he was right. He has never again caught such a magnificent fish as the one he landed that night long ago. But he does see that same fish—again and again—every time he comes up against a question of ethics.

一生的收获

他已经11岁了。只要一有机会，他就会到新汉普郡湖心岛上他家小屋的码头钓鱼。

鲈鱼季节开放的那天晚上，他和父亲早早地开始垂钓，用蠕虫作诱饵钓太阳鱼和鲈鱼。他系上银色的小诱饵，练习抛线。诱饵击在水面，在夕阳中荡起金色的涟漪。随后，当月亮冉冉升上湖面时，涟漪又变成了银色。

当鱼竿向下弯时，他知道线的另一端一定钓到了一条大鱼。父亲看着他动作熟练地在码头边钓鱼，眼中露出了赞赏的神情。

最后，他小心翼翼地将筋疲力尽的鱼拎出了水面。这是他见过的最大的一条鱼，但是一条鲈鱼。

男孩和父亲看着这条漂亮的鱼，鱼鳃在月光下一张一合的。父亲点燃一根火柴，看了看手表。已经是夜里10点了，离开放还有两个小时。他看了看鱼，然后又瞧了瞧男孩。

"儿子，你得把它放回去。"他说。

"爸爸！"男孩叫道。

"还会有其他鱼的。"父亲说。

"不会有这条大的。"男孩叫道。

他看了看湖四周。月光下没有其他的渔民或船只。他又看了一眼父亲。从父亲明白无误的口气中,他知道这个决定没有商量余地,即使没有人看到他们,也无从得知他们什么时候钓到了这条鱼。他慢慢地将鱼钩从大鲈鱼的嘴唇上取下来,然后将它放回了黑幽幽的水里。

鱼摆动着有力的身躯,消失在了水里。男孩想,他可能再也见不到这么大的一条鱼了。

那是 34 年前的事了。如今,男孩是纽约市一位功成名就的建筑师。他父亲的小屋仍在湖心岛上。他常常带着自己的儿女在同一个码头钓鱼。

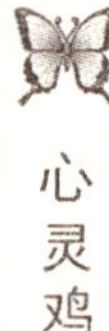

而且他想得没错。他再也没有见过很久以前那天夜里钓到的那么大的鱼。但他每次面临道德难题时,他的眼前总是一次次浮现出那条鱼。

The Roses and Thorns

The twin sisters went into the rose garden. Soon afterwards, one of the girls ran back to her mother and said, "Mama, this is a bad place!"

"Why, my child?"

"Because there're thorns below each flower."

After a while, the other girl ran to her mother and said, "Mama, this is a good place."

"Why, my child?"

"Because there're flowers on each thorn in here."

On hearing this, the mother was lost in thought.

Everything in the world both has a good side and a bad side; the key lies in from which point of view you will look at it.

玫瑰与荆棘

一对孪生小姑娘走进玫瑰园。不多久,其中一个小姑娘跑回来对母亲说:"妈妈,这里是个坏地方!"

"为什么呢,我的孩子?"

"因为这里的每朵花下面都有刺。"

不一会儿,另一个小姑娘跑来对母亲说:"妈妈,这里是个好地方。"

"为什么呢,我的孩子?"

"因为这里的每丛刺上都有花。"

母亲听了,沉思起来。

世间万物既有好的一面又有坏的一面,关键在于你从哪个角度去看。

When the Moon Follows Me

Each of my sons made the discovery early. We would be riding in the car at night, and the little voice would call out from the back seat, "Hey, the moon is following us!" I would explain that the moon was not actually gliding along with our car. There would be another period of critical observation and the final verdict, delivered more quietly this time: "But it really is moving. I can see it."

I thought of that one evening as I was driving. The moon, one day short of fullness, rode with me, first gliding smoothly, then bounding over the bumpy stretches, now on my right, then straight ahead, the silver light washing over dry grasses in open fields, streaking along through black branches, finally disappearing as the road wound its way through the hills.

When I crested the hill in the village, there it was again—grown suddenly immense, ripe, flooding the town with a sprawling light so magical I began to understand why it is said to inspire "looniness." I could hardly wait to get back home to show the boys.

Robert was in the bathtub, so I grabbed John. "Close your eyes and come see what followed me home," I said, hoping to increase the dramatic impact. I led him out into the night. "Okay. Open! Isn't it beautiful?"

John blinked a few times and looked at me as if I might be loony. "Mom, it's just the moon. Is this the surprise?" I suppose he was hoping for a puppy.

I should have realized that, being only ten, he was probably too young to know how much we sometimes need the magic and romance of moonlight—a light that is nothing like the harsh glare of the sun that it reflects. Moonlight softens our faults; all shabbiness dissolves into shadow. It erases the myriad details that crowd and rush us in the sunlight, leaving only sharp outlines and highlights and broad brushstrokes—the fundamental shape of things.

Often in the soothing, restorative glow we stare transfixed, bouncing out ambitions and hopes and plans off this great reflector. We dream our dreams; we examine the structure of our lives; we make considered decisions. In a hectic, confusing world, it helps to step out into a quiet, clear swash of moonlight, to seek out the fundamentals and eschew the incidentals.

The night after I showed John the moon, he burst breathlessly through the door, calling, "Mom, come out for a minute!" This time, he led me, coatless and shivering. The driveway gravel crunched underneath our sneakers. From somewhere in the woods beyond the pond, the plaintive calls of geese honked and died away.

Past the row of pine trees that line the road, the sky opened up with the full moon on it, suspended so precariously close that it might come hurtling toward us—incandescent, even larger and more breathtaking than the night before, climbing its motionless climb over the molten silver of our pond. Even a ten-year-old could see this wasn't just the moon. This was The Moon.

When I turned around, John was grinning, expectant, studying my face intently to see if he had pleased me. He had. I knew that now the moon was following him too.

月随人走

我的每个儿子早就发现了。我们夜里驾车回家，后座常常传来一声叫喊，"嘿，月亮在跟着我们！"我向他们解释说，月亮并不是真的随着我们的车子滑行。又经过了一段时间的审慎观察，做出了最后的裁定。这次声音更平静了："它真的在移动。我可以看得到。"

我记得那天晚上我驾车的情景。那是一轮亏月，始终伴我前行，起初是平稳滑行，然后在崎岖不平的路上开始跳跃，时而在我右侧，时而又在我正前方，银色的月光洒在空旷的草地上，飞快地穿过黑黢黢的树枝。最后，当道路沿着群山蜿蜒盘行时，月亮便消失了。

我到达村里的山顶时，月亮再次出现，这次突然变得硕大、圆满，月光匍匐着洒满了整个镇子，是那样变幻莫测，我才开始明白了为什么月亮能激发“狂想”。我迫不及待想赶回家让孩子们观看。

罗伯特正在浴缸里洗澡，所以我飞快地拎起约翰。“闭上眼睛，看看谁跟着我一起回家了，”我说，希望增加戏剧性的效果。我领着他走进了夜幕。“好了。睁开吧！是不是漂亮极了？”

约翰眨了几下眼睛，然后看着我，好像我是个疯子。“妈妈，这不过是一轮月亮罢了，有什么大惊小怪的?”我猜他希望是一只小狗。

我早该意识到，他才 10 岁，年纪还太小，无法知道有时我们是多么需要月光的魅力和浪漫——一道太阳折射出的耀眼光芒。月光减轻了我们的过失；所有的罪孽都溶解在月影之中。它擦去了阳光下充斥我们的无数细枝末节，仅留下了鲜明的轮廓、强光部分和宽宽的线条——事物基本的形态。

我们常常沐浴在心旷神怡的光里，目不转睛地看着，将我们的抱负和希望从这个大反射器上跳开。我们异想天开；我们审视生活结构；我们深思熟虑做出决定。在这个熙来攘往的世界，月光帮助我们步入了宁静亮堂的地带，寻找生活真谛，避开繁文缛节。

我领着约翰看过月亮后的那天夜里，他从门口气喘吁吁地喊道：“妈妈，出来一会儿！”这次，他领着未穿外衣、瑟瑟发抖的我。我们的运动鞋踩在车道的沙砾上嘎吱嘎吱响个不停。从池塘边的树林里传来一群大雁的鸣叫，然后又渐渐消失了。

穿过路边的那排松树，天空开阔，中天悬挂着一轮满月。月亮近在咫尺，岌岌可危，像要冲我们猛撞过来——闪闪发亮，比昨晚的更大、更惊人，笼罩着整个池塘，波光粼粼，犹如熔化的银子。就连一个 10 岁的孩子都能看出这不仅仅是一轮月亮。这是一个月球。

我转过身后，只见约翰笑眯眯的，充满了期待，热切地注视着我，看看是否让我感到高兴。他如愿以偿。我知道现在月亮也在跟着他了。

A Big Tree and a Young Tree

A young father asked an elderly neighbor how strict parents should be with their children.

The old man pointed to a rope between a big tree and a young one, saying, “Untie the rope.”

The young father did so and at once the young tree bent. Then the old man asked the young man to tie it again, and immediately the young tree stood upright as it used to.

Now the old man said, “There, it is the same with children. You must be strict with them for their healthy growth. But sometimes you must let them stand alone to see if they are strong enough. Being strict with them is for the sake of their independence development."

大树和小树

一位年轻父亲问一位上年纪的邻居,父母亲应该如何严格对待自己的孩子。

老人指着一根绑在一棵大树和一棵小树之间的绳子说:"解开绳子。"

年轻父亲解开绳子,小树马上弯下了腰。随后,老人让年轻父亲又绑好了绳子,小树马上又像先前那样站得笔直了。

这时,老人说道:"瞧,这和养孩子一样。为了他们健康成长,你必须严格要求他们。但有时,你必须让他们自立,看他们是否足够强壮。严格要求他们,是为了他们独立发展。"

A Young Apple Tree

A poor farmer had a friend who was famous for the wonderful apple he grew.

One day, his friend gave the farmer a young apple tree and told him to take it home and plant it. The farmer was pleased with the gift, but when he got home he did not know where to plant it.

He was afraid that if he planted the tree near the road, strangers would steal the fruit. If he planted the tree in one of his field, his neighbors would come at night and steal some of the apples. If he planted the tree near his house, his children would take the fruit. Finally he planted the tree in his wood where no one could see it. But without sunlight and good soil, the tree soon died.

Later the friend asked the farmer why he had planted the tree it such a poor place. "What's the difference?" the farmer said angrily. "If I had planted the tree near the road, strangers would have stolen the fruit. If I had planted the tree in one of my fields, my neighbors would have come at night and stolen some of the apples. If I had planted it near my house, my own children would have taken the fruit."

"Yes," said the friend, "but at least someone could have enjoyed the fruit. Now you not only have robbed everyone of the fruit, but also you have destroyed a good apple tree!"

一棵小苹果树

一个穷困的农夫有一个朋友,这个朋友因为种了神奇的苹果树而远近闻名。

有一天,农夫的这个朋友送给他一棵小苹果树。农夫对这个礼物非常高兴。但当他回到家时,却不知道将它栽什么地方。

他担心如果把苹果树栽在路边,陌生人就会偷树上的苹果;如果把树栽在自己的一块地里,邻居们夜里就会过来偷苹果;如果把树栽在自己的房边,他的孩子们就会摘苹果。最后,他把那棵树栽在了林子里,那里没人能看见。但没有阳光和沃土,树不久就死了。

后来，朋友问农夫他为什么把树栽在那样贫瘠的地方。“那有什么不一样？”农夫生气地说。“我把苹果树栽在路边，陌生人就会偷树上的苹果。我把树栽在自己的一块地里，邻居们夜里就会过来偷苹果。我把树栽在自己的房边，我自己的孩子们就会摘苹果。”

“是的，”他的朋友说。“但至少可能有人来分享这些果实。现在你不仅剥夺了每个人的果实，也毁了一棵好苹果树！”

The Power of a Bee

One afternoon a few summers ago, I had been clearing brush in the mountains for several hours and decided to reward myself with lunch. Sitting on a log, I unwrapped a sandwich and surveyed the rugged scenery. Two turbulent streams joined to form a clear, deep pool before roaring down a heavily wooded canyon.

My idyll would have been perfect had it not been for a persistent bee that began buzzing around me. The bee was of the common variety that plagues picnickers. Without thinking, I brushed it away.

Not the least intimidated, the bee came back and buzzed me again. Now, losing patience, I swatted the pest to the ground and crunched it into the sand with my boot.

Moments later I was startled by a minor explosion of sand at my feet. My tormentor emerged with its wings buzzing furiously. This time I took no chances. I stood up and ground the insect into the sand with all my 210 pounds.

Once more I sat down to my lunch. After several minutes I became aware of a slight movement near my feet. A broken but still living bee was feebly emerging from the sand.

Beguiled by its survival, I leaned down to survey the damage. The right wing was relatively intact, but the left was crumpled like a piece of paper. Nevertheless, the bee kept exercising the wings slowly up and down, as though assessing the damage. It also began to groom its sand-encrusted thorax and abdomen.

Next the bee turned its attention to the bent left wing, rapidly smoothing the wing by running its legs down the length. After each straightening session, the bee buzzed its wings as if to test the lift. This hopeless cripple thought is could still fly!

I got down on my hands and knees to better see these futile attempts Closer scrutiny confirmed the bee was finished—it must be finished. As a veteran pilot, I knew a good deal about wings.

But the bee paid no attention to my superior wisdom. It seemed to be gaining strength and increasing the tempo of its repairs. The bent veins that stiffened the gossamer wing were nearly straight now.

At last the bee felt sufficiently confident to attempt a trial flight. With an audible buzz it released its grip on the earth—and flew into a rise in the sand not more than three inches away. The little creature hit so hard that it tumbled. More frantic smoothing and flexing followed.

Again the bee lifted off, this time flying six inches before hitting another mound. Apparently the bee had regained the lift in its wings but had not mastered the directional controls. Like a pilot learning the peculiarities of a strange airplane, it experimented with short hops that ended ignominiously. After each crash the bee worked furiously to correct the newly discovered structural deficiencies.

Once more it took off, this time clearing the sand but heading straight toward a stump. Narrowly avoiding it, the bee checked its forward speed, circled and then drifted slowly over the mirror-like surface of the pool as if to admire its own reflection. As the bee disappeared, I realized that I was still on my knees, and I remained on my knees for some time.

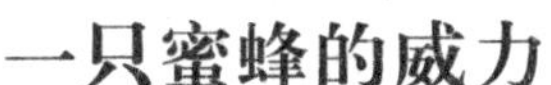

一只蜜蜂的威力

几年前夏天的一个下午，我在清理山上的灌木丛，连续干了好几个小时后，决定吃午饭犒劳一下自己。我坐在一根圆木上，打开一块三明治，观察着层峦叠嶂的山景，只见两条汹涌的小溪呼啸着流过林木茂密的峡谷后汇合成一泓清澈见底的深潭。

要不是一只固执的蜜蜂一直在我身边嗡嗡乱叫，我的田园生活情趣本应是非常完美的。这是那种干扰野餐者的普通蜜蜂。我不假思索就将它赶跑了。

蜜蜂毫不畏惧，又飞回来朝我嗡嗡叫了起来。这次，我失去耐心，猛地把这个害虫拍到地上，并用靴子将它踩进了沙地里。

过了一会儿，发现脚下沙地微微响了一声，我吃了一惊，折磨我的这个东西拼命扇着翅膀又钻了出来。这次，我不再给它机会了。我站起来，用我210磅的体重将这只昆虫踩进了沙地里。

我再次坐下来吃午饭。几分钟后，我感到到脚边又微微动了一下。只见那只受伤却仍活着的蜜蜂又从沙里有气无力地钻了出来。

我被它的生命力迷住了，弯下腰去查看它受的伤势。右边的翅膀相对完整，但左边的翅膀被压得像一张纸一样。不过，这只蜜蜂一直在慢慢地上下拍动着翅膀，好像要确定一下自己的伤势。同时，它也开始修整起沙土包裹的胸部和腹部。

接下来，蜜蜂把注意力转向了左边被弄弯了的翅膀，迅速用腿在翅膀上滑动捋平翅膀。每捋一段时间后，蜜蜂就嗡嗡嗡扇动翅膀，似乎要测试它的提升力。这只没有希望的瘸子还以为自己能飞呢！

为了更好看清它无效的努力，我双膝两手趴在地上；进一步细查之后，证实这个蜜蜂完了，它肯定不行了。作为一名富有经验的飞行员，我对翅膀了如指掌。

但蜜蜂对我的超人智慧并不在意。它似乎在积蓄力量，并加快了修复的速度。由于翅脉弯曲，使它轻而薄的翅膀变得僵硬，但现在几乎又平展起来了。

最后，蜜蜂感觉有足够的信心可以试飞一次了。随着一阵清晰可闻的嗡嗡声，它离开了地面，然后飞到了距离不足3英寸的一个沙丘上。小东西撞得太猛，所以翻滚了几下。接着是拼命捋翅和收缩屈伸。

蜜蜂再次飞起，这次飞了6英寸，然后撞到了另一个土墩上。显然，蜜蜂已经得到了启动翅膀的力量，但还掌握不住方向。像飞行员在学习掌握一架奇怪飞机的特性一样，它在试飞几个短途，最后落得很不光彩。每次坠落后，蜜蜂都拼命动作，以纠正新发现的结构上的不足。

它再次起飞，这次清除了身上的沙子，径直朝着一个树桩飞去。它偏了一点，躲过树桩，检查了前飞的速度，绕了一圈，慢慢地飞过镜子般明亮的湖面，仿佛是要欣赏自己的倒影。蜜蜂消失后，我才意识到自己仍跪在地上；之后，我又跪了好一阵子。

The Boy and the Walnuts

A boy once found a jar full of walnuts and raisins in his mother's kitchen and he put his hand in to help himself to hold as many as he could. When he tried to take his hand out of the jar, however, he found that the opening was too small for his clenched fist to pass through.

"What shall I do?" he wailed. "My hand will be stuck in this jar for ever."

Just then his mother came in.

"Really," she said. "there's nothing to make such a fuss about. Try taking half as many as walnuts and raisins you have in your hand and you'll find it will come out of the jar quite easily."

男孩与核桃

有一次，一个小男孩在他妈妈的厨房里发现了一个装满核桃和葡萄干的罐子，便将手伸进去，想尽可能多抓一把。然而，他设法抽出手时，却发现罐口太小，他抓着核桃的手怎么也通不过去。

"我怎么办呢?"他大声哭道。"我的手会永远被卡在这个罐子里的。"

正在这时，他的妈妈走了进来。

"其实，"她说。"这没有什么可大惊小怪的。试着抓一半的核桃和葡萄干，你的手轻而易举就会出来了。"

First Snow

He wasn't sure what had awakened him. Perhaps the child had made some small noise in his sleep. But as he peeked from beneath the covers, his gaze was drawn not to the cradle but to the window.

It was then that he realized what had sneaked through the shield of his slumbers. It was the sense of falling snow.

Quietly, so as not to disturb the child's mother, he rose from the bed and inched toward the cradle. Reaching down, he gently lifts the warm bundle to his shoulder. Then, as he tiptoed from the bedroom, she lifted her head, opened her eyes and—daily does of magic—smiled up at her dad.

He carried her downstairs, counting the creaks on the way. Together, they settled in at the kitchen table, and adult in him slipped away. Two children now, they pressed their noses against the glass.

The light from the street lamp on the corner filtered down through the birch trees, casting a glow as green as a summer memory upon the winter-brown backyard. From the distance can the endless echo of the stoplight, flashing in ruby message, teasing like a dawn that would not come.

The flakes were falling thick and hard now, pouring past window, a waterfall of mystery. Occasionally, one would stick to the glass, as if reluctant to tumble to its fate. Then, slowly, slipping and sliding down the glass, it would melt, its beauty fleeting gone.

Within an hour, a white table was spread up on the lawn. And as gray streaks of dawn unraveled

along the bleak seam of the distant hills, father and daughter watched the new day ripple across the neighborhood.

A porch light came on. A car door slammed. A television flickered.

Across the street, a family scurried into gear. But this day was different. Glimpsed through undraped windows as they darted from room to room, the slim figures of the children seemed to grow ever father until, finally, the kitchen door flew open and out burst three awesomely bundled objects that set instantly to rolling in the snow.

He wonders where they had learned this behavior. Even the littlest one, for whom this must have been the first real snowfall, seemed to know instinctively what to do.

They rolled in it, they tasted it, they packed it into balls and tossed it at one another. Then, just when he thought they might not know everything, they set about shaping a snowman on the crest of the hill.

By the time the snowman's nose was in place, the neighborhood was fully awake. A car whined in protest, but skidded staunchly out of its driveway. Buses ground forward like Marines, determined to take the hill. And all the while, the baby sat secure and warm in his arms.

He knew, of course, that she wouldn't remember any of this. For her there would be other snowfalls to recall. But for him, it was her first. Their first. And the memory would stay, cold and hard, fresh in his thoughts, long after the snowman melted.

第一场雪

他拿不准是什么把他从睡梦中唤醒的，也许是孩子在梦里发出的一些小小的声响吧。但当他从被子下面伸出头悄悄向外看时，吸引他的目光的不是摇篮，而是窗户。

这时，他才意识到是什么偷偷穿过了自己的梦境。是他感觉到了落雪纷飞。

为了不惊醒孩子的母亲，他默默地从床上起来，一步一步走向摇篮，俯下身轻轻地抱起暖烘烘的襁褓，然后蹑手蹑脚走出卧室，她抬起头，睁开眼睛，对爸爸露出了微笑，她每天都这样妙不可言。

他抱着她下楼，小心翼翼，惟恐弄出响声。他们一块在厨房的餐桌边停下来。他心中那种成人感悄悄溜走。现在是两个孩子将鼻子贴在玻璃上。

街角路灯的光透过白桦树照下来，犹如在冬天褐色的后园投下一道夏日记忆一样的绿光。红色尾灯从远处源源不断地照过来，闪动着红宝石般的讯号，就像迟迟不来的黎明在逗人。

现在雪花越下越密、越下越大了，纷纷扬扬飘过窗户，就像神秘的瀑布似的。有时，一片雪花会粘在玻璃上，好像是不甘于命运，于是顺着玻璃慢慢滑落、融化，它的美丽转瞬即逝。

不到一小时，草坪就铺上了一块雪白的台布。随后，一道道灰蒙蒙的曙光沿着远山黯淡的接缝铺散开来，父女俩目不转睛地望着新的一天波纹状穿过街坊四邻。

一盏门廊灯亮了起来。一扇车门咚地关上。一台电视闪了起来。

街对面的一家匆匆拉开了窗帘。但今天不一样，透过拉开窗帘的窗户，只见那家的几个孩子在几个房间里跑来跑去，瘦小的身影似乎变得越来越胖，最后厨房门飞快地打开，突然蹦出来3个包裹得严严实实的东西，立刻在雪地里打起滚来。

他不知道他们是在哪里学的这种举止。即便是那个最小的孩子似乎本能地知道该

干什么，因为这肯定是他真正经历的第一场降雪。

他们在雪地里打滚，他们把雪放在嘴里品尝，他们团起雪球打起了雪仗。随后，正在他想他们不可能什么都知道时，他们开始在斜坡顶上堆起了雪人。

待他们堆好雪人的鼻子时，邻居们全都醒了。一辆汽车呜呜叫着，以示抗议，但还是坚定地滑到了一边。公共汽车像舰队似的旋转向前，决定爬上前面的斜坡。而他的宝宝却一直安全可靠暖暖地坐在他的怀里。

当然，他知道，她不会记住这一切。对她来说，还会有别的雪景去回忆。但对他来说，这是她的第一场雪，是他们的第一场雪。就是那个雪人融化后很久，这场雪也会带着阵阵寒意，让他记忆犹新。

The Revelation of Lilacs

"I can't believe it. These blooms have lasted so long this year," my wife said.

"I hadn't really thought about it, but you are right. As much as I love lilacs, they come and go so fast," I said.

It has been incredibly exciting this year here in my backyard. Our lilac tree has produced the most blooms I have ever seen. The scent is so wonderful that I spend a lot of time just standing on our small deck breathing it all in.

Many of the branches are hollow and cracked leaving me to believe it has seen many springs. A few winters ago one of the biggest branches crashed to the ground under the weight of melting snow. It broke my heart. I guess I wasn't expecting much from the old thing this year. But it is magnificent!

Since we have been experiencing so much rain lately the flowers have become heavier. The once tall bush seems to be under a lot of pressure. I can relate to that.

Sadly, today I noticed the first bunch of flowers turning brown. It won't be long until they are all gone. But here's what I've learned from it.

Some people are like fragrant flowers. They come into our lives ever so briefly and leave behind a scent that remains embedded in our being. They brighten your day by just having had contact with them even if for a moment. If kindness would have scent it would remind you of them.

Like when I smell pine, all the best Christmas memories rush through my mind. When I smell roses I think of romantic, moon-filled evenings.

Some people, having given so much to you, remain a part of who you are forever. You cannot possibly go through a day without thinking about them. Their beautiful spirit gently nudges your heart each time you hear their name. The very thought of them stirs within your soul like the sweet fragrance of a thousand roses.

Loved ones who have passed on, having given their lives to you, having stayed in bloom through a lifetime of eternal spring, are like these lilacs. Although my heart is saddened having discovered that they are dying, I will not remember them that way. I will forever see a thousand blooms each time I think of them. In the coldest, darkest days of the winter of my life, the memory of them will get me through it all. Even the slightest fragrance will bring a smile to my face and my heart will pound remembering the love.

I'm thankful every day not only for the beauty of the people in my life, but for the lingering fragrance and everlasting memories of ever having loved them at all.

Loving them and life means I will have spring forever in my heart.

紫丁香的启示

“我无法相信。今年这些花开了这么久，”妻子说。

“我确实没有想过，但你说得对。我喜欢紫丁香，它们来去匆匆，”我说。

今年我家后院的景象让人无比兴奋，我们的紫丁香树从来没有开过这么多花。紫丁香芬芳四溢，我好多时候都站在小露台上尽情呼吸它的香气。

紫丁香的好多枝条已经中空裂开，这使我相信这棵紫丁香树已经历了好多个春天。几年前的一个冬天，由于积雪融化，这棵树上最大的一个枝条被压落到了地上。这让我很伤心。我以为今年这棵老树没有多大指望了。但它太棒了！

我们这里最近雨水一直很多，所以紫丁香花开得越来越多。从前高大的树丛似乎承受了很大压力。我能理解那种情况。

让我伤心的是，今天我注意到第一丛花渐渐变成了褐色，过不了多久它们就会全部凋谢。但我从中也有所领悟。

有些人就像芬芳的鲜花。他们在我们的生活中是那样短暂，却留下一缕清香，深深地嵌入我们的生命。即使和他们只有瞬间的接触，这些人也会照亮我们的人生。如果友善具有芳香，它会使你想起这些人。

就像我一闻到松树的香气，圣诞节最美好的回忆便会一下子涌上心头。我闻到玫瑰的芳香时，便会想起月华满天的浪漫之夜。

有些人给了你这么多便成了你永恒的一部分。如果你不想他们，就可能过不了某一天。每次听到他们的名字，他们美丽的灵魂都会轻轻触及你的心灵。你灵魂深处对他们的想念犹如千朵玫瑰那样甜蜜芬芳。

那些你爱的把生命传给你的人绽放在生命永恒的春天里，就像这些紫丁香一样。尽管我发现这些花快要凋谢，感到伤心，但我不会那样回忆它们。每次想起它们时，我都会永远看到百花绽放的情景。在生命里最寒冷、最黑暗的冬天，一想起它们，我就会挺过去。哪怕是最细微的芳香，也能让我露出笑脸，让我在怦然心动中想起爱。

我每天充满感激，不仅是因为我身边那些好人，也因为爱他们而产生的袅袅芳香和永久回忆。

爱他们、爱人生就意味着我将在心里拥有永恒的春天。

The Apple Bitten by God

My fingers can still move; my brain can still think; I have the ideal I pursue all my life; I have the relatives and friends who love me and whom I love; Right, I still have one heart of thanksgiving... Who can imagine this open-minded and wonderful words was written by a handicapped man who's been in the wheelchair more than 30 years with high paralysis.

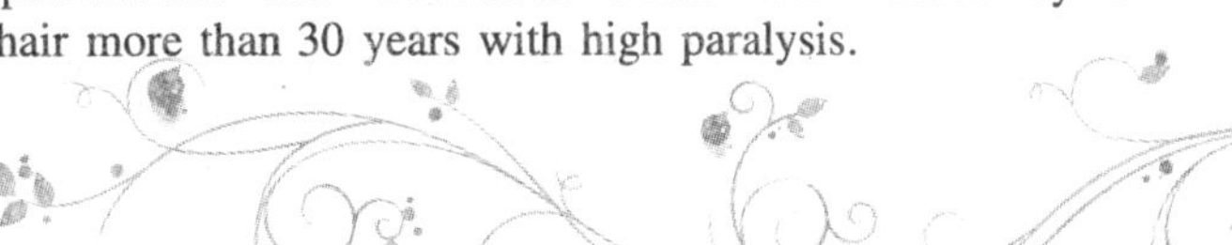

Who is this handicapped man? He is Stephen W. Hawking, great master of world science. Once, at the end of the academic report, a young female reporter asked compassionately, "Mr. Hawking, the disease has fixed you in the wheelchair forever. Don't you think the fate makes you lose too much?" In the face of such a somewhat unexpected and sharp question, Hawking was so calm, his face still smiling. He tried to type on the keyboard with difficulty to write the above-mentioned words.

For Hawking, the fate is so harsh: he can neither speak with his mouth nor stand on his legs nor move his body that he's lost a lot of most essential living conditions ordinary people have. However, Hawking still feels he's very rich, for example, a finger that can move, a brain that can think... all these make him content and grateful to life.

Some people say everyone is the apple bitten by God. Only because God particularly likes the fragrance of someone, he bites him terribly hard. Hawking is such an apple. God gives him a mutilated body but leaves him a soul of fragrance.

It won't be too little that life gives everyone. As long as you treasure it and keep creating it at pains, you can have the fragrance of life.

上帝咬过的苹果

我的手指还能活动；我的大脑还能思维；我有终生追求的理想；我有爱我和我爱着的亲人与朋友；对了，我还有一颗感恩的心……谁能想到，这段豁达而美妙的文字，竟是出自一位在轮椅上生活了30多年高位瘫痪的残疾人。

这位残疾人是谁？他就是世界科学巨匠斯蒂芬·W. 霍金。一次，在学术报告结束之际，一位年轻女记者不无怜悯地问："霍金先生，疾病已将你永远固定在轮椅上，你不认为命运让你失去太多了吗？"面对这个有些突兀和尖锐的提问，霍金显得很平静，他的脸依然带着微笑。他用那根还能活动的手指，艰难地敲击键盘，敲出了以上的那段文字。

对霍金来说，命运非常苛刻：他口不能说，腿不能站，身不能动，失去了许多常人拥有的最基本的生存条件。可是，霍金仍感到自己很富有，比如，一根能活动的手指，一颗能思维的大脑……这些都让他感到满足并对生活充满了感恩。

有人说，每个人都是被上帝咬过后的苹果，只因上帝特别喜爱某些人的芬芳，所以才对他咬得特别重。霍金就是这样一只苹果，上帝给了他残缺的肢体，却让他拥有了一个芳香的心灵。

生活给予每个人的都不会太少。只要好好珍惜，不断用心打造，你就能拥有生命的芬芳。

Mahogany

The open ground in front of my home in the countryside was leased to the other to plant mahogany seedlings. After the seedlings planted, the man who planted the trees would always water them every other day. The number of days he came had no rules, sometimes three days, sometimes five days, sometimes more than ten days. The quantity of watering was not steady, sometimes more, sometimes less. The mahogany sometimes suddenly withered, so when he came, he always brought some seedlings to replant.

Initially, I thought he was so lazy that he would water the trees as a long time passed. But how would a lazy man know how many trees had withered? He said, "Planting the trees is the foundation of 100 years, so the trees have to learn to find the water in the earth. I water, just to imitate God's rain that is not exactly calculated. If they cannot grow in this uncertainty by drawing water, the seedlings will naturally wither. But as long as they find the water in this uncertainty and struggle to take roots, they will grow into the trees of 100 years out of question," the man said in earnest. "If I pour a certain amount of water every day, the seedlings will become dependent on me, and their roots will grow on the surface and cannot go deep into the ground, so once I stop watering, the seedlings will wilt even more. The seedlings that have survived will collapse when they encounter a violent storm."

What he said moved me very much. I think that it is not only a tree, but also human beings. In the uncertainty, we will develop an independent mind, turn the tiny nutrients into the huge energy and try to grow.

桃花心木

乡下老家前面的空地租给人家种桃花心木的树苗。树苗种下来后,植树人总是隔几天才来浇水。他来的天数并没有规则,有时三天,有时五天,有时十几天来一次。浇水的量也不一定,有时浇得多,有时浇得少。桃花心木有时就莫名地枯萎了,所以他来时总会带几株树苗补种。

我起先认为他太懒,隔那么久才为树浇水。但懒的人怎么会知道有几棵树枯萎了呢?他说:"种树是百年基业,所以树木自己要学会在土地里找水源。我浇水只是模仿老天下雨,老天下雨是算不准的。如果无法在这种不确定中汲水生长,树苗很自然就枯萎了。但只要在不确定中找到水源、拼命扎根,长成百年的大树就不成问题了。"种树人语重心长地说。"如果我每天都来定量浇水,树苗就会养成依赖的心,根就会浮生在地表上,无法深入地底,一旦我停止浇水,树苗会枯萎得更多。幸而可以存活的树苗,遇到狂风暴雨,也是一吹就倒了。"

植树者言,使我非常感动,想到不只是树,人也是一样。在不确定中,我们会养成独立自主的心,把很少的养分转化为巨大的能量,努力生长。

Beyond the Beautiful

On the Gobi Desert in Africa, there is a small flower, whose florescence is so short that it only exists for two days and dies with its mother plant.

However, who can imagine, for such two days' short bloom, this small flower pays out what hard work and efforts?

On the Gobi, the plants with huge roots can grow while the small flower has only one root winding and twisting deep into the ground. This work usually takes it five years to complete the insertion of the root, and then it gathers the nutrients bit by bit. In the sixth spring, it can turn verdant and bloom a small four-colored flower.

Only blooming two days, this small flower pays out its lifetime about six years.

From this small flower, I see that the instantaneous beauty and the ephemeral success actually need a long wait and a lifetime efforts.

美丽背后

非洲戈壁滩上有一种小花,它的花期很短,仅仅两天时间,便随母株一起香消玉殒。

然而,谁能想象,为了这两天短暂的开放,小花付出了多少艰辛和努力?

在戈壁滩上,根系庞大的植物才能生长,而小花的根却只有一条,蜿蜒盘曲着插入地底深处,通常它要花费5年时间来完成根茎的穿插工作,然后一点点积蓄养分,第6年春天才在地面上吐绿绽翠,开出一朵小小的四色鲜花。

这朵仅仅开放两天的小花为此付出了一生6年的时光。

从这种小花身上,我看到了瞬间的美丽和短暂的成功原来需要漫长的等待和一生的努力!

The Pointless Competition

The monkey found the tiger walking towards the mountain, thinking that there must be a delicious peach grove on the mountain, or the tiger wouldn't leave his home and struggle to climb the mountain.

The monkey took a shoot, darting ahead of the tiger. After he crossed a mountain, sure enough, there was a peach grove coming in view. The monkey was afraid that the tiger ran to compete with him for eating peaches, rapidly climbed up the tree, grasped the peach branches to shake off all the peaches, and then shifted them to the thicket.

The monkey hid behind a big tree close by, spying the activity of the tiger. But when passing here, the tiger was still walking steadily. The monkey thought, there must be a better peach grove ahead, or will the tiger still keep walking on?

The monkey once again took the shortest route, speeding ahead of the tiger. As expected, a bigger and better peach grove came into sight. He shook the peaches off the tree quickly and hid in the bush...

The tiger was still walking on step by step. On an open ground of the mountain, the tiger stopped, looked around, taking a panoramic view of the activities of all the animals on and below the mountain. He picked the target he was going to hunt for, the angle and the timing, pouncing on it like a storm...

At this moment, the monkey hiding nearby to peep came to understand: it turned out that what the tiger was going to find was not the peaches. So the monkey scurried back along the same route. But stacks of peaches concealed in the bushes had been ravaged by the ants and insects, and some had been removed by the other animals and some had been rotten by the rainwater.

In life, we shouldn't waste our energy in the pointless competition, for it will make us lose some fruit that we may have gotten.

无谓的竞争

猴子发现老虎向山上走去，心想，山上一定有鲜美的桃林，否则老虎就不会离开家园，不辞辛苦地向山上爬。

猴子抄近路，飞一般抢在了老虎前面。翻过一座山后，果然有一片桃林出现在眼前。猴子怕老虎跟上来与它争吃桃子，赶快爬到了树上，抓着树枝把桃子全摇落下来，然后把它们转移到了草丛中。

猴子躲藏在一旁的大树后面，偷偷观察着老虎的行动。而老虎从这里经过时仍是一步一个脚印地走着。猴子心里想：前面一定有更美好的桃林，要不，老虎还会继续前行吗？

猴子又抄近路，飞一般抢在了老虎前面。果然，又一片更大更好的桃林出现在它眼前。它赶快摇落了树上的桃子，藏在草丛中……

老虎仍然一步一步地走着自己的路。在一座四周开阔的山头上，老虎停下来，四下张望，山上山下所有动物的活动情况都尽收眼底。它选准了自己要猎取的目标、角度和时机，如风暴般扑了上去……

这时，躲在不远处偷看的猴子才明白：原来老虎要寻找的并不是桃子。因此，猴子赶快顺着原路往回跑。可是，那藏在草丛中的一堆堆桃子已被蚂蚁、虫子糟蹋得不成了样子，有的已被别的动物搬走了，有的已被雨水腐烂了。

在生活中，实在不该把精力浪费在无谓的竞争中，反而使自己失去了一些原本可能得到的成果。

Life Is Like a Piece of Cake

A little boy is telling his grandma how everything is going wrong. Meanwhile, Grandma is baking a cake. She asks her grandson if he would like a snack, which, of course, he does.

"Here, have some cooking oil." "Yuck," says the boy. "How about a couple of raw eggs?" "Disgusting, Grandma!" "Would you like some flour then? Or maybe baking soda?" "Grandma, those are all yucky!"

Grandma replies, "Yes, all those things seem bad all by themselves. But when they are put together in the right way, they make a wonderfully delicious cake! God works the same way. Many times we wonder why he would let us go through such difficult times. But God knows that when he puts these things all in his order, they always work for good! We just have to trust him. Eventually, they will all make something wonderful! I hope your day is a piece of delicious cake."

生活就像一块蛋糕

小男孩正在对他的奶奶说一切都不顺心。此刻，奶奶正在烤蛋糕。她问孙子是不是想吃一块蛋糕。他当然想吃。

“喂,来点儿油。”“呸,”男孩说。“来几个生鸡蛋怎么样?”“恶心,奶奶!”“那你喜欢面粉?或者喜欢发酵粉吗?”“奶奶,那些东西都令人恶心!”

奶奶回答说:“是的,所有那些东西单独看起来似乎并不好,但当它们以适当方式放在一起时,就成了美味无比的蛋糕!上帝就是这样做的。很多时候,我们抱怨他常常让我们经历这样的艰难时刻。但上帝知道,当他以自己的顺序把这些东西在一起时,它们总是会一劳永逸地发挥作用。我们得相信他。最终,它们就会成为美妙的东西!我希望你的每一天都是一块美味可口的蛋糕。”

The Only Attitude Is Gratitude

Around twenty years ago I was living in Seattle and going through hard times. I could not find satisfying work and I found this especially difficult as I had a lot of experience and a Masters degree. To my shame I was driving a school bus to make ends meet and living with friends. I had lost my apartment. I had been through five interviews with a company and one day between bus runs they called to say I did not get the job. I went to the bus barn like a zombie of disappointment.

Later that afternoon, while doing my rounds through a quiet suburban neighborhood I had an inner wave—like a primal scream—arise from deep inside me and I thought"Why has my life become so hard?" "Give me a sign, I asked..."

Immediately after this internal scream I pulled the bus over to drop off a little girl and as she passed she handed me an earring saying I should keep it in case somebody claimed it. The earring was stamped metal, painted black and said, "BE HAPPY". At first I got angry—yeah, yeah, I thought. Then it hit me. I had been putting all of my energies into what was wrong with my life rather than what was right! I decided then and there to make a list of 50 things I was grateful for.

At first it was hard, then it got easier. One day I decided to up it to 75. That night there was a phone call for me at my friend's house from a lady who was a manager at a large hospital. About a year earlier I had submitted a syllabus to a community college to teach a course on stress management. She asked me if I would do a one-day seminar for 200 hospital workers. I said yes and got the job.

My day with the hospital workers went very well. I got a standing ovation and many more days of work. To this day I KNOW that it was because I changed my attitude to gratitude.

Incidentally, the day after I found the earring the girl asked me if anyone had claimed it. I told her no and she said, "I guess it was meant for you then."

I spent the next year conducting training workshops all around the Seattle area and then decided to risk everything and go back to Scotland where I had lived previously. I closed my one-man business, bought a plane ticket and got a six-month visa from immigration. One month later I met my wonderful English wife and best friend of 15 years now. We live in a small beautiful cottage, two miles from a paved road in the highlands of Scotland.

"THE ONLY ATTITUDE IS GRATITUDE" has been my motto for years now and completely changed my life.

感激是唯一的态度

大约20年前,我住在西雅图,正经历着坎坷。我经验丰富,拥有硕士学位,却找不到满意的工作,感到特别难受。让我羞愧的是,当时我驾驶一辆校车勉强度日,和朋友住在一起。要知道,我失去了自己的房子。我应聘一家公司,经历了五轮面试。一天,我就要出车时,对方打来电话说我没应聘上。我向车库走去时,失魂落魄。

那天下午晚些时候,我开着校车转到一片安静的郊区的居民区时,内心闪过了一个念头——像精神病患者的早期治疗——来自我的内心深处。我想:“为什么自己的生活变得如此艰难?”“给我一个征兆,我请求过……”

很快,我把车停住,一个小姑娘要下车。她经过我身边时,递给我一只耳饰,说保管住,以防有人认领。耳饰上面压有金属印,被漆了黑色,写的是“一定要幸福”。起初,我很生气——是啊,是啊,我想。接着,它让我忽然明白了。我一直一门心思用在想我的生活出的问题上,而不是我的生活的美好!我当即决定列出50件感激的事情。

一开始,很难列出来,后来就变得容易了。我决定将这个习惯坚持到75岁。有天晚上,一个电话打到了我朋友的家中要求找我,是一家大医院的女经理打来的。大约一年前,我向一所社区大学递交过一份课程提纲,要求去教一门成功应对压力的课程。她问我是否愿意给200名医院职工做一场为期一天的讲习会。我答应了,得到了这份工作。

我跟那家医院的职工们相处得很融洽。我受到了长期欢迎,获得了更多天的工作。直到今天,我都非常清楚,那全是因为我转变为感激生活的态度。

顺便提一下,我找到那个耳饰后第二天,那个小姑娘问我是否有人认领。我告诉她没有,她说:“我猜当时它是为你准备的。”

接下来的一年,我一直都在西雅图各地给车间工人们做培训,后来决定冒着一切风险回到我以前生活过的苏格兰。我关掉了只有我一个人的生意,买了一张飞机票,从移民局获得了半年签证。一个月后,我见到了我那漂亮的英国妻子和交了15年的挚友。现在我们住在一所漂亮的小别墅,距离苏格兰高地的一条道路两英里。

多年来,“感激是唯一的态度”已经成为我的座右铭,彻底改变了我的人生。

Look downward and Look upward

After making some slight achievements, a young man began to be self-satisfied and despised other people.

One day, the young man walked along with a wise man. On the way the young man spread himself astrut, but the wise man was silent. When they reached a peak, the wise man asked, “Look downward, what do you see?” “I see the woods, farmlands, houses, and the people as small as ants working in the fields.”

“Then what do you feel?” “Everything is all below me. I look like the one who dominates the earth.”

“If looking upward, what will you see?” “I see higher mountains, the white clouds on these mountains and the blue sky above the white cloud.”

“Then what do you feel?” The young man fell silent for a moment. “A person who knows to look upward can clearly understand his position; a person who knows the blue sky is always overhead won't be foolish to put himself on a sovereign position.”

The young man was suddenly enlightened, so since then he became studious and modest and made more progress.

向下看与向上看

一个年轻人小有成就，便开始自我满足，看不起人。

有一天，年轻人和一位智者结伴而行。一路上，年轻人夸夸其谈、趾高气扬，而智者却沉默不语。当他们到达一个山顶时，智者问："向下看，你看到了什么？""我看到了树林、农田、房舍，还有像蚂蚁般大小在田间劳作的人们。"

"那你有什么感受呢？""万物都在我之下，我好像就是大地的主宰。"

"如果向上看，你会看到什么呢？""我看到了更高的高山、高山上的白云、白云上的蓝天。"

"那你又有什么感受呢？"年轻人一时语塞。"一个懂得向上看的人，才能清醒地认识自己所处的位置；一个明白头顶永远是一片蓝天的人，才不会愚蠢地把自己摆到至高无上的地位。"

年轻人恍然大悟，从此变得好学上进、谦虚待人。

The Blind Boy

The park bench was deserted as I sat down to read under an old willow tree. Disillusioned by life with good reason to frown, for the world was intent on dragging me down.

Then a young boy out of breath approached me, all tired from play. He stood right before me with his head tilted down and said with great excitement, "Look what I found!"

In his hand was a flower, its petals all withered. I faked a small smile and then shifted away.

But instead of retreating he sat next to me and placed the flower to his nose and declared, "It sure smells sweet and it's beautiful too. That's why I picked it; here it's for you."

The wildflower before me was dying or dead without vibrant colors like orange, yellow, or red. But I knew I must take it, or he might never leave. So I reached for the flower, and replied, "Just what I need."

But instead of him placing the flower in my hand, he held in the midair. It was then that I noticed for the very first time that boy was blind.

I heard my voice quiver, tears shining like the sun as I thanked him for picking the very best one. "You're welcome," he smiled, and then ran off to play, unaware of the impact he'd had on my day.

I sat there and wondered how he managed to see a self-pity woman under an old willow tree. How did he know of my self-indulged plight? Perhaps from his heart, he'd been blessed with true sight.

Through the eyes of a blind child, at last I could see the problem was not with the world; the problem was me. And for all of those times I myself had been blind, I vowed to see the beauty in life and cherish every second that's mine.

And then I held that wilted flower up to my nose, breathed in the fragrance of a beautiful rose and smiled.

盲人指路

我在一棵老柳树下坐下来看书时，公园那条长椅空无一人。我对生活的幻想破灭了，完全有理由愁眉不展，因为这个世界抱定决心要把我拖向深渊。

这时，一个气喘吁吁的小男孩玩得筋疲力尽，走到我跟前。他站在我面前，歪着头，非常激动地说："看我找到了什么！"

他手里拿着一朵花，花瓣都已经蔫了。我假装微微一笑，然后移开了视线。

但他没有走，而是在我身边坐下来，把花放到鼻子边，大声说道："这花确实香，也很漂亮。这就是我采这朵花的原因。现在送给你。"

我眼前的这朵野花就要死了或早已死了，没有橙色、黄色或红色这样鲜艳的颜色。但我知道我必须接住，否则他也许永远都不会离开。于是，我伸手去接花，回答说："正是我想要的。"

但是，他没有把花放在我手里，而是出人意料地把它举在了空中。就在这时，我第一次注意到男孩是个盲人。

我听到自己声音颤抖感谢他采了一朵最好的花时，泪光闪闪。"不用谢，"他笑着说，然后跑去玩了，不知道他对我这一天产生的影响。

我坐在那里，纳闷他是怎样看到老柳树下有一个顾影自怜的女人的。他又是怎么知道我自暴自弃的呢？也许他内心深处具有真正的洞察力。

通过一个失明孩子的眼睛，我终于能够明白问题和这个世界无关，问题在于我自己。尽管我曾多次"失明"过，但我发誓要去注意生命中的美，珍惜属于自己的每一秒钟。

随后，我举起那朵枯萎的花，放到鼻子边，闻到了一朵漂亮玫瑰的芬芳，脸上露出了微笑。

The Secret behind a Painting

Once there was a beggar sleeping on the street. One day, he met a painter down and out. Soon the painter fell sick owing to excessive worry. Before his death, the painter gave a beggar a painting, on which there were a pair of hands and a smiling face. The beggar was wild with joy because he heard some painters became famous after death. So he started waiting for one day to sell the painting a large amount of money. One year passed, two years passed, and he had waited for many years, but the painter didn't become famous. Later, the beggar left this world with regret.

Dramatically, there was also a beggar getting a painter's painting, on which there were also a pair of hands and a smiling face. The beggar came to understand the painting. He hadn't much fantasy, but laughed happily for a whole day instead. Since then, he no longer begged from others, but began making money with his hands. After a few years, he had owned his house, his family and a smiling face.

In fact, sometimes wealth is not necessarily money; it may be beside us. But if you don't know to discover it and dig it in the ordinary life, you might be "poor" all your life.

一幅画背后的秘密

从前,有一个露宿街头的乞丐。一天,他认识了一个贫困潦倒的画家。不久,画家积郁成疾。临终前,画家送给乞丐一幅画。画的是一双大手和一张微笑的脸,乞丐欣喜若狂,因为他曾听说过一些画家死后出名的事。于是,他便开始等着某一天用这幅画卖一大笔钱。一年过去了,两年过去了,他等了许多年,画家没有出名。后来,乞丐带着遗憾离开了人间。

富有戏剧性的是,也有一个乞丐得到了一位画家的一幅画,画的同样是一双大手和一张微笑的脸。乞丐看懂了这幅画,他没有太多空想,只是痛快地笑了一整天。从此,他不再向别人乞讨,开始用自己的双手赚钱。几年后,他有了房子,有了家庭,有了一张微笑的脸。

其实,有时财富不一定就是金钱,它可能就在我们身边。但如果你不懂得在平凡的生活中去发现它、挖掘它,那么你有可能一辈子都是个"穷人"。

Please Help Tie It

In the middle school, I was a student living on campus. The school I studied in required the students to bring their own rice.

Once back to school, the school bus carried a few people, a young man wearing glasses next to me was. I put my rice bag on an empty seat beside him. Perhaps because of tiredness, I fell asleep as soon as I got on the bus. When I woke up, I found the rice bag mouth loosed, grains of rice rolled out into a pile of whiteness.

When I exclaimed involuntarily, a cold glance cast at me, and I saw a face, full of disdain, as if telling me he saw the entire process of the rice falling. In an instant, I flew into a rage, how could he leave me in the lurch indifferently? I squatted in front of that young man and lay back the rice handful by handful into the bag with my hands.

Thereafter, I have been surrounded by the rage and bewilderment that I had never had, so I began to suspect something and re-examine all around me.

When I went home again and related what I encountered on the bus that day, I was still angry, cursing the young man on the same bus with the ugliest words.

Unexpectedly, my mother said calmly, "My child, you can feel aggrieved, or even complain, but you have no right to ask the other to assume your own responsibility and fault; as a mother, I hope my daughter can help tie the other's rice bag mouth when it looses."

请帮忙系上

中学时,我是住校生。我所就读的中学要求学生自己带米。

有一次返校,校车上人很少,我的旁边只有一个戴眼镜的年轻人。我把那袋米放在

那年轻人旁边的一个空位上，也许是因为疲劳，我一上车就昏昏入睡了。等我醒来，我发现不知何时，米袋口松开了，一粒粒的米顺着袋口滚落下来，流成了一堆白色。

当我失声惊叫时，一个冷漠的眼神从旁边斜射过来，我看见一张脸，写满了不屑，仿佛在告诉我，他看到了米滑落的整个过程。刹那间，我的整个肺都气炸了，他怎么可以这样漠不关心、见死不救？我蹲在那个年轻人的面前，用双手一捧一捧地把米送回了袋子。

此后，我一直被一种从未有过的愤怒和惘然所包围，开始怀疑一些东西，重新审视身边的一切。

当我又一次回到家里，讲述那天车上的遭遇时，我余怒未消，用最丑恶的字眼来诅咒同车的那个年轻人。

不料，母亲却平静地说："孩子，你可以觉得委屈，甚至可以埋怨，但你没有权利要求别人去承担你自己的责任和过失；作为一位母亲，我希望我的女儿在别人的米袋口松开时，能帮忙系上。"

The Meaning of Life

An eight-year-old boy approached an old man in front of a wishing well, looked up into his eyes, and asked: "I understand you're a very wise man. I'd like to know the secret of life."

The old man looked down at the youngster and replied, "I've though a lot in my lifetime, and the secret can be summed up in four words:

"The first is think. Think about the values you wish to live your life by.

"The second is believe. Believe in yourself based on the thinking you've done about the values you're going to live your life by.

"The third is dream. Dream about the things that can be, based on your belief in yourself and the values you're going to live by.

"The last is dare. Dare to make your dreams become reality, based on your belief in yourself and your values."

And with that, Walter E. Disney said to the little boy: Think, believe, dream and dare.

人生的意义

一个 8 岁的小男孩走到一眼许愿井旁边的一位老人身边，抬头望着他的眼睛问道："我知道你是一个非常有智慧的人，我想知道人生的真谛。"

老人看着小男孩答道："我在一生中想了很多，生活的真谛可以概括为四个词：

"首先是思考，思考你生活的价值观。

"其次是信任，对自己的信任基于你已经找到自己一生依赖生存的价值观。

"其三是梦想，梦想那些可以基于你一生遵循的价值观和对自己的信任的事情。

"最后是勇敢，在你的价值观和对自己信任的基础上，勇敢地让梦想变成现实。"

最后，沃尔特·E·迪斯尼对这个小男孩说：思考、信任、梦想和勇敢。

Don't Think Highly of Yourself

There was an American writer who related such a story on many occasions:

It was at an exhibition of the artists' works organized by the Red Cross. I was invited as a special guest to participate in the exhibition. During this period, two cute girls of 16 or 17 years old came to me and asked me for my autograph devoutly.

"I haven't brought my fountain pen. Is the pencil okay?" Actually, I knew they wouldn't refuse. I just wanted to show a well-known writer's great demeanor modestly to the common readers.

"Certainly," the young girls readily agreed. I could see they were very excited. Of course, their excitement also made me feel more gratified. One of the girls handed her exquisite notebook to me. I produced my pencil, wrote a few words of encouragement naturally and unrestrainedly, and signed my name. The girl read my signature, frowned, looked at me carefully and asked, "Aren't you Robert Charboss?"

"No," I told her conceitedly, "I'm the author of Alice Adams, the winner of two Pulitzer Prizes."

The young girl turned to another one, shrugged and said, "Mary, lend your rubber to me."

At that moment, all my conceit and pride turned into a bubble instantly. Since then, I always warn myself: no matter how outstanding you are, don't think highly of yourself.

别太把自己当回事

有一位美国作家在多种场合讲述过这样一个故事：

那是在红十字会举办的艺术家作品展览会上，我作为特邀的贵宾参加了展览会。其间，有两个可爱的十六七岁小女孩来到我面前，虔诚地向我索要签名。

"我没带自来水笔，用铅笔可以吗？"我其实知道她们不会拒绝，我只是想表现一下一位著名作家谦和地对待普通读者的大家风范。

"当然可以。"小女孩们果然爽快地答应了。我看得出她们很兴奋，当然她们的兴奋也使我倍感欣慰。一个女孩将她非常精致的笔记本递给我。我取出铅笔，潇洒自如地写上了几句鼓励的话语，并签上了我的名字。女孩看过我的签名后，皱了皱眉，仔细看了看我，问道："你不是罗伯特·查波斯啊？"

"不是，"我非常自负地告诉她，"我是《爱丽丝·亚当斯》的作者，两次普利策奖得主。"

小女孩将头转向另一个女孩，耸了耸肩，说："玛丽，把你的橡皮借我用用。"

那一刻，我所有的自负和骄傲瞬间化为了泡影。从那以后，我都时刻告诫自己：无论自己多么出色，都别太把自己当回事。

Human Beings Have Choices

It takes both rain and sunshine to create a rainbow. Lives are no different. There is happiness and

sorrow. There is the good and the bad; dark and bright spots. If we can handle adversity, it only strengthens us. We cannot control all the events that happen in our lives, but we can decide how we deal with them.

Richard Blechnyden wanted to promote Indian tea in St. Louis World Fair in 1904. It was very hot and no one wanted to sample his tea. Blechnyden saw that all the other iced drinks were doing flourishing business. It dawned on him to make his tea into an iced drink, mix in sugar and sell it. He did and people love it. That was the introduction of iced tea to the world.

When things go wrong, as they sometimes will, we can react responsibly or resentfully.

Human beings are not like an acorn which has no choice. An acorn cannot decide whether to become a giant tree or to become food for the squirrels. Human beings have choices. If nature gives us a lemon, we have a choice: either cry for grace or make lemonade.

人生可以选择

彩虹是雨和阳光共同创造的。生活也是这样，有喜有悲、有好有坏、有明有暗。如果我们能战胜不幸，就会增强我们的力量。尽管我们无法控制生活中发生的所有事情，但可以决定如何处理它们。

1904 年，理查德·布莱克尼登在圣路易斯世界博览会上推销印度茶。当时天气很热，没人想品尝他的茶。布莱克尼登看到其他冰镇饮料都生意兴隆，于是就想到了一个主意，将茶做成冰镇饮料，加上糖，再卖。他这样做后，人们非常喜欢。冰茶就是这样介绍给世人的。

事情有时会出错，我们既可以积极回应，也可以愤愤不平。

人不像无从选择的橡子。一粒橡子无法决定是长成参天大树，还是成为松鼠的食物。人则有选择的余地。如果大自然给我们一颗柠檬，那我们就可以做出选择：要么感恩而泣，要么将它做成柠檬汁。

The Boys and the Sticks

A father's sons were always fighting. He had no way to stop them, so he decided to teach them a lesson.

He told his sons to bring him a bunch of sticks. He took the sticks, gave them to his eldest son and asked him to break them. The eldest son tried with all his might but was not able to do it. The other sons tried their best and were also unsuccessful.

The father then separated the sticks and put one into each son's hand. He asked his sons again to try and break the sticks. They broke them easily.

The father said, "My sons, if you are of one mind, and unite to assist each other, you will be like these sticks together; but if you are divided among yourselves, you will be broken as easily as a single stick."

男孩与木棍

父亲的一群孩子总喜欢吵架，但他想不出什么办法来阻止他们，于是决定给他们上一课。

他吩咐孩子们抱来一捆木棍。他拿起这捆木棍，递给大儿子，让他把它们折断。大儿子用尽全力，也没能做到。其他的儿子努力了半天，也没有成功。

于是，父亲把那些木棍分开，将它们各自放进了每个儿子的手里。他再次要求他们用力折断那些木棍。这次，他们轻而易举便将它们折断了。

父亲说："儿子们，要是齐心协力、团结互助，你们就会像这捆木棍一样；但要是各自为政，你们就会像这单根木棍一样容易折断。"

The Mahogany Piano

Many years ago, when I was a young man in my twenties, I worked as a salesman for a St. Louis piano company. We sold our pianos all over the state by advertising in small town newspapers and then, when we had received sufficient replies, we would load our little trucks, drive into the area and sell the pianos to those who had replied.

Every time we would advertise in the cotton country of Southeast Missouri, we would receive a reply on a postcard which said, "Please bring me a new piano for my little granddaughter. It must be red mahogany. I can pay $10 a month with my egg money." The old lady scrawled on and on and on that postcard until she filled it up, then turned it over and even wrote on the front—around and around the edges until there was barely room for the address.

Of course, we could not sell a new piano for $10 a month. No finance company would carry a contract with payments that small, so we ignored her postcards.

One day, however, I happened to be in that area calling on other replies, and out of curiosity I decided to look up the old lady. I found pretty much what I expected: The old lady lived in a one-room sharecroppers cabin in the middle of a cotton field. The cabin had a dirt floor and there were chickens in the house. Obviously, the old lady could not have qualified to purchase anything on credit—no car, no phone, no real job, nothing but a roof over her head and not a very good one at that. I could see daylight through it in several places. Her little granddaughter was about 10, barefoot and wearing a feed sack dress.

I explained to the old lady that we could not sell a new piano for $10 a month and that she should stop writing to us every time she saw our ad. I drove away heartsick, but my advice had no effect—she still sent us the same postcard every six weeks. Always wanting a new piano, red mahogany, please, and swearing she would never miss a $10 payment. It was sad.

A couple of years later, I owned my own piano company, and when I advertised in that area, the postcards started coming to me. For months, I ignored them—what else could I do?

But then, one day when I was in the area something came over me. I had a red mahogany piano on my little truck. Despite knowing that I was about to make a terrible business decision, I delivered the piano to her and told her I would carry the contract myself at $10 a month with no interest, and that would mean 52 payments. I took the new piano in the house and placed it where I thought the roof would be least likely to rain on it. I admonished her and the little girl to try to keep the chickens off of it, and I left—sure I had just thrown away a new piano.

But the payments came in, all 52 of them as agreed—sometimes with coins taped to a 3 × 5 inch card in the envelope. It was incredible!

So, I put the incident out of my mind for 20 years.

Then one day I was in Memphis on other business, and after dinner at the Holiday Inn, I went into the lounge. As I was sitting at the bar having an after-dinner drink, I heard the most beautiful piano music behind me. I looked around, and there was a lovely young woman playing a very nice grand piano.

Being a pianist of some ability myself, I was stunned by her virtuosity, and I picked up my drink and moved to a table beside her where I could listen and watch. She smiled at me and asked for requests. When she took a break she sat down at my table.

"Aren't you the man who sold my grandma a piano a long time ago?"

It didn't ring a bell, so I asked her to explain.

She started to tell me, and I suddenly remembered. My Lord, it was her! It was the little barefoot girl in the feed sack dress!

She told me her name was Elise and since her grandmother couldn't afford to pay for lessons, she had learned to play by listening to the radio. She said she had started to play in church where she and her grandmother had to walk over two miles, and that she had then played in school, had won many awards and a music scholarship. She had married an attorney in Memphis and he had bought her that beautiful grand piano she was playing.

Something else entered my mind. "Elise," I asked. "It's a little dark in here. What color is that piano?"

"It's red mahogany," she said. "Why?"

I couldn't speak.

Did she understand the significance of the red mahogany? The unbelievable audacity of her grandmother insisting on a red mahogany piano when no one in his right mind would have sold her a piano of any kind? I think not.

And then the marvelous accomplishment of that beautiful, terribly underprivileged child in the feed sack dress? No, I'm sure she didn't understand that either.

But I did, and my throat tightened.

Finally, I found my voice. "I just wondered," I said. "I'm proud of you, but I have to go to my room."

And I did have to go to my room, because men don't like to be seen crying in public.

一架桃花心木钢琴

很多年前，我还是20多岁的小伙子，当时我是圣路易斯钢琴公司的一名推销员。我们的钢琴销售遍及整个州，我们通常是先在各小镇的报纸上做广告，然后等到收到足够的回单，我们就给我们的一辆辆小卡车装货，开到那个地方，把钢琴卖给那些回单的人。

每次在密苏里州东南部棉花产地打广告，我们都会收到一张明信片，上面写着："请给我的小孙女带一架新钢琴。必须是红色桃花心木的。我可以用每月卖鸡蛋的钱支付10美元。"这位老太太字迹潦草，直到写满了一张明信片，甚至写到了正面——边边角角都写满了，直到差不多没地方写地址为止。

当然，我们不会把一架把钢琴分期每月卖10美元，没有哪家信贷公司会以这么小的分期付款签合同，所以我们没有理睬她的那些明信片。

然而，有一天，我碰巧要在那个地方拜访其他客人。出于好奇，我决定去探访那位老太太。我发现大大出乎我的意料：老太太住在棉花田中央的一个佃农单间小屋里。小屋是泥土地面，而且还养了鸡。显然，老太太没有资格赊购任何东西：她没有车，没有电话，没有真正的工作，只有头上的房顶，就连房顶也不是很好。我可以看到有好几处地方漏光。她的小孙女大约10岁，赤着双脚，身穿饲料袋改做的衣服。

我向老太太解释说，我们不能以每月10美元分期出售新钢琴，她不要再每次看到广告给我们写信了。我驱车离开时，感到心痛，但我的建议没有奏效——她仍然每隔6周就给我们寄去一张相同的明信片。总是想买一架新钢琴，红色桃花心木的，求求你们了，她还发誓绝不遗漏每次10美元付款。这真让人伤心。

两三年后，我拥有了自己的钢琴公司；而当我去那个地方打广告时，那些明信片开始源源不断地寄给我。有好几个月，我都对它们熟视无睹。我还能做什么呢？

但后来有一天，我在那个地区活动时，一件东西引起了我的注意。我的小卡车上装了一架红色桃花心木钢琴。尽管我知道这是一桩糟糕的买卖，但我还是把这架钢琴运到了她家，并告诉她我亲自签署这个每月付10美元没有利息的合同，而这将意味着要付52次款。我把钢琴送进屋里，把它放在一个最不可能淋到雨的地方，告诫她和小女孩尽量让鸡远离钢琴，随后我便离开了——我肯定是扔掉了一架新钢琴。

可是，那些钱一笔一笔地寄来了，正如合同上约定的那样，整整52笔——有时硬币粘在信封里一张3.5英寸大的卡片上。真不可思议！

于是，我便把这件事忘在了脑后，转眼就是20年。

后来有一天，我在孟斐斯做其他买卖。我在防洪堤上的假日旅馆吃完饭后，走进了休闲室。我坐在酒吧里喝餐后饮料时，听到身后传来最美妙的钢琴曲。我环顾四周，看见一个可爱的年轻女子弹奏一架非常漂亮的大钢琴。

我总是自信有钢琴家的才干，一下子被她的精湛演技震住了。我端起饮料，走到她身边的一张桌子，我在那里可以倾听欣赏。她朝我微微一笑，发出了邀请。她中场休息时，在我这张桌边坐下。

“你不就是很久以前卖给我祖母一架钢琴的那个人吗？”

我一时想不起来，于是便请她解释一下。

她开始向我说起来，我突然想起来了。我的上帝，是她！是那个赤着脚、穿着饲料袋改做的衣服的小女孩！

她告诉我她的名字叫伊莉斯，因为她的祖母没有钱供她上钢琴课，所以她学弹钢琴是靠听收音机。她说她开始演奏是在教堂里，她和祖母要步行两英里走到那里。她后来在学校演奏，多次获奖，还获得了一次音乐奖学金。她嫁给了孟斐斯的一位律师，刚才弹奏的那架漂亮的大钢琴就是他给她买下的。

这时，我想到了别的东西。“伊莉斯，”我问道，“这里光线有点儿暗，你那架钢琴是什么颜色？”

“是红色桃花心木的，”她说。“怎么了？”

我说不出话来。

她明白红色桃花心木的意义吗？她明白她祖母是怎样执意要买一架红木钢琴而做

出的那些惊人举动吗？当时头脑正常的人不会把钢琴卖给她。我想不会。

还有，那个取得非凡成就的漂亮而穷困的小女孩呢？不，我确信她也不会明白。

但我明白，我的喉咙哽咽了。

最后，我又能说话了。“我当时只是好奇，”我说，“我为你感到骄傲，但我得去自己的房间了。”

我确实得去自己的房间，因为男人们是不喜欢当众流泪的。

The Boy and the Nail

Once there was a little boy who had a bad temper. His father gave him a bag of nails and told him that every time he lost his temper, he must hammer a nail into the fence.

The first day the boy hammered 37 nails into the fence. Over the next few weeks, as he learned to control his anger, the number of nails hammered daily dwindled down. He discovered it was easier to hold his temper than to drive those nails into the fence.

Finally the day came when the boy didn't lose his temper at all. He told his father about it and the father suggested that the boy now pull out one nail for each day that he was able to hold his temper.

The days passed and one day the young boy told his father that all the nails were gone. The father took his son by the hand and led him to the fence. The fence would never be the same. "When you say things in anger, they leave a scar just like those nails," his father said.

男孩和钉子

从前，有一个小男孩，他的脾气很坏。他的父亲送给他一袋钉子，告诉他说，他每发一次火，就必须将一颗钉子钉在栅栏上。

第一天，男孩将37颗钉子钉进了栅栏。又过了几周，随着他学会控制自己的怒火，钉子的数目日益减少。他发现控制自己的脾气要比往栅栏上钉那些钉子容易。

最后，男孩再也不发火的日子终于来了。他把这件事告诉了他的父亲。他的父亲建议他现在每天能控制住自己的脾气，就拔掉一颗钉子。

又过去了好几天。有一天，男孩对他的父亲说，所有的钉子都没有了。男孩的父亲拉住他的手，将他领到了栅栏边。栅栏再也不是从前的样子了。“当你生气地说出事情时，它们就像那些钉子一样留下了伤疤。”他的父亲说。

The Next Step to Life

"A journey of a thousand miles must begin with a first step," a Chinese sage once said. Our first

step was to rent a pop-up trailer so our family of five could try camping. The trip was a success. To pull the trailer on subsequent trips, we had to buy a bigger station wagon. Sundry equipments followed: sleeping bags, stove, lantern, grill, pup tent, cooler and so on. Eventually, when we went camping, we looked like the Grand Army of the Republic.

Now we were clamoring for a canoe. I placed an ad in the paper: "Wanted, canoe for young family on limited budget. Please call after 6 p. m."

We waited for days by a silent phone. Then one night came—THE CALL. "Are you the family looking for a canoe?" asked an elderly voice.

"Yes, we are, ma'am." I replied.

"I may have what you are looking for. First, tell me about your family and your plans for the canoe."

So I told her how our family had enjoyed camping that summer, and how we especially liked remote places near lakes. I told her that a canoe seemed like the next step for us.

Apparently I'd said the right things, for the woman invited us to come to look at a canoe. On the following Sunday, the whole family drove to her house. We rang the bell, and a frail woman with white hair invited us in.

Once we were seated around the kitchen table, she proceeded to engage each of us in conversation. She made it clear that the canoe was special to her. She wanted it to go to a family with love and care.

It seems we passed the test, because she invited us out to the garage. It was empty, except for a wooden rack on which rested—THE CANOE.

It was 18 feet long, with high, curved bow and stern; green-painted canvas seats, one with a cedar backrest; and two cushions stuffed with balsam-fir needles. A portrait of an Indian chief had been wood-burned on a hand-carved paddle.

The canoe was magnificent. It was almost too much to hope that such a glorious thing could be ours.

Dazzled, we followed the woman back to the house. She opened an old album and showed us a picture of a smiling couple on a porch swing. We recognized our hostess. The young man was handsome.

She turned the page, and we recognized the canoe. The young man was in the stern, holding the Indian head paddle. In the bow sat a young woman wearing a straw hat. "My husband courted me in that very canoe," the woman explained. She told us about some of the outings they had enjoyed long ago.

We feared the canoe was beyond our grasp. My wife and I had agreed that we could go as high as $100. This canoe was clearly worth more than that. Timidly we inquired how much she was asking.

"How much will you prepare to spend?" she asked.

"Seventy-five dollars," I stammered, leaving room for negotiation.

"Tsk," said the woman. "With your young family, I couldn't possibly accept more than $35." We shook hands fervently.

Our treasured canoe has taken us on many adventures—island-hopping on a Maine lake, blueberrying expeditions, moonlit paddles to listen for loons. True to our word, we have treated it with love and care.

When our children outgrew family camping, my daughter took the canoe to college. At the campus woodworking shop, she made a new center thwart to replace the old one.

A workman there pointed out a small brass plaque, which we had overlooked for years. Thus we found out that our canoe had been manufactured in 1907 by the Morris Canoe Company in Veazie, Maine. A fire a few years later put Morris out of business.

So today our canoe is a collector's item, valued in the thousands of dollars. But the real value, for us, lies in the adventures our family had, and the memories we now treasure. We'll never forget our friend, the woman who shared her memories and helped us take the next step to life.

人生的第二步

中国一位圣人曾经说过："千里之行，始于足下。"我们的第一步是从租赁一辆蹩脚的拖车开始的，这样一家5口人便可一块去野营了。旅行取得了成功。在后来的旅行中，为了拉那辆拖车，我们不得不买了一辆旅行车。接下来是各种各样的装备：睡袋、炉子、提灯、烤肉架、三角小帐篷、冷却器等。最终出去野营时，我们浩浩荡荡，看上去就像共和国大军。

现在，我们家嚷嚷着想要一只独木舟。我在报纸上刊登了一条广告："征求启事：年轻家庭欲购独木舟，资金有限。请下午6点后打电话。"

我们等了好几天都不见有电话。后来有一天夜里，电话突然响了起来。"是你们家想要独木舟吗？"一个苍老的声音问道。

"是的，是我们家，太太。"我回答说。

"我也许有你们要找的那种独木舟。首先，给我谈谈你们家的情况和你们要独木舟的打算。"

于是，我就把那年夏天我们家一道野营的事儿告诉了她，同时还告诉她说，我们尤其喜欢湖附近的偏远地方。我对她说，独木舟好像是我们下一步计划的关键。

显然，我的话正中下怀，因为老太太邀请我们去看独木舟。第二个星期天，我们全家驱车赶到了她的家。我们按响门铃，随后一位白发苍苍、弱不禁风的老妇人将我们迎了进去。

我们一在她的餐桌边落座，她就开始跟我们每个人攀谈了起来。她明确表示说，独木舟对她不同寻常，她想要独木舟归属到一个充满爱心和关怀的家庭。

似乎我们通过了考试，因为她请我们进了她的车库。那里空荡荡的，只有一个木架，上面放着一只独木舟。

独木舟长18英尺，船头和船尾弯弯的高高翘起；绿色油漆帆布座，其中一个座上带有雪松木靠背；而且两个垫子装有胶枞针叶；一幅印第安首领的头像浇铸在雕花船桨上。

独木舟美观大方，简直难以想象这样一件贵重东西会归我们所有。

我们晕晕乎乎跟随老太太回到屋里。她打开一本旧相册，让我们看一张一对夫妇面带笑容坐在门廊秋千上的照片。我们认出了我们的女主人。那个小伙子非常英俊。

她翻过那页，然后我们就看到了那只独木舟。那个小伙子手握那只刻着印第安首领头像的船桨坐在船尾。一个年轻姑娘头戴草帽坐在船头。"我的丈夫就是在那只独木舟上向我求爱的。"老太太解释说。她给我们说起了多年前他们外出郊游的情景。

我们担心买不起这只独木舟。我和妻子商定最高出价100美元。独木舟明显不止这个价。我们不好意思地问她要价多少。

"你们准备花多少钱？"她问。

"75美元。"我结结巴巴地说，留下了砍价的余地。

"啧啧，"老太太说，"像你们这样年轻的家庭，超过35美元我是不可能接受的。"我们热情地握了握手。

这只心爱的独木舟曾载着我们经历过许多次的冒险——在缅因州一个湖上越岛作战,去冒险采摘过蓝莓,在月光下泛舟湖倾听潜鸟的吟唱。说实在话,我们对独木舟充满了爱心和关怀。

当我们的子女都长大不适合家庭野营时,我们的女儿将独木舟带到了大学。在学校的木工店,她做了一块新的中横坐板,换下了那块旧板。

店里的木匠无意间发现了一个小铜饰板,这么多年我们一家人谁也没有注意到。于是,我们发现我们的独木舟是1907年由缅因州维基市莫里斯轻舟公司生产的。几年后的一场大火使该公司变成了一片废墟。

因此,眼下我们的独木舟摇身一变,价值几千美元,成了收藏品。但对我们来说,独木舟的真正价值在于,我们家共同分享过的奇趣和珍藏在心间的回忆。我们将终生难忘我们的朋友——那位老太太,不仅她自己留下了点点滴滴的回忆,而且帮助我们走向了人生的第二步。

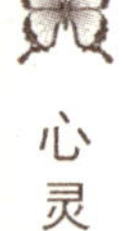

Good Medicine

"What are you busy with yourself, Mother?" the girl of less than six years old asked her mother curiously. "Making dinner for the neighbor's aunt." "Why?" "Because the other day the aunt lost her dear daughter and is so sad now. We must take good care of her these days."

"Why need our care?" "Because from then on the aunt cannot do what they liked to along with her daughter. She is very pitiful. In her distress, making dinners and doing chores are also becoming so difficult. My dear, can you help Mother hit an idea to help the aunt in other ways?"

At her mother's proposal, the girl thought for a long while. All of a sudden, she went to the neighbor's house and knocked at the door.

The neighbor with a look of haggardness and tiredness opened the door. "What can I do for you?" asked the neighbor. "I heard my mother say you're very distressed for losing your daughter..." The girl timidly handed the band-aid tightly held in her hand to the neighbor.

The neighbor suddenly choked with sobs, her tears gushing from her eyes. She hugged the girl and said, "Thank you. This band-aid will cure my wound."

灵丹妙药

"妈妈,您在忙什么呢?"还不到6岁的女孩好奇地问妈妈。"给邻居家的阿姨做饭。"

"为什么?""前几天阿姨失去了心爱的女儿,现在很伤心。我们这几天要好好照顾她。"

"为什么需要我们照顾呢?""阿姨以后不能和她女儿一起做她们喜欢做的事了,很可怜。人在极度悲伤时,做饭和料理家务也会变得很难。女儿,你能不能也帮妈妈想想其他能帮助阿姨做的事呢?"

女孩听到妈妈的提议，认真地思考了很久，突然走到邻居家敲响了门。一脸憔悴和疲惫的邻居开了门。“有什么事吗？”邻居问道。“听妈妈说，您因为失去了女儿，非常痛苦……”女孩羞涩地把攥在手里的创可贴递给了邻居。

邻居突然哽咽起来，泪水夺眶而出。她抱住女孩，说：“谢谢，这个创可贴一定会治好我的伤口。”

A Lesson for Living

"Everything happens for the best," my mother said whenever I faced disappointment. "If you carry on, one day something good will happen."

Mother was right, as I discovered after graduating from college in 1932, I had decided to try for a job in radio, then work my way to a sports announcer. I hitchhiked to Chicago and knocked on the door of every station and got turned down every time.

In one studio, a kind lady told me that big stations couldn't risk hiring an inexperienced person. "Go find a small station that'll give you a chance," she said.

I thumbed home to Dixon, Illinois. While there were no radio-announcing jobs in Dixon, my father said Montgomery Ward had opened a store and wanted a local athlete to manage its sports department. Since Dixon was where I had played high-school football, I applied. The job sounded just right for me. But I wasn't hired.

My disappointment must have shown. "Everything happens for the best," Mom reminded me. Dad offered me the car to job hunt. I tried WOC Radio in Davenport, Iowa. The program director, a wonderful Scotsman named Peter MacArthur, told me they had already hired an announcer.

As I left his office, I asked aloud, "How can a fellow get to be a sports announcer if he can't get a job in a radio station?"

I was waiting for the elevator when I heard MacArthur calling, "What was that you said about sports? Do you know anything about football?" Then he stood me before a microphone and asked me to broadcast an imaginary game.

The preceding autumn, my team had won a game in the last 20 seconds with 65-yard run. I did a 15-minute build-up to that play, and Peter told me I would be broadcasting Saturday's game!

On my way home, as I have many times since, I thought of my mother's words: "If you carry on, one day something good will happen."

I often wonder what direction my life might have taken if I'd gotten the job at Montgomery Ward.

人生的教训

“一切都会好的。”每当我面临失望时，母亲都会说。“如果你坚持下去，总有一天好事会出现。”

1932年大学毕业时，我才发现母亲说的没错。当时，我决定在电台找一份工作，然后通过奋斗，当一名体育播音员。我搭便车来到芝加哥，敲了每一家电台的门，每次都被拒之门外。

在一家演播室，一位好心的女士告诉我说，大电台都不可能冒风险去聘用没有经验的人。“找一家小电台，它会给你一个机会的。”她说。

我搭便车回到家乡伊利诺伊州迪克森。迪克森没有无线电播音的工作。父亲告诉我说，蒙哥马利·沃德开了一家商店，想在当地聘用一位运动员管理体育部。因为迪克森是我中学曾打过橄榄球的地方，所以我就提出了申请。这份工作对我正合适，但我还是没被雇佣。

我的失望之情一定是露了出来。“一切都会好的。”妈妈提醒我说。爸爸将车给我，让我去找工作。我去了衣阿华州达文波特 WOC 电台试了试。节目主管是一个名叫彼得·麦克阿瑟的了不起的苏格兰人。他告诉我说他们已经雇佣了一名播音员。

我离开他的办公室时，大声问道：“一个在广播电台都找不到工作的人怎么能成为一名体育播音员呢？”

我等电梯时，听到麦克阿瑟朝我喊道：“你说的体育是怎么回事？你知道橄榄球吗？”于是，他让我站在麦克风前，请我为一场假想的比赛解说。

在前一年的秋天，我的球队在最后 20 秒以 65 码的距离赢得了一场球。我对那场球赛做了 15 分钟的精彩解说。彼得告诉我可以为星期六的比赛解说！

在回家的路上，我想到了母亲的那番话，从此多次都是这样：“一切都会好起来的。如果你坚持不懈，好事总有一天会到来。”

我常常想，如果得到了蒙哥马利·沃德的那份工作，我的人生会通向何方。

The Sculpture of Life

A sculptor was absorbed in his work in which he was carving and polishing an unshaped marble with the graver in his hand while a small boy close by was looking at him with curiosity.

After a while, the sculpture gradually took shape: head, shoulders, arms, limbs, then hair, eyes, nose, mouth... A beautiful woman appeared before them.

The small boy felt extremely surprised and asked the sculptor, “How did you know she hid in it?”

The sculptor told the boy with a haw-haw, “There was nothing in the stone. I just moved the woman in my heart here with my graver.”

人生的雕塑

一位雕刻家正在全神贯注地工作，用手中的刻刀一刀一刀地琢磨一块尚未成形的大理石。一个小男孩好奇地在一旁看着他。

不一会儿，雕像逐渐成形：头部、肩膀、手臂、身躯，接着头发、眼睛、鼻子、嘴巴……，一个美丽的女人出现在了面前。

小男孩万分惊讶，问雕刻家：“你怎么知道她藏在里边的呢？”

雕刻家哈哈大笑，对孩子说："石头里原本什么也没有，只不过是我把我心中的女人用刻刀给搬到这里来了。"

Don't Quit

Wishing to encourage her young son's progress on the piano, a mother took her boy to a Paderewski concert.

After they were seated, the mother spotted a friend in the audience and walked down the aisle to greet her. Seizing the opportunity to explore the wonders of the concert hall, the little boy rose and eventually explored his way through a door marked "NO ADMITTANCE".

When the house lights dimmed and the concert was about to begin, the mother returned to her seat and discovered that the child was missing. Suddenly, the curtains parted and spotlights focused on the impressive Steinway on stage. In horror, the mother saw her little boy sitting at the keyboard, innocently picking out "Twinkle, Twinkle Little Star."

At that moment, the great piano master made his entrance, quickly moved to the piano and whispered in the boy's ear, "Don't quit. Keep playing." Then, leaning over, Paderewski reached down with his left hand and began filling in the bass part. Soon his right arm reached around to the other side of the child and he added a running obbligato.

Together, the old master and the young novice transformed the frightening situation into a wonderfully creative experience. And the audience were mesmerized.

Whatever our situation in life and history, there is the voice deep within our beings, "Don't quit. Keep playing. You are not alone. Together we will transform the broken patterns into a masterwork of my creative art. Together, we will mesmerize the world."

不要停

一位母亲想鼓励小儿子好好练琴，就带着他去看巴岱莱夫斯基的音乐会。

他们坐好后，这位母亲在观众席里发现了一位朋友，便走过去和她打招呼。小男孩抓住这个机会，好奇地离开了座位，走进了音乐厅一扇标有"禁止入内"的门。

当观众席的照明灯暗下来、音乐会就要开始时，这位母亲回到了自己的座位，发现孩子不见了。突然，帷幕拉开了，聚光灯照在了舞台上那架显眼的施泰韦钢琴上。这位母亲惊恐地发现自己的小儿子坐在键盘边，凭记忆天真地弹奏起了《闪闪小星星》。

此时，那位伟大的钢琴师入场，快步走到钢琴边，低声对小男孩说道："不要停。接着弹。"随后，巴岱莱夫斯基弯下腰，伸出左手，开始补全低音部分。不久，他的右臂绕到了小男孩的另一侧，补全了伴奏部分。

年长的大师和年幼的新手一起将那令人担心的情景变成了极具创意的演出。而且观众们如痴如醉。

无论我们现在和过去的境遇如何，我们的内心深处总会有一个声音说："不要停，接着弹。你不是独自一人。我们一起将破碎的音符变成具有创意的杰作。我们一起倾倒整个世界。"

Enjoy What You Have

People who are satisfied appreciate what they have in life and don't worry about how it compares to what others have. Valuing what you have over what you do not or cannot have leads to greater happiness.

Four-year-old Alice runs to Christmas tree and sees wonderful presents beneath it. No doubt she has received fewer presents than some of her friends, and probably she has not received some of the things she most wanted. But at that moment, she doesn't stop to think why aren't there more presents or to wonder what she may have asked for that she didn't get. Instead, she marvels at the treasures before her.

When we think about our lives, too often we think about what we don't have and what we didn't get. But such a focus denies us pleasure. You wouldn't sit next to the Christmas tree and remind Alice that there were presents she didn't receive. Why remind yourself of the things in life you don't have when you could remind yourself of what you do have?

People who have the most are only as likely to be happy as those who have the least. People who like what they have, however, are twice as likely to be happy as those who actually have the most.

享受自己所有

知足的人感激生活中拥有的一切,不会因为和别人比较而担心。珍惜自己拥有的东西胜于自己没有或不能拥有的东西,将会给你带来更大的快乐。

4 岁的爱丽丝跑到圣诞树边,看到了树下漂亮的礼物。毫无疑问,她收到的礼物比她的一些朋友的要少,而且也许没有收到她最想要的一些东西。但此时此刻,她想到的并不是这里为什么没有更多的礼物,或者自己还能得到什么未曾拥有的东西。相反,她对眼前这些的宝物感到惊奇。

我们在回想生活时,常常回想自己并未得到的东西。但这种专注会让我们失去快乐。你不会坐在圣诞树边提醒爱丽丝她没有收到有些礼物。当你能让自己想起眼前拥有的东西时,为什么又要提醒自己去想那些不曾拥有的东西呢?

最富的人可能和最穷的人一样快乐。然而,喜欢自己所有的人可能比实际最富的人快乐一倍。

A Wonderful Present

It was a cold December afternoon. A girl of about eight or nine stood in front of a shop on a small street. Her face was close to the shop window. Inside the window there were lots and lots of beautiful things. With large and serious eyes, the girl looked at the jewels and carefully studied each of them. Then a smile came across her face, and she stepped back from the window and entered the shop.

There was not much light inside the shop. But the girl could see that the shop was full of wonderful things. In the counter, there were more jewels. And there were also many other things for which she did not even know their names.

Pete Richards was standing behind the counter when the girl came in. He was about thirty years old. He looked very lonely. His eyes were cold as he looked at the little girl. "Please," she said to Pete, "would you let me look at the necklace in the window?"

Pete took the necklace from the window and held it up for the girl to see. It was a very beautiful necklace. It was a string of blue beads.

"It is just right," said the girl. "Will you wrap it up in pretty paper for me please?" Pete looked at the girl with cold eyes. "Are you buying it for someone?" he asked. "For my sister. She takes care of me. You see, this will be the first Christmas since our mother died. I've been looking for a wonderful present for her."

"How much money do you have?" asked Pete. From the pocket of her coat, the girl took a handful of pennies and put them on the counter. "This is all I have," she explained simply. "I have been saving money for my sister's present."

For a moment Pete Richards was silent. He looked at the girl again. She was a pretty girl. Her hair was yellow as the sunlight, and her eyes were blue as the sea. And now there was a happy look in her blue eyes. It struck him. Then he removed the price mark on the necklace so that the girl could not see it. How could he tell her the price?

"Just a moment," Pete went to the back of the shop. "What is your name, little girl?" he called out to her as he was busy about something.

"Jean Grace," answered the girl.

When Pete returned, he held a package in his hand. It was wrapped in pretty Christmas paper and tied with green ribbon. "There you are," he said. "Don't lose it on the way home."

The girl smiled happily at him, and then turned and ran out of the shop. Through the big shop window Pete watched her until she was lost among crowds of people. Jean Grace reminded Pete of his old grief. A few years ago, Pete loved a girl. Her hair and eyes were of the same colors as Jean Grace. And the necklace was meant for her. But on a rainy night, the girl was knocked down and killed in a car accident. Pete was filled with grief and began to live a lonely life. Sometimes he talked with the people who came to his shop, but after the business hours he was left alone with his grief.

Now the blue eyes of Jean Grace made him remember again all that he had lost. The pain was so great that sometimes he even wanted to run away from the people who came to buy Christmas presents in his shop in the next ten days.

Christmas Eve came. The last customer left his shop. Pete sat down behind his counter and soon was deep in thought.

All at once the door opened and a young woman came in. Pete looked up and was surprised. He felt he had seen this woman somewhere before. Her hair was sunlight yellow and her eyes were sea blue.

The young woman came up to Pete Richards, and without saying anything she put on the counter a package wrapped in pretty Christmas paper. From her pocket she took some green ribbon and put it with the package. When Pete opened the package he saw the string of blue beads.

"Did this come from your shop?" she asked.

"Yes," Pete answered.

"Are the stones real?"

"Yes. They are not the best in the world, but they are real."

"Can you remember to whom you sold them?"

"A small girl. Her name was Jean Grace. She wanted the necklace for her sister's Christmas present."

"How much was it?"

"Sorry, I can't tell you that," Pete said. "The seller never tells anyone else what a buyer pays."

"But Jean Grace never had more than a few pennies. How could she pay for such a necklace?"

Pete started to wrap the necklace in the Christmas paper and tie the package with the green ribbon. He was as careful as he had been ten days earlier. Then he said to the young girl, "Jean Grace paid the biggest price she could. She gave all she had."

He handed the package to her. For a moment there was no sound in the little shop. Then somewhere in the city, the church bells began to ring. It was midnight, and the beginning of another Christmas Day.

"But why did you do it?" the girl asked.

There was no answer. It seemed Pete Richards was not listening.

"But why did you do it?" she asked again in a soft voice. "There is no one else to whom I can give a Christmas present," Pete said quietly. "It is already Christmas morning. Will you let me take you to your home? I would like to wish you and your little sister Jean Grace a Merry Christmas at your door."

And so, to the sounds of church bells, Pete Richards and a young girl whose name he had not yet learned walked out. They walked out into the Christmas morning and into the hope and happiness of a new Christmas Day.

神奇的礼物

12月的一个寒冷的下午。一个大约八、九岁的小女孩站在一条小街的一家商店门前。她的脸紧贴着商店橱窗。橱窗里有好多好多漂亮东西。小女孩睁着大大的眼睛认真地看着那些珠宝，仔细地一一打量着。随后，她露出了微笑，从橱窗边走开，走进了那家商店。

商店里没有多少光亮。但小女孩能看得到商店里琳琅满目。柜台里还有更多的珠宝。而且还有好多其他的东西，她甚至都叫不上它们的名字。

小女孩进来时，皮特·理查兹正站在柜台后面。他大约30岁，看上去非常孤独。他在看小女孩时，目光冰冷。她对皮特说："请你让我看看橱窗里的项链好吗？"

皮特从橱窗里拿出项链，举起来让小女孩看。这是一条非常漂亮的项链，上面串着一串蓝色的珠子。

"正合适，"小女孩说。"请你给我用漂亮的纸给我包裹一下好吗？"皮特用冰冷的目光看着小女孩，问道："你是为某个人买吗？""是为我的姐姐买的。她常常关照我。你明白，这将是我们的妈妈去世以来的第一个圣诞礼物。我一直在为她找一件神奇的礼物。"

"你有多少钱？"皮特问。小女孩从上衣口袋里掏出了一把便士，将它们放在柜台上。"我就有这么多，"她简明地解释说。"我一直为给姐姐买礼物攒钱。"

皮特·理查兹沉默了一会儿。他又看了小女孩一眼。她是一个漂亮女孩，她的头发像阳光一样金黄，眼睛像大海一样湛蓝，而且蓝色的眼睛里总洋溢着快乐的神情。这一下子打动了他。随后，他将项链上的价格标签取下来，这样小女孩就看不到了。他怎么能告诉她价格呢？

"请等一会儿，"皮特走到商店的后部。"你叫什么名字，小姑娘？"他一边忙着某件事，一边向她大声问道。

"琼·格雷斯。"女孩回答说。

当皮特回来时，他一只手里拿着一个包裹。那是用漂亮的圣诞纸包着，还扎着绿丝带。"给你，"他说。"别在回家的路上丢了哟。"

小女孩冲他开心地微微一笑，然后转过身，跑出了商店。皮特透过大橱窗望着她，直到她消失在茫茫人海中。琼·格雷斯使皮特想起了他伤心的往事。几年前,皮特爱一个女孩。她的头发和眼睛的颜色跟琼·格雷斯的一模一样,而且她也是想要那种项链。但在一个雨夜,那个女孩被一辆汽车撞死了。皮特充满了悲伤,开始过起了一种孤独生活。有时他跟来商店的人说话,但下班后,他就一个人与悲伤相伴。

现在,琼·格雷斯的蓝眼睛使他又想起了他所失去的一切。痛苦是那样巨大,在接下来的10天里,他甚至想从来他的店里买圣诞礼物的人身边逃走。

圣诞节前夜来临了。最后一个顾客离开了他的商店。皮特在柜台后面坐下来,很快就陷入了沉思。

突然,门开了。一个年轻女人走了进来。皮特抬起头,吃了一惊。他感到以前曾在什么地方见过这个女人。她的头发像阳光般金黄,眼睛像大海一样湛蓝。

年轻女人走到皮特·理查兹的身边,没说一句话,将一个用漂亮的圣诞纸包着的包裹放在柜台上。她从口袋里掏出一些绿丝带,和包裹放在一起。当皮特打开包裹时,他看到了那串蓝色的珠子。

"这是你店子里的东西吗?"她问。

"是的。"皮特回答说。

"这些宝石是真的吗?"

"是的。它们不是世界上最好的,但它们是真的。"

"你能记得是把它们卖给谁的吗?"

"一个小女孩。她的名字叫琼·格雷斯。她想把这条项链作为圣诞礼物送给她的姐姐。"

"这价值多少钱?"

"对不起,这我不能告诉你。"皮特说。"卖主从来不透露给别人买主付了多少钱。"

"可是,琼·格雷斯从来没有超过几便士以上的钱。她怎么能买得起这样一条项链呢?"

皮特用圣诞纸包起那条项链,并用绿丝带扎住包裹。他像10天前那样做得小心翼翼。随后,他对那个年轻女孩说:"琼·格雷斯已经付了她能付的最高价格。她拿出了自己所有的积蓄。"

他将那个包裹递给她。小小的店里好一阵子没有声音。随后,在城市的某个地方,响起了教堂的钟声。现在是午夜,又一个圣诞节已经开始了。

"可是,你为什么这样做?"女孩问。

没有回音。好像皮特·理查兹没在听。

"可是,你为什么这样做?"她又柔声问道。"我没有圣诞礼物可送给别人,"皮特轻声说道。"已经是圣诞节早上了。你让我把你送回家好吗?我想在你们家门口祝你和你的小妹妹琼·格雷斯圣诞节快乐。"

于是,伴随着教堂的钟声,皮特·理查兹和一个他还不知道名字的年轻女孩走出了店门。他们走进了圣诞节的早晨,走进了一个新圣诞节的希望和幸福里。

The Grace of Life

A girl was dissatisfied with her mother's chattering, so in rage she rushed out of her home and wandered in the street alone full of grievance.

Just as she was hungry and thirsty, an old man beckoned her to his home and gave her a bowl of meal. The girl was moved to tears and told him about her grievance.

With that, the old man shook his head and said, "While you're being grateful to me for my giving you a bowl of meal, have you thought of the person who've been giving you?" the girl became speechless at once.

At times, when a person thanks the others for their offering a bit of bounty, he or she always forgets the maximum kindness he or she gets.

人生的恩惠

一个女孩子因为不满母亲的唠叨,一气之下跑出了家门,怀着满肚子委屈,孤独地走在大街上。

正当她又饥又渴时,一位老人把她叫到了自己家里,给她盛了一碗饭。女孩感激得哭了,并向他讲述了自己的委屈。

老人听后,摇了摇头说:"你在感激我给你一碗饭的同时,可想过那一直给你做饭的人!"女孩顿时无言。

往往有时候,人在感激别人给自己的一点小恩惠时,却忘记了自己得到的最大恩惠。

The Tiger's Whisker of Life

A young woman by the name of Yun Ok came one day to the house of a mountain hermit to seek his help. The hermit was a sage of great renown and a maker of charms and magic potions.

When Yun Ok entered his house, the hermit said without raising his eyes from the fireplace into which he was looking. "Why are you here?"

Yun Ok said, "Oh, Famous Sage, I am in distress! Make me a potion!"

"Yes, yes, make a potion! Everyone needs potions! Can we cure a sick world with a potion?"

"Master," Yun Ok replied, "if you do not help me, I am truly lost!"

"Well, what is your story?" the hermit said, resigned at last to listen.

"It is my husband," Yun Ok said. "He is very dear to me. For the past three years he has been away fighting in the wars. Now that he has returned, he hardly speaks to me, or to anyone else. If I speak, he doesn't seem to hear. When he talks at all, it is roughly. If I serve him food not to his liking, he pushes it aside and angrily leaves the room. Sometimes when he should be working in the rice field, I see him sitting idly on top of the hill, looking toward the sea."

"Yes, so it is sometimes when young men come back from the wars," the hermit said. "Go on."

"There is no more to tell, Learned One. I want a potion to give my husband so that he will be

loving and gentle, as he used to be."

"Ha, so simple, is it?" the hermit asked. "A potion! Very well, come back in three days and I will tell you what we shall need for such a potion."

Three days later, Yun Ok returned to the home of the mountain sage. "I have looked into it," he told her. "Your potion can be made. But the most essential ingredient is the whisker of a living tiger. Bring me this whisker and I will give you what you need."

"The whisker of a living tiger!" Yun Ok said. "How could I possibly get it?"

"If the potion is important enough, you will succeed," the hermit said. He turned his head away, not wishing to talk any more.

Yun Ok went home. She thought a great deal about how she would get the tiger's whisker. Then one night when her husband was asleep, she crept from her house with a bowl of rice and meat sauce in her hand. She went to the place on the mountainside where the tiger was known to live. Standing far off from the tiger's cave, she held out the bowl of food, calling the tiger to come and held out the bowl of food, calling the tiger to come and eat. The tiger did not come.

The next night Yun Ok went again, this time a little bit closer. Again she offered a bowl of food. Every night Yun Ok went to the mountain, each time a few steps nearer the tiger's cave than the night before. Little by little, the tiger grew accustomed to seeing her there.

One night Yun Ok approached to within a stone's throw of the tiger's cave. This time the tiger came a few steps toward her and stopped. The two of them stood looking at one another in the moonlight. It happened again the following night, and this time they were so close that Yun Ok could talk to the tiger in a soft, soothing voice. The next night, after looking carefully into Yun Ok's eyes, the tiger ate the food that she held out for him. After that when Yun Ok came in the night, she found the tiger waiting for her on the trail. When the tiger had eaten, Yun Ok could gently rub his head with her hand. Nearly six months had passed since the night of her first visit. At last one night, after caressing the animal's head, Yun Ok said, "Oh, Tiger, generous animal, I must have on of your whiskers. Do not be angry with me!"

And she snipped off one of the whiskers.

The tiger did not become angry, as she had feared he might. Yun Ok went down the trail, not walking but running, with the whisker clutched tightly in her hand.

The next morning she was at the mountain hermit's house just as the sun was rising from the sea. "Oh, Famous One!" she cried, "I have it! I have the tiger's whisker! Now you can make me the potion you promised so that my husband will be loving and gentle again!"

The hermit took the whisker and examined it. Satisfied that it had really come from a tiger, he leaned forward and dropped it into the fire that burned in his fireplace.

"Oh, sir!" the young woman called in anguish. "What have you done with it!"

"Tell me how you obtained it," the hermit said.

"Why, I went to the mountain each night with a little bowl of food. At first I stood afar, and I came a little closer each time, gaining the tiger's confidence. I spoke gently and soothingly to him, to make him understand I wished him only good. I was patient. Each night I brought him food, knowing that he would not eat. But I did not give up. I came again and again. I never spoke harshly. I never reproached him. And at last one night he took a few steps toward me. A time came when he would meet me on the trail and eat out of the bowl that I held in my hands. I rubbed his head, and he made happy sounds in his throat. Only after that did I take the whisker."

"Yes, yes," the hermit said, "you tamed the tiger and won his confidence and love."

"But you have thrown the whisker in the fire!" Yun Ok cried. "It is all for nothing!"

"No, I do not think it is all for nothing," the hermit said. "The whisker is no longer needed. Yun Ok, let me ask you, is a man more vicious than a tiger? Is he less responsive to kindness and understanding? If you can win the love and confidence of a wild and blood-thirsty animal by gentleness and patience, surely you can do the same with your husband?"

Hearing this, Yun Ok stood speechless for a moment. Then she went down the trail, turning over in her mind the truth she had learned in the house of the mountain hermit.

人生的虎须

一天，一个名叫云鸥的年轻女子来到山中一位隐士住的地方寻求帮助。这位隐士是一个大名鼎鼎的圣人，会施魔法、做魔液。

云鸥走进他的屋里时，隐士没抬眼睛，盯着壁炉，问道："你为什么来这里？"

云鸥说："噢，大圣人，我非常苦恼！给我做一杯魔液吧！"

"好，好，做一杯魔液！人人都需要魔液！我们能用魔液普度众生吗？"

"大师，"云鸥答道。"你若不帮我，我真要迷失方向了！"

"好吧，是什么事？"最后，隐士总算愿意听她讲了。

"是我的丈夫。"云鸥说。"他对我非常恩爱。过去3年里，他离开家，一直驰骋疆场。如今他回来了，既不怎么和我说话，也不和别人说话。就是我说话，他似乎也充耳不闻。就是他说话，也是三言两语。如果我做的饭菜不合他的口味，他就把饭菜推到一边，忿忿离开房间。有时，该下稻田干活了，我却看见他无所事事地坐在山顶上，望着大海。"

"是的，从战场回来的年轻人有时就是这样。"隐士说。"接着往下说。"

"没有要说的了，大圣人。我要魔液是想送给我的丈夫，好让他能像从前那样钟情温柔。"

"哈，这么简单，是吗？"隐士问。"一杯魔液！很好，3天后你再来，到时我会告诉你酿造这么一杯魔液需要什么。"

3天后，云鸥再次来到山中圣人的住处。"我已经研究过了，"他告诉她说。"你的魔液可以酿成。但最重要的成分是一只活虎的胡须。你要把这根胡须拿来，我就可以把你需要的东西给你。"

"活虎的胡须！"云鸥说。"我怎么可能拿到手呀？"

"如果魔液举足轻重，你就会成功。"说着，隐士转过头，不愿再多谈。

云鸥回到了家，苦思冥想，怎么才能得到老虎的胡须呢？后来有一天夜里，待丈夫睡着后，她手端一碗肉米饭悄悄出了家门，来到老虎经常出没的山腰处。她远离老虎洞站在那里，捧出了那碗肉米饭，呼唤老虎过来吃。老虎没有过来。

第二天夜里，云鸥又到了那里，这次站的离老虎洞稍微近了些。她再次捧出一碗饭。每天晚上，云鸥来山中一次，每次都要比前一天夜里靠近老虎洞几步。渐渐地，老虎对她的出现就习以为常了。

一天夜里，云鸥距离老虎洞只有几步远了。这一次，老虎朝她迈了几步，又停住了脚步。他们两个就这样站在月光下互相打量着对方。第二天晚上，出现了同样的情形，只是这一次，他们离得更近了。云鸥已经能够用软语轻声跟老虎说话。第三天夜里，待仔细看了云鸥的眼睛后，老虎吃掉了她捧上的饭食。从那以后，云鸥每次晚上过来，就会发现老虎在道上迎候她。等老虎吃过饭，她总能用手轻轻抚摸他的头。从她第一次探望老虎，将近半年过去了。终于，有一天晚上爱抚过老虎的头后，云鸥说："噢，老虎，慷慨的伙伴，我必须取你一根胡须，你可别生我的气啊！"

随后，她便剪了一根老虎的胡须。

老虎没有像她担心的那样生气。云鸥顺着山路下来了，这个时候她不是行走，而是奔跑了起来，手里紧紧攥着老虎的那根胡须。

第二天早上，她来到山中隐士住的地方，这时太阳刚好从海上冉冉升起。“噢，大圣人！”她大声喊道，“我拿到了！我有老虎的胡须了！现在你可以给我做你事先答应过的魔液了吧，这样我的丈夫就会重新钟情温柔。”

隐士接过那根胡须，仔细瞧了瞧。看到那确实是老虎的胡须，他感到非常满意，就倾身向前把那根胡须丢进了壁炉里正在燃烧的火中。

“噢，先生！”年轻女子痛苦地叫道。“你这是做什么呀！”

“告诉我你是怎么拿到的，”隐士说。

“唉，天天晚上我端一小碗饭上到山腰。起先，我远远地站在那里，后来我一次一次逐渐靠近，赢得了老虎的信任。我轻声柔语，安慰他，使他明白我对他只有好意。我很有耐心，每天晚上都给他送去食物。尽管我知道他不会吃，但我没有放弃。我跑了一趟又一趟，从不说苛刻的话，也从不责怪他。终于，有一天夜里，他向我迈了几步。有一段时间，他开始在道上迎接我，并愿意就着我端的碗吃。我轻轻地抚摸起他的头，他的喉咙里不时发出愉悦的声音。我就是这个时候取走了它的胡须。”

“好，好，”隐士说。“你驯服了老虎，赢得了他的信任和爱。”

“可你已经把那根胡须扔进了火里！”云鸥叫道。“一切都完了！”

“不，我认为一切都没有完，”隐士说。“那根胡须已经没有必要了。云鸥，我来问你，一个男人比一只老虎凶残吗？哪一个更不善解人心？如果你能通过温柔和耐心赢得一只嗜血成性的野兽的爱和信任，你肯定也能对丈夫做到吧？”

听了这番话，云鸥站在那里，默然无语。过了一会儿，她便沿着小路下山了。她一直在脑海里思考着山中隐士在屋里对她的那些点化。

One-dollar Tip

In a dirty and messy waiting room, a tired old man sat on the seat by the door. When the train pulled in, the ticket-punching began. The old man stood up in no hurry, ready to go to the ticket-punching entrance. Suddenly, a fat old lady entered the waiting room. She carried a large suitcase, obviously riding this train. But the suitcase was so heavy that she was out of breath. Seeing the old man, the fat old lady shouted at him, "Hi, old chap, carry the suitcase for me and I'll give you a tip awhile." The old man carried the suitcase and headed for the entrance with the fat old lady.

Hardly were the tickets punched and they just got on when the train had started. The fat old lady wiped off the sweat and said luckily, "Thanks to you, or I'll surely miss the train." Then, she fished out one dollar and handed it to the old man, who took it with a smile. At that moment, the conductor went along. "Hi, Mr. Rockefeller, welcome to ride this train. What can I do for you, please?"

"No, thanks, I just made a three-day hiking, and now I'm going to return to New York headquarters," the old man replied politely.

"What, Rockefeller!" the fat old lady exclaimed, "My God, I even let oil tycoon Mr. Rockefeller carry the suitcase for me and gave him one-dollar tip. What was I doing?" She hurriedly apologized to Rockefeller and pleaded him to give back the tip to her in awe.

"Madam, you needn't apologize, for you did nothing wrong at all," Rockefeller said with a smile, "this one dollar was what I earned, so I took it." With the words, Rockefeller put the dollar into his pocket solemnly.

The real great people are the ones who are at the top, but still know how to be the common people.

一美元小费

在一个又脏又乱的候车室，靠门的座位上坐着一个满脸疲惫的老人。列车进站，开始检票了。老人不急不忙地站起来，准备往检票口走。突然，候车室走进来一个胖太太，她提着一个很大的箱子，显然也是赶这班列车，可箱子太重了，累得她呼呼直喘。胖太太看到了那个老人，冲他大喊："喂，老头，你给我提一下箱子，我一会儿给你小费。"那个老人拎过箱子，就和胖太太向检票口走去。

他们刚刚检票上车，火车就启动了。胖太太抹了一把汗，庆幸地说："还真多亏了你，不然我非误车不可。"说着，她掏出一美元，递给了那个老人。老人微笑着接了过去。这时，列车长走了过来。"洛克菲勒先生，您好，欢迎您乘坐本次列车，请问我能为您做点什么吗?"

"谢谢，不用了，我只是刚刚做了一个为期 3 天的徒步旅行，现在我要回纽约总部了。"老人客气地回答。

"什么，洛克菲勒!"胖太太惊叫起来。"上帝，我竟让洛克菲勒先生给我提箱子，居然还给了他一美元小费，我这是在干什么啊!"她忙向洛克菲勒道歉，并诚惶诚恐地请洛克菲勒把那一美元小费退给她。

"太太，你不必道歉，你根本没做错什么。"洛克菲勒微笑着说。"这一美元是我挣的，所以我收下了。"说着，洛克菲勒把那一美元郑重地放进了口袋里。

真正的大人物是那种身在高位、仍懂得如何去做平常人的人。

Movement and Quietude

An athlete was debating with an old monk.

"Life lies in movement," the athlete roared.

"Life lies in quietude," the old monk whispered.

"Quietude is idleness!" the athlete said plausibly.

"Movement is fickleness!" the old monk didn't give in.

"Quietude is a pool of backwater!" "Movement is a gust of dark wind!"...

For the essence of life, the two of them argued heatedly among themselves. So far each of them sticks to his own version, unable to convince the other of accepting the definition of life.

In fact, they may completely think from the angle of the other and completely abandon the dispute, for life not only lies in movement, but also quietude.

A flower in silent bloom is a kind of beauty, so is a bird in swift flight.

动与静

一个运动员跟一个老和尚辩论。

“生命在于运动。”运动员大声吼道。

“生命在于宁静。”老和尚低声说道。

“宁静就是懒惰！”运动员振振有词。

“运动等于浮躁！”老和尚毫不相让。

“宁静是一潭死水！”“运动是一阵黑风！”……

对于生命的本质，他们二人吵得不可开交，至今仍然各执一词，谁也无法说服对方，让对方接受自己对于生命的定义。

其实，他们完全可以站在对方的角度想一想，完全放弃争吵，因为生命既在于运动，也在于宁静。

一朵悄悄开放的花，是一种美丽；一只匆匆飞过的鸟，也是一种美丽。

Are You a Carrot, an Egg or Coffee Bean

A daughter complained to her father about her life, saying everything was so difficult. She didn't know how to cope with her life, so she wanted to abandon herself to despair. She had been tired of struggle and endeavor, as if a problem was just resolved and a new problem emerged again.

Her father was a cook. He took her to the kitchen, first poured some water into the three pots, and then put them on the roaring fire to burn. Pretty soon, the water began boiling. He put some carrots into the first pot, an egg into the second one and coffee bean ground into powder into the third. He cooked them in the boiling water without a word.

His daughter smacked her lips, impatiently waiting and wondering what her father was doing. About 20 minutes later, he closed the fire, scooped the carrot out into a bowl, the egg into another bowl and coffee into a cup. After doing these, he turned to his daughter and asked, "Honey, what did you see?" "Carrots, an egg and coffee," she answered.

He let her close up and touch the carrots with her hands. After touching them, she felt they turned soft. Her father let his daughter take up the egg and break it. After shelling it, he saw it was a cooked egg. Finally, he let her drink the coffee. Tasting the savory coffee, her daughter smiled. She asked, "Father, What does this mean?"

He explained that these three things faced the same adversity—the boiled water, but their reactions were different. The carrots were strong and solid, without weakness before into the boiling water, but after into it, they softened and weakened. The egg was originally fragile, its thin shell protecting the liquid insides; but after being boiled, its insides turned hard. And the powdered coffee beans was very unique, for entering the boiling water, they changed the water. "Which one is you?" he asked his daughter. "When you encounter the adversity, how will you react? Are you a carrot, an egg or coffee bean?"

His daughter was lost in thought.

你是胡萝卜、鸡蛋还是咖啡豆

一个女儿对父亲抱怨她的生活,抱怨事事都那么艰难。她不知该如何应付生活,想要自暴自弃。她已厌倦抗争和奋斗,好像一个问题刚解决,新的问题就又出现了。

她的父亲是一位厨师,他把她带进厨房。他先往三只锅里倒入一些水,然后把它们放在旺火上烧。不久,锅里的水就烧开了。他往一只锅里放些胡萝卜,第二只锅里放只鸡蛋,最后一只锅里放入碾成粉末状的咖啡豆。他将它们浸入开水中煮,一句话也没说。

女儿咂咂嘴,不耐烦地等待着,纳闷父亲在做什么。大约20分钟后,他闭了火,把胡萝卜捞出来放入一个碗里,把鸡蛋捞出来放进另一个碗里,然后又把咖啡舀到了一个杯子里。做完这些后,他才转过身问女儿:"亲爱的,你看见什么了?""胡萝卜、鸡蛋、咖啡。"她回答说。

他让她靠近些,并让她用手摸摸胡萝卜。她摸了摸,注意到它们变软了。父亲又让女儿拿那只鸡蛋并打破它。她剥掉壳后,看到的是一只煮熟的鸡蛋。最后,他让她喝了咖啡。品尝到香浓的咖啡,女儿笑了。她问道:"爸爸,这意味着什么?"

他解释说,这三样东西面临同样的逆境——煮沸的开水,但其反应各不相同。胡萝卜入锅之前强壮结实、毫不示弱;但进入开水后,它变软变弱。鸡蛋原来是易碎的,薄薄的外壳保护着呈液体的内脏;但经开水一煮,它的内脏变硬了。而粉状咖啡豆则很独特,进入沸水后,却改变了水。"哪个是你呢?"他问女儿。"你遇到逆境时,该如何反应?你是胡萝卜、鸡蛋还是咖啡豆?"

他的女儿陷入了沉思。

Please Bury Me Shallowly

During World War II, a Nazi concentration camp imprisoned many Jews, most of whom were women and children, suffering from the Nazis' ruthless torture and slaughter.

There was a naive lively little girl, who was put in the concentration camp with her mother. One day, her mother and some other women were taken away by the Nazi soldiers and never returned to her side. People knew they must have been killed. When the girl asked the grown-ups where her mother had gone and why she hadn't come back for such a long time, they shed tears in silence. Later, they fooled the little girl, saying that your mother went to look for your father and would return soon. The little girl believed it, so she stopped weeping and asking, but sang the children's songs her mother had taught her, one after another, echoing as a breeze in the dismal concentration camp. She climbed onto the small window to look out of it from time to time, hoping to see her mother walking from a distance.

The little girl didn't wait for her mother to come back. On one morning, the Nazi soldiers drove her and dozens of thousands of Jews to the execution ground with the bayonets. On the execution ground a huge pit had been dug earlier. They would be buried alive here. The people were silent, the death impending over every life so veritably. Faced with the death, the people couldn't make any voice in trepidation.

One by one, the Nazi soldiers cruelly pushed the people into the pit. When one of the Nazi soldiers went to her and stretched out to push her into the pit, the little girl widened her beautiful eyes and said to the Nazi soldier, "Uncle, please bury me shallowly, will you? Or when my mother comes to look for me, she won't find me."

The Nazi soldier's outstretched hand froze in the air.

请把我埋得浅一点

二战时期,一座纳粹集中营里关押着很多犹太人,他们大多是妇女和儿童,遭受着纳粹无情的折磨和杀害。

有一个天真活泼的小女孩,和她的母亲一起被关押在集中营里。一天,她的母亲和另一些妇女被纳粹士兵带走了,从此再也没有回到她身边。人们知道,她们肯定是被杀害了。当小女孩问大人们她的妈妈哪里去了,为什么这么久还不回来时,大人们沉默着流泪了。后来,他们就骗小女孩说,你的妈妈去找你的爸爸了,不久就会回来的。小女孩相信了,她不再哭泣和询问,而是唱起了妈妈教她的儿歌,一首接一首地唱着,像轻风一样回荡在阴沉的集中营。她还不时爬上小窗,向外张望,希望看到妈妈从远处走来。

小女孩没有等到妈妈回来。就在一天清晨,纳粹士兵用刺刀驱赶着,将她和数万名犹太人逼上了刑场。刑场上早就挖好了很大的深坑,他们将一起被活埋在这里。人们沉默着,死亡是如此真实地逼近每一个生命。面对死亡,人们在恐惧中发不出任何声音。

纳粹士兵把人们一个接一个残忍地推下了深坑。当一个纳粹士兵走到小女孩跟前,伸手要将她推进深坑时,小女孩睁大漂亮的眼睛对纳粹士兵说:"叔叔,请你把我埋得浅一点好吗?要不,等我妈妈来找我时,就找不到我了。"

纳粹士兵伸出的手僵在了半空中。

God's Boxes

I have in my hands two boxes God gave me to hold.

He said, "Put all your sorrows in the black box, and all your joys in the gold one."

I did as he told, and in the two boxes both my joys and sorrows I stored. But though the gold box became heavier each day, the black one was as light as before. Out of curiosity, I opened the black box; I wanted to find out why. And I saw, in the base of the box, a hole my sorrows had fallen out by.

I showed the hole to God, and mused, "I wonder where my sorrows could be."

He smiled gently and said, "My child, they are all here with me."

I asked God why he gave me the boxes, one the gold, and the other the black with the hole.

"My child, the gold is for you to count your blessings; the black is for you to let go."

上帝的盒子

我手里拿着上帝让我拿的两只盒子。

他说："把你所有的悲伤放进黑盒里，把所有的快乐放进金盒里。"

我按照他说的做了，在两只盒子里存放了我的快乐和悲伤。可是，尽管每天金盒越来越重，那只黑盒却像从前一样轻。由于好奇，我打开黑盒，想找到原因。我看到盒底有一个洞，我的悲伤已经从那里掉了出去。

我让上帝看那个洞，然后沉思道："我不知道我的悲伤可能去了哪里。"

他温和地微微一笑说："我的孩子，它们都在我这里。"

我问上帝为什么他给我的盒子一个是金色的、另一个是黑色有洞的。

"我的孩子，金盒是让你清点祝福，黑盒是让你放走悲伤。"

Life Is Like Water

There was a man who came down in the world and couldn't achieve his ambition. So he was recommended to a sage.

The sage thought for a long time, silently scooped up the water and asked, "What is the shape of the water?" the sage poured the water into the glass before he could answer. The man took a tumble, "I know, water is like a glass shape." The sage said nothing and poured the water into the vase nearby. The man realized it, "I know, water is like a vase." The sage shook his head, gently carried the vase in both hands and poured the water into the pot filled with sand. The clear water disappeared into the sand.

The man was lost in thought.

The sage bent down to grasp a handful of sand and sighed, "Look, the water died away like this; this is a lifetime!"

The man said happily, "I know, you tell me the society is like various containers everywhere, so man should be like water. When you are in a certain container, you will become its shape and easily die in a regular container, just like the water, disappearing rapidly and suddenly; and nothing can change!" with the words, the man stared at the sage's eyes, for he was eager to be affirmed.

"Yes," then the sage added, "No!" the sage went out of the house while the man followed. Under the eaves, the sage bent over, touched the flagstone steps for a while and stopped. The man reached out his hand to where the sage had just touched and saw a concave, but he didn't know what secret the cavity on the flat stone step hid.

The sage said, "In rainy days, the rain water would fall from the eaves, so the concave is the result the water falls."

The man came to see light. "I understand people may be put into the regular containers, but they should be like the little drop of water, holing the hard flagstones, until changing the containers."

The sage said, "Right, this concave will turn into a hole!"

Life is like water, so we must not only make every effort to adapt to the environments, but also we should try to change the environments to realize our own value. We should have more tenacity and bend and turn when necessary because it is too hard, it will easily break. Only those who are not only stiff but also have more flexibility and resilience can they overcome more difficulties and setbacks.

人生如水

有一个人总是落魄不得志，便有人向他推荐智者。

智者深思良久，默然舀起水，然后问：“这水是什么形状?”智者没等回答，又把水倒入杯子。这人恍然大悟：“我知道了，水的形状像杯子。”智者无语，把杯子中的水倒入旁边的花瓶。这人悟道：“我知道了，水的形状像花瓶。”智者摇头，轻轻端起花瓶，把水倒入一只盛满沙土的盆子。清水便一下融入沙土不见了。

这个人陷入了沉思。

智者弯腰抓起一把沙土，叹道：“看，水就这么消逝了，这也是一生!”

这个人高兴地说：“我知道了，您是告诉我，社会处处像一个个规则的容器，人应该像水一样，盛进什么容器就是什么形状，而且人还极可能在一个规则的容器中消逝，就像这水一样，消逝得迅速、突然，而且一切无法改变!”这人说完，眼睛紧盯着智者的眼睛，他现在急于得到智者的肯定。

“是这样。”智者转而又说，“又不是这样!”说完，智者出门，这人随后跟着。在屋檐下，智者伏下身子，手在青石板台阶上摸了一会儿，然后顿住。这人把手伸向刚才智者所触之地，看见有一个凹处。他不知道这本来平整的石阶上的“小窝”藏着什么玄机。

智者说：“一到雨天，雨水就会从屋檐落下，这个凹处就是水落下的结果。”

此人大悟：“我明白了，人可能被装入规则的容器，但又应该像这小小的水滴，击穿这坚硬的青石板，直到改变容器。”

智者说：“对，这个窝就会变成一个洞!”

人生如水，我们既要尽力适应环境，也要努力改变环境，实现自我。我们应该多一点韧性，能够在必要时弯一弯、转一转，因为太坚硬容易折断。唯有那些不只是坚硬、而且更多一些柔韧和弹性的人，才能克服更多困难，战胜更多挫折。

What Is the Best in Life?

There was a young man who had a strange disease-he was depressed all day long.

One day, he paid a visit to a wise man for effective prescription. The wise man told him, "What do you think is the best thing that will make you happy?" He looked around and could not find the best thing. So he decided to look for it.

The young man packed his luggage, said goodbye to his family and started his journey.

The first day he met a politician, he asked, "Sir, do you know what is the best thing in the world?" The politician answered with a bureaucratic tone, "The best thing in the world is power." He reflected for a moment and found that power did not attract him much. As a result, he continued his journey.

The second day, he ran into a beggar and asked him the same question. Narrowing his eyes, the beggar said casually, "The best thing? It must be the delicious food." After consideration, he decided that he had little longing for food, so it was not the answer he wanted.

The third day he met a woman and brought forward that question once again. She blurted out joyfully, "Of course it is the upscale and beautiful garment from Paris!" He was not interested in garment and left at last.

The fourth day he saw two men in serious disease. When asked the best thing in their minds, they said with regret, "Isn't it obvious? It's health!" The man disagreed, "How come health is the best thing? I own it every day but I don't think it is the best thing."

The fifth day he met a child playing under the sunshine. When the child naively said, "The best thing is to have as many toys as I can," the man shook his head and kept on his journey.

The following days he successively ran into an old woman, a merchant, a painter, a prisoner, a mother and a young man.

The old woman said, "Youth is the best thing."

The merchant said, "Profit."

The painter said, "Color."

The prisoner said, "Freedom."

The mother said, "My precious child."

The young man said, "The smile of my beloved girl."

None of these answers had satisfied him. He kept moving forward and encountering different people. Finally, he came back to the wise man with all kinds of answers.

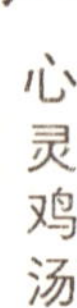

The wise man seemed to have known his experience and his disappointment, so he rubbed his gray beard and said, "Stop looking for the answer as you will never find a precise and unique one. Think about it. Is there anything or scene that you like most now?"

Through the long and wearisome journey the man had suffered hunger and cold with dust covered all over his body. He thought for a while and told the wise man, "I have been out for a long time. I missed my wife and lovely kids. I missed the scene that my whole family sat around the stove talking and laughing in winter nights," he could not help but sighed, "That's my favorite picture now!"

The wise man patted him on the shoulder and said, "Go home. The best thing is in your home now. It will cheer you up."

The man was not convinced, "But I left from my home!"

The wise man smiled, "You didn't know what you like before the journey, but now you must have known what you are fond of."

He was right: The best thing in the world is what we like most.

No matter what you have owned or have not, no matter it is complicated or simple, no matter it is cheap or expensive, as long as you like it, it is bound to be the best thing in the world.

人生最美好的是什么?

有一个年轻人得了一种怪病:他一天到晚都郁郁寡欢。

有一天,他去拜访一位智者寻求良方。智者对他说:"你认为世界上让你快乐的最好东西是什么?"年轻人环顾四周,无法找到最好的东西。于是,他决定去寻找。

年轻人打点行装,告别家人,踏上了旅途。

第一天,他遇到了一位政客,他问:"先生,你知道世界上最好的东西是什么吗?"政客打着官腔说:"世界上最好的东西是权力。"年轻人想了一会儿,发现权力对他没有多大吸引力。因此,他又继续寻找。

第二天,他碰到了一个乞丐,就问了同一个问题。乞丐眯起眼睛,漫不经心地说:"最好的东西?那一定是美食。"年轻人想了想,认为自己对食物不太渴望,所以这不是他想要的答案。

第三天,他遇到了一个女人,又一次提出了那个问题。那个女人兴高采烈地脱口说道:"当然是巴黎高档漂亮的时装了!"年轻人觉得自己对时装不感兴趣,最后就离开了。

第四天,他看到了两个重病的人。当他问他们认为世界上最好的东西是什么时,他们悔恨地说:"这不明摆着吗?是健康。"年轻人不同意这个看法:"健康怎么会是最好的东西呢？我每天都拥有，但我认为它不是最好的东西。”

第五天，他遇到了一个在阳光下玩耍的孩子。当那个孩子天真地说“最好的东西就是有好多好多的玩具”时，这个人摇了摇头，继续赶路。

接下来的几天，他又先后遇到了一位老太太、一个商人、一名画家、一个囚犯、一位母亲和一个年轻人。

老太太说：“年轻是最好的东西。”

商人说：“利润是最好的东西。”

画家说：“色彩是最好的东西。”

囚犯说：“自由是最好的东西。”

母亲说：“我的宝贝孩子是最好的东西。”

年轻人说：“我心爱姑娘的微笑是最好的东西。”

没有一个回答让他满意。他继续向前走，遇到了各种各样的人。最后，他带着五花八门的答案回到了智者身边。

智者似乎已经知道他的体验和失望，就捋着花白胡子说：“不要去寻找答案了，因为你永远找不到一个准确无二的答案。想一下，你现在有什么最喜欢的东西或情景吗？”

这个人经过长途跋涉，疲惫不堪、饥寒交迫、灰尘满身。他想了一会儿，对智者说：“我出门已经很长时间了。我想念妻子和可爱的孩子，想念全家人冬夜围着火炉谈笑风生的情景。”说到这里，他禁不住感叹道.“那是我现在最喜欢的画面！”

智者轻轻地拍了拍他的肩膀，说：“回去吧。最好的东西在你的家里。它会让你快乐起来的。”

这个人不相信：“可我就是从家里离开的！”

智者笑道：“出来前，你不知道自己喜欢什么，但现在你一定已经知道自己喜欢什么了。”

他说的对：世界上最好的东西就是我们最喜欢的东西。

无论是你拥有的还是未曾拥有的，无论它是复杂的还是简单的，无论是便宜的还是昂贵的，只要你喜欢，那它肯定就是世界上最好的东西。

Mary’s Smile

When Mary opened the door, she found a man with a knife glowering at her ferociously. Mary hit a bright idea and said with a smile, “Pal, what a joke! Marketing the kitchen knife? I like it and I buy it...” she said as she let the man inside the house, then went on saying, “You’re the very image of my former kind-hearted neighbor. So glad to see you. Would you like coffee or tea...”

The gangster with a murderous look gradually became bashful.

He stammered, “Thank you, oh, thank you!”

At last, Mary did “buy” the shining kitchen knife; the strange man took the money, hesitated for a while and did leave her. On turning to go, he said, “Miss, you will change all my life!”

玛丽的微笑

玛丽打开门时，发现一个持刀的男人正恶狠狠地看着自己。玛丽灵机一动，微笑着说："朋友，你真会开玩笑！是推销菜刀吧？我喜欢，我要一把……"她一边说，一边让男人进屋，接着说："你很像我过去的一位好心的邻居，看到你真的好高兴，你要咖啡还是茶……"

本来面带杀气的歹徒渐渐腼腆了起来。

他结结巴巴地说："谢谢，噢，谢谢！"

最后，玛丽真的"买"下了那把明晃晃的菜刀，陌生男人拿着钱迟疑一会儿，真的走了，他在转身离去时说："小姐，你将会改变我的整个一生！"

Thank the Hand of Life

Thanksgiving Day was near. The first grade teacher gave her class a fun assignment—to draw a picture of something for which they were thankful.

Most of the class would celebrate the holiday with turkey and other traditional goodies of the season. These, the teacher thought, would be the subjects of most of her student's art. And they were.

But Douglas made a different kind of picture. He was a different kind of boy. As other children played at recess, Douglas was likely to stand close by her side.

Yes, his picture was different. When asked to draw a picture of something for which he was thankful, he drew a hand. Nothing else. Just an empty hand.

His abstract image captured the imagination of his peers. Whose hand could it be? One child guessed it was the hand of a farmer because farmers raise turkeys. Another suggested that of a police officer because the police protect and care for people...

The teacher paused at Douglas' desk, bent down and asked him whose hand it was.

The little boy murmured, "It's yours, teacher."

She recalled the times she had taken his hand and walked with him. How often had she said, "Take my hand, Douglas, we'll go outside." "Let me show you how to hold your pencil." "Let's do this together."

Brushing aside a tear, she went on with her work.

In fact, people might not always say "thanks". But they'll remember the hand that reaches out.

感谢人生的援手

感恩节即将来临。一年级老师给学生们布置了一道有趣的作业，就是画一幅他们感谢某事的图画。

大多数学生常常用火鸡和其他传统季节美食来庆祝节日。老师认为，这将是大多数学生艺术创作的主题。而且确实是这样。

但是，道格拉斯画了一幅与众不同的画。他是一个与众不同的男孩。其他孩子课间休息做游戏时，他十有八九都站在老师身边。

是的，他的画与众不同。当老师要求画一幅感谢某事的图画时，他画了一只手。别的什么也没有。仅仅是一只空手。

他这张抽象画引起了同学们的想象力。这会是谁的手呢？有一个孩子猜那是农夫的手，因为农夫们养火鸡。另一个孩子猜那是警察的手，因为警察保护和照顾人们……

老师在道格拉斯的课桌边停住了脚步，弯下腰，问他那是谁的手。

小男孩低声说道："老师，那是您的手。"

她回忆起了自己曾拉着他的手一起散步的一次次情景。她常常说："道格拉斯，拉着我的手，我们到外面去。""让我给你示范一下怎样握铅笔。""让我们一起做。"

她擦去眼角的一滴泪，继续讲起了课。

其实，人们可能并不总是感恩，但他们会铭记伸出的援手。

It Is As You Will

There was once a wise old woman who lived back in the hills. All the children used to come back and ask her questions. She always gave the right answers.

There was a naughty little boy among the children. One day he caught a tiny bird and held it in his cupped hands. Then he gathered his friends around. He said, "Let's trick the old woman. I'll ask her what I'm holding in my hands. Of course, she'll answer that I have a bird. Then I'll ask her if the bird is living or dead. If she says the bird is dead, I'll open my hands and let the bird fly away. If she says the bird is alive, I'll quickly crush it and show her the dead bird. Either way, she'll be wrong."

The children agreed that this was a clever plan. Up the hill they went to the old woman's hut.

"Granny, we have a question for you," they all shouted.

"What's in my hands?" asked the little boy.

"Why, it must be a bird," replied the old woman.

"But is it living or dead?" demanded the excited boy.

The old woman thought for a moment and then replied, "It is as you will, my child."

你来决定

从前，有一位博学的老妇人，她住在后山。过去所有的孩子都经常来找她问问题。她总是有求必应。

其中有一个调皮的小男孩。有一天，他抓到一只小小鸟，双手捧住，然后把伙伴们叫到身边，说："咱们去骗一下那个老太太。我要问她我手里握着什么东西。她肯定会回答说我握的是小鸟。然后，我问她小鸟是活的还是死的。如果她说鸟是死的，我就张开手让小鸟飞走。如果她说小鸟是活的，我就马上用劲一捏，让她看到那只死鸟。不管用什么方法，她都说不对。"

孩子们都异口同声地说这是一个聪明的计划。他们爬上山，来到了老妇人的小屋。

"奶奶,我们要问您一个问题。"他们都大声说道。

"我手里是什么东西?"那个小男孩问道。

"噢,肯定是一只小鸟。"老妇人回答说。

"可是活的还是死的呢?"小男孩兴奋地问道。

老妇人想了一会儿,然后回答说:"这由你来决定,孩子。"

Love of a Lifetime

A teacher and his student lay down under the big tree near the grass. Then suddenly the student asked the teacher, "Teacher, I'm confused, how do we find our soul mate? Can you help me?"

Silent for a few seconds, the teacher then answered, "Well, it's a pretty hard and easy question."

The teacher continued, "Look that way. There is a lot of grass. Why don't you walk there? Please don't walk backwards, just walk straight ahead. On your way, try to find a blade of beautiful grass and pick it and then give it to me. But just one."

The student said, "Well, OK then... wait for me..." and walked straight ahead to the grass.

A few minutes later the student came back.

The teacher asked, "Well, I don't see a beautiful blade of grass in your hand."

The student said, "On my journey, I found quite a few beautiful blades of grass, but I thought that I would find a better one, so I didn't pick it. But I didn't realize that I was at the end of the field, and I hadn't picked any because you told me not to go back, so I didn't go back."

The teacher said, "That's what will happen in real life."

What is the message of this story?

In the story, grass is the people around you, the beautiful blade of grass is the people that attract you and the grassy field is time.

In looking for your soul mate, please don't always compare and hope that there will be a better one. By doing that, you'll waste your lifetime because time never goes back.

一生的爱

一位老师和他的学生躺在草地边的大树下。这时,学生突然向老师问道:"老师,我很困惑,我们怎么找到情投意合的伴侣呢?您能帮帮我吗?"

老师沉默了一会儿,然后回答说:"噢,这是一个既很难又简单的问题。"

老师接着说:"看那边。有很多,你何不到那里走走?请不要后退,一直向前走。路上,尽力找一棵美丽的草,把它拔下来,然后交给我。但只能拔一棵。"

学生说:"噢,好吧……等着我……"然后径直向草地走去。

几分钟后,学生返回。

老师问道:"唉,我没有看见你手里有漂亮的草呀。"

学生回答说:"我在路上发现了好多漂亮的草,但我认为自己会找到更好的草,就没有拔。但我没有意识到自己走到了地头,因为你告诉我不要后退,所以我一棵也没拔。"

老师说:"现实生活就是这样。"

这个故事的教训是什么呢？

在这个故事里，草就是你周围的人，漂亮的草就是吸引你的人，草地就是时间。

在寻找情投意合的伴侣时，请不要总是比较，希望会有更好的伴侣。如果这样做，你就会浪费一生的时间，因为时间一去不复返。

Life is Like the Heart of a Torch

At that time, I was in the dark period of life.

"My son, let's look at the burning torch in the darkness." My father lit a torch. My father held high the torch and asked, "Look, what's property of the flame?" "It's burning upwards," I said.

My father turned the torch upside down and asked, "What's property of the flame now?" "It is still burning upwards."

"What's the flame like?" "A heart."

"Yes, the flame is the heart of a torch, a heart upward forever," my father said, "whether in prosperity or adversity, whether on the peak or in the valley, the flame always burns upwards, raising the radiance of life. My son, I also hope you can have a heart of torch."

Thank my father and his edification, for it is he who let me have a heart of torch on the long journey of life in future, a heart upward forever.

人生如火炬心

那时，我正处在人生的黑暗时期。

“孩子，让我们来看看黑暗中燃烧的火炬。”父亲点亮了一支火炬。父亲高举起火炬，问：“看，火焰有什么特点呢？”“它在向上燃烧。”我说。

父亲把火炬向下，又问：“现在火焰有什么特点呢？”“它仍是向上燃烧。”“这火焰像什么呢？”“像一颗心。”

“是的，火焰就是火炬的一颗心，一颗永远向上的心。”父亲说。“无论处于顺境，还是逆境，是身在高峰，还是身陷低谷，火焰总是向上燃烧，向上升起生命的光芒。孩子，我也希望你能拥有一颗火炬的心。”

感谢父亲，感谢父亲的教诲，他让我在以后漫漫人生长路上拥有了一颗火炬的心，一颗永远向上的心。

What Will Matter in Life

Ready or not, someday it will come to an end. There will be no more sunrises, no days, no hours or minutes. All the things you collected, whether treasured or forgotten, will pass to someone else.

Your wealth, fame and power will turn to irrelevance. It will not matter what you owned or what you were owed.

Your grudges, resentments, frustrations and jealousies will finally disappear. So, too, your hopes, ambitions and plans will all expire. The wins and losses that once seemed so important will fade away.

It won't matter where you came from, or on what side of the tracks you lived. It won't matter whether you were beautiful or brilliant. Your gender, skin color and race will be irrelevant.

So what will matter? How will the value of your days be measured?

What will matter is not what you bought, but what you built; not what you got, but what you gave.

What will matter is not your success, but your significance.

What will matter is not what you learned, but what you taught.

What will matter is every act of integrity, compassion, courage and sacrifice that encouraged others.

What will matter is not your competence, but your character.

What will matter is not how many people you knew, but how many will feel a lasting loss when you're gone.

What will matter is not your memories, but the memories of those who loved you.

What will matter is how long you will be remembered.

Living a life that matters doesn't happen by accident.

It's not a matter of circumstance but of choice.

Choose to live a life that matters.

人生重要的是什么

无论是否做好准备,总有一天会结束。日出、日子、时分不再会有。你搜集的所有一切,无论是值得珍惜还是应该忘记的,都会传给别人。

你的财富、名声和权力都会变得无关。你拥有的和亏欠的都不再重要。

你的怨恨、不满、沮丧和嫉妒最后都会消失。所以,你的希望、抱负和计划也会统统终止。曾对你看似非常重要的得失也会渐渐消失。

你来自哪里或曾生活在轨道的哪一边不再重要。你是美丽大方还是才华横溢不再重要。你的性别、肤色和种族也不再重要。

那什么才重要的呢?你该如何衡量自己的人生价值呢?

重要的不是你买的,而是你建的,不是你得到的,而是你给予的。

重要的不是你的成功,而是你的意义。

重要的不是你学会了什么,而是你教会了什么。

重要的是你用正直、同情、勇气和牺牲鼓舞他人的每一次举动。

重要的不是你的能力,而是你的品质。

重要的不是你认识多少人,而是你去世时,会有多少人久久失落。

重要的不是你的记忆,而是那些爱你的人的回忆。

重要的是你会被铭记多久。

过一种重要的人生并非偶然。

那不是环境问题,而是选择问题。

选择过一种重要的人生吧。

幸福点亮人生

The Direction of Happiness

A young man was walking by the lakeside when he suddenly saw a piece of gold glittering in the water. He was so happy that he jumped into the water to fish for it. But he couldn't reach it on matter how he tried his best. Being wet, dirty and tired, he had to disembark for a rest. Unexpectedly, after the water became placid, the gold appeared again.

He jumped into the water again unwillingly, but in vain, so he had to disembark again to sit beside the lake. He thought, "Where is the gold coin in the water on earth? I have seen it clearly, why can't I find it even though I have tried so hard?" After the water became placid, the gold coin appeared once again. So once again he jumped into the water to fish for it. He did it again and again, but in vain, which made him really unwilling to accept.

At that moment, his father came to look for him. Seeing his son wet and dirty, he asked, "What happened in the world? Why are you so embarrassed?"

His son answered, "I see a piece of gold coin in the water clearly, but I can't get it anyway!"

His father saw a gold coin seemed on the placid water, so he looked up at the tree and said to his son, "Look! It's not a gold coin but the reflection of the sheet metal that is hung on the tree."

Ordinary people are always busy running about honorary and illusory things while all these just consist in greed, which eclipses our ability of telling right from wrong. Some people think life is hard and we must find a way of releasing at once! So they turn to seek for religious belief; but if religious belief has no right understanding, suggestions or ideas, you will go astray. So we should choose the right direction of life, get rid of evil and cultivating good and comprehend truth.

Worldly substance is illusory like the reflection of the water, so we should often have a contented mind and can understand, tolerate and thank everything, which will reach perfection. In this way, you'll be even-tempered and good-humored every day and have a happy life.

幸福的方向

一位年轻人走到湖边散步，突然看到水中有一块闪闪发亮的金币。他很高兴，就赶快跳进水里捞取。但是，任凭他怎么努力，都捞不到金币。他浑身湿脏、疲倦，只好上来坐在岸边休息。没想到湖水平静之后，金币又显现了出来。

他很不甘心地又跳下水，结果还是没捞到，只得再上来坐着。他心想："水中的金币到底在哪里呢？我明明看到了，为什么费了这么大劲儿还捞不到呢？"等水面又恢复平静后，金币再次出现。于是，他又跳下去捞，如此反复都徒劳无功，他实在很不甘心。

这时，父亲出来找他。看到儿子全身湿淋淋脏兮兮的，就问他："到底发生了什么事？你为什么会如此狼狈？"

儿子回答说："我明明看到水中有金币，可怎么捞都捞不到！"

父亲看到平静的水面上好像真有一个金币，又抬头看看树上，就对儿子说："你看！哪是什么金币，那是挂在树上的金属片，投射在水中呈现的幻影罢了！"

凡夫总是为名利、空幻的东西在奔波、辛劳，而这一切都只在于一贪念，而贪念往往会蒙蔽我们辨别是非的能力。有的人认为，人生很苦，要赶快找解脱的方法，因此转而寻求宗教信仰；但是，如果信仰没有正知、正见、正念，路就会走偏了。所以，我们应该要选

择正确的人生方向,断恶修善,体悟真理。

世间的物质不过如水中倒影般虚无,因此要常怀知足之心,对人生事物能善解、包容、感恩,凡事就能圆融,这样就能天天过得心平气和,拥有一个幸福的人生。

The Uncared-for Happiness

In a painter's house, I saw a very special painting, which was a piece of mounted white paper, on the left middle of which there was a black stain.

I didn't understand what gifted pen such a black stain was that the painter hung it on the most prominent position right in the middle of the wall. I kept pondering for a long time, but my mind was still a complete blank.

I asked the artist for advice.

The painter said, "This painting of mine is called 'Happiness.'"

"Happiness? I don't understand." In my memory, no artist could paint happiness.

The painter said, "The black stain in the middle stands for pain. When every person sees this painting of mine, he or she only sees this painful black stain, but can't see the happiness in the background. Isn't our life in this way? How much happiness we turn a blind eye to, but we are shut out by the minimal pain."

I said, "In your mind, this painting should be a piece of white paper."

He said, "Without pain, we won't even more see happiness."

I come to see that we always focus on the pain while the happiness is often the part we have overlooked.

被忽略的快乐

在一位画家的屋里,我见到了一幅非常特别的画。那是一张被装裱起来的白纸,在中间偏左上的位置有一块黑渍。

我不明白这块黑渍到底算什么生花妙笔,被画家挂在了墙壁正当中最为显眼的位置上。我琢磨了很长时间,头脑里仍然是一片空白。

我向画家请教。

画家说:"我的这幅画叫'快乐'。"

"快乐?我不明白。"在我的记忆中,没有哪个画家能画出快乐来。

画家说:"中间这块黑渍是痛苦,每个人看到我的这幅画时,都是只看到这块痛苦的黑渍,却看不到背景里的快乐。我们的生活不是这样吗?多少快乐,我们都视而不见,却被微小的痛苦遮住了双眼。"

我说:"按照你的说法,这张画应该是一张白纸。"

他说:"没有痛苦,我们更见不到快乐。"

我明白了,我们总是盯着痛苦,而快乐常常是被我们忽略的那部分。

The Catalogue of Happiness

"On my head pour only the sweet waters of serenity. Give me the gift of the untroubled mind."

Once, as a young man full of exuberant fancy, I undertook to draw up a catalogue of the acknowledged happiness of life. As other men sometimes tabulate lists of properties they own or would like to own, I set down my inventory of earthly desirable: health, love, beauty, talent, power, riches and fame.

When my inventory was completed, I proudly showed it to a sage who had been the mentor and spiritual model of my youth. Perhaps I was trying to impress him with my precocious wisdom. Anyway, I handed him the list. "This," I told him confidently. "is the sum of mortal happiness. If a man could possess them all, he would be as a god."

"An excellent list," he said thoughtfully. "But it appears, my young friend, you have omitted the most important element of all. You have forgotten the one ingredient, lacking which each possession becomes a hideous torment."

"And what," I asked, "is that missing ingredient?"

With a pencil stub he crossed out my entire tabulation and wrote down: peace of mind. "This is the gift God reserves," he said.

"Talent and beauty He gives to many. Wealth is commonplace, fame not rare. But peace of mind-that is His final guerdon of approval, the fondest insignia of His love. Most men are never blessed with it; others wait all their lives—yes, far into advanced age—for this gift to descend upon them."

人生幸福的目录

"只将宁静蜜汁醍醐灌顶,赐我以无忧心境。"

我年轻时曾充满丰富的幻想,着手起草了一份被公认为人生幸福的目录。就像他人有时会把他们拥有或想拥有的财产列成表那样,我把世人想要的东西——健康、爱情、美丽、才能、权力、财富和名誉——列了一个详细目录。

我列完这个详细目录后,自豪地让一位智者过目,他曾是我少年时代的辅导老师和精神楷模。也许我是想以自己早熟的智慧给他留下深刻印象。总之,我把那张目录递给了他。我充满自信地对他说:"这是人类幸福的总和。一个人能拥有所有这些,就和神一样了。"

他若有所思地说:"是一张出色的目录。可是,我年轻的朋友,你遗漏了最重要的一个要素。你忘记了一个因素,缺少了它,每项财产都会变成可怕的痛苦。"

我问道:"那遗漏的这个因素是什么?"

他用铅笔头划掉了我的整张表格,写下了:心静。"这是上帝保留的礼物。"他说。

"他把才能和美丽赐予许多人。财富是平凡的,名望也不稀罕,但心静才是他恩准的最后赐赏,是他最温柔的爱的象征。多数人从来没有这种福气,有些人则等了一辈子——是的,一直等到了老态龙钟,才等到这个赏赐降临到他们身上。"

Happiness Is a Choice

Are you happy? Do you remember a time when you were happy? Are you seeking happiness today?

Many have sought a variety of sources for their feeling of happiness. Some have put their heart and efforts into their work. Too many turned to drugs and alcohol. Untold numbers have looked for it in the possession of expensive cars, exotic vacation homes and other popular "toys". Most of their efforts have a root in one common fact: people are looking for a lasting source of happiness.

Unfortunately, I believe that happiness evades many because they misunderstand the process and journey of finding it. I have heard many people say, "I'll be happy when I get my new promotion," or "I'll be happy when I lose that extra 20 pounds." This thinking is dangerous because it presupposes that happiness is a response to having, being or doing something.

In life, we all experience stimulus and response. Stimulus is when a dog barks at you and bares his teeth. Response is when your heart beats faster, your palms get sweaty and you prepare to run. Today, some people think that an expensive car is stimulus. Happiness is a response. A great paying job is stimulus. Happiness is a response. A loving relationship is stimulus. Happiness is a response. This belief leaves us thinking and feeling, "I'll be happy when..."

It has been my finding that actually the opposite is true. I believe that happiness is a stimulus and response is what life brings to those who are truly happy. When we are happy, we tend to have more success in our work. When we are happy, people want to be around us and enjoy loving relationships. When we are happy, we more naturally take better care of our bodies and enjoy good health. Happiness is not a response-rather, it is a stimulus.

Happiness is a conscious choice we make every day of our lives. For unknown reasons to me, many choose to be miserable, frustrated and angry most of the time. Happiness is not something that happens to us after we get something we want—we usually get things we want after we choose to be happy.

I have made only one simple rule for my own happiness: every day above ground is a good day. Therefore, I tend to have a lot of good and happy days in succession.

幸福是一种选择

你感到幸福吗？你还记得过去幸福的时光吗？现今天你在寻找幸福吗？

许多人已经找到了让他们幸福的各种各样的源泉。有的人全身心地投入工作，也有许多人迷上毒品和酒精。还有数不清的人从豪华汽车、异国风情的度假屋和其他流行的“玩具”中寻找幸福。他们的努力大多数是植根于一个共同的事实：人们都在寻找一种持久的幸福源泉。

不幸的是，我认为，幸福之所以躲避很多人，是因为他们误解了寻找幸福的过程和旅程。我曾听到很多人说：“如果能得到新的提升，我就会幸福。”或者“如果减掉那多余的 20 磅，我就会幸福。”这种想法很危险，因为它预示着幸福就是拥有什么、成为什么或做什么的一种反应。

在生活中，我们都能感受到刺激和反应。刺激就是一条狗龇牙咧嘴朝你狂叫，反应则是你心跳加速、掌心出汗、准备跑走。如今，有些人认为，高档汽车是一种刺激，幸福则是一种反应。一份高薪工作是一种刺激，幸福则是一种反应。相亲相爱是一种刺激，幸福则是一种反应。这种想法会让我们有"当……我就会幸福"这样的想法和感觉。

我发现其实恰恰相反。我相信幸福是一种刺激,反应则是生活带给那些真正幸福的人的东西。当我们感觉幸福时,往往在事业上能取得更大的成功。当我们感觉幸福时,人们都想来到我们身边一起分享融融情意。当我们感觉幸福时,我们会更加自然地好好保重自己的身体,享受健康的乐趣。幸福不是一种反应,更准确地说是一种刺激。

幸福是我们对自己生命中每一天做出的有意选择,因为某些我无法知道的原因,很多人在大部分时间选择痛苦、沮丧和愤怒。幸福不是我们拥有自己想要的东西后才能出现的东西,常常是我们先选择让自己幸福、然后才能得到的东西。

为了让自己幸福,我只制定了一个简单的法则:在世的每一天都好好过,因此我常常拥有一个又一个幸福的好日子。

Don't Keep Happiness away from Us

A college student once told me,"I don't need to be happy—just successful."

It's an odd juxtaposition. She needn't be happy-"just successful." She places one in opposition to the other.

Students are today's expressions of tomorrow's practices.

I remember from my own undergraduate years of a headline in my campus newspaper, "Why Aren't We Happy?" As the headline suggested, we fell short of leading joyful lives. Yet at least we are still looking for happiness. Like my success-seeking student, why do many of us want to give up happiness?

I've often failed to enjoy Sunday because of my schedule on Monday. At bottom, it was simply anticipatory anxiety over the work of the week ahead—I fear that there would be unexpected complications or that I would fail to measure in some way. Usually, when Monday came, I did quite well. Much of what I worried about never happened.

Happiness has its own underpinning. There's completeness to happiness that does not allow us to exclude our sense of the person we should be. Pleasure is certainly possible in less-than-honorable actions. But the experience of happiness requires more; it is pleasure taken in worthy things.

True happiness requires choices that develop into habits that evolve into character. And that's work we can't delegate.

So the essential first step is trying to lessen the anxiety—one that can avoid it. It requires us to brave everything unexpected and face all the annoyances of life calmly.

别让幸福远离我们

一名大学生曾告诉我说:"我不需要幸福,只要成功。"

这是一个奇怪的交叉对比。她不需要幸福,"只要成功"。她把这两者对立了起来。

学生今日之言就是明日之行。

我记得上大学时,校报上有一篇文章的标题是:"为什么我们不幸福?"这个标题是说:我们缺少快乐的生活。然而,我们至少仍在寻找幸福。为什么我们中的许多人像那个追求成功的学生一样要放弃幸福呢?

我常常不能去享受星期天,是因为星期一的工作进度。实际上,这仅仅是提前对未来一周的工作感到忧虑,我担心会发生难以预料的麻烦,要么是担心自己在某些方面无法进行估量。通常,星期一来临时,我做得还不错。我担心的很多事情从来没有发生过。

幸福自有其道德基础。幸福的完整性让我们不得不考虑自己应该做什么样的人。当然,一些不怎么光彩的行为也可能会产生快乐。但要想体验幸福,需要付出更多;正是快乐让我们体会到了事物的价值。

真正的幸福需要做出选择,这些选择可以形成习惯,从而发展成为性格。这是我们无法越俎代庖的工作。

因此,获取幸福的首要一步就是尽量减少忧虑,这关键的第一步能让我们避开忧虑。它要求我们勇于接受毫无预想的一切,坦然面对生活中的一切烦恼。

The Secret of Happiness

There was a businessman, who sent his son to the most wise man in the world to ask for the secret of happiness. After going through all hardships for 40 days, this boy finally found the wise man's beautiful castle.

When he entered the castle, the boy didn't meet a saint, but witnessed an unusually lively scene: businesspeople came in and out, in every corner people were talking with each other and a small band was playing gentle music. The local delicacies was placed on a table. The wise man was talking with all the people one by one, so the boy had to wait for two hours for his turn.

The wise man attentively listened to the boy's reason for the visit, but he said at this point he didn't have time to explain the secret of happiness to him. He suggested the boy go around the palace and returned to see him after two hours.

"At the same time I ask you to do one thing," the wise man said as he handed a spoon to the boy and dripped two drops of oil into it, "When you walk, take this spoon and do not let the oil spill."

The boy began walking up and down the steps of the palace, his eyes always focusing on the spoon. Two hours later, he returned to the wise man.

"Have you seen the Persian carpets of my restaurant? Have you seen my garden the gardening master spent 10 years creating? Have you noticed those beautiful sheepskin volumes of my library?" the wise man asked.

The boy was very embarrassed, admitting he didn't see, for what he was only concerned about was the thing the wise man entrusted to him—namely, not to let the drops of oil in the spoon spill.

"Then you go back to see all kinds of rare things in here," the wise man said, "If you don't know a person's home, you won't be able to trust him."

Feeling more easily, the boy picked up the spoon and walked back into the palace. This time, he noticed all the artworks hung on the ceiling and walls, viewed the garden and the surrounding mountain scenery and saw the delicate flowers. When he returned to the wise man again, the boy dwelt on all he saw.

"But where's the two drops of oil I gave you?" the wise man asked.

Looking at the spoon, the boy found the oil had all been spilled.

"So this is the only warning I want to give you," the wise man said, "the secret of happiness lies in enjoying all the wonders of the world and at the same time never forget the two drops of oil in the spoon."

幸福的秘密

有位商人把儿子派往世界上最有智慧的人那里,去讨教幸福的秘密。这位男孩历尽艰辛,走了40天,终于找到了智者的美丽城堡。

男孩走进城堡,没有遇到一位圣人,相反却目睹了一个热闹非凡的场面:商人们进进出出,每个角落都有人在交谈,一支小乐队在演奏轻柔的乐曲。一张桌子上摆满了当地的美味佳肴。智者正一个个同所有的人谈话,所以男孩必须要等两个小时才能轮到。

智者认真地听了男孩所讲的来访原因,但说此刻他没有时间向男孩讲解幸福的秘密。他建议男孩在他的宫殿里转上一圈,两个小时后再来找他。

"与此同时,我要求你办一件事,"智者边说边把一个汤匙递给男孩,并在里面滴进了两滴油。"当你走路时,拿好这个汤匙,不要让油洒出来。"

男孩开始沿着宫殿的台阶上上下下,眼睛始终盯着汤匙不放。两小时后,他回到了智者面前。

"你看到我餐厅里的波斯地毯了吗?看到园艺大师花了十年心血创造出来的花园了吗?注意到我图书馆那些美丽的羊皮卷文献了吗?"智者问道。

男孩感到十分尴尬,承认他什么也没看到,他当时唯一关注的只是智者交付给他的事,也就是不要让汤匙里的两滴油洒出来。

"那你就转回去见识一下我这里的种种珍奇之物吧,"智者说道。"如果你不了解一个人的家,你就不能信任他。"

男孩轻松多了,他拿起汤匙重新回到宫殿里漫步。这一次,他注意到了天花板和墙壁上悬挂的所有艺术品,观赏了花园和四周的山景,看到了娇嫩的花儿。当他再回到智者面前时,男孩仔细地讲述了他所见到的一切。

"可是,我交给你的两滴油在哪里呢?"智者问道。

男孩向汤匙望去,发现油已经洒光了。

"那么,这就是我要给你的唯一忠告,"智者说道,"幸福的秘密在于欣赏世界上所有的奇观异景,同时永远不要忘记汤匙里的两滴油。"

The Law of Happy Life

It is okay to make mistakes. Making mistakes is something we all do, and I'm still a fine and worthwhile person when I make them. There is no reason for me to get upset when I make a mistake. I am trying, so even if I make a mistake, I am going to continue trying. I can handle making a mistake. It is okay for others to make mistakes, too. I will accept mistakes in myself and in others.

Everybody doesn't have to love me. Not everybody has to love me or even like me. I don't necessarily like everybody, I know, so why should everybody else like me? I enjoy being liked and being loved, but if somebody doesn't like me, I will still be okay. I cannot make somebody like me, as somebody cannot get me to like them. I don't need approval all the time. If someone does not approve of me, I will still be okay.

I don't have to control things. I will survive if things are different than what I want them to be. I can accept things the way they are, people the way they are and myself the way I am. There is no reason to get upset if I can't change things to fit my idea of how they ought to be. There is no reason why I should have to like everything. Even if I don't like it, I can't live with it.

I'm responsible for my day. I'm responsible for how I feel and what I do. Nobody can make me feel anything. If I have a rotten day, I'm the one who allows it to be that way. If I have a great day, I'm the one who deserves credit for being positive. It is not the responsibility of other people to change so that I can feel better. I'm the one who is in charge of my life.

I can handle it when things go wrong. I don't need to watch out for things to go wrong all the time. Things usually go just fine, and when they don't, I can handle it. I don't have to waste my energy worrying. The sky won't fall in; things will be okay.

I can do it. I don't need someone else to take care of my problem. I can do it. I can take care of myself. I can make decisions for myself. I can think for myself. I don't have to depend on somebody else to take care of me.

I can play to the score. There is more than one way to do something. More than one person has had good ideas that will work. There is no one and only "best" way. Everybody has ideas that are worthwhile. Some may take more sense to me than others, but everyone's ideas are worthwhile while everyone has something worthwhile to contribute.

幸福生活的定律

犯错误也没什么大不了的。我们都会犯错误。就是犯错误，我还是一个恪尽职守的人才。我犯错误后，完全没有理由忐忑不安。因为我一直在努力，所以即使犯了错误，也会继续努力。我能正确对待犯错误。别人犯错误也没关系。我会接受自己犯错误，也会接受别人犯错误。

并不是人人都得爱我。不是每个人都得爱我或喜欢我。我不一定喜欢我认识的每一个人，所以为什么其他每个人都应该喜欢我呢？尽管我乐意被人喜欢或被人爱，但如果有人不喜欢我，我仍会好好的。我无法迫使某个人喜欢我，就像某个人也不能迫使我喜欢他一样。我不需要时时刻刻得到认可。如果有人不认可我，我仍会好好的。

我不必事事都控制。就是事情和我想的不一样，我也照样活着。我能接受事情本来的样子，接受人们本来的面貌，接受本真的我。如果我不能让事情成为我想要的样子，也没有什么理由忐忑不安。我没有理由要喜欢所有的一切。即使不喜欢，我仍能忍受。

我对自己的每一天负责。我对自己的感觉和自己的所为负责。没有人能强迫我对一切事情的感觉。如果我一天过得很糟，那是我对自己的放任自流。如果我一天过得很棒，那是我态度积极，应该受到赞扬。其他人没有责任为了让我感觉更好而改变。我是掌握自己人生的主人。

出了问题，我能处理。我不必时刻担心事情会出错。事情常常会顺利进行，就是不能顺利进行，我也能处理好。我不必浪费时间去杞人忧天。天不会塌下来，一切都会 OK。

我能行。我不需要别人来处理我的问题。我能行。我能照顾好自己，能自己做出决

定,能自己思考。我不必依靠别人来照顾我。

我能随机应变。做事方法不止一种。不止一个人有奏效的妙方。也没有哪一种方法"无懈可击"。每个人都有值得一试的主意。有些可能对我更有帮助,但每个人的主意都有可取之处,每个人都能想出一些好办法。

The Ways of Happiness

I live in the land of Disney, Hollywood, where the sun shines all the year. You may think people in such a glamorous place brimming over with fun are happier than others. If so, you have some mistakes about the nature of happiness.

Many intelligent people still equate happiness with fun. The truth is that fun and happiness have little or nothing in common. Fun is what we experience during an act. Happiness is what we experience after an act. It is a deeper, more abiding emotion.

The way people firmly believe that life full of joy and away from pain equaling happiness actually diminishes their chances of ever attaining real happiness. If fun and pleasure are equated with happiness, pain must be equated with unhappiness. But in fact, the opposite is true: more times than not, things that lead to happiness involve some pain.

As a result, many people avoid the very endeavors that are the source of true happiness. They fear the pain inevitably brought by such things as marriage, raising children, professional achievement, religious commitment, civic or charitable work and self-improvement.

Ask a bachelor why he resists marriage even though he finds dating to be less and less satisfying. If he's honest, he will tell you that he is afraid of making a commitment. For commitment is in fact quite painful. The single life is filled with fun, adventure and excitement. Marriage has such movement, but they are not its most distinguishing features.

Similarly, couples who choose not to have children are in favor of painless fun over painful happiness. They can dine out whenever they want, travel wherever they want and sleep as late as they want. Couples with infants are lucky to get a whole night's sleep or a three-day vacation. I don't know any parents would choose the word fun to describe raising children.

But couples who decide not to have children never experience the pleasure of hugging them or tucking them into bed at night. They never know the joy of watching a child grow up or of playing with a grandchild.

But these forms of fun do not contribute in any way to my happiness. Writing, raising children, creating deep relationship with my wife and trying to do good in the world will bring me more happiness.

Understanding and accepting that true happiness has nothing to do with fun is one of the most liberating realizations we can ever come to. It liberates time: now we can devote more hours to activities that can genuinely increase our happiness. It liberates money: buying that new car or those fancy clothes won't increase our happiness now. And it liberates us from envy: we now understand that all those rich and glamorous people we were so sure are happy because actually they are not be happy at all.

The moment we understand that fun doesn't bring happiness, we will begin to lead our lives differently. The effect can be surely life-transforming.

幸福的方式

我住在好莱坞迪斯尼乐园,那里一年四季阳光普照。你也许以为生活在那样富有魅力、充满乐趣的地方一定比别的地方的人幸福。假如这样的话，你就对幸福的真谛有些误解。

很多聪明人仍把幸福和乐趣相提并论。其实，乐趣和幸福几乎或根本没有共同之处。乐趣是我们行为过程中的体验。幸福是我们行为过后的体验。它是一种更深刻、更持久的感情。

人们坚信充满欢乐、远离痛苦的生活方式就等于幸福，其实减少了他们获得真正幸福的机会。如果欢乐和愉快等同幸福，那痛苦就一定等同不幸。但事实上恰恰相反：多数情况下，能带来幸福的事物常常包含一些痛苦。

因此，许多人避开的那些努力正是真正幸福的源泉。他们害怕那些必定会带来痛苦的事情，比如结婚、抚养子女、专业成就、承担宗教义务、社会或慈善事业以及自我改善。

即使一个单身汉对约会越来越不满意，你问他为什么不想结婚时，如果他诚实，也会告诉你，他害怕承担义务。因为承担义务确实非常痛苦。独身生活充满乐趣、冒险和激情。尽管婚姻也有这样的活动，但大为逊色。

同样，选择不要孩子的夫妇都赞成没有痛苦的快乐，而不要痛苦的幸福。他们可以随时出去吃饭，随便到什么地方旅游，想睡多晚就睡多晚。有小孩子的夫妻能睡一晚上或有 3 天假期，算是幸运的了。我不知道什么夫妇会用“乐趣”这个词来形容抚养孩子。

可是，决定不要孩子的夫妇绝不会体会到拥抱孩子或晚上给孩子掖被子时的乐趣。他们绝不会明白看着孩子长大或逗弄孙子孙女的喜悦。

不过，这些形式的乐趣无论如何都不是我说的幸福。写作、抚养孩子、加深和妻子的感情和尽力做善事会给我带来更多的幸福。

理解并接受真正的幸福和娱乐无关，我们就能获得最大限度的解放。它解放时间：现在我们可以把更多时间用于那些能真正增加我们幸福的活动。它解放金钱：买那辆新车或那些时尚衣服现在不会增加我们的幸福。而且它把我们从嫉妒中解放出来：我们现在理解了那些我们确信幸福、令人向往的富人，因为他们其实根本不幸福。

我们懂得了娱乐不会带来幸福，就会开始以不同的方式生活。其效果肯定会改变人生。

The Door to Happiness

Happiness is like a pebble dropped into a pool to set in motion an ever-widening circle of ripples. As Stevenson said, “Being happy is a duty.”

There is no exact definition of the word—happiness. Happy people are happy for all sorts of reasons. The key is not wealth or physical well-being, for we find beggars, invalids and so-called failures are extremely happy.

Being happy is a sort of unexpected dividend5. But staying happy is an accomplishment, a triumph of soul and character. It is not selfish to strive for it. It is, indeed, a duty to us and others.

Being unhappy is like an infectious disease; it causes people to shrink away from the sufferer. He soon finds himself alone, miserable and embittered. There is, however, a cure that seems ridiculous but simple: if you don't feel happy, pretend to be!

It works. Before long you will find that instead of repelling people, you attract them. You will discover how deeply rewarding it is to be the center of wider and wider circles of goodwill.

Then the make-believe becomes a reality. You possess the secret of peace of mind and can forget yourself in being of service to others.

Being happy, once it is realized as a duty and established as a habit, opens door into mysterious gardens thronged with grateful friends.

幸福之门

幸福就像掉进池塘里的一枚鹅卵石，渐渐荡起一圈圈涟漪，不断向外扩散。就像史蒂文森所说：“幸福是一种责任。”

“幸福”这个词没有确切的定义，幸福的人之所以幸福，有各种各样的理由。关键不在财富或健康，因为我们发现乞丐、残疾人和所谓的失败者都特别快乐。

幸福是一种意想不到的红利。但保持幸福是一种成就，是灵魂和品格的成功。追求幸福并不是自私，其实是对自己和他人的一种责任。

郁郁寡欢就像传染病，这使人们常常对郁郁寡欢的人退避三舍。他很快会发现自己孤独、痛苦和难过。然而，有一种治疗方法看似荒唐，其实简单：如果你觉得不幸福，就假装幸福！

这很管用。不久，你会发现，自己会吸引他人，而不是令人不快。你会发现以善意为中心、越来越宽广的交际圈是多么有益，深得人心。

于是，假装的幸福就成了一种事实。你拥有内心平静的秘诀，就能在帮助他人时忘记自我。

一旦意识到保持幸福心境是一种责任并形成一种习惯，就能打开神秘花园的门，那里聚集着满怀感激的朋友们。

Happiness Doesn't Need a List

A man and his girlfriend were married. It was a large celebration.

All of their friends and family came to see the lovely ceremony and to partake of the festivities and celebrations. All had wonderful time.

The bride was gorgeous in her white wedding gown and the groom was very dashing in his black tuxedo. Everyone could tell that the love they had for each other was true.

A few months later, the wife came to the husband with a proposal, "I read in a magazine, a while ago, about how we can strengthen our marriage. Each of us will write a list of the things that we find a bit annoying with the other person. Then, we can talk about how we can fix them together and make our lives happier together."

The husband agreed. So each of them went to a separate room in the house and thought of the things that annoyed them about the other. They thought about this question for the rest of the day and wrote down what they came up with.

The next morning, at the breakfast table, they decided that they would go over their lists.

"I'll start," offered the wife. She took out her list. It had many items on it. Enough to fill 3 pages, in fact. As she started reading the list of the little annoyances, she noticed that tears were starting to appear in her husband's eyes.

"What's wrong?" she asked.

"Nothing," the husband replied. "Keep reading your list."

The wife continued to read until she had read all three pages to her husband. She neatly placed her list on the table and folded her hands over the top of it.

"Now, you read your list and then we'll talk about the things on both of our lists," she said happily.

Quietly the husband stated, "I don't have anything on my list. I think that you are perfect the way that you are. I don't want you to change anything for me. You are lovely and wonderful and I wouldn't want to try and change anything about you."

The wife, touched by his honesty and the depth of his love for her and his acceptance of her, turned her head and wept.

In life, there are enough times when we are disappointed, depressed and annoyed. We don't really have to go looking for them. We have a wonderful world that is full of beauty, light and promise. Why waste time in this world looking for the sad, disappointing or annoying when we can look around us, and see the wondrous things before us?

幸福不需要列单子

一个男人和他的女朋友喜结连理，举行了一场盛大庆典。

所有的亲朋好友都来亲眼目睹这场迷人的典礼，同喜同贺，大家都非常开心。

新娘一袭雪白婚纱，光彩照人；新郎一身黑色礼服，英气逼人。大家都能看出来，他们彼此相爱是出于真心。

几个月后，妻子向丈夫提出了一个建议："我刚才在杂志上看到一篇文章，说的是我们如何能巩固我们的婚姻。我们各自列出使对方有点儿生气的事情，然后可以商量一下看如何一起解决，这会使我们的生活更加幸福。"

丈夫表示同意。于是，他们各自到自己的房间里想使对方生气的事情。那天剩下的时间，他们都在想这个问题，并把想起来的事情写了下来。

第二天早上吃早饭时，他们决定仔细看了一下对方写的。

"我先来吧，"妻子主动说道。她拿出自己列的单子，上面确实写了满满 3 页。她开始念丈夫那些小毛病时，注意到丈夫的眼里涌出了泪水。

"怎么了？"她问道。

"没什么，"丈夫答道。"继续念你的单子吧。"

妻子接着念，直到向丈夫念完 3 张纸后，才把单子整齐地放在桌子上，两手交叉放在上面。

"现在，你念自己的单子吧。你念完后，我们来谈谈双方单子上列的那些事情，"妻子开心地说道。

丈夫平静地说:“我在单子上什么也没写。我认为你现在非常完美。我不想让你为我改变什么。你可爱迷人,我不想设法改变你所有的一切。”

丈夫的诚实、深爱和容忍感动了她。她转过头,哭了起来。

生活中,很多时候,我们都会感到失望、沮丧和苦恼。我们不必较真去寻找它们。我们拥有一个充满美丽、光明和希望的奇妙世界。我们环顾四周,就可以看到这些奇妙事情,为什么要把时间浪费在寻找伤心、失望和苦恼上呢?

Happiness Lights Your Life

Ten things are necessary for happiness in this life, the first being a good digestion, and the other nine—money; so at least it is said by our modern philosophers. Yet the author of A Gentle Life speaks more truly in saying that the Divine Creation includes thousands of superfluous joys which are totally unnecessary to the bare support of life.

He alone is the happy man who has learned to extract happiness—not from ideal conditions, but from the actual ones about him. The man who has mastered the secret will not wait for ideal surroundings; he will not wait until next year, next decade, until he gets rich, until he can travel abroad, until he possesses everything, but he will make the most of life today.

Paradise is everywhere, but you must take your joy, or you will never find it.

It is after business hours, not in them, that people relax themselves. When finishing their work, people must, like Philip Amour, unlock the doors of some wholesome recreation at once. Dr. Lyman Beecher used to divert himself with a violin, relieving the great strain put upon him.

"A man," says Dr. Johnson, "should spend part of his time laughing."

Humor was Lincoln's life-preserver, as it has been of thousands of others. "If it were not for this," he used to say, "I should die." His jests and quaint stories lit the gloomy hours of the nation.

"Next to virtue," said Agnes Strickland, "the fun in this world is what we can least spare."

"I have fun from morning till night," said the editor Charles A. Dana to a friend who was growing prematurely old. "Do you read novels, play billiards and walk a great deal?"

Gladstone early formed a habit of looking on the bright side of things and never lost a moment's sleep by worrying about public business.

There are many out-of-door sports, and the very presence of nature is to many a great joy. How true it is that, if we are cheerful and contented, all nature smiles with us-the air seems more balmy, the sky more clear, the earth has a brighter green, the trees have a richer foliage, the flowers are more fragrant, the birds sing more sweetly, and the sun, moon and stars all appear more beautiful. "It is a grand thing to live—to open the eyes in the morning and look out upon the world, to drink in the pure air and enjoy the sweet sunshine and to feel the pulse throb; it is a good thing to be alive simply, and it is a good world we live in in spite of the abuse we're fond of giving it."

Each of us has joy mines that aren't prospected. And he who goes "prospecting" to see what he can daily discover is a wise man, who is training his eyes to see beauty in everything and everywhere.

"One ought, every day," said Goethe, "at least to hear a little song, read a good poem, see a fine picture, and, if it were possible, to speak a few reasonable words." And if this be good for one's self, why not try the song, the poem, the picture and good words on someone else?

Shall music and poetry die out of you while you are struggling for that which can never enrich the character, nor add to the soul's worth? Shall a disciplined imagination fill the mind with beautiful pictures? He who has intellectual resources to fall back upon won't lack daily recreation most wholesome...

It is a remark of Archbishop Whately that we ought to cultivate the cornfields of the mind, but the pleasure grounds also. A well-balanced life is a cheerful life; a happy union of fine qualities and unruffled temper, a clear judgment, and well-proportioned faculties. In a corner of his desk, Lincoln kept a copy of the latest humorous work; and it was frequently his habit, when fatigued, annoyed or depressed, to take this up and read a chapter with great relief. Honesty, sagaciousness or wit—anything to provoke mirth and make a man jollier—this, too, is a gift from heaven.

幸福点亮人生

这一生要幸福，必须具备十个条件，首先要有良好的消化能力，其他九个则都是金钱。至少这是我们当代的哲学家这样说的。不过，《温柔生活》的作者说得更为现实，他说这种神圣产物包含成千上万的多余快乐。这对毫无生活能力的人来说完全是多此一举。

他自己就是一个幸福的人，他已经学会了如何找到幸福，不是来自理想的状态，而是来自身边的实际生活。领悟了这个秘密的人，就不会等待理想的环境，不会等到下一年、下一个十年，不会等到自己成为富人，不会等到自己能去国外旅行，也不会等到自己拥有一切，而是充分利用今天。

天堂无处不在，但你必须带着快乐，否则你将永远找不到。

人们应在上班时间后，而不应在上班时间内，放松自己。人们必须像菲利普·阿穆尔那样，在完成工作时，马上打开有益于健康的娱乐之门。莱曼·比彻博士经常用一把小提琴自得其乐，以此来缓解巨大的紧张感。

约翰逊博士说："一个人应花一部分时间欢笑。"

和成千上万的人一样，幽默是林肯的人生秘诀。他常常说："要不是因为这样，我就应该死。"他的笑话和有趣故事点亮了处于低潮时期的国家。

"除了美德，"艾格尼丝·斯特里克兰说。"乐趣也是世界上我们能分享的最少东西之一。"

"我一天到晚都很快乐，"编辑查尔斯·达纳问一个未老先衰的朋友。"你看小说、打台球、经常散步吗？"

英国首相格拉德斯通很早就养成了一种乐观看待事物的习惯，从来没有因担心公务而失眠过。

许多户外活动和自然景象都可以让人获得许多快乐。确实，如果我们愉快满足，大自然都会同我们微笑——空气似乎比平常更加和煦，蓝天更加晴朗，大地更加翠绿，树木更加茂盛，鲜花更加芬芳，小鸟唱得更加甜美，太阳、月亮和星星更加美观。

"活着的感觉真棒——清晨睁开眼睛，望着窗外的世界，呼吸着纯净的空气，享受着可爱的阳光，感受着脉跳；简单地活着就是一件好事；尽管我们动不动就骂这个世界，但我们仍然生活在一个美好的世界里。"

我们每个人身上都有"尚未开采的快乐宝藏"。

每天都去"采矿"并能有新发现的人才是真正的智者，因为他让自己的眼睛训练有素，从每件事和每个地方中看到美。

歌德说："一个人应该每天至少听一首小曲、咏一首好诗、赏一幅美画，而且如果可能的话，说几句有道理的话。”

如果这对一个人有益的话，何不试着去听歌、咏诗、赏画，对他人说有道理的话呢？

当你为既不能充实性格又不能增添心灵价值的东西奋斗时，音乐和诗歌会从你的心中消失吗？循规蹈矩的想象力怎能让你的脑海里充满美丽的画面？一个心智健全的人每天都不缺少有利身心健康的娱乐活动……

沃特利大主教说，我们应该耕种心灵的麦田，也应该培养精神的游乐场。意识健全的生活是一种愉快的生活；是优秀品质、温和性情、清晰判断和适当能力的一种幸福结合。林肯总是在桌角放一册最近的幽默作品，每当疲乏、烦恼或沮丧时，他就常常习惯地拿起这册书，带着极大安慰看上一章。诚实、睿智或风趣都能带来欢笑，使人更加开心，这也是上天赐予的礼物。

Where Is Happiness?

A bird went to look for its happiness in the distance.

It flew and flew when it suddenly saw a little wilting flower, whose face was full of smile. Not knowing why, the bird asked the little flower, "You're going to die. Why are you still so happy?"

"Because my dream will come true," said the little flower.

"What kind of dream do you have?"

"To bear luscious fruit."

Then the little bird saw it: happiness is a hope in the heart.

The little bird kept flying; it flew and flew when it suddenly saw a lame duck, which was singing a song. Not knowing why, it asked the duck, "The fate treats you so unfairly. Why are you still so happy with yourself?"

"Because I saw a little duck fall," said the duck.

"So are you happy because you saw it trip over itself?"

"No, I'm happy because I help it stand up again."

Then the little bird saw it: happiness is a love in the heart.

The bird kept flying; it flew and flew when it suddenly saw a spider climbing up a slippery wall. The spider fell off the wall midway, but it kept climbing again and fell off again. This didn't discourage the spider; it kept climbing over and over again. Not knowing why, the little bird asked the spider, "You failed again and again, why don't you have pain but happiness on your face?"

"As long as I keep making my efforts, there is still hope to climb up it. Because of this, I'm so delighted," said the spider.

The little bird saw it: happiness is a faith in the heart.

So the little bird pursued happiness no longer because it had seen the truth: happiness is not in the distance but in your own heart.

幸福在哪里？

一只小鸟去远方寻找幸福。

它飞啊飞，突然看到了一朵快要枯萎的小花，但小花笑容满面。小鸟不解何故，便问小花:“你快要死了,为什么你还这样开心呀?”

“因为我的梦想就要实现了。”小花说。

“什么梦想?”

“长出甜美的果实。”

小鸟明白了:幸福是心中的一个希望。

小鸟向前飞;它飞啊飞,突然看到了一只瘸腿鸭。鸭子正哼着歌儿。小鸟不解何故,便问鸭子:“命运对你这样不公,为什么你还这样开心呀?”

“因为我看到一只小鸭摔倒了,”鸭子说。

“你是见到小鸭摔倒而开心吗?”

“不是。我开心,是因为我帮小鸭站了起来。”

小鸟明白了:幸福是心中的一份爱。

小鸟继续向前飞;它飞啊飞,突然看到了一只蜘蛛正在爬一面滑溜溜的墙。蜘蛛中途摔了下来,但它又向上爬,爬到中途,又摔了下来,但蜘蛛一点也不泄气,继续向上爬。小鸟不解何故,便问蜘蛛:“你一次次失败,为什么你的脸上没有痛苦而是快乐呢?”

“只要我不断努力,总有希望爬上去。正因为这样,我非常开心。”蜘蛛说。

小鸟明白了:幸福心中的一种信念。

于是,小鸟不再去远方寻找幸福,因为它已经开始懂得,幸福不在远方,而在自己心里。

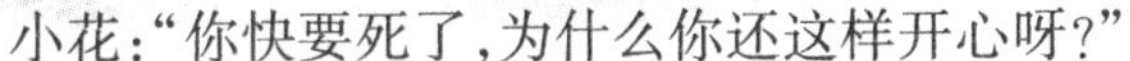

I Choose to Be Cheerful

At the beginning of my 8:00 a. m. class one Monday at college, I cheerfully asked my students how their weekend had been. One young man said that this weekend had not been very good. He'd had his wisdom teeth extracted. The young man then proceeded to ask me why I always seemed to be so cheerful.

His question reminded me of something I'd read somewhere before, "Every morning when you get up, you can have a choice about how to spend that day." I said to the young man, "I choose to be cheerful."

"Let me give you an example," I continued. The other students in the class ceased their chatter and began to listen to our conversation. "In addition to teaching here at college, I teach at the community college, about seventeen miles down the freeway from where I live. One day, a few weeks ago, I drove those seventeen miles to that college. I exited the freeway and turned onto College Drive. I only had to drive another quarter-mile down the road to the college. But just then my car died. I tried to start it again, but the engine wouldn't turn over. So I put my flashers on, grabbed my books and marched down the road to the college.

"As soon as I got there I called AAA and asked them to send a tow truck. The secretary in the Provost's office asked me what had happened. 'This is my lucky day,' I replied, smiling.

"'Your car breaks down and today is your lucky day?' She was puzzled. 'What do you mean?'

"'I live seventeen miles from here,' I replied. 'My car could have broken down anywhere along the freeway. It didn't. Instead, it broke down in the perfect place: off the freeway, within walking distance of here. I'm still able to teach my class, and I've been able to arrange for the tow truck to meet me after class. If my car was meant to break down today, it couldn't have been arranged in a more convenient fashion.'

"The secretary's eyes opened wide, and then she smiled. I smiled back and headed for class."

After ending my story to the students, I scanned the sixty faces in the lecture hall with a smile. Obviously, my story had touched them.

我选择快乐

星期一早上8点我在大学授课时,兴高采烈地问学生们周末过得怎么样。一位年轻人说这个周末过得不很好,因为他拔掉了智齿。年轻人随后问我为什么总是看起来这样快乐。

他的问题使我想起了以前在什么地方看过的一句话:"每天早上起床时,你可以选择如何度过这一天。"我对年轻人说:"我选择了快乐。"

"我给你举个例子,"我接着说。班上其他同学也不再叽叽喳喳说话,开始听我们谈话。"除了在这里授课,我还在社区学院授课。顺着高速公路,距离我住的地方有17英里车程。几周前的一天,我开车去那个学院授课。我下了高速公路,拐到学院快车道上。我再开四分之一英里就到那个学院了。但就在这时,我的车熄火了。我试着重新发动车子,但发动机没有起动。于是,我打开闪光灯,一把抓起书,大步流星朝学校走去。

"我一到那里,就给美国汽车协会打电话,让他们派一辆拖车来。教务处的秘书问我发生了什么事儿。我面带微笑地回答说:'今天是我的幸运日。'

"'你的车坏了,今天是你的幸运日?'她迷惑不解。'你是什么意思?'

"我回答说:'我住的地方离这里有17英里。我的车子本可能坏在高速公路上的任何地方,但它并没有,而是坏在了一个非常理想的地方:下了高速公路,刚好可以步行到这里。我仍能授课,而且我已经安排好拖车下课后来接我。如果我的车子今天想坏,它安排的方式是再方便不过了。'

"秘书睁大了眼睛,然后露出了微笑。我也对她微笑了一下,就上课去了。"

讲完故事后,我面带微笑扫视着报告厅里的60张面孔。显然,我的故事已经打动了他们。

The Mystery of Happiness

In Jerusalem, I met such a young man, who was extraordinarily optimistic, so I asked him what the secret of his happiness was. He said to me, "At the age of 11, I accidentally received a thing.

"That day I rode a bicycle in the street when a gust of wind blew me to the center of the street. An approaching truck from the opposite direction knocked me down and rolled my leg.

"When the blood kept oozing, I realized I would live for the rest of my lifetime with only one leg. I was extremely frustrated, but I quickly realized my sadness and frustration couldn't exchange my

lost leg, so I decided that I could never waste my time in sorrow and grief in the future.

"When my parents rushed to the hospital, they were both shocked and saddened.

"I told them, 'I have adapted to all this. It's time for you to adapt to the situation that I spare one leg.'

"From then on, seeing my friends feel sad and dismayed at some trifles, I will tell them to smile on life and enjoy life."

At the age of 11, this young man has understood that it is a waste to put time and energy on things that have lost, whereas the secret of happiness is to enjoy and cherish what we have now owned.

幸福的奥秘

我曾在耶路撒冷遇到这样一个年轻人，他有着非同寻常的快乐性格，因此我问他快乐的秘密是什么，他对我说："11 岁时，我意外地收到了一样东西。

"那天，我在街上骑着自行车，一阵大风把我吹到街中央，这时迎面驶来一辆大货车，把我撞倒在地，轧伤了我的一条腿。

"血不断地流，那时我意识到，我的下半生将会在只有一条腿的情况下度过，当时我沮丧万分，但我很快意识到，悲伤沮丧都无法换回失去的那条腿。因此，我决定，以后绝不能把时间浪费在悲伤、难过中。

"我父母赶到医院时，他们既惊愕又难过。我对他们说：'我已经适应了这一切，这次轮到你们来适应我只剩下一条腿的境况。'

"从此以后，看到我的朋友们因一些小事而难过、沮丧时，我都会告诉他们要笑对人生、享受生活。"

这个年轻人 11 岁时就已经明白把时间和精力用在已经失去的事物上是一种浪费，而快乐、幸福的秘密就是享受并珍惜现在所拥有的。

Make Way for the Others' Happiness

That morning, a bus was rolling on. On it were the people going to work. Suddenly, a car rushed out from the road nearby; the bus stopped with an urgent brake. It was a car for taking photographs of the wedding, followed by a long wedding motorcade. The passengers started to complain that they would go to work late, but the bus driver sat in his seat quietly and rang the horn from time to time.

Someone said to the driver, "No use ringing the horn; they won't make way for you. You'd better rush through the gap between the motorcade."

The driver turned back and said with a smile, "I ring the horn not to urge them to make way for me, but to bless them." After a pause, he added, "Marriage is a happy thing, so we have a chance to make ways for the others' happiness, isn't it a happy thing?"

The passengers on the bus calmed down instantly.

It is a happy thing to make way for others' happiness while the one who has such a mood is certainly a happy person.

给别人的幸福让道

那天早上，一辆公交车正在行驶，车上都是去上班的人。突然，一旁的路上冲出一辆车，公交车一个急刹后停住了。那是一辆婚礼的摄像车，后面是一列长长的迎亲车队。乘客开始抱怨上班要迟到了，公交车司机却静静地坐在位子上，不时按一下喇叭。

有人对司机说："你只按喇叭不行，他们不会给你让道的，不如从车队的空隙冲过去。"

司机回过头，笑着说："我按喇叭不是催他们给我让道，我是为他们祝福呢！"顿了顿，他又说："别人结婚是一件幸福的事儿，我们有机会为别人的幸福让一次道，这不也是一件幸福的事儿吗？"

满车的乘客霎时安静了下来。

给别人的幸福让道，是一件幸福的事儿；有这种心情的人，必定也是一个幸福的人。

The Power of a Smile

I placed the items on the moving belt. Slowly, my packages moved towards the cash register.

The cashier was tired. I could see it on her face. It was towards the end of her shift. She had no doubt been standing and ringing the cash register all day. I know the cash registers don't ring anymore, for they are computerized, but when I worked as a cashier, they rang.

My two-year-old son, Josees, was with me.

She performed her job with all her weary spirit she could summon.

Josees stood in front of her across the belt. His tiny frame was inches below the top of the moving belt. I don't know what made him move away from me and stand there. Children can at times move more on instinct than logic.

He stood there looking up.

Sensing something, she looked down. "Oh thank God, look at that smile!" she exclaimed.

She changed. The tiredness left. The dreariness left. She appeared as fresh as if she had just walked through the door.

Josees continued standing and smiling. She continued to revive.

I saw not the power of a child, but the power of a pure smile.

Remember, you have the same power.

Each day you will meet someone who is tired, weary and dreary. For many, the tired, weary, dreary person you meet will be in the mirror.

Even in the mirror, the power of a smile still works.

When you smile, the muscles of your face contract on a special gland in the brain which release a hormone in the brain that eases stress and causes a slight euphoric high.

Smile right now and see if that gland is in your brain, too.

She was still bubbling as we walked out of the store.

Josees never said a word. He only smiled.

Remember Josees when you meet your weary person each day. Remember someone needs smile.

微笑的力量

我把要买的商品放在传送带上。慢慢地,我那些东西移向收银员。

收银员一脸倦容,我从她的脸上看得出来。她轮班的时间要到了。她肯定一直在那里站着按了一天的收银机。我知道收银机不再响铃了,因为它们都电脑化了,但我做出纳时,收银机都响铃。

两岁的儿子乔西斯和我在一起。

收银员强打精神工作着。

乔西斯随着传送带站在她面前,他矮小的身材离传送带顶还有几英寸。我不知道是什么让他离开我站在了那里。孩子们有时更多的是依靠本能,而不是逻辑,进行活动。

他站在那里,仰起头。

收银员感觉到了什么,低下头。"噢,天哪,看那微笑!"她惊叫道。

她像变了个人,疲倦和低落一扫而光,看上去就像刚开始工作似的神采奕奕。

乔西斯继续站在那里微笑着。她继续精神抖擞。

我明白那不是一个孩子的力量,而是一个纯真微笑的力量。

记住,你也拥有这样的力量。

每天你都会遇到某个疲惫、厌烦和低落的人。对许多人来说,镜子里的那个疲惫、厌倦、低落的人正是自己。

即便是在镜子里,微笑的力量仍会发生作用。

你微笑时,面部肌肉会因大脑里的某个特定的腺体而收缩,分泌荷尔蒙来减轻压力,产生一种轻微的快感。

马上微笑吧,看你的大脑里是否也有这样的腺体。

我们走出商店时,收银员还是喜气洋洋。

乔西斯一句话没说,只是微笑。

每天当你遇到疲惫的人时,记住乔西斯。记住有人需要微笑。

What Does Happiness Come from?

This story is about a beautiful, well-dressed lady who complained to her psychiatrist that she felt her whole life was empty and meaningless.

So the doctor called over the old lady who cleaned the office floors, and then said to the rich lady, "I'm going to ask Mary here to tell you how she found happiness. All I want you to do is to listen."

So the old lady put down her broom and sat on a chair and told her story, "Well, my husband died of malaria and three months later my only son was killed by a car. I had nobody... I had nothing left. I couldn't sleep; I couldn't eat; I never smiled at anyone; I even thought of taking my own life. Then one evening a kitten followed me home from work. Somehow I felt sorry for that kitten. It was cold outside, so I decided to let the kitten in. I got it some milk, and it licked the plate clean. Then it rubbed against my leg, and for the first time in months, I smiled. Then I stopped to think: if helping a kitten could make me smile, maybe doing something for people could make me happy.

"So the next day I baked some biscuits and took them to a neighbor who was sick in bed. Every day I tried to do something nice for someone. It made me so happy to see them happy. Today, I don't know of anybody who sleeps and eats better than I do. I've found happiness, by giving it to others."

When she heard that, the rich lady cried. She had everything that money could buy, but she had lost the things which money couldn't buy.

幸福来自什么?

这个故事说的是一个衣着华贵的美丽女士。她对心理医生抱怨说她感到生活空虚、毫无意义。

于是,医生叫来负责打扫办公室地板的老太太,然后对这个富有的女士说:"我让玛丽告诉你她是怎样发现快乐的。我要你做的就是好好听。"

于是,老太太放下扫帚,坐在一张椅子上,讲起了她的故事:"噢,我丈夫死于疟疾,三个月后我唯一的儿子也被汽车撞死了。我失去了亲人……一无所有。我睡不好,吃不下,对谁也没有个笑脸。我甚至想寻短见。后来有一天晚上,我下班时,一只小猫跟我回了家。不知怎么的,我很可怜那只小猫。外面很冷,所以我决定小猫进屋。我给了它一些牛奶,它把碟子舔得一干二净,然后蹭起了我的腿。几个月里,我第一次露出了笑脸。于是,我就停下来想,如果帮助一只小猫就可以让我微笑,也许帮助别人会让我快乐。

"于是,第二天我烤了一些小点心,送给一位卧病在床的邻居。每天,我都试着为别人做一些好事。看到别人快乐,我也非常开心。今天,我不知道还有谁会比我吃得好、睡得香。通过奉献他人,我找到了幸福。"

听了老太太的话,富有的女士哭了。尽管她拥有钱能买到的一切东西,但她却失去了钱无法买到的那些东西。

Happiness Is a Flow of Air

A merchant prince collected many precious antiques, calligraphy and paintings, various pearls, emeralds and the like. In order to prevent theft, he installed a tight security system and rarely went to enjoy them every day, only as part of his personal wealth to show off.

One day, seized by a whim, the rich merchant decided to let the building dustman widen his view.

When he entered, the dustman didn't reveal his envy, but slowly looked through them one by one and enjoyed them carefully. Out of the thick steel door, the businessman couldn't help flaunting, "What about them? Having seen so many good things, aren't you well worth your lifetime?"

The dustman said, "Yes, I now feel myself as rich as you, and happier than you."

The businessman was extremely puzzled, looking unhappy.

"I have seen all your treasures, so am I not rich as you? And I don't have to worry about those things, so am I not happier than you?"

To appreciate is often happier than to possess.

快乐是一种流动的空气

一位富商花费巨资收藏了许多珍贵的古董、字画以及各种珍珠、翡翠等。为防失窃，他安装了严密的保安系统，平日很少进去欣赏，只当成个人财富的一部分用来炫耀。

一天，富商忽然心血来潮，决定让大厦清洁工进去开开眼界。清洁工进去后，并未流露出艳羡之色，只是慢慢地逐一浏览，细细欣赏。待步出厚厚的铁门时，富商忍不住炫耀说："怎么样？看了这么多的好东西，不枉此生了吧？"那个清洁工说："是啊，我现在自觉与你一样富有，而且比你更快乐。"

那富商大惑不解，面露不悦。

"你所有的宝贝我都看过了，不就是与你一样富有了吗？而且我又不必为那些东西担心，岂不比你更快乐？"

能够欣赏，常常比实际拥有更快乐。

The Source of Happiness

Life is like a heavy truck, so happiness and sorrow are like the two wheels. No cross, no crown. No pain, no joy. There are two different minds. One is that to live a day is to leave a day. The other is that to live a day is to enjoy a day. Just one word difference, it has reflected the complete reverse state of psychology. Life is like the course that is investing all the time. Therefore, in a sense, life is the capital.

Life is like a book. There are two pens that can write this book. One is writing growth while the other is writing caducity. One is describing success while the other is describing failure. In other words, one is depicting happiness and the other is showing sorrow as well.

When you have it, you should utilize it well and make it develop great actions. Please remember, the active attitude creates wonderful life while the negative attitude waste lifetime.

One noon, a rich lady went to visit a poor but happy family. When she was about to knock at the door, she heard someone speaking in the room.

A little girl said, "Would you like some braised pork today?"

Another girl said, "No. I would like some toasted chicken."

Following the words, the lady knocked at the door and went into the room. She saw them sitting at a table. Surprisingly, there were only some pieces of thin and dry bread, two cold potatoes and a jar of water on the table. The lady asked them what the matter was. They said that they imagined that, so poor food was turned into many kinds of delicious food.

One girl said, "When you consider it as pancakes, the bread will be very tasty."

Another girl said, "If you consider bread as ice-cream, it will be more delicious."

When the lady left the family, she had a new understanding of happiness. She found that the source of happiness is not substance, but human's heart. Where is the happiness in our life? It is in our heart.

幸福之源

生活就像一辆载重卡车,喜与悲有如两个车轮。没有苦难,就没有王冠。没有痛苦,就没有欢乐。有两种不同的思想:一种过一天少一天,另一种是过一天享受一天。仅一字之差,就反映出了截然不同的心态。生活就像不断投资的过程。因此,就某种意义来说,生活就是资本。

生活如同一本书,谱写这本书可以有两支笔。一支描写成长,另一支描写衰老。一支描写成功,另一支描写失败。换句话说,一支在描述幸福,另一支在表现悲伤。

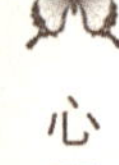

当你拥有生命时,就应该好好利用它,使之变成伟大的行动。请记住,积极的态度创造精彩的人生,而消极的态度则虚度人生。

一天中午,一位富有的女士去拜访一个贫穷但幸福的家庭。她正要敲门时,听到屋里有人在说话。

一个小女孩说:“今天你想吃炖肉吗?”

另一个女孩说:“不,我想吃烤鸡肉。”

听到这里,那位女士敲门,进了屋里。她看到她们坐在桌边。让她吃惊的是,桌子上只有几片又薄又干的面包、两个凉土豆和一罐水。那位女士问她们这是怎么回事。她们说她们是那样想象的,这样可怜的食物就变成了各种各样的美食。

一个女孩说:“当你把这面包想成薄煎饼时,它就会美味可口。”

另一个女孩说:“如果你把这面包想成冰淇淋,它就会更香甜可口。”

那位女士离开这家人时,对幸福有了新的理解。她发现幸福的源泉不在物质,而在人心。我们生活中的幸福在哪里呢?它在我们的心里。

Happiness is a Feeling

When a friend and I were standing in line at the grocery store the other day, I told her how lazy my children were. After I had come in from work that day, my house was in a mess like most times.

"I believe children nowadays are just out for what they can get. I bend over backwards for them, but they can't even help keep our house clean. Even if it doesn't bother me so, the other women will laugh at me when they find my house is in a mess."

"Do you know how blessed you are?" a woman behind us asked. "I'd love to go home and find my house a mess. I won't mind my carpet being ruined or the dishes left everywhere. I won't mind the dirty clothes being piled or many socks to match. I won't even mind anyone talking about my dirty home. As a matter of fact, I'd love it. I'd dearly love to tell my children how much I love them. You see, my two children were killed in a car accident and now it's just my husband and me. My house stays clean.

"There are no fingerprints on my walls, no mysterious spots on my carpets. There're no voices of arguing, no slamming doors, no laughter, no I love you Mom. So you see, you're very blessed. What you're disgusted about now is just what I wish to get. How I'd love to hold my kids, wipe away their tears and share their dreams. Or just to watch them play. If I had my children, I wouldn't care how my house looked. I'd be happy just to have them."

Now if you come into my house and see a big old mess, you can think bad thoughts if you want, but I feel greatly blessed.

幸福是一种感觉

前几天，我和一位朋友在食品杂货店排队买东西时，我对她说自己的孩子们是多么懒。那天我下班回家后，家里像大多数时候那样乱得不成样子。

“我认为现在的孩子只是伸手索取。我为他们竭尽全力，可他们连帮我保持房间干净都做不到。就是我不烦，别的女人看到我的家又脏又乱也会笑话我。”

“你知道自己有多幸福吗？”我们身后的一个女人说。“我真想回到家，看到家里乱得不成样子。我不会介意地毯弄坏、碟子乱放。我不会介意脏衣服成堆、好袜子不成对。就是什么人对我脏兮兮的家说三道四，我也不会介意。事实上，我喜欢这样。我真想告诉自己的孩子们我是多么爱他们。你明白，我的两个孩子在一次车祸中死了，现在就剩下我和丈夫了。我的家里总是很干净。

“墙上没有手指印，地毯上没有莫名其妙的污点。没有吵闹声，没有重重的关门声，没有笑声，也没有人说‘我爱你，妈妈’。所以，你明白，你非常幸福。你现在讨厌的一切正是我渴望得到的啊。我多么希望能抱着自己的孩子，擦去他们的眼泪，分享他们的梦想。或者只是看着他们玩。如果我还有孩子，我是不会介意自己的家里是什么样子的。只要拥有他们，我就会幸福的。”

现在，如果你来我家里，看到还是那么乱七八糟，你怎么往坏处想都可以，但我感到非常幸福。

Bring Happiness Home

When I went to a guest at a friend's house, I found a wooden sign hung on the door. It read, "Before entering, please shuck off your trouble; when returning, bring back your happiness."

After entering the house, I saw the host and hostess were both harmonious, two children were generous and polite and warmth and harmony filled the house.

I naturally asked the wooden sign. The hostess looked at the host with a smile, "You tell the story."

The host then gently looked back at the hostess, "You say because it was your creativity."

Finally, the hostess said gently and slowly, "Once when I got home, I was shocked to see a sleepy gloomy face in the elevator mirror, with the frowned eyebrows and the worried eyes. So I thought when my children and husband faced this worried sullen face, what would they feel? If I also faced such a face, what would I react? Then, I imagined expect my children's silence and my husband's indifference at the dinner table... The next day, I wrote a wooden sign and nailed it on the door to remind myself. It turned out that it not only reminded myself but also the whole family. The miracle occurred in this way. Moreover, not only our family but also the guests to our house always become happy..."

带快乐回家

到一个朋友家去做客，我见门口赫然挂着一块小木牌，上书："进门前，请脱去烦恼；回家时，带快乐回来。"

进屋后，果见男女主人一团和气，两个孩子大方有礼，温馨和谐充盈着整个屋子。

我自然询问起那块木牌，女主人笑着望向男主人："你说。"

男主人则温柔地望着女主人："还是你说，因为这是你的创意。"

最终，女主人轻缓地说道："有一次，我回家，在电梯的镜子里看到了一张困倦灰暗的脸，一双紧拧的眉毛，烦恼的眼睛……把我自己吓了一大跳。于是，我想，当孩子、丈夫面对这样愁苦阴沉的面孔时，会有什么感觉？假如我面对的也是这样的面孔又会有什么反应？接着，我想到孩子在餐桌上的沉默、丈夫的冷淡……第二天，我就写了一块小木牌钉在门上，以提醒自己。结果，提醒的不只是我自己，而是一家人。奇迹就这样出现了。而且，不仅是我们一家人，到我家的客人也都变得欢欢喜喜……"

Happiness is a Bowl of Water

Once upon a time, a rich man and a poor man talked about what happiness was.

The poor man said, "All that at present is happiness."

Observing the poor man's shabby cottage and clothes, the rich man sneered, "How can this be called happiness? My happiness is a luxurious house with a hundred rooms and a thousand servants!"

On the very night, a big fire burnt down the rich man's hundred-room house into pieces. And his servants each went his own way. The rich man became a beggar overnight.

One day, it was extremely hot. He, a beggar now, came to ask for some water to drink when he passed by the poor man's cottage. The poor man brought him a big bowl of cool and fresh water, asking, "What do you think happiness is now?"

The beggar said anxiously, "Happiness is the bowl of water in your hands now."

Happiness is essentially all that at present. One can enjoy happiness in all his lifetime only by stringing all these present moments together.

幸福是一碗水

从前，一个富人和一个穷人谈论什么是幸福。

穷人说："幸福就是现在。"

富人望着穷人的茅舍和破旧的衣着，轻蔑地说："这怎么能叫幸福呢？我的幸福可是百间豪宅、千名奴仆啊。"

当晚，一场大火把富人的百间豪宅烧得片瓦不留，奴仆们各奔东西。一夜之间，富人

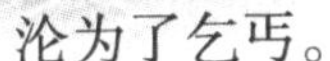

沦为了乞丐。

一天，酷暑难熬，这乞丐路过穷人的茅舍，想讨口水喝。穷人端来一大碗清凉的水，问他："你现在认为什么是幸福。"

乞丐眼巴巴地说："幸福就是此时你手中的这碗水。"

幸福本来就是现在。只有将一个个现在串起来，才有一生一世的幸福。

The Light of a Smile

About ten years ago I was stuck in an abusive relationship. The relationship lasted 10 years and during that time all my thoughts were negative and circled around how I was going to get out of that relationship alive and with my children. The negativity had pulled me so far away from the truth that I was blind towards anything good.

Then one day I went to the bank. I was standing in line and as usual I was totally caught up in my thoughts about survival. I suddenly had the feeling that someone was watching me. I looked up and saw a man with his son standing in line in front of me. The man and the child were looking at me, then looking at each other and looking at me again. Both of them had a light around them that I had never seen before, they did not say a word, but smiled. I don't recall but I probably did not smile back. I was too stunned. I forgot everything around me, my life, the bank and all happenings. As soon as I was done with my transaction at the bank I ran outside to see where they were heading. But they were gone. But the smile was deeply imbedded into my soul. I found the strength to leave the relationship and start a new life. For me those two "visitors" were angels.

When I think back at this beautiful experience that helped me to change my life, I feel blessed for all it took was a smile and I have plenty of them now to give away.

An old saying goes, "If you don't have something positive to say, don't say anything at all." I would like to rephrase that saying to, "If you don't have something positive to say, at least smile." The truth is not what is said in words, but the words unsaid in a smile.

微笑的光芒

大约10年前，我处在受到虐待的家庭关系中。这种关系持续了10年。在此期间，我所有的想法都很消极，整天思来想去的都是如何带着孩子们摆脱这种关系。这种消极的想法已经让我远离现实，所以我对一切美好的事情也都熟视无睹。

后来，有一天，我去银行办事。我站在那里排队时，和平常一样全神贯注地想着如何生存下去。我突然感觉仿佛有人在目不转睛地看着我。我抬起头，看到一个男人带着儿子排在我前面。那人和孩子正在看着我，然后他们相互看了看，又看着我。他们俩周围有一种我以前从未见过的光，他们一言不发，只是微笑着。我现在想不起来了，但我可能没有对他们微笑。我当时目瞪口呆，忘记了周围的一切，我的生活、银行和所有正在发生的事情。我一办完事，就跑出银行，去看他们朝哪里去了。可是，他们已经不见了踪影。而那种微笑却深深地嵌入了我的脑海。我找到了离开那种虐待关系的力量，开始了一

种新的生活。对我来说，那两个“客人”就是天使。

我回想这段帮助我改变人生的美好经历时，感到非常幸运，尽管得到的仅仅是一个微笑，但我现在却把很多微笑送给他人。

一句古话说：“你若不知该说什么好，就什么也别说。”我想可以改为：“你若不知该说什么好，至少微笑一下。”其实不在于说了什么，而在于微笑不语中。

The Essence of Happiness

There was a man who tried his best to make money in youth, finally attained his goal in middle age and became a millionaire. But the rich substance didn't make him happy for his attained dream. Instead, one of his senior high school classmates who ran a vanilla garden lived an ordinary but happy life, always with a smile on the face. He was very puzzled about it.

One day, he was reluctant to ask his classmate, "My money can buy 100 vanilla gardens, but why am I not as happy as you?"

Pointing to the window next to them, his classmate asked, "From the window what have you seen?"

The rich man said, "I've seen many people strolling in the garden."

The classmate asked again, "What have you seen in the mirror?"

Seeing he was so haggard in the mirror, he said, "I only see myself."

The classmate asked, "Which landscape is vaster?"

The rich man said, "Of course it is through the window."

The classmate said with a smile, "Just because you live in the world of a mirror! When you try to take off the quicksilver on the back of the mirror, you will see the world."

Happiness comes from share and devotion. The essence of the meaning of life does not lie in the possession, but in the share. The one who shares happiness with others will always enjoy the countless happiness.

幸福的本质

有个人年轻时拼命赚钱，中年时终于实现了自己的梦想，成为一个富翁。可是，物质丰富的他其实并没有因为达到梦想而感到幸福。他的一个经营香草园的高中同学反而过着平凡却幸福的生活，时常可以看见他那愉快的笑脸。对此，他十分不解。

有一天，他很不甘心地请教这位同学：“我的钱可以买100个香草园，可为什么我没有你幸福？”

同学指着旁边的窗户问：“从窗外你看到了什么？”

富翁说：“我看到很多人在逛花园。”

同学又问：“那你在镜子前又看到了什么呢？”

富翁看到镜子里憔悴的自己说：“我看到了我自己。”

同学问：“哪一个风景更辽阔呢？”

富翁说:“当然是通过窗户看得远了。”

同学微笑道:“就因为你活在镜子的世界里!当你试着将镜子后面的那层水银剥掉,你就会看到全世界。”

幸福来自分享与付出。生命意义的本质不在于拥有,而是分享。与人分享幸福的人,永远都有享不尽的幸福。

He Who Can Be Moved Will Be Happy

"We can be moved everywhere, as if spring is the nourishment of life, but we always hurry on, suffering from thirst."

Going to work every day, I cross the zebra crossing at the east entrance of the university and go on eastwards to my office building. Most of the time when I just come to the junction, the red light at the crosswalk lights up and I have to wait. It was the same that day that I occasionally turned around when I suddenly saw beside the enclosure of the expansion site of the campus remaining the two old willow trees, whose huge green crowns glitter in the morning sun and undulate with the breeze, perfectly beautiful.

At that moment, I was deeply moved.

That night, I wrote in the diary, "It was an intolerable red light when I rushed to work, but surprisingly, an occasional turning round gave me one whole day's happiness, or even the sense of happiness reviving the memory of the willow trees any time in my lifetime."

In this world sometimes we are mentally tired, sometimes we are physically tired, and sometimes life seems a hard journey faraway. However, the sudden pigeon whistle passing overhead surprise us, and this is the advent of being touched unexpectedly. As if the pure cotton protecting our body and mind, being moved makes us dwell in the homes of considerate happiness.

Whether the natural beauty of the survived willow trees, or the minor details of a child growing up, or the conscientious assistance that human suffering arouses, is all the branches that the flower that we are moved blooms and bear the fruit of happiness for us.

He who can be moved will be happy.

人能感动,就能幸福

“感动无处不在,仿佛泉水,是滋养生命的。但是,我们却匆匆走过,忍受着干渴。”

每天上班,我都要在大学东门过斑马线,再往东走到单位。多数时候,都是刚到路口,人行横道的红灯就亮起来,我只有等待。那天也一样,只是我偶然回了一下头。我忽然看到大学校园扩建工地围墙边被留存下来的两棵老柳树,那巨大的绿色树冠在朝阳下熠熠闪光,随着微风荡漾,美到了极致。

那一刻,一种感动深深袭击了我。

那天晚上,我在日记中写道:“本是匆忙上班时一次难耐的红灯,偶然的回头,给我的竟是一整天的幸福,甚至是一生中任何时候对柳树的回忆重复唤起的幸福感觉。”

在这个世界上有时心累,有时身累,有时人生仿佛就是天涯苦旅。但是,头顶的鸽哨突然掠过，让人顿感一丝惊喜，这就是意想不到的感动。感动，仿佛纯棉呵护我们的身心，让我们常住在体贴入微的幸福家园之中。

无论是幸存柳树的自然之美、一个幼儿长大成人的细枝末节，还是人间辛酸唤起的良知援助，都是感动之花开放的枝桠，都为我们结出幸福的果实。

人能感动，就能幸福。

Happiness of Saying Thanks

In our life, we have rarely expressed our gratitude to the one who'd lived those years with us. In fact, we don't have to wait for anniversaries to thank the ones closest to us—the ones so easily overlooked. If I have learned anything about giving thanks, it is this: give it now! While your feeling of appreciation is alive and sincere, act on it. Saying thanks is such an easy way to add to the world's happiness.

Saying thanks not only brightens someone else's world, it brightens yours. If you're feeling left out, unloved or unappreciated, try reaching out to others. It may be just the medicine you need.

Of course, there are times when you can't express gratitude immediately. In that case don't let embarrassment sink you into silence—speak up the first time you have the chance.

Once a young minister, Mark Brian, was sent to a remote parish of Kwakiutl Indians in British Columbia. The Indians, he had been told, did not have a word for thank you. But Brian soon found that these people had exceptional generosity. Instead of saying thanks, it is their custom to return every favor with a favor of their own, and every kindness with an equal or superior kindness. They do their thanks.

I wonder if we had no words in our vocabulary for thank you, would we do a better job of communicating our gratitude? Would we be more responsive, more sensitive, more caring?

Thankfulness sets in motion a chain reaction that transforms people all around us—including ourselves. For no one ever misunderstands the melody of a grateful heart.

感谢的快乐

在我们的生活中，我们很少向和我们共同生活了多年的人表达感激之情。事实上，我们不必去等待周年纪念去感谢那些最亲近却又容易被我们忽略的人。如果说我学到了表达感谢的东西，那就是现在就去感谢！当你仍然存在感激之情并出自真心时，要马上行动。道谢是一种非常容易给世界增添幸福的方法。

道谢不仅能点亮他人的世界，也会点亮你的世界。如果你觉得失落、不被关爱、不被欣赏，那就试着向他人敞开你的心灵，也许这正是你需要的良药。

当然，有时你无法及时表达感谢。在这种情况下，不要让困窘使你陷入沉默，用你抓住的第一次机会大声说出来。

从前，有一位年轻牧师，叫马克·布赖恩，他被派到加拿大不列颠哥伦比亚省夸丘特尔印第安的一个遥远的教区。有人告诉他，这些印第安人的语言中没有一个词用来表达“谢谢你”。但是，布赖恩不久便发现，这些印第安人非常慷慨。他们不去道谢，而是习惯通过帮助别人来回报每一个帮助自己的人，而且每一个善行都会得到同等或更多的回报。他们是以行动来感谢。

我不知道，如果我们的词汇里没有道谢的词语，我们会在相互传达感谢时做得更好吗？我们会更有责任感、更能善解人意、更体恤他人吗？

表达感激会产生一连串反应，改变我们周围的人，包括我们自己，因为没有人会误解来自感激之心的悦耳音调。

Keeping Pleasant

"He is a fool who cannot be angry, but he is really a wise man who won't."

The habit of keeping pleasant is indeed better than an income of a million dollars a year. The life without cheerfulness is like the severe winter without the sun.

We all love cheerful company, but we are apt to forget that cheerfulness is a habit which can be cultivated by all.

We find it very difficult to be gay when we are in distress. It requires great courage. We should never forget that to be cheerful when it is not easy to be cheerful shows greatness. Thorny may be our way, but how happy is the conqueror's song!

The perfection of cheerfulness consists in the happy frame of mind. It is displayed in good temper and kind behavior. It arises partly from personal goodness and partly from belief in the goodness of others. It can make people see the glory in the grass and the sunshine on the flower. It encourages happy thoughts, and lives in an atmosphere of peace. It costs nothing, and yet it is invaluable. It blesses its possessor, and affords a large measure of enjoyment to others.

To light up other's heart, one's own heart must be lit first.

保持快乐

"不会生气的人是笨蛋，但不生气的人是真正的智者。"

保持快乐的习惯确实比年薪百万美元的收入强。生活没有快乐，就像严冬没有阳光。

我们都喜欢快乐的伙伴，但我们却容易忘记快乐是每个人都可以培养的一种习惯。

我们发现悲伤时很难快乐起来，那需要有极大的勇气。我们永远也不要忘记，不快乐时能够快乐起来是一件了不起的事儿。也许前方的道路充满荆棘，但胜利者的歌是多么快乐！

快乐的极致在于快乐的心境。它表现在良好的性情和得体的举止上。它一部分来自个人的善良，一部分来自对他人善良的信赖。它能使人看到绿草间的美丽光辉和花朵上的灿烂阳光。它可以促进快乐的思想，然后生活在和平的氛围中。它分文不花，却是无价之宝。它会祝福其所有者，并会给别人带来无穷的快乐。

要照亮别人的心，首先必须照亮自己的心。

Happiness Is Like the Sunshine

"There's the dearest little old gentleman," says James Buckham, "who goes into town every morning on the 8:30 train. I don't know his name, and yet I know him better than anybody else in town. He just radiates cheerfulness as far as you can see him. There is always a smile on his face, and I never heard him open his mouth except to say something kind, courteous, or good-natured. Everybody bows to him, even strangers, and he bows to everybody. If the weather is fine, his jolly compliments make it seem finer; and if it is raining, the merry way in which he speaks of it is as good as a rainbow."

"The inborn geniality of some people," says Whipple, "amounts to genius." There are those whose very presence carries sunshine with them wherever they go; a sunshine which means pity for the poor, sympathy for the suffering, help for the unfortunate and benignity toward all.

Everybody loves the sunny soul. His very face is passport anywhere. All doors fly open to him. He disarms prejudice and envy, for he bears good will to everybody. He is as welcome in every household as the sunshine.

"He was quiet, cheerful, genial," says Carlyle in his "Reminiscences" concerning Edward Irving's sunny helpfulness. "Irving's voice was to me one of blessedness and new hope."

And to William Wilberforce the poor Southey paid his tribute, "I never saw any other man who seemed to enjoy such perpetual serenity and sunshine of spirit."

When Goldsmith was in Flanders he discovered the happiest man he had ever seen. At his toil, from morning till night, he was full of song and laughter. Yet this sunny-hearted being was a slave, maimed, deformed, and wearing a chain. How well he illustrated that saying, if there is no bright side, to polish up the dark one!

The first prize at a flower show was taken by a pale, sickly little girl, who lived in a close, dark court in the east of London. The judges asked how she could grow it in such a dingy and sunless place. She replied that a little ray of sunlight came into the court; as soon as it appeared in the morning, she put her flower beneath it, and, as it moved, moved the flower, so that she kept it in the sunlight all day.

"Water, air and sunshine, the three greatest hygienic agents, are free, and within the reach of all. Twelve years ago," says Walt Whitman, "I came to Camden to die. But every day I went into the country, bathed in the sunshine, lived with the birds and squirrels and played in the water with the fishes, I received my health from nature."

"It is the unqualified result of all my experience with the sick," said Florence Nightingale, "that second only to their need of fresh air is their need of light; that, after a close room, what most hurts them is a dark room; and that it is not only light, but direct sunshine they want."

The sun, making all living things grow, exerts its happiest influence in cheering the mind of man and making his heart glad. If a man has sunshine in his soul, he will go on his way to happiness, content to look ahead under a cloud, not bating one jot of heart or hope if for a moment cast down, and not only happy himself, but giving happiness to others.

幸福像阳光一样

詹姆斯·巴克汉说:"有一位非常可爱的老先生,他每天早上坐8点半的火车进城。我不知道他的名字,但我比城里任何人都熟悉他。无论离多远,只要你能看到他,他就会露出快乐的神情。他的脸上总是带着微笑,他只要一开口,所说的话都是那样亲切、谦恭、愉快。所有人都向他鞠躬致敬，就连陌生人也是这样；他也向所有人鞠躬致敬。如果天气晴好，他那令人愉快的问候会使天气显得更加晴好；如果是雨天，他讨论天气时的乐观语气则像彩虹一样美丽。”

惠普尔说：“有些人具有天生的亲切感。”那些人无论走到哪里，都会带来阳光；这里所说的阳光是指对穷人的怜悯、对痛苦者的同情，对不幸者的帮助和对所有人的善行。

每个人都喜欢快乐的人。他那张脸就是前往各地的通行证，所有的大门都对他敞开。他常常消除偏见和嫉妒，因为他总是把好意带给每个人。他像阳光一样受到所有家庭的欢迎。

卡莱尔在他的《回忆录》里说到了爱德华·欧文乐观助人的性格：“他平静、乐观、亲切。欧文的话语对我来说就是一种充满幸福和新希望的声音。”

绍迪对威廉·威尔伯福斯这样赞美道：“我从来没有见过其他任何人能像他这样享受永久的平静和精神的阳光。”

戈德史密斯在佛兰德斯时，发现了一个他所见过的最快乐的人。这个人干活时从早到晚歌声和笑声不断。然而，这个性情乐观的人是一个奴隶，残废、丑陋、戴着脚镣。他充分证明了那句话：如果没有光明的一面，就去改善阴暗的一面！

在一次花展上，一个苍白病弱的小女孩夺得了一等奖。她住在伦敦东区的一个狭窄、阴暗的庭院里。评委问她是怎样在这样一个肮脏、阴暗的地方种出了如此美丽的花。她回答说，是一小缕阳光照进了庭院，每天早上太阳一出现，她就把花放在这缕阳光下，随着光线移动，她也移动花盆，这样她就可以让花儿一整天在阳光下。

“水、空气和阳光这三种最有益健康的因素是免费的，人人都能得到，”沃尔特·惠特曼说，“12 年前，我来到卡姆登想死。但我每天走进乡村，沐浴在阳光下，和小鸟与松鼠共同生活，和那些鱼儿在水里嬉戏时，我从大自然中得到了健康。”

弗洛伦斯·南丁格尔说：“在我照顾病人的所有经历中，有一种观点说病人对灯光的需要仅次于对新鲜空气的需要，这是一个不合格的结论。在一个封闭的房间里，对病人伤害最大的是房间的阴暗；他们需要的不仅是灯光，而且他们需要阳光的直射。”

太阳使万物生长，同时发挥着最令人愉快的影响，使人精神振奋、心情愉快。如果一个人心里拥有阳光，他就会走上幸福之路；在压力下也愿意向前看，即使有片刻沮丧，也不会减少一丝精神或希望；不仅自己幸福，而且把幸福送给他人。

Happiness is the Scent of Soul

Once a relative offered them two baskets of peaches. One basket of peaches were just ripe while the other were already overripe and would go bad at once.

The father asked, "Which way of eating can avoid wasting a peach?"

The eldest son said, "Of course, we should eat those overripe, for they can't be kept for three days."

"But after you eat up those, the peaches in the other basket will go bad!" Obviously, the father was not satisfied with the eldest son's advice.

The second son thought for a while and said,"We should eat the peaches just ripe. Choose the good ones!"

"If so,won't the overripe peaches be wasted in vain? Don't you think it pity?"

The father turned to the youngest son."What good idea do you have?"

"I feel,"thinking for a while,the youngest son said,"we'd better mix them together,give some of them to the neighbors,let them help us eat,so that we won't waste a peach."

Hearing this,the father nodded and said with a smile,"OK. It is really a good way. Then let's do it by your way."

Roman Roland said,"Happiness is the scent of soul."This feeling is very unique. If you don't experience by yourself,you won't savor the pleasure and the satisfaction of spirit. Because when we choose to give,we harvest the comfort and warmth in mind.

幸福是灵魂的香味

有一次,亲戚送给他家两筐桃子。一筐是刚刚成熟的;一筐是已经完全熟透,马上就会变质。

父亲问:"选择怎样的吃法,才能不浪费一个桃子?"

大儿子说:"当然是先吃熟透的,这些放不过三天。"

"可等你吃完这些后,另外那筐也要开始腐烂了。"父亲显然不满意大儿子的建议。

二儿子想了想,说:"应该吃刚好熟的那筐,拣好的吃!"

"如果这样,熟透的那筐桃子不是白白浪费了吗?你不觉得可惜吗?"

父亲把目光转向了小儿子。"你有什么好办法吗?"

"我觉得,"小儿子想了一下说,"我们最好把这些桃子混在一起,然后分给邻居们一些,让他们帮着我们吃,这样就不会浪费一个桃子了。"

父亲听了,点了点头,笑道:"不错,这的确是个好办法,那就按你的想法去做吧。"

罗曼·罗兰说:"幸福是灵魂的香味。"这种感觉很独特,如果不是亲身经历,就根本无法体会其中的愉悦和精神上的满足,因为在选择给予的同时,我们收获了心灵上的慰藉和温暖。

Pleasure Is a Freedom Song

Pleasure is a freedom song,but it is not freedom. It is the blossoming of your desires,but it is not their fruit;it is a depth calling unto a height,but it is not the deep or the high;it is the caged bird taking wing,but it is not space encompassed. Ay,in very truth,pleasure is a freedom song. And I fain would have you sing it with fullness of heart;yet I would not have you lose your hearts in singing.

Some of your youth seek pleasure as if it was all,and they are judged and rebuked. I would not judge nor rebuke them. I would have them seek,for they shall find pleasure,but not her alone;seven are her sisters,and the least of them is more beautiful than pleasure. Have you not heard of the man who was digging in the earth for roots and found a treasure?

And some of your elders remember pleasures with regret like wrongs committed in drunk. But regret is the beclouding of the mind and not its chastisement. They should remember their pleasures with gratitude, as they would the harvest of a summer. Yet if it comforts them to regret, let them be comforted.

And there are among you those who are neither young to seek nor old to remember; and in their fear of seeking and remembering they shun all pleasures, lest they neglect the spirit or offend against it.

But even in their foregoing is their pleasure.

And thus they too find a treasure though they dig for roots with quivering hands.

But tell me, who is he that can offend the spirit?

Shall the nightingale offend the stillness of the night, or the firefly the stars? And shall your flame or your smoke burden the wind?

You think the spirit is a still pool which you can trouble with a staff. Oftentimes in denying yourself pleasure you do but store the desire in the recesses of your being.

Who knows but that which seem omitted today, waits for tomorrow? Even your body knows its heritage and its rightful need and won't be deceived.

And your body is the harp of your soul, and it is yours to bring forth sweet music from it or confused sounds.

And now you ask in your heart, "How shall we distinguish that which is good in pleasure from that which is not good?" Go to your fields and your gardens and you shall learn that it is the pleasure of the bee to gather honey of the flower, but it is also the pleasure of the flower to yield its honey to the bee, for to the bee a flower is a fountain of life, and to the flower a bee is a messenger of love, and to both, bee and flower, the giving and the receiving of pleasure is a need and an ecstasy.

Be in your pleasures like the flowers and the bees.

快乐是一首自由的歌

快乐是一首自由的歌，但它不是自由。它是你们的欲望的绽放，但不是它们的果实；它是深谷对高峰的呼唤，但它既不深沉也不高耸；它是囚禁在笼里的展翅的小鸟，但不是环抱的空间。哎，快乐的确是一首自由的歌。我愿意让你们全心全意地歌唱它，而不愿让你们在歌唱时丧失信心。

你们年轻人中有些追求快乐，好像它是所有的一切，他们遭到了判决和谴责。我不会判决他们，也不会谴责他们。我会让他们去寻找，因为他们要找到快乐，而不仅仅是快乐；快乐有七个姐妹，她们中最小的也比快乐美。你们没听说过有人在刨树根时发现了宝藏吗？

你们中有些老年人遗憾地回忆快乐，就像酒醉时做的错事。但遗憾会让心灵蒙上阴影，而不是惩罚。他们应以感恩之心回忆自己的快乐，就像回忆夏天的收获。然而，如果遗憾能给他们安慰，那就让他们得到安慰吧。

你们中的一些人既不是追寻的年轻人，也不是回忆的老年人；他们在追寻和回忆的恐惧中避开一切快乐，唯恐自己忽视或冒犯了灵魂。但是，他们在前行中也有快乐。所以，尽管他们用颤抖的双手挖掘树根，也会找到宝藏。

可告诉我，谁敢冒犯灵魂？是夜莺会扰乱夜的宁静，还是萤火虫会冒犯繁星？你们的火焰或烟雾会给风增加负担吗？

你们以为灵魂是用一根木棍就能搅乱的一潭静水。你们通常拒绝快乐，你们只是把快乐的欲望藏在心间。

谁知道今天忽略的事情会等到明天吗？就连你们的身体也知道它的本性和合理需求，不会受到欺骗。

你们的身体是灵魂的竖琴，它或奏出甜美的乐曲，或发出杂音，这全在你。

现在你们扪心问一下："我们将怎样区别快乐中的善与恶？"去你们的田野和花园，你们就会认识到蜜蜂的快乐在于采集花蜜，对花朵来说，给蜜蜂提供花蜜就是快乐。因为对蜜蜂来说一朵花就是生命之泉；对花朵来说，一只蜜蜂就是爱的使者；对蜜蜂和花朵两者来说，给予和接受的快乐是一种需要和狂喜。

像花朵和蜜蜂那样享受快乐吧。

World of Smiles

About ten years ago when I was in college, I was working as an intern at my University's Museum of Natural History. One day while working at the cash register in the gift shop, I saw an elderly couple come in with a little girl in a wheelchair.

As I looked closer at this girl, I saw that she was kind of perched on her chair. I then realized she had no arms or legs, just a head, neck and torso. She was wearing a little white dress with red polka dots.

As the couple wheeled her up to me I was looking down at the register. I turned my head toward the girl and gave her a wink. As I took the money from her grandparents, I looked back at the girl, who was giving me the cutest, largest smile I have ever seen. All of a sudden her handicap was gone and all I saw was this beautiful girl, whose smile just melt me and almost instantly gave me a completely new sense of what life was all about. She took me from a poor, unhappy college student and brought me into her world: a world of smiles, love and warmth.

That was ten years ago. I'm successful person now. And whenever I get down and think about the troubles of the world, I think about that little girl and the remarkable lesson about life that she taught me.

微笑的世界

大约10年前，我上大学时，在学校的自然历史博物馆做实习生。有一天，我正在礼品店的收银台工作，看到一对老夫妇推着一个坐轮椅的小女孩走进店里。

我贴近看时，只见她坐在轮椅上有点儿不稳。随后，我意识到，她没有手臂和双腿，只有脑袋、脖子和躯干。她穿着一身雪白的红色圆点小连衣裙。

当那对夫妇推着她向我走来时，我正低头看着收银机。我把头转向那个女孩，向她眨了眨眼。我接过老夫妇的钱时，回头看那个女孩，只见她正朝我微笑，那是我有生以来见过的最可爱、最灿烂的微笑。突然间，她的缺陷消失了，我所看到的是一个美丽的女孩。她的微笑感化了我，几乎马上给了我一种生命的全新感觉。她把我这样一个郁郁寡欢的穷大学生带进了她的世界：一个充满微笑、爱和温暖的世界。

那是10年前的事了。如今，我功成名就。每当我萎靡不振，想起世间的种种烦恼时，就会想起那个小女孩和她教给我的人生的非凡一课。

The Value of Smile

You must have a good time meeting people if you expect them to have a good time meeting you.

I have asked thousands of people to smile at someone every hour of the day for a week and then come to class and talk about the results. How did it work? Let's see... here is a letter from William B. Steinhardt, a New York stockholder. His case isn't isolated. In fact, it is typical of hundreds of cases.

"I have been married for over eighteen years," wrote Mr. Steinhardt, "and in all that time I seldom smiled at my wife or spoke two dozen words to her from the time I got up until I was ready to leave for business. I was one of the worst grouches who ever walked down Broadway.

"When you asked me to make a talk about my experience with smiles, I thought I would try it for a week. So the next morning, while combing my hair, I looked at my glum mug in the mirror and said to myself, 'Bill, you are going to wipe the scowl off that sour puss of yours today. You are going to smile. And you are going to begin right now.' As I sat down to breakfast, I greeted my wife with a 'Good morning, my dear,' and smiled as I said it.

"You warned me that she might be surprised. Well, you underestimated her reaction. She was bewildered. She was shocked. I told her that in the future she could expect this as a regular occurrence, and I kept it up every morning.

"This changed attitude of mine brought more happiness into our home in two months since I started than there was during the last year.

"As I leave for my office, I greet the elevator operator in the apartment house with a 'Good morning' and a smile; I greet the doorman with a smile. I smile at the cashier in the subway booth when I ask for change. As I stand on the floor of the Stock Exchange, I smile at people who until recently never saw me smile.

"I soon found that everybody was smiling back at me, I treat those who come to me with complaints or grievances in a cheerful manner, I smile as I listen to them and I find that adjustments are accomplished much easier. I find that smiles are bringing me dollars, many dollars every day.

"I share my office with another broker. One of his clerks is a likable young chap, and I was so elated about the results I was getting that I told him recently about my new philosophy of human relations. He then confessed, when I first came to share my office with his firm he thought me a terrible grouch—and only recently changed his mind. He said I was really human when I smiled.

"I have also eliminated criticism from my system. I give appreciation and praise now instead of condemnation. And these things have literally revolutionized my life. I am a totally different man, a happier man, a richer man, richer in friendships and happiness—the only things that matter much after all."

You don't feel like smiling? Then what? Two things. First, force yourself to smile. If you are alone, force yourself to whistle or hum a tune or sing. Act as if you were already happy, and that will tend to make you happy.

Everybody in the world is seeking happiness—and there is one sure way to find it. That is by controlling our thoughts. Happiness doesn't depend on outward conditions. It depends on inner conditions.

It isn't what you have or who you are or where you are or what you are doing that makes you happy or unhappy. It is what you think about it. For example, two people may be in the same place, doing the same thing; both may have about an equal amount of money and prestige—and yet one may

be miserable and the other happy. Why? Because of a different attitude. I have seen just as many happy faces among the poor peasants toiling with their primitive tools in the devastating heat of the tropics as I have seen in air-conditioned offices in New York, Chicago or Los Angeles.

"There is nothing either good or bad," said Shakespeare, "but thinking makes it so."

Abe Lincoln once remarked, "Most folks are about as happy as they make up their minds to be." He was right.

Whenever you go out-of-doors, draw the chin in, carry the crown of the head high; drink in the sunshine; greet your friends with a smile, and put soul into every handclasp. Do not fear being misunderstood and do not waste a minute thinking about your enemies.

Try to fix firmly in your mind what you would like to do; and then, without veering off direction, you will move straight to the goal. Keep your mind on the great and splendid things you would like to do, and then, as the days go sliding away, you will find yourself unconsciously seizing upon the opportunities that are required for the fulfillment of your desire. Picture in your mind the able, earnest, useful person you desire to be, and the thought you hold is hourly transforming you into the particular individual... Thought is supreme. Preserve a right mental attitude—the attitude of courage, frankness, and good cheer. To think rightly is to create. All things come through desire and every sincere prayer is answered.

Some years ago, a department store in New York City, in recognition of the pressures its sales clerks were under during the Christmas rush, presented the following homely advertisement:

THE VALUE OF A SMILE AT CHRISTMAS

It costs nothing, but creates much. It enriches those who receive, without impoverishing those who give. It happens in a flash and the memory of it sometimes lasts forever. It brings the rest to the weary, the daylight to the discouraged and the sunshine to the sad. Yet it can't be bought, begged, borrowed, or stolen, for it is something that is no earthly good to anybody till it is given away. And if the last-minute rush of Christmas buying some of our salespeople should be too tired to give you a smile, may we ask you to leave one of yours? For nobody needs a smile so much as those who have none left to give!

微笑的价值

如果你希望别人愉快接见你，你必须愉快会见别人。

我曾要求数千人时刻对某人微笑，持续一周后，到班里来说说结果。它会起怎样的作用呢？我们来看一下……这是纽约股票经纪人威廉·B. 斯坦因哈特写的一封信。他的情况并不是孤立的。事实上，它在数百案例中具有代表性。

"我已经结婚18年多了，"斯坦因哈特先生写道。"在此期间，我从起床到准备去上班，很少对妻子微笑，也很少说二十几个词。我是那些走在百老汇大街的人当中最糟糕的一个。

"当你要我谈一下自己微笑的经验时，我认为我要尝试一星期。所以，第二天早上梳头时，我看看镜子里自己哭丧着脸，就对自己说：'比尔，你今天要把脸上的愁容一扫而光。你要微笑，马上就开始。'当我坐下来吃早饭时，我向太太招呼说：'早安，亲爱的，'而且一边说，一边对她微笑。

"你曾提醒过我，她可能大吃一惊。噢，你低估了她的反应。她不知所措，大为震惊。我告诉她说，她以后可以把这看成平常的事情，而且我每天早上都要这样做。这种改变的态度两个月里给我们家带来的快乐比去年一年的还要多。

“我离开家去办公室时,会对公寓大楼的电梯员微笑说‘早上好!’我还微笑着和看门人打招呼。我在地铁售票处兑换零钱时,也会向出纳员微笑。我站在证券交易所时,向那些从未见过我微笑的人微笑。我发现每个人也都对我微笑。我用一种愉快的方式对待那些向我抱怨或诉苦的人。我一边微笑一边听他们说,我发现调解起来要容易得多。我发现微笑给我带来金钱,每天都财源滚滚。

“我和另一位经纪人共用一间办公室。他的一个职员是可爱的小伙子。我为自己取得的成效洋洋得意,最近就把自己人际关系的新人生观告诉了他。后来,他承认说,我起初和他的公司共用办公室时,他还以为我是一个郁郁寡欢的人呢,直到最近才改变了看法。他说,我微笑时的确有人情味。

“我也改掉了批评别人的习惯。现在,我总是欣赏和赞扬,而不是指责。而且这些东西实际上已经彻底改变了我的生活。我完全变成了另一个人,一个更快乐、更充实的人——毕竟这才是真正重要的东西。”

你不想微笑吗?那怎么办?做两件事。首先强迫自己微笑。如果你一人独处,就强迫自己吹口哨、哼小曲或唱歌,装作自己非常快乐的样子,这样就会让你快乐起来。世界上每个人都在追求快乐,找到快乐只有一个可靠的方法,那就是控制我们的思想。快乐并不依靠外在条件,而是依靠内在条件。

决定你快乐不快乐的不是你有什么、你是谁、你在何处或你正在做什么,而是你有什么想法。比如,两个人也许在同一个地方做同样一件事,两个人也许拥有同样多的金钱和声望,但其中一个也许很痛苦,另一个则很快乐。为什么?因为想法不一样。我曾看到贫穷的农夫在热带酷热难当的地方用原始工具辛苦劳作,但他们的笑脸和我在纽约、芝加哥或洛杉矶的办公室里看到的笑脸一样多。

“事情没有好坏之分,”莎士比亚说。“只是思想不同。”

亚伯·林肯曾说过:“大多数人的快乐是因为他们决定快乐。”他说的对。

无论何时你出门,要收下巴,头抬高,吸收阳光,用微笑来问候朋友们,每一次握手都要注入灵魂。别怕误解,别浪费一分钟去想自己的敌人。

尽力下定决心去做你喜欢做的事情,然后不要偏离方向,直达自己的目标。聚精会神做你喜欢做的伟大美好的事情。然后,随着岁月流逝,你会发现自己不知不觉抓住了实现自己心愿所需要的机会。你在心里把自己想象成你渴望做的干练、认真、有用的人,你心里的想法每时每刻都在把你变成你所希望的那种不同寻常的人……思想至高无上。保持一种正确的人生态度,一种勇敢、坦率和乐观的态度。思想正确就是创造。一切事情都源于希望,每个真诚的祈祷都会实现。

几年前,纽约市一家百货商店为缓解圣诞节高峰期店员们的压力,展出了下面这个亲切的广告:

圣诞节微笑的价值

它分文不花,却创造多多。它让得到者富有,付出者也不会贫穷。它在瞬间发生,有时却给人留下永恒的回忆。它给疲惫者带来休息,给沮丧者带来光明,给悲伤者带来阳

光。但它买不到，讨不来，借不了，偷不走，因为你把它送给别人才会有好处。在圣诞节最后一分钟的高峰期，如果我们的售货员太累没有向你微笑，请你留下一个微笑好吗？因为那些无法给予微笑的人更需要微笑！

Smile at Strangers

Have you ever noticed or thought about how little eye contact most of us have with stranger? Why? Are we afraid of them? What keeps us from opening our hearts to people we don't know?

I don't really know the answers to these questions, but I do know that there is virtually always parallel between our attitude toward strangers and our overall level of happiness. In other words, it's unusual to find a person who walks around with her head down, frowning and looking away from people, who is secretly a peaceful, joyful person.

I'm not suggesting it's better to be outgoing than introverted, that you need to expend tons of extra energy trying to brighten others' days, or that you should pretend to be friendly. I'm suggesting, however, that if you think of strangers as being a little more like you and treat them not only with kindness and respect, but with smiles and eye contact as well, you'll probably notice some pretty nice changes in yourself. You'll begin to see that most people are just like you—most of them have families, people they love, troubles, concerns, likes, dislikes, fears, and so on. You'll also notice how nice and grateful people can be when you're the first one to reach out. When you see how similar we all are, you begin to see the innocence in all of us. In other words, even though we often mess up, most of us are doing the best that we know how with the circumstances that surround us. Along with seeing the innocence in people comes a profound feeling of inner happiness.

对陌生人微笑

你曾注意到或想到我们中的大多数人和陌生人的目光接触是多么少吗？为什么？是我们害怕他们吗？是什么阻挡了我们向陌生人敞开心扉的呢？

我确实不知道怎样回答这些问题，但我知道，其实在我们对待陌生人的态度和我们总体幸福水平之间总有一种类似的东西。换言之，发现一个低头皱眉、眼望别处的人内心安详而又快乐，是不同寻常的。

我并不是说，性格外向就比性格内向好，为了使别人生活得更愉快，你需要浪费额外的精力，或者说，你必须要假装友好。我是说，如果你把陌生人看成是你自己的一点影子，然后不仅用善意和尊重对待他们，而且要用微笑和目光接触，你也许会注意到一些非常美好的变化会发生在你身上。你会开始看到多数人都和你一样——他们多数人都有家庭、烦恼、忧虑、喜恶、恐惧等。你还会注意到，当你第一个伸出援手时，他们是多么友好和感激。当你看到他们都是多么相似时，你会开始看到我们所有人身上的单纯率直。换言之，即使我们常常陷入困境，我们多数人会竭尽全力去应对我们周围的环境。看到人们的单纯率直，随之而来的则是来自内心深处的一种幸福感。

第四卷

每个人都会成功

The Gold Watch in the Barn

A farmer carelessly lost an expensive gold watch in the barn on the farm, where he searched for everywhere but in vain.

So he put a notice on the gate of the farm: whoever finds the gold watch will be rewarded 100 dollars.

Facing the temptation of the handsome reward, people tried their best to look for everywhere. However, the grain was piled like a hill along with bales of straw, so if they wanted to find the gold watch, it would be like fishing for a needle in the ocean.

When the sun set, the gold watch was not found yet. They took pains but found nothing. So they began complaining the watch was too small, the barn was too large and the straw was too thick. It was getting dark that they were still unable to find it. So they gave up the temptation of 100 dollars one by one.

But only a small boy in shabby clothes was still not discouraged but kept looking for it in the grain. He had nothing to eat throughout the day. In order to solve the family problem, he was eager to find the gold watch and let his parents, brothers and sisters have a full meal.

The night was already getting late; the boy was also tired. He was lying in the straw to have a rest when he heard a strange "tick-tock".

He immediately held his breath and listen attentively.

It was quieter in the barn while "tick-tock" sounded clearly. The boy followed the sound, found the gold watch buried in the depths of the grain and finally got the 100 dollars.

Like the gold watch in the barn, success has existed around us and spread in every corner of life. Only we are calm and firmly look for it can we find it.

谷仓里的金表

一个农场主不慎将一只名贵的金表丢失在了农场的谷仓里。他到处搜寻,结果毫无踪迹。

于是,就在农场门口贴上了一条告示:凡是找到金表的,奖赏100美元。

面对重赏的诱惑,人们竭尽全力四处寻找,无奈谷仓内谷粒成山,还有成捆成捆的稻草,想在其中找回金表如同大海捞针。

太阳落山了,金表还是杳无踪迹。大家费尽心机,一无所获,开始抱怨金表太小了,谷仓太大,稻草太厚。天渐渐暗了下来,更是无法寻找。于是,一个个放弃了100美元的诱惑。

但是,只有一个衣衫褴褛的小男孩依然毫不气馁,继续在谷堆里寻找。他已经整整一天没有吃饭了。为了解决家庭的困难,他渴望能找到金表,能让父母和兄弟姐妹吃上一顿饱饭。

夜已深了,男孩也累了。他躺在稻草堆里想歇一会儿,突然,他听见了一个奇特的"滴答滴答"声。

他顿时屏住了呼吸,认真倾听。

谷仓更加安静了,"滴答"声更加清晰了。男孩循着声音找到了埋藏在谷堆深处的金表，最终得到了100美元。

成功如同谷仓内的金表，早已存在于我们周围，散布于人生的每个角落，只有我们静下心来，执著地去寻找，才能发现。

The Goal of Life

A father went to hunt for hares with his three sons to the grassland. Upon arrival at the destination, all well prepared, before they took action, their father asked three sons a question, "What do you see?"

The eldest son replied, "I saw the shotguns in our hands, the hares running on the prairie and the endless stretch of grassland." His father shook his head and said, "You're wrong."

The second son answered, "I saw our father, eldest brother, younger brother, shotguns, hares and the boundless grassland." The father again shook his head and said, "You're wrong."

The youngest only answered, "I can only see hares." Then their father said, "You're right."

Only can a definite goal point out the right direction of action and less detour on the road to achieving the objective. In fact, the indiscriminate or excessive goals will impede our progress, so in order to achieve what we have in our mind, if unrealistic, we may ultimately accomplish nothing.

人生的目标

父亲带着三个儿子到草原上猎杀野兔。在到达目的地、一切准备得当、开始行动之前，父亲向三个儿子提出了一个问题："你看到了什么？"

老大回答道："我看到了我们手里的猎枪、在草原上奔跑的野兔、还有一望无际的草原。"父亲摇摇头说："不对。"

老二回答："我看到了爸爸、大哥、弟弟、猎枪、野兔，还有茫茫无际的草原。"父亲又摇摇头说："不对。"

而老三的回答只有一句话："我只看到了野兔。"这时，父亲才说："你答对了。"

有了明确的目标，才会为行动指出正确的方向，才会在实现目标的道路上少走弯路。事实上，漫无目标或目标过多都会阻碍我们前进，要实现自己的心中所想，如果不切实际，最终可能一事无成。

The Most Successful Lesson

I grew up in Estepona. I was 16 when one morning, Dad told me I could drive him to Mijas, on the condition that I took the car in to be serviced at a nearby garage. I readily accepted. I drove Dad to Mijas, and promised to pick him up at 4 p.m., then dropped off the car at the garage. With several hours

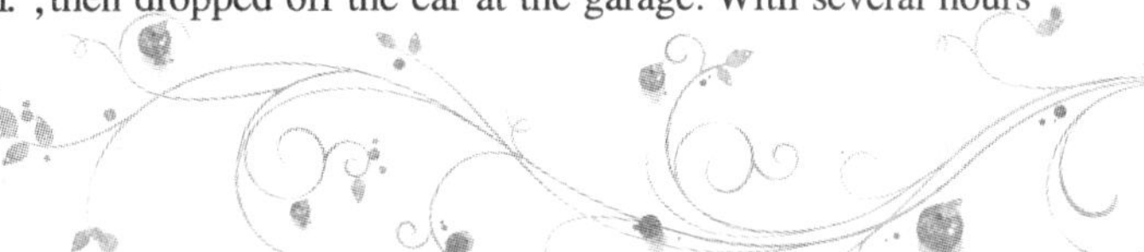

to spare, I went to a theater. However, when the last movie finished, it was six. I was two hours late!

I knew Dad would be angry if he found out I'd been watching movies. So I decided not to tell him the truth. When I hurried there I apologized for being late, and told him I'd come as quickly as I could, but the car had needed some major repairs. I'll never forget the look he gave me.

"I'm disappointed you feel you have to lie to me, Jason," Dad looked at me again. "When you didn't turn up, I called the garage to ask if there were any problems, and they told me you hadn't yet picked up the car."

I felt ashamed as I weakly told him the real reason.

A sadness passed through Dad as he listened attentively. "I'm angry with myself. I realize I've failed as a father. I'm going to walk home now and think seriously about where I've gone wrong all those years."

"But Dad, it's 18 miles!" My protest and apologies were useless.

Dad walked home that day. I drove behind him, begging him all the way, but he walked silently.

Seeing Dad in so much physical and emotional pain was my most painful experience. However, it was also the most successful lesson. I have never lied since.

最成功的一课

我在埃斯特普纳长大。我16岁的一天早上，爸爸对我说，我可以开车把他送到米加斯，条件是我要把车开到附近的一家修车厂保养一下。我欣然答应，就把爸爸送到了米加斯，并许诺下午4点来接他，然后便开车去了修车厂。因为还剩有好几个小时，所以我就去了一家电影院。然而，最后一场电影结束时，已经6点了。我迟到了两个小时！

我知道，如果发现我一直看电影，爸爸一定会生气。于是，我决定不对他说实话。我匆匆赶到那里，道歉说自己来晚了，然后告诉他说我要尽快赶来，但汽车需要一些大修。我永远难忘他看我的眼神。

"詹森，我对你认为自己不得不对我撒谎感到失望，"爸爸又看着我。"你没有回来时，我给修车厂打电话问是否有什么问题，他们告诉我说你还没有取车。"

我把真实原因告诉他时，底气不足，羞愧难当。

爸爸一边仔细听，一边感到忧伤。"我对自己生气。作为父亲，我发现自己已经失败。我现在要走回去，认真想一下这些年自己都错在了哪里。"

"可是，爸爸，这有18英里啊！"我的反对和道歉毫无用处。

那天，爸爸走回了家。我开车跟在后面，一路都在求他，但他默默地走着。

看着爸爸身心受到如此痛苦的折磨是我最痛苦的一次经历。然而，这也是最成功的一课。从此以后，我再也没有撒过谎。

Do One Thing Every Day

There was a painter, who held over a dozen of painting shows. Regardless of the number of visitors, he always smiled.

I once asked him, "Why are you have so happy every day?"

He told me one thing, as a boy, I had a lot of interests and was very eager to excel. Painting, playing the accordion, swimming or playing basketball, I must be the first. This, of course, was impossible. So I felt so depressed that my learning plummeted.

When my father learned about it, he took a funnel and a handful of corn seeds, let me put my hands under the funnel to take, picked up one seed and threw it into the funnel, when the seed slipped down the funnel and dropped on my hands. My father threw more than 10 times, so my hands had more than 10 seeds. Then, my father grasped a full handful of corn seeds and put them into the funnel. The seeds jostled each other and no one dropped.

My father said to me, "This funnel represents you; if you can finish one thing every day, you will harvest a seed and happiness. But when you want to hold everything together to do, you won't harvest one seed."

每天做好一件事

有一位画家,举办过十几次个人画展。开始无论参观者多少,他脸上总是挂着微笑。有一次,我问他:"你为什么每天都这么开心呢?"

他给我讲了一件事:小时候,我兴趣非常广泛,也很要强。画画,拉手风琴,游泳,打篮球,必须都得第一才行。这当然是不可能的。于是,我心灰意冷,学习成绩一落千丈。父亲知道后,找来一个漏斗和一捧玉米种子,让我双手放在漏斗下面接着,然后捡起一粒种子投到漏斗里面,种子便顺着漏斗滑到了我的手里。父亲投了十几次,我的手中也就有了十几粒种子。然后,父亲一次抓起满满的一把玉米粒放在漏斗里面,玉米粒相互挤着,竟然一粒也没有掉下来。

父亲对我说:"这个漏斗代表你,假如你每天都能做好一件事,每天你就会有一粒种子的收获和快乐。可是,当你想把所有的事情都挤到一起来做,反而连一粒种子也收获不到了。"

Think Highly of Yourself

A boy who lived in an orphanage often asked the dean pessimistically and sentimentally, "No one wants me, so what's the point of living on earth?"

The dean always smiled but didn't reply.

One day the dean handed a stone to the boy and said, "Tomorrow morning take this stone to the market for sale, but not for 'true sale'. Remember, no matter how much money other people offer, you can't absolutely sell it."

The next day the boy squatted in one corner of the market. Unexpectedly, many people wanted to buy him the stone, and the price they offered was higher and higher.

Back to the orphanage, the boy excitedly reported to the dean. The dean smiled and ordered him to hawk in the gold market tomorrow. In the gold market, some people even offered the price 10 times higher than that of yesterday to buy the stone.

Finally, the dean ordered the boy to display the stone in the gem market. As a result, the price of

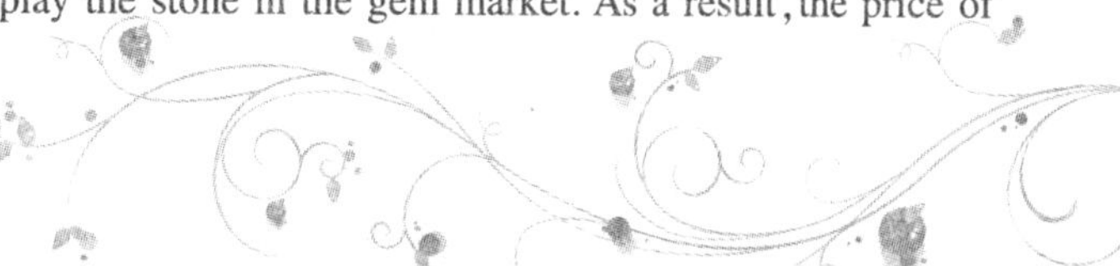

the stone rose 10 times than that of yesterday. Because the stone wasn't sold at any cost, it was spread as a "rare gem".

Excitedly, the boy went back to the orphanage holding the stone in both hands and reported all this to the dean.

Looking at the boy, the dean said slowly, "The value of life, like this stone, will have a different significance in a different environment. As long as you think highly of yourself, self-value and self-love, your life will be meaningful and valuable."

看重自己

一个生长在孤儿院的男孩常常悲观伤感地问院长:“像我这样没人要的孩子,活着究竟有什么意思呢?”

院长总是笑而不答。

一天,院长交给男孩一块石头说:“明天早上,你拿这块石头到市场上去卖,但不是‘真卖’。记住,无论别人出多少钱,绝对不能卖。”

第二天,男孩蹲在市场角落。出人意料的是,有许多人向他买那块石头,而且价钱越出越高。

回到院里,男孩兴奋地向院长报告,院长笑笑,要他明天拿到黄金市场上去叫卖。在黄金市场,竟有人出比昨天高10倍的价钱要买那块石头。

最后,院长叫男孩把石头拿到宝石市场上去展示。结果,石头的价钱较昨天又涨了10倍,由于给多少钱都不卖,竟被传扬为“稀世珍宝”。

男孩兴冲冲地捧着石头回到孤儿院,将这一切禀报院长。

院长望着男孩,慢慢道:“生命的价值就像这块石头一样,不同的环境会有不同的意义。只要看重自己,自珍自爱,生命就有意义、有价值。”

Get a Thorough Understanding of Yourself

In one's lifetime it is oneself that one spends the most time being with or dealing with. But it is precisely oneself that one has the least understanding of.

When you are going uphill in life, you tend to overestimate yourself. It seems that everything you seek for is within your reach; luck and opportunities will come your way and you are overjoyed that they constitute part of your worth.

When you are going downhill, you tend to underestimate yourself, mistaking difficulties and adversities for your own incompetence. You think it wise for yourself to know your place and stay aloof from worldly success. In doing so you are actually wearing a mask of cowardice, behind which the flow of sap in your life will be retarded.

To get a thorough understanding of yourself is to gain a correct view of yourself and be a sober realist—aware of both one's strength and shortage. You may look forward hopefully to the future but be sure not to expect too much, for ideals can never be fully realized. You may be courageous to meet challenges but it should be clear to you where to direct your efforts. That's to say, as long as you have

a perfect knowledge of yourself there won't be difficulties you can't overcome, nor obstacles you can't surmount.

To get a thorough understanding of yourself needs self-appreciation. Whether you liken yourself to a towering tree or a blade of grass, whether you think you are a high mountain or a small stone, you represent a state of nature that has its own raison d'etre. If you earnestly admire yourself you'll have a real sense of self-appreciation. As soon as you gain full confidence in yourself you'll be able to overcome any adversity.

To get a thorough understanding of yourself also requires doing yourself a favor when it's needed. In time of anger, do yourself a favor by giving vent to it in a quiet place so that you won't be hurt by its flames; in time of sadness, do yourself a favor by sharing it with your friends so as to change a gloomy mood into a cheerful one; in time of tiredness, do yourself a favor by getting a good sleep or taking some tonic.

To get a thorough understanding of yourself is to get a full control of your life. Then you will find your life full of color and fragrance.

彻悟自己

人的一生中,和自己相处时间最长或打交道最多的是自己,但最不了解自己的也正是自己。

人生得意时,你往往高估自己。你追求的一切好像都触手可及。好运和机遇会和你一路同行,你对它们成了你自身价值的一部分而狂喜。

人生失意时,你往往低估自己,错把困难和不幸看成是自己的无能。你认为了解自己的处境、与世无争是明智之举。这样做,你其实给自己戴上了胆小的面具,并会在以后的生命流动中妨碍自己的发展。

要彻悟自己就是正确看待自己,做一个清醒的现实主义者,认识到自己的实力和不足。也许你在充满希望地盼望未来,但一定不要期望值太高,因为理想永远不能完全实现。你也许能勇敢地面对挑战,但你应该清楚自己努力的目标在哪里。也就是说,只要你完全了解自己,没有困难不可以克服,没有障碍不可以逾越。

要彻悟自己需要自我欣赏。无论你是把自己比作参天大树还是比作一叶小草,无论你认为自己是一座高山还是一块小石头,你都代表一种自然状态,都有自己存在的理由。如果你能认真地欣赏自己,就能获得自我欣赏的真实判断力。你一拥有充分的自信,就能战胜一切不幸。

要彻悟自己,也需要适当关心自己。生气时,在宁静的地方发泄一下,以免被火气烧伤;悲伤时,告诉你的朋友,让沮丧的心情欢快起来;疲惫时,好好睡一觉或滋补一下。

要彻悟自己,就是完全控制自己的生命。这样,你会发现生命充满了色彩和芬芳。

Another Secret to Success

A sculptor got a marble with very fine texture. He felt the marble was so suitable for carving a portrait. So he picked up the chisel. Not knowing the tension or excessive force, only a chisel, he knocked off a large chunk of debris. The sculptor stopped immediately. After three days' thought, he decided to abandon the sculpture he had designed because he realized he was hard to manage this valuable material. Later, this marble was presented to the sculptor Michelangelo, who used this marble to carve the unparalleled masterpiece—David Statue.

The careful viewers pointed to an obvious streak of scar on David's back, slightly regretted for its not 100% perfection and sighed for the former previous sculptor's temerity in a sort of way.

Michelangelo corrected, "The gentleman has been very careful. If he's temerarious and hasty, this special material has been long gone, and my David Statue will never come into being."

"So, would you also like to thank the sculptor?" some people were puzzled.

"Yes, I would like to thank him for his rare seriousness, because his sculpture and abandon are extremely serious. Furthermore, I would like to thank him for the scar he left. It always reminds me that I must be extremely careful of each of my carving and chiseling, without any slightest carelessness."

Michelangelo told another secret to highlight his success with respect—learn from the lessons of others and accomplish everything at hand with the greatest seriousness.

成功的另一个秘诀

一位雕塑家得到一块质地非常精美的大理石。他觉得大理石非常适合雕刻一个人像。于是,他拿起了凿子。不知是因为紧张还是用力过重,只那么一凿,他就敲掉了一大块碎屑。雕塑家立刻停下来,经过3天思索,他决定放弃构思好的雕塑,因为他意识到自己难以驾驭这块宝贵的材料。后来,这块大理石被赠送给雕塑家米开朗琪罗。米开朗琪罗用这块大理石雕刻出了旷世杰作——大卫像。

细心的观赏者指着大卫背上的一道明显的伤痕,为其不能百分之百的完美而略感惋惜,并慨叹先前的那位雕塑家有些冒失。

米开朗琪罗纠正道:"那位先生已经相当慎重了,如果他冒失草率的话,这块特别材料早就不复存在了,而我的大卫像也就无从产生了。"

"这么说,你还要感谢那位雕塑家?"有人困惑不解了。

"是的,我要感谢他难得的认真,他的雕刻和放弃都是极其认真的。另外,我还要感谢他留下的那块伤痕,它总是在提醒着我,让我的每一刀、每一凿都千百倍细心,不能有丝毫疏忽大意。"

米开朗琪罗充满敬意地道出了他获得成功的另一个秘诀:汲取别人的教训,以最大的认真去做好手头的每一件事。

Load and You Won't Fall

After unloading, a cargo ship returned when it suddenly encountered a hurricane. Panic-stricken, the sailors were on tenterhooks with anxiety. The old captain ordered decisively, "Open all the cargos and pour water into them immediately." The sailors were worried, "It will double the risk. Aren't we

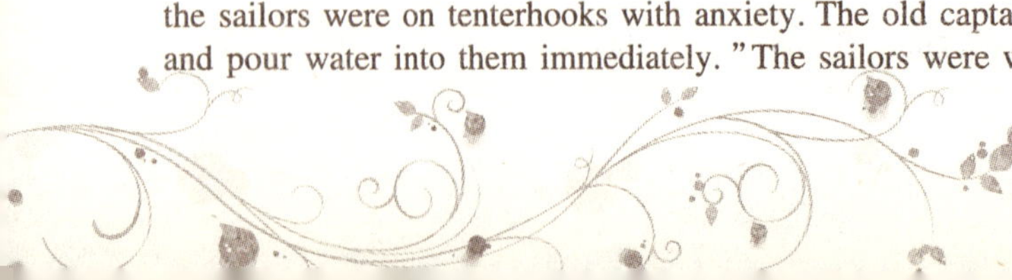

destroying ourselves?" The captain said calmly, "Have you seen the deep-rooted trees with thick trunks are knocked down by storms? It is the small trees without roots that are knocked down."

The sailors did suspiciously as they were told. Though the storm and swells were still so fierce, but with the water of the cargos increasing, the freighter gradually calmed down.

The captain told the crew who felt great relief, "An empty cask is easily overturned by the wind, but if filled with water, it won't be knocked down. When loading, the ship is safest while it is most dangerous when empty."

People are also like this. Those people who muddle along and waste the time are like an empty cask without filling water, often completely knocked down by the storm of life.

负重,才不会跌倒

一艘货轮卸货后返航,在浩瀚的大海上突然遭遇巨大风暴。惊慌失措的水手们急得团团转。老船长果断下令:"打开所有货仓,立刻往里面灌水。"水手们担忧:"险上加险,不是自找死路吗?"船长镇定地说:"大家见过根深干粗的树被暴风刮倒过吗?被刮倒的是没有根基的小树。"

水手们半信半疑地照着做了。虽然暴风巨浪依旧那么猛烈,但随着货仓里的水越来越满,货轮渐渐平稳了。

船长告诉那些松了口气的水手:"一只空木桶是容易被风打翻的,如果装满水,风是吹不倒的。船上负重时最安全,空船时才最危险。"

人何尝不是呢?那些得过且过、空耗时光的人,就像一个没有盛水的空木桶,往往一场人生的风雨便把他们彻底打翻了。

I Can Make It Happen

History abounds with tales of experts who were convinced that the ideas, plans and projects of others could never be achieved. However, success favored those who believed, "I can make it happen."

The Italian sculptor Agostino D'Antonio worked diligently on a large piece of marble. Unable to produce his desired masterpiece, he lamented, "I can do nothing with it."

Other sculptors also worked on this piece of marble, but to no avail.

Michelangelo discovered the stone and visualized the possibilities in it. His "I-can-make-it-happen" attitude resulted in one of the world's masterpiece—David.

Even the great Thomas Edison discouraged his friend, Henry Ford, from pursuing his rudimental idea of a motorcar. Convinced of the worthlessness of the idea, Edison invited Ford to come and work for him.

However, Ford tirelessly pursued his dream. Although his first attempt resulted in a vehicle without reverse gear, Henry Ford knew he could make it happen. And, of course, he did.

Let's not forget our friends Orville and Wilbur Wright. Journalists, friends, armed forces specialists, and even their father laughed at the idea of an airplane.

"What a silly and insane way to spend money. Let the birds fly in the sky," they jeered.

"Sorry," the Wright brothers responded. "We have a dream, and we can make it happen."
You can also make it happen.

我能做到

历史上有很多深信别人的想法、计划和方案根本无法实现的专家的故事。然而，成功却青睐那些相信"我能做到"的人。

意大利雕刻家阿高斯提诺·丹东尼奥对一块巨大的大理石上勤奋雕刻。当他无法雕刻出理想的作品时，悲叹道："我对它无能为力。"

另一些雕刻家也在这块大理石上费了一番工夫，但无济于事。

米开朗基罗发现了这块巨石，并使其中的所有可能性都显现了出来。他的"我能做到"的态度最终成就了世界名作的《大卫像》。

就连伟大的托马斯·爱迪生也劝阻他的朋友亨利·福特放弃制造机车的初步想法。爱迪生深信这个想法没有任何价值，邀请福特过来为他工作。

然而，福特不屈不挠地追求自己的梦想。尽管初次尝试的结果是一辆没有倒车挡的汽车，但亨利·福特知道他能做到。而且，他的确取得了成功。

我们不要忘记我们的朋友奥维尔·怀特和威尔伯·怀特。新闻记者、朋友们、军事专家，甚至他们的父亲都嘲笑他们对飞机的构想。

"这样花钱真是愚蠢疯狂！让小鸟在天空飞吧，"他们嘲笑说。

"对不起，"怀特兄弟回答说，"我们有一个梦想，而且我们能让它实现。"

你也能把梦想变成现实。

The Most Severe Punishment

Cliff Baros was a pastor, who related a story he educated his children.

When very small, his son Bobby and daughter Betty went wrong. Cliff warned if they recommitted next time, he would punish them. The next day when he came back from work, Cliff found the children recommitted. He was irritated, but seeing the children were so poor, his heart softened, so he didn't have the heart to punish them.

Cliff said to me, "Bobby and Betty were very small. I called them into the room, undid my belt, took off my shirt, knelt at the bed with baring my back and made each of them whip me 10 times with the belt.

"You can't imagine how sad they cried, which were heartfelt, remorseful tears. They didn't want to lash their father, but we made clear beforehand that whoever made a mistake would be punished. I told them the punishment was inevitable, but as a father, I decided to replace them to bear. I insisted they lash me hard for 20 times. The two children cried as they were beating me, even more grieved than they received the most severe punishment.

"Since then, I even never beat Bobby and Betty because they knew I loved them, but I wouldn't ignore their mistakes for it. So they were always very obedient, not afraid of being punished, but respected and loved me."

最严厉的惩罚

克利夫·巴罗斯是一名牧师。他讲述了自己教育子女的一个故事。

当时他的儿子博比和女儿贝蒂还很小,做了错事。克利夫警告说,如果下次再犯,就要处罚他们。第二天下班,克利夫发现一对儿女故伎重演。克利夫很恼火,但看着孩子们可怜的样子又心软了,他不忍心处罚他们。

克利夫对我说:"博比和贝蒂都很小。我把他们叫进房间,然后解下自己的皮带,脱下衬衫,光着脊梁跪在床前,让他们每人用皮带抽我 10 下。

"你想象不到他们哭得有多伤心,那是发自内心的、悔恨的眼泪。他们不想抽打自己的父亲,但我们有言在先,犯了错就要受惩罚。我告诉他们,处罚是不可避免的,但作为父亲,我决定替他们承受。我坚持要他们用力打满 20 下。两个孩子一边打我,一边痛哭,比受到最严厉的惩罚时还难过。

"从那以后,我甚至再没打过博比和贝蒂,因为他们知道我爱他们,但不会因此而忽视他们的错误。所以,他们总是非常听话,不是怕被罚,而是出于对我的尊重和爱。"

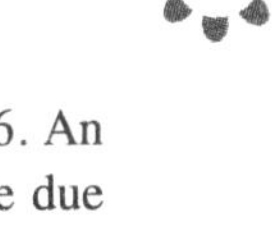

Without the Excuse to Abandon the Efforts

A man suffered two tragic accidents in his life. The first misfortune occurred at the age of 46. An air crash made more than 65% of his skin burnt. In the 16 surgeries, his face became a color plate due to the skin graft, his fingers missing and his legs particularly small and couldn't move but only paralyzed in a wheelchair. Who can imagine after six months, he personally piloted a plane into the blue sky!

Four years later, evil befell him again: the plane he piloted his suddenly crashed back to the runway when it took off, his 12 vertebrae were all crushed and forever paralyzed below the waist. But he didn't take such disasters as the reason for his depression. He said, "Before paralysis I can do 10,000 things, but now I can only do 9,000, so I can still focus on the 9,000 things I can do. I have suffered two major setbacks in my life, so I can only choose not to take the setbacks as an excuse to abandon efforts."

This strong man in life was Mitchell. Because never giving up his efforts, he eventually became a millionaire, a public orator and an entrepreneur and won a position in the political arena.

一生没有放弃努力的借口

有个人在他的一生中遭受过两次惨痛的意外事故。第一次不幸发生在他 46 岁时。一次飞机意外事故使他身上 65% 以上的皮肤都被烧坏了。在 16 次手术中,他的脸因植

皮而变成了一块彩色板。他的手指没有了，双腿特别细小，而且无法行动，只能瘫在轮椅上。谁能想到，6 个月后，他亲自驾驶着飞机飞上了蓝天！

4 年后，命运再一次把不幸降临到他的身上，他驾驶的飞机在起飞时突然甩回了跑道，他的 12 块脊椎骨全部被压得粉碎，腰部以下永远瘫痪了。但他没有把这些灾难当作自己消沉的理由，他说："我瘫痪前可以做一万种事，现在我只能做九千种，我还可以把注意力放在能做的九千种事上。我的人生遭受过两次重大的挫折，所以我只能选择不把挫折拿来当成自己放弃努力的借口。"

这位生活的强者就是米切尔。正因为他永不放弃努力，最终成了百万富翁、公众演说家和企业家，还在政坛上获得了一席之地。

The Danger of Success

A young novice climber prepared to climb the Alps in the border of Swiss. This was the first time he would climb the mountains in the true sense, so he invited the two experienced guides to keep company.

That was a very dangerous steep mountain road, but protected by the two excellent guides around him, he did not feel any danger.

They climbed a long road, and when they were out of breath exhausted, the summit was close at hand. The guide walking ahead was willing to let the novice first stand on the peak and enjoy the feeling of "seeing the mountains around and below are wee," so he moved aside and let the young climber walk ahead.

At this moment, charmed by the honor, the young climber who had climbed up the peak forgot the strong gust that would blow on the peak at any time and excitedly jumped up cheering his victory.

Just at this moment, the guide caught up with him and pulled him down to the ground.

"Kneel on the ground quickly!" he snapped, "For the position you are now on, no gesture is safe, unless kneeling on the ground!"

There are too many times we want to stand up tall and enjoy the success and glory that belong to us. But it is in these moments that we most easily disappear in the gale.

成功的危险

有一位年轻的登山新手，准备去攀登瑞士境内的阿尔卑斯山。这是他第一次攀登真正意义上的高山，所以他邀请了两名经验丰富的向导陪同。

那真是一段危险陡峭的山路，但有一前一后两名优秀向导的保护，他并没有觉得自己有什么危险。

他们攀登了很长的山路，就在他们筋疲力尽气喘吁吁之时，顶峰到了眼前。走在前面的向导愿意让新手第一个站到山巅，享受"一览众山小"的感觉，于是挪向一边，让年轻的登山者走在了前面。

这时，在荣誉的魔力下，爬到峰顶的年轻登山者，竟然忘记了山峰上随时可能刮起猛烈的阵风,他兴奋地跳起来,欢呼自己的胜利。

就在这时,向导赶上前来,一把将他拉倒在地。

“跪到地上,快!”他厉声说道。“你现在所处的这个位置上,没有什么姿势是安全的,除非跪在地上!”

有太多的时刻,我们想要高高站起,享受属于我们的成功与荣耀。可就是在这些时刻,我们最容易消失在狂风之中。

Will Inspired Life

The little country schoolhouse was heated by an old-fashioned pot-bellied coal stove. A little boy had the job of coming to school early each day to start the fire and warm the room before his teacher and classmates arrived.

One morning they arrived to find the schoolhouse engulfed in flames. They dragged the unconscious little boy out of the flaming building more dead than alive. He had major burns over the lower half of his body and was taken to a nearby county hospital. From his bed the semi-conscious little boy faintly heard the doctor talking to his mother. The doctor told his mother that her son would surely be dead,for the terrible fire had devastated the lower half of his body.

But the brave boy didn't want to die. He made up his mind that he would survive. Somehow,to the amazement of the physician,he did survive. When the mortal danger was past,he again heard the doctor and his mother speaking quietly. The mother was told that since the fire had destroyed so much flesh in the lower part of his body that he was doomed to be a lifetime cripple.

Once more the brave boy made up his mind. He would not be a cripple. He would walk. But unluckily from the waist down,he had no motor ability. His thin legs just dangled there,all but lifeless. Ultimately,he was released from the hospital.

Every day his mother would massage his little legs,but there was no effect. He was either in bed or confined to a wheelchair. Yet his determination that he would walk was as strong as ever.

One sunny day his mother wheeled him out into the yard to get some fresh air. This day,instead of sitting there,he threw himself from the chair. He pulled himself across the grass,dragging his legs behind him. He worked his way to the white picket fence bordering their lot. With great effort,he raised himself up on the fence. Then,stake by stake,he began dragging himself along the fence, resolved that he would walk.

He started to do this every day until he wore a smooth path all around the yard beside the fence.

Ultimately,through his daily massages,his persistence and his resolute determination,he did develop the ability to stand up,first to walk haltingly,then to walk by himself—and then—to run.

He began to walk to school,then to run to school,to run for the sheer joy of running. Later in college he made the track team. Still later in Madison Square Garden this young man who was not expected to survive,who would surely never walk,who could never hope to run—Dr. Glenn Cunningham,ran the world's fastest mile!

意志激励人生

小乡村校舍靠一个老式大肚煤炉取暖。小男孩负责每天一早在师生到校前赶来生

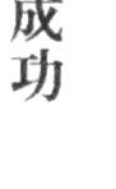

起炉火、温暖教室。

一天早晨，师生们发现校舍被大火吞没了。他们把昏迷的小男孩从燃烧的房子里拽出来时，他已经半死不活了，下半身严重烧伤，被送到了附近的一家县医院。半昏迷的小男孩在病床上模糊听到了医生对他妈妈的谈话。医生对小男孩的母亲说，她的儿子肯定会死，因为可怕的大火已经烧坏了他的下半身。但勇敢的小男孩不想死。他下定决心要活下来。不知何故，让医生惊愕的是，他真的活了下来。致命的危险过后，他又听到医生在低声对母亲说话。医生告诉男孩的母亲说，大火已经烧坏了他下半身的大部分肌肉，所以他注定要终生残废。

勇敢的小男孩又一次下定了决心，他不会残废，他要走路。但不幸的是，他腰部以下根本没有了运动神经能力，细腿只是在那里摇晃，几乎毫无知觉。最后，他终于出院了。

每天，妈妈都会按摩他的双腿，但毫不见效。他每天不是待在床上，就是坐在轮椅上。然而，他想行走的决心仍是那样坚强。

一个阳光灿烂的日子，妈妈把他推进院子里呼吸新鲜空气。这天，他没有坐在那里，而是从轮椅上扑下来，拖着双腿爬过草地，努力爬到那个地方边界的白色尖桩篱栅边，用了很大劲儿扶着篱笆站了起来。随后，他开始顺着篱笆的一个个木桩向前拖行，下定决心一定要行走。

渐渐地，他每天都这样做，直至把院子里沿着篱笆的院子磨出了一条平滑的小路。终于，通过每天按摩、坚持不懈和坚定决心，他确实养成了站起来的能力，起初步履蹒跚，后来独立行走，最后竟跑了起来。

他开始步行上学，然后跑步上学，跑步成了他的一大乐趣。后来上大学时，他参加了田径队。再后来，这个曾被认为不能活下来、再也不会行走、更没有希望跑步的年轻人格伦·坎宁汉博士，在麦迪逊广场花园跑出了世界上最快的速度！

A Creed to Live by

Don't determine your worth by comparing yourself with others because each of us is special.

Don't set your goals by what other people deem important. Only you know what is best for you.

Don't take for granted the things closest to your heart. Cling to them as you would your life, for without them life is meaningful.

Don't let your life slip through your fingers by living in the past or the future. Treasure each day in your life and you will have all the days of your life.

Don't give up before you try your best. Nothing is really over until the moment you stop trying.

Don't be afraid to admit that you are less than perfect. It is this fragile thread that binds us to each other.

Don't be afraid to encounter risks. It is by taking chances that we learn how to be brave.

Don't shut love out of your life by saying it's impossible to find. The quickest way to receive love is to give love; the fastest way to lose love is to hold it too tightly; and the best way to keep love is to give it wings.

Don't abandon your dreams. To be without dreams is to be without hope; to be without hope is to be without purpose.

Don't run through life so fast that you forget not only where you've been, but also where you're going. Life is not a race, but a journey to be savored each step of the way.

人生的信条

不要通过和他人比较来确定自己的价值,因为我们每个人都与众不同。

不要以别人认为重要来确立自己的目标。只有你知道什么对你最好。

不要想当然地认为最贴近你心灵的东西。要像对自己的生命一样紧紧地抓住它们,因为没有它们,生命就毫无意义。

不要生活在过去或未来而让生命从指尖溜走。珍视生活中的每一天,你就会拥有生命的全部日子。

不要在竭尽全力之前就放弃。直到你停止努力,一切才会真正结束。

不要害怕承认自己还不完美。维系我们之间关系的正是这根脆弱的细线。

不要害怕遭遇风险。只有抓住这种机会,我们才能学会如何勇敢。

不要说找不到爱而把生命中的爱拒之门外。得到爱的最快方式就是付出爱;失去爱的最快方式就是把爱抓得太紧;保持爱的最佳方式就是给爱一双翅膀。

不要放弃自己的梦想. 生活没有梦想,就没有希望;没有希望,就没有意义。

不要让生命的脚步跑得太快,这样你不仅会忘记自己曾到过什么地方,而且会忘记自己要去什么地方。人生不是一次赛跑,而是一段旅程,途中的每一步都要细细品味。

No Road Is Longer Than Your Feet

It was a 24-member expedition to the virgin forest at the upper reaches of the Amazon River. Due to the special climate of tropical rainforests, many members lost contact with the expedition for their serious physical discomfort.

Until two months later, all the circumstances of this expedition were made it clear: among the 24 people, 23 of them died unluckily in the primeval forests; only one created the miracle of survival. He was the famous explorer John Borusen.

In the primeval forests, Borusen suffered from severe asthma. He kept groping in the vast forests on an empty stomach for three days and nights. In this process, he lost consciousness more than ten times, but the strong desire to survive made him time and again stand up and continued struggling tenaciously. He insisted step by step, explored step by step and the miracle of life was born in such insistence and grope!

Later, when many reporters rushed to interview John Borusen, one question they asked most frequently was, "Why could you survive luckily alone?" He said, "There is no mountain higher than people, nor is the road longer than feet."

There is always a way out. As long as we have our feet, we'll have a road. This is the faith that supported him to survive.

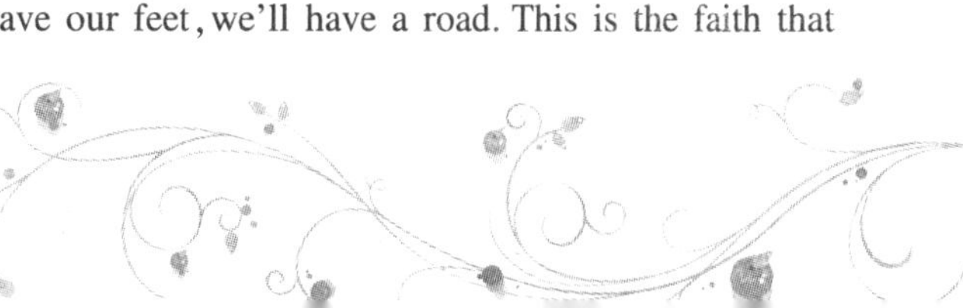

没有比脚更长的路

那是一支24人组成的探险队，到亚马逊河上游的原始森林去探险。由于热带雨林的特殊气候，许多人因身体严重不适，相继与探险队失去了联系。

直到两个月后，才彻底搞清了这支探险队的全部情况：在他们24人当中，有23人在原始森林中不幸遇难，只有一个人创造了生还的奇迹，这个人就是著名探险家约翰·鲍卢森。

在原始森林中，约翰·鲍卢森患上了严重的哮喘病，他饿着肚子在茫茫林海中坚持摸索了3天3夜。在此过程中，他昏死过去十几次，但强烈的求生欲使他一次又一次地站了起来，继续顽强抗争。他一步一步地坚持，一步一步地摸索，生命的奇迹就这样在坚持与摸索中诞生！

后来，许多记者争先恐后地采访约翰·鲍卢森，问得最多的一个问题是："为什么唯独你能幸运地死里逃生？"他说："世界上没有比人更高的山，也没有比脚更长的路。"

天无绝人之路。只要有脚，就会有路。这就是支撑他死里逃生的信念。

The Secret of Becoming Rich

Ayer lived a rich life, so his friends wanted to know the secret of his wealth. One day, Ayer would go to the market to handle affairs, when one of his friends happened to go the same way. So they went along.

It was terribly sultry. When they went halfway, they were so tired and thirsty that they stopped and sat down under a big tree by the roadside.

Ayer took out two bowls from his backpack, placed before them, then untied the water bag and filled the bowls with water.

They carried the bowls and were about to drink off when a gust of wind suddenly blew, making them not open their eyes.

After the wind stopped, his friend found a lot of sand dropped in his bowl, even with some leaves on it. The friend frowned, poured away the water in the bowl without hesitation, picked up Ayer's water bag conveniently, poured himself another bowl and drank off without a break.

When he put down his bowl, he found Ayer's bowl was also muddy, but Ayer only carefully picked up the fallen leaves, threw them off and put the bowl on the ground.

After a while, the water was gradually clean and clear, when Ayer carried the bowl and drank slowly.

His friend laughed at his misery, for he even regarded a bowl of water as a treasure.

After hearing that, Ayer said with a smile, "Each bowl of water is drawn by me from the well, which I took pains to dig. How can't I regard it as a treasure?"

When sand and leaves dropped into a bowl, what Ayer's saw was still the water, but what his friend was nothing but the sand and leaves. Maybe it was the secret of Ayer's wealth.

致富的秘诀

阿伊尔生活富裕，朋友们很想知道他致富的奥秘。有一天，阿伊尔要到集市上办事，他的一位朋友正好同路。于是，俩人结伴而行。

天气十分闷热。行至一半，俩人又累又渴，就停下脚步，在路边的一棵大树下坐了下来。

阿伊尔从随身携带的背囊里取出两只碗，摆放在两人面前，然后解下水囊，向碗里倒满了水。

他们端起碗，刚要一饮而尽，突然刮来了一阵风，吹得人睁不开眼。

风停后，朋友发现碗里落了不少沙子，水面上还多了几片树叶。朋友皱了皱眉，没多想，就把碗里的水倒了，顺手拿起阿伊尔的水囊，给自己重新倒了一碗，一口气就喝干了。

等他放下手中的碗时，发现阿伊尔的碗里也是一片浑浊，但阿伊尔只是小心地拈起碗里的落叶扔掉，再把碗放到地上。

过了一会儿，水渐渐澄清了，阿伊尔这才端起碗，慢慢地喝了起来。

朋友笑阿伊尔吝啬，连一碗水都当成宝贝似的。

阿伊尔听完，微微一笑说："每碗水都是我从井里打上来的，而井又是我辛辛苦苦亲手挖的。我怎么能不把它当成宝贝呢？"

一碗水落进了沙子和树叶，在阿伊尔的眼中，看到的还是水，而在朋友的眼里，看到的却只是沙子和树叶，这或许就是阿伊尔致富的奥秘。

Life Lies in Believing in Yourself

There may be days when you get up in the morning and things aren't the way you had hoped they would be.

That's when you have to tell yourself that things will get better. There are times when people let you down.

But those are the times when you must remind yourself to trust your own judgments and opinions, to keep your life focused on believing in yourself.

There will be challenges to face and changes to make in your life, and it is up to you to accept them.

Constantly keep yourself headed in the right direction for you. It may not be easy at times, but in those times of struggle you will find a stronger sense of who you are.

So when the days come that are filled with frustration and unexpected responsibilities, remember to believe in yourself and all you want your life to be.

Because the challenges and changes will only help you to find the goals that you know are meant to come true for you.

人生在于相信自己

你或许会有这样的日子:早晨起来,却发现事情并不像自己原来希望的那样。

这个时候,你必须告诉自己:情况一定会好起来。总会有人们让你失望和沮丧的时候。

但这个时候,你必须提醒自己,要相信自己的判断和看法,提醒自己一生都要始终相信自己。

生活中总会要面对挑战,总会要发生改变。你要接受挑战和改变。

始终让自己朝适合自己的正确方向前进。也许时有不易,但一次次奋斗,你都会更强烈地意识到自己是谁。

因此,当充满沮丧和意外责任的日子来临时,要记住相信自己,要记住你想要的人生是什么样。

因为挑战和改变唯一能帮你找到你明白对你来说一定会实现的目标。

Life Lies in Choosing

When he was still young, everything was possible, for the world was just before him.

One morning, God came to him, "What wish do you have? Tell me and I can make it come true for you, for you're my pet. But remember, you can only tell one."

"However," he said unwillingly. "I have a lot of wishes."

God slowly shook his head, "There're too many beautiful things in the world, but life is limited, so no one can possess all. Once you make a choice, you will give up others. Come on, choose carefully, with no regrets."

Surprised, he asked, "Will I regret?"

God said, "Who knows. Choose love and you will have to put up with the emotional torment; to choose wisdom means pains and loneliness; choose money and you will have the trouble it brings along. There're too many people who regret that they should virtually take another way after they've gone one way. Think about it carefully, what do you really want in your lifetime?"

He thought and thought, all desires pouring in and fluttering around him. Which one was the one he couldn't give up? Finally, he said to God, "Let me think, let me think."

God said, "But you should be quick, my son."

Since then, his life was filled with the constant comparisons and balances. He used half the time of his life to make lists and the other half to tear them up because he always found himself to leave out something.

Day after day, year after year, he was no longer young. God came to him again. "My child, haven't you decided your wish yet? But you only have five minutes left."

"What?" he exclaimed. "Over the years, I haven't enjoyed the joy of love, I haven't accumulated wealth and haven't received wisdom; I haven't gotten all I want. My God, how can you take away my life at this time?"

Five minutes later, no matter how painfully he pleaded, God couldn't help but take him away.

Life is like this: everywhere is alive with choices. Since it is impossible to have everything, you should learn to make a choice; if you're greedy for everything, perhaps you can only achieve nothing in the end.

人生在于选择

那时他还年轻,凡事都有可能,世界就在他面前。

一个清晨,上帝来到了他身边。“你有什么心愿吗? 说出来,我都可以为你实现,你是我的宠儿。但你记住,你只能说一个。”

“可是,”他不甘心地说。“我有许多的心愿啊。”

上帝缓缓地摇了摇头。“这世间的美好实在太多,但生命有限,没有人可以拥有全部,有选择,就有放弃。来吧,慎重选择,永不后悔。”

他惊讶地问:“我会后悔吗?”

上帝说:“谁知道呢。选择爱情就要忍受情感的煎熬;选择智慧就意味着痛苦和寂寞;选择钱财就有钱财带来的麻烦。这世上有太多的人走了一条路后,懊悔自己其实该走另一条路。仔细想一想,你这一生真正要什么?”

他想了又想,所有的渴望都纷至沓来,在他周围飞舞。哪一件是他不能舍弃的呢? 最后,他对上帝说:“让我想想,让我再想想。”

上帝说:“但要快一点啊,我的孩子。”

从此,他的生活就是不断比较和权衡。他用生命中一半的时间来列表,用另一半的时间来撕毁这张表,因为他总发现自己有所遗漏。

一天又一天,一年又一年,他不再年轻了。上帝又来到了他面前。“我的孩子,你还没有决定自己的心愿吗? 可你的生命只剩下 5 分钟了。”

“什么?”他惊叫道。“这么多年来,我没有享受过爱情的快乐,没有积累过财富,没有得到过智慧,我想要的一切都没有得到。上帝啊,你怎能在这个时候带走我的生命呢?”

5 分钟后,无论他怎么痛苦求情,上帝还是无奈地带走了他。

人生就是这样,无处不是在选择。既然无法拥有一切,那就学会有所取舍;如要贪全,恐怕最后只能是一无所得。

The Teacher Changed His Life

Steve, a twelve-year-old boy with alcoholic parents, was about to be lost forever, by the U. S. education system. Remarkably, in spite of his reading skills, Steve was failing. He had been failing since first grade. Steve looked more like a teenager than a twelve year old, but he went unnoticed... until Miss White.

Miss White was a smiling, young, beautiful redhead, and Steve was in love! For the first time in his young life, he couldn't take his eyes off his teacher; yet he still failed. He never did his homework, and he was always in trouble with Miss White. His heart would break under her sharp words, and when he was punished for failing to turn in his homework, he felt just miserable! Still, he did not study.

In the middle of the first semester, the entire seventh grade was tested for basic skills. Steve hurried through his tests, and continued to dream of other things, as the day wore on. His heart was not in school, but in the woods, where he often escaped alone, trying to shut out the sights, sounds and smells of his alcoholic home. No one checked on him to see if he was safe. No one knew he was gone because no one was sober enough to care.

One day, Miss White's impatient voice broke into his daydreams.

"Steve!" Startled, he turned to look at her.

"Pay attention!"

Steve locked his gaze on Miss White with adolescent adoration as she began to go over the test results for the seventh grade.

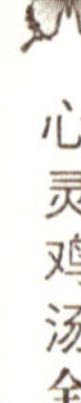

"You all did pretty well," she told the class, "except for one boy, and it breaks my heart to tell you this, but... " She hesitated, pinning Steve to his seat with a sharp stare, her eyes searching his face.

"... The smartest boy in the seventh grade is failing my class!"

She just stared at Steve, as the class spun around for a good look. Steve dropped his eyes and carefully examined his fingertips.

After that, it was war! Steve still wouldn't do his homework. Even as the punishments became more severe, he remained stubborn.

"Just try it! ONE WEEK!" He was unmoved.

"You're smart enough! You'll see a change!" Nothing fazed him.

"Give yourself a chance! Don't give up on your life!" Nothing.

"Steve! Please! I care about you!"

Wow! Suddenly, Steve got it! Someone cared about him? Someone, totally unattainable and perfect, CARED ABOUT HIM!

Steve went home from school, thoughtful, that afternoon. Walking into the house, he took one look around. Both parents were passed out, and the stench was overpowering! He quickly gathered up his camping gear, a jar of peanut butter, a loaf of bread, a bottle of water, and this time... his schoolbooks. Grim and determined, he headed for the woods.

The following Monday he arrived at school on time and waited for Miss White to enter the classroom. She walked in, all sparkle and smiles! God, she was beautiful! He yearned for her smile to turn on him. It did not.

Miss White immediately gave a quiz on the weekend homework. Steve hurried through the test, and was the first to hand in his paper. With a look of surprise, Miss White took his paper. Obviously puzzled, she began to look it over. Steve walked back to his desk, his heart pounding within his chest. As he sat down, he couldn't resist another look at the lovely woman.

Miss White's face was in total shock! She glanced up at Steve, then down, then up.

Suddenly, her face broke into a radiant smile. The smartest boy in the seventh grade had just passed his first test!

From that moment nothing was the same for Steve. Life at home remained the same, but life still changed. He discovered that not only could he learn, but also he was good at it!

He discovered that he could understand and retain knowledge, and that he could translate the things he learned into his own life. Steve began to excel! And he continued this course throughout his school life.

After high school, Steve enlisted in the Navy and had a successful military career. During that time, he met the love of his life, he raised a family, and he graduated from college magna cum laude. During his navy career, he inspired many young people, who without him, might not have believed in themselves. Steve began a second career after the Navy, and he continued to inspire others, as an adjunct professor in a nearby college Miss White left a great legacy. She saved one boy who has changed many lives.

You see, it's simple, really. A change took place within the heart of one boy all because of one teacher who cared.

老师改变了他的一生

史蒂夫是一个12岁的美国男孩，他的父母都是酒鬼，他快要辍学了。值得注意的是，尽管他有阅读技巧，但他总是考试不及格。从一年级开始，他就一直不及格。史蒂夫看上去比12岁的孩子要大，但他常被人忽略……直至怀特小姐到来。

怀特小姐年轻漂亮，满面笑容，一头红发。史蒂夫一下就喜欢上了她！他长这么大还是第一次无法将目光从她身上移开，但他还是考试不及格。他从来不做家庭作业，而且总是给怀特小姐找麻烦。他常因她尖刻的话语而伤心，而且每当因为没有交作业而被处罚时，他感觉好痛苦！然而，他还是学不进去。

第一学期期中，整个七年级检测的都是基本技能。史蒂夫匆匆应付完那些考试，就继续想着其他的东西。他的心不在学校，而是在树林里，他常常独自逃到那里，尽力把在充满酒精气味家看到、听到和闻到的东西排除在外。没有人去查看他是否安全，没有人知道他离开了学校，因为没有人清醒到去在意。

有一天，怀特小姐不耐烦的声音闯进了他的白日梦。

"史蒂夫！"他吃了一惊，回头看着她。

"注意！"

当怀特小姐开始仔细检查七年级测试结果时，史蒂夫将充满青春期崇拜的目光盯在她身上。

"你们都做得很好，"她开始对全满同学讲道，"除了一个男生，而告诉你们这个让我伤心，但……"她迟疑了一会儿，犀利的目光将史蒂夫定在了他的座位上，眼睛搜寻着他的脸。

"……七年级中最聪明的男孩在我的班里不及格！"

她只是盯着史蒂夫，这时全班学生马上转过来仔细看着。史蒂夫垂下目光，仔细查看着自己的手指尖。

之后，是对立的状态！史蒂夫仍不愿做作业。甚至处罚越来越严重时，他仍然顽固不化。

"请尝试一下！就一周！"

他不为所动。

"你够聪明的！你会看到变化的！"

什么都影响不了他。

"给你自己一个机会！不要放弃自己的人生！"

仍然没有任何改变。

"史蒂夫！请！我担心你！"

哇！突然，史蒂夫心里一动！有人担心他？有人担心他，简直无法想象，不敢奢望！

那天下午，史蒂夫放学回家，若有所思。走进家门，他扫了一下四周。他的父母亲都

喝醉了，酒气冲天！他很快收拾了自己的露营用品、一罐花生酱、一条面包、一瓶水，这次还有他的教科书。他脸色冷峻，毅然决然朝树林奔去。

下周一，他按时到校，等待怀特小姐走进教室。她进来时，神采奕奕，面带微笑！天哪，她太美了！他渴望她的微笑能转向他。但没有。

怀特小姐马上对周末作业进行测验。史蒂夫匆匆完成了测试，第一个交卷。怀特小姐面带惊奇，接过他的试卷。她显然迷惑不解，开始查看试卷。史蒂夫回到了自己的课桌，心咚咚直跳。他坐下来时，禁不住又看了一眼这个可爱的女人。

怀特小姐的脸完全震惊了！她抬头瞥了一眼史蒂夫，然后垂下目光，接着又抬头看了一眼。

突然，她露出了灿烂的笑容。七年级中最聪明的男孩刚才已经通过了第一次测验！

从那个时刻起，史蒂夫的一切都大不一样了。尽管家里的生活仍然一样，但生活还是发生了改变。他发现自己不但会学习，而且善于学习！

他发现自己能理解知识、保存知识，而且可以将他学到的东西应用到生活中去。史蒂夫开始脱颖而出！他要继续自己的学习生涯。

中学毕业后，史蒂夫报名参加了海军，并度过了一段成功的军旅生涯。在那段时间，他遇到了他的爱人，组建了家庭，并以优异成绩从大学毕业后。他在海军生涯中鼓舞了很多年轻人，如果没有他，那些人可能不会相信自己。从海军复原后，史蒂夫开始了他的第二职业，同时继续激励他人，担任附近一所大学的副教授，怀特小姐给这所大学留下了一大笔财产。她挽救了一个男孩，他已经改变了许多人的生命。

你明白，其实这很简单。一个男孩内心之所以发生改变，全是因为一位关心他的老师啊。

心态改变命运

The Boy Who Cupped the Sunshine in His Hands

One morning in Philadelphia, the sun slanted through all the dense jungles and the lofty churches. John, 6, wearing the shabby clothes, walked from afar, his dark small hands holding a piece of stolen bread.

John stopped for a moment at the entrance to the solemn church and then left tightly holding the bread.

He was an orphan, whose parents were killed in World War II leaving him alone in the orphanage for five years. Like many children in the orphanage, he had a lot of free time. Mostly no one took care of them, so they had to learn how to steal those they wanted.

John believed that the existence of God, so every Sunday morning in any case he would go to the church to have a look and listen to those people singing inside or reciting the Bible. He felt only at this moment he was the child of God and so close to God. But he couldn't enter because his clothes was so dirty. John himself knew it.

John was quietly counting. This was his 45th Sunday at the entrance to the church. He stood on tiptoe for a while and walked away.

As time passed, the pastor noticed John and learned from the others that he was the small boy who liked stealing things in the orphanages.

On the 46th Sunday, the sun was shining and John came, still holding a piece of bread with his dark small hands. When he just stood there, the pastor came out. He felt like running away, but he was carried along by the pastor's amiable smile.

The pastor walked up to John and clearly saw his small hands trembling.

"Are you John?"

John didn't answer, but looked at the pastor and nodded.

"Do you believe in God?" the pastor petted John on his head stained with dust.

"Yes, I do!" This time John told him loudly.

"So you believe in yourself?"

John looked at the pastor, without a word.

The pastor went on saying, "At the first sight of you, I find you're different from other kids because you have a good heart."

Blushed, John said timidly, "In fact, I'm a thief." With that, he lowered his head.

The pastor didn't speak, but held John's dark small hands, slowly opened them and put them against his wrinkled face.

"Ah!" Just at the same time, John exclaimed and was about to take out his dark small hands. Yet the pastor tightly held his small hands and spread them out in the sun.

"Do you see, John?"

"What?"

"You're cupping the sunshine in your hands."

John looked at his hands blankly: when did they become so beautiful?

"In God's eyes, all children are the same. When they take the initiative to spread out their hands to greet the sun, the sun will naturally shine on them. And you have two things more than they do. The first is fortitude and the second is kindness." With that, the pastor led him into the church.

It was the first time that John went into this sacred place, and at this moment he didn't feel inferior and cowardly, but the unquenchable warmth.

On that morning embracing the sunshine, John found himself again, along with the confidence, satisfaction, happiness, dreams he had never had...

20 years have passed. Now the boy who ever tightly held the bread with his dirty hands has been the most famous chef in Philadelphia and made many popular dishes.

Every Sunday morning, he would personally send the bread he baked to the orphanage. Those children who greeted him with cheers were used to consciously spreading their palms before they got the bread.

Because they all knew when we take the initiative to spread out our hands to greet the sunshine, the sun will naturally shine on us.

手捧阳光的男孩

费城的一天清晨，阳光斜射过整个的密林和高大的教堂。6岁的约翰身穿破旧的衣服从远处走来，黑乎乎的小手里还捏着一块刚偷来的面包。

约翰在庄严的教堂门口站了一会儿，紧捏着面包又走了。

他是个孤儿，父母在二战中身亡，留下他在孤儿院里寂寞地生活了5年。他和很多孤儿院里的孩子一样，有很多的空闲时间。而更多的空闲时间，他们都无人照料，只好学着如何去偷那些他们想要的东西。

约翰相信上帝的存在，所以每个星期日的早上无论如何他都会到教堂门口去看一看，听一会儿那些人在里面唱歌或朗诵《圣经》。他觉得，只有在这个时刻他才是上帝的孩子，他原来离上帝是那么的近。可是，他不能进去，因为他的衣服很脏，这点约翰自己也知道。

约翰默默地数着，这是他第45个星期日站在这个教堂门口了。他踮着脚看了看，又站了一会儿，走开了。久而久之，牧师注意到了约翰，也从旁人的口中得知他就是那个喜欢在孤儿院里偷东西的小男孩。

第46个星期日，阳光明媚，约翰依旧用他那双黑乎乎的小手捏着一块面包来了。他刚站在那里，牧师便走了出来。他当时想跑，但却被牧师和蔼的笑容吸引住了。

牧师走到他身边，清楚地看到约翰的小手在发抖。

“你是叫约翰吗？”

约翰没有回答，只是看着牧师点了点头。

“你相信上帝吗？”牧师抚摸着约翰沾满灰尘的脑袋。

“相信，我相信！”这次约翰大声地告诉了他。

“那你相信自己吗？”

约翰看着牧师，没有说话。

牧师接着说：“从看到你第一眼时，我就觉得你和其他孩子不一样，因为你有一颗善良的心。”

约翰脸红了，怯生生地说：“其实，我是个小偷。”说完便低下了头。

牧师没有说话，而是握住了约翰黑乎乎的小手，缓慢地打开，放在了自己布满皱纹的脸上。

“啊！”就在同时，约翰惊呼着要抽开污黑的小手。可是，牧师却把他的小手紧紧地抓住，在阳光下摊开。

“看到了吗，约翰？”

“什么？”

“你的手里捧着阳光。”

约翰呆呆地看着自己的双手,它们何时变得如此美丽?

“在上帝的眼中,所有的孩子都一样。当他们主动摊开双手迎接阳光时,阳光自然就会照到他们。而你比他们多了两样东西,一是坚强,二是善良。”说完,牧师便将他领进了教堂。

这是约翰生平第一次走进这种神圣的地方,而此时他的内心已不是自卑和怯懦,而是无法泯灭的温暖。在那个怀抱阳光的早上,约翰找回了自己,还有从来不曾有过的自信、满足、幸福、梦想……

转眼20年过去了,这个曾用脏手紧握面包的男孩如今已经成了费城最有名的厨师,做出了许多受人喜爱的菜肴。每个星期日的上午,他都会亲自去孤儿院送上自己烤出的面包。而那些欢呼而来的孩子们都习惯在拿到面包之前自觉地摊开手掌。因为他们都知道,当我们主动摊开双手迎接阳光时,阳光自然就会照到我们。

Where the Sun Always Rises

“Get up! Get up!” my mother whispers. My eyes flash open in the predawn gray. Sleepily, I look around the screened-in porch of our family's log cabin, where we spend our summer weeks.

I take in the dock-green porch swing, the birch-leg table, the twin bed where my sister sleeps, the smoky gloss of the kerosene lantern. My face feels the coolness of the early-morning air.

I relax and curl deeper beneath the blankets' warmth. “Get up!” my mother whispers again. “The sunrise is glorious!” Careful not to let the screen door slam, she sets off down to the lake.

Get up to see the sunrise? The last thing this 14-year-old wants to do is leave a warm bed to see the sun rise. It's freezing out there.

My 17-year-old sister pushes back her covers and sits up. I make a supreme effort and struggle out too. We grab my father's World War II army blankets and wrap them tightly around our cotton nighties. Our pace is quick. One of us misses catching the screen door. It slams.

Carefully, we pick our way over slippery rocks and prickly pine needles, down 49 dew-covered log steps to the shore. We catch our breath and look up. Across the lake, a sliver of brilliant red crests the top of the shadowed forest. It outlines our mother on the lakeshore, the first light catching the soft red of her hair.

Hues of purplish, rose and amber begin to pulsate in the sky. High above, in the soft blue, a lone star still sparkles. Silver mist rises gently from the lake. All is still.

Suddenly, the curve of a brilliant sun bursts through the dark forest. The world begins to awaken. A blue heron rises from a distant shore and gently fans its way over the water. Two ducks make a rippled landing near our dock, while a loon skims along the edge of a nearby island, hunting its morning food.

Breathing the chill air, the three of us draw our blankets closer. At last, the soft hues of dawn turn bright with the new day. The star fades. My sister and I took one more look and race back to bed.

My mother is reluctant to leave the sunrise amphitheater. It is a while before I hear her reach the top step and gently close the porch door.

太阳总在那里升起

“起床喽！起床喽！”母亲低声喊道。我一下子睁开眼睛，闪现在眼前的是黎明前的灰暗。我睡眼惺忪地环顾着我们家小木屋的那个安着屏风的门廊。这里就是我们度过数周夏日时光的地方。我欣赏着草绿色的门廊秋千、白桦木腿桌、姐姐睡的成对单人床，还有那烟熏的煤油灯罩。我感到脸上掠过凉爽的晨风。

我伸了伸腰，又往温暖的毛毯里拱了拱身子。“起来吧！”母亲又小声喊道。“日出多么壮观！”母亲小心翼翼，不让屏门发出任何响声，然后向湖边走去。

起床就为了看日出？对一个 14 岁的孩子来说，最不想做的就是离开暖被窝去看日出。外面冻死人了。

17 岁的姐姐掀被坐起，我也一鼓劲钻了出来。我们俩一把拽起父亲二战时用过的军用毛毯，紧紧地裹在棉睡衣外面，匆匆跑了出去。我们俩都忘了带上门。门砰地关了上去。

我们小心翼翼地走过滑溜溜的岩石，绕过那些山地松针，沿着露水打湿的 49 级木台阶向湖岸走去。我们喘了口气，抬头望去。只见在湖对岸，一抹耀眼的红色爬上了树影婆娑的林梢，映衬出了母亲在湖岸的身影；第一缕阳光照在了她柔红色的头发上。

淡紫色的、玫瑰色的和琥珀色的光波开始在天空中微微颤动起来。苍穹之上，柔蓝之中，一颗孤星仍在闪烁。银雾从湖面上冉冉升起。四周万籁俱寂。

突然，一道灿烂的阳光射过黑黝黝的森林。整个世界开始苏醒。一只蓝苍鹭从远处的湖岸振翅飞起，在湖面上轻轻抖动着向前飞去。在我们的码头附近，两只鸭子荡起涟漪上了岸。一只潜鸟掠过附近一个小岛的边缘，在猎食早餐。

我们仨呼吸着习习凉气，将毛毯裹得更紧了。终于，黎明时那种朦胧的色调随着新的一天的到来变得明亮。那颗孤星退隐而去。我和姐姐又看了一眼，便又飞快地钻进了被窝。

母亲舍不得离开那蔚为壮观的日出美景。过了好一会儿，我才听到她迈上门前最高一级台阶，轻轻合上了门廊的门。

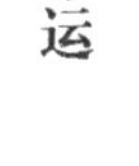

Keep Walking in Sunshine

I hadn't walked across our old farm in fifteen years. Yet the sensations came flooding back. I could smell the freshness of new mown alfalfa. I could feel the sun's sudden warmth on my wet shoulders when it reappeared after a brisk July thunderstorm.

Rain or shine, I used to walk this path each day to see Greta. She always made me smile, even after Sis and I had just had a big squabble. I would help Greta with her chores. Then we would visit over a generous helping of her delicious homemade chocolate cookies and ice cream. Being confined to

a wheel chair didn't stop Greta from being a fabulous cook.

Greta gave me two of the greatest gifts I've ever received. First, she taught me how to read. She also taught me that when I forgave Sis for our squabbles, it meant I wouldn't keep feeling like a victim. Instead, I would feel sunny.

Mr. Dinking, the local banker, tried to foreclose on Greta's house and land after her husband passed away. Thanks to Pa and Uncle John, Greta got to keep everything. Pa said that it was the least he could do for someone talented enough to teach me to read!

Soon folks were coming from miles around to buy Greta's homemade cakes, pies, bread, cookies, cider, and ice cream. Hank, the grocery store man, came each week to bring Greta supplies and stock his shelves.

Greta even had me take a big apple pie to Mr. Dinking who became one of her best customers and friends. That's just how Greta was. She could turn anyone into a friend!

Greta always said, "Dear, keep walking in sunshine!"

No matter how terrible my day started, I always felt sunny walking home from Greta's house—even beneath the winter starlight.

I arrived at Greta's house today just after sunset. An ambulance had stopped a few feet from her door. When I ran into the old house, Greta recognized me right away.

She smiled at me with her unforgettable twinkling blue eyes. She was almost out of breath when she reached out and softly touched my arm. Her last words to me were, "Dear, keep walking in sunshine!"

I'm sure that Greta is walking in the brightest sunshine she's ever seen. And, I'm sure that she heard every word I read at her memorial service.

I chose a beautiful verse by Leo Buscaglia. It's one that Greta taught me to read many years ago.

"Love can never grow old.
Locks may lose their brown and gold.
Cheeks may fade and hollow grow.
But the hearts that love will know,
Never winter's frost and chill,
Summer's warmth is in them still."

常常走在阳光里

我已经15年没有走过我们的老农场了。然而,那些感情又潮水般涌来。我可以闻到新割的紫花苜蓿的清新气息,可以感觉到7月的一场清新的暴风雨过后阳光突然暖暖地照在湿湿的肩膀上。

无论雨天还是晴天,我每天沿着这条小路去看格丽塔。即使我刚和姐姐大吵了一架,她也总让我露出微笑。我常常帮格丽塔做家务。然后,我们常常放开肚子,吃她亲手做的巧克力饼干和冰淇淋。坐轮椅并不能阻止她成为一名出色的厨师。

格丽塔送给我两件有生以来最了不起的礼物。首先,她教会了我念书。她还教会我,我们争吵时要原谅姐姐,这意味着我不再感到委屈,而会感到快乐。

格丽塔的丈夫去世后,当地银行家丁金先生曾想取消她抵押给银行的房产的赎回权。幸亏爸爸和约翰叔叔帮忙,格丽塔才保住了所有的一切。爸爸说,他对一位能教会我念书的人只能这样尽他所能帮忙了!

很快,方圆几英里的人们都来买格丽塔做的蛋糕、馅饼、面包、饼干、苹果酒和冰淇淋。食品杂货店老板汉克每周都会给格丽塔送来供应品并从她这里进货。

格丽塔甚至让我给丁金先生送去一个大苹果馅饼。他也成了她最好的顾客和朋友。格丽塔就是这样做的。她可以把任何人都变成朋友！

格丽塔总是说："亲爱的，要经常走在阳光里！"

无论每天开始时多么糟糕，从格丽塔的小屋走回家时，即使是披着冬夜的星光，我总会感觉心情愉快。

今天太阳刚下山，我就来到了格丽塔家。一辆救护车已经停在她门前几英尺的地方。我跑进老房子时，格丽塔立刻认出了我。

她那双令人难忘的蓝眼睛闪动着向我微笑。当她伸手轻抚我的手臂时，她几乎上气不接下气。她最后对我说的话是："亲爱的，要常常走在阳光里！"

我相信格丽塔正走在她所见过的最明媚的阳光里。而且，我也相信她听到了我在她的追悼仪式上念的每一个字。

我选的是利奥·巴斯卡格里亚的一首优美的诗。这正是格丽塔多年前教我念的一首诗。

"爱从来不会衰败。
秀发会失去原有的光彩。
脸颊会日渐黯淡消瘦。
但有爱的心中，
从来没有冰霜寒冬，
夏天的温热永远依旧。"

Sunshine on a Rainy Day

Have you ever had a day when everything seemed to go wrong? Not too long ago I was having one of those days. I was discouraged, weary and sad. My focus was on me, me, me. After all, no one else was experiencing the same trials as I was.

I expressed my downcast state to my mother, hoping for some pity. Instead, she said, "I heard Jamie was having a difficult day, too. Why don't you make her some cookies and we will take them to her this afternoon?" I didn't really want to, but I decided that I didn't want to go back to my other problems just yet. I made the cookies and arranged them on a little plate. Then I made a card with a sunflower on it and wrote a small note of comfort.

That afternoon we dropped by my friend's house. I went to the door and rang the bell. Soon, Jamie came to the door and looked at me in surprise for my unexpected visit. Before she could say anything, I rushed, "I heard you were having a hard day and decided to bring you something. I hope your day goes better." The look that came over Jamie's face was one that I could never put into words. It was as if a darkened sky was suddenly lit with the golden rays of the sun; it was as if in that small act her day was brightened.

I got back into the car and for some amazing reason, I felt a lot better myself. That day I experienced the truth that James Barrie attempted to describe. "Those who bring sunshine to the lives of others cannot keep it from themselves."

雨天的阳光

你曾有过事事不顺的一天吗？不久以前，我就过了这样一天。我感到沮丧、厌倦和伤心，一门心思想的都是自己。毕竟，没有人经历过和我这样的磨难。

我把自己沮丧的心情告诉了母亲，希望得到一些同情。可是，她说："我听说杰米也过了艰难的一天。你何不给她做一些饼干，今天下午送给她呢？"我真不想做，但我决定不再去想其他问题，所以就去做饼干了，把做好的饼干摆在一只小盘子上，然后还做了一张画着太阳花的卡片，在上面写了一句安慰话。

那天下午，我们去我的朋友家拜访。我去按门铃。很快，杰米来到门口，吃惊地望着我，没想到我会来看她。还没等她开口说话，我就马上说道："我听说你今天很难过，就决定送你一些东西。我希望你这一天好起来。"当时，杰米的表情让我难以言表，就像是阴暗的天空突然被一道道金色的阳光照亮一样，也像是我那个小小的举动照亮了她的一天。

我回到车里，惊奇地发现自己的心情也好多了。那天，我体会到了詹姆斯·巴利试图描述的一条真理："给别人的生活带去阳光的人，也会给自己带来阳光。"

The Sunshine Within

A man traveled to the Sahara desert with his two boys.

Having seen the immense desert, one of the boys said with disdain, "What a barren land with such a large desert and so much sand!" while the other said excitedly, "What a huge treasure with such a large desert and so much sand!"

The traveler asked the first boy, "Why don't you like this large desert?"

The boy replied, "Except these useless sand, it has no tree, no grass, no water, so who will like it?"

The other rectified at once, "It has no tree, no grass, no water, but it has gold. Haven't you heard the 'gold hidden in the sand'? How much gold hidden in such a huge desert!"

What soul you have, what world you will have; what soul you have, what kind of life you will have. If your heart is clouded, your fate will be dark and gloomy; if you have the sunshine within, your life will be bright and happy.

胸藏阳光

一个人带着他的两个男孩到撒哈拉沙漠去旅行。

见到无边无垠的大沙漠后，一个男孩不屑地说："这么大的沙漠，这么多的沙子，真是一个不毛之地啊！"而另一个男孩则兴奋地说："这么大的沙漠，这么多的沙子，真是一

笔巨大的财富啊!”

旅人问他的男孩:“你为什么不喜欢这片大沙漠呢?”

男孩说:“除了这些没用的沙子,没有树,没有草,没有水,谁喜欢这沙漠啊?”

另一个男孩立刻纠正说:“虽说沙漠里没有树,没有草,也没有水,但它有金子。难道你没听说过‘沙里藏金’吗?这么大的沙漠,该藏着多少金子啊!”

有怎样的心灵,就有怎样的世界;有怎样的心灵,就有怎样的人生。心有阴霾,命运将会黯淡无光;胸藏阳光,生活将会明媚而幸福。

The Sunshine in the Dew

I remember the early morning streamed with dew everywhere. The girl cupped a blade of leaf and gently sucked the dew on it. In the misty morning, I seemed to see a fairy that didn't belong to this world, so I dare not make any sound, afraid the worldly noise would disturb her.

I deeply gazed at her and the amiable dewdrops close to her.

She moved a little, only combing her hair with her hand. I thought she should fly away. Behold! How light her feather was!

Seeing me, she smiled at me.

"Are you a fairy?" I asked, rubbing my eyes.

She smiled broadly, luring the sun here right off. The sun stretched itself and vied with her for the dew.

"If only I were really a fairy. Then when I leave, Mom won't be so sad. "Her voice was light and gentle, as if talking to herself.

"Leave? Where are you going?"

"To heaven. Mom and Dad don't tell me what illness I've got, but I know it is an incurable disease. They say as long as I keep drinking the dew every morning, I will recover. For one year, I've always been coming here before the sun. If it is too late, the dew will be drunk up by the sun. "With that she resumed her high spirits once more.

I dare not imagine this pure-hearted beautiful girl was mortally ill. What a beautiful cloud in the world she was! She reminded me of the birth of a baby, so pure, so serene. At this moment, her pure soul was going like the wind against the grass. In any case it was impossible for anyone to believe that Death was chasing her.

It was the last day of my seven-day holiday that my life became unusually lively. I had come to evade the troubles, wishing to beat a rumor with the seven-day holiday. Now, I felt all the troubles had been washed off by the dew, savoring the freshness and cheerfulness of life. The girl said, "I have outlived six months more than the doctors had predicted. I have created a myth, so why am I unhappy?"

The girl eventually passed away, so poetically going to heaven to date God. If we explain the death with the girl's optimism, I think she would say, "If I'm late, the steps to heaven will be covered with lichenes."

On that morning she passed away, I finally sucked the dewdrops. At this moment the most limpid water filled those simple pottery within me.

I went to her grave, sprinkling the dew I gathered drop by drop onto it. I wanted the drops of water close to the girl to escort her pure soul to arrived in the garden of God safe and sound.

At that moment, I seemed to see the girl's angelic presence and smiling face that would never fade, but I was laden with sorrow. Now, I knew, to awaken my years withered and gradually wizened

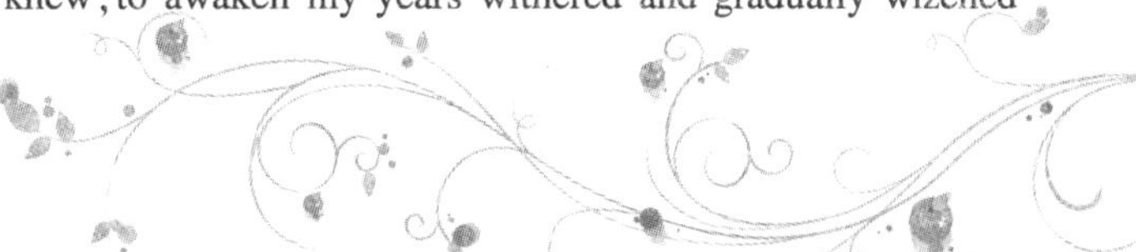

only needed her lips to gently call my name before the sun faded.

Unexpectedly, she responded to me! Against the sunny sky, a cloud sailed along, bringing a drizzle. I knew those raindrops must be the words she would soothe, light and gentle, but full of vitality.

Well, why should I evade troubles one after another on earth? Moreover, the dialogue between us has never been disconnected—

I ask her, "Why is the morning sun always so fresh?"

She says, "Because the sun is washing its face with the dew every morning."

露水里的阳光

我想起了那个到处都沾满露水的清晨。少女捧着一片叶子,轻轻吮吸叶片上的露水。在雾蒙蒙的清晨,我仿佛看见了一位不食人间烟火的精灵,我不敢发出声响,怕尘俗的喧嚣惊扰了她。

我深深地注视她和她身边一滴滴亲切的露水。

她动了动,只是用手拢了一下头发。我还认为她要飞走,看,她的羽毛有多轻啊!

她看到我了,冲我微笑。

"莫非你是个精灵?"我揉了揉眼睛问道。

她灿烂地笑起来,把阳光一下子引到了这里。太阳伸着懒腰,和她争抢着露水。

"我真是个精灵就好了。那样,等我走时,妈妈就不会那么伤心了。"她的声音又轻又细,仿佛自言自语。

"走?你要去哪里?"

"去天堂啊,爸爸妈妈不告诉我得了什么病,但我知道自己得的是绝症。他们说只要我每天早晨坚持喝露水,病就会好的,一年了,我总是赶在阳光出来之前来到这里,来晚了,露水就会被太阳喝光的。"她又恢复了快乐的情绪。

我不敢想象,眼前这个美丽得一尘不染的少女竟然身患绝症。她是人世间多么美丽的一朵云啊!她让我想起了婴儿的诞生,那么纯净,那么安详。此刻,她纯净的灵魂正贴着草叶飞驰,无论如何也无法让人相信,死亡正在身后追赶着她。

这是我7天假日的最后一天,我的生命因为这一天而变得异常鲜活起来。我是来躲避烦恼的,想用7天假日去击败一个流言。现在,我感觉到所有的烦恼都被露水洗掉了,同时感受到生命的清新和愉悦。少女说:"我已经比医生预测的死亡时间多活了6个月,我已经创造了神话,我为什么不开心呢?"

少女最终还是去了,很诗意地到天堂去赴上帝的约会了。如果用少女的乐观思想解释死亡的话,我想她一定会说:"去晚了,通往天堂的台阶会生满青苔。"

她走的那个早晨,我吸了最后一口露滴,这最清澈的水,在这个时候,注满了我身体内部那些简朴的陶罐。

我来到她的墓前,把自己采集来的露水一滴一滴地洒了下去。我想让少女身边的这一滴滴水,护送她那颗纯净的灵魂,安然抵达上帝的花园。

那一刻,我仿佛看到了少女天使般的身影和永不褪色的笑脸,而我却忧伤了。现在我知道，要唤醒我那凋谢的、逐渐枯萎的年华，只需她的嘴唇，在阳光隐遁之前，轻轻地唤出我的名字。

她竟回应了我！晴朗的天空下，一朵云悠悠飘过，带来一场又轻又细的雨，我知道，那些雨滴一定是她安慰我的话语，又轻又细，但饱含生命的力量。

那么，我还有什么理由躲闪尘世中一个个接踵而至的烦恼呢？况且，我们之间的对话从来就没有间断过——

我问她："为什么每天早晨的太阳总是如此新鲜？"

她说："因为太阳每个早晨都在用露水洗脸。"

The Sunshine over Their Heads

When a farmwife grew the soybean, because of drought and field mice, she buried the seeds so deep. After a few days, the farmwife took her six-year-old son to look about. When she turned over the earth, they found many of the seeds had sprouted long stems, on whose top were two-segment yellow tender buds. The delicate life was spiraling up in the gaps of the soil and soon would break ground.

Her son asked in surprise, "Mom, have the sprouts eyes?"

"No."

"But how do they know to grow up and not down?"

"Because it wants to look for the sun and without the sun they will die eventually."

Her son asked her again, "Mom, without the sun will I die?"

The answer was yes, but the farmwife dare not answer in this way, so she had to say to him, "My son, be at ease. It won't be without the sunlight."

In fact, human life often loses sunny days, as the seeds buried in the earth. The seeds buried deep seeds are undoubtedly hard to grow, but after they grow up, they will be surely well established and vigorously developed and able to brave the storm.

Though they have no eyes, the upward seeds tell us the sun is over our heads...

阳光就在自己头顶

一位农妇种黄豆，因天气干旱和田鼠为患，她把种子埋得很深。过了几天，农妇带上年仅6岁的儿子去察看，翻开土壤，他们发现很多种子都长出了长茎，顶是两瓣黄黄的嫩芽，这柔弱的生命正在土壤的空隙中七弯八拐地往上生长着，很快将要破土而出。

儿子惊讶地问："妈妈，小苗长眼睛了吗？"

"没有。"

"那它们怎么都知道要往上长，而不往下长呢？"

"因为它要寻找太阳，没有阳光它们最终会死的。"

儿子又问农妇："妈妈，我要是没有阳光会死吗？"

答案是肯定的，但农妇不敢这样回答，只好对他说道："孩子，你放心，不会没有阳光的。"

其实，人的生命里时常会有失去阳光的日子，就像种子被埋在土里一样。埋得很深的种子固然生长艰难，但长大后必定根深叶茂，能经风雨。

种子没长眼睛，但向上的种子告诉我们，阳光就在自己的头顶……

Push the Sun to Set

A boatman rowed a boat on the sea, the waves surging against the boat ceaselessly. The boat slightly swayed with the waves. A seagull sat on the boatman's shoulder and said to him, "How happy you are! The sea is swaying you, as you are on a swing."

Hearing this, the boatman shook his head and said with a smile, "No, I'm swaying the sea! Look, the waves of the sea are being swayed up."

The so – called bigness and smallness, strength and weakness often depend on people's senses and habits. As long as you're unwilling to show the impression of weakness, you will never be weak.

Facing the setting sun, the frustrated are often depressed while those positive and optimistic would say, "When I walk one step forward to the remotest corners of the earth, it will go one step backward. The sun didn't set by itself, but I drove it down. Look, how strong I am!"

推太阳下山

一个船夫摇着一只小船在大海中行驶。浪花不断向小船涌来。小船随着波浪微微荡漾。一只海鸥栖在船夫的肩头，对他说："你多幸福啊，大海摇荡着你，就像在打秋千似的。"

船夫听了，摇摇头笑着说："不对，是我在摇荡着大海！你看，大海的波涛都被我摇起来了。"

所谓的大与小、强与弱，很多时候都是依照人们的感官和习惯定论的。只要你不甘示弱，那弱小又从何谈起呢？

面对即将坠落的夕阳，失意的人往往怅惘沮丧不已。而那些积极乐观的人却会说："我向天涯走一步，天涯向后退一步。太阳不是自己落下山去的，而是我把它赶下去的，看看我的力量有多大！"

The Love of a Hunchback

Moses Mendelssohn, the grandfather of the well-known German composer, was far from being handsome. Along with a rather short stature, he had a grotesque hunchback.

One day he visited a merchant in Hamburg who had a lovely daughter named Frumtje. Moses fell hopelessly in love with her. But Frumtje was repulsed by his misshapen appearance.

When it was time for him to leave, Moses gathered his courage and climbed the stairs to her room to take one last opportunity to speak with her.

She was a vision of heavenly beauty, but caused him deep sadness by her refusal to look at him. After several attempts at conversation, Moses shyly asked, "Do you believe marriages are made in heaven?"

"Yes," She answered, still looking at the floor. "And do you?"

"Yes I do," He replied. "You see, in heaven at the birth of each boy, the Lord announces which girl he will marry. When I was born, my future bride was pointed out to me. Then the Lord added, 'But your wife will be humpbacked.'"

"Right then and there I called out, 'Oh Lord, a humpbacked woman would be a tragedy. Please, Lord, give me the hump and let her be beautiful.'"

Then Frumtje looked up into his eyes and was stirred by some deep memory. She reached out and gave Mendelssohn her hand and later became his devoted wife.

驼背的爱情

德国著名作曲家门德尔松的祖父摩西·门德尔松一点儿也不英俊。他不仅身材非常矮小,而且还长着奇形怪状的驼背。

有一天,他去汉堡拜访一位商人。这个商人有一个可爱的女儿,名叫弗鲁姆叶。摩西无可救药地爱上了她。但因为他相貌丑陋,弗鲁姆叶一口拒绝。

快要离开时,摩西鼓起勇气,爬上楼梯,来到她的房间,想利用这最后一次机会和她说说话。

她美若天仙,却让他非常伤心,因为她连看都不看他一眼。摩西连试了几次,才畏畏缩缩地问道:"你相信婚姻是天作之合吗?"

"相信,"她回答说,眼睛仍然看着地板。"你呢?"

"是的,我也相信。"他回答说,"你明白,天堂里每个男孩出生时,上帝便宣布他要娶哪个女孩。我出生时,上帝也为我指出了未来的新娘。接着,上帝补充道:'但你的妻子会是一个驼背。'"

"我当场就大声叫道:'噢,上帝,一个驼背女人将是一场悲剧。上帝,求求您,把驼背给我,让她变漂亮吧。'"

于是,弗鲁姆叶抬起头,望着他的眼睛,她被深深地打动了。她伸出手,答应了门德尔松的求婚,后来成了他忠诚的妻子。

The Star Pillow

In the autumn, a little girl walked in the woods. She picked up the red leaves blown off by the wind and put them into an exquisite bamboo basket, which was filled with the red leaves, shaped like the eyes, the palms or the stars.

"What are you picking these fallen leaves for?" I asked her curiously.

"To stuff my pillow," replied she excitedly.
"What a beautiful pillow filled with the red leaves!" I lauded.
"No. It's the pillow filled with stars!" The little girl picked up her head, seriously correcting me as an adult for my fault.

星星枕头

秋天，一个小女孩在林间漫步。她把被风吹落在地的红叶捡起来，装进一个精致的竹篮里面。眼睛形的红叶，手掌形的红叶，星形的红叶，装了满满一竹篮。

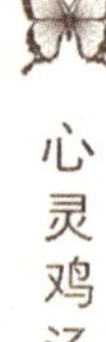

"拣这些落叶干什么？"我好奇地问她。

"装枕头呀。"她兴奋地回答。

"多么美丽，一个装满红叶的枕头！"我赞美道。

"不，是装满星星的枕头！"小女孩昂起头，认真地纠正了我作为一个成人的错误。

The Smile Penetrating the Soul

An Africa volcano erupted, the landslides raging down and rushing to a small village not far from the foot of a hill. Farms, fields and woods—everything didn't escape the catastrophe of being destroyed.

The torrential landslides awakened a 14-year-old girl in her sleep. The landslides flowing into the room had risen to her neck, only her arms, neck and head showing up. The rescue workers who arrived in time gathered around her but could find no way out because the girl was black and blue and each pull would be a greater harm. Now, the house had collapsed, her parents were killed by the landslides and she was one of the few survivors in the village.

When a reporter focused the video camera on her, she had never uttered a word suggesting she was in pain, but gritted her teeth with a smile and kept thanking the rescue workers with her arms shaping a V. She firmly believed that the rescue workers sent by the government would be able to save her. However, the rescue workers did their best and couldn't save her from the impregnable landslides. The little girl always waved her hands with a smile and was submerged by the landslides bit by bit.

In the last moment of her life, she had a smile on her face, her arms shaping a V. That moment was like a century; the people on the spot witnessed this solemn but tragic scene tearfully.

The world was deadly quiet, only the soul dancing alone.

Death can destroy a person's life, but never destroy the faith and spirit contained in the V on the verge of life and death! The power that rocks the world often contained on the edge of life makes all the tribulations of life drift like film.

穿透灵魂的微笑

非洲的一座火山爆发了，随之而来的泥石流狂泻而下，迅速扑向了坐落在山脚下不远处的一个小村庄。农庄、良田、树林，一切的一切都没有躲过被冲毁的劫难。

滚滚而来的泥石流惊醒了睡梦中的一个14岁的小女孩。流进屋内的泥石流已上升到了她的颈部。小女孩只露出双臂、颈部和头部。及时赶来的营救人员围着她一筹莫展，因为对遍体鳞伤的她来说，每一次拉扯无疑是一种更大的伤害。此刻，房屋早已倒塌了，她的双亲也被泥石流夺去了生命，她是村里为数不多的幸存者之一。

当记者把摄像机对准她时，她始终没有叫一个“疼”字，而是咬着牙微笑着，不停地向营救人员致谢，两臂做出了表示胜利的“V”字形。她坚信政府派来的营救人员一定能救她。可是，营救人员倾尽全力，也没能从固若金汤的泥石流中救出她来。小女孩始终微笑挥手，一点一点地被泥石流淹没了。

在生命的最后一刻，她脸上流露着微笑，手臂一直保持着“V”字形。那一刻漫长得像一个世纪，在场的人含泪目睹了这庄严而又悲惨的一幕。

世界静极了，只见灵魂独舞。

死神可以夺去人的生命，却永远夺不去生死关头那个“V”字所蕴含的信念和精神！常常在生命边缘蕴含着震撼世界的力量，让人生所有的苦难如轻烟般飘散。

View in the Heart

There was a temple at the foot of Nanshan Mountain and an old banyan was in front of the temple.

One morning, a young monk got up to clean the courtyard and saw the fallen leaves from the old banyan were everywhere, when he couldn't help feeling sad and looking at the tree with a sigh.

He couldn't hold back his sorrow, threw down the broom, rushed to his master's room and knocked on the door to plea for an interview.

On hearing the knocking, his master opened the door. When he saw the disciple's worried look, he thought something must have happened. So he hurried to ask him, "My disciple, why are you worried so much in the early morning?"

The disciple told his master doubtfully, "Master, you always admonish us to work hard, cultivate our moral character, grasp the truth and seize the hour. But even if I understand this truth, it is impossible to escape death. Till that time, won't I or so-called Tao be just like the fallen leaves in autumn or the deadwood in winter? Won't they be alike to be buried by a heap of loess?"

After hearing it, the old monk pointed at the old banyan and said to the young monk, "My disciple, you needn't worry about this. In fact, the fallen leaves in autumn and the deadwood in winter will climb back to the trees silently, become the flowers in spring, grow into the leafy profusion in summer, dance in the wind in autumn and return to the earth with the snowflakes of cold winter."

"Why don't I see it?"

"Because you haven't any view in your heart, you can't see their beautiful youth."

Fixing on the withered fallen leaves and imagining they will be in bud in the earth, your daily life will be sunny and full of vitality.

As long as you have the view in your heart, are you still hard to enjoy the path full of fragrance of flowers?

心中有景

南山脚下有一座庙，庙前有一棵老榕树。

一天早晨，一个小和尚起床后开始打扫庭院，看见满地都是榕树的落叶，禁不住开始伤感起来，望着榕树直叹气。

小和尚的伤心越发无法控制，干脆扔掉扫帚冲向师傅的房间，叩门恳求师傅召见。

师傅闻声打开门，看到徒弟一脸忧虑，知道一定发生了什么事情，就急忙问道："我的徒儿，一大早的什么事情让你如此着急呢？"

徒弟充满疑惑地对师傅说："师傅，你总是告诫我们要勤奋努力，培养品德，掌握真理，只争朝夕。可是，即使我懂得了这个道理，也是无法避免死亡。到了那个时候，无论是我，还是所谓的道，不就像秋天的落叶和冬天的枯枝吗？它们不是一样会被一堆黄土埋葬吗？"

听完这番话，老和尚指着那棵老榕树对小和尚说："我的徒儿，对此你不必担心。事实上，无论秋天的落叶还是冬天的枯枝，会悄悄爬回树干，春天成为花朵，夏天枝繁叶茂，秋天随风舞动，最后伴着寒冬的雪花又回到土地。"

"为什么我没有看到呢？"

"因为你的心中没有任何风景，当然就看不到它们美丽的青春了。"

凝望枯萎的落叶，想象着它很快又会在泥土中萌芽，每一天的生活都会充满阳光和蓬勃的朝气。

只要心中有景，要欣赏到花香满径还会难吗？

Painting with the Feet

One day, the famous French painter Gayle attended a banquet. At the banquet a short man went up to him, made a deep bow and asked to be his disciple. Gayle looked at the man, found he was a disabled man missing two arms, declined him and said, "I' m afraid you will be inconvenient to paint?"

But the man didn' t mind and immediately said, "No, though I have no hands, I still have two feet." Then, he asked the host to bring the paper and brush, sat down on the floor and began to paint with his toes holding the brush. He painted with their feet, but he did very well.

His spirit touched the guests present, including Gayle. Gayle was very pleased to accept him as a disciple.

Since he acknowledged Gayle as his teacher, the short man worked harder. Few years later, he had become well known all over the world. He was the famous painter Ducina with no arms.

用脚画画

有一天,法国名画家纪雷参加一个宴会。宴会上有个身材矮小的人走到他面前,向他深鞠一躬,请求他收为徒弟。纪雷朝那人看了一眼,发现他是个缺了两只手臂的残废人,就婉转拒绝他,并说:"我想你画画恐怕不太方便吧?"

可是,那个人并不在意,立刻说:"不,我虽然没有手,但还有两只脚。"说着,便请主人拿来纸和笔,坐在地上,就用脚趾头夹着笔画了起来。他虽然是用脚画画,但画得很好。

在场的客人(包括纪雷)都被他的精神感动了。纪雷很高兴,马上收他为徒弟。

这个矮个子拜纪雷为师后,更加用心学习,没几年便名扬天下。他就是有名的无臂画家杜兹纳。

Polish the Stone in Your Heart

A man couldn't get along with the crowd. He heard there lived a sculptor with mighty self-restraint by the sea, so he went to pay a formal visit. He said to the sculptor, "Why is my temper so bad? Can I change it?"

The sculptor said with a smile, "Yes, you can." He gave the man a bag of fist-sized stones and told him, "Each time you lose your temper, polish the edges and corners of one stone."

The man returned home with the stones. He remembered the sculptor's words: each time you lose your temper, polish the edges and corners of one stone. Day after day, the stones in the bag were getting fewer and fewer while his temper had changed a lot.

A few years later, he went to see the sculptor with the stones. The sculptor let him recall, as long as he forgot an unpleasant thing, he would put a stone on the beach. The man tried to think hard, but he had no idea of the story of many unpleasant things. So the smooth stones filled the beach.

The sculptor said, "Look at these stones, which had edges and corners but a few years later were almost the same as pebbles. In fact, the pebbles initially had edges and corners but became smooth after years of ebb and flow."

With the words, the sculptor picked up a stone, pointed to the print on the beach and said, "The bigger edges and corners the stones have on the beach, the deeper their prints will leave. Similarly, people are like stones: each time you lose your temper, you will leave a print in the heart of the other side; the more acute the stone is in your heart, the harsher your words are and the more serious harm the other side will suffer. So you have to learn to polish the stones in your heart..."

磨平心底的石头

一个人不合群,他听说海边住着一位极有涵养的雕刻家,就前往拜见。他对雕刻家说:"为什么我的脾气这么坏?能改变吗?"

雕刻家笑了笑说："能。"雕刻家送给这个人一袋子拳头大小的石头，并对他说："以后你每发一次脾气，就把一块石头的棱角磨平。"

这个人带着石头回去了。他记着雕刻家的话：每发一次脾气，就拿出一块石头打磨。日复一日，袋子中的石头少了，他的脾气也改了许多。

几年后，他带着那些石头去见雕刻家。雕刻家让他回忆，每忘记一件不愉快的事就把一块石头摆在沙滩上。这个人开始极力地想，许多不愉快的事已想不出来龙去脉了。于是，沙滩上摆满了光滑的石头。

雕刻家说："你看这些石头，本来是有棱有角的，几年后就和鹅卵石差不多了。其实，鹅卵石起初也有棱有角，经过了多年的潮起潮落，才变得光滑。"

说完，雕刻家拿起一块石头，指着沙滩上的印痕说："石头在沙滩上，棱角越大，印痕越深。同样，人也和石头一样，你每发一次脾气，就会在对方的心灵上留下一次印痕，你心底的石头越尖锐，你的言语就越刻薄，对方所受的伤害就会越大。所以，你要学会把心底的石头磨平……"

The Enlightenment of the Four Lights

In my mind kept the picture of a U. S. campus advertising, on which there were four lights, arranged in file from left to right. The left one was very bright and the right was a lamp without light. Among these four lights, every two adjacent lights had a dialogue, which affected the light and the shade of the lights.

The dialogue behind the first light was, "I have an idea. I want to do it. " The answer was, "Can it be done?"

The second light dimmed a little. The dialogue behind the lamp was, "I have a try. " The answer was, "It may be hard!"

The third lamp became dimmer. The dialogue behind the lamp was, "Many people don't agree with me to do so. " The answer was, "Forget it then!"

The fourth lamp finally went out.

In reality, to put out an idea is much easier than to ignite it. In fact, looking back the life for decades, the most fruitful years are the journeys of tumbling instead.

四盏灯的启迪

我的脑海里一直浮现出一个美国校园广告的画面，广告上有四盏灯，从左到右依次排列着，左边那盏灯非常明亮，右边的则是一盏无光灯。这四盏灯每相邻的两盏间都有一段对话，它们影响着灯的明暗度。

第一盏明灯后的对话是："我有个想法，想去做。"回话说："可以做到吗？"

第二盏灯稍暗了些，灯后的对话是："我试试看。"回话说："很难吧！"

第三盏灯变得更加昏暗了，灯后的对话是："周围的人都不同意我去做。"回话说：

“那就算了吧!”

第四盏灯最终熄灭了。

现实中,熄灭想法总要比点燃想法容易得多。其实,回首几十年走过的人生之旅,最有收获的岁月反而是“摔倒”的几段路。

No One But Yourself Can Defeat You

A young painter resided in a small narrow house, living on painting portraits before he became famous.

One day, a rich man came by and found the painter paint so meticulously that he liked it and asked him to draw a portrait. They agreed on the remuneration of 10, 000 dollars.

After a week, the portrait was done. The rich man came to take the painting as agreed on. At this moment, the rich man hit on an evil idea of bullying the unknown young artist, so he refused to pay the remuneration.

The rich man thought, “The man in the painting is me. If I don't buy this painting, no one will buy it. Why should I pay so much money for it?” So the rich man said, “I will only pay 3, 000 dollars to buy this painting.”

The young artist was stunned, for he had never come across such things. He strongly argued on just grounds, expecting the rich man to abide by the agreement and to be a trustworthy man.

“I can only pay 3, 000 dollars to buy the painting. Speak no more.” The rich man thought he had won, “I ask you at last, will you sell it 3, 000 dollars or not?”

The young artist knew the rich man deliberately went back on his word, so he felt indignant. He said in a firm tone, “No. I would prefer not to sell the painting rather than to be humiliated by you. Today you break your word and someday you must pay 20 times.”

“What a joke! 20 times will be 200, 000! I won't be stupid to pay 200, 000 dollars to buy the painting!”

“Well, we'd better wait and see,” the young artist said to the rich man who left angrily.

After the stimulation of such an incident, the painter moved out of this sad place, anew formally acknowledged teachers to work hard night and day.

More than a dozen years later, he finally blazed a new way and became popular in the circle of art.

After he left the studio, the rich man had forgotten the artist's painting and words the next day. Until one day, some friends of the rich man simultaneously came to tell him, “Something is so strange! We paid a visit to a famous artist's exhibition of paintings, in which one painting is marked 200, 000 dollars and the man in the painting looks exactly the same as you. It is so ridiculous that the title of the painting is Thief.”

It came to him a terrible blow. He immediately thought of what had happened to the painter more than a dozen years before. If the painting were really the one he broke his promise that year, it would be terrible to him. He went to find the young painter the same night right away. As expected, the painting titled as Thief was no other than that one he had broken his word that year. He quickly apologized to the artist and paid 200, 000 dollars to buy back the portrait.

With an undefeated ambition, the young painter made the rich man bend his head. This young man was Pablo Picasso.

除了你自己，没人能打败你

有一位青年画家，成名前住在一间狭窄的小房子里，靠画人像为生。

一天，一个富人经过，看他的画工细致，很喜欢，便请他帮忙画一幅人像。双方约好酬金是一万元。

一个星期后，人像完成了。富人依约前来取画。这时，富人心里起了歹念，欺画家年轻又未成名，不肯按约定支付酬金。

富人心想："画中的人是我，这幅画如果我不买，那绝不会有别人买。我又何必花那么多钱来买呢？"于是，富人说："我只愿花 3000 元买这幅画。"

青年画家愣住了，他从来没碰到过这种事，费了许多口舌向富人据理力争，希望富人能遵守约定，做个守信用的人。

"我只能花 3000 元买这幅画，你别再罗嗦了。"富人认为他居上风，"我最后再问你一句，3000 元卖不卖？"

青年画家知道富人故意赖账，心中愤愤不平。他以坚定的语气说："不卖。我宁可不卖这幅画，也不愿受你的屈辱。今天你失信毁约，将来一定要你付出 20 倍的代价。"

"笑话，20 倍，是 20 万啊！我才不会笨得花 20 万买这幅画呢！"

"那我们等着瞧好了。"青年画家对悻悻离去的富人说。

经过这一事件的刺激后，画家搬离了这个伤心地，重新拜师学艺，日夜苦练。

十几年后，他终于闯出了一片天地，成了艺术界一位知名人物。

离开画室后，那个富人第二天就把画家的画和话忘到了脑后。直到有一天，富人的几位朋友不约而同地来告诉他："有件事好怪！我们去参观一位著名艺术家的画展，其中有幅画标价 20 万，画中的人跟你长得一模一样。好笑的是，这幅画的标题竟然是贼。"

富人好像当头一棒，立刻想起了十多年前画家的事。如果这幅画正是自己当年赖账的那幅画，那么这件事对自己的影响可就太坏了。他立刻连夜赶去找青年画家，果然不出所料，这幅标题为《贼》的画，正是自己当年赖账的那幅画。他赶紧向画家道歉，并花 20 万买回了那幅人像画。

凭着一股不服输的劲头，青年画家终于让富人低下了头。这个年轻人就是帕布罗·毕加索。

The World Will Make Way for You

Eel Prague was the first black journalist who won the Pulitzer News Prize in the history of the United States. Brave and hardworking, he made outstanding achievements and created a miracle in the history of the American news. Recalling his own childhood experiences, he said, "Our family was so poor that my parents made a living by toiling for others. At that time, my father was a sailor, who would have to go between the ports on the Atlantic Ocean. I always thought the black people humble like us couldn't have any prospect, so perhaps we would wander about aimlessly like the ships where my father worked."

One day when he was nine, his father took him to visit Van Gogh's former residence. In front of the creaky small wooden bed and the pair of cracked leather shoes, Prague, asked his father curiously, "Since Van Gogh was the world's greatest painter, wasn't he a millionaire?" His father answered, "Van Gogh was a poor man who even didn't afford to marry a wife."

Once, his father took him to Denmark. At Hans Christian Andersen's home with the stained walls, Prague was confused to ask, "Didn't Andersen live in the royal palace?" His father replied, "Andersen was a shoemaker's son, who had lived in this broken attic before his death. The royal palace only appeared in his fairy tales."

Since then, Prague's life had changed completely. He said, "I'm fortunate enough to have a good father, who let me know Van Gogh and Andersen. And these two great artists also told me the success of people has nothing to do with poverty."

In real life, we often see such a group of people, they would decide their own future and living patterns because of their poor born environment; they often dialogue with the world in a pitiful voice due to their humble roles; They always abandon their childhood dreams for the temporary living predicament; they always lower their heads alive with wisdom because they are discriminated for their plain features.

In fact, God is fair; he would sometimes put those intelligent creatures among the poor and lowly people, making them poor and humble so that they keep away from money and power, and making them wander in a dark cave at birth and see no light. But God will surely favor some of the poor, who have the strong sense of survival, the resolute courage, the unyielding character and the superior talent. God will make them come to the fore and fill the bill in a certain valuable field.

Don't dialogue with the world in a pitiful voice. As long as a person knows where he or she is going, the world will make way to him or her.

世界会为你让路

伊尔・布拉格是美国历史上第一位荣获普利策新闻奖的黑人记者，他勇敢勤奋、功绩卓越，创造了美国新闻史上的一个奇迹。他在回忆自己童年经历时说："我们家很穷，父母都靠卖苦力为生。那时，我父亲是一名水手，他每年都要往返于大西洋各个港口之间。我一直认为，像我们这样地位低微的黑人是不可能有什么出息的，也许一生都会像父亲所工作的船只一样，漂泊不定。"

他9岁那年，有一天，父亲带他去参观梵高的故居。在那张吱嘎作响的小木床和那双龟裂的皮鞋面前，布拉格好奇地问父亲："梵高是世界上最著名的大画家，他不是百万富翁吗？"父亲回答说："梵高是一个连妻子都娶不上的穷人。"

一次，父亲带着布拉格去了丹麦。在安徒生墙壁斑驳的故居，布拉格困惑地问："安徒生不是生活在皇宫里吗？"他的父亲答道："安徒生是一个鞋匠的儿子，他生前就住在这栋破阁楼里。皇宫只在他的童话里才出现。"

从此，布拉格的人生完全改变了。他说："我庆幸有一位好父亲，他让我认识了梵高和安徒生，而这两位伟大的艺术家又告诉我，人能否成功与贫穷无关。"

现实生活中，我们常常看到有这样一群人，他们会因自己穷困的出生环境而判定自己未来的生活格局；他们常因自己角色的卑微而用垂怜的声音与世界对话；他们总是因暂时的生活窘迫而放弃儿时的梦想；他们总是因其貌不扬被人歧视而低下了充满智慧的头颅。

其实，上天是公平的，他有时会把那些聪慧的宠儿放在贫贱的下等人中间，让他们家世贫穷、出身卑贱，让他们远离金钱和权势，让他们一出生就在黑暗的洞穴中徘徊，看不到光明。但上天一定会青睐某些穷人——他们有着坚强的生存意识、果敢的斗志、不屈的傲骨和出众的天赋。上天会在某个有价值的领域让他们脱颖而出并出类拔萃。

别用垂怜的声音与世界对话。一个人只要知道上哪里去，全世界都会给他让路。

The Clear Spring of Soul

A prisoner picked up 1, 000 yuan in the course of building the road outside the prison. He handed it out without hesitation. However, someone in charge of the prison said to him in contempt, "Stop cheating! With your own money, play such a trick to bribe me; what you want to gain back is the reduced sentence; people of your sort are not honest."

In total despair, the prisoner believed that no one in the world would trust him any more. So he escaped from prison that night.

On his way to flight, he plundered money and values without restraint. After plundering enough pelf, he took a train bound for the border. The carriages were so crowded that he had to stand close to a water closet. At this moment, a quite beautiful girl walked into the closet, and found that the latch was broken when she closed the door. She stepped out and whispered to him, "Sir, could you guard the door for me?"

In a daze for a second, he, looking into the pure eyes of the girl, nodded his head. The girl went into the closet with a blush; and he guarded the door tightly like a loyal guard.

At that very moment, he changed his mind suddenly. At the next stop he got off the train, and went to give himself up to the police at the train station.

Trust is the most precious thing in this world. It cannot be bought, or gained by lure or force. It comes deep from one's soul, and lives in the clear spring of a soul. It can redeem the soul and make the heart full of purity and confidence.

灵魂的清泉

有一个劳改犯人在外出修路的过程中，在路上捡到了 1000 元钱，他不假思索地把它交了上去。可是，负责监狱的某个人却轻蔑地对他说："你别来这一套，拿自己的钱，变着花样贿赂我，想换减刑的资本，你们这号人就是不老实。"

囚犯万念俱灰，心想，这世界上再也不会有人相信他了。晚上，他越狱了。

在亡命的途中，他大肆抢劫钱财，准备外逃。在抢得足够的钱财后，他乘上开往边境的火车。火车上很挤，他只好站在厕所旁。这时，有一位十分漂亮的姑娘走进了厕所，关门时却发现门扣坏了。她走出来，轻声对他说："先生，你能为我把门吗？"

他一愣，看着姑娘纯洁的眼神，他点了点头，姑娘红着脸进了厕所。而他像一个忠诚的卫士一样，严守着门。

在那一刹那，他突然改变了主意。到了下一站，他下车了，到车站派出所投案自首。

在这世界上，信任是一种弥足珍贵的东西，没有人能用金钱买得到，也没有人可用利诱和武力争取得到，它来自一个人的灵魂深处，也活在灵魂里的清泉，它可以拯救灵魂，让心灵充满纯洁和自信。

The Twelve Smiles

A passenger told an air hostess that he needed a cup of water to take his medicine when the plane just took off. She told him that she would bring him the water in ten minutes.

Thirty minutes later, when the passenger's ring for service sounded, the air hostess flew in a flurry. She was kept so busy that she forgot to deliver him the water. As a result, the passenger was held up to take his medicine. She hurried over to him with a cup of water, but he refused it.

In the following hours on the flight, each time the stewardess passed by the passenger she would ask him with a smile whether he needed help or not. But the passenger never paid heed to her.

When he was going to get off the plane, the passenger asked the stewardess to hand him the passengers' booklet. She was very sad. She knew that he would write down sharp words, but with a smile she handed it to him.

Off the plane, she opened the booklet, and cracked a smile, for the passenger put it, "On the flight, you asked me whether I needed help or not for twelve times in all. How can I refuse your twelve sincere smiles?"

That's right! Who can refuse twelve sincere smiles from a person?

12 次微笑

飞机刚刚起飞，一位乘客向空姐要一杯水吃药。空姐告诉他等飞机起飞后 10 分钟就为他送来。

30 分钟后，客人要求服务的铃声响了，空姐慌了神，原来在忙碌中她忘了为客人送水，耽误了客人吃药。她马上给客人送去一杯水，但客人拒绝了。

在此后几小时的飞行中，空姐每次经过客人身边都要微笑着问客人需要什么服务，但客人从不理睬她。

要下飞机了，客人叫空姐拿来留言簿，空姐很伤心，她知道客人要写下批评的话，但她仍微笑着把留言簿递给了客人。

下了飞机，空姐打开留言簿，她笑了，因为客人写道："在飞行中，你微笑着问我需不需要服务，一共有 12 次，我怎么能拒绝你 12 次真诚的微笑呢？"

是啊！谁能拒绝别人 12 次真诚的微笑呢？

The Old Man Who Planted Oak Trees

A young traveler was exploring the Alps. He came upon a vast stretch of barren land. It was desolate. It was the kind of place you hurry away from.

Then, suddenly, the young traveler stopped dead in his tracks. In the middle of this vast wasteland was a bent-over old man. On his back was a sack of acorn. In his hand was a four-foot length of iron pipe.

The old man was using the iron pipe to punch holes in the ground. Then from the sack he would take an acorn and put it in the hole. Later the old man told the traveler. "I've planted over 100, 000 acorns. Perhaps only tenth of them will grow. " The old man's wife and son had died, and this was how he chose to spend his final years. "I want to do something useful," he said.

Twenty-five years later the now-not-as-young traveler returned to the same place. What he saw amazed him. He could not believe his own eyes. The land was covered with a beautiful forest two miles wide and five miles long. Birds were singing, animals were playing, and wild flowers perfumed the air.

The traveler stood there recalling the desolation that once was; a beautiful oak forest stood there now—all because someone cared.

种橡树的老人

一个年轻的旅行者在阿尔卑斯山探险。他来到一块一望无际的不毛之地。那里荒无人烟,是一种让人急欲离开的地方。

后来,年轻的旅行者突然停住了脚步。只见辽阔的荒地中央一位老人正在弯腰播种。他背着一大袋橡子,手里拿着一根 4 英尺长的铁管。

老人用那根铁管在地上打洞,然后从袋子里掏出一颗橡子,放进洞里。后来,老人告诉那个旅行者:"我已经种了 10 万颗橡子。大概只有十分之一的橡子能够成长。"老人的妻儿都已经死去,而这就是他选择度过晚年的一种方式。"我想做一些有用的事儿。"他说。

25 年后,那个已不再年轻的旅行者又故地重游。而眼前的景象却让他惊叹不已。他无法相信自己的眼睛。那块土地覆盖上了 5 英里长、两英里宽的美丽森林。那里,小鸟歌唱,动物嬉戏,野花飘香。

旅行者站在那里,回忆着它以前的荒凉;一片美丽的橡树林现在之所以耸立在那里,都是因为某个人的关心啊。

The People Standing at the Peak

Once, Einstein gave a lecture in a university, where the large classroom was full of teachers and students who respected him. After his speech, the audience on the scene started to ask questions.

A girl got up and asked, "You're known as a giant of science. Do you think you're a giant?"

Einstein said with a smile, "A giant isn't a person who is tall in height. You see I'm so small, how can I have an image of a giant? Maybe I see a bit farther, only because I stand higher!"

Then a boy asked, "You mentioned you stand higher than others, it reminds me that you had a long talk with a lady on the peak of the Alps. I don't want to ask what you talked, but I want to know whether you realized you have been a peak in the history of science when you stood on the peak."

Looking at the boy carefully, Einstein asked, "Do you think I'm like a peak? Anyhow, my height cannot become a peak. And what's more, there is no peak that no one can conquer, so we don't want to be a peak, but we want to be a person to climb the summit!"

Then, he took up a piece of chalk and wrote on the blackboard, "Standing on the peak, you are not tall, but even smaller!"

He then turned to the audience and said, "Although I stand tall, in the eyes of the world I'm still small! Finally, I can tell you a sentence, which was the last one I told the lady on the peak of the Alps: 'Any peak can be conquered, for there is no giant in the world but the one who stands higher!'"

A storm of applause sounded. The lady who listened to Einstein's instruction on the Alps that year was no other than Madam Curie!

站在峰顶的人

有一次,爱因斯坦在一所大学演讲,大教室里坐满了对他充满崇敬之情的师生。演讲完毕,由现场人员开始自由提问。

一位女生站起来问:"您被誉为科学界的巨人,您认为自己是巨人吗?"

爱因斯坦微笑着说:"巨人并不是长得高大的人。大家看我如此瘦小,怎么能有巨人的形象呢? 也许我看得远一些,那也只是因为我站得高一些而已!"

一个男生接着问:"您提到比别人站得高一些,我想起了不久前您在阿尔卑斯山的高峰之巅曾和一位女士长谈过一次。我不想问您谈话的内容,只想知道站在山顶的那一刻,您是否意识到在科学史上自己也已站成一座山峰。"

爱因斯坦仔细地看了看发问的人,问:"你看我像一座山峰吗? 我这个身高不管怎么站都成不了山峰。而且,没有一座高峰不是被人征服的,我们不要做高峰,而要做登上山顶的人!"

说着,他拿起粉笔在黑板上写下一行字:"站在山顶,你并不高大,反而更加渺小!"

随后,他转过身,对台下的人说:"我虽然站得高,可在世人的眼中依然是渺小的!最后,我可以告诉大家一句话,这句话也是我在阿尔卑斯山绝顶之上对那位女士讲的最后一句:'任何一座高峰都是可以征服的,世上从来没有巨人,只有站得更高的人!'"

台下掌声一片。当年在阿尔卑斯山上聆听爱因斯坦教诲的那位女士正是居里夫人!

The Pavilion in the Heart

For his honesty and trustworthiness, Mexican President Vicente Fox, was respected by the people. The principle he conducted himself all his life was honesty. It was the personality that made him a country's president from an ordinary salesman.

Once, Fox was invited to a university to give a lecture. A student asked him, "The political arena is always filled with fraud. In your experience in politics have you lied?"

Fox said, "No, never."

The students whispered among themselves and some of them were chuckling because every politician always expresses himself. They always vow, saying he has never lied.

Fox wasn't angry. He said to the college students, "Boys and girls, in this society, perhaps it is very hard to prove that I'm an honest man, but you should believe that, in this world there's honesty, which is always around us. I want to tell you a story. Perhaps after hearing it, you will forget it, but this story means a lot to me.

"There was a father who was a farmer. One day, he felt the pavilion in the garden was too worn-down, so he had it dismantled. His son was so interested in dismantling the pavilion that he said to his father, 'Daddy, I want to see how you have the pavilion dismantled, so can you have it dismantled until I come back from the boarding school to take a vacation?'

"His father agreed.

"However, after the boy left, the workers quickly dismantled the pavilion.

"After the boy returned from school, he found the old pavilion had disappeared. He said in low spirits to his father, 'Dad, you told me a lie.'

"His father looked at the boy in surprise. The boy went on, 'You said the old pavilion would be dismantled until I came back.' His father said, 'My boy, I'm wrong, and I should keep my promise.'

"The father called in the workers again and had them re-build a pavilion in the shape of the old one. After the pavilion made, he called in his son and said to the workers, 'Now, please dismantle it.'

"I know the father, who was not rich, but kept his promise in front of his child."

Hearing this, the students asked, "What's the father's name, please? We hope to know him."

Fox said, "He has died, but his son is still alive."

"Then, where's his son? He should be an honest man."

Fox said calmly, "His son is now standing here. It's me. I want to tell you is I'd like to treat this country and everyone of it like my father treating me."

A storm of applause thundered in the audience.

Dismantling and building a pavilion twice won't only satisfy a boy's wish, but also the moral requirement of an adult's self-improvement.

Dismantling a pavilion in the garden will build a pavilion in the heart of a boy. This pavilion is a faith-in trustworthiness.

心中的亭子

墨西哥总统福克斯以诚实守信的品德受到国人的尊重，他一生做人的原则就是两个字：诚实。正是这样的人格品质，使他从一个普通的推销员成为一个国家的总统。

一次，福克斯受邀到一所大学演讲，一个学生问他："政坛历来充满欺诈，在你从政的经历中有没有撒过谎？"

福克斯说："不，从来没有。"

大学生在下面窃窃私语，有的还轻声笑出来，因为每一个政客都会这样表白。他们总是发誓，说自己从来没有撒谎。

福克斯并不气恼，他对大学生说："孩子们，在这个社会上，也许我很难证明自己是个诚实的人，但你们应该相信，这个世界上还有诚实，它永远都在我们的周围。我想讲一个故事，也许你们听过就忘了，但这个故事对我却很有意义。

"有一位父亲是个农场主。有一天，他觉得园中的那座亭子已经太破旧了，就安排工人们准备将它拆掉。他的儿子对拆亭子这件事很感兴趣，于是对父亲说：'爸爸，我想看看你们怎么拆掉这座亭子，等我从寄宿学校放假回来再拆好吗？'

"父亲答应了。

"可是，等孩子走后，工人们很快就把亭子拆掉了。

"孩子放假回来后，发现旧亭子已经不见了。他闷闷不乐地对父亲说：'爸爸，你对我撒谎。'

父亲惊异地看着孩子。孩子继续说：'你说过的，那座旧亭子要等我回来再拆。'父亲说：'孩子，爸爸错了，我应该兑现自己的诺言。'

"这位父亲重新召来工人，让他们按照旧亭子的模样在原来的地方再造一座亭子。亭子造好后，他把孩子叫来，然后对工人们说：'现在，请你们把它拆掉。'

"我认识这位父亲，他并不富有，但他却在孩子面前兑现了自己的承诺。"

学生们听后问道："请问这位父亲叫什么名字？我们希望认识他。"

福克斯说："他已经过世了，但他的儿子还活着。"

"那他的孩子在哪里？他应该是一位诚实的人。"

福克斯平静地说："他的孩子现在就站在这里，就是我。我想告诉大家的是，我愿意像父亲对我一样对待这个国家，对待这个国家的每一个人。"

台下掌声雷动。

将一座亭子拆建两次，绝不仅仅为了满足一个孩子的愿望，更是为了满足一个成人自我完善的道德要求。

在园子里重新拆掉一座亭子，就在孩子的心里重建了一座亭子，这座亭子就是一个信念——对诚信的信念。

Spring Is Coming and I Cannot See It

One day there was a blind man with a hat at his feet and a sign that read, "I am blind. Please help."

A man was walking by him and stopped to observe—he only had a few coins in his hat. The man dropped a few more coins in his hat and without asking for his permission took the sign, turned it round, and wrote another announcement. He placed the sign by the blind man's feet and left. That afternoon the man passed by the blind man again and noticed that his hat was full of bills and coins. The blind man recognized his footstep and asked if it was him who had rewritten his sign and he wanted to know what he wrote on it.

The man responded,"I just rewrote your sign differently."He smiled and went on his way. The sign read,"Spring is coming and I cannot see it."

春天就要来了,我却无法看到

一天,有一个盲人,脚边放了一顶帽子和一个告示,上面写道:"我是瞎子。请帮帮我。"

一个人经过他身边,停下来观看,只见他的帽子里只有几枚硬币。那人又向帽子里丢了几枚硬币,然后未经允许就拿住告示,翻过来,又写了一张告示,放在盲人的脚边,就离开了。那天下午,这个人又路过盲人的身边,注意到帽子里放满了钞票和硬币。盲人听出了他的脚步声,问是不是他又写了告示并想知道他在上面写了什么。

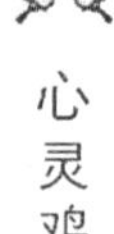

这个人回答说:"我只是用不同的方式写出了你的告示。"他微微一笑,就走了。

告示上写的是:"春天就要来了,我却无法看到。"

The Oasis in the Heart

A young man called Cindy came to an oasis, where he met an old man.

Cindy asked,"What about here?"

The old man asked,"What about your hometown?"

Cindy replied,"It's horrible! I loathe it."

The old man went on,"Well, hurry away. It's as horrible as your hometown."

Later came a young man called Rockery. He asked the same question and the old man also countered with the same question.

Rockery replied,"My hometown is so good. I miss its people, flowers and things..."

The old man said,"It's equally good here."

The listener was so surprised that he asked the old man why his answer was different from the first one.

The old man said,"What you want to look for is what you will find!"

If you're enterprising, you will live in the oasis. If you reach for what's beyond your grasp and reap without sowing, the oasis of life will become the desert.

心里的绿洲

一个名叫辛迪的青年来到一片绿洲。他碰到一位老人。

辛迪问:"这里如何?"老人反问说:"你的家乡如何?"辛迪回答:"糟透了!我很讨厌。"老人接着说:"那你快走,这里同你家乡一样糟。"

后来又来了一个名叫罗加瑞的青年,他问了同样的问题,老人家也是同样的反问。

罗加瑞回答说:"我的家乡很好,我很想念家乡的人、鲜花和事物……"

老人便说:“这里也是同样的好。”

旁听者觉得诧异,问老人为什么前后说法不一致。

老人说:“你要寻找什么,你就找到什么!”

如果有进取心,生活则处处是绿洲。如果好高骛远、不劳而获,生活中的绿洲就会变成沙漠。

Spring Is Always Within

This past April while visiting my parents on the farm I'd grown up on, I wandered outside to drink in the feel of "home", a comfort I really needed right then. I was used to sunny Southern Californian mornings, and the brisk early-morning Iowan air nipped at my nose, ears and bare hands.

With my father's fleece-lined jacket wrapped around me, and my hands snuggled deep in its well-worn pockets, I meandered around the spacious homestead when the unexpected sweet scent of lilacs suddenly called to me. Turning toward the bountiful hedge of lilacs in the distance, I spotted what looked like blooms. I hurried over.

The lavender lilacs were indeed in glorious bloom! I pulled a plentiful clump to my face and inhaled the intoxicating scent, as I had done every spring throughout my childhood. A warm delight seeped through my chilled bones, and I smiled at the thought that spring had arrived!

Strolling back to the house, the promise of springtime-warmth, renewal and beauty-journeyed right along with me.

My father sat at the kitchen table, poring over the morning market reports.

"It's spring! The lilacs are in bloom!" I announced joyously.

"Lilacs in bloom or not, it isn't spring until winter is gone," he contradicted. "We'll get a bit of cold weather yet."

But my heart refused to let the optimism that the lilacs had brought to me fade. Immediately, I recalled the card my mother had sent me just that past week—one that had subconsciously inspired this trip home. My mother knew that I was feeling down. On the cover of the card she sent me was a photo of a single flower emerging from a desolate barren slope of rock. The exquisite flower willed itself to have life, in spite of the conditions around it. Inside were the words "In the midst of winter, I found within me an eternal spring," followed by my mother's words:

"Spring has always been your favorite time of year. As always, it's within."

These are words that my mother, ever the optimist, lives by. Even in the midst of winter, she finds spring.

"It's pouring rain!" Dad once said.

"Everything smells so fresh after a rain!" Mom responded.

"But I'd wanted to get the yards mowed today," he replied, obviously disappointed.

"We need the rain," she countered. "Now everything will be greener."

"But the forecast is rain for the entire day," Dad moaned.

"Then we should go to the movies this afternoon," Mom smiled.

"It's so expensive," he retorted.

"That's precisely why we should go to the matinee," she countered. "Three of the kids can get in free, and it's only half-price for the rest of us."

Recalling this Rockwell scene of a Sunday afternoon when I was twelve, I'm reminded that for my mother torrential rains produced a rainbow.

Throughout my childhood and over the course of my adult years, when I met with success, my mother presented me with a bouquet of lilacs. And on the days when the lemons were so bitter they simply couldn't be made into lemonade, no matter how much sugar was added, like the day a good friend passed away; like the day when a long-standing love relationship ended... lilacs arrived from my mother with a note of understanding to match their beauty and sweet fragrance.

"Spring has always been your favorite time of year," she always reminded. "As always, it's within."

Even so, it was the lilacs made her words ring true. With the sight and fragrance of that April morning's came the realization of why a trip home was necessary. I needed to assuage my sadness, my feelings of loneliness and melancholy. I was pining. My dear daughter, now an adult, had moved into a place of her own. She now lives many states and many miles away. While happy for her, I mourn the loss of her nearness...

That morning, the sight of the lilacs brought my mother's words back to life. They reminded me that in the midst of an internal winter, a winter that is within, I must recall the beauty of springtime and the scent of the lilacs. So I won't see her as having gone away, but rather as taking part in new and wondrous experiences in a world that has as many springs as winters.

"Dad, the lilacs are in bloom. It's spring!" I assured my father that day.

"Hmm," he said, glancing at me, his expression skeptical. Noting my frown, his features softened. "Of course it's possible that spring has arrived," he placated, smiling. "After all, like you said, the lilacs are in bloom."

Oh, for the every renewing beauty of springtime! And the sweet and irrepressible scent of the lilacs to remind us that spring is found within.

春天总在心里

过去的这个4月，我去自己从小在那里长大的那个农场探望父母亲。我漫步在屋外，沉浸在"家"的感觉中，我当时确实需要家的慰藉。我习惯了加州南部阳光明媚的早晨，依阿华州清晨凛冽的空气刺痛了我的鼻子、耳朵和没戴手套的双手。

我将父亲的一件羊毛衬里夹克裹在身上，两手深深地插进破破烂烂的口袋里，在宽阔的农场上遛达。突然，紫丁香的芬芳出乎意料地向我袭来。我转向远处一丛丛茂密的紫丁香，注意到好像是花朵。我匆匆跑了过去。

淡紫色的丁香花确实在漂亮地怒放着！我将一大丛拉到面前，吮吸着那醉人的花香，就像我童年时每年春天做的那样。一股暖暖的喜悦之情穿过了我冰冷的身体。一想到春天已经来临，我露出了微笑。

我信步回到房里，春天的希望——温暖美丽、万物复苏——一路伴随着我。

父亲坐在餐桌边，仔细看着早晨行情报道。

"春天来了！紫丁香花开了！"我欢快地宣布道。

"紫丁香开不开花，只有等冬天过去，才是春天，"他反驳说，"冷天还要持续一阵。"

但我的内心不愿让紫丁香带给我的乐观消失。我马上想起上周母亲刚送给我的一张卡片。正是那张卡片促使我这次下意识地回了家。母亲知道我情绪低落。她送给我的那张卡片的正面是一张照片，照片上是一朵花从一块岩石荒芜贫瘠的斜面上露出来。尽管周围环境恶劣，但这朵精美的花朵却努力活着。卡片里写着："在隆冬季节，我在自己的内心找到了永恒的春天。"后面还有母亲的一句话："春天总是你最爱的季节。春天总在心里。"

这就是我一向乐观生活的母亲的话语。即使是在隆冬季节，她也总能找到春天。

“大雨倾盆了！”有一次，爸爸说。

“雨后的一切都是那样清新好闻！”妈妈回答说。

“可我今天本来想割院子里的草，”父亲回答说，显然感到失望。

“我们需要这场雨，”她反驳说，“现在一切都会更加青翠。”

“可预报说，一天都有雨。”爸爸抱怨说。

“那我们今天下午就去看电影。”妈妈笑着说。

“太贵了。”他反驳道。

“那正是我们应去看日场的原因，”她反驳说。“3 个孩子可以免票入场，我们其他人只需半价。”

回忆起我 12 岁那年一个星期天下午的这种罗克韦尔画风的情景，我想到，在母亲看来，倾盆大雨过后会出现一道彩虹。

在我童年时期和成年历程中，每当我取得成功时，母亲都会送给我一束紫丁香。而在柠檬苦涩，无论加多少糖也做不成柠檬汁时，比如好友去世那天，长久爱情关系结束那天……母亲也会送来紫丁香，上面写着一张与紫丁香的美丽芬芳相媲美的默契的纸条。

“春天总是你最爱的季节。”她总是提醒说。“春天总在心里。”

虽然如此，还是紫丁香让我感到她的话是真的。我从那个 4 月的早晨看到的紫丁香和闻到的芳香意识到，这次回家为什么必要。我需要缓解悲伤、孤独和忧郁。我在思念。我的爱女现在已经长大成人，搬到了一个属于自己的地方。她现在住的相隔好多州，离我有好多英里。我为她感到高兴的同时，也为她不在身边而忧伤。

那天早晨，看到那些紫丁香，使我又想起了母亲的话。它们提醒我，即使内心处在隆冬季节，我也必须记起春天的美丽和紫丁香的芳香。所以，我不再把她看成是远走高飞，而宁愿看成是进入了一个富有精彩体验的新世界。那个世界，春天和冬天一样多。

“爸爸，紫丁香开了！春天来了！”我那天对父亲断然说道。

“嗯，”说着，他瞥了我一眼，一副怀疑的神情。他看到我皱眉，表情变得温和起来。“当然，有可能春天已经来了。”他微笑着安抚说。“毕竟，像你说的那样，那些紫丁香已经开了。”

噢，为春天每年回归的美丽而喝彩！而且紫丁香抑制不住的芬芳提醒我们，春天在我们心里就能找到。

To Be a Lake

When I was young, I was always frustrated, almost everything ending in failure. I became utterly disheartened, sighing miserably all day. Having seen me like that, my father decided to enlighten and cheer me up.

One day, he gave me a cup of water and asked me to taste it. I found it salty. My father said he just put one small spoonful of salt in the cup. And then, he led me to a lake, where he scattered a big handful of salt into the lake, scooped up a spoonful of water and let me taste it again.

He asked, "Does it still taste salty?" "Not at all," I said.

My father said, "Now, you may know the root of your pains: you are just a cup of water, but not a lake. To be a lake and you won't feel miserable any more."

I came to understand my father's motive: That I feel miserable is because my heart is as small as a cup of water without grand ideals and ambitions as a lake.

To be a lake with great ideals and ambitions, your pains of failures and frustrations will be dissolved and melted instantly like the salt scattered into the lake.

做一片湖

年轻时,我处处受挫,几乎做每一件事都以失败而告终。我变得灰心丧气,整日长吁短叹,痛苦不堪。父亲见我这副样子,决定开导我,让我振作起来。

有一天,父亲给了我一杯水,让我尝尝。我尝过后,感觉咸了。父亲说,他只在杯里放了一小勺盐。然后,父亲又带我来到了湖边,在湖里撒了一大把盐后,舀起一勺水,再让我尝尝。

父亲问:"还咸吗?""一点也不咸了。"我说。

父亲说:"现在,你大概知道自己痛苦的根源了,那就是你只是一杯水,而不是一片湖。去作一片湖,你就不会有痛苦的感觉了。"

我终于明白了父亲的良苦用心:自己之所以痛苦,就是因为自己的心还狭小得像一杯水,心中没有湖一样宏大的理想和抱负。

去做一片湖,心怀远大的理想和抱负,失败和挫折的痛苦,就会像撒入湖里的盐一样,瞬间得到化解和消融。

The Candlewick

After moving into a new residence, there was a sudden blackout and darkness in the house before the hostess tidied up.

The hostess just touched the candle and matches when a tap at the door came from outside.

Opening the door, she found it was a small girl, who picking up her little face and asked, "Auntie, is there a candle in your home?"

How so? The first day I just moved the neighbor sent for their boy to borrow something. Weren't they bullying the newcomer? Today I lend them a candle and maybe they would come to borrow onion or garlic. No. No way! So the hostess said, "Oh dear, unluckily, your aunt just moved here and don't prepare the candle." After that, she was about to close the door.

"Auntie, look, my mother asked for me to send it." The small girl, like a conjurer, drew her hand from behind and raised high two thick candles.

Facing the crystal-clear eyes of the girl, the hostess was shocked, weakly leaning on the door with her hands covering her face and having no nerve to look at the girl...

烛 芯

乔迁新居，女主人还没收拾完毕，突然停电了，室内一片漆黑。

女主人刚摸到蜡烛和火柴，门外便传来了"笃笃"的敲门声。

打开门一看，原来是一个小女孩，她仰着小脸问道："阿姨，你家有蜡烛吗？"

怎么？我刚搬来第一天邻家就支使孩子来借东西，这不是欺侮新来的吗？今天借给她家蜡烛，说不定明天又来借葱、借蒜，不，不行！女主人便说："哎呀，真不巧，阿姨刚搬来，没准备蜡烛。"说完，她就准备关门。

"阿姨，你看，我妈妈让我送来的。"小女孩变戏法似的从背后抽手，高高地举着两根粗粗的蜡烛。

面对孩子清莹的眼睛，女主人一下惊呆了，继而无力地倚着门，双手捂面，不敢与孩子对视……

Courage

A father was worried about his son, who was sixteen years old but had no courage at all. So the father decided to call on a Buddhist monk to train his boy.

The Buddhist monk said to the boy's father, "You should leave your son alone here. I'll make him into a real man within three months. However, you can't come to see him during this period."

Three months later, the boy's father returned. The Buddhist monk arranged a boxing match between the boy and an experienced boxer. Each time the fighter struck the boy, he fell down, but at once the boy stood up; and each time a punch knocked him down, the boy stood up again. Several times later, the Buddhist monk asked, "What do you think of your child?"

"What a shame!" the boy's father said. "I never thought he would be so easily knocked down. I needn't have him left here any longer."

"I'm sorry that that's all you see. Don't you see that each time he falls down, he stands up again instead of crying? That's the kind of courage you wanted him to have."

勇 气

一位父亲为儿子担心。儿子16岁了，却没有一点勇气。于是，父亲决定去拜访一位禅师，请他训练儿子。

禅师对男孩的父亲说："你应该让他单独留在这里。不出3个月，我要让他成为一个真正的男子汉。不过，在这段时间，你不能来见他。"

3个月后，男孩的父亲又来见禅师。禅师安排这个男孩和一位经验丰富的拳师进行拳击比赛。拳师每次一出手，男孩就倒在地上，但男孩又马上站起来；每次将他击倒，他

就又站起来。几个回合后，禅师问道："你认为自己的孩子怎么样？"

"真丢人！"男孩的父亲说。"我决没想到他这样不堪一击。我不需要他再留在这里了。"

"很遗憾，你只看到这一点。难道你没看到他每次倒下后并没有哭泣，而是重新站起来了吗？这才是你想要他拥有的那种勇气。"

Gifts from the Heart

A young man while roaming the desert came across a spring of delicious crystal – clear water. The water was so sweet he filled his leather canteen so he could bring some back to a tribal elder who had been his teacher. After a four – day journey he presented the water to the old man who took a deep drink, smiled warmly and thanked his student lavishly for the sweet water. The young man returned to his village with a happy heart.

Later, the teacher let another student taste the water. He spat it out, saying it was awful. It apparently had become stale because of the old leather container. The student challenged his teacher: "Master, the water was foul. Why did you pretend to like it?" The teacher replied, "You only tasted the water. I tasted the gift. The water was simply the container for an act of loving – kindness and nothing could be sweeter."

I think we understand this lesson best when we receive innocent gifts of love from young children. Whether it's a ceramic tray or a macaroni bracelet, the natural and proper response is appreciation and expressed thankfulness. After all, gifts from the heart are really gifts of the heart.

来自内心的礼物

一个小伙子途径沙漠偶遇一泓泉水：水晶般清澈，甘甜可口。于是，他灌了满满一皮水壶，以便也能给曾做过他老师的同族中的一位长者捎些回去。经过4天跋涉，他将水呈给了那位老人。老人畅饮了一口，衷心地笑了，同时大大感谢他这位学生为他捎来这甘甜的泉水。年轻人心情愉快地返回了自己的村子。

老师让另外一名学生品尝这水。这名学生一口吐了出来，说难喝死了。显然，由于那个皮水壶的缘故，水已经变了味。学生去问老师："师傅，那水明明是馊的，你为什么假装喜欢呢？"老师回答道："你尝的只是这水。我尝的是份礼物。那水只不过是表达爱的载体，没有什么比这更甘甜的了。"

我想当我们收到小孩子们表达爱的无恶意的礼物时最能理解老者的话。无论收到的礼物是一只陶盘还是一只通心面做的手镯，自然恰当的反应是欣赏和致谢。毕竟，来自内心的礼物才是真正的礼物。

Tolerance Is Gold

On August 23, 2004, the Athens Olympic horizontal bar final was going on vehemently. Russian Nemov, 28, entered the arena third. He won the audience with the very difficult movement of rising high in the air and grabbing the bar, but when landing, he made a flaw—moving a step forward, so the referee only scored him 9.725 points.

At this moment, in the history of the Olympic Games, a rare instance appeared: the whole audience kept shouting "Nemov," "Nemov," and all rose, brandishing their arms and shooing their outrage to the referee long and loud. The competition was suspended. The fourth player, American Paul Ham, though ready, could only stand on the spot in embarrassment.

Faced with such a scenario, Nemov who had withdrawn stood up from his seat, waved and greeted to the audience hailing him, bowed deeply and thanked them for their love and support. Nemov's magnanimity further kindled the audience's dissatisfaction. More boos rang while some of the audience even threw out their fists with thumbs down making indecent moves.

Against this enormous pressure, a referee was forced to score Nemov 9.762 points. However, such a score could not only appease the audience's discontent, but boos sounded again.

Upon this, Nemov displayed his charisma and magnanimity. He returned to the game and raised his right arm to pay tribute to the audience and deeply bowed to express his gratitude. After that, he extended his right index finger to make a gesture for silence, and then pressed his hands down to request and soothe the audience to remain calm and give Paul Ham a quiet condition.

Nemov's tolerance set the interrupted game for over minutes going on.

In that game Nemov didn't get a gold medal, but he was still a "champion" in the eyes of the audience; he didn't defeat the opponents, but he won the audience with his own tolerance.

宽容是金

2004年8月23日，雅典奥运会男子单杠决赛正在激烈进行。28岁的俄罗斯名将涅莫夫第三个出场。他以连续腾空抓杠的高难度动作征服了全场观众，但在落地时，他出现了一个小小的失误——向前移动了一步，裁判因此只给他打了9.725分。

此刻，奥运史上少有的情况出现了：全场观众不停地喊着"涅莫夫"、"涅莫夫"，而且全都站了起来，不停地挥舞手臂，用持久而响亮的嘘声表达自己对裁判的愤怒。比赛被迫中断，第四个出场的美国选手保罗·哈姆虽已准备就绪，却只能尴尬地站在原地。

面对这种情景，已退场的涅莫夫从座位上站起来，向朝他欢呼的观众挥手致意，并深深地鞠躬，感谢他们对自己的喜欢爱和支持。涅莫夫的大度进一步激发了观众的不满，嘘声更响了，一部分观众甚至伸出双拳，拇指朝下，做出不雅的动作。

面对如此巨大的压力，裁判被迫重新给涅莫夫打了9.762分。可是，这个分数不仅未能平息观众的不满，反而使嘘声再次响成一片。

这时，涅莫夫显示出了他非凡的人格魅力和宽广胸襟。他重新回到赛场，举起右臂向观众致意，深鞠一躬，表示感谢；接着，他伸出右手食指做出噤声的手势，然后将双手下压，请求和劝慰观众保持冷静，给保罗·哈姆一个安静的比赛环境。

涅莫夫的宽容，让中断了十几分钟的比赛得以继续进行。

在那次比赛中，涅莫夫虽然没有拿到金牌，但他仍是观众心目中的“冠军”；他没有打败对手，但他以自己的宽容征服了观众。

To Leave the Grudge Behind

Mandela was put into prison for leading to fight against the whites' policy of apartheid. The white ruler imprisoned him in a deserted Ruben Island in the Atlantic Ocean for 27 years. At that time Mandela was already old, but the white ruler still cruelly maltreated him like a young prisoner.

Mandela was detained in a"zinc-sheeted room' of the total concentration camp. In the daytime he smashed the large blocks into the stone stocks in the quarry. Sometimes he went into the icy sea to fish for kelp or mined the lime—every morning he lined up with the other prisoners to the quarry, and then was untied the fetters and dug the limestone with a sharp pick and shovel in the large quarry. Because he was an important criminal, Mandela had three guards altogether. They were not friendly, always finding various reasons to maltreat him.

No one imagined after he was out of prison and elected president in 1991, Mandela's action in his inauguration shocked the whole world.

After the presidential inauguration began, Mandela got up and addressed to welcome the guests. He in turns introduced the political leaders from the countries of the world, then he said he was deeply honored to receive so many distinguished guests, but what he was most pleased was the three guards who guarded him first in Ruben Island prison also turned up. Immediately, he invited them to get up and introduced them to all the guests.

Mandela's open mind and spirit of tolerance made those white people who had cruelly maltreated him for 27 years ashamed while all the people present were filled with deep esteem. Watching the aged Mandela stood up slowly and respectfully saluted the three guards who had guarded him. All the guests present and the whole world calmed down.

Later, Mandela explained to his friends that when he was young, he was quick-tempered and irascible. It was the life in prison that made him learn how to control his emotion, so he could survive. The years in prison gave him time and encouragement and made him learn how to deal with the pains he had encountered. He said that thanksgiving and tolerance often originate from the pain and tribulation, so we must train through the terribly strong willpower.

On the day he was released, he was calm, "When I walk out of the prison to the prison gate leading to freedom, I have made it clear that if I can't leave the grief and grudge behind, in fact I are still in prison. "

把怨恨留在身后

曼德拉因为领导反对白人种族隔离的政策而入狱，白人统治者把他关在荒凉的大西洋小岛罗本岛上达27年。当时曼德拉年事已高，但白人统治者依然像对待年轻犯人一样残酷虐待他。

曼德拉被关在总集中营一个“锌皮房”里，白天将采石场的大石块碎成石料。他有时要下到冰冷的海水里捞海带，有时干采石灰的活儿——每天早晨排队到采石场，然后被解开脚镣,在一个很大的石灰石场里用尖镐和铁锹挖石灰石。因为曼德拉是要犯,所以有三个看守。他们对他并不友好,总是寻找各种理由虐待他。

谁也没想到,1991 年曼德拉出狱当选总统后,在就职典礼上的一个举动震惊了整个世界。

总统就职仪式开始后,曼德拉起身致辞,欢迎来宾。他依次介绍了来自世界各国的政要,然后说,能接待这么多尊贵的客人,他深感荣幸,但他最高兴的是,当初在罗本岛监狱看守他的 3 名狱警也能到场。随即,他邀请他们起身,并把他们介绍给大家。

曼德拉的博大胸襟和宽容精神,令那些残酷虐待了他 27 年的白人汗颜,也让所有到场的人肃然起敬。看着年迈的曼德拉慢慢站起,恭敬地向三个曾关押他的看守致敬,在场的所有来宾以至整个世界,都静了下来。

后来,曼德拉向朋友们解释说,自己年轻时性子很急,脾气暴躁,正是狱中生活使他学会了控制情绪,因此才活了下来。牢狱岁月给了他时间与鼓励,也使他学会了如何处理自己遭遇的痛苦。他说,感恩与宽容常常源自痛苦与磨难,必须通过极强的毅力来训练。

获释当天,他心情平静:“当我走出牢房,迈过通往自由的牢门时,我已经清楚,如果自己不能把悲痛与怨恨留在身后,那我其实仍在牢里。”

Sand and Stone

Two friends were walking through the desert. During some point of the journey they had an argument, and one friend slapped the other one in the face.

The one who got slapped was hurt, but without saying anything, wrote in the sand, "Today my best friend slapped me in the face."

They kept on walking until they found an oasis, where they decided to take a bath. The one who had been slapped got struck in the mire and started drowning, but the friend saved him.

After he recovered from the near drowning, he wrote on a stone, "Today my best friend saved my life."

The friend who had slapped and saved his friend asked him, "After I hurt you, you wrote in the sand and now you write on a stone. Why?"

The other friend replied, "When someone hurts us, we should write it down in the sand where winds of forgiveness can erase it away. But when someone does something good for us, we must engrave it in stone where no wind ever erases it."

沙与石

两个朋友穿越沙漠。途中,他们发生了争执。其中一位朋友打了另一位朋友一耳光。

被打的人非常伤心,但他什么也没有说,只是在沙地上写道:“今天我最好的朋友扇了我一耳光。”

他们继续前行，终于发现了一片绿洲。他们决定在那里洗个澡。被打过耳光的那位朋友陷入了泥潭，眼前就要被淹死，但那位朋友救了他。

缓过劲来后，他在一块石头上写道：“今天我最好的朋友救了我一命。”

那位打过耳光又救了他的朋友问：“我伤害了你，你把字写在了沙地上，现在你却把字刻在了石头上。这是为什么？”

另一位朋友回答说：“当某人伤害我们时，我们应该把它写在沙子里，宽恕的风会把它抹去。但当某人为我们做好事时，我们必须把它刻在石头上，任何风都不会将它抹去。”

The Precious Stone Within

A wise woman who was traveling in the mountain found a precious stone in a stream.

The next day she met another traveler who was hungry, and the wise woman opened her bag to share her food. The hungry traveler saw the precious stone and asked the woman to give it to him. She did so without hesitation.

The traveler left, rejoicing in his good fortune. He knew the stone was worth enough to give him security for a lifetime.

But a few days later he came back to return the stone to the wise woman. "I've been thinking," he said. "I know how valuable this stone is, but I give it back in the hope that you give me something even more precious. Give me what you have within you that enabled you to give me this stone."

Sometimes it's not the wealth you have but what's inside you that others need.

内心的宝石

一个聪明的女人在山里旅行时在山涧里发现一颗宝石。

第二天，她遇到了另一个饥饿的旅行者。聪明女人打开包，和他分享自己的食物。饥饿的旅行者看到了那颗宝石，让那女人把宝石送给他。她毫不犹豫就送给了他。

那个旅行者离开后，对自己的好运乐不可支。他知道那颗宝石足够他一辈子高枕无忧。

但几天后，他又回来把宝石还给了这个聪明的女人。“我一直在想，”他说，“我知道这颗宝石是多么珍贵，但我把它归还，希望你给我更珍贵的东西。我想要你把宝石给我时你内心拥有的那种东西。”

有时，别人需要的并不是你的财富，而是你内心拥有的东西。

A Beautiful Prayer

I asked God to take away my habit.
God said, "No. It is not for me to take away, but for you to give up."
I asked God to make my handicapped child whole.
God said, "No. His spirit is whole while his body is only temporary."
I asked God to grant me patience.
God said, "No. Patience is a byproduct of tribulations; it isn't granted, it is learned."
I asked God to give me happiness.
God said, "No. I give you blessings; happiness is up to you."
I asked God to spare my pain.
God said, "No. Suffering draws you apart from worldly cares and brings you closer to me."
I asked God to make my spirit grow.
God said, "No. You must grow on your own! But I will prune you to make you fruitful."
I asked God for all things that I might enjoy life.
God said, "No. I will give you life, so that you may enjoy all things."
I asked God to help me LOVE others, as much as He loves me.
God said, "Ah, you have the idea at last."
This day is yours. Don't throw it away. You will be blessed.

美丽的祈祷

我请求上帝带走我的习惯。
上帝说:"不,不是我来带走,而是你要放弃。"
我请求上帝让我残疾的孩子完整无损。
上帝说:"不,他的精神完整,身体是暂时的。"
我请求上帝赐给我耐心。
上帝说:"不,耐心是磨难的副产品,它不是赐予,而是学来的。"
我请求上帝给我幸福。
上帝说:"不,我给你祝福,幸福取决于你。"
我请求上帝免除我的痛苦。
上帝说:"不。痛苦让你远离尘世的烦恼,离我更近。"
我请求上帝让我的灵魂成长。
上帝说:"不,你必须自己成长!但我会给你剪枝,让你硕果累累。"
我请求上帝给我一切,让我能享受人生。
上帝说:"不,我会给你生命,以便你能享受一切。"
我请求上帝帮我爱别人,就像他爱我一样。
上帝说:"啊,你终于有了主意。"
这一天是你的,不要抛弃它,你就会幸福。

The Real Meaning of Peace

There once was a king who offered a prize to the artist who would paint the best picture of peace. Many artists tried. The king looked at all the pictures. But there were only two he really liked, and he had to choose between them. One picture was of a calm lake. The lake was a perfect mirror for peaceful towering mountains all around it. Overhead was a blue sky with fluffy white clouds. All who saw this picture thought that it was a perfect picture of peace.

The other picture had mountains, too. But these were rugged and bare. Above was an angry sky, from which rain fell and in which lightning played. Down the side of the mountain tumbled a foaming waterfall. This did not look peaceful at all.

But when the king looked closely, he saw behind the waterfall a tiny bush growing in a crack in the rock. In the bush a mother bird had built her nest. There, in the midst of the rush of angry water, sat the mother bird on her nest—in perfect peace. Which picture do you think won the prize? The king chose the second picture. Do you know why?

"Because," explained the king, "peace does not mean to be in a place where there is no noise, trouble, or hard work. Peace means to be in the midst of all those things and still be calm in your heart. That is the real meaning of peace."

宁静的真谛

从前有一个国王,悬赏能画出最好的宁静画的画家。很多画家都进行了尝试。国王看了所有的作品,但只有两幅,他真正喜欢,他必须从中选择。一幅画中是一片宁静的湖,四周群山环绕,湖泊就是一面完美的镜子。蓝天之上白云飘飘,每个看到这幅画的人都认为这真是一幅完美的宁静画。

另一幅画也有山脉。但这些山脉崎岖不平,光秃秃的。上面是乌云滚滚的天空,大雨如注,闪电雷鸣,一条飞瀑从山的一侧倾泻而下。这看起来一点都不宁静。但国王仔细看时,却看到瀑布后面在岩石的一条裂缝中长着一个小小的灌木丛。灌木丛中,一只母鸟极其安静地卧在巢上。你认为哪幅画能赢得悬赏?国王选择了第二幅。你知道为什么吗?

国王解释说:"这是因为宁静并不是指这个地方没有噪音、烦恼和辛劳。宁静就是置于所有那些东西之中,你心里仍然平静。这才是宁静的真谛。"

I'm the White Cloud and You're the Blue Sky

At the age of three, she unexpectedly began to care about life and death. One day, she stared at her mother worriedly in the bathroom, "After you're old someday, you will die soon, won't you?"

Her mother was first stunned and then turned to comfort her, "It's still quite far away!"

The next morning she woke and looked around worriedly, "Mom, if you die, grandparents die and

I die, too, how about this room? Will it be empty? Who else will move in?"

"Your baby can live in it," said her mother.

She drew inferences smugly, "Oh, I see. After my baby dies, my baby's baby can live on in!"

She felt a sense of relief until her mother forced a nod...

She grew up happily and joyfully as if she had forgotten this subject. At the age of four and a half years, she resumed that talk. That day tipping her little head, she asked her mother in the car, "Where will people go after they die?"

"Their bodies descend to earth while their souls ascend to the heaven."

"Mom, you go to the heaven at first when you die. And when I die, I go to the heaven, too. Then I can find you there."

"Alright."

"Mom, you're a gray cloud. I'm a white cloud. We can play hand in hand in the sky watching birds flying."

"But after I ascend to the heaven, you'll go there after a long time. How can you find me?"

"I will knock at the clouds one by one asking, 'Are you my mom?' If you hear my voice, you won't surely have the heart to ignore me."

"Very good!" her mother responded vaguely.

But this little girl went on saying, "Mom, otherwise, I'm the white cloud and you're the blue sky, which is so vast that I can be in your arms as soon as I go up there!"

Her mother couldn't restrain herself any longer and took her daughter tightly in her arms...

At her age of four, we have lived for many four-years. Can we look for our mothers cloud by cloud?

我是白云，你是蓝天

3岁时，她突然开始关心生死问题。一天，她在卫生间担心地看着妈妈："将来你老了，很快就会死的，是吗？"

妈妈一愣，转而安慰她："那还是很远很远的事呢！"

第二天早晨一醒来，她忧心忡忡地环顾四周："妈妈，如果你死了，爷爷奶奶死了，我也死了，这间屋怎么办呢？不是空了吗？谁来住呢？"

妈妈说："你的宝宝可以住呀！"

她自鸣得意地举一反三："噢，我知道了，等我的宝宝死了，我宝宝的宝宝还可以住！"

妈妈勉强点了点头，她这才如释重负……

她快快乐乐地成长着，好像忘掉了这个话题。到了4岁半时，她又旧话重提。那一天，坐在车上，她歪着脑袋问妈妈："人死了，会去哪里呢？"

"身体入土，灵魂上天。"

"妈妈，你死了先上天，等我死了也上天，就可以找到你了。"

"好吧。"

"妈妈，你是一朵灰色的云。我是一朵白色的云。我们手拉手在天上玩，看鸟飞。"

"可是，妈妈上天后，你要过很久很久才上天，怎么找到我呢？"

"我会一朵云、一朵云地敲门问：'你是我的妈妈吗？'你要是听到了，肯定不忍心不理我。"

妈妈含糊地应着："真好！"

可是，那小姑娘还意犹未尽："妈妈，要不，我是白云你是蓝天吧。蓝天很大很大，我一上去就在你怀里了！"

妈妈实在忍不住，一把将女儿紧紧抱在了怀里……

她4岁，而我们已经过了好多个4岁，我们会一朵云一朵云地去找妈妈吗？

Roses Are the Smiling Face of the Earth

All over my garden I've planted nothing but roses, fragrant and ablaze with color like sunset clouds when looked at from afar. I'd be very happy if anyone of my visiting friends should desire to pick and take some for their homes. I trust that any friend of mine carrying the rose would vanish into the distance feeling that his emotions had been rekindled.

A close friend came for a visit the other day. I know her to be a lover of flowers and plants. And for that reason I told her at her departure that she should pick a bunch of roses to grace her boudoir. I promised that the scent of the roses would be wafted far, far away.

Tiptoeing into the garden in high spirits, the girl friend of mine sniffed here and smelt there, but in the end she didn't pick a single rose. I said, "There are so many of them that she can pick as many as she'd like to; I'm not a florist and don't make a living out of them." With that I raised the scissors.

"It hurts me to cut such beautiful roses," with her hands clutching at my sleeves, she exhorted me. "Never cut them. Roses are the smiling face of the earth, so who can be so iron-hearted as to destroy a smile so intoxicating?

My mind was thoroughly boggled: the ugly earth, the humble earth, the plain earth—it is only because of the roses that it reveals an amazing and bright smile, and it is for the sake of that smile that it wins the care and pity of people.

玫瑰是泥土的笑脸

我在花园里种了芬芳的玫瑰花，远远望去，像一片燃烧的晚霞。我想等朋友们来做客时，让他们带一些玫瑰回家。我相信朋友们捧着火红的玫瑰渐渐消失在远方，一定能被重新点燃往日的情怀。

有一天，一位非常要好的女友来探望我，我知道她平常最喜爱花花草草。她临别时，我告诉她说，采一束玫瑰，点缀你的闺房吧。我保证这些玫瑰肯定会芳香四溢。

女友轻手轻脚，跨进了花园，东闻闻西嗅嗅，神采飞扬，就是不肯采摘。我说："没关系，多的是，我又不是花店老板，不靠玫瑰赚钱的。"说完，我就举起了剪刀。

"这么美丽的玫瑰剪下来，让人心疼。"她抓紧我的袖子叮咛。"千万不能剪啊，玫瑰是泥土的笑脸，谁能忍心毁坏美得醉人的微笑呢？"

我的灵魂猛然一惊：丑陋的泥土、卑微的泥土、朴素的泥土，因为玫瑰，露出了惊艳一笑，正因为这一笑，才赢得了人们的爱惜。

I Have a Dream

I say to you today, my friends, that in spite of the difficulties and frustrations of the moment, I still have a dream. It is a dream deeply rooted in the American dream.

I have a dream that one day this nation will rise up and live out the true meaning of its creed: "We hold these truths to be self-evident: that all men are created equal."

I have a dream that one day on the red hills of Georgia the sons of former slaves and the sons of former slave owners will be able to sit down together at a table of brotherhood; I have a dream that one day even the state of Mississippi, a desert state, sweltering with the heat of injustice and oppression, will be transformed into an oasis of freedom and justice.

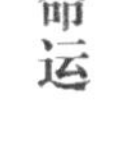

I have a dream that my four children will one day live in a nation where they won't be judged by the color of their skin but by the content of their character.

I have a dream today.

I have a dream that one day the state of Alabama, whose governor's lips are presently dripping with the words of interposition and nullification, will be transformed into a situation where little black boys and black girls will be able to join hands with little white boys and white girls and walk together as sisters and brothers.

I have a dream today.

I have a dream that one day every valley shall be exalted, every hill and mountain shall be made low, the rough places will be made plain, and the crooked places will be made straight, and the glory of the Lord shall be revealed, and all flesh shall see it together.

This is our hope. This is the faith with which I return to the South. With this faith we will be able to hew out of the mountain of despair a stone of hope. With this faith we will be able to transform the jangling discords of our nation into a beautiful symphony of brotherhood. With this faith we will be able to work together, to pray together, to struggle together, to go to jail together, to stand up for freedom together, knowing that we will be free one day. This will be the day when all of God's children will be able to sing with a new meaning, "My country, 'tis of thee, sweet land of liberty, of thee I sing. Land where my fathers died, land of the pilgrim's pride, from every mountainside, let freedom ring." And if America is to be a great nation, this must become true.

So let freedom ring from the prodigious hilltops of New Hampshire. Let freedom ring from the mighty mountains of New York. Let freedom ring from the heightening Alleghenies of Pennsylvania! Let freedom ring from the snowcapped Rockies of Colorado! Let freedom ring from the curvaceous peaks of California! But not only that; let freedom ring from Stone Mountain of Georgia! Let freedom ring from Lookout Mountain of Tennessee! Let freedom ring from every hill and every molehill of Mississippi. From every mountainside, let freedom ring.

When we let freedom ring, when we let it ring from every village and every hamlet, from every state and every city, we will be able to speed up that day when all of God's children, black men and white men, Jews and Gentiles, Protestants and Catholics, will be able to join hands and sing in the words of the old Negro spiritual, "Free at last! Free at last! Thank God Almighty, we are free at last!"

我有一个梦想

朋友们，今天我对你们说，尽管我们会遇到种种困难和挫折，但我仍有一个梦想，它深深地扎根在美国人的梦想中。

我梦想有一天，这个国家会站立起来，真正表现出其信条的真谛："我们信奉的真理不言自明:人人生而平等。”

我梦想有一天,在佐治亚州的红山上,奴隶的后代与奴隶主的后代能兄弟般坐在一起;我梦想有一天,甚至密西西比这个正义匿迹、压迫成风、热浪逼人的地方,也将变成自由与公正的绿洲。

我梦想有一天,我的4个孩子将在一个不是根据他们的肤色、而是根据他们的品行来衡量他们的国度里生活。

今天我有一个梦想。

我梦想有一天,种族歧视行为泛滥的阿拉巴马州能有所改变,尽管该州州长仍然满口异议反对联邦法令,但有朝一日,那里的黑人男孩和女孩将能和白人的男孩和女孩亲密无间、携手并进。

今天我有一个梦想。

我梦想有一天,幽谷上升,高山下降,崎岖之路变成通途,圣光披露,满照人间。

这就是我们的希望。我怀着这种信念回到南方。有了这个信念,我们将能从绝望之巅劈出一块希望之石。有了这个信念,我们将能把这个国家种族不和的喧嚣变成一曲展现兄弟情义的优美乐章。怀着这个信念,我们将能共同努力、共同祈祷、共同斗争、共同坐牢、共同维护自由;因为我们知道,终有一天,我们会自由。在自由到来的那一天,上帝的所有儿女们将以全新的意义共同歌唱这支歌:“我的祖国,美丽的自由之乡,我为你歌唱,你是我父辈逝去的地方,你是最初移民的骄傲,让自由之声响彻每一座山峦。”如果美国要成为一个伟大的国家,必须实现这个梦想。

让自由之声从新罕布什尔州的巍巍山顶上响起来!让自由之声在纽约州的茫茫群山上响起来!让自由之声从宾夕法尼亚州高耸入云的阿勒格尼山上响起来!让自由之声从科罗拉多州白雪覆盖的落基山上响起来!让自由之声从加利福尼亚州崎岖不平的山地上响起来。不仅如此,还要让自由之声从佐治亚州的石山上响起来!让自由之声从田纳西州的了望山上响起来!让自由之声在密西西比州的每一座丘陵响起来!让自由之声从每一个山坡响起来!

当这一天来临,当我们让自由之声回响,让自由之声从每一个大大小小的村落、每一个州和每一座城市响起来时,我们将能够加速这一天的到来。到那时,上帝的所有儿女们,黑人和白人,犹太人和异教徒,新教徒和天主教徒,都将携手合唱古老的黑人灵歌:“终于自由了!终于自由了!感谢万能的上帝,我们终于自由了!”

The Gold in the Orchard

There was once a farmer who had a fine olive orchard. He was very hardworking, and the farm always prospered under his care. But he knew that his three sons despised the farm work, and were eager to make wealth, through adventure.

When the farmer was old, and felt that his time had come to die, he called the three sons to him and said, “My sons, there is a pot of gold hidden in the olive orchard. Dig for it, if you wish it.”

The sons tried to get him to tell them in what part of the orchard the gold was hidden; but he would tell them nothing more.

After the farmer was dead, the sons went to work to find the pot of gold; since they did not know where the hiding-place was, they agreed to begin in a line, at one end of the orchard, and to dig until one of them should find the money.

They dug until they had turned up the soil from one end of the orchard to the other, round the tree-roots and between them. But no pot of gold was to be found. It seemed as if someone must have stolen it, or as if the farmer had been wandering in his wits. The three sons were bitterly disappointed to have all their work for nothing.

The next olive season, the olive trees in the orchard bore more fruit than they had ever given; when it was sold, it gave the sons a whole pot of gold!

And when they saw how much money had come from the orchard, they suddenly understood what the wise father had meant when he said, "There is gold hidden in the orchard. Dig for it, if you wish it."

果园里的金子

从前有一个农民,他有一座漂亮的橄榄园。他非常勤劳,而且农场在他的照管下蒸蒸日上。可他知道自己的三个儿子瞧不起农活,都迫不及待想通过冒险发家致富。

这个农民上了年岁,感到死期快要来临时,将三个儿子叫到身边说:"儿子们,橄榄园里藏有一罐金子。想要就去挖吧。"

儿子们想让父亲告诉他们金子藏在果园的哪一块地方,可他什么也没再给他们说。

那个农民死后,三个儿子就开始挖地,想找到那罐金子;因为他们不知道金子藏在什么地方,所以他们一致同意排成一行从果园的一头开始挖起,直到其中一人挖到金子为止。

他们挖啊挖,从果园的一头一直挖到了另一头,果树周围和果树之间也都挖到了,可还是没有找到那罐金子。看来一定是有人已经把那罐金子偷走了,要么就是他们的父亲一直在异想天开。三个儿子对他们白干了一场,感到大失所望。

到了第二年的橄榄季节,果园里的橄榄树结出的果子比以往的都多;卖完果子后,三个儿子赚了整整一罐金子!

他们从果园里得到这么多钱后,突然明白了聪明的父亲所说的"果园里藏有金子,想要就去挖吧"这句话的含义。

The Weight of a Snowflake

"Tell me the weight of a snowflake," a titmouse asked a wild dove.

"Nothing more than nothing," was the answer.

"In that case I must tell you a marvelous story," the titmouse said.

"I sat on the branch of a fir tree, close to its trunk, when it began to snow-not heavily, not in a

raging blizzard—no, just like a dream, without a sound and without any violence. Since I did not have anything better to do, I counted the snowflakes settling on the twigs and needles of my branch. Their number was exactly 8, 865, 220. When 8, 865, 221st dropped onto the branch, nothing more than nothing, as you say—the branch broke off."

Having said that, the titmouse flew away.

The dove, since Noah's time an authority on the matter, thought about the story for a while, and finally said to herself, "Perhaps there is only one person's voice lacking for peace to come to the world."

雪花的重量

"告诉我雪花有多重。"一只山雀问野鸽子。

"几乎没什么重量。"鸽子回答说。

"那样的话,我必须告诉你一件不可思议的事儿。"山雀说。

"我卧在冷杉树上,离树干很近。这时,天开始下起了雪,不是很大,不是狂风暴雪,不是,就像一个梦似的,悄无声息,一点都不厉害。因为无事可做,我就数起了落在树杈枝叶上的雪花。它们的确切数目是 8865220 片。你说雪花几乎没什么重量,但当第 8865221 片雪花落在树枝上时,树枝就折断了。"

说完,山雀就飞走了。

从诺亚时期就已是各种问题权威人士的鸽子,想了一会儿这个故事,最后自言自语说:"也许让和平来到世上,再有一个人的声音就够了。"

Four Seasons of a Tree

There was a man who had four sons. He wanted his sons to learn to not judge things too quickly. So he sent them each on a quest, in turn, to go and look at a pear tree that was a great distance away. The first son went in the winter, the second in the spring, the third in summer, and the youngest son in the fall.

When they had all gone and come back, he called them together to describe what they had seen. The first son said that the tree was ugly, bent, and twisted. The second son said no. It was covered with green buds and full of promise. The third son disagreed. He said it was laden with blossoms that smelled so sweet and looked so beautiful, it was the most graceful thing he had ever seen. The last son disagreed with all of them. He said it was ripe and drooping with fruit, full of life and fulfillment.

The man then explained to his sons that they were all right, because they had each seen but one season in the tree's life.

He told them that you cannot judge a tree, or a person, by only one season, and that the essence of who they are and the pleasure, joy, and love that come from that life can only be measured at the end, when all the seasons are up.

If you give up when it's winter, you will miss the promise of your spring, the beauty of your summer, and fulfillment of your fall. Don't let the pain of one season destroy the joy of all the rest.

树的四季

从前一个人有四个儿子。他想让儿子们学会不对事情匆匆作出判断，就让儿子们轮流去远方观察一棵梨树。大儿子冬天去，二儿子春天去，三儿子夏天去，小儿子秋天去。

当他们都已看过回到家时，父亲把他们叫到一起，让他们描述一下看到的情形。大儿子说那棵树很难看，弯弯扭扭的。二儿子说不是这样，树上满是绿芽，充满了希望。三儿子意见不一，说那棵树开满了花，芳香扑鼻，非常漂亮，那是他见过的最美的东西。小儿子不同意他们三人的看法，他说梨树成熟了，上面缀满了果实，充满了生机和成就感。

父亲向儿子们解释说他们说的都对，因为他们每人看到的只是那棵树一生中的一个季节。他告诉他们，不要仅凭一个时段来判断一棵树或一个人，他们的本质生命中的快乐、喜悦和爱只能到最后，当所有的季节都结束时才能去评判。

如果你在冬天就放弃，那将会错过春天的希望、夏天的美丽和秋天的收获。不要让一个季节的痛苦毁掉一年所有其他的欢乐。

The Upwind Fragrance

One day, Ananda sat quietly alone in the garden when he suddenly smelled the scent of flowers wafting with the evening wind.

When the wind usually blows the scent of flowers, you can't always smell the fragrance because you're unsteady in mood. While you calm down, the wind doesn't necessarily come, so you can't smell any scent.

Then one evening, Ananda was particularly quiet in mind, and it was spring—the season with the most fragrant flowers, and spring breeze was slowly wafting along. So with so many concerted reasons, Ananda smelt the most beautiful floral scent in his lifetime.

The fragrance encircled Ananda, running through him, and then flowing to an unknown distance. These scent kept him sit still from leaving from dusk to night and made him so moved.

In such a sensation, Ananda felt his heart wafting up with the scent; he thought of some problems that had never been considered: plants are fragrant when they are in bloom; are there the fragrant plants even without blossoming? Flowers are restricted to a short-lived karma and are there flowers often fragrant? Even if the spring flowers waft so far, they also have an extension and are there scents pervading all over the world? All flowers all waft downwind and are there fragrance that can be wafted upwind?

Thinking about these problems, Ananda was so enthralled that he couldn't be calm in the next few days. One day, Ananda sat spellbound in the fragrance of flowers when Buddha passed by where he sat quietly and asked, "Why are you not at ease?" Ananda asked his teacher of the abstruse questions that puzzled him.

Buddha replied, "The one who keeps to mitzvah is not necessarily fragrant in bloom and fruit and who will be also fragrant even without the flower of wisdom. The heart lost in Buddhist meditation needn't seek for fragrance in the karma, for he forever keeps merry fragrance within himself. The one

who blooms wisdom will permeate his fragrance all over the world, not to be confined by seasons. A person who develops sila, meditation and prajna through his own heart can waft the fragrance of his personality even in adversity."

At this, Ananda was so moved.

Buddha said affably, "Not only do devotees smell the fragrance of the garden but also blossom in their hearts—the fragrance with virtue. Thus no matter where he lives, in the city or in the mountains, all the people will smell his scent!"

If our mind is a garden, isn't any day in our life the most beautiful blooming season?

If our hearts are filled with spring breeze, isn't anytime in our life the best spring?

逆风飘香

有一天,阿难独自在花园里静坐,突然闻到了随着黄昏吹来的风飘过来的一阵阵花香。

平常有风吹着花香时,由于心绪波动,不一定能闻到花香。当心静下来时,又不一定有风吹来,所以也闻不到花香。

那个黄昏,阿难的心情特别宁静,又是春天——花朵最香的时节,正好春风缓缓吹送。在这么多原因的配合下,阿难闻到了有生以来最美妙的花香。

花香围绕着阿难,花香穿流过他的身心,然后流向不可知的远方。这些花香使阿难从黄昏静坐到夜里舍不得离开,这些花香也使得阿难非常感动。

在感动中,阿难宁静的心也随花香飘动起来,他想到了一些从未想过的问题:草木都是开花时才会香,有没有不开花就会香的草木呢?花朵送香都限定在一个短暂的因缘里,有没有经常芬芳的花朵呢?春花的香再远也有一个范围,有没有弥漫全世界的香呢?所有的花都是顺风飘送,有没有逆风飘香呢?

阿难想着这些问题,想到入神,竟然使他在接下来的几天无法静心。有一天,阿难又坐在花香中出神,佛陀走过他静坐的地方,就问他:"你的心情波动,到底是为了什么呢?"阿难就把自己苦思而难解的问题请教了老师。

佛陀说:"守戒律的人,不一定要开花结果才有芬芳,即使没有智慧之花,也会芳香。有禅定的心,就不必要在因缘里寻找芬芳,他的内心永远保持喜悦的花香。智慧开花的人,他的芬芳会弥漫整个世界,不会被时节范围所限制。一个透过内在培养戒、定、慧的品质的人,即使在逆境里也可以飘送人格的芬芳!"

阿难听了,感动不已。

佛陀和蔼地说:"修行人不只要闻花园的花香,也要在自己的内心开花——有德行的香。这样,不管他居住在城市或山林,所有的人都会闻到他的花香!"

如果我们的内心就是一个花园,人生的哪一天不是最美的花季呢?

如果我们的内心春风洋溢,人生的哪个时候不是最好的春天呢?

The Moon Still Shines

Shirley worked in Chicago. Every day she commuted between the suburban home and the office. She noticed the driver was a particular man. Whenever the passengers got on the bus, he would smile at them. All the people smiled back at him wonderfully.

However, Shirley also noticed there was a passenger never smiled back at the driver. He wore a bushy beard; he often coughed rudely as he got on the bus and forced the other to offer the seat to him in a loud voice.

All this didn't make the driver stop his smile at the passengers. Instead, the "bearded" man seemed never to see the smile.

This aroused Shirley's interest. Once, she asked the driver, "Sir, may I ask why don't you throw that damned 'bearded' man out of the bus?"

The driver looked at Shirley and said, "He's my guest."

"Then you take back your smile at least. Don't be so kind to him!"

"Let me tell you about my puppy," the driver said patiently, "each time the moon shines, the puppy would bark at it incessantly."

Hearing this, Shirley was puzzled and asked, "What can this dog and the moon account for?"

The driver said, "It keeps barking, but the moon still shines."

月光依然照耀

雪莉在芝加哥工作。每天,她搭乘公共汽车往返于工作单位和城郊的家。她注意到司机是个很特别的人,每当有乘客上车,他都朝他们微笑。大家都回敬那位司机一个个美好的笑容。

然而,雪莉也注意到,有一个乘客始终没有朝司机笑过。他留着浓密的大胡子,常常一边上车一边粗鲁地咳嗽,还大着嗓门强迫别人给他让座。

这一切都没让司机停止送上他的微笑。相反,"大胡子"男人似乎从来看不见那笑容。

这引起了雪莉的兴趣。有一次,她问司机:"先生,请问您为什么不把那讨厌的'大胡子'男人扔出车外?"

司机望着雪莉,说:"他是我的客人。"

"那您至少收回您的笑容,别对他那么和善呀!"

"让我来告诉您我家小狗的事吧,"司机很有耐心地说,"那小家伙每次有月光照耀,都会对月亮吠个不停。"

雪莉听了很疑惑,问:"这狗和月亮的事又能说明什么呢?"

司机说:"虽然它一直吠叫,但月光依然照耀啊。"

Looking for the Gold

At one time Andrew Carnegie was the wealthiest man in America. He came to America from his native Scotland when he was a small boy, did a variety ofodd jobs, and eventually ended up as the largest steel manufacturer in the United States. At one time he had forty - three millionaires working for him. In those days a millionaire was a rare person; conservatively speaking, a million dollars in those days would be equivalent to at least twenty million dollars today.

One reporter asked Carnegie how he came to hire forty - three millionaires.

Carnegie responded, "You got to remember that those men have not been millionaires when they started working for him but have become millionaires only as a result."

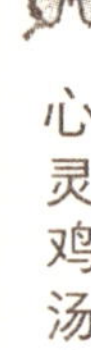

The reporter's next question was, "Well, how did you develop these men to become so valuable to you that you paid them that much money?"

Carnegie replied, "People are developed the same way gold is mined. When gold is mined, several tons of dirt and stone must be moved first to get an ounce of gold; but one goes into the mine not looking for dirt but gold."

Like everything else, the more good qualities we look for in our people, the more good qualities we are going to find.

寻找金子

安德鲁·卡内基曾是美国最富有的人。他小时候从故乡苏格兰来到美国，打过各种零工，最终成为全美最大的钢铁制造商。43 名百万富翁曾为他工作过。当时，百万富翁如凤毛麟角。保守来说，当时的一百万美元至少相当于今天的两千万美元。

一名记者问卡内基是怎样雇佣 43 位百万富翁的。

他回答说："你要记住，那些人开始为我工作时并不是百万富翁，但为我工作后就成了百万富翁。"

记者又问道："那你是怎样培养这些人，使他们成为有用之才，并付给他们那么多钱的呢？"

卡内基回答说："培养人才就像淘金。淘金时，先要洗去几吨泥石，才能淘到一盎司金子。但到矿山要找的不是污泥，而是金子。"

像所有其他事情一样，我们从自己身上寻找的优良品质越多，找到的优良品质就越多。

The Fate of the Two Trees

The farmer planted two fruit seedlings of the same size at the same time. The first one tried its best to absorb nutrients from underground, reserved, moistened every branch, accumulated its strength and quietly planned how to improve itself and grow up. The other also tried to absorb nutrients from

underground, condensed and planned how to bloom and bear fruit.

The following spring, the first tree burst into the delicate sprouts and grew up with all its might. When the second one just burst into the tender leaves, it jumped at squeezing out the buds. The first had the clear target and strong endurance, so it luxuriated quickly. The second bloomed and bore fruit each year. At first the farmer was really surprised to appreciate it very much. But because when not yet ripe, it took the responsibility of blooming and bearing fruit, this tree was exhausted to bend itself, its fruit was sour and often brought a group of children's stone attacks. Furthermore, the children would climb onto its frail body to damage its self-esteem and trunk when they were plundering the fruit.

Time flew by, and finally one day, the strong tree that hadn't bloomed for a long time breezily burst out the buds. Because of adequate nutrients and strong body, it bore the large and sweet fruit. Meanwhile, the tree that had been eager to bloom and bear fruit had become dead wood. The farmer sighed in surprise, cut down the thin dead wood and used it as firewood.

Sometimes the people who are not eager to project themselves are precisely the most competitive, most dynamic and most promising ones.

两棵树的命运

农夫在地里同时种了两棵一样大小的果树苗。第一棵树拼命地从地下吸收养料，储备起来，滋润每个枝干，积蓄力量，默默地盘算着怎样完善自身，向上生长。另一棵树也拼命地从地下吸收养料，凝聚起来，开始盘算着开花结果。

第二年春天，第一棵树便吐出了嫩芽，憋着劲向上长。另一棵树刚吐出嫩叶，便迫不及待地挤出花蕾。第一棵树目标明确，忍耐力强，很快就长得身材茁壮。另一棵树每年都要开花结果。刚开始，着实让农夫吃了一惊，非常欣赏它。但由于这棵树还未成熟，便承担开花结果的责任，累得弯了腰，结的果实也酸涩难吃，还时常招来一群孩子石头的袭击。更有甚者，孩子会攀上它羸弱的身体，在掠夺果子的同时，损伤它的自尊心和肢体。

时光飞转，终于有一天，那棵久不开花的壮树轻松地吐出了花蕾，由于养分充足、身材强壮，结出了又大又甜的果实。而此时那棵急于开花结果的树却成了枯木。农夫诧异地叹了口气，砍下那根瘦小的枯木，烧火用了。

有时不急于表现自己的人恰恰是最富有竞争力、生命力最强、最有前途的人。

Dig the Clear Spring of Wisdom

When the children born in Jewish families are just sensible, their mothers would apply the honey on the books and make them lick.

The only purpose to do so is to let the children build up such a notion: the books are sweet and have wisdom in them. When the children grow up a little bit more, almost every Jewish mother would take the same question for their children to guess.

If one day you encounter a fire unluckily and your house is surrounded by the fire, what is you

can't forget most when you run for your life?

After denying a lot of answers, the mothers would tell them, what they will bring with themselves isn't money and valuables but a priceless treasure called wisdom.

In the eyes of smart Jews, life is like a tree. If you want to thrive and luxuriate, you must keep digging the deep well of wisdom and water your life with sweet and clear spring. In the process of growing, life needs keep absorbing nutrients, in which wisdom is an absolutely essential kind.

挖掘智慧的清泉

生在犹太人家庭的孩子刚刚懂事时,母亲就会将蜂蜜抹在书本上,让孩子去舔书本上的蜜。

这样做,目的只有一个,那就是让孩子从小树立这样一种观念:书本是甜的,而且书里有智慧。孩子再长大点儿,几乎每个犹太母亲都会拿同样一个问题让孩子猜。

假如有一天你不幸遭遇火灾,你的房子被大火包围,你逃命时,最不能忘记携带的是什么?

在否定了许多答案之后,母亲就会告诉他们:应该携带的不是金银财宝,而是一种无价之宝,它的名字叫智慧。

在聪明的犹太人眼里,生命宛如一棵树,要想茁壮成长、枝繁叶茂,就必须不断挖掘智慧的深井,用那甘爽清冽的泉水浇灌生命。生命在成长过程中要不断吸收养料,智慧是其中必不可少的一种。

Observe the Sky with Salt

An elderly man led the villagers night and day to convey the salt to some place for barley to overwinter. One night, they slept in the wilderness, studded with stars in the sky. With the method passed down by the ancestors, the elderly man fumbled out three grains of salt block to throw into the bonfire for divining the change of the weather in the mountains...

Everyone was waiting for the elderly man's "weather forecast": if they heard the salt block cracking in the fire, it would be the omen of a fine day; without sound, it symbolized the weather would go bad and the rain and wind would come at any time.

The elderly man looked serious because the salt block made no sound in the fire. He thought it was infelicitous, affirming that they must at once hurry on with their journey after daybreak. But a young man in their team thought that "Observe the sky with salt" was a superstition, so he argued against setting out in haste.

Sure enough, the following afternoon the weather changed unexpectedly, with the blinding snowstorm, when the young man realized the elderly man's sagacity. In fact, with the scientific explanation of today, the elderly man was also right: whether the salt block will make any sound is concerned with the humidity of the air. In other words, when the storm threatened, the temperature would go up and the salt block would be affected with damp and fall silent when it was put into the fire.

Young people often look down on the philosophy of the elderly, thinking one – sidedly that they

are outdated and useless. In fact, some philosophy of life is like sea salt; old as it is, it is still a kind of crystallization.

以盐窥天

一位长者带领村民日夜兼程，要把盐运送到某地换成大麦过冬。有天晚上，他们露宿荒野，星空灿烂。长者依然用世代祖先传下来的方法取出三粒盐块投入营火，占卜山间天气的变化……

大家都在等待长者的"天气预报"：如果听到火中盐块发出的"噼里啪啦"的声响，那就是好天的预兆：如果毫无声息，那就象征天气即将变坏，风雨随时来临。

长者神情严肃，因为盐块在火中毫无声息。他认为不吉利，主张天亮后马上赶路。可是，队伍中一位年轻人认为"以盐窥天"是迷信，反对匆忙启程。

第二天下午，果然天气骤变，风雪交加，坚持晚走的年轻人这才领悟长者的睿智。其实，用今天的科学解释，长者也是对的，盐块在火中是否发出声音，与空气中的湿度相关。换句话说，当风雨逼近，温度就会上升，盐块受潮，投入火中自然喑哑无声。

年轻人往往看不起老人的哲学，片面认为他们都是过时的、无用的。其实，一些人生理念如同海盐，尽管它很老，但仍是一种结晶。

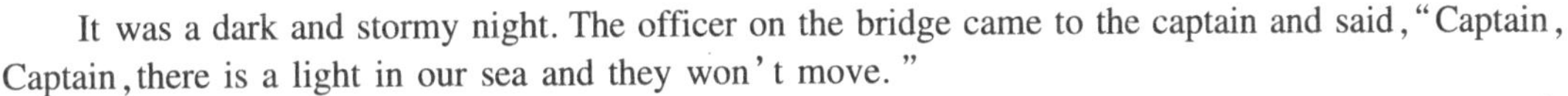

Do You Have a Lighthouse in Your Heart?

It was a dark and stormy night. The officer on the bridge came to the captain and said, "Captain, Captain, there is a light in our sea and they won't move."

"What do you mean they won't move? Tell them to move. Tell them to starboard right now."

The signal was sent out, "Starboard, starboard." The signal came back, "Starboard yourself."

"I can't believe this. What's going on here? Let them know who I am."

The signal was sent out. "This is the mighty Missouri, starboard." The signal came back, "This is the lighthouse."

My friends, correct principles are lighthouses, they do not move. They are natural laws. We cannot break them. We might as well learn them, accommodate them, utilize them and be grateful for them. Then it enlarges us, emancipates us and empowers us.

Eliot once said, "We shall never cease striving, and the end of all our striving will arrive where we began and know the place for the first time."

你心中有灯塔吗？

那是一个漆黑的暴风雨之夜。驾驶台上的驾驶员走到船长身边说："船长，船长，我们的海道上有一个发光物，他们不愿移开。"

“你说‘他们不愿移开’是什么意思？告诉他们移开。告诉他们马上右偏。”

信号发了出去：“右偏，右偏。”信号返回：“你自己右偏。”

“我无法相信。这里是怎么了？告诉他们我是谁。”

信号又发了出去：“这是密苏里号巨轮，右偏。”信号返回：“这是灯塔。”

我的朋友们，正确的原则就像灯塔，它们不会移动。它们是自然法则。我们无法打破。我们不妨去学习它们、适应它们、利用它们、感激它们。然后，它们会让我们扩展、解脱，并使我们得到使用的能力。

艾略特曾说过：“我们将永不停止奋斗，经过全力以赴的奋斗后，我们将到达出发地，并第一次认识这个地方。”

真诚赞美的力量

Give the Defeated Opponent Flowers

In a television program of the world pro boxing championship, I watched some warm details.

The athletes were two American pro boxers: the older was called Kaphera, 35; the younger Barrera, 28. They played six rounds in the first half, ending in a tie for their equivalent strength. In the seventh round of the second half, Barrera repeatedly hit veteran Kaphera in the head, so that the latter was badly battered.

At the interval, Barrera genuinely apologized to Kaphera. He first used the clean towel in his hand to wipe the bloodstain off Kaphera's face bit by bit, and then showered the mineral water on his head. Barrera looked apologetic, as if he himself was injured. Then they proceeded with their boxing. Perhaps older or weaker, Kaphera was knocked down over and over by Barrera.

According to the rules, after the opponent was knocked down and the referee called three times in a row, if the boxer who collapsed couldn't get up, he would be defeated. Kaphera struggled to his feet. The referee began to count, "One, two. . . " Before "three" could be uttered, Barrera came up and pulled Kaphera up. The referee was very surprised, for such a scene in the boxing field was extremely rare. Barrera explained to the referee, "I fouled, but you didn't see it, so I didn't win in this round." After Barrera helped Kaphera up, they clapped their hands each other with a smile and went on to box.

Finally, Barrera defeated Kaphera at the score of 110 to 108. The audience flooded to Barrera hailing and presenting him with flowers and gifts. Barrera pushed his way through the crowd, went straight towards veteran Kaphera unfrequented and sent him the flowers. Both of them hugged and kissed each other's hit parts, as if they were close brothers. Kaphera sincerely congratulated on Barrera with a heartfelt smile. He held Barrera's hand, raised it high over their heads and paid tribute to the whole audience.

Kafeila was defeated, but he was gentlemanly; Barrera won, and he was magnanimous.

When you win, give your defeated opponent flowers; it is a great success in personality and realm.

把鲜花送给失败的对手

在一档世界职业拳王争霸赛电视节目中，我看到了几个暖人的细节。

比赛的是两个美国职业拳手，年长的叫卡菲拉，今年 35 岁；年轻的叫巴雷拉，今年 28 岁。上半场两人打了 6 个回合，实力相当，难分胜负。在下半场第 7 个回合，巴雷拉接连击中老将卡菲拉的头部，使他鼻青脸肿。

短暂休息时，巴雷拉真诚地向卡菲拉致歉，他先是用自己手中干净的毛巾一点一点擦去了卡菲拉脸上的血迹，然后把矿泉水洒在了卡菲拉头上。巴雷拉一脸歉意，那神情仿佛受伤的是自己。接下来，两人继续交手。也许是年纪大了，也许体力不支，卡菲拉一次又一次被巴雷拉击倒。

按规则，对手被打倒在地上后，由裁判连喊三声，如倒地的拳手起不来就算输了。卡菲拉挣扎着起来，裁判开始报数，“一、二……”，三字还没出口，巴雷拉却上前把卡菲拉拉了起来。裁判感到很吃惊，这样的情景在拳场上极为少见，巴雷拉向裁判解释说：“我犯规了，只是你没有看见，这局不算我赢。”巴雷拉扶起卡菲拉后，他们微笑着击掌，继续交战。

最终，巴雷拉以 108 比 110 打败了卡菲拉。观众潮水般涌向了巴雷拉，向他献花、致敬、送礼物。巴雷拉拨开了人群，径直走向了被冷落的老将卡菲拉，把鲜花送给了卡菲拉。

两人紧紧地抱在一起，相互亲吻被击中的部位，俨然一对亲兄弟。卡菲拉真诚地向巴雷拉祝贺，一脸由衷的笑容。他握住巴雷拉的手，高高地举过了头顶，向全场观众致敬。

卡菲拉虽然败了，但败得很有风度。巴雷拉赢了，赢得十分大度。

在自己胜利时，把鲜花送给失败的对手，这是一种人格和境界上的大成功。

The Flowers That Can Speak

A 6-year-old girl asked her mother, "Can flowers speak?"

"Oh, my dearie, if flowers can't speak, how lonely the spring is, who will look around it?"

The little girl smiled with satisfaction.

At the age of 16, the girl asked her father, "Can the stars in the sky speak?"

"Oh, my daughter, if the stars can speak, the sky will be noisy, who will yearn towards the serene paradise?"

The little girl smiled with satisfaction again.

At the age of 26, the girl had become a full-blown female. One day she asked in private her husband, a diplomat, "At the banquet of the previous evening, was the way I behaved and spoke appropriate?"

"Great!" the diplomat had no intention of flattering, "When you spoke, it was like the tinkling spring or the melodious music; though you spoke so much, it was not unnecessary; when you were silent, you were like a fragrant lotus or an elegant crane; though quiet, it involved everything... Sweetheart, can you tell me how you cultivate yourself?"

His wife said with a smile, "At the age of , I learned from my mother as a teacher how to dialogue with Nature. At the age of 16, I learned from my father as a writer when to speak and when not. Before I saw you, I learned from historians, philosophers, writers, musicians, painters and diplomats what kind of speech I should make when I meet different kinds of people. Honey, I have also received thoughts, wisdom, courage, views and love from you!"

会说话的花儿

一个6岁的小女孩问妈妈："花儿会说话吗？"

"噢，孩子，花儿如果不会说话，春天该是多么寂寞，谁还对春天左顾右盼呀？"

小女孩满意地笑了。

小女孩长到16岁，问爸爸："天上的星星会说话吗？"

"噢，孩子，星星若能说话，天上就会一片嘈杂，谁还会向往天堂静穆的乐园呢？"

小女孩又满意地笑了。

女孩到了26岁，已是一个成熟的女性。一天，她悄悄地问做外交官的丈夫："昨晚宴会上，我的举止言谈合适吗？"

"棒极了！"外交官毫无吹捧之意。"你说话时，像叮咚的泉水、悠扬的乐曲，虽千言而不繁；你静处时，似浮香的荷、优雅的鹤，虽静音而传千言……亲爱的，能告诉我你是怎样修炼的吗？"

妻子笑道："6岁时，我从当教师的妈妈那里学会了和自然界对话。16岁时，我从当作家的爸爸那里学会了什么时候该说话、什么时候不该说话。见到你前,我从史学家、哲学家、文学家、音乐家、画家、外交家那里学会了和什么样的人谈什么样的话。亲爱的,我还从你那里得到了思想、智慧、胆量、看法和爱!”

The Flowers on the Ruins

A long time ago, in order to open up new streets, many old buildings were pulled down in London. However, owing to various reasons, new roads couldn't start working and the ruins of the old buildings were exposed to the sun and rain.

One day, a group of natural scientists came here and found weeds and wild flowers even grew on the ruins. Amazingly, some of the plants had never been seen in Britain, for they usually grow in the countries bordering the Mediterranean. These buildings pulled down were mostly built when the ancient Romans attacked Britain along the Thames.

It was mostly at that time when the seeds of these plants were taken here. They were wedged under the heavy stones and tiles year after year, losing the chance to grow and sprout. Once they saw the sunshine, they immediately resumed their vitality and bloomed beautiful flowers.

In fact, so is life. On the journey of life, we often encounter all kinds of setbacks and failures. At this time, don't be disappointed or give up easily. As long as you have a firm belief in your heart and try to look for it, you will always find "a ray of sunshine" that helps you pull through.

废墟上的花朵

很久以前,为了开辟新街,伦敦拆除了许多旧楼房。然而,因为种种原因,新路久久没能开工,旧楼房的废墟晾在那里,任凭日晒雨淋。

有一天,一群自然科学家来到了这里,发现在这一片废墟上竟长出了一片野花野草。令人惊奇的是,其中有一些花草在英国从来没有见到过的,它们通常只生长在地中海沿岸国家。这些被拆除的楼房大多都是在古罗马人沿着泰晤士河进攻英国时建造的。这些花草的种子多半就是那个时候被带到了这里的,它们被压在沉重的石头砖瓦下,一年又一年,丧失了生长发芽的机会。而一旦见到阳光,它们就立即恢复了勃勃生机,绽开了一朵朵美丽的鲜花。

其实,人的生命也是如此。在生命的旅途中,我们常常遭遇各种挫折和失败。这时,不要心灰意冷,不要轻易言败。只要心中有一个坚定的信念,努力去找,总会找到帮助自己渡过难关的“一缕阳光”。一旦有了阳光照耀,一定能萌发出新的生机,绽放出新的美丽。

Lilies Valley

In a remote mountain valley, there is a cliff with the height of a thousand feet. Nobody knows when on the precipice a small lily began to exist.

When the lily was born, it was entirely alike with the weed. But in its heart she knew she was not a weed.

In the depth of her heart, there was an intrinsic innocent thought: "I am a flower called lily, not a weed. The only method to prove myself is to start out beautiful flowers."

With this thought, the lily diligently took up water and the sunlight, got deeply rooted and stood straight.

Finally in an early spring morning, the crown of the lily tied the first calyx.

In the lily's heart she was very happy, but the neighbor weeds disdained it very much. They were laughing at the lily in secret: "This fellow is obviously the grass, but she insists that she is a flower. On her head, it is not a calyx, but a brain lump."

Even in public situation, they ridiculed the lily: "Don't dream any more. Even if you really can blossom, in this wild your value is the same as ours."

Occasionally, bees, butterflies and birds also urged the lily not to bloom so hard: "On this precipice, even if you start out the most beautiful flower in the world, people cannot appreciate you!"

The lily said, "I must blossom because I know I have the beautiful flower. I want to blossom to fulfill my dignified life as a flower; I must blossom to prove my own existence. No matter who will appreciate, no matter how others look at me, I must and will blossom!"

Though despised by all others, the wild lily released her inner feelings diligently. One day, she finally blossomed. With that intelligent white and graceful bearing, it became the most beautiful one on the cliff.

At this time, all other plants and insects didn't dare to ridicule her. The lily was being in full bloom. On the flowers there were crystal-like water drops every day. The wild grasses thought that they were dew. Only the lily knew that they were tears of extreme happiness. Every spring, the wild lily tried its best to bloom year after year. Its seeds along with the wind flew into nearby mountain valleys, prairie and cliff. And then, there were wild lilies everywhere.

Dozens of years later, people in cities and countryside hundred of miles away from the cliff came to appreciate these lilies. Many kids bend down to smell their fragrance. Many lovers hug each other and swear that they will stay together forever. Countless people are moved into tears, for their pure and tender hearts are touched by this beauty that they have never seen before. Later on, that place was called "Lilies Valley".

In spite of others' appreciation, lilies all over the mountain still remember the first lily's teaching by heart, that is, "We should bloom with all our mind, never argue with others and prove our existence with blooms."

百合山谷

遥远的山谷里有一个高达千尺的悬崖。没有人知道什么时候悬崖上开始长出了一朵小百合。

百合诞生时，完全和杂草一样。但她在心里知道自己不是一棵野草。

她内心深处本来就有一个天真的想法："我是一朵名叫百合的鲜花，不是一棵野草。唯一能证明我自己的方法就是开出美丽的鲜花。"

百合怀着这个念头坚持不懈地吸收水分和阳光，深深扎根，终于，在一个春天的早晨，百合的花冠上结出了第一个花萼。

百合的心里非常高兴，但附近的杂草却都不屑一顾。他们在私下嘲笑着百合："这家伙显然是草，她却坚持说自己是一朵花。她头上结的不是花萼，而是一颗脑瘤。"

他们甚至在公开场合奚落百合："别再做梦了。即使你真的会开花，在这荒野你的

价值也和我们的一样。”

偶尔，蜜蜂、蝴蝶和小鸟也劝百合不要那样用力开花：“在这悬崖上，即使你开出世界上最美丽的花朵，人们也无法欣赏你！”

百合说：“我必须开花，因为我知道自己有美丽的花朵。我想开花，是为了实现自己作为一朵花的高贵人生；我必须开花，以证明自己的存在。无论有没有人欣赏，无论别人怎样看我，我都必须而且一定会开花！”

尽管受到了其他所有花草的鄙视，但野百合坚持不懈地释放内心的情感。有一天，她终于开花了。她因聪慧、洁白和风姿绰约而成为悬崖上最美丽的花朵。

此时，所有其他的花草和昆虫都不敢嘲笑她了。百合花在盛开着。花朵上每天都有晶莹的水珠。野草们都以为那是露水。只有百合知道那是狂喜的泪滴。年复一年，每到春天，百合都竭尽全力地开花。她的种子随风飞落在附近的山谷、草原和悬崖。而且此时，到处都开满了野百合花。

几十年后，距离悬崖数百里的城市人和乡下人都赶来欣赏这些百合花。好多小孩弯下腰去闻百合花的芳香。好多情侣互相拥抱，山盟海誓说要永远厮守在一起；无计其数的人感动得掉下了眼泪，因为看到这从未见过的美，他们纯净温柔的心受到了触动。后来，那个地方被人称为“百合山谷”。

不管别人怎样欣赏，满山遍野的百合花都仍然铭记着第一朵百合花的教导：“我们应该全心全意地开花，绝不要和别人争论，要以鲜花来证明自己的存在。”

To Be a Flower's Bosom Friend

I have a neighbor who plants a lot of potted flowers. Every morning he would sing a song as he waters the flowers. One day I asked, "you're always very pleased with yourself. Do you always have good news every day?" He said with a smile, "Look, how beautiful and pleasing these flowers are, making me live in the spring. Can't I be happy?"

On a Valentine's Day, I bought a bouquet of roses from an old woman for my sweetheart. But because of our irreparable rift, she threw down the flowers in the presence of me. Unexpectedly, the old woman caught up with us, gave back the money to me and immediately picked up the abandoned flowers from the ground.

She gently stroked the rose petals, whisked off every grain of dust from them and said piteously, "I have made a vow to each bouquet of flowers, with my sincere blessing! Why did you throw it away? You're not qualified to be master of the bouquet of flowers."

I looked at my sweetheart, speechless. We not only hurt a bouquet of flowers, but also a protector of flowers.

On another occasion, it was a sunny day, with the surging crowds and a lot of traffic. In the middle of the street lay a handful of red roses. A boy was anxious to go to pick it up, but he was unable to go forward for the busy traffic. When it was his turn, he raced ahead, but the roses had been rolled to pieces. The boy picked it up, bit by bit, the remains of the flowers, slowly cupped those injured petals, held them in his hands for a long time and broke into tears in the street.

Until now, I'm still often moved for that scene.

One day, British writer Oscar Wilde walked into a florist's and asked to have some of the flowers

taken out of the shop window. The shop clerk did as he told and asked how many he would buy. Wilde said, "I don't want to buy the flowers, but I think they're too crowded, afraid they would be crushed, so I want them to take it easy."

Knowing their sorrows and joys and caring for their pains, they are the bosom friends of flowers. They will neither miss a butterfly flying in the sleeve nor waste each beautiful scene of life. To be the bosom friend of a flower is to live in the spring of the soul.

做一朵花的知己

我有一个邻居,养了很多盆花。每天早上,他都会一边浇花一边哼着小曲。有一天,我问:"你总是美滋滋的,天天有喜事吗?"他笑着说:"你看看,这花儿又美又喜人,让我每天都生活在春天里,能不乐吗?"

有一次过情人节,我从一位老妇人那里买了一束玫瑰送给我的情人。但因为我们之间的裂痕无法弥补,所以她当着我的面扔掉了那束花。没想到老妇人竟从后面赶上来,把钱退给了我,马上从地上捡起那束被遗弃的花儿。

她轻轻摩挲着玫瑰花瓣,掸掉花上每一粒灰尘,无比怜惜地说:"我给每一束花都许过愿,都有真心的祝福啊! 你们怎么就扔了呢? 你们不配做那束花的主人。"

我和情人面面相觑。我们不仅伤害了一束花,也伤害了一位护花使者。

还有一次。那天阳光灿烂,人潮涌动,车流不息。大街的中央,躺着一捧鲜红的玫瑰。一个少年焦急地要去将它拾捡起来,但车来车往,他无法前行。终于等到机会,他抢步过去,玫瑰已被轧碎。少年一点一点拾捡着满地的花骸,慢慢地捧起那些受伤的花瓣,久久地握在手心,竟然当街痛哭。

直到现在,我仍然时常为这个场景怦然心跳。

有一天,英国作家王尔德走进一家花店,要求把橱窗里的花取出一部分。店里的人照着他的要求去做,并问他要买多少。王尔德说:"我不想买花,只是我看它们太拥挤了,怕它们被挤坏,想让它们轻松一下。"

懂得花的悲欢,体恤花的疼痛,他们是花的知己。他们不会错过钻入衣袖的一只蝴蝶,也不会浪费人生每一幅美景。做一朵花的知己,就是住进心灵的春天。

The Poor Man's Jasmines

When he first arrived in India, my friend saw an old man peddling some cheap gadgets in the street of Bombay. The old man was one of the poor people in Bombay and virtually there was no difference from beggars. Most of them were some lone old people, whose life had no support.

My friend was a kind-hearted man, so he didn't hesitate to pocket some changes to him. The old man motioned him to pick some from the gadgets as he pleased. My friend took a fancy to those things, so he left without choosing.

But unexpectedly the old man drew in the gadgets and followed him closely.

At first, my friend didn't think a lot, just supposing he packed up the gadgets to go home. But when he went out very far and saw the old man still following him, he was a bit tired, thinking the old man must feel he was benevolent and wanted to beg more money from him.

My friend turned back, gesticulated to the old man and told him not to follow him because he hadn't much money. But the old man seemed not to understand what he meant, mumbling something and still following him obstinately. The bundle on his back made him sweating all over.

My friend happened to meet his Indian colleague in the street and heard his story. The colleague turned to ask why the old man was following his friend.

The old man gasped, "My son, you gave me money, but didn't want my things, so I have to give you something. I see you are a foreigner, likely not to be up on here. I just want to follow you and show you the way. All I can do for you is this. . . "

My friend's heart was shocked. He said he didn't know why, when he felt the old man was just like his father, affable and warm.

穷人的茉莉花

朋友刚到印度时，在孟买的大街上看到一位老人在兜售一些不值钱的小玩意。老人是孟买的穷人，其实和乞丐没有什么区别。他们大多是一些孤寡老人，生活上无依无靠。

朋友是个心地善良的人，毫不犹豫地从兜里掏出零钱给他。老人便示意朋友在他的那些小玩意里随便选些东西。那些东西没有朋友看上眼的，所以他没有选就走了。

可是，没想到那个老人竟然收起那堆小玩意，紧紧地跟在他身后。

刚开始，朋友没想那么多，只以为他要收摊回家。可是，当他走出去很远，看到老人仍跟着他时，他便有些厌烦了，心想那老人一定是觉得他是个善心人，想从他那里再讨些钱吧。

朋友转过身对老人比划着，告诉他自己身上没多少钱，别再跟着了。可是，老人好像完全没有理解他的意思，嘴里嘟囔着什么，仍然执拗地跟着他，背上那个偌大的包袱压得他汗流浃背。

朋友恰巧在街上遇见了印度的同事，听说了朋友的遭遇。同事转过身，问那个老人为什么跟着朋友。

老人气喘吁吁地说："孩子，你给了我钱，却没有要我的东西，我总得给你点什么呀。我看你是外国人，可能对我们这里不太熟悉，我只想跟着你，为你指指路，我能为你做的只有这个了……"

朋友的心灵受到了震动，他说不知为什么，那一刻他感觉那个老人很像自己的父亲，亲切而温暖。

A Boy and Flowers

On a country road, a small boy was bending to talk with the roadside flowers. I couldn't follow what he was talking. I asked him, "What are you talking to the flowers?" He couldn't hear me clearly, so I had to squat down to say again.

He said, "I told the flowers, how beautifully you're blooming!"

He also told me: if I want to talk to the flowers, I must squat down to whisper in their ears so that they can hear me.

What the boy said made me stand at the roadside for a long time, thinking: if we can't squat down to look at the same level, you can neither understand the boy nor see the roadside flowers, just as we will never know its temperature if we don't put our bare feet into the stream.

男孩与鲜花

乡路上,一个小男孩正低下身子,和路边的花说着一些我听不明白的话。

我问他:"你对花说些什么呢?"

他听不清,我只好蹲下来对他又说一次。

他说:"我对花说:你今天开得真好看!"

他还告诉我说,如果我要对花说话,一定要蹲下来在花边耳语,花才能听见。

小孩的话使我在路边呆立了很久,想着:如果我们不能蹲下平视,就不能了解孩子,也不能看清路旁的花;如同我们不赤足踏进溪水,就永远不会知道溪水的温度。

The Flower Never Minds

Recently I visited a friend who had a greenhouse. As she showed me her flowers, I came to the most beautiful one of all, a golden chrysanthemum in full bloom. But to my great surprise, it was growing in an old, dented and rusty bucket.

I thought to myself, "If this were my plant, I'd put it in the loveliest flowerpot I had!"

My friend changed my mind. "I ran short of pots," she explained, "and knowing how beautiful this one would be, I thought it wouldn't mind starting out in this old pail. It's just for a little while, till I can put it out in the garden."

Aren't we the same as flowers? The important is not where we are from or what position we are in now, but where we are going.

花儿不会介意

最近,我拜访了一位有花房的朋友。她带我参观她那些花儿,我来到一株最美丽的花儿前,那是一株盛开的金菊。但让我大为吃惊的是,它长在一个坑坑洼洼、锈迹斑斑的旧桶里。

我暗自想道:"如果这是我养的花儿,我会把它种在最漂亮的花盆里!"

朋友的话改变了我的想法。"种花的罐子用完了,"她解释说。"而且我知道这株金菊肯定会艳压群芳,就想着它不会介意在这个旧桶里开始成长。过一阵子,我就能把它移到花园里了。"

我们和花儿不是一样吗?重要的不是我们来自哪里,也不是我们现在的位置,而是

我们将去何方。

The Lily Can Also Bloom in the Cursed Clay

On the morning of the New Year's Day, a villager opened his door and found an earthen pot used for loading bone ashes.

He knew this was his neighbor's curse because they were hostile to each other generation after generation.

He didn't go to that neighbor's in rage, but took the pot to load some clay in the field and planted a lily...

One day, the lily bloomed. He quietly sent the pot of flower to the enemy's doorway.

And on the very day, his enemy blushingly went to apologize to the magnanimous villager.

People are easily moved, so we have to know how to move them. Even the lily can also bloom in the cursed clay.

诅咒的泥土也能开出百合

有个乡人,大年初一早晨打开门,发现门前有一个装骨灰的陶罐。

他知道这是邻居对他的诅咒,两家世代有仇。

他没有怒气冲冲地找上门去,而是拿着陶罐,到田里装了泥土,并种了一棵百合花……

有一天,花开了,他悄悄地把这盆花送到了仇人的家门口。

就在那一天,仇人羞愧地来到这位大度的乡人家里道歉。

人心很容易感动,要懂得怎样去打动它,诅咒的泥土也能开出百合。

The Sound a Flower Blooms

The florist says, "Almost all white flowers are fragrant. The more colorful the flowers are, the less fragrance."

Like flowers, the simpler and purer the people are, the more beauty they have in their heart.

The florist says, "In fact, evening primroses are also fragrant in the daytime, but very few people smell their aroma."

Because people are impetuous in the daytime, they can't smell evening primroses' faint aroma. If a person is also quiet in the daytime, they will discover evening primroses and sweet osmanthus are also fragrant even in the torrid noon.

The florist says, "When you buy lotus flowers, you must pick those in bloom."

Morning is the best time for lotus flowers to bloom. If a lotus flower doesn't bloom in the morning, it may not at noon and night. It's just as we read a person: if he is unpromising as youth, he

will be harder at middle age or old age.

The florist says, "The more expensive flowers, the more likely they wither."

We should treasure our youth because it is the most expensive flower, which will be lost most easily.

The florist says, "Each rose has thorns."

Like everyone, he always has part of his character you can't stand. To love a rose doesn't mean to try to eradicate its thorns, but learn not to be hurt by its thorns and learn to keep your thorns from scratching the one you love.

As long as you keep your eyes open and don't cast too much worldly dust on your mind, you can hear the voice of wisdom even in a grain of sand or a sparkling star.

花开的声音

花卉专家说:“几乎所有的白花都很香,越是颜色艳丽的花越是缺乏芬芳。”

人也是一样,越朴素单纯的人,越有内在美。

花卉专家说:“夜来香其实白天也很香,但很少有人闻得到。”

因为白天人心浮躁,闻不到夜来香的幽幽香气。如果一个人白天的心也很沉静,就会发现夜来香、桂花即使在酷热的中午也是香的。

花卉专家说:“清晨买莲花一定要挑那些盛开的。”

早晨是莲花开放最好的时间,如果一朵莲花早晨不开,可能中午和晚上都不开了。我们看人也是一样,一个人年轻时没有作为,中年或晚年就更难有作为了。

花卉专家说:“越是昂贵的花越容易凋谢。”

要珍惜青春,因为青春是最名贵的花,最容易失去。

花卉专家说:“每一株玫瑰都有刺。”

正如每个人一样,性格中都有你不能容忍的部分。爱护一朵玫瑰,并不要非得努力把它的刺根除,只要学会如何不被它的刺弄伤;同时还要学会如何不让自己的刺划伤爱你的人。

只要留心,只要思想不蒙上过多世俗的灰尘,即使在一粒沙、一颗闪烁的星星里,都能听见智慧的声音。

A Bouquet of Flowers at the Door

Early one morning I gathered a beautiful bouquet of sweet - smelling long - stemmed roses for myself. The roses were definitely a delight for my eyes. Then a calm and gentle voice said in my heart, "Give them to your friend."

I went straight into the house and arranged the roses in a vase. Then I wrote this note as small as I could, "For my friend." I went across the street to my neighbor's, who is also one of my closest friends, and I left the bouquet at the front door.

Later that day my friend called to thank me. She said the flowers were a true blessing. Late the

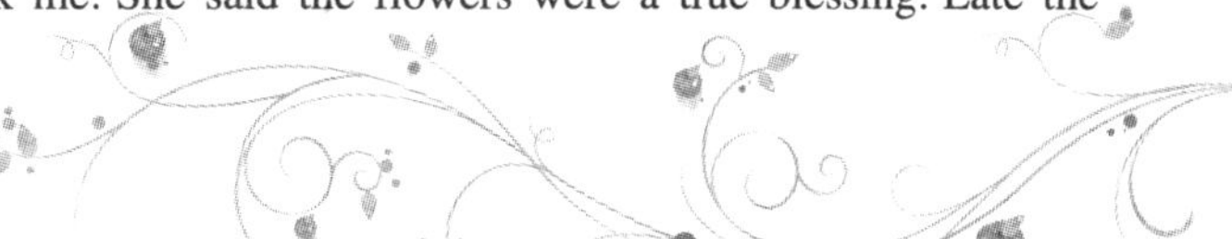

night before she had been arguing with one of her children. Being cruel, as teenagers can sometimes be, her child said to her, "You have no friends."

What a surprise when she went to leave for work that morning and found not just the blessing of the bouquet of flowers, but the tiny note which simply said, "For my friend."

放在门口的一束鲜花

一天清晨,我为自己采摘了一束芳香四溢的长茎玫瑰花。这些玫瑰花确实让我赏心悦目。这时,一个平静温和的声音在我的心里说道:"把它们送给你的朋友。"

我径直走进屋里,把那些玫瑰花插入花瓶,然后尽可能小地写了这样一张纸条:"送给我的朋友。"我穿过大街,走到我的邻居、也是我最亲密的一个朋友家门口,然后把那束花放在那里。

那天晚些时候,我的朋友打电话向我道谢。她说那些鲜花是一种真正的祝福。昨天深夜,她一直和她的一个孩子争吵。她的孩子才十几岁,有时说话无情无义,这样对她说道:"你根本没有朋友。"

那天早晨,她去上班时,不仅在门口发现了那束表示祝福的鲜花,还发现了那张小小的纸条,上面简单地写着"送给我的朋友",她是多么惊喜!

The Postman Who Planted Flowers

In a small village there was a middle-aged postman, who just turned 20 years old and started delivering all kinds of happy or sad stories to the residents' homes day after day for 50 kilometers. 20 years flew by, and so many changes took place, but the road from the post office to the village always hadn't had any tree and nothing but the flying dust as could be seen.

"How long shall I go along this deserted road?"

As soon as he thought he must spend his life pedaling the bike on the dusty road with no flower or tree, he felt somewhat sorry.

One day when he finished delivering the letters and was ready to return worriedly, he happened to pass by a florist's. "Right, that's it!" He walked into the shop, bought a handful of wild flower seeds, and from the next day on scattered these seeds along the roadside. Thus, after one day, two days, one month, two months... he always kept scattering the wild flower seeds.

Before long on the lonely road he had come and gone for 20 years bloomed a lot of little flowers, in full bloom in all seasons endlessly.

For the villagers, the seeds and the scent were more pleasing than any mail the postman delivered in all his life.

On the road without dust but full of petals, the postman whistled and pedaled his bike, feeling lonely and anxious no more.

种花的邮差

小村里有位中年邮差,他刚满 20 岁便开始每天往返 50 公里的路程,日复一日将悲喜故事送到居民的家中。就这样20年一晃而过，物换星移，唯独从邮局到村庄的这条道路，从过去到现在，始终没有一枝半叶，触目所及，唯有飞扬的尘土。

“这样荒凉的路还要走多久呢？”

他一想到必须在这无花无树、充满尘土的路上，踩着脚踏车度过自己的人生时，心中总是有些遗憾。

有一天，他送完信，心事重重准备回去，刚好经过了一家花店。“对了，就是这个！”他走进花店，买了一把野花的种子，并从第二天起把这些种子撒在往来的路上。就这样，经过一天、两天、一个月、两个月……他始终持续散播着野花种子。

没多久，那条已经来回走了20年的荒凉道路，居然开起了许多小花，四季盛开，永不停歇。

种子和花香对村庄里的人来说，比邮差一辈子送达的任何一封邮件更让他们开心。

在不是充满尘土而是铺满花瓣的道路上吹着口哨，踩着脚踏车的邮差，不再孤独，也不再愁苦了。

The Rose Root

There's life underground and on the ground, where there're a group of creatures knowing love and hate.

One day, the streamlet encountered the rose and said, "My root neighbor, I've never seen anyone as ugly as you. Whoever meets you will say it must a monkey inserted its long tail into the earth, threw it down and left. It seems that you want to imitate the earthworm, but you didn't learn its elegant and round movement, only learned to drink my blue juice. As soon as I met you, I was half drunk by you. Ugly, you say, what are you doing?"

The lowly root said, "Yes, my streamlet brother, in your eyes I certainly have no appearance. The long touch with the soil made me dark gray; the overtiredness deformed me, as a worker's deformed arm. I'm also a worker, who work for my extension to the sun. I absorbed juice from you, transmitted it to her and made her fresh and lovely; after you left, I would go afar to look for the juice to sustain life. My streamlet brother, one day, you will go to the place where the sun shines. Then, you can go to see how beautiful my part in the sunlight is."

The streamlet didn't believe that, but out of caution, he didn't say anything, thinking to himself, wait and see.

When his trembling body gradually grew up into the light, the first thing he did was to look for the extension the root had said. Gosh! Everywhere he could see the radiant and enchanting spring scenery while where the root took, a rose graced the land more beautiful.

On thc branches hung the heavy flowers, whose intoxicating fragrance was filling the air.

The streamlet flowed across the grass with the blooming flowers, "My God, I haven't thought such an ugly root even stretching such a beauty!"

玫瑰花根

地下同地上一样有生命，有一群懂得爱憎的生物。

有一天，细流遇到玫瑰花根，说：“花根邻居，像你这么丑的，我从来没有见过呢。谁见了你都会说,准是一只猴子把它的长尾巴插在地里,扔下不管,径自走了。看来你想模仿蚯蚓,但没有学会它优美圆润的动作,只学会了喝我的蓝色汁液。我一碰上你,就被你喝掉了一半。丑八怪,你说,你这是干什么?"

卑贱的花根说:"不错,细流兄弟,在你眼里我当然没有模样。长期和泥土接触,使我浑身灰黑;过度劳累,使我变了形,正如变形的工人胳臂一样。我也是工人,我替身体见到阳光的延伸部分干活。我从你那里吸取了汁液,就是输送给她的,让她新鲜娇艳;你离开后,我就到远处去寻找维持生命的汁液。细流兄弟,总有一天,你会到太阳照耀的地方。那时候,你去看看我在阳光下的部分是多么美丽。"

细流并不相信,但出于谨慎,没有做声,暗忖道,等着瞧吧。

当他颤动的身躯逐渐长大,到了亮光下时,他干的第一件事就是去寻找花根所说的延伸部分。天哪!他看到了到处是一派明媚的春光,花根扎下去的地方,一株玫瑰把土地装点得分外美丽。

沉甸甸的花朵挂在枝条上,在空气中散发着醉人的芳香。

细流穿过了鲜花盛开的草地。"天哪,想不到丑陋的花根竟然延伸出美丽!"

Flowers and Hope

When World War II ended, there were ruins everywhere. American sociologist David Popenoe visited a German family living in the basement.

After leaving there, one of the people going the same way asked Popenoe, "Do you think they can rebuild their home?"

"Surely!" Popenoe answered verily.

"Why did you answer so surely?"

"What did you see they put on the table in the basement?"

"A vase of flowers."

"Right," Popenoe said, "any nation in such a plight that has not yet forgotten the love of beauty must be able to rebuild her homes on the ruins."

This story tells us how admirable and inspiring the people in despair who could still pursue the flower of hope were!

鲜花与希望

第二次世界大战结束,到处是一片废墟。美国社会学家戴维·波普诺去访问一户住在地下室里的德国居民。

离开那里之后,同行的人问波普诺:"你看他们能重建家园吗?"

"一定能!"波普诺肯定地回答。

"为什么回答得这么肯定呢?"

"你看到他们在地下室的桌上放着什么吗?"

"一瓶鲜花。"

"对,"波普诺说。"任何一个民族,处在这样困苦的境地,还没有忘记爱美,那就一定能在废墟上重建家园。"

在绝望中仍能追寻希望之花的人,是多么令人敬佩与振奋!

A Young Flower in the Desert

There was a young flower in the desert where all was dry and sad-looking. She grew there alone, enjoyed every day and said to the sun, "When shall I grow up?"

The sun would say, "Be patient—Each time I touch you, you will grow a little."

She was so pleased because she would have a chance to bring beauty to this corner of sand... and this was all she wanted to do—to bring a little bit of beauty to this world.

One day the hunter came by and stepped on her. She was going to die—and she felt so sad. Not because she was dying but because she would not have a chance to bring a little bit of beauty to this corner of the desert.

The great spirit saw her and heard her. Indeed, he spoke it out. She should be alive... and he reached down, touched her and gave her life.

Later, she grew up to be a beautiful flower. This corner of the desert became so beautiful because of her.

沙漠里的一朵小花

遍地干旱、满目凄凉的沙漠中有一朵小花。她独自生长在那里,享受着每一天,对太阳说:"我什么时候才能长大呀?"

太阳总是说:"要耐心。我每次抚摸你,你都会长大一点。"

她非常开心,因为她也有机会为沙漠的这个角落带来美丽……而且这是她唯一想做的事情,为这个世界带来一点美丽。

有一天,一位猎人经过,正好踩在她身上。她快要死了,感到非常伤心。并不是因为她即将死去,而是因为她再没有机会为沙漠的这个角落带来一点美丽了。

伟大的精灵看到了她,并听到了她的心声。事实上,他说了出来。她应该活着。于是,他俯下身,抚摸着她,给了她生命。

后来,她长成了一朵美丽的花。沙漠的这个角落因她而变得非常美丽。

The Rose Within

A man planted a rose and watered it faithfully and before it blossomed, he examined it.

He saw the bud that would soon blossom, but noticed thorns upon the stem and he thought, "How can any beautiful flower come from a plant burdened with so many sharp thorns?" Saddened by this thought, he neglected to water the rose, and just before it was ready to bloom it died.

So it is with many people. Within every soul there is a rose. The noble qualities planted in us at birth grow amid the thorns of our faults. Many of us look at ourselves and see only thorns, the defects. We despair, thinking that nothing good can possibly come from us. We neglect to water the rose within us, and eventually it dies. We never realize our potential.

Some people do not see the rose within themselves; someone else must show it to them. One of the greatest gifts a person can possess it to be able to reach past the thorns of another and find the rose within them.

This is one of the characteristic of love: look at a person and, knowing his faults, recognize the nobility in his soul, and help him realize that he can overcome his faults. If we show him the rose within himself, he will conquer the thorns. Only then will he blossom times over.

心中的玫瑰

有个人种了一株玫瑰，一丝不苟地给它浇水。在玫瑰将要开花前，他仔细看了看。他看到花蕾马上就要绽放，但注意到花茎上的刺，心里想道：“长了这么多尖刺的一棵植物怎么能开出美丽的花朵呢?”想到这个，他伤心起来，不再给花浇水了。就在准备开花时，这株玫瑰却死了。

许多人也是这样。每个人的心里都有一株玫瑰。我们出生时植根在我们体内的那些高贵品质生长在我们像尖刺般的缺点中。我们许多人在审视自己时，只看到刺，只看到缺点。我们丧失信心，认为自己不可能做出什么好事。我们疏于浇灌内心的玫瑰，所以它最后死去。我们从未意识到自己的潜力。

有些人看不到自己内心的玫瑰，其他人必须告诉他。一个人所能具备的其中一个最伟大的天赋就是能忽略他人的尖刺，发现他们内心的玫瑰。

这就是爱的其中一个特性：看一个人，知道他的缺点，同时也认识到他灵魂中的高尚品质，帮助他认识到他可以克服自己的缺点。如果我们让他知道他内心的玫瑰，他就会克服那些尖刺。只有到那个时候，他的玫瑰才会再次绽放。

Your Mind is a Garden

Some time ago, Sophia and I were visiting some friends in the country. We were staying at a beautiful little cabin, surrounded by fruit trees, flowers and even a few goats. Painted above the doorway in brightly colored, flowing letters were the words:

Your mind is a garden.
Your thoughts are the seeds.
You can grow flowers or
You can grow weeds.

Little did we know it at the time, but this little poem was to have a profound affect both on our thought patterns as well as our artworks.

It started almost as a kind of game. We decided to make a real effort to watch our thoughts and see exactly what it was that we were planting in our own "Mind Gardens."

We gradually came to see how so many of the problems and difficulties we were encountering in our lives had their beginnings in the seeds of doubt, fear and anxiety we were continually planting in our minds.

As we become more and more aware of these negative thoughts we are able to say, "No, I won't plant this weed in the garden of my mind."

I will consciously choose to plant something better. The results are truly spectacular.

When you start to consciously cultivate your own mind garden, you will truly be amazed at the changes, which begin to happen in your life. Things that you once thought were either impossible or very far away will suddenly come into view.

Any garden is an ongoing process. It's not enough to just plant a single seed of happiness and forget about it. Weeds would soon choke your frail little seedling. It is necessary to continuously pull out and throw away those seeds of fear, doubt and anxiety as soon as they appear.

Love, happiness and tranquility are all contagious. People who keep planting these seeds in their own mind are also planting them in others'. Remember:

Your mind is a garden.
Your thoughts are the seeds.
You can grow flowers or
You can grow weeds.

So ask yourself, what are you going to grow in the florid garden of your mind?

Fill your life with love and happiness.

心是花园

不久前，我和索菲娅去乡下拜访一些朋友，我们住在一座漂亮的小木屋里。小屋外果树和鲜花环绕，还有几只山羊。小屋门上方用颜色鲜艳、行云流水的字体写着：

心是花园，思想是种。可以种花，或种杂草。

尽管我们当时不大明白，但这首小诗会给我们的思维模式和艺术作品带来深远的影响。

开始时几乎就像一场游戏。我们决定真正努力观察自己的思想，要看一下我们自己的"思想花园"里种的到底是什么。

我们最终渐渐发现，我们在生活中遇到的许多问题和困难正是源于我们不断在心里种的怀疑、恐惧和忧虑的种子。

当我们越来越多地认识到这些消极思想时，我们就会说："不，我不会把这颗野草种在自己的心灵花园。"

我会有意识地选种一些更好的东西，结果确实激动人心。

当你开始有意识地耕种自己的心灵花园时，生活中发生的改变也确实会让你大吃一惊。你曾认为不可能或遥远的东西会突然进入你的视野。

任何花园都处在不断变化中。只种下一粒幸福的种子，然后忘在脑后是不够的。杂草很快就会困死你的弱不禁风的幼苗。恐惧、怀疑和忧虑的杂草一出现，必须不断拔除、扔掉。

爱、幸福和宁静都会传染。那些不断在自己的心灵花园种下这些种子的人也正把爱、幸福和宁静种进别人的心田。记住：

心是花园，思想是种。可以种花，或种杂草。

所以，你问一下自己，你打算在自己绚丽的心灵花园种什么？

让你的生活充满爱和幸福。

The Praise That Changed the Life

When he was small, Hill was an acknowledged bad boy.

At the age of 9, his father married his stepmother. At that time they lived poor in the countryside while his stepmother was from a wealthy family.

His father introduced Hill to his stepmother as he said, "Dear, I hope you notice in the entire shire this is the worst boy, who has made me have no other way. Maybe before tomorrow morning he will throw a stone at you, or do a bad thing you will never imagine."

To Hill's surprise, his stepmother went up to him with a smile, held up his head and looked at him carefully. She then turned around to tell her husband, "You're wrong. He is not the worst boy in the entire shire, but the most intelligent and creative boy. Only he doesn't find a place to vent his passion."

His stepmother's words warmed his heart, his tears almost rolling down. With this, he started building friendship with his stepmother. And this became the drive of his life, making him create 28 successful golden rules, which helped tens of thousands of ordinary people set foot on the road to success and prosperity.

Before his stepmother came, no one praised him smart, and his father and neighbors identified him as a bad boy. However, his stepmother's words changed his life's destiny.

When Hill was 14 years old, his stepmother bought him a used typewriter and said to him, "I believe you will become a writer." Hill accepted his stepmother's gift and expectation, and started contributing to a local newspaper. He understood and enjoyed his stepmother's enthusiasm while he saw with his own eyes she had changed his family with her enthusiasm. Therefore, he would live up to her.

The strength from his stepmother aroused Hill's imagination, inspired his creativity, helped him link with a lot of wisdom and made him a rich man and famous writer in the United States and one of most influential figures in the 20th century.

Praise will never be superfluous, especially for children. A sincere praise may be better than 10,000 severe reproaches.

改变一生的赞美

拿破仑·希尔小时候是一个公认的坏男孩。

他9岁时,父亲把继母娶进了家门。当时,他们还是居住在乡下的贫苦人家,而继母则来自富有的家庭。

父亲一边向继母介绍拿破仑·希尔,一边说:"亲爱的,希望你注意这个全郡最坏的男孩,他已经让我无可奈何。说不定不到明天早上,他就会拿石头扔向你,或者做出你完全想不到的坏事。"

出乎拿破仑·希尔意料的是,继母微笑着走到他面前,托起他的头认真地看着他。接着,她回头对丈夫说:"你错了,他不是全郡最坏的男孩,而是全郡最聪明、最有创造力的男孩。只不过他还没有找到发泄热情的地方。"

继母的话说得拿破仑·希尔心里热乎乎的,眼泪几乎滚落下来。就是凭着这一句话,他和继母开始建立友谊。也就是这一句话,成为激励他一生的动力,使他日后创造了成功的28项黄金法则,帮助千千万万的普通人走上成功和致富的道路。

在继母到来之前，没有一个人称赞过他聪明，他的父亲和邻居认定他就是坏男孩。但是，继母就只说了一句话，便改变了他一生的命运。

拿破仑·希尔14岁时，继母给他买了一部二手打字机，并对他说："相信你会成为一名作家。"拿破仑·希尔接受了继母的礼物，理解了她的期望，并开始向当地的一家报纸投稿。他了解继母的热忱，也很欣赏她的那股热忱，他亲眼看到她用自己的热忱改变了他们的家庭。所以，他不愿意辜负她。

来自继母的这股力量，激发了拿破仑·希尔的想象力，激励了他的创造力，帮助他获得了很多智慧，使他成了美国的富豪和著名作家，成了20世纪最有影响的人物之一。

赞美永远都不多余，尤其是对孩子。一次真诚的赞美，可能胜过一万次严厉的责备。

The Power of the Violin

At noon that day, I drove back to the villa. Just as I entered the living room, I heard a slight sound coming from the bedroom upstairs-it was the sound of my favorite violin.

"Thief!"

I dashed upstairs. Sure enough, as expected, a boy of about 12 years old was petting my violin. The boy had disheveled hair and a thin face, his unfitting coat bulging, seemingly stuffed with something. At first glance, I found a new pair of shoes at the bed missing. It seemed he was surely a thief.

Then, I saw his eyes full of fear and despair. My anger was immediately replaced by a smile, I asked, "Are you Mr. Ram's nephew Rubens? I'm his butler. Two days ago I heard Mr. Ram say he has a nephew living in the countryside to come. It must be you. You're really like him!"

On hearing my words, the boy was first stunned, but then quickly said, "Has my uncle gone out? I think I'd better first go out for a walk and visit him again in a while."

I nodded and asked the boy who was preparing to put down the violin, "Do you like to play the violin so much?"

"Yes, but I'm so poor that I can't afford it," the boy replied.

"Then, I give this violin to you." The boy looked at me questioningly, but he picked up the violin. Going out of the living room, he suddenly saw on the wall my huge color photo I performed in the Grand Theater of Sydney. He involuntarily shivered for a moment and ran out without looking back.

I was sure that the boy had understood what happened because no master would decorate the living room with the butler's photo.

A few years later, at a music competition of senior high school students in Melbourne, I was invited to judge the final. Finally, a violin player called Merritt won the first prize with his solid strength!

After the award, Merritt ran to me holding a violin box, his face crimson, asked, "Mr. Brian, do you still know me? You have given me a violin, which I have been treasuring, until today! Today, I can give back this violin to you without regret..."

It turned out that he was "Mr. Ram's nephew Rubens"!

Tears welled up in my eyes.

小提琴的力量

那天中午，我驾车回到了别墅。刚进客厅门，我就听见了楼上的卧室里有轻微的响声，是我最喜欢的那把小提琴发出的声音。

“有小偷！”

我一个箭步冲上楼，果然不出所料，只见一个大约12岁的少年正在那里抚摸我的小提琴。那个少年头发蓬乱，脸庞瘦削，不合身的外套鼓鼓囊囊，里面好像塞了某些东西。我一眼瞥见自己放在床头的一双新皮鞋失踪了，看来他是个小偷无疑。

这时，我看见他的眼里充满了惶恐和绝望。我愤怒的表情顿时被微笑所代替，我问道：“你是拉姆先生的外甥鲁本吗？我是他的管家，前两天我听拉姆先生说他有一个住在乡下的外甥要来，一定是你了，你和他长得真像啊！”

听见了我的话，少年先是一愣，但很快说道：“我舅舅出门了吗？我想我还是先出去转转，待会儿再来看他吧。”

我点了点头，然后问那位正准备将小提琴放下的少年：“你很喜欢拉小提琴吗？”

“是的，但我很穷，买不起。”少年回答说。

“那我把小提琴送给你吧。”少年疑惑地看了我一眼，但还是拿起了小提琴。临出客厅时，他突然看见了墙上挂着一张我在悉尼大剧院演出的巨幅彩照，不由得颤栗了一下，然后头也不回地跑远了。

我确信那位少年已明白了是怎么回事，因为没有哪位主人会用管家的照片来装饰客厅。

几年后，在墨尔本市高中生的一次音乐比赛中，我应邀担任决赛评委。最后，一名叫梅里特的小提琴选手凭借雄厚的实力夺得了第一名！

颁奖大会结束后，梅里特拿着一只小提琴盒跑到我面前，脸色绯红地问：“布赖恩先生，您还认识我吗？您曾送过我一把小提琴，我一直珍藏着，直到有了今天！今天，我可以无愧地将这把小提琴还给您了……”

原来他就是“拉姆先生的外甥鲁本”！

我的眼里涌起了泪花。

The Warm Pebbles

Once a rusty tin jar was ploughed out by a farmer and he found an ancient book in it. It was so old that the papers were rotten and most of them became broken as turned. He read it over and again carefully and later, he discovered it was a book on magic, stating that on the Black Sea shores existed a pebble that could turn anything into gold. This pebble, unlike all the others, was warm to touch. Suddenly a strong desire stuck deep roots in his mind: he would go to search the shores for the pebble.

From dawn to dusk he would pick up pebbles and feel them. To ensure he did not pick the same pebble twice, he would throw every picked pebble far out into the sea.

Searches lasted days, weeks and then months. A year and then another, every pebble he picked up was as cold as ice and he would throw them away as fast as he could. Now he had become so experienced at it that he could pick up a pebble and cast in with one smooth action.

At last he was bored with such endless searches and nearly disappointed, doubting whether there was really such a pebble.

One evening as he was dragging his worn-out legs, and leaving the beach after a whole day's aimless search, he was a common pebble in front of him. "This will be the last one!" said the man hopelessly. With a sigh he bowed and picked it up with his spent hand. Not until he gathered all his strength and threw it farther into the sea did he realize that it was warm and even a little hot, but it was too late.

温暖的鹅卵石

从前，一只生锈的锡罐被一个农民犁了出来，他发现里面有一本古书。这本书太旧了，纸张已经腐烂了，大部分一翻就碎了。他一遍又一遍仔细读着这本书，后来发现那是一本魔法书，书上说：在黑海的海岸上，有一块可以将任何东西变成金子的鹅卵石。这块鹅卵石和其他所有的石头不一样，它摸起来温暖。突然一种强烈的欲望在他的心里深深地扎下了根：他要去那些海岸寻找这块鹅卵石。

从早到晚，他拣鹅卵石、摸鹅卵石。为了确保不重复拣起同一块鹅卵石，他常常把每一块拣过的鹅卵石都远远地扔进了海里。

日复一日，周复一周，月复一月，年复一年，他拣过的每一块鹅卵石都像冰一样冷，他常常尽可能快地扔掉它们。现在他已经富有经验，麻利地拣起鹅卵石，又马上扔掉。

最后，他厌倦了这种没完没了的寻找，快要失望了，怀疑是否真的有这样一块鹅卵石。

一天晚上，漫无目的地搜索了一天后，当他拖着疲惫的双腿要离开海岸时，看到面前有一块普通的鹅卵石。"这将是最后一块了！"他一筹莫展地说。他叹了口气，弯下腰，筋疲力尽地伸手拾起了那块鹅卵石。直到他用尽全力把它远远地扔进了大海，才意识到这块鹅卵石是温暖的，甚至还有点儿热，但已经太晚了。

Send You a Moon

One night, a Buddhist monk who cultivated himself in the mountain walked from the woods path in the bright moonlight and went back to his cottage, when he happened to run into a thief there. He was afraid to startle the thief, so he kept waiting at the door...

The thief couldn't find any valuable thing. When he turned to leave, he saw the monk. He was in a panic, but the monk said, "Since you came from afar to visit me, after all I can't let you back empty-handed!" With that, he undressed his cloak. "It's chilly in the night, so you can go with this cloak."

Then, the monk draped the clothes over the thief. Out of his wits, the thief slipped away with his head bowed.

Seeing off the thief, the monk said with emotion, "Poor man, I wish I could send you a moon!"

The next day the warm sun shone. The monk opened his eyes and saw the cloak he had draped over the thief the previous night was neatly folded on the doorstep. The monk was very pleased and said, "I finally sent him a moon..."

送你一轮明月

一天夜里，一位在山中修行的禅师从皎洁月光下的林间小路上散完步，回到自己的茅屋时，正碰上有个小偷光顾，他怕惊动小偷，一直站在门口等候……

小偷找不到值钱的东西，返身离去时看到了禅师，正感到惊慌时，禅师说："你走老远的山路来探望我，总不能让你空手而回呀！"说着，脱下了身上的外衣，"夜里凉，你带着这件衣服走吧。"

说着，禅师就把衣服披在了小偷身上。小偷不知所措，低着头溜走了。

禅师看着小偷的背影，感慨说："可怜的人呀，但愿我能送一轮明月给你！"

第二天，暖阳照耀。禅师睁开眼睛，看到昨晚披在小偷身上的那件外衣整齐地叠着，放在了门口。禅师非常高兴，喃喃说道："我终于送了他一轮明月……"

Put down the Parcel and Hurry on

A young man with a large parcel on his back came from afar for Master Wuji. He said, "Master, I'm so lonely and so painful that the long trek makes me tired out, my shoes worn-out, my feet cut by the thorns, my hands also injured and bleeding and my voice hoarse due to the long shouting... why can't I find the sun in the heart?"

The master asked, "What do you put in your large parcel?"

The young man said, "It is very important to me, inside it including the suffering each time I fall, the weeping each time I'm hurt, the trouble each time I feel lonely... relying on it, I can come to you here."

So Master Wuji took the young man to the river, where they crossed in a boat. Ashore, the master said, "Hurry on your journey shouldering the boat!"

"What, shouldering the boat?" the young man was surprised, "it is so heavy. How can I shoulder it?"

"Yes, my son, you can't carry it," the master just smiled and said, "when you cross the river, the boat is useful. But after crossing it, you will put down the boat and hurry on. Otherwise, it will become a burden. Suffering, loneliness and tears-all these are useful to life. They can sublimate life, but if you don't forget them all the time, they will become the burden in life. Put it down! My son, life can't bear a heavy burden."

The young man put down his parcel and hurried on. He felt his pace was easy and merry, and much faster than before.

It turns out that life is not necessarily so heavy.

放下包裹赶路

一名青年背着一个大包裹千里迢迢跑来找无际大师，他说："大师，我是那样孤独和痛苦，长途跋涉使我疲倦到了极点；我的鞋子破了，荆棘割破了双脚；手也受伤了，流血不止；嗓子因长久的呼喊而喑哑……为什么我还不能找到心中的阳光呢？"

大师问:“你的大包裹里装的什么?”

青年说:“它对我非常重要。里面是我每一次跌倒时的痛苦,每一次受伤后的哭泣,每一次孤寂时的烦恼……靠它,我才能走到您这里来。”

于是,无际大师带青年来到河边,他们坐船过了河。上岸后,大师说:“你扛着船赶路吧!”

“什么,扛着船赶路?”青年很惊讶,“它那么沉,我扛得动吗?”

“是的,孩子,你扛不动它。”大师微微一笑,说:“过河时,船是有用的。但过了河,就要放下船赶路。否则它会成为包袱。痛苦、孤独、眼泪,这些对人生都是有用的。它们能使生命得到升华,但须臾不忘,就成了人生的包袱。放下它吧!孩子,生命不能太负重。”

青年放下了包袱,继续赶路,他发觉自己的步子轻松而愉悦,比以前快多了。

原来,生命可以不必如此沉重。

The Miracle of the Spring

When spring came to the city of Cleveland, Ohio, it did not change Gates Avenue. The people who lived on the pretty streets near Gates Avenue were making gardens, painting their houses and getting their lawn mowers ready for the summer. But Gates Avenue continued to look dirty and ugly.

Gates Avenue was a short street. But it seemed long because it was so ugly, most of the families who lived there had very little money. They never expected to have much more.

Sometimes the men had jobs and sometimes they didn't. Their houses had not been painted in many years and did not even have running water. The Gates Avenue families carried their water from the hydrants on the street corners.

The street itself was ugly, too. It had no pavement and no streetlight. The railway at one end of Gates Avenue added noise and dirt.

Most of the little girls in the school near Gates Avenue wore pretty new clothes that spring. But the little girl from Gates Avenue wore the same dirty dress that she had worn all winter. It was probably the only dress she owned.

Her teacher sighed. The little girl was so nice! She always worked hard in school; she was always polite and friendly. But her face was dirty and her hair was untidy.

One day the teacher said, "Will you wash your face before you come to school tomorrow morning? Please do that for me." The teacher could see that girl was pretty under the dirt.

The next morning the child's pretty face had been washed. Her hair was clean and tidy, too. Before the little girl went home that afternoon, the teacher said, "Now, dear, please ask your mother to wash your dress."

But the little girl continued to wear the dirty dress. "Her mother is probably not interested in her," the teacher thought. So she bought a bright blue dress and gave it to the little girl. The child took the present and hurried home as fast as she could.

The next morning she came to school in the new blue dress, and she was clean and tidy. She told the teacher, "My mother was surprised when she saw me this morning in my new dress. My father wasn't at home; he had gone to work. But he will see me at supper this evening."

When her father saw her in the new blue dress, he was surprised to find that he had a pretty little girl. When the family sat down to eat supper, he was even more surprised to find a cloth on the table. The family had never used a tablecloth before. "What is the cloth for?" he asked.

"We're going to be more tidy here," his wife said. "It isn't nice to have a house that dirty and untidy when our daughter is so clean."

After supper the mother started to wash the floors. Her husband watched for a little while without saying anything. Then he went outside into the backyard and began to repair the fence. The next evening, with the family's help, he started digging for a garden.

During the next week, the man who lived in the next house watched what the little girl's family was doing. Then he started to paint his house for the first time in ten years.

A few days later the young minister of a church near Gates Avenue passed the two houses and saw the men working. He noticed that there was no pavement on Gates Avenue and no streetlight. He knew the houses had no running water. "People who are trying so hard to have clean homes and tidy yards on a street like this should be helped," the minister said to himself.

He went to see the men who were at the head of the city government. And he went to see important businessmen and the leaders of the churches and schools. He asked them to help the families living on Gates Avenue.

A few months later Gates Avenue looked like a different street. There was pavement now on the avenue. There was a street light on the corner. The houses had running water. Six months after the little girl got her new blue dress, Gates Avenue was a tidy street of friendly homes where respectable families lived.

People who knew about the changes called it the "Gates Avenue Cleanup." Everywhere the young minister went, he told the story of this miracle.

Other cities heard of the "cleanup," and began to organize their own "cleanup" campaign. Since 1997, thousands of U. S. towns and cities have organized campaigns for painting and repairing homes. For the people who live in the homes, life has been made better.

Who knows what miracles may happen when a teacher gives a little girl a new blue dress?

春天的奇迹

春天来到俄亥俄州克利夫兰市时，没有改变盖茨大道。住在盖茨大道附近那些漂亮街道上的人们正在建花园、漆房子，而且为夏天准备好了草坪锄草机。但盖茨大道看上去还是那样肮脏丑陋。

盖茨大道是一条短街。但它显得很长，因为它很丑陋，住在那里的大多数家庭都没多少钱。他们压根就没想赚更多的钱。

有时男人们有活做，有时则没有。他们的房子已经好多年没有油漆过了，甚至连自来水都没有。住在盖茨大道的家庭是从街角的水龙头上接水。

街道本身也很丑陋。既没有人行道，也没有街灯。盖茨大道一端的铁路增加了噪音和灰尘。

盖茨大道附近学校的大多数小学女生那年春天都穿着漂亮的新衣服。但来自盖茨大道的那个小女孩还是穿着她已经穿了一冬天的那件脏衣服。大概她只有这一件衣服吧。

她的老师叹了口气。小女孩长得非常漂亮！她在学校总是非常用功；她总是礼貌友好。但她的脸很脏，头发也不整洁。一天，老师说："明天早上你上学前把脸洗一下好吗？请为我洗一下。"老师能看出那女孩洗去灰尘是非常漂亮的。

第二天早上，小女孩的漂亮脸蛋果然已经洗了。她的头发既干净又整洁。那天下午小女孩回家前，老师说："听着，宝贝，让你妈妈洗一下你的衣服。"

但小女孩还是穿着那件脏衣服。"她的妈妈可能对她不感兴趣吧。"老师心里说。

于是，她买了一件鲜蓝色连衣裙，送给了小女孩。小女孩接住礼物，飞快地跑回了家。

第二天早上，她穿着新买的蓝色连衣裙来到了学校，而且打扮得干净整洁。她告诉老师说："今天早上妈妈看到我穿上新买的蓝色连衣裙时，吃了一惊。爸爸不在家；他上班去了。但今天吃晚饭时他会看到我的。"

她的父亲看到女儿穿着新买的蓝色连衣裙，吃惊地发现小女儿是那样漂亮。当一家人坐下来吃晚饭时，他甚至更加吃惊地发现桌子上铺了一块台布。一家人以前从来没有使用过桌布。"垫布做什么用？"他问。

"我们这里要比以前更加整洁，"他的妻子说。"当我们的女儿这样干净时，让我们的房子这样脏乱不好。"

饭后，小女孩的妈妈开始擦洗地板。她的丈夫看了一会儿，没说一句话。随后，他走出门，来到后院，开始修整篱笆。第二天傍晚，在一家人的帮助下，他开始挖建花园。在接下来的一个星期里，住在隔壁的那个人看到了小女孩一家人的行动。随后，他开始油漆房子，这是10年以来的第一次。

几天后，盖茨大道附近一座教堂的一名年轻牧师从两家的房边经过，看到两个男人在那里忙活着。他注意到盖茨大道上既没有人行道，也没有街灯。他知道房子里没有自来水。"街上像这样竭尽全力想拥有干净住宅和整洁院子的人们应该得到帮助。"牧师自言自语说。

他去见市政府的那些头头们，随后又去见商界要人和教堂与学校的领导。他要他们帮助住在盖茨大道上的那些家庭。

又过了几个月后，盖茨大道看上去像换了一条街，现在已经有了人行道。街角安上了路灯。房子里有了自来水。小女孩穿上她新买的蓝色连衣裙后的6个月，盖茨大道成了一条整洁的街道，那里的住户都友好相处，那里住着受人尊敬的家庭。

知道这些变化的人们称之为"盖茨大道大清扫。"年轻牧师每到一处，都讲述这个神奇的故事。其他城市听说了这个故事，随后也开始组织起自己的"大清扫"运动。自1997年以来，几千座美国乡镇和城市都组织起了粉饰和修补住宅的活动。对住在家里的人来说，生活已经变得更好了。

当一名老师送给一个小女孩一身新连衣裙时，谁知道会发生什么奇迹呢？

Bright Heart

Last year around Halloween, I was invited to participate in a carnival for Tuesday's Child, an organization that helps children with the AIDS virus. I was asked to attend because I'm on a television show; I went because I care. I don't think that most of the kids recognize me as a celebrity. They just thought of me as a big kid who came to play with them for the day. I think I like it better that day.

At the carnival they had all kinds of booths. I was drawn to one in particular because of all the children that had gathered there. At this booth, anyone who wanted to could paint a square. Later that square was going to be sewn together with the others, to make a quilt. The quilt would be presented to a man who had dedicated his life to this organization and would soon be retiring.

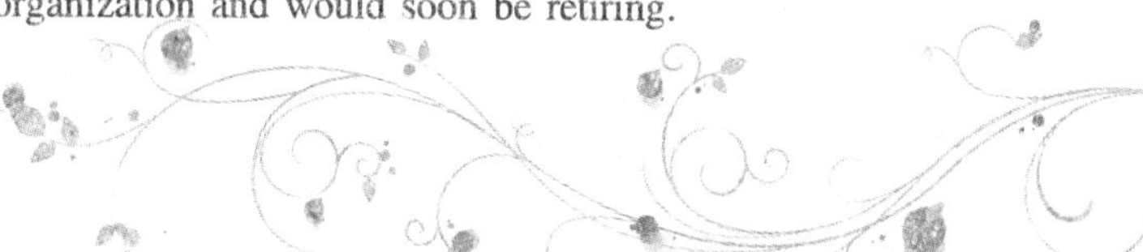

They gave everyone fabric paints in colors and asked the kids to paint something that would make the quilt beautiful. As I looked around at all the squares, I saw pink hearts and bright blue clouds, beautiful orange sunrises, green leaves and purple flowers. The pictures were all bright, positive and uplifting. All except for one.

The boy sitting next to me was painting a heart, but it was dark, lifeless. It lacked the bright, vibrant colors that his fellow artists had used.

At first I thought maybe he took the only paint that was left and it just happened to be dark. But when I asked him about it, he said his heart was that color. I asked him why and he told me that he was very sick. Not only was he very sick, but his mom was very sick as well. He looked straight into my eyes and said, "There's nothing anyone can do that will help."

I told him I was sorry that he was sick and I could certainly understand why he was so sad. I could even understand why he had made his heart a dark color. But... I told him, "It isn't true that there is nothing anyone can do to help. Other people may not be able to make him or his mom better, but we can do things like giving a hug, which in my experience can really help when you are feeling sad." I told him that if he would like, I would be happy to give him one so he could see what I meant. He instantly crawled into my lap and I thought my own heart would burst with the love I felt for this sweet little boy.

He sat there for a long time and when he had had enough, he jumped down to finish his coloring. I asked him if he felt any better and he said that he did, but he was still sick and nothing would change that. I told him I understood. I walked away feeling sad, but recommitted to this cause. I would do whatever I could to help.

As the day was coming to an end and I was getting ready to head home, I felt a tug on my jacket. I turned around and standing there with a smile on his face was the little boy. He said, "My heart is changing colors. It's getting brighter... I think those hugs really do work."

On my way home I felt my own heart and realized it, too, had changed to a brighter color.

明亮的心

去年万圣节前夕，我应邀参加了"星期二孩子"的狂欢节。"星期二孩子"是一个帮助感染艾滋病的儿童的组织。我应邀参加，是因为我主持电视节目；我赴约，是因为我关心。我想，大多数孩子不会把我当作名人，只会把我当作一个过来陪他们玩的大孩子。我想我更喜欢这样。

在狂欢节上，他们有各种各样的棚子。所有孩子都聚在一个棚子下面，我被吸引了过去。在这个棚子里，大家都画了一个棉蕾。随后，棉蕾要和别的棉蕾缝在一起，做成一条被子。这被子将送给一个将其一生奉献给这个组织的人，因为他马上就要退休。

他们把各色颜料发给每个孩子，让孩子们把被子画得漂亮一些。我围绕着所有的棉蕾看着，只见有粉红色的心，鲜蓝色的云，美丽的橘黄色旭日，翠绿的叶子和紫色的花朵。所有的图案都是那样鲜亮、积极、向上。只有一幅例外。

坐在我旁边的那个男孩正在画一个心形图案，但这颗心黑糊糊的，毫无生气，缺乏伙伴们使用的那些明亮活泼的色彩。

起初，我还以为他只是随便画画，碰巧画成了黑色。但当我问他时，他说他的心就是这种颜色。我问他为什么，他告诉我说他病得很重。不仅他病得很重，他妈妈病得也很重。他望着我的眼睛说："谁也无能为力。"

我告诉他说，我对他生病感到难过，当然能明白他为什么那样伤心，甚至能明白他为什么把心画成黑色。可是……我告诉他说："谁也无能为力是不对的。其他人也许无法使他们母子康复，但我们可以做一些事，比如给一个拥抱，根据我的经验，你感到伤心时，这确实能有帮助。”我告诉他，如果他愿意，我很高兴拥抱他一下，这样他就能明白我的用心了。他马上爬到我的膝间。我想我自己的心为这个可爱的男孩而一下子充满了爱。

他在我的膝间坐了好一阵子。当他感到满足时，才跳下去，继续涂起了画。我问他是不是感觉好了些。他说是的，但他仍然有病，什么也改变不了。我告诉他说我明白。我离开时感到伤心，但会为这件事再做努力，尽自己所能来帮助他。

当一天快要结束我准备回家时，我感到有人在拽我的夹克。我回头一看，只见面带微笑站在那里的是那个小男孩。他说：“我的心正在改变颜色，它会变得越来越亮……我想那些拥抱确实有用。”

回家的路上，我摸了摸自己的心，感到它也变得越来越亮了。

The Reason of Einstein's Success

At the age of 16, Einstein failed in several courses because he mixed with a group of mischievous kids. One weekend morning, Einstein held a fishing rod and was about to fish with those kids, his father stopped him and said to him calmly, "Einstein, you're so fond of playing all the day that you failed in the examination. I'm so worried about your future with your mother."

"What are you worrying about? Jack and Robert also failed, but don't they go fishing as usual?"

"My boy, you can't think so." Looking at Einstein, his father said lovingly, "There goes a fable in our hometown. I hope you can listen to it carefully.

"There were two cats playing on the roof. Once off guard, a cat fell into the chimney holding another one. When the two cats climbed out of the chimney, a cat's face was stained with the soot while the other's face was clean. Seeing the soot-faced cat, the clean cat thought its face was dirty and ugly, so it quickly ran to the riverside and washed its face. The soot-faced cat saw the clean-faced cat, thinking its face was also clean, so it swaggered in the street.

"Einstein, no one can be your mirror. Only you are your own mirror. Taking other people to be your mirror, even a genius may become a fool."

Hearing this, Einstein was ashamed to lay down his fishing rod and returned to his small room.

Since then, Einstein often took himself as a mirror to examine and reflect, and kept hinting himself: I was unique, so I needn't be as mediocre as others. This was why Einstein succeeded.

1,000 people have 1,000 kinds of lifestyles with 1,000 kinds of wishes in life. Different ways and wishes will produce different attitudes towards life. You can consult the other people's attitude to determine your own, but you can never follow others to do so.

You must see yourself clearly, and know you're your pursue is. Your future doesn't depend on how others do, but on how you are going to do.

爱因斯坦成功的原因

16岁那年，爱因斯坦整天同一群调皮贪玩的孩子在一起，几门功课都不及格。一个周末的早晨，爱因斯坦正拿着钓鱼竿准备和那群孩子一起去钓鱼，父亲拦住了他，心平气和地对他说："爱因斯坦，你整日贪玩，功课不及格，我和你的母亲很为你的前途担忧。"

"有什么可担忧的？杰克和罗伯特他们也没及格，不照样去钓鱼吗？"

"孩子，你千万不能这样想。"父亲充满关爱地望着爱因斯坦说。"在我们故乡流传着这样一个寓言，我希望你能认真听一听。

"有两只猫在屋顶上玩耍。一不小心，一只猫抱着另一只猫掉到了烟囱里。当两只猫从烟囱里爬出来时，一只猫的脸上沾满了黑烟，而另一只猫的脸上却干干净净。干净猫看见满脸黑灰的猫，以为自己的脸也又脏又丑，便快步跑到河边洗了脸。而黑脸猫看见干净猫，以为自己的脸也是干净的，就大摇大摆地上街闲逛去了。

"爱因斯坦，谁也不能成为你的镜子，只有自己才是自己的镜子。拿别人做自己的镜子，天才也许会照成傻瓜的。"

听后，爱因斯坦羞愧地放下鱼竿，回到了自己的小屋里。

从此，爱因斯坦时常拿自己作为镜子来审视和映照自己，并不断地自我暗示：我是独一无二的，我没有必要像别人一样平庸。这就是爱因斯坦成功的原因。

一千个人有一千种生活方式，有一千种生活的愿望。不同的方式和愿望，就会产生不同的生活态度。你可以参照别人的态度确定自己的态度，但你永远不能照着别人那样做。

你必须看清自己，并清楚自己想追求什么。你的未来如何，不取决于别人怎样做，而是取决于你自己怎样做。

To Be Your Own Goddess of Mercy

A man went under the eaves to stay away from the rain when he saw Goddess of Mercy passing by holding an umbrella. This man said, "Goddess of Mercy, release all flesh. Can you take me along?"

Goddess of Mercy said, "I'm in the rain and you're under the eaves. There is no rain under the eaves, so you don't need my release."

The man immediately jumped out from under the eaves and stood in the rain. "Now I'm also in the rain. Should I be released?"

Goddess of Mercy said, "You're in the rain, so am I. I am not caught in the rain because I have an umbrella. And you're caught in the rain because you have no umbrella. Therefore, it is not I but the umbrella that released myself. If you want to be released, don't need to find me, please find an umbrella for yourself!" With that she was gone.

The next day, the man got into trouble, so he went to the temple to ask for Goddess of Mercy. Entering the temple, he found there was a person worshiping in front of the image of Goddess of Mercy. That person just looked like Goddess of Mercy.

The man asked, "Are you Goddess of Mercy?"

That person replied, "I am."

The man asked again, "Why do you worship yourself?"

Goddess of Mercy laughed, "I also got into trouble, but I know to ask for others is less than to ask for myself."

做自己的观音

有个人在屋檐下躲雨,看见观音正撑伞走过。这人说:"观音菩萨,普度一下众生吧,带我一段如何?"

观音说:"我在雨里,你在檐下,而檐下无雨,你不需要我度。"

这人立刻跳出檐下,站在雨中:"现在我也在雨中了,该度我了吧?"

观音说:"你在雨中,我也在雨中,我不被淋,因为有伞;你被雨淋,因为无伞。所以,不是我度自己,而是伞度我。你要想度,不必找我,请自找伞去!"说完便走了。

第二天,这人遇到了难事,便去寺庙里求观音。走进庙里,才发现观音像前也有一个人在拜,那个人长得和观音一模一样,丝毫不差。

这人问:"你是观音吗?"

那人答道:"我正是观音。"

这人又问:"那你为何还拜自己?"

观音笑道:"我也遇到了难事,但我知道求人不如求己。"

If You Can See It, You Can Be It

Arnold Schwarzenegger was not that famous in 1976 when he met with a newspaper reporter.

The reporter asked Schwarzenegger, "Now you've retired from bodybuilding, what do you plan to do next?"

Schwarzenegger answered very calmly and confidently, "I'm going to be the No. 1 movie star in Hollywood."

The reporter was shocked and amused at Schwarzenegger's plan. At that time, it was very hard to imagine how this muscle-bound bodybuilder, who was not a professional actor and who spoke poor English with a strong American Austrian accent, could ever hope to be Hollywood's No. 1 movie star.

So the reporter asked Schwarzenegger how he planned to make his dream come true, Schwarzenegger said, "I'll do it the same way I became the No. 1 bodybuilder in the world. What I do is to create a vision of whom I want to be, then I start living like that person in my mind as if it were already true." Sounds almost childishly simple, doesn't it? But it worked! Schwarzenegger did become the No. 1 highest-paid movie star in Hollywood!

Remember: "If you can see it, you can be it."

你能看到,就能做到

阿诺德·施瓦辛格1976年遇到一位新闻记者时还不是那样有名。

记者问施瓦辛格:"你现在从健美运动中退出,下一步打算做什么?"

施瓦辛格非常平静而自信地回答说:"我打算成为好莱坞头号电影明星。"

记者听到施瓦辛格的打算既震惊又可笑。当时,很难想象这位肌肉结实的健美运

动员既不是职业演员，英语说得又差劲，还带有很重的奥地利口音，怎么可能有希望成为好莱坞头号电影明星呢？

所以，当记者问施瓦辛格如何打算梦想成真时，施瓦辛格说："我会像当初成为世界头号健美运动员那样去做。我要做的就是创造一个自己想做的那个人的形象，然后像我心里想的那个人那样开始生活。"听起来是不是幼稚简单？但发挥了作用！施瓦辛格真的成了好莱坞收入最高的电影明星！

记住："你能看到，就能做到。"

Dig Three Feet Deeper

There's a story about the California gold rush that tells of two brothers who sold all they had and went prospecting for gold. They discovered a vein of the shining ore, staked a claim, and proceeded to get down to the serious business of getting the gold ore out of the mine. All went well at first, but then a strange thing happened. The vein of the gold ore disappeared! They had come to the end of the rainbow, and the pot of gold was no longer there. The brothers continued to pick away, but without success. Finally they gave up in disgust.

They sold their equipment and claim rights for a few hundred dollars, and took the train back home. Now the man who bought the claim hired an engineer to examine the rock strata of the mine. The engineer advised him to continue digging in the same spot where the former owners had left off. And three feet deeper, the new owner struck gold.

A little more persistence and the two brothers would have been millionaires themselves.

That's gold in you too. Do you need to dig three feet farther?

再挖三英尺

有个故事讲的是加州淘金潮时，有两个兄弟卖掉了他们所有的家产去加州淘金。他们发现了一个金光闪闪的矿脉，于是买下了这个矿藏的开采权，一定要把矿藏中的金子挖出来卖钱。开始进展得很顺利，但后来发生了一件奇怪的事情。金矿脉突然消失了！他们的幻想破灭了，金矿不在了！兄弟俩开始继续挖着，但仍然没有发现矿脉。最后，他们气急败坏地放弃了。

他们以几百美元的价格卖掉了自己的设备和开采权，然后坐着火车回到了家乡。现在那个买了他们的金矿开采权的人雇了一个工程师去勘查了这个金矿的岩层结构。这个工程师建议他继续在那两个兄弟上次挖到的地方挖下去。于是又挖了三英尺后，这个人发现了金子。

如果那兄弟俩再多一点点坚持的话，也许现在已经是百万富翁了。

你本身也藏有金矿，你需要再多挖三英尺吗？

予人玫瑰，手留余香

We All Can Become Angels

When I was a middle school student, a memorable thing occurred.

It was a Friday. On the way home from school I saw a classmate called Kyle, who carried a thick pile of books in his arms. I thought, "Why does he carry all the books home? He must be a bookworm."

Kyle was just transferred to our class. I shrugged and went on walking, when I suddenly saw a large group of children deliberately knocked down the books in his hands, and even some of them tripping Kyle, he immediately fell to the ground.

His glasses flying off, Kyle raised his head. I read the painful expression from his eyes and felt my heart tightened, so I ran to him. He was groping for his glasses on the ground. I handed his glasses to his hands. He thanked me with a smile on his face, which was the smile of gratitude from the bottom of his heart.

I learned where we lived was not far away from each other. So we returned home together. As I thought he was not bad and asked whether he took interest in playing soccer together on Saturday, he accepted.

Throughout the weekend we all mixed together and he made a very good impression on my friends and me.

It was Monday again. On the way to school, I once more saw Kyle carrying a pile of books in his arms.

Since then Kyle and I became best friends.

Years later, Kyle specially invited me to attend his graduation. In his speech, he said, "The graduation is the best moment to express his gratitude for those who have helped us. I would like to take this opportunity to thank my best friend."

Then, he began to talk about the story we had known each other. I was surprised to widen my eyes. Until the day I knew: that weekend many years ago, he had intended to commit suicide! He said he had carried all his books home, so that after his death his mother wouldn't have to specially go to the school to arranging his things left behind. Having said that, he looked at me sitting in the audience with a smile on his face and went on, "However, I was so lucky that my friend pulled me back from the brink of death."

At that moment, I truly understood what he said, "Never underestimate the power your behavior can produce, for your little action may change the fate of another person. Heaven makes each of us face and influence another life in some way."

Some people love to illuminate the lives of others with their own happiness and love. It is always worthwhile to do so. When we break our wings and can't fly, the friends around us are the angels who embrace us in their arms.

予人玫瑰,手留余香

我还是一名中学生时,发生了一件难忘的小事。

那是一个星期五,我在放学回家的路上看到了一个名叫凯尔的同学,他怀里抱着一摞厚厚的书。我想:"为什么要把所有书都带回家呢?他一定是个书呆子。"

凯尔刚转到我们班上。我耸耸肩继续往前走。这时,我突然看到,一大帮孩子故意把他手中的书打翻在地,还有人在凯尔脚下使了个绊儿,他随即倒地。

凯尔的眼镜飞了出去,他抬起头看了看,我从他眼中读出了痛苦的神情,我的心随之一紧,然后朝他跑去。他趴在地上摸索着找眼镜。我把眼镜递到了他手上。他向我道谢,脸上浮现出了笑容,那是发自肺腑的感激的笑容。

我得知,原来我们住的地方相距不远。于是,我们结伴回了家。我觉得他这个人还不错,就问他是否有兴趣周六一起去踢球,他欣然同意了。

整个周末,我们都混在一起,他给我和我的朋友们留下了非常好的印象。

周一又到了,上学路上,我又看到了怀抱一摞书的凯尔。

此后,我和凯尔成了最好的朋友。

多年后,凯尔特别邀请我去参加他的大学毕业典礼。他在致辞中说:"毕业典礼是对帮助过我们的人表达谢意的最好时刻。我要借这个机会,感谢我最好的朋友。"

接着,他开始讲我们认识的故事,我惊讶得睁大了眼睛。直到那天我才知道:多年前的那个周末,他原来是打算自杀的!他说自己把所有的书都抱回了家,这样妈妈在他死后就不必特意去学校整理他的遗物。说到这里,他看着坐在台下的我,脸上展现出了笑容,他接着说:"然而,我很幸运,是我的朋友把我从死亡的边缘拉了回来。"

那一刻,我才真正理解了他的话:"永远不要低估你的行为能够产生的力量,你一个小小的举动就可能改变另一个人的命运。上天让我们每个人都要面对另一个生命,让我们以某种方式去影响另一个生命。"

有人乐于用自己的快乐和爱心去照亮他人的生活,这样做永远都是值得的。当我们的翅膀折断、无力飞翔时,身边的朋友就是把我们拥入怀中的天使。

The Boy and the Huge Rock

This story happened in a small village. One day there was an earthquake. Nothing was destroyed and no one was hurt. But a huge rock fell from a nearby mountain and stopped in the middle of the road.

When the earthquake stopped, many people came to the road and saw the huge rock. Some of the strongest men tried to lift the rock out of the road. But they couldn't move it. They tried to push in but failed. They tried to pull it with ropes but nothing worked.

"Well," they all agreed, "There's nothing we can do about it. We'll have to change the road."

At this time a boy about 12 years old said, "I think I can help you to move the rock."

"You?" they shouted. "What are you talking about?" The men all laughed at the boy.

The next morning some people came into the street. One of them shouted, "The rock is gone!" More people ran out to see. It was true. The rock wasn't in the road any more. It wasn't even near the road.

"This is impossible," they said. "Where did it go?"

The boy stood in the street, smiling, "I told you I could move it last night."

The boy walked over to where the rock had been and uncovered some dirt with shovel. "I buried it," he said.

The people looked surprised.

"You see," he said, "I dug a deep hole next to the rock and I dug a small incline up to the rock and the rock rolled down into the hole by itself. I covered it with dirt."

The crowds shouted,"Clever boy! Clever boy!"
And some of them said,"Why haven't we thought of this good method?"

男孩和巨石

这个故事发生在一个小村里。有一天发生了地震。什么东西也没有遭到破坏,也没有人员受到伤害。但一块巨石从附近的山上滚落下来,挡在了路中央。

当地震停止时,许多人来到路边,看到了这块巨石。有几个最身强力壮的人想设法把石头从路上搬开。但他们怎么也搬不动。他们设法向里推,无济于事。他们用绳子用力拉,也不起一点作用。

"唉,"他们都异口同声地说。"我们对此无能为力了。我们必须得改路了。"

这时,一个大约12岁的男孩说:"我想我可以帮你们把石头移走。"

"你?"他们齐声喊道。"你在说什么呀?"他们都嘲笑起这个男孩。

第二天早上,有人来到街上。其中一个人大声叫道:"巨石不见了!"越来越多的人跑出来看。石头果真不见了。路上也不见了石头,甚至也不在路边。

"这不可能,"他们说。"石头到哪里去了呢?"

那个男孩站在路中央,微微笑道:"昨天晚上我就告诉你们我能移动石头。"

男孩走到巨石原来所在的地方,用铁铲掀起一些土。"我把它埋在了这里。"他说。

人们露出了惊讶的表情。

"你们明白,"他说。"我贴近巨石边挖了一个深坑,又在岩石上方挖了一个小斜坡,岩石自动就滚进了坑里。然后,我用土盖住了它。"

人们大声喊叫起来:"聪明孩子! 聪明孩子!"

随后,有些人说:"为什么我们没有想到这个好方法呢?"

A Coin Can Also Make You Succeed

Two young men hunted for jobs together, one Englishman, the other Jew.

A coin lay on the ground. The English young man went on without looking but the Jewish young man picked it up excitedly.

The English young man scorned the Jewish young man, thinking: what a good-for-nothing, even picking up a coin!

Watching the English young man from behind, the Jewish young man sighed with emotion in his heart, what a good-for-nothing, letting the money slip away from him!

The two men walked into a company at the same time. The company was so small that any employee had to work hard at a low salary, but the English young man was pleased to stay.

Two years later, the two men met on the street, when the Jewish young man had become a boss but the British young man was still looking for a job. The English young man was puzzled and said, "You were so unpromising, how can you get rich so quickly?"

The Jewish young man said,"Because I didn't stride over one coin like a gentleman as you. You even didn't want a coin, so how will you make a fortune?"

The English young man did want money, but what he was staring at the pound instead of the penny, so his money was always in future. It was the answer to the question.

一枚硬币也能成功

两个年轻人一同寻找工作,一个是英国人,一个是犹太人。

一枚硬币躺在地上,英国青年看也不看就走了过去,犹太青年却激动地将它捡起。

英国青年对犹太青年的举动露出鄙夷之色:一枚硬币也捡,真没出息!

犹太青年望着远去的英国青年心生感慨:让钱白白从身边溜走,真没出息!

两个人同时走进一家公司。公司很小,工作很累,工资也低,英国青年不屑一顾地走了,犹太青年却高兴地留了下来。

两年后,两人在街上相遇,犹太青年已成了老板,英国青年还在寻找工作。英国青年对此不可理解,说:"你这么没出息的人怎么能这么快地发了呢?"

犹太青年说:"因为我没有像你那样绅士般从一枚硬币上迈过去。你连一枚硬币都不要,怎么会发大财呢?"

英国青年并非不要钱,可他眼睛盯着的是大钱而不是小钱,所以他的钱总在明天。这就是问题的答案。

A Real One Who Panned the Gold

Two Mexicans went along the Mississippi for panning. When they came to a mouth of the river, they parted because one thought he could pan more gold in the Arkansas and the other thought he would have a greater chance in the Ohio River.

Ten years later, the man who went to the Ohio River really made a fortune. There he not only found a lot of gold sand but also built the docks and roads while he made the place where he stayed a large market town. Now the business prosperity and industrial development of Pittsburgh along the Ohio River are thanks to all his pioneering and early development.

The man who went to the Arkansas seemed not to be so lucky, for there was no news about him since they parted. Some said he had gone to Davy Jones' locker and some said he had returned to Mexico. Until 50 years later a nugget of 2. 7 kilograms caused a stir in Pittsburgh, so people had come to know about him. At that time, a reporter of Pittsburgh Newsweek wrote, "The largest nugget in U. S. A. came from Arkansas. A young man in the fish pound behind his house picked it up. From the diaries his grandfather left, this nugget was thrown into the pound by his grandfather.

Afterwards, the "Newsweek" published the grandfather's diaries, one of which wrote: Yesterday, I again found a piece of gold in the stream, greater than the piece of gold panned last year. Will I go into the city to sell it? Then there will be hundreds of people swarming here. The log shed my wife and I built with our own hands, the garden and the pond behind the house we opened up sweating all over, along with the campfire at nightfall, the loyal hound, the delicious stewed meat, the chickadees, the trees, the sky, the grassland as well as the precious peace and freedom will no longer exist. I would

rather see the spray when it is thrown into the pound than just sit watching all these disappear from my eyes.

The 1760s were the age that the United States began to create millionaires, so everyone was in a frenzied pursuit of money. But this gold miner threw away the panned gold. A lot of people thought it an incredible story. Until now some people still doubt its authenticity. However, I always believe it is true because in my mind this gold miner was a real one who panned the gold.

真正的淘金人

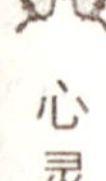

两个墨西哥人沿密西西比河淘金，到了一个河叉分了手，因为一个人认为阿肯色河可以淘到更多的金子，一个人认为去俄亥俄河发财的机会更大。

10年后，入俄亥俄河的人果然发了财，他在那里不仅找到了大量的金沙，而且建了码头，修了公路，还使他落脚的地方成了一个大集镇。现在俄亥俄河岸边的匹兹堡市商业繁荣，工业发达，起因无不和他的拓荒与早期开发有关。

进入阿肯色河的人似乎没有那么幸运，自分手后就没了音讯。有的说已经葬身鱼腹，有的说已经回了墨西哥。直到50年后，一个重2.7公斤的自然金块在匹兹堡引起轰动，人们才知道他的一些情况。当时，匹兹堡《新闻周刊》的一位记者写道："这颗全美最大的金块来源于阿肯色，是一位年轻人在他屋后的鱼塘里捡到的，从他祖父留下的日记看，这块金子是他的祖父扔进去的。

随后，《新闻周刊》刊登了那位祖父的日记。其中一篇是这样的：昨天，我在溪水里又发现了一块金子，比去年淘到的那块更大，进城卖掉它吗？那就会有成百上千的人涌向这里，我和妻子亲手用一根根圆木搭建的棚屋，挥洒汗水开垦的菜园和屋后的池塘，还有傍晚的火堆、忠诚的猎狗、美味的炖肉、山雀、树木、天空、草原、大自然赠给我们的珍贵的静谧和自由都将不复存在。我宁愿看到它被扔进鱼塘时荡起的水花，也不愿眼睁睁地望着这一切从我眼前消失。

18世纪60年代正是美国开始创造百万富翁的年代，每个人都在疯狂地追求金钱。可是，这位淘金者却把淘到的金子扔掉了。有很多人认为这是天方夜谭，直到现在还有人怀疑它的真实性。可是，我始终认为它是真的，因为在我的心中，这位淘金者是一位真正淘到金子的人。

The Seeds of Hope

One year, a newspaper of the United States published an announcement the horticultural institute offered a reward at a high price for the pure white marigold. The high reward attracted so many people, but in the kaleidoscopic nature, besides golden, the marigold is brown, but it is not easy to cultivate3 the white one. So after they were excited for a time, many people had forgotten the announcement.

20 years flew away. One normal day after 20 years, the horticultural institute that had published the announcement accidentally received a zealous letter and 100 seeds of pure white marigold. On that day the news spread like wildfire.

It turned out to be an old woman of over 70 years old. The institute had always been hesitating over the fact that the letter asserted with certainty that the seeds could bloom pure white marigold, and the need for verification became the focus of the debate. Whether they would make an experimental verification became the focus of controversy at one time.

Some said you would never live up to the old man's wish. Those seeds finally took root in the earth. The miracle appeared after one year: large patches of pure white marigold swayed in the breeze. Accordingly, the old woman who was always unknown to the public became a new focus.

Originally, the old woman was an out-and-out flower-lover. When she occasionally read the announcement 20 years ago, her heart kept thumping. But her eight children unanimously opposed her decision. After all, a woman who never knew the seed genetics couldn't complete what the experts could never accomplish, so her thought was only a lunatic raving!

Still, the old woman didn't change her mind and went on working without hesitation. She scattered some of the most common seeds and took good care of them. A year later, when the marigold bloomed, she chose one faintest from those golden and brown flowers and made it wither naturally in order to get the best seed. The next year, she again grew them and chose the faintest from these flowers to plant... day after day, year after year, through many cycles of spring sowing and autumn harvest, the old woman's husband died, her children flew far and high, a lot of things happened in her life, but only the desire to grow the pure white marigold took root in her heart.

Finally, after 20 years on the day we all know, in the garden she saw a marigold, which was not nearly white, but as white as silver or snow.

A problem even experts couldn't cope with was readily solved by an old woman who didn't understand genetics. Wasn't it a miracle? To take root in the heart, even the most common seed, can grow into a miracle!

希望的种子

当年，美国一家报纸曾刊登了一则园艺所重金悬赏征求纯白金盏花的启事。高额赏金让许多人趋之若鹜，但在千姿百态的自然界中，金盏花除了金色的，就是棕色的，能培植出白色的不是一件易事。所以，激动了一阵后，许多人就把那则启事抛到了九霄云外。

一晃20年过去了。20年后很平常的一天，当年那家曾刊登启事的园艺所意外地收到了一封热情的应征信和100粒"纯白金盏花"的种子。当天，这件事不胫而走。

寄种子的原来是一位年已古稀的老人。对信中言之凿凿能开出纯白金盏花的种子，园艺所一直举棋不定，该不该验证一时成了争论的焦点。

有人说：绝不应该辜负了一位老人的心意。那些种子终于落土生根。奇迹是在一年之后才出现的，大片大片纯白色的金盏花在微风中摇曳。一直默默无闻的老人因此成了新的焦点。

原来，老人是一个地地道道的爱花人。当她20年前偶然看到那则启事后，便怦然心动。她的决定却遭到了8个儿女的一致反对。毕竟，一个压根就不懂种子遗传学的人，一件让专家都不能完成的事，她的想法岂不是痴人说梦！

老人还是痴心不改，义无反顾地干了下去。她撒下了一些最普通的种子，精心侍弄。

一年后，金盏花开了，她从那些金色的、棕色的花中挑选了一朵颜色最淡的，任其自然枯萎，以取得最好的种子。次年，她又把它们种下去，然后再从这些花中挑选出颜色最淡的花的种子栽种……日复一日，年复一年，春种秋收，周而复始，老人的丈夫去世了，儿女远走了，生活中发生了很多事情，但唯有种出白色金盏花的愿望在她的心中生了根。

终于，在我们今天都知道的那个20年后的一天，她在那片花园中看到一朵金盏花，它不是近乎白色，而是如银如雪的白。

一个连专家都解决不了的问题，在一位不懂遗传学的老人手中迎刃而解，这不是奇迹吗？种在心里，即使一粒最普通的种子，也能长出奇迹！

The Secret of Success

A wise man was asked, "How can we succeed, please?"

The wise man smiled and handed him a peanut. "Pinch it forcibly."

The man pinched the peanut so hard that its shell broke, with only a kernel left.

"Rub it further," said the wise man.

The man did it as he was told. The red seed capsule was rubbed off, only leaving the white fruit.

"Pinch it again with your hands," said the wise man.

The man pinched it so hard, but he couldn't ruin it anyway.

"Rub it again with your hands," the wise man said.

Of course, nothing was rubbed off.

"Despite repeated setbacks, it has a strong and indomitable heart; it is the secret to success," said the wise man.

成功的秘密

有人问一位智者："请问，怎样才能成功呢？"

智者笑笑，递给他一颗花生。"用力捏捏它。"

那人用力一捏，花生壳碎了，只留下花生仁。

"再搓搓它。"智者说。

那人又照着做了，红色的种皮被搓掉了，只留下白白的果实。

"再用手捏它。"智者说。

那人用力捏着，却怎么也没法把它毁坏。

"再用手搓搓它。"智者说。

当然，什么也搓不下来了。

"虽然屡遭挫折，却有一颗坚强的百折不挠的心，这就是成功的秘密。"智者说。

Reaching the Summit

Whenever the sun dropped and the blue sky came up, my father and I used to climb the mountain near my house. Walking together, my father and I used to have a lot of conversations through which I learned lessons from his experiences. He always stressed to me, "You should have objectives and capacity like the mountain."

This has largely influenced my life. If we didn't enjoy mountain climbing, we couldn't have had enough time to spend together because my father was very busy. I believe mountaineering is really beneficial. It gave me time to talk with my father and to be in deep contemplation as well as develop my patience. I loved scaling mountains to get away from the noise and pollution of the city and breathe the fresh air.

One time we climbed a very high mountain. It was so challenging for me because I was only ten years old. During the first few hours of climbing, I enjoyed the fresh air, the birds' singing, and the beautiful dances of butterflies; but as time passed, I got a pain in both of my legs. At that moment, I wanted to quit climbing. Actually, I hated it at that moment, but my father said to me, "Spring is a season when everything comes to life again. The mountain and fields where we're standing are embroidered with flowers and trees. You can always see a beautiful sky at the top of the mountain, but you can't see it before you reach the top. You can always enjoy the scenes of many waterfalls and countless peaks and valleys at the top of the mountain, but you can't when you are halfway up. Only there at the top can you embrace all of those things, just like in life."

At that time, I was too young to understand his thoughts, but after that, I got new hope and confidence. Finally, I found myself standing at the top of the mountain. And there, I could see the whole of the sky, which was as clear as crystal.

攀登峰顶

每当夕阳西下、天空湛蓝时，我和父亲常常去爬我家附近的那座山。我和父亲爬山时，总会有好多话题；通过交谈，我从父亲的经历中学到了很多东西。他总是对我强调说："你应该像大山一样有目标和气量。"

这已经在很大程度上影响了我的人生。要不是我们俩都喜欢爬山，不可能有那么多时间在一起，因为父亲很忙。我相信登山确实有益。它给了我与父亲交谈的时间，并让我能够沉思和培养耐心。我爱登山，以便远离城市的噪音和污染，呼吸新鲜的空气。

有一次，我们去爬一座很高的山。对我来说，那真是一个挑战，因为那时我只有 10 岁。在爬山的最初几个小时，我享受到了清新的空气、小鸟的歌唱和蝴蝶的美丽舞姿。但随着时间过去，我的双腿开始酸痛。此刻，我想放弃爬山。实际上，我此刻讨厌爬山，但父亲对我说："春天是万物复苏的季节。我们脚下的山和田野都长满了花草树木。你在山顶总能看到美丽的天空，但到达山顶前，你无法看到。你在山顶总能欣赏到许多瀑布，看到无数的山峰和山谷，但你在半山腰，无法看到。就像生活中一样，只有到达峰顶，你才能拥抱所有那一切。"

那时，我还太小，无法理解他的想法，但那以后，我获得了新的希望和信心。最后，我登上了山顶。在那里,我可以看到像水晶般透明的整个天空。

A Bag of Seeds

Ford as Motor Magnate was not a closehanded man, but he rarely donated. He stubbornly believed that the value of money was not its amount but how to use. What worried him most was that the people who weren't good at using them often used the donations. Once, Schoolmaster Marsha Betty of Georgia came to ask Ford for donations, but he refused her.

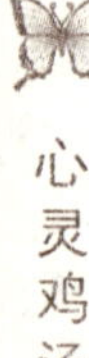

She said, "So please donate me a bag of peanut seeds." Upon that, Ford bought her a bag of peanut seeds. Ford later forgot it. Unexpectedly, a year later, Ms. Betty visited him and handed him 600 dollars. It turned out that her students planted the bag of peanut seeds, and this was the harvest of one year. Ford said nothing, but took out six million dollars and handed it to Betty.

What Ford was worried about was not unnecessary because if the money is easy to get, the people who get it are hard to feel the hardship and wisdom hidden behind the money. I more appreciate Betty's highest respect for a little bit favor. What she led the children to sow was virtually enough to prove that they had the qualification to receive the benefaction from others.

一袋种子

汽车大王福特不是一个吝啬的人,但他却很少捐款。他顽固地认为,金钱的价值并不在于多寡,而在于使用方法。他最担心的就是捐款经常会落到不善于运用它们的人手里。有一次,佐治亚州的玛莎·贝蒂校长为了扩建学校来请求福特捐款,福特拒绝了她。

她说:"那么就请捐给我一袋花生种子吧。"于是,福特买了一袋花生种子送给了她。福特后来就忘了这件事。没想到一年后,贝蒂女士又是上门了,交给了他 600 美元。原来学生们播种了当初的那袋花生种子,这就是一年的收获。福特什么都没说,立即拿出了 600 万美元交给了贝蒂。

福特的担心绝不是多余的,太轻易得来的金钱往往很难让受施者感受到金钱后面潜藏着的苦与智。我更赞赏贝蒂对点滴施与的至高尊重,她带领孩子们撒播下的其实足以证明他们有领受他人恩惠的资格。

Wait a Little Longer in Despair

An old woman grew a large patch of corn behind her house.

A full corn said, "On the day of harvest, the old lady will certainly pick me first because I'm the best corn this year!" But on the harvest day, the old woman didn't pick it.

"Tomorrow, tomorrow she will definitely pick me!" the best corn comforted itself. The next day the old woman got in some other corn but the best one.

"Tomorrow, the old lady will surely pick me!" the best corn still comforted itself...

But since then, the old woman never came until one day the best corn became disappointed. The original full grain became dried and hard, its whole body seemed to be cracking, so it prepared to rot with the corn stalk.

Just at this moment the old woman came. She said as she was picking it, "This is the best corn this year. As seeds, they will certainly grow better corn next year!"

Perhaps you're always very confident, but do you have the patience to wait a little longer when you're in despair?

绝望时再等一下

一位老太太在屋子后面种了一大片玉米。

一个颗粒饱满的玉米说:"收获那天,老太太肯定先摘我,因为我是今年长得最好的玉米!"可收获那天,老太太并没有把它摘走。

"明天,明天她一定会把我摘走!"很棒的玉米自我安慰道。第二天,老太太又收走了其他一些玉米,唯独没有摘这个玉米。

"明天,老太太一定会把我摘走!"棒玉米仍然自我安慰着……

可从此以后,老太太再也没有来过,直到有一天,玉米绝望了,原来饱满的颗粒变得干瘪坚硬,整个身体像要炸裂一般,它准备和玉米秆一起烂在地里。

就在这时,老太太来了,一边摘下它,一边说:"这可是今年最好的玉米,用它作种子,明年肯定能种出更棒的玉米!"

也许你一直都很相信自己,但你是否有耐心在绝望时再等一下?

The Sound of Waterfalls

A young man who reveled in painting and calligraphy wanted to acknowledge a great artist as teacher, so with the painting he completed with one whole year he went to see the artist. The artist looked at it and gently shook his head. "Not bad. But you couldn't have drawn the sound of waterfalls!"

A year later, the young man again begged for an audience offering the better waterfall painting who flattered himself to the artist. The artist shook his head again. "What a pity. You did the same!"

Another year later, so confidently, the young man again requested an interview holding the smugly perfect waterfall painting to the artist. The artist shook his head again. "Young man, you did just the same!"

The young man felt perplexed and said, "Master, as your pupil I don't see light. Please point me out a pathway!"

The artist picked up a paintbrush, drew on the young man's painting, on which standing across the shores of the pool under the waterfalls were two people, one of whom was shouting with his hands cupping his mouth while the other one was all ears. The young man came to get over how to paint the

sound of the waterfalls.

瀑布的声音

一位酷爱书画的年轻人想拜在书画大师门下。于是,他带着自己花费了整整一年工夫才画成的一幅画去求见大师。大师看了看,轻轻地摇了摇头,说:“还好,只是没能画出瀑布的声音!”

一年后,年轻人再次求见大师,将一幅自以为更好的瀑布画捧给大师。大师看了看,又摇了摇头说:“遗憾,还是没能画出瀑布的声音!”

又过了一年,年轻人颇有信心地再次求见大师,将一幅自以为完美无缺的瀑布捧给大师。大师再次摇了摇头说:“年轻人,你还是没能画出瀑布的声音!”

年轻人困惑了,说:“大师,晚辈确实不能悟出其中道理,求您明示!”

大师提起画笔,在年轻人的画上作起了画。他在瀑布下水潭的岸上画上两个相对而站的人,其中一个正双手拢在嘴边大声喊,另一个正伸着耳朵仔细听。年轻人终于明白怎样才能画出瀑布的声音了。

The Wisdom at the Cliff

Sawhill, a famous British painter, was once at the invitation of the UK Queen to draw a large mural in the Royal Palace. In order to finish this great work, he put up a three – story – high scaffolding.

The queen led a group of Minister to come and watch. At that moment, Sawhill was standing at the edge of scaffolding, without sensing the hand of Death was already touching him!

The queen and the ministers were all stunned, but none dared to utter a word. All of them knew, whoever uttered a word, Sawhill would be startled and fell to the ground dead.

Just then, Sawhill's assistant had quick wits in the emergency, rushed to the mural at a stride, picked up the paintbrush and began scrawling and smearing on it. Seeing this, Sawhill flew into a rage, hurriedly ran forward to snatch the paintbrush from the hands of his assistant. So Sawhill was saved.

When a person is forced in a desperate place by some reason, wisdom will bloom suddenly. This phenomenon is called the“wisdom at the cliff.”

悬崖边的智慧

英国著名画家索希尔有一次应英国女王的邀请,在皇宫里画一幅大壁画。为画这幅巨作,他搭起了一个三层楼高的脚手架。

女王率领一批大臣前来观看。当时,索希尔正站在脚手架的边缘,丝毫没有觉察到死神的手已经触摸到他!

女王和大臣们全都吓呆了,但谁也不敢出声。大家知道,谁要是喊出声来,索希尔一定会受到惊吓,掉到地上摔死。

这时,索希尔的助手急中生智,大步冲到壁画前,拿起画笔在壁画上乱涂乱抹起来。索希尔见状勃然大怒,急忙奔上前去抢夺助手手里的画笔。这样,索希尔得救了。

当一个人被某种缘由逼入绝地时,智慧就会突然开花。这种现象被人称为“悬崖边的智慧”。

Stand in the Proper Position

Accidentally, a lily seed dropped in the wheat field. The seed budded, shot out the slender stems and leaves, grew the buds and bloomed the pure white flowers. Looking at the uniform wheat seedlings surrounding it, the lily was so proud, “Look, you' re all ordinary wheat seedlings and your value is to yield several ears of wheat and become the food of mankind. As for me, I' m the noble lily, who is the symbol of purity, so you can' t compare with me. . . ”

The lily was so pleased with itself while the wheat seedlings remained silent. At this moment, a farmer went over. He took no interest in flowers. He only had the crops in his eyes, so the beautiful lily was only a weed. He pulled out the lily right away and threw it off on the ridge of the field.

The lily was insolated by the scorching sun and gradually withered.

I believe you are so excellent and the people around you are not as good as you. Perhaps you are a lily, but are you wrong to grow in the wheat field? The lily growing in the wheat field is a weed. You' d better consider in earnest where your proper position is.

站到适合你的位置上

一粒百合花籽意外地落在麦田里。花籽发芽了,抽出了修长的茎和叶,又孕育出了花蕾,开出了洁白的花。看看周围都是千篇一律的麦苗,百合非常骄傲:“看看你们,都是凡俗的麦苗,你们的价值也就是结出几穗麦子,成为人类的食物。而我呢,是高贵的百合,是纯洁的象征,你们谁都不能跟我相提并论……”

百合洋洋自得,麦苗却一言不发。这时,一个农夫走了过来。他对花卉没有兴趣,眼里只有他的庄稼,美丽的百合对于他不过是一株杂草。他随手拔掉百合,扔到了田埂上。

百合被烈日暴晒着,渐渐枯萎。

我相信你很优秀,你周围的人都比不上你。也许你是一株百合,但你是不是错长在了麦田里?长在麦田里的百合,就是杂草。还是认真想一下,适合自己的位置在哪里吧。

Christmas Morning

A light drizzle was falling as my sister Jill and I ran out of the Methodist Church, eager to get home and play with the presents that Santa had left for us and our baby sister, Sharon. Across the street from the church was a Pan-American gas station where the Greyhound bus stopped. It was closed for Christmas, but I noticed a family standing outside the locked door, huddled under the narrow overhang in an attempt to keep dry. I wondered briefly why they were there but then forgot about them as I raced to keep up with Jill.

Once we got home, there was barely time to enjoy our presents. We had to go off to our grandparents' house for our annual Christmas dinner. As we drove down the highway through town, I noticed that the family was still there, standing outside the closed gas station.

My father was driving very slowly down the highway. The closer we got to the turnoff for my grandparents' house, the slower the car went. Suddenly, my father U-turned in the middle of the road and said, "I can't stand it!"

"What?" asked my mother.

"It's those people back there at the Pan-Am, standing in the rain. They've got children. It's Christmas. I can't stand it."

When my father pulled into the service station, I saw that there were five of them: the parents and three children—two girls and a small boy.

My father rolled down his window. "Merry Christmas," he said.

"Howdy," the man replied. He was very tall and had to stoop slightly to peer into the car.

Jill, Sharon, and I stared at the children, and they stared back at us.

"You waiting on the bus?" my father asked.

The man said that they were. They were going to Birmingham, where he had a brother and prospects of a job.

"Well, that bus isn't going to come along for several hours, and you're getting wet standing here. Winborn's just a couple miles up the road. They've got a shed with a cover there, and some benches," my father said. "Why don't y'all get in the car and I'll run you up there."

The man thought about it for a moment, and then he beckoned to his family. They climbed into the car. They had no luggage, only the clothes they were wearing.

Once they settled in, my father looked back over his shoulder and asked the children if Santa had found them yet. Three glum faces mutely gave him his answer.

"Well, I didn't think so," my father said, winking at my mother, "because when I saw Santa this morning, he told me that he was having trouble finding all, and he asked me if he could leave your toys at my house. We'll just go get them before I take you to the bus stop."

All at once, the three children's faces lit up, and they began to bounce around in the back seat, laughing and chattering.

When we got out of the car at our house, the three children ran through the front door and straight to the toys that were spread out under our Christmas tree. One of the girls spied Jill's doll and immediately hugged it to her breast. I remember that the little boy grabbed Sharon's ball. And the other girl picked up something of mine. All this happened a long time ago, but the memory of it remains clear. That was the Christmas when my sisters and I learned the joy of making others happy.

My mother noticed that the middle child was wearing a short-sleeved dress, so she gave the girl Jill's only sweater to wear. My father invited them to join us at our grandparents' for Christmas dinner, but the parents refused. Even when we all tried to talk them into coming, they were firm in their decision. Back in the car, on the way to Winborn, my father asked the man if he had money for bus fare. His brother had sent tickets, the man said.

My father reached into his pocket and pulled out two dollars, which was all he had left until his next payday. He pressed the money into the man's hand. The man tried to give it back, but my father

insisted. "It'll be late when you get to Birmingham, and these children will be hungry before then. Take it. I've been broke before, and I know what it's like when you can't feed your family."

We left them there at the bus stop in Winborn. As we drove away, I watched out the window as long as I could, looking back at the little girl hugging her new doll.

圣诞节的早晨

细雨霏霏,我和姐姐吉尔跑出了卫理公会教堂,渴望回家玩圣诞老人留给我们和小妹妹莎伦的礼物玩具。教堂对面是一家泛美加油站,灰狗长途汽车会在那里中途停站。因为是圣诞节,加油站没开,但我注意到一家人站在那扇紧锁的门外,他们挤在狭小的挑檐下,想尽量不让雨淋湿。我一时间不知道他们为什么站在那里,但当我飞奔着去赶吉尔时,就把他们忘到了脑后。

我们一回到家,几乎没有时间去享受礼物了。我们必须得去爷爷奶奶家吃一年一度的圣诞大餐。我们驱车经过刚才那条公路时,我注意到那家人仍站在加油站紧闭的门外。

爸爸的车在公路上开得很慢。越接近去爷爷奶奶家的岔道,车子就越慢。突然,爸爸在途中来了个反向转弯,说:"我真不忍心!"

"什么?"妈妈问道。

"就是那些雨中站在泛美加油站那里的人。他们带着小孩。都圣诞节了。我真不忍心啊。"

爸爸把车开到油站,我看见那一家有5个人:父母亲和三个孩子——两个女孩和一个小男孩。

爸爸摇下车窗,说:"圣诞快乐!"

"你好,"那人答道。他长得很高,必须得稍微弯下腰,才能朝我们车里看。

我和吉尔、莎伦盯着那几个孩子,他们也盯着我们。"你们在等汽车吗?"爸爸问道。男人回答说是,他们准备去伯明翰,他有个哥哥在那里,而且期望能找到一份工作。

"噢,汽车好几个小时都来不了,站在这里你们会淋湿的。向前两三英里就是温邦站,那里有个棚屋,还有一些长凳。"爸爸说。"你们何不都上车,我送你们到那里。"

男人想了一会儿,然后向他的家人招手。他们钻进车里。他们没有任何行李,只有身上穿着的衣服。他们一坐好,爸爸就转过头问那几个孩子,圣诞老人是否找到了他们。三张闷闷不乐的脸给了他无声的回答。

"噢,我想不是这样,"爸爸向妈妈眨了眨眼说。"因为早上我看到圣诞老人时,他对我说他很难找到所有的人,然后他问我是否能把给你们的玩具放到我的房里。我们这就就去拿礼物,然后我再送你们去车站。"

三个孩子顿时神采奕奕,开始在后排座位又蹦又跳、有说有笑。

到了我们家,我们钻出车子,那三个孩子跑过前门,直奔摆在圣诞树下的那些玩具。其中一个女孩发现了吉尔的洋娃娃,马上把它抱在了胸前。我记得那个小男孩飞快地抓起莎伦的球,另一个女孩拿起了一件我的东西。这些都是很久以前的事了,回

忆起来却仍是如此清晰。我和姐妹们正是在那个圣诞日领会到了让别人快乐而得到的喜悦。

妈妈注意到他们家的老二穿着短袖裙,就把吉尔仅有的毛线衣送给了她穿。爸爸邀请他们跟我们一起去爷爷奶奶家吃圣诞大餐,但他们夫妇谢绝了。回到车里,在去温邦的路上,爸爸问那男人是否有钱买车票。那人说他的哥哥已经寄来了车票。

爸爸将手伸进口袋,掏出仅剩下的两美元,那本来是我们要熬到下次发工资那天的。他把钱塞进了那人手里。那人想尽力把钱推回来,但爸爸坚持让他收下。“你们到伯明翰时间会很晚,这些孩子不到那时就会饿的。收下吧。我以前也曾身无分文,我知道让家人吃不饱是什么滋味。”

我们把他们送到了温邦公共汽车站。我们驱车离开时,我从车窗回望了很久,回望着那个抱着新洋娃娃的小女孩。

Thank Poverty

In a small village on Ruyacy Plateau of Ethiopia, a small boy with his textbooks tucked under his arm ran barefoot to school and back home, whose home was good 10 kilometers away from the school. The poor family circumstances made the small boy impossible take the bus to go to school. So in order not to be late for classes he could only run to school. Every day the boy ran all the way accompanied by the cool morning dew and the splendid plateau sunset glow, as well as the wind whizzing by his ears.

Now, some years later, the boy who had run to school with the textbooks tucked under his arm has broken 15 world records and become the world's best long-distance runner in the race. He is Haile Gebrselassie. Because he had run with the textbooks tucked under his arm in his early years, in the subsequent tournaments, one of his arms was always lifted a bit higher than the other one, and closer to his body-and still retains the posture of running with the textbooks tucked.

If he hadn't been poverty-stricken, it wouldn't have made the world champion of today. Now, when recalling his early youth, Haile Gebrselassie said with emotion, "I'd like to thank poverty. Other children's parents had cars, which could take them to school, to the cinema or to a friend's house. And because of poverty, running to school was my only choice, but I like the feeling of running, which is a kind of happiness."

感谢贫穷

在埃塞俄比亚鲁西高原上的一个小村庄里,有一个小男孩每天腋下夹着课本,赤脚跑步上学和回家,他家离学校足足有10公里远的路程。贫穷的家境使小男孩不可能有坐车去上学的奢望。于是,为了上课不迟到,他只能选择跑步上学。每天小男孩都一路奔跑,与他相伴的除了清晨凉爽的朝露和高原绚丽的晚霞,还有耳边呼啸而过的风声。

若干年后的今天,这个曾夹着课本跑步上学的小男孩在世界长跑比赛中,先后15次打破了世界记录，成为当今世上最优秀的长跑运动员。他就是海尔·格布雷西拉西耶。由于早年经常夹着课本跑步，因此他在后来的比赛时，一只胳膊总要比另一只抬得要稍高一些，而且更贴近身体，依然保留着少年时夹着课本跑步的姿势。

如果不是贫穷，也成就不了今天的世界冠军。今天，海尔·格布雷西拉西耶回顾自己那段少年时光时，不无感慨地说："我要感谢贫穷。其他孩子的父母有车，可以接送他们去学校、电影院或朋友家。而我因为贫穷，跑步上学是我别无选择的，但我喜欢跑步的感觉，那是一种幸福。"

The Boy and a Drop of Dew

One morning, a small boy was squatting motionless on the grass in the garden for a long time.

His mother felt so odd that she walked close to see what had happened. The boy, in earnest, squatted in front of a blade of grass, on which a round dew in the sun gave a colorful light, exceedingly beautiful. As he enjoyed the dew, the small boy put his hands under the grass in silence.

Seeing his mother walk over to him, the boy said sadly, "Mother, the dew's dying."

The mother said to her son with a smile, "Even if you put your hands under the grass, you cannot stop the dew disappear from this world."

The boy said, "Mother, I'm only thinking not to throw it in pain when it falls."

男孩与露珠

一天早上，一个小男孩蹲在花园的草地上，久久不动。

母亲觉得蹊跷，便凑上前看个究竟。只见男孩非常认真地蹲在一片草叶面前。草叶上，一颗圆圆的露珠，在太阳的照射下，正幻出七彩的光芒，格外美丽。小男孩一边欣赏着这滴露珠，一边把双手摊开，静候在草叶下。

看到妈妈走过来，男孩忧伤地说："妈妈，露珠快要死了。"

母亲微笑着对儿子说："你就是把双手放在草叶下面，还是阻止不了露珠在这个世界上消失的命运啊。"

男孩说："妈妈，我只是想，它落下来时，别摔疼了它。"

Put up a Banner for Yourself

Roger Rolls was the first black governor in the history of New York State, USA. He was born in one of New York's notorious slums. The children born here rarely did decent work after they grew up. However, Roger Rolls was an exception, for he was not only admitted to the university, but also he

became a governor.

At his inaugural press conference, a reporter asked him, "What made you become the governor?" Faced with more than 300 journalists, Rolls did not mention his struggle but only spoke of his primary school schoolmaster—Pierre Paul.

In 1961, Pierre Paul was engaged as the director and principal of Nobita Primary School. When he entered this school, he found the children here did not cooperate with the teachers. Pierre Paul thought up many ways to guide them, but no one was effective. Later, he found these children were very superstitious, so when he gave lectures, he added a program of palm reading as a means of fortune-telling, with which he encouraged the students.

When Rolls jumped from the hathpace and walked to the platform with his small hands stretched out, Pierre Paul said, "As soon as I see your slender little fingers, I know you will be the governor of New York State in future." At that moment, Rolls was shocked because only his grandmother inspired him once, saying that he could become the captain of a five-ton ship. This time, Pierre Paul said he could become the governor of New York State, so he remembered that remark and believed him.

From that day on, the "New York State Governor" was like a banner that constantly inspired him to study energetically and make progress. Rolls no longer stained his clothes with mud, nor did he spoke in foul language. He began to straighten his back when he was walking. In the next more than 40 years, he demanded himself according to the identity of a governor. At the age of 51, he finally became the governor of New York State.

Put up a banner of faith for yourself and you will have the drive to struggle and the vitality of life!

给自己树一面旗帜

罗杰·罗尔斯是美国纽约州历史上第一位黑人州长，他出生在纽约一个声名狼藉的贫民窟。这里出生的孩子长大后很少有人从事体面的职业。然而，罗杰·罗尔斯是个例外，他不仅考入了大学，而且成了州长。

在他就职的记者招待会上，一位记者向他问道："是什么让你当上了州长？"面对三百多名记者，罗尔斯对自己的奋斗史只字未提，只谈到了他上小学时的校长皮尔·保罗。

1961 年，皮尔·保罗被聘为诺必塔小学的董事兼校长。他走进这所小学时，发现这里的孩子不与老师合作。皮尔·保罗想了很多办法来引导他们，但没有一个奏效。后来，他发现这些孩子很迷信，于是他上课时就多了一项给孩子看手相的内容。他用这个办法来鼓励学生。

当罗尔斯从高台跳下，伸着小手走向讲台时，皮尔·保罗说："我一看你修长的小拇指，就知道你将来是纽约州的州长。"当时，罗尔斯大吃一惊，因为只有他奶奶让他振奋过一次，说他可以成为 5 吨重的小船的船长。这一次，皮尔·保罗竟说他可以成为纽约州的州长。他记下了这句话，并相信了他。

从那天起，"纽约州州长"就像一面旗帜，不断激励他发奋向上。罗尔斯不再让衣服沾满泥土，说话时也不再污言秽语。他开始挺起腰杆走路。在以后的 40 多年间，他每天都按州长的身份要求自己。51 岁那年，他终于成了纽约州的州长。

给自己树一面信念的旗帜，你就有了奋斗的动力和生命的活力！

The Mystery of Success

At 50, Socrates had been bald and wrinkled on his forehead, coupled with the deep eye sockets.

However, an 18 – year – old beautiful girl madly fell in love with him and eventually became his wife.

Someone couldn't help making a secret inquiry of Socrates about the secret of success, "Sir, what method did you use to get the young girl?"

Socrates said, "I don't really have time to study this question, just focusing on doing my own things."

The man didn't believe and went on asking, "What a beautiful girl! If you didn't pursue her, how would she love you?"

Looking up at the sky, Socrates said, "Please look at the moon in the sky. The more you try to follow her, the more she doesn't allow you to catch up; but when you hurry on with your journey wholeheartedly, she will follow you closely."

成功的奥秘

苏格拉底50岁时,头顶已经秃顶,额头上布满皱纹,眼窝深陷。

然而,一个18岁的漂亮姑娘却疯狂地爱上了他,并且最终成了他的妻子。

有个人忍不住向苏格拉底刺探成功的奥妙:"先生,你是用什么方法把小姑娘追到手的?"

苏格拉底说:"我实在没有功夫研究这个问题,我只是专心致志地做自己的事。"

那人不相信,继续穷追不舍:"这么漂亮的姑娘,你不追她,她怎么会爱上你呢?"

苏格拉底抬头望着天空,说:"请看看天上的月亮吧。你越是拼命地追她,她越是不让你追上;而当你一心一意地赶自己的路时,她却会紧紧地跟着你。"

The Mountain Doesn't Come and I'll Go to It

A master led several disciples to meditate.

The disciples said, "Master, we have heard many magic arts. Can you show us?"

The master said, "Alright. I will show you a great art of moving the mountain here." Then, the master began to sit in meditation.

An hour later, the mountain was still across them.

The disciples said, "Master, why does the mountain come here?"

The master said unhurriedly, "Now that the mountain doesn't come here, I'll go to it." Then, he stood up and went over to the opposite mountain.

When we do something, we might as well change the way of thinking from a new angle if a method can't work.

The journey of life is like sailing on the ocean. Maybe we can't change the direction of the wind,

but we can change the direction of the sails.

山不过来，我就过去

一位大师带领几位徒弟参禅悟道。

徒弟说："师父，我们听说您会很多法术，能不能让我们见识一下？"

师父说："好吧，我就给你们露一手'移山大法'，把对面那座山移过来。"说着，师父开始打坐。

一个时辰过去了，对面的山仍在对面。

徒弟们说："师父，山怎么不过来呢？"

师父不慌不忙地说："既然山不过来，那我就过去。"说着，他站起来，走到了对面的山上。

做一件事情，当我们用一种方法难以奏效时，不妨换一种思维方式，换一种角度。

人生的旅程正如在大海上行船一样，也许我们无法改变风的方向，但我们可以改变帆的方向。

Please Focus on Me

I had never noticed her. She was not the kind of girl who could draw attention. She was not tall and just plain. In class, she liked sitting at the back, reading or taking notes. It was once I asked her to read aloud the text that I looked at her with new eyes when I heard her standard American pronunciation. Later on, the National College English Speech Contest would be held. Our school had a quota of one student allowed to attend. I thought it over and filled in her name with a smile. I red-penciled her manuscript of speech, corrected her pronunciation, and even adjusted her body language. At that time, we busied ourselves with such work till night.

However, I was always kind of worried because she was too introvert and too quiet. Could she seize this rare opportunity?

On the night of the contest, I sat in the front row of the auditorium very early. I told her, take it easy. Blushed, she looked at me and said nothing.

My heart sank. It seemed that she did tense up. I patted her and let her go to draw lots. As a result, what she drew was No. 9 while No. 8 was a recognized English master-hand.

Sure enough, the English master-hand was fairly successful in the speech with his humor, jocosity and highly personal style. The whole audience would make a warm applause almost every 30 seconds until she appeared on the stage, still talking over his speech with excitement.

My palms began to sweat. I sat there, with no courage to look at her. It was the first time that she went up the stage, so I couldn't blame her for any slips. But at that moment, I found I was so scared of her failure.

The strong spotlight and empty auditorium made her so small and so insignificant that nobody seemed to notice she had been on the stage. I said to myself, no hope.

But the moment that shocked me occurred. She did say good evening to the audience as we had arranged. I clearly heard a voice, a very loud voice, "Now, please focus in on me."

Three times in all. Louder and louder. Earsplitting.

The whole audience fell silent.

I could hardly believe that resonant voice came from the girl who was usually soft-voiced and didn't draw attention at all. Then I heard her sweet voice lingering in the air, more attractive than a nightingale.

After her speech ended for a long while, a thunderous applause sounded in the whole audience and I unwittingly clapped my hands until my tears welled up. Yes, I think I will never forget that it was my student after years who taught me the most touching lesson in life, namely, never underestimate the power of the silent, for sometimes a tremendous energy originates from the silent accumulation.

请把焦点对准我

我从来都没注意过她。她也不是那种能引人注目的女孩。她个子不高,长相仅仅一般。上课时,她喜欢一个人坐在后排,看书或记笔记。有一次叫她读课文时,听到她标准的美式发音,我才对她刮目相看。后来,全国高校英语演讲比赛,我们学校有一个名额,我想了想,微笑着填上她的名字。改稿,纠正发音,甚至到肢体语言的处理。那段时间,我们每天都忙到很晚。

可是,我总是隐隐有些担心,因为她太内向、太安静,她能抓住这个难得的机会吗?

比赛那天晚上,我很早就坐在了大礼堂的前排。我对她说,别紧张。她看着我,脸红红的,什么也没说。

我的心一沉,看来她确实紧张。我拍拍她,让她去抽签。结果,她抽到的是第 9 号,而前面一位选手,是公认的英语高手。

果然,英语高手的演讲相当成功,幽默诙谐,充满个人风格。全场几乎每隔半分钟就会响起一次热烈的掌声,直到她上台,大家还在兴奋地讨论着他的演讲。

我的手心沁出汗水,我在台下,不敢望向她。她是第一次上台,出现任何差错我都不能怪她。可是,在那一刻我才发现,我是那么害怕她失败。

强烈的镁光灯,空旷的大礼堂,她显得那么小,那么微不足道。似乎没有人注意到她已经走上了台。我在心里说,没希望了。

但让我震惊的一刻发生了。她并没有像我们安排好的那样问大家晚上好。我清清楚楚地听到了一个声音,很响亮的声音:"现在,请把焦点对准我。"

一共三遍。一遍比一遍响亮,震人耳鼓。

全场鸦雀无声。

我不敢相信,那么洪亮的声音是那个平时说话细声细气、毫不起眼的小姑娘发出来的。接下来我听到她婉转的声音在空中盘旋,比夜莺更动听。

她的演讲结束良久,全场才响起雷鸣般的掌声,我不知不觉拍手拍到热泪盈眶。是的,我想我永远不会忘记,是我的学生若干年后教会了我生命里最动人的一课,那就是,千万不要低估沉默者的力量,有时巨大的能量源自无声无息的蕴积。

Wait for Three Days

A Chinese female writer who visited the United State met an old woman selling flowers in the street of New York. The old woman wore shabby clothes, looking very fragile, but her face was peaceful and happy. The writer chose one flower and said, "You look very happy."

"Why not? All is so beautiful."

"Don't you mind your plight at all?" the writer blurted out.

The old woman's answer shocked the writer, "It was the worst day when Jesus was crucified on Friday, but three days later it was Easter. So when I'm in trouble, I will wait for three days, for after three days it will go back to normal."

"Wait for three days." What an ordinary and philosophical way of life, for it throws off boredom and pain and harvests happiness with might and main.

等待三天

访美的一位中国女作家在纽约街头遇到了一位卖花的老太太。这位老太太穿着相当破旧,身体看上去也很虚弱,但脸上却很祥和、高兴。女作家挑了一朵花说:"您看起来很高兴。"

"为什么不呢?一切都这么美好。"

"您对自己的处境一点也不在乎吗?"女作家随口说道。

老太太的回答让女作家大吃一惊:"耶稣在星期五被钉上十字架时,是全世界最糟糕的一天,可三天后就是复活节。所以,当我遇到不幸时,就会等待三天,三天后一切都恢复正常了。"

"等待三天。"多么平凡而又充满哲理的一种生活方式,它把烦恼和痛苦抛下,全力去收获快乐。

Open Your Mind

A few decades ago in New York, there was a girl named Emily, whose ideal was like each young girl's: to find a handsome ideal lover to marry and live to old age. But the girls around her had married successively and she was still alone. She was always full of remorse all day, firmly believing that her dream would never come true.

After her family's persuasion, Emily went to see a famous psychologist. When they shook hands, her cold fingers made the psychologist quiver, and her sad eyes and pale gaunt face were telling him, "I'm hopeless, and what way will you have?"

After pondering for a long while, the psychologists said, "Emily, I want to ask you to help me. I really need your help, can you?" Emily nodded doubtfully.

"My family will have an evening party on Tuesday, but my wife has more work than she can cope with alone. You come to help me entertain the guests. Tomorrow morning, you first go to buy a new set of clothes, and then do your hair. You will help me entertain the guests, saying that you welcome them on behalf of me and help them, particularly the lonely people." Emily looked uneasy, so the psychologist encouraged her, "It doesn't matter. In fact, it is very simple. For example, when you find someone doesn't carry a cup of coffee, hand it to him or her; if it is too sultry, open the window or something." Emily finally agreed to try it.

On Tuesday, Emily came to the party with decent hairstyle and dress. According to the psychologist's requirement, she fulfilled her duty, doing nothing but to help others. Her eyes lively and smiling, she completely forgotten her worry and became the most popular one at the evening party. After the party, three young men offered to escort her home.

Week by week, the three young men were pursuing Emily ardently. She eventually agreed with the proposal of one of them. The psychologist was invited as a guest to attend their wedding. Looking at the happy bride, the people said that the psychologist created a miracle.

If you don't go into the other people's mind, they won't enter your world because you keep the door closed.

Against this, the psychologist's prescription is: try opening the closed door of mind, look at whether the light you project on others will be reflected on your own body a hundred times.

敞开心扉

几十年前,纽约有一位名叫埃米丽的姑娘,她的理想跟每一位妙龄姑娘一样:找一位潇洒的白马王子结婚,白头偕老。可周围的姑娘们都先后成家了,她还是独身一人。她整天自怨自艾,认定自己梦想永远不可能实现了。

埃米丽在家人的劝说下去找一位著名的心理学家。握手时,她那冰凉的手指让人心颤,还有那伤感的眼神、苍白憔悴的面孔,都在向心理学家说:"我没指望了,你会有什么办法呢?"

心理学家沉思良久,说道:"埃米丽,我想请你帮我一个忙,我真的很需要你的帮忙,可以吗?"埃米丽将信将疑地点了点头。

"我家星期二要开个晚会,但我妻子一个人忙不过来,你来帮我招呼客人。明天一早,你先去买一套新衣服,然后去做个发型。你要帮我去招呼客人,说是代表我欢迎他们,要注意帮助他们,特别是显得孤单的人。"埃米丽一脸不安,心理学家鼓励她说,"没关系,其实很简单。比如说,看谁没咖啡就端一杯,要是太闷热了,就开开窗户什么的。"埃米丽终于同意试一试。

星期二这天,埃米丽发式得体,衣衫合身,来到了晚会上。按照心理学家的要求,她尽职尽力,只想着帮助别人。她眼神活泼,笑容可掬,完全忘掉了自己的心事,成了晚会上最受欢迎的人。晚会结束后,有三个青年都提出要送她回家。

一周又一周,三个青年热烈地追求着埃米丽,她最终答应了其中一位的求婚。心理学家作为被邀请的贵宾,参加了他们的婚礼。望着幸福的新娘,人们说心理学家创造了一个奇迹。

你走不进别人的心里,别人也走不进你的世界,那是因为你自己把门关上了。

对此,心理学家开出的处方是:试着把封闭的心扉敞开,看看你投射在别人身上的光芒,会不会一百倍地射回你自己的身上。

Appreciation Is a Kind of Goodness

In the autumn of 1852 when he hunted in Spasskoye, Turgenev accidentally picked up a magazine called "Modern". He turned over a few pages at random and was attracted by a story entitled "Childhood", whose author was a novice nobody, but Turgenev appreciated and cherished so much.

He asked about the author' residence, finally learned he lost his mother at the age of two and his father at the age of seven, raised by his aunt single-handedly; in order to get out of the muddy way of life, the author went to the Caucasian forces as soon as he graduated from school. Turgenev even more showed great sympathy and concern and after several twists and turns, he found the author's aunt and expressed his appreciation and affirmation for the author.

The aunt quickly wrote a letter telling her nephew, "Your first story has caused a great sensation in Valeryan, and even the great writer Turgenev praises you on every occasion. He said, 'If he can keep writing, this young man must have a boundless prospect!'"

Receiving his aunt's letter, the author was wild with joy. He wrote it just because he was depressed for his life to kill his loneliness, without the wild fancy of being a writer. The famous writer Turgenev's appreciation suddenly lit the flame in his mind and helped him find the self-confidence and the value of life, so he kept writing unrestrictedly and eventually became an artist and thinker with the world prestige.

He was Lev Tolstoy, the author of "War and Peace", "Anna Karenina" and "Resurrection."

欣赏是一种善良

1852年秋天，屠格涅夫在斯帕斯科耶打猎时，无意间在松林中拣到了一本皱巴巴的《现代人》杂志。他随手翻了几页，竟被一篇题名为《童年》的小说吸引住了，作者是一个初出茅庐的无名小辈，但屠格涅夫却非常欣赏，钟爱有加。

他四处打听作者的住处，最后得知作者两岁丧母，7岁丧父，由姑母一手养大。为了走出生命途中的泥泞，作者刚跨出校门，便去高加索部队当兵。屠格涅夫更是倾注了极大的同情和关注，几经周折，找到了他的姑母，表达了他对作者的欣赏与肯定。

姑母很快就写信告诉侄儿："你的第一篇小说在瓦列里扬引起了很大轰动，连大作家屠格涅夫逢人就称赞你。他说：'这位青年人如能继续写下去，他的前途一定不可限量！'"

收到姑母的信后，作者欣喜若狂，他本是因为生活的苦闷而信笔涂鸦打发心中寂寥，并无当作家的妄念。由于名家屠格涅夫的欣赏，竟一下子点燃了他心中的火焰，帮他找回了自信和人生价值，于是他一发不可收地写了下去，最终成了享有世界声誉的艺术家和思想家。

他就是《战争与和平》、《安娜·卡列尼娜》和《复活》的作者列夫·托尔斯泰。

He Opened My Mind

He sat on the lawn, a hard cardboard lying before him, his dog squatting beside him. On the cardboard it wrote, "I'm in trouble, feeling very hungry and begging for your help."

I was a woman who was easily moved when I saw someone need help. For my peculiarity, my husband both loved and hated. I pulled over our van, watching the man and his dog from the rearview mirror. He was still very young, perhaps only 40 years old. He wrapped his head with a large handkerchief, just like a motorcyclist or a pirate. He was dirty with a scraggly beard. All he had was only a small parcel. No one stopped for him. I saw other drivers only see him once and looked away immediately.

It was hot outside. From the man's deep blue eyes, I saw his frustration, boredom and exhaustion, sweat streaming down his face.

I reached into my wallet and produced a banknote of 10 dollars. My 12-year-old son Nick immediately knew what I was going to do. "Can I bring it to him, Mom?"

"Be careful, dear," I warned him as I handed the money to him. From the rearview mirror I watched him running quickly to the man and gave him the money with a shy smile. I saw the man was shocked to stand up, take the money and put it into his pocket. "Great," I thought, "at least he can eat a warm dinner tonight." I felt satisfied and proud. Now I would go for my business.

When returning to the car, Nick looked at me with his sad and pleading eyes. "Mommy, his dog looks so hot. The man is really good." I thought I had to do something else.

"Go back to tell him waiting there for a while until we come back in 15 minutes," I told Nick. He jumped off the car and ran to tell that stranger. Then, we drove to the nearest store and carefully chose gifts. "The things cannot be too heavy," I explained to the kids, "they must be the ones that he can carry." We finally bought something, a bag of dog food and two bottles of water (one was for the dog and the other for the man) as well as some fast food for the man.

We quickly went back and found he was still there waiting for us. No one stopped for him yet. With trembling hands, I grabbed the shopping bags and moved out of the car, followed my four children, each of them with a gift. When we were walking towards him, I felt a flash of fear thrilling through my mind, hoping that he was not a serial killer, or any other dangerous man. I looked into his eyes and saw he was trying to hold back his tears like a small boy.

I told him that I hoped these things were not too heavy for him, and showed him all the things we bought. When I took out the plate for water, he snatched it from my hand, as if it was made of gold. He told me before that he had no way to give his dog water. He put it down carefully, poured the bottle of water into it, stood up and looked straight into my eyes. His eyes were so blue, so nervous; when he said, "Madam, I don't know what to say," my eyes brimmed over with tears. Then, he held his head wrapped with a large handkerchief in both hands and broke into tears.

Tearfully, I said with a smile, "You don't have to say anything."

When we boarded our van and drove on, he knelt on the grass, held his dog with his arms and kissed its nose with a smile. I waved my hand cheerfully, and then allowed my tears to course down.

At this moment, my daughter Brandy turned to me and said in the sweetest voice of a little girl, "I feel really great now."

On the surface it seems that we helped him, but in fact he gave me a gift I would never forget-it had impacted on my children profoundly.

In the following years, my children had all grown up and become useful people to the society. At a charity speech, my son Brundy told this story to the audience. He concluded in the end, "It influenced me so greatly that it made me know that regardless of a person's appearance, their mind should get goodwill, compassion and acceptance. It was the stranger who opened my mind."

他打开了我的心灵

他坐在草地上，面前摆着一张硬纸板，他的狗蹲伏在旁边。硬纸板上写着："我陷入了困境，感到很饿，恳求得到帮助。"

我是一个看到有人需要帮助就容易动心的人。丈夫对我这一特性既爱又恨。我把我们的有篷货车开了过去，从后视镜里注视着那人和狗。他还很年轻，也许只有40岁。他用一条大手帕裹住头，就像摩托车手或海盗。他身上很脏，胡子拉碴。他所有的东西只是一个小包裹。没有人为他停留。我看见别的司机只对他看了一眼，就立即把目光移向了别处。

外面很热。我从那人深蓝色的眼睛里看出了他的沮丧、厌倦和疲惫，汗水如溪流般从他的脸上流了下来。

我把手伸进钱包，抽出了一张10美元的钞票。12岁的儿子尼克立刻知道我要做什么了。"我能把它拿去送给他吗，妈妈？"

"小心点，亲爱的。"我一边警告他，一边把钱递给了他。我从后视镜里注视着他飞快地向那人跑去，然后带着羞涩的微笑把钱递给他。我看见那人震惊地站起来，接过钱，把它放进自己的口袋。"好极了，"我心想。"至少，他今晚可以吃一顿热饭了。"我感到既满意又骄傲。现在我要去办自己的事了。

尼克回到汽车里时，眼含悲伤和恳求看着我。"妈妈，他的狗看起来是那么热，那人真的很好。"我想我还得再做一些事。

"回去告诉他在那儿等一会儿，我们15分钟后就回来。"我告诉尼克。他跳下汽车，跑过去告诉那个陌生人。然后，我们开车来到了最近的一家商店，仔细挑选礼物。"东西不能太重。"我向孩子们解释。"必须是他能拿得动的才行。"我们终于买好了东西，一包狗食、两瓶水（一瓶是给狗的，一瓶是给那人的），还为那人买了一些快餐食品。

我们迅速返回，他还在那儿等着我们。仍然没有人为他停留。我颤抖着双手，抓起购物包，走出了汽车，四个孩子都跟在我身后，每个人都拿着礼物。当我们向他走去时，我的心里闪过一瞬间的恐惧，希望他不是一个连环杀人犯或其他什么危险人物。我望着他的眼睛，只见他正像小男孩一样在竭力忍住自己的泪水。

我告诉他，我希望这些东西对他来说不是太重，并把我们买的东西拿给他看。当我取出那个盛水的盘子时，他一把将它从我的手里抓过去，好像它是用金子做成的似的。他告诉我，此前，他没办法给他的狗水喝。他小心翼翼地将它放下，把我们买的那瓶水倒在里面，站直身子，直直地看着我的眼睛。他的眼睛是那么蓝、那么紧张，当他说"夫人，我不知道该说什么"时，我的眼睛里充满了泪水。然后，他用两手抱着他那用大手帕裹着的头，哭了起来。

我含着眼泪，微笑着说："你什么也不必说。"

当我们登上车继续前进时，他在草地上跪下来，用胳膊搂着他的狗，亲吻它的鼻子，微笑着。我高高兴兴地挥了挥手，然后任由泪水流淌。

这时，我的女儿布兰迪转身面对我，用最甜美的小女孩的声音说："我现在感觉真的好极了。"

虽然从表面上看，似乎是我们帮助了他，但实际上他却给了我一件令我永远难忘的礼物——这件事对我的孩子们的影响意义深远。

在其后的数年里，我的孩子们都陆续长大成人，成了对社会有用的人。在一次慈善演讲会上，我的儿子布伦迪向听众们讲述了这个故事。他在最后总结时说道："那件事对我影响很大，它让我懂得，不管一个人的外表怎样，他们的内心都应该得到善意、同情和认可。是那个陌生人打开了我的心灵。"

Play it Again, Dad

From second grade on, there was one event I dreaded every year: the piano recital. A recital meant I had to practice a boring piece of music and perform in front of strangers who, I was sure, knew the notes much better than I. It also meant wearing a crinkly crinoline dress and enduring the bright lights of a movie camera as I swished across the church stage. Each year I would ask my father if I could skip the recital "just this once". And each year he'd say no, muttering something about building self-confidence and working toward a goal.

So it was with great satisfaction that I stood in church one recent Sunday, video camera in hand, and watched my father sweat in his shirt and tie before rising to play the piano in his very first recital.

Eight-year-old Patrick Gumery led off the event, followed by Susannah Thomson, nine. Then came my 68-year-old dad, Robert Sessions, who sat down at the Kawai grand piano and taught me more about courage and persistence than all the words he used those 30-plus years ago.

From the time he was small, my father had longed to play music. His mother, a factory worker, couldn't afford lessons, so a kindly couple in the small Arkansas town where he lived offered to pay. But he soon stopped after being teased by other boys his age. "I quit and always regretted it." He recalled.

He could have gone on regretting it, as too many of us do. But though he was rooted in his past, he wasn't stuck there. Three years ago, when he retired from the faculty at the University of Richmond, he asked his church music director, Charles Staples, to take him as a student. Staples had the good grace not to laugh. Just before the recital, he told me my dad was playing "the best I've ever seen him. I keep waiting for him to reach his peak, but he hasn't yet."

For a moment after my father sat down at the keyboard to play, he simply stared down at his fingers, and I wondered whether he would even begin. He had tried to keep the event quiet, telling my stepmother she didn't need to come. But she had every intention of coming, and also invited my sisters and me as well as my dad's three golfing partners who, much to his dismay, showed up.

As we waited those few seconds, I knew he was worrying that his music would sound juvenile—that we'd expect more from a 68-year-old than an eight-year-old, even someone who had been playing for so short a time. His sense of dignity was on the line. He's forgotten the notes, I worried, remembering those split seconds decades ago when my mind would go blank and my fingers would freeze.

But then the sure, poignant strains of Aram Khachaturian's "Melody" emerged, from the same large fingers that once baited my fishing lines, and I realized he had been doing what music teachers always tell their novitiates to do: focus on the music and pretend the rest of us aren't there.

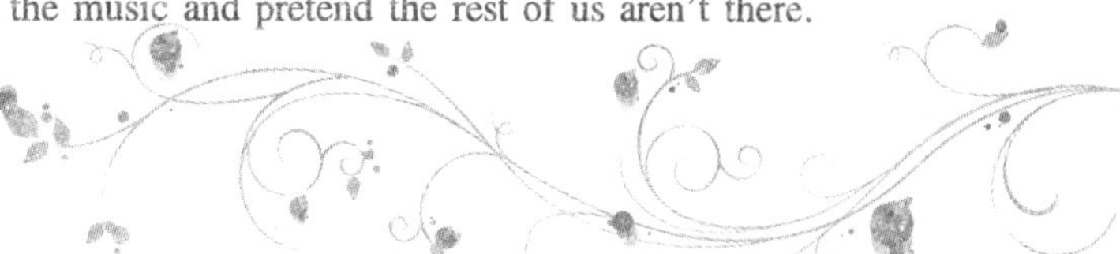

Also in the audience was my 11-year-old son Jeff. My father has taught his grandson how to play hearts, pitch a tent, cast a fishing rod, swing a golf club and compose music on the computer. He encouraged Jeff to start the piano even when the boy insisted he would never play in a recital, two years ago, Dad was there when Jeff did what he said he would never do. So somehow it was fitting to hear Jeff offer my father some advice about performing. "Just remember, if you make a mistake, it's not the end of the world," my son told him, "Probably no one won't notice it anyway."

My dad made it through "Melody" and sailed through Burgmuller's "Arabesque". What he lacked in precision, he more than made up for in feeling. He then rose, turned to his audience and curtsied.

"So what did you think about your granddad?" I asked Jeff later.

"He was great," Jeff replied, "I'm glad he did it. And I bet he is too."

"I'm proud of him for starting something new at his age," I said.

"Yeah, and doing it so well," Jeff added, "It would be like Dr. Spock taking up baseball at 90. I guess he could do it, but it would be hard."

T. Berry Brazelton, the pediatrician and author, said grandparents show grandchildren the mountaintops, while parents teach the drudgery of how to get there. My father may not have reached his peak musically, but as far as his grandson is concerned, he's at the top of the mountain.

再弹一次,爸爸

从二年级起,有一件事我每年都非常害怕,那就是钢琴独奏会。独奏会意味着我必须得练习一首无聊的乐曲,并在许多陌生人面前演奏,我敢肯定,这些人远比我熟悉那些音符;同时也意味着我要穿上飒飒作响、四周鼓出的裙子,忍受电影摄像机耀眼的灯光,飕飕走过教堂的舞台。我每年都求父亲能不能略过独奏会,"就这一次"。他每年都说不行,同时咕哝着说要树立自信、向目标努力这样的话。

所以,最近的一个礼拜日,我站在教堂里,手持摄像机,望着衬衣和领结都汗津津的父亲准备第一次钢琴独奏时,感到非常高兴。

8 岁的帕特里克·加梅里首先独奏,接着是 9 岁的苏珊娜·汤姆森,随后就是我 68 岁的爸爸罗伯特·塞森斯。他在佳威牌平台钢琴前坐下,他的勇气和恒心比他 30 多年来教给我的要多。

我父亲从小就渴望弹奏乐曲。他的母亲是一名工人,拿不起学费,于是他所住的阿肯色州一个小镇的一对好心夫妇自愿掏钱。但被其他同龄的男孩们取笑后,他不久就停了下来。"我放弃学琴,总是感到遗憾。"他回忆说。

他本可能继续遗憾,像我们这样的人太多了。但尽管他对过去念念不忘,却没有沉湎其中。3 年前从里士满大学的教职上退休后,他请教堂的音乐指挥查尔斯·斯坦普尔斯收他做学生。斯坦普尔斯温文尔雅,没有发笑。就在独奏会前,他告诉我说,我爸爸弹得"从来没有这样好过。我一直在等着他达到演奏的顶点,但他还在进步。"

我父亲在钢琴键盘前坐下准备演奏后,他一时间只是低头看着自己的手指,我不知道他会不会开始弹。他一直隐瞒这件事,吩咐继母不必来听。但她一心想来,不仅请了我和姐妹们,还请了我爸爸的 3 个高尔夫球友。那三个球友到场时,爸爸大为惊慌。

我们等了几秒钟,我知道他在担心他弹的琴声会非常幼稚,担心我们会期望 68 岁的人比8岁的人弹得好，即便是他学了这么短的一段时间。他的尊严感正经受着考验。我担心他已经忘了那些音符，同时想起了几十年前我好多次一时间脑海里一片空白、手指僵硬的情景。

但艾拉姆·哈恰图良的坚定、生动的《旋律》的音符从那些曾给我的钓鱼线装诱饵的粗大手指上流了出来，我意识到他正在按照音乐老师对初学者的吩咐去做：对乐曲聚精会神，装作我们其他人都不在场。

听众当中还有我11岁的儿子杰夫。我父亲教过外孙怎样玩红心牌、搭帐篷、投钓竿、挥高尔夫球棒和在电脑上作曲。他鼓励杰夫弹钢琴，即使当时那男孩坚持说绝不在独奏会演奏。两年前，杰夫做了他曾坚持说绝对不做的事，爸爸也去听了。所以，不管怎样，听杰夫给我父亲提一些有关演奏的忠告是合适的。"请记住，就是你弹错了，也不是世界末日。"我儿子对他说。"也许根本没人会注意到这一点。"

爸爸弹完了《旋律》，又弹起了伯格穆勒的《阿拉伯风格曲》。尽管他的演奏缺乏精确，但他能用情感去弥补。随后，他站起身，转向听众，屈膝行礼。

"那你认为外公怎么样?"我后来问杰夫。"他当时真棒。"杰夫回答说。"我很高兴他那样做。我敢说他也很高兴。""他这样的年龄开始新的东西，我为他感到自豪。"我说。"是的，而且做得是那样好，"杰夫补充说。"这就像斯波克医生90岁才打棒球。我想他能行，但会不容易。"

儿科医生兼作家T.贝利·布里兹顿说，祖父母把山顶指给孙子孙女，父母亲教子女怎样克服困难到达那里。我父亲也许还没有登上音乐的顶峰，但对他的外孙来说，他已经站在了山顶上。

The Spring Will Come

I remember one winter my dad needed firewood, and he found a dead tree and sawed it down.

In the spring, to his dismay, new shoots sprouted around the trunk.

He said, "I thought sure it was dead. The leaves had all dropped in the wintertime. It was so cold that twigs snapped as if there were no life left in the old tree. But now I see that there was still life at the taproot." He looked at me and said, "Bob, don't forget this important lesson. Never cut a tree down in the wintertime. Never make a negative decision in the low time. Never make your most important decisions when you are in your worst mood. Wait. Be patient. The storm will pass. The spring will come."

春天一定会来

我记得有一年冬天爸爸需要柴火。随后，他就找到了一棵枯树，将它锯下来。

第二年春天，让他吃惊的是，树干周围发出了新芽。

他说："我还以为它肯定死了呢。冬天树叶都掉光了。天这样冷，小树枝一折就

断，好像老树没有了生命。但现在我看到主根还有生命。”他看着我说，“鲍勃，别忘了这个重要教训。千万别在冬天把一棵树砍倒。千万别在运气低谷时作出消极决定。千万别在情绪最糟时作出最重要的决定。要等待。要耐心。风暴会过去。春天一定会来。”

The Discovery at the Bend

A young man travelled by train. As the train was rumbling across a wilderness, the passengers looked out of the windows idly and aimlessly.

When it approached a bend, the train slowed down and then an unadorned house came into view. It was so conspicuous against the desolate landscape that everybody on the train turned to admire it with eyes wide open. Some passengers even began a discussion about it.

The young man was also impressed by the scene. On his return he got off the train at the nearest station and found his way to the house. Its owner told him that troubled by the noise of the train he wanted to sell the house but nobody would buy it.

Soon after the young man spent thirty thousand dollars for the house, regarding it as a favorable site for advertisement. It was facing the railway bend where the train had to slow down and the weary passengers would cast their eyes at the house to refresh themselves.

He managed to get access to big companies and tried his best to convince them of the advantage of the place for advertisement. Finally, the Coca Cola Company took a lease on it to put up promotion signs. The young man was paid 180 thousand for a three - year rent.

The story is absolutely true. It proves that any discovered potential may lead to success.

拐弯处的发现

有一位年轻人乘火车旅行。当火车隆隆驶过一片荒野时，乘客们都百无聊赖、毫无目的地望着车窗外。

接近一个拐弯处时，火车放慢了速度。随后，一座没有装饰的房子进入了视野。它和荒凉的地貌形成了鲜明对照，车上的人都睁大眼睛欣赏起来。有的乘客甚至开始对这座房子讨论了起来。

那个年轻人也对这座房子留下了深刻的印象。回程时，他在离那座房子最近的站点下了车，找到了通向那座房子的路。房子的主人告诉他说，由于火车噪音困扰，他想卖掉房子，但没人愿意买。

年轻人把这座房子看作是广告的有利场所，不久以后便花3万美元买了下来。房子面对着铁路拐弯处，火车在那里不得不减速，疲惫的乘客常常会把目光投向这座房子上，来消除疲劳。

他设法和一些大公司取得了联系，尽力使他们相信用那个地方做广告的优势。最后，可口可乐公司租用那里，竖起了促销的招牌，付给了年轻人18万美元租金，租期3年。

这个故事绝对真实。它证明，只要发现有可能，就会走向成功。

Acres of Diamonds

There was a farmer in Africa who was happy and content. One day a wise man came to him and said, "If you had a diamond the size of your thumb, you could have your own city; if you had a diamond the size of your fist you could probably own your own country." And then he went away. That night the farmer couldn't sleep. He was unhappy because he was discontent, and he was discontent because he was unhappy.

The next morning he made arrangements to sell off his farm, took care of his family and went in search of diamonds. He looked all over Africa and couldn't find any. He looked all through Europe and couldn't find any. When he got to Spain, he was emotionally, physically and financially broke. He got so disheartened that he threw himself into the Barcelona River.

Back home, the man who had bought his farm was watering the camels at a stream that ran through the farm. Across the stream, the rays of the morning sun hit a stone and made it sparkle like a rainbow. He thought it would look good on the mantelpiece. He picked up the stone and put it in the living room. That afternoon the wise man came and saw the stone sparkling. He asked, "Is Hafiz back?" The new owner replied, "No, why do you ask?" The wise man said, "Because that is a diamond. I recognize one when I see one." The man said, "No, that's just a stone I picked up from the stream. Come, I'll show you. There are many more." They went and picked some samples and sent them for analysis. Sure enough, the stones were diamonds. They found that the farm was indeed covered with acres and acres of diamonds.

What is the moral of this story?

When our attitude is right, we realize that we are all walking on acres and acres of diamonds. Opportunity is always under our feet. We don't have to go anywhere else. All we need to do is recognize it.

钻石宝地

非洲有一位快乐而满足的农夫。有一天，一位智者走到他身边，说："如果你拥有一块拇指大的一块钻石，你就能拥有一座自己的城市；如果你拥有拳头大的一块钻石，你就可能拥有一个自己的国家。"说完，他就离开了。那天夜里，农夫难以入眠。他因不满足而闷闷不乐，也因为闷闷不乐而不满足。

第二天早上，他安排卖掉了自己的农场，安顿好了家人，就去寻找钻石了。他找遍了非洲，一无所获。他找遍了欧洲，也一无所获。他到达西班牙时，已经身心疲惫、一文不名了。他心灰意冷，纵身跳进了巴塞罗纳河。

此时在他的家乡，买下他农场的那个人正在潺潺流过农场的小溪边给骆驼饮水。小溪对面，晨阳照射在了一块石头上，使那块石头像一道彩虹那样闪耀。他想：这块石头摆在壁炉架上一定非常好看。他捡起了石头，把它放到了客厅里。当天下午，那个智者又来了，看到那块石头在闪闪发光，便问道："哈非兹回来了吗？"新主人回答说："没有，你为什么这样问?"智者说:"因为那是一块钻石。我一眼就能认出来。"那人说:"不,那只是我从小溪边捡起的一块石头。过来,我领你去看。那里还有更多呢。"他们走到了小溪边,挑了一些样品,将它们送去分析。那些石头果然是钻石。他们发现这整个农场确实蕴藏着大量钻石。

这个故事的寓意是什么呢?

我们态度端正时,就会意识到我们都走在广阔的钻石地上。机会总在我们脚下。我们不必到其他地方去寻找。我们需要做的就是加以识别。

The Mountain Spring and the Gold Sand

A small mountain spring ran tinkling down the narrow stone crevices. Many years passed. An egg – sized shallow hole was washed out on the rock. Strangely, the mountain spring anyhow brought some bright yellow gold sand and got to fill the small hole.

One day, an old woodcutter hit on this secret. To his amazement, he cupped the gold sand carefully.

Since then, the old man furtively fetched the gold sand once every half a month or so, so he became rich soon.

When discovering his father's secret, his son advised: If they widened the stone crevice for more mountain spring, more gold sand could be washed here. The old man thought it over and felt it advisable. So the father and son chiseled the narrow stone crevice so widely that the mountain spring was several times than ever. But unexpectedly, the gold sand didn't increase but disappeared ever since.

They felt puzzled: Where had the gold sand gone?

山泉与金砂

一股细细的山泉沿着窄窄的石缝叮叮咚咚往下流淌,也不知过了多少年,竟然在岩石上冲刷出了一个鸡蛋大小的浅坑。奇异的是,山泉不知从哪里冲来了黄澄澄的金砂,渐渐地填满了小坑。

有一天,一位砍柴的老汉偶然发现了这个秘密,惊喜之下,他小心翼翼地捧走了金砂。

从此,老汉过个十天半月就偷偷来取一次金砂,日子很快富裕了起来。

老汉的儿子发现了父亲的秘密,他建议:拓宽石缝,扩大山泉,不是能冲来更多的金砂吗?老汉想了想,觉得有理,父子俩就把窄窄的石缝凿宽了,山泉比原来大了几倍,谁知金砂不但没有增多,反而从此消失得无影无踪了。

父子俩百思不解:金砂到哪里去了呢?

Just Choose One Chair to Sit on

Pavarotti was a well – known world music superstar.

Each time he was asked for advice about the secret of success, he mentioned his father's words.

Graduating from a normal university, Pavarotti asked his father, "Will I be a teacher or a singer?"

Thinking for a moment, his father said, "If you want to sit on two chairs, you may drop from the gap between the two chairs. Life requires you to choose one chair to sit on."

Finally, Pavarotti chose singing.

After seven years' failures and efforts, he first performed on stage.

Then, after another seven years, he stepped on the stage of the Metropolitan Opern at last.

只坐一把椅子

帕瓦罗蒂是众所周知的世界歌坛超级巨星。

当有人向他讨教成功的秘诀时，他每次都提到他父亲说过的一段话。

在从师范学院毕业之际，帕瓦罗蒂问父亲："我是去当教师还是去做个歌唱家？"

父亲沉思了片刻说："如果你想坐在两把椅子上，你可能会从两把椅子中间掉下去。生活要求你必须要有选择地坐到一把椅子上去。"

帕瓦罗蒂最终选择了歌唱。

经过7年的失败与努力，他首次登台演出。

又过了7年，他终于登上了大都会歌剧院的大雅之堂。

Success and a Twig

There is a kind of bird who can fly ten thousands of miles across the Pacific Ocean. While what it needs is just a twig. The bird holds a twig in its mouth as it flies. When it feels tired, it drops the twig onto the water, flies down and rests on it for a while; when hungry, it stands on it and catches fish; when sleepy, it stands on it to sleep.

Who can imagine the little bird succeeds in flying across the Pacific Ocean only depending on a simple twig?

If it doesn't hold a twig in its mouth but take all the things needed on its trip such as its nest, food and so on, can the bird fly up?

If one blindly asks too much for the conditions to succeed, even the best condition will turn to be his burden like the gold tied to the wings.

Success is to create the conditions when needed, just as that kind of bird flies across the Pacific Ocean with a simple twig to base itself on for survival and flight.

成功与一截树枝

有一种鸟，它能飞行几万里，飞越太平洋，而它需要的只是一小截树枝。它把树枝衔在嘴里，累了把那截树枝扔到水面上，然后飞落在树枝上休息一会儿，饿了它就站在那截树枝上捕鱼，困了它就站在那截树枝上睡觉。

谁能想到小鸟成功地飞越了太平洋，靠的却仅是一小截简单的树枝！

如果小鸟在嘴里衔的不是树枝，而是把鸟窝、食物等旅途中所需要的用品，一股脑儿全带在身上，那小鸟还飞得起来吗？

如果一味地苛求成功的条件，再好的条件也会成为一种负担，成为绑缚在翅膀上的黄金。

成功就是在没有条件时去创造，就像那种飞越太平洋的小鸟，靠一小截简单的树枝立足、生存和飞翔。

The Golden Window

A small boy lived on a farm that seemed so far away from everywhere. He needed to get up before sunrise every morning to start his chores and out again later to do the evening ones.

During sunrise he would take a break and climb up on the fence so in the distance he could see the house with golden windows. He thought how great it would be to live there and his mind would wander to imagine the modern equipment and appliances that might exist in the house. "If they could afford golden windows, then there must have other nice things." He then promised himself, "Someday I will go there and see this wonderful place."

Then one morning his father told him to stay at home and his father would do the chores. Knowing that this was his chance, he packed a sandwich and headed across the field towards the house with the golden windows.

As the afternoon went on, he began to realize how he misjudged the distance and something else was very wrong. As he approached the house, he saw no golden windows but instead a place with in bad need of a painting surrounded by a broken down fence. He went to the tattered screen door and knocked. A small boy very close to his age opened the door.

He asked him if he had seen the house with the golden windows. The boy said, "Sure, I know," and invited him to sit on the porch. As he sat there, he looked back from where he just came where the sunset turned the windows on his home to gold.

金色窗户

有一个小男孩住在一个农场，这个农场好像离所有的地方都很远。每天早上太阳出来以前，他需要起床做杂务，晚些时候再出来做一次晚上的杂务。

太阳升起时，他会休息一下，爬上篱笆，这样他就可以看到远处那座有金色窗户的房子。他认为住在那里是非常了不起的事儿，他常常想象着房子里的现代化设备和电器。“要是他们能装得起金色窗户，那肯定还有其他好东西。”随后，他向自己许诺说，“总有一天，我要到那里去看这个了不起的地方。”

后来有一天早上，他父亲让他呆在家里，自己要去做这些杂务。他知道这是一个机会，就带上一块三明治，穿过田野，朝那座有金色窗户的房子走去。

下午来临时，他开始意识到自己错估了到那座房子的距离，其他事情也大相径庭。当走近那座房子时，他没有看到金色窗户，而是看到了一个急需粉刷、四周篱笆坏掉的地方。他走到那扇破屏门前，敲了敲。一个和他年龄非常接近的男孩打开了门。

他问那男孩是否见过那个有金色窗户的房子。那男孩说：“我当然知道，”并请他坐在门廊上。他坐在那里，回头向自己刚才来的方向望去，只见落日把他的家染成了金色。

Two Acorns

If you want to understand adversity, take two identical acorns from the same oak tree and plant them in two different locations. Plant the first in the middle of a dense forest, and the other on a hill by itself.

Here's what will happen. The oak standing on a hillside is exposed to every storm and gale. As a result its roots plunge deep into the earth and spread in every direction, even wrapping themselves around giant boulders. At times it may seem the tree isn't growing fast enough – but the growth is happening underground. It's as if the roots know they must protect the tree from the threatening elements.

What about the acorn planted in the forest? It becomes a weak, frail sapling. And since it is protected by its neighbors, the little oak doesn't sense the need to spread its roots for support.

Don't be afraid of adversity! Welcome it! That's your surefire route to ultimate success.

两个橡果

如果你想理解什么是逆境，就去拿两个从同一棵树上摘下来的相同的橡树果，并把他们种到不同的地方。第一颗种在浓密的树林当中，而另外一颗则单独种在一座山上。

事情的结果便是这样。那棵长在山上的橡树经历了大风大雨，结果它的根深深地扎进了泥土中，并不断向四周扩张，甚至把自己置身于巨大的石块中。有时它可能看起来长得不是很快，但这时它却在地下悄悄生长着，好像它的根知道自己必须快速生长，以免树木受自然危害的影响。

而种在树丛中的橡树果是什么样子的呢？它变成了一棵虚弱的小树苗。因为有周围树丛的保护，所以这棵小树苗便不知道要把自己的根扎得更深。

不要害怕困难！要欢迎它！那是你最终成功的必经之路。

Pinkie Victory Over Big Iron Hammer

The world No. 1 salesman was asked to share his secret of success upon his retirement. 2, 500 salesmen came to listen to his speech. He set a very big iron ball and a big hammer on the stage.

Then he asked, "Who can move this iron ball?" One man in the audience said, "I want to try." He went on the stage and knocked at the big iron ball once with the hammer.

It didn't budge.

Then came more men. The iron ball still didn't move. At this time the speaker said, "Now I will teach you the secret." He then poked the iron ball every 5 seconds with his pinkie. The iron ball began to move a little after 40 minutes. But the iron ball swung fiercely after 50 minutes.

He then asked, "Who can stop the iron ball on the stage?"

The people down the stage all said it couldn't be done.

The world No. 1 salesman said, "This is my secret of success. I visit customers every day until they give in. You see, they just can't block me when I succeed."

以小搏大的成功之道

世界头号推销员退休时接受邀请,分享他的成功秘诀。2500 名推销员来听他演讲。他在台上放了一只很大的铁球和一把大铁锤。

随后,他问道:"谁能移动这只铁球?"台下有个人说:"我想试一下。"那人上台,用铁锤敲了一下大铁球。

铁球没有动。

随后,又上来几个人。铁球还是没有动。这时,演讲者说:"现在我来教给你们其中的秘诀。"接着,他就每过 5 秒钟用小手指捅一下大铁球。40 分钟后,铁球微微移动。但 50 分钟后,铁球剧烈晃动起来。

他接着问:"谁能上台停住铁球?"

台下的人都说这做不到。

世界头号推销员说:"这就是我成功的秘诀。我每天都拜访顾客,直到他们让步。你看到了吧,我成功时,谁都挡不住。"

I Will Run to the Goal

It was a classic night. The noisy Mexico City gradually calmed down. The main stadium of Olympic track and field competition was enveloped in the darkness.

After he finished making the scenes the marathon winners received the trophies and marked the victory, Greenspan, the world famous newsreel producer, found the stadium empty. It was time for him to return to the hotel for a rest. He was about to leave when he suddenly saw a bandaged man with his

right leg stained with the blood ran into the stadium. This man ran lamely out of breath, but he didn't stop. After he ran along the runway for a circle and got to the goal, he collapsed on the ground...

Greenspan guessed this was a marathon athlete. Out of curiosity, he went over to ask why the athlete wanted to run to the goal with such a difficulty.

The young man called Kowari from Tanzania replied gently, "That my country sent me here from more than 20,000 kilometers is not let me get off the mark in the competition, but makes me complete the game. I want to run to the goal, though I have fallen behind all other runners, but I have a sacred goal like them: I will run to the goal. Though the audience won't cheer me any more, my motherland is watching me intently from behind..."

Tears welled up in Greenspan's eyes. Soon, he spread the most touching scene in the history of the Olympic Games to every corner of the world.

Life should have a dream of reaching the peak, yet we should understand not everybody has the ability to do it. The most important is not whether we can reach the peak but whether we have made the greatest efforts-to reach the goal in the mind is a success.

我要跑向终点

那是一个经典的夜晚，喧嚣的墨西哥城终于渐渐安静下来，奥运会田径比赛的主体育场被笼罩在夜色中。

享誉国际的纪录片制作人格林斯潘将当天马拉松比赛优胜者们领取奖杯、庆祝胜利的镜头制作完毕，才发现体育场内已空无一人，自己该回宾馆休息了。他刚要离开体育场，突然看到一个右腿沾满血污，绑着绷带的人跑进体育场。这个人一瘸一拐地跑着，气喘吁吁，却没有停下来。他顺着跑道跑了一圈，抵达终点后，一下瘫倒在地……

格林斯潘猜想，这是一名马拉松运动员。在好奇心的驱使下，他走了过去，询问这名运动员为什么要这么吃力地跑到终点。

这位来自坦桑尼亚、名叫埃克瓦里的年轻人轻声回答说："我的国家从两万多公里外送我来这里，不是叫我在这场比赛中起跑，而是派我来完成这场比赛的。我要跑向终点，尽管我已经落在奔跑队伍的最后面，但我有着和他们一样神圣的目标：我要跑到终点，尽管不再有观众为我加油，但我身后有祖国的凝望……"

格林斯潘泪光盈盈。很快，他就用镜头将奥运史上这最动人的一幕传递到世界上的每个角落。

人生应该拥有登临峰顶的梦想，但更应该懂得不是每个人都有到达峰顶的能力。最重要的不是能否到达峰顶，而是是否尽到了最大努力——到达心中的目标，便是一种成功。

Move Back Is Also a Success

When he just went to hold the post in the new parish, a pastor encountered a hot potato: there was a garden in front of the pastor gate and a number of children would cross the garden to school, so the

flowers were picked from time to time.

That spring, the flowers of the garden were in full bloom. One early morning, the pastor stood in the garden waiting for the children going to school. Soon, some of them came along; a little boy asked the pastor, "Can I snap a flower?"

"Which one do you want?" the pastor asked genially. The boy chose a tulip.

The pastor said, "Very good. It belongs to you now. However, if you leave the flower here, it can still bloom for several days; if you pick it now, you can only play for a little while. You are a smart kid, so you choose by yourself."

The little boy thought for a while and said, "Then I leave it here. I will come back to see it until class is over."

On that day, more than 20 children agreed to leave the flowers in the garden until they wilt.

That spring, the pastor left the whole garden to the people, but he had never lost one.

退一步也是成功

一位牧师刚到新教区任职,便碰到了一个棘手的问题:教区门前有一个花园,每天不少孩子上学都要横穿花园,因此鲜花被摘的现象时有发生。

那年春天,花园的鲜花开得格外茂盛。这天,牧师一大早就站在了花园中,等待着上学的孩子们。不一会儿,有几个孩子走过来,其中有一个小男孩开口问牧师:"我能折枝花吗?"

"你想要哪一枝?"牧师和蔼地问道。小男孩选了一枝郁金香。

牧师说:"好啊,这花归你了。不过,如果你把花儿留在这里,它还能开好几天;如果你现在折了它,那就只能玩一会儿了。你是个聪明的孩子,你自己作个选择吧。"小男孩想了想,说:"那我就把它留在这里,等我放学回来再看。"

那天,有 20 多个孩子都同意把花儿留在花园里,直到它们枯萎。

那年春天,牧师把整个花园的花全给了人,却没有丢一枝。

The Strength of Success

After the rain, a spider crawled hard to the frayed web. Because the wall was so damp, it slipped down as it crawled at a certain height. It still crawled up again and again when it dropped down...

The first person saw it, saying to himself with a sign, "Isn't my life is like this spider's? I'm always busy but get nothing." Then he was downhearted day by day.

The second person saw it, saying, "What a stupid spider! Why not move around and crawl from the dry wall nearby? I shouldn't be as foolish as it in future." Then he became more intelligent.

When the third person saw it, the spirit of the spider who suffered repeated defeats but continued to struggle moved him right away. Then he became stronger.

Spirits of success can always detect the strength of success.

成功的力量

雨后，一只蜘蛛艰难地向墙上已经支离破碎的网爬去，由于墙壁潮湿，它爬到一定的高度，就会掉下来。它一次次地向上爬，又一次次地掉下来……

第一个人看到了，他叹了口气，自言自语说："我的一生不正如这只蜘蛛吗？忙忙碌碌而无所得。"于是，他日渐消沉。

第二个人看到了，说："这只蜘蛛真愚蠢，为什么不从旁边干燥的地方绕一下爬上去？我以后可不能像它那样愚蠢。"于是，他变得聪明起来。

第三个人看到了，他立刻被蜘蛛屡败屡战的精神感动了。于是，他变得坚强起来。

成功的心态总能发觉成功的力量。

Confidence Is the Key of Success

Confidence is the key of success. When you're truly and justifiably confident, it radiates from you like sunlight, and attracts success to you like magnet.

It's so important to believe in yourself. Believe that you can do it under any circumstances. Because if you believe you can, you really will. That belief just keeps you searching for the answers, and you can get it pretty soon.

Confidence is more than an attitude. It comes from knowing exactly where you are going, exactly how you are going to get there. It comes from acting with integrity and a strong sense of purpose. It comes from a strong commitment to take responsibility, rather than just let life happen.

One way to develop self - confidence is to do the thing you fear and get the successful experiences from it.

Confidence is compassionate and understanding. It is not arrogant. Arrogance is born out of fear and insecurity. Confidence comes from strength and integrity.

Confidence is not just believing you can do it. Confidence is knowing you can do it. Knowing that you are capable of accomplishing anything you want, and live your life with confidence.

Anything can be achieved through focused, determined effort, commitment and self - confidence. If your life is not what you want it to be, you have the power to change it. But you must change it step by step. Live each moment with your goals and your plan of action. Live each moment with your priorities in your heart. Act with your own purpose and you will have the life you want.

自信是成功的钥匙

自信是成功的钥匙。当你真正有足够的理由自信时，自信会像阳光一样从你身上散发出来，并像磁铁一样把成功吸引到你身边。

相信自己非常重要。在任何情况下都要相信自己能行。因为如果你相信自己能行，你就会真正做到。那种信念正好使你不断寻找答案，然后很快你就能得到答案。

自信不仅仅是一种态度。自信来自你准确知道自己去哪里，准确知道你如何到达那里。自信来自正直诚实的行动和坚定的目标感。自信来承担责任的坚定承诺，而不是仅仅随波逐流。

发扬自信的一个方法就是去做你害怕做的事情，从中获取成功的体验。

自信富于同情和理解。自信不是傲慢自大。傲慢自大来自害怕和缺乏安全感。自信来自力量和诚实。

自信不仅仅是相信你能行。自信是知道自己能行。知道你有能力完成自己想做的一切，从而充满自信地生活。

通过明确坚定的努力、承诺和自信，任何事情都能做到。如果你的生活不如意，你有力量去改变它。但你必须一步步地改变。每时每刻都带着目标和行动计划去生活。每时每刻心里都要带着轻重缓急去生活。有的放矢地行动，你就会得到自己想要的生活。

最伟大的亲情

Mother's Hands

Night after night, she came to tuck me in, even long after my childhood years. Following her longstanding custom, she'd lean down and push my long hair out of the way, then kiss my forehead.

I don't remember when it first started annoying me—her hands pushing my hair that way. But it did annoy me, for they felt work-worn and rough against my young skin. Finally, one night, I shouted out at her, "Don't do that anymore—your hands are too rough!" She didn't say anything in reply. But never again did my mother close out my day with that familiar expression of her love.

Time after time, with the passing years, my thoughts returned to that night. By then I missed my mother's hands, missed her goodnight kiss on my forehead. Sometimes the incident seemed very close, sometimes far away. But always it lurked in the back of my mind.

Well, the years have passed, and I'm not a little girl anymore. Mom is in her mid-seventies, and those hands I once thought to be so rough are still doing things for me and my family. She's been our doctor, reaching into a medicine cabinet for the remedy to calm a young girl's stomach or soothe the boy's scraped knees. She cooks the best fried chicken in the world and gets stains out of blue jeans like I never could...

Now, my own children are grown and gone. Mom no longer has Dad, and on special occasions, I find myself drawn next door to spend the night with her. So it was late on Thanksgiving Eve, as I slept in the bedroom of my youth, a familiar hand hesitantly run across my face to brush the hair from my forehead. Then a kiss, ever so gently, touched my brow.

In my memory, for the thousandth time, I recalled the night my young voice complained, "Don't do that anymore—your hands are too rough!" Catching Mom's hand in hand, I blurted out how sorry I was for that night. I thought she'd remember, as I did. But Mom didn't know what I was talking about. She had forgotten—and forgiven—long ago.

That night, I fell asleep with a new appreciation for my gentle mother and her caring hands. And the guilt that I had carried around for so long was nowhere to be found.

母亲的手

夜复一夜，她都过来给我掖被子，甚至在我的童年过去很久之后还是那样。这种习惯由来已久，她常常俯下身，拨开我的长发，然后吻我的前额。

我不记得最初从什么时候开始讨厌她用手拨开我的头发。但那的确让我讨厌，因为她长期劳作的手摸在我细嫩的皮肤上是那样粗糙。终于，有一天夜里，我朝她大声喊道："不要再这样做了——你的手太粗糙了！"她什么也没有说。但母亲再也没有用那种熟悉的爱的方式来结束我的一天。

光阴荏苒，日月如梭，许多年后，我的思绪又回到了那天夜里。那时我想念母亲的手，想念她留在我前额上的晚安之吻。有时这情景似乎很近，有时又似乎很远。但它总是潜伏在我的脑海深处。

噢，时光流逝，我不再是小姑娘了。母亲也已经七十四五岁了，那双我曾认为粗糙的手仍在为我和我的家庭做事。她是我们的医生，常常伸手去药箱里给我胃疼的女儿找药或为我的儿子擦伤的膝盖敷药。她能做出世界上味道最美的炸鸡，能洗掉牛仔裤上我永远洗不掉的污点……

现在,我自己的孩子都已经长大成人,离开了家。爸爸也撒手而去了。在那些特殊时刻,我常常情不自禁地走到隔壁,和她一起过夜。因此,一次感恩节前夕,到了深夜,我睡在年轻时的卧室里时,一只熟悉的手迟疑地滑过了我的脸,拨开了我前额的头发,随后一个吻触在了我的前额上,是那样轻柔。

我在记忆里无数次回想起那天夜里我年轻气盛发的牢骚:"不要再那样做了——你的手太粗糙了!"我握住母亲的手,脱口说出了我是多么后悔那天夜里自己所说的话。我以为她会像我一样记得这件事。但妈妈不知道我在说什么。她早已忘记了这件事,也早已原谅了我。

那天夜里,我带着对温柔母亲和她体贴双手的新的感激之情进入了梦乡。而且我长久以来的内疚感也消失得无影无踪了。

Are You Cold, Mother?

On a heavy snowy day in winter, the two men walked along a valley. After trudging for one whole day, they came to a grave.

The grave was covered with the thick snow, the tombstone looking very simple. The older man said to the young man, "This is your mother's grave..." The young man knelt down on the snow.

The story took place in 1952. In order to save the Korean War from losing, the "UN forces" reinforced a group of soldiers, among whom Wilson was. At that time the most intense fighting occurred here.

The strong offensive of the People's Army made the "UN forces" retreat in defeat successively. On the way to retreat, Wilson was farther and farther away from the troops. At this moment, he suddenly heard a baby's cry, which came from the snow hole. Wilson instinctively dug up the snow, immediately shocked by what he saw.

In a mother's arms, the infant was crying aloud. What was even more shocking was the mother was naked. It turned out that when the mother carried her baby on the back to take refuge, they were trapped in this valley, for it started snowing heavily. In order to save her baby, the mother gave all her clothes to her child and then tightly held the baby in her arms. Though the naked mother had been dead, the baby in her arms survived.

Wilson was deeply moved by such an unexpected scene. He dug a pit with the field-operation tools in the frozen snow, buried the mother and then held the crying baby to pursue the troops.

After the war, he adopted this child and took him to the United States to bring up. When the child grew up slowly, Wilson told him what happened that year and took him to the valley to look for his mother.

The young man kneeling at the grave burst into tears.

After a while, the young man got to his feet and started to clean the snow on the grave. After cleaning the snow around, he undressed his clothes, covered the grave, then threw himself on the grave and spoke out the words concealed in his heart for long, "Mom, how cold you are for so many years!"

妈妈,你冷吗?

一个大雪纷飞的冬日,山谷里来了两个人。走了一整天后,他们来到了一座坟墓前。

坟上积了厚厚的雪，墓碑看起来非常简陋。年长者对年轻人说："这就是你妈妈的坟墓……"年轻人跪倒在了雪地上。

故事发生在1952年。为了挽回朝鲜战争败局，"联合国军"增援了一批士兵，威尔逊就是其中一员，当时最激烈的一次战斗就发生在这里。

人民军的强烈攻势使"联合国军"节节败退。撤退途中，威尔逊离大部队越来越远了。就在这时，他突然听到了婴儿的哭声，哭声是从一个雪窟窿里传出来的。威尔逊本能地扒开积雪，顿时被眼前的景象惊呆了。

在一个母亲的怀里，婴儿大声地哭着。更令人吃惊的是，母亲一丝不挂。原来，这位母亲背着孩子避难时，被困在了这个山谷里，天下起了大雪。为了救活自己的孩子，母亲把自己所有的衣服都给了孩子，然后把孩子紧紧抱在怀里。虽然赤裸的母亲已经死去，但她怀中的孩子却活了下来。

威尔逊被这意外的景象深深感动了。他用野战工具在冰冻的雪地上挖了个坑，把这位母亲埋葬了，然后抱着大哭的婴儿追赶大部队去了。

战争结束后，他领养了这个孩子，并把他带到美国去抚养。孩子慢慢长大了，威尔逊把当年发生的事告诉了他，并带着他来到山谷里找妈妈。

跪在坟前的年轻人痛哭失声。

过了一会儿，年轻人站起身，开始清理坟墓上的积雪。他把周围的积雪都清理完，把衣服一件件脱下来盖在了坟墓上，然后扑到坟墓上，说出了久藏在心里的话："妈妈，这么多年你多冷啊！"

The Potential of Love

On the way home, when she would be home immediately, a young woman looked at her balcony on the fourth floor while her lovely son was also expecting her mother to come back on the balcony. When he saw his mother, his son started waving his hand. At this moment the young woman was also consciously waving her hand. Suddenly, she realized this might be dangerous, but it was already late because her son wanted to greet her, leaned forward, suddenly lost his balance and turned over from the balcony. Then the people in the room were so shocked that all of them rushed to the balcony shouting. When finding her son falling down, she dashed ahead regardless of her safety to save her son. Perhaps God was moved; the son was met by his mother and unharmed. People found it very strange how a young woman ran so fast and could catch her son because according to her running speed she should have broken the 100 – meter world record.

Later, people asked the 100 – meter world champion to do a test: whether he could meet the object with the same weight falling from the balcony in the same distance. The result was he couldn't make it anyway. Let the young woman test again, but the result was that she couldn't break the 100 – meter world record. Finally, people summarized: the power of love is great.

This story illustrates that love can also inspire the potential.

爱心的潜能

一位少妇在回家的路上,马上要到家时,习惯地看了一下4楼自家的阳台,可爱的儿子也正在阳台上期待着妈妈回来。当看到妈妈时,儿子开始招手,这时少妇也有意识地招手,突然她意识到这样可能会有危险,但已经晚了。因为儿子要迎妈妈,所以身体前倾,突然失去平衡,从阳台上坠了下来。这时,房间里的人惊呆了,纷纷跑到阳台上呼叫。妈妈发现儿子掉下来,就奋不顾身地去救儿子,也许是感动了上帝,儿子被妈妈接住了,并且安然无恙。人们都觉得很奇怪,一个少妇怎么跑得那样快,并能接住自己的儿子,因为按当时少妇跑的速度应该已打破了百米世界记录。

后来,人们找百米世界冠军做了一个试验:同样的距离,从阳台上掉下同样重量的物体,看能否接得住。结果是无论如何也接不住。再让这位少妇试,结果也是再也没有看到打破百米世界记录的速度。最后,人们总结为:爱的力量是伟大的。

这个故事说明:爱心同样可以激发潜能。

A Rose for Her Mother

A gentleman stopped his car at the door of a flower shop. He wanted to order a bunch of flowers and asked them to deliver them to his mother. who was far in his hometown.

He saw a girl crying on the road when he was about to enter the shop. The gentleman walked to the little girl and asked her, "Little girl, why are you crying?"

"I want to buy a rose for my mother, but I haven't enough money," said the girl.

Hearing that, the gentleman felt sympathetic to the girl. "It was so. . . " Then he grasped the girl's hand and entered the flower shop. He first ordered the bouquet for his mother and bought a rose for the girl.

Walking out of the shop, the gentleman proposed driving the girl home.

"Would you really drive me home?"

"Of course!"

"Then drive me to my mother. But uncle, the place where my mother lives is very far from here."

Following the way the girl showed, the gentleman drove out of the urban district along the winding mountain road and finally came to the cemetery.

The little girl put the flower close to a new grave. In order to present a rose to her mother who just passed away a month ago, she took a long journey.

The gentleman drove the girl to her home, then he return to the flower shop. He cancelled the flower bunch to her mother but bought a big bunch of fresh flower instead. He drove directly to his mother's home, five-hour drive from here. He would present the flower to his mother in person.

送给母亲的玫瑰

有位绅士在花店门口停下了车，他打算向花店订一束花，请他们送去给远在故乡的母亲。

绅士正要走进店门时，发现有个小女孩坐在路上哭，便走到小女孩面前问她说："孩子，为什么坐在这里哭？"

"我想买一朵玫瑰花送给妈妈，可我的钱不够。"孩子说。

绅士听了，感到心疼。"这样啊……"于是，绅士牵着小女孩的手走进花店，先订了要送给母亲的花束，然后给小女孩买了一朵玫瑰花。

走出花店时，绅士向小女孩提议，要开车送她回家。

"真的要送我回家吗？"

"当然啊！"

"那你送我去妈妈那里好了。可是，叔叔，我妈妈住的地方离这里很远。"

绅士照小女孩说的一直开了过去，没想到走出市区大马路之后，随着蜿蜒山路前行，竟然来到了墓园。

小女孩把花放在一座新坟旁边。她为了给一个月前刚过世的母亲，献上一朵玫瑰花，而走了一大段远路。

绅士将小女孩送回了家中，然后再次返回花店。他取消了要寄给母亲的花束，而改买了一大束鲜花，直奔离这里有5小时车程的母亲家里，他要亲自将花献给妈妈。

A Daughter's Love for Her Mother

Dear Mom,

I haven't written many letters to you before, as we've almost always been able to just pick up the phone and have a chat, so it's hard to know how to start.

Of course, all the usual things apply—we all miss you and hope you're all right wherever you are.

When you left us, it took a little for it to sink in that I would never see you again. I guess I was a bit like you being away on a trip or those times when we didn't find the time to even speak on the phone for a week or so.

I realize now there are too many things left unsaid and too many questions unasked.

Dad is finding life difficult without you and his loneliness is almost unbearable to me, as there's so little I can do to help him. I think in time he'll find some interests and make a new kind of life. But at the moment he seems only to look forward to the time when he can join you again.

Emily and I are feeling a little better each day and, in a way, your going has brought us closer together. We seem to understand each other better at the moment and maybe eventually we'll have the sort of relationship that really close sisters enjoy.

We've both found strengths in each other over the past weeks, and these are a huge comfort. Perhaps we never needed to look for them before because we had you to be strong for us.

I guess I'm lucky to have my own children to keep me so busy. I don't have much time to dwell on my sadness but sometimes I crave the peace to just have a private think about you.

For a couple of weeks after you died, my brain seemed to go crazy, searching through its memory banks for something I could keep in my heart which was special to you and me. One day it came to me—the tour we made of some special garden.

Remember the day it poured with rain the whole time but we were determined to make the most of it? I enjoyed just being with you by myself, without the children clamoring for your attention. The gardens were beautiful despite the rain and you bought me a rose I'd admired for my own garden.

For a while after your death, I expected to feel your presence around me as Dad and Emily seem to do with such ease. When I was out walking, I would look at the sky and wonder whether you could see me, or whether you were with me. At night I wondered whether you'd become a star, as some people believe.

But as time passes, I think I'm closer to finding the truth. You're with me every time I comfort one of the children or try to find the right words to gently chastise them. I listen for your words of wisdom and they come from within me because your greatest gift to me was teaching me how to be a good mother to my own children.

And although you're no longer here with us, I know in times of sadness or pain the children feel your arms around them just as I sense that I feel your arms around me, too. In years to come I hope your gift to me will be passed to my own children's children. And I know it's your voice telling me in these changing times the best thing we can give our children is love, because love is eternal and love doesn't die. So long for now, and thank you from all of us.

Happy Mother's Day, mom.

. Love Carol

母女情怀

亲爱的妈妈：

我以前没有给您写过多少封信，因为我们几乎总能拿起电话聊天，所以很难知道怎么开始写起。

当然，可以用那些老生常谈——我们都想念您，希望您无论在什么地方都万事如意。

您离开我们时，有一小段时间我陷入了永远无法再见您的思念。我想那有点儿像您出门旅行了，要么就像我们有时一周左右都没时间通电话。

我现在意识到还有太多的话没说，还有太多的问题没问。

没有了您，爸爸发现生活难过，他的孤独让我几乎无法忍受，因为我几乎帮不了他什么忙。我想他最后会找到一些有兴趣的事儿，开始一种新的生活。但是，他现在似乎只盼望能和您再次相聚。

我和埃米莉的感觉渐渐好转。从某种意义上说，您的离去使我们更加亲密。我们此时似乎彼此更加了解，也许最终我们会享有亲密姐妹们享有的那种关系。

在过去的几周里，我们已经从彼此身上找到了力量，这是极大的安慰。也许我们以前从不需要寻求这种力量，因为我们有您做坚强后盾。

我想幸运的是我自己有孩子，使我忙得团团转，没有多少时间沉湎于悲伤，但有时我渴望安静，可以私下去思念您。

在您去世后的两三周里，我的大脑好像发了疯似的，拼命在记忆库里寻找珍藏在我心里的某件事——某件对您我二人都特别亲密的事情。有一天，我终于想起来了——就是我们到一个特别花园进行的那次游览。

还记得那天一直大雨倾盆，但我们打定主意要尽情玩玩一下的情景吗？我就喜欢单独和您在一起，没有孩子们大声吵闹使您分心。尽管下着雨，但花园很美。您给我买了一枝玫瑰，我曾希望自己的花园种有这种玫瑰。

您去世后的一段时间，我期望能感到您就在我身边，因为爸爸和埃米莉好像轻松自如就能感受到。我在外面散步时，常常仰望天空，想知道您是不是能看到我，或者您是不是和我在一起。夜里，我常常想，您是不是就像有些人相信的那样变成了一颗星星。

但随着时间流逝，我想我越来越近地找到了真实的感觉。每当我安慰一个孩子或要找出合适的词语来轻轻责打他们时，您都和我在一起。如果我留神倾听您的智慧话语，它们就会从我的内心传来，因为您留给我最伟大的礼物就是教会我如何给自己的孩子当一个好妈妈。

尽管您不再和我们一起生活在这里，但我知道在悲伤和痛苦时，孩子们能感到您环抱着他们，就像我感到您环抱着我一样。在未来的岁月里，我希望把您留给我的礼物传给我的子孙们。而且我知道那是您的声音在告诉我，在这变化的时代，我们能留给我们孩子们的最好东西就是爱，因为爱是永恒的，爱不会死去。就此再见了，我们都衷心感谢您。

母亲节快乐，妈妈！

爱您的卡罗尔

The Hair in the Box Meal

In those years of poverty, many classmates often couldn't bring decent box meal to school, so did my deskmate. His meal was always the black fermented soybean while mine was often ham and fried egg, completely different from his. Moreover, every time my classmate would first pick the hair from his box meal and eat it as if nothing had happened. This discomfortable discovery continued all along.

"Obviously his mother is so lousy that even her hair drops in the meal." My classmates talked about it secretly. I felt it was too dirty but I couldn't show that for the sake of his self-respect. So my impression on him began to decline greatly.

One day after school, he called me and said, "Would you like to go to my home if you're free?"

Though reluctant, I found it awkward to refuse because this was his first invitation since we were in the same class. Following my friend, we arrived at a poor village located at the Seoul's steepest place.

"Mum, I bring my friend home."

Hearing my classmate's excited voice, his aged mother opened the door and appeared. "My son's friend comes. Let me have a look." But his mother, who had walked out of the door, was only touching the door's beam column with her hands. It turned out that she was blind.

I felt sad without a word. My classmate's box meal was as usual the fermented soybean every day, but it was his blind mother who carefully prepared for him. It was not only a lunch, but also a mother's brimming love, and even the hair mixed in it was the mother's love.

午饭盒里的头发

在那个贫困的年代,很多同学往往连带个像样的午饭盒到学校上课的能力都没有,我邻座的同学就是如此。他的饭菜永远是黑黑的豆豉,我的午饭盒却经常装着火腿和荷包蛋,两者有着天壤之别。而且这个同学每次都会先从午饭盒里捡出头发后,再若无其事地吃。这个令人浑身不舒服的发现一直持续着。

"可见他妈妈有多邋遢,竟然每天饭里都有头发。"同学们私下议论着。为了顾及同学自尊,又不能表现出来,总觉得好脏,因此对这同学的印象也开始大打折扣。

有一天,学校放学后,那同学叫住了我:"如果没什么事,就去我家玩吧。"

虽然心中不太愿意,但自从同班以来,他第一次开口邀请我到家里玩,所以我不好意思拒绝,就随朋友来到了位于汉城最陡峭地形的某个贫民村。

"妈,我带朋友来了。"

听到同学兴奋的声音后,他年迈的母亲打开了房门,出现在了门口。"我儿子的朋友来啦,让我看看。"可是,走出房门的同学母亲只是用手摸着房门外的梁柱。原来她是盲人。

我感到一阵心酸,一句话都说不出来。同学的午饭菜虽然每天如常都是豆豉,却是眼睛看不到的母亲小心翼翼帮他装的,那不只是一顿午餐,更是母亲满满的爱心,甚至连掺杂在里面的头发也一样是母亲的爱。

Mom Charged Zero Dollar

Texas has a law: any 14-year-old children must share the household chores for the parents, such as washing dishes, scrubbing the floor and mowing the lawns.

One Sunday night, smart Tom wrote a bill to his mother:

Tom helped Mom buy the food in the supermarket, so Mom should pay five dollars;

Tom got up and folded his quilt, so Mom should pay two dollars;

Tom scrubbed the floor, so Mom should pay three dollars;

Tom is an obedient good boy, so Mom should pay 10 dollars.

The total is 20 dollars.

After that, Tom pressed the note on the table and went to bed. When his mother saw it, she smiled tolerantly, added a few lines on it and put it beside Tom's pillows.

When Tom woke up, he saw such a bill:

Mom was pregnant with Tom for 10 months, so Tom should pay 0 dollar;

Mom taught Tom to speak and walk, so Tom should pay 0 dollar;

Mom made good food for Tom every day, so Tom should pay 0 dollar;

Mom accompanied Tom to the children's playground every weekend, so Tom should pay 0 dollar;

Mom prays for Tom every day, hoping he becomes an angelic lovely little boy, so Tom should pay 0 dollar.

The total is 0 dollar.

Now this note is still treasured by Tom. It tells Tom that the real love can't be measured by money.

Mother is so generous because she loves too genuinely; Mother is so tolerant because she loves too deeply. When we have such a genuine and deep love in our hearts as Mother, we won't ask for reward, either.

妈妈只收零美元

得克萨斯州有一条法律：凡年满 14 岁的孩子必须为父母分担家务，比如洗碟子、擦地板和剪草坪。

一个星期天的晚上，聪明的汤姆给妈妈写下了一份账单：

汤姆帮妈妈到超级市场买食品，妈妈应付 5 美元；

汤姆自己起床叠被，妈妈应付 2 美元；

汤姆擦地板，妈妈应付 3 美元；

汤姆是一个听话的好孩子，妈妈应付 10 美元。

合计:20 美元。

写完后，汤姆把纸条压在餐桌上，便上床睡觉去了。妈妈看到这张纸条后，宽容地笑了笑，随手在上面添了几行字，放到汤姆的枕边。

汤姆醒来后，看到了这样的一张账单：

妈妈怀了汤姆 10 个月，汤姆应付 0 美元；

妈妈教汤姆说话和走路，汤姆应付 0 美元；

妈妈每天为汤姆做好吃的食物，汤姆应付 0 美元；

妈妈每个周末陪汤姆去儿童乐园，汤姆应付 0 美元；

妈妈每天为汤姆祈祷，希望他成为天使般可爱的小男孩，汤姆应付 0 美元。

合计:0 美元。

这张纸条至今仍被汤姆珍藏着。它告诉汤姆，真正的爱是无法用金钱计量的。

妈妈为什么如此慷慨，因为她爱得太真；妈妈为什么如此宽容，因为她爱得太深。等我们心中有了妈妈那样真那样深的爱时，我们也会不图报酬。

Prayer for My Mother

Now that I am no longer young, I have friends whose mothers have passed away. I have heard these sons and daughters say they never fully appreciated their mothers until it was too late to tell them.

I am blessed with the dear mother who is still alive. I appreciate her more each day. My mother doesn't change, but I do. As I grow older and wiser, I realize what an extraordinary person she is. How sad that I am unable to speak these words in her presence, but they flow easily from my pen.

How does a daughter begin to thank her mother for life itself? For the love, patience and just plain hard work that go into raising a child? For running after a toddler, for understanding a moody teenager, for tolerating a college student who knows everything? For waiting for the day when a daughter realizes her mother really is?

I don't know how, dear God, except to bless her as richly as she deserves and to help me live up to the example she has set. I pray that I will look as good in the eyes of my children as my mother looks in mine.

为母亲祈祷

我不再年轻,一些朋友的母亲已经去世了。我曾听这些子女们说过,他们从来没有向自己的母亲充分表示过感激之情,直到想告诉她们时为时已晚。

我庆幸自己亲爱的母亲仍然健在。我对她的感激与日俱增。母亲没有变,但我却变了。随着年龄的增长,我越来越懂事,我认识到她是一个多么非凡的人。我对自己在她面前说不出这些话感到难过,但这些话却能轻松地流诸笔端。

一个女儿如何开口感谢她的母亲给予的生命呢?是感谢她在抚养孩子时付出的爱、耐心和平常的辛劳?是感谢她跟在蹒跚学步的孩子身后奔跑,对喜怒无常的少女的理解和对一个自以为是的大学生的宽容?还是感谢她等待女儿认识到她是一位真正母亲的这一天?

亲爱的上帝,我不知道该如何表达,除了你好好保佑她——她应该得到——并帮助我做到以她为榜样。我祈祷,在自己的孩子们的眼里,我会像母亲在我的眼里一样好。

You Thanked Mother

When you came into the world, she held you in her arms.
You thanked her by weeping your eyes out.
When you were 1 year old, she fed you and bathed you.
You thanked her by crying all night long.
When you were 2 years old, she taught you to walk.
You thanked her by running away when she called.

When you were 3 years old, she made all your meals with love.

You thanked her by tossing your plate on the floor.

When you were 4 years old, she gave you some crayons.

You thanked her by coloring the kitchen table.

When you were 5 years old, she dressed you for the holidays.

You thanked her by plopping into the nearest pile of mud.

When you were 6 years old, she walked you to school.

You thanked her by screaming, "I'm not going!"

When you were 7 years old, she bought you a baseball.

You thanked her by throwing it through the next – door – neighbor's window.

When you were 8 years old, she handed you an ice cream.

You thanked her by dripping it all over your lap.

When you were 9 years old, she paid for piano lessons.

You thanked her by never even bothering to practice.

When you were 10 years old, she drove you all day, from soccer to gymnastics to one birthday party after another.

You thanked her by jumping out of the car and never looking back.

When you were 11 years old, she took you and your friends to the movies.

You thanked her by asking to sit in a different row.

When you were 12 years old, she warned you not to watch certain TV shows.

You thanked her by waiting until she left the house.

When you were 13, she suggested a haircut that was becoming.

You thanked her by telling her she had no taste.

When you were 14, she paid for a month away at summer camp.

You thanked her by forgetting to write a single letter.

When you were 15, she came home from work, longing for a hug.

You thanked her by having your bedroom door locked.

When you were 16, she taught you how to drive her car.

You thanked her by taking it every chance you could.

When you were 17, she was expecting an important call.

You thanked her by being on the phone all night.

When you were 18, she cried at your high – school graduation.

You thanked her by staying out partying until dawn.

When you were 19, she paid your college tuition, drove you to campus, carried your bags.

You thanked her by saying good – bye outside the dorm so you wouldn't be embarrassed in front of your friends.

When you were 20, she asked whether you were seeing anyone.

You thanked her by saying, "It's none of your business."

When you were 21, she suggested certain careers for your future.

You thanked her by saying, "I don't want to be like you."

When you were 22, she hugged you at your college graduation.

You thanked her by asking whether she could pay for a trip to Europe.

When you were 23, she gave you furniture for your first apartment.

You thanked her by telling your friends it was ugly.

When you were 24, she met your fiancé and asked about your plans for the future.

You thanked her by glaring and growling, "Muuhh – ther, please!"

When you were 25, she helped to pay for your wedding, and she cried and told you how deeply she loved you.

You thanked her by moving halfway across the country.

When you were 30, she called with some advice on the baby.

You thanked her by telling her, "Things are different now."

When you were 40, she called to remind you of a relative's birthday.

You thanked her by saying you were "really busy right now."
When you were 50, she fell ill and needed you to take care of her.
You thanked her by reading about the burden parents become to their children.
And then one day she quietly died.

报答母亲

你来到人世,她将你抱在怀里。

你报答她,哭得死去活来。

你1岁时,她喂你,给你洗澡。

你报答她,整夜号哭。

你2岁时,她教你走路。

你报答她,她一叫你就跑。

你3岁时,她充满爱心为你做饭。

你报答她,把盘子摔在地上。

你4岁时,她送给你几支蜡笔。

你报答她,给餐桌涂上了颜色。

你5岁时,她给你穿上节日盛装。

你报答她,扑通跌进了最旁边的泥堆里。

你6岁时,她步行送你上学。

你报答她,尖叫着:"我不去!"

你7岁时,她给你买了一只棒球。

你报答她,把棒球扔到了邻居的窗户上。

你8岁时,她递给你一块冰淇淋。

你报答她,把膝盖上滴得到处都是。

你9岁时,她掏钱让你学钢琴。

你报答她,从不操心去练。

你10岁时,她整天开车,从足球场赶到健身房,又从一个生日宴会赶到另一个生日宴会。

你报答她,跳下车,头也不回。

你11岁时,她带你和朋友去影院。

你报答她,让她坐到另一排。

你12岁时,她警告你不要看某些电视节目。

你报答她,等她一离开你就去看。

你13岁时,她建议你把发型剪得体。

你报答她,对她说没有品位。

你14岁时,她掏了一个月钱送你去夏令营。

你报答她,一封信也忘了写。

你15岁时，她下班回家，渴望拥抱。
你报答她，锁住了卧室门。
你16岁时，她教你学开车。
你报答她，一有机会就开车。
你17岁，她在等一个重要电话。
你报答她，打了一夜电话。
你18岁中学毕业时，她痛哭失声。
你报答她，在外面聚会通宵达旦。
你19岁时，她为你缴纳大学学费，开车送你到校，为你拎包。
你报答她，在宿舍门外说再见，这样你就不会在朋友们面前现难堪。
你20岁时，她问你是否在约会。
你报答她，说："这不关你的事。"
你21岁时，她为你将来的事业提建议。
你报答她，说："我不想和你一样。"
你22岁大学毕业时，她拥抱你。
你报答她，问她能不能掏钱让你到欧洲兜风。
你23岁时，她为你的第一套公寓送去家具。
你报答她，告诉朋友家具难看。
你24岁时，她遇到你的未婚夫，问你们将来有什么打算。
你报答她，对她怒目而视、大声吼叫："妈——妈，求你了！"
你25岁时，她花钱帮你筹办婚礼，哭诉爱你是多么深。
你报答她，把家迁到了千里外。
你30岁时，她打电话为宝宝抚养提忠告。
你报答她，告诉她："现在情况不一样。"
你40岁时，她打电话提醒你，记住亲戚的生日。
你报答她，说你"现在实在忙。"
你50岁时，她病倒在床，需要你照顾她。
你报答她，说父母成了子女们的负担。
后来有一天，她悄然而去。

I Think of My Mother Far－off

My mother doesn't read a word, but she would read each of my letters for several times, even in the middle of the night. My mother is at pains to read her son's days away from home. My mother would worry about my each voice for coughing that she couldn't eat or sleep for three days and three nights; and she would worry about one of my cold for an entire winter.

As I grow up day by day, my mother would speak less and less. All the days and nights are elongating the distance between mother and me. When I speak, she would listen to me quietly by the side; when I change my clothes, she would take it to wash quietly; when the wind blows, she would get up in the moonlight, close the doors and windows carefully and walk on tiptoe out of my room; when it is cold, she would put one of my clothes on my bed silently.

But I once ignored my mother's existence. Until one day I knew my mother sitting on the threshold far - off and listening to my news, rain or sunshine. Mother, please don't release your hand, for in front of you I'm a child who will never grow up. On the road to a long journey, I still have too much confusion and hesitation, so I need your hands to guide me.

Since then, when I fall silent, I would think of my mother.

我想起远方的母亲

母亲不认识一个字，但我的每一封信她都要看几遍，甚至在半夜，母亲是用心去阅读儿子在外的日子。母亲会为我的一声咳嗽担心得三天三夜吃不下、睡不着，会为我的一次感冒担心整整一个冬季。

随着我的日益长大，母亲的话越来越少，所有的日日夜夜都在拉长我和母亲之间的距离。我说话，她就在一旁默默地听；我换下衣服，她就默默地拿去洗；起风了，她就会摸着月色爬起来，小心翼翼地关好门窗，然后蹑手蹑脚地走出我的房间；天冷了，她就会拿一件衣服默默地放在我的床边。

而我却一度忽略了母亲的存在，直到有一天才知道，远方有我的母亲坐在门槛上，从风里雨里聆听我的消息。母亲，请你不要松开你的手，在你面前，我是一个永远长不大的孩子，远行的路上，我还有太多的迷惘与彷徨，需要你的双手牵引。

从此，沉默的时候，我就会想起母亲。

Mother's Strength

There were two warring tribes in the Andes, one that lived in the lowlands and the other high in the mountains.

One day the mountain people invaded the lowlanders, and as part of their plundering of the people, they kidnapped a baby of one of the lowlander families and took the infant with them back up into the mountains.

The lowlanders didn't know how to climb the mountain. They didn't know any clue of the path that the mountain people used, and they didn't know where to find the mountain people or how to track them in the steep terrain.

Even so, they sent out their best party of fighting men to climb the mountain and bring the baby home. The men tried first one method of climbing and then another. After several days of efforts, however, they had climbed only a couple of hundred feet. Feeling hopeless and helpless, the lowlanders decided that the cause was lost, and they prepared to return to their village below. As they were packing their gear for the descent, they saw the baby's mother walking toward them. They realized that she was coming down the mountain that they hadn't figured out how to climb. And then they saw that she had the baby strapped to her back. How could that be?

One man greeted her and said, "We, the strongest and most able men in the village, couldn't climb this mountain. How did you do this?"

The mother shrugged her shoulders and said, "It isn't your baby."

As long as you have love in your heart, no mountain you cannot climb.

母亲的力量

安第斯山有两个敌对的部落,一个部落住在低地,另一个住在高山上。

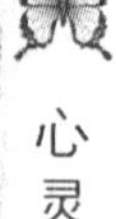

有一天,山上部落侵略山下部落。在对山下部落抢劫中,他们绑架了一户人家的婴儿,并把婴儿带上了山。

山下部落的人不知道怎么才能爬上山。他们不知道山上部落走的山道的任何线索,也不知道在哪里找到山上部落,更不知道怎样在陡峭的山地跟踪追击。

尽管如此,他们仍然派自己部落中最优秀、最勇敢的战士爬上山,把孩子抢回来。战士们尝试了一个又一个方法。然而,努力了好几天之后,他们仅仅爬了几百英尺。山下部落的战士们感到绝望无助,认为没办法爬到山上去,准备回到山下的村庄。正当他们收拾工具准备返回山下时,只见那个婴儿的母亲正朝他们走来。他们意识到她下来的那座山正是他们不知道怎样爬的那座山。随后,他们看到她背着那个婴儿。这怎么可能呢?

一个战士跟她打招呼说:"我们是部落中最强壮、最能干的男人,都爬不上山。你是怎么做到的呢?"

孩子的母亲耸了耸肩,说:"那不是你们的孩子。"

只要心中有爱,没有爬不过去的高山。

The Most Fragrant Smell of Medicine

That year I jobbed at a Chinese traditional medicine store whose business was not bad and who decocted medicinal herbs for patients. So the store was filled with the heavy herbal smell, which made the passer-bys cover their noses.

I found, without knowing from which day, a boy of thirteen or fourteen years old sat on the stairs before the store for a while every day, which I felt so unusual.

One day, I asked him, "Do you like the herbal smell?"

He said gently, "I grew up in this kind of smell!" He said his mother took herbal medicines year after year, so he was able to decoct herbs for his mother when he was very young. He decocted herbs with deep affection, hoping his mother would recover as soon as possible.

I asked, "Is your mother fully recovered?" He shook his head and said, "My mother passed away three years ago!" I felt depressed for a moment.

Gazing far away, he went on, "When I first passed by here and smelled the herbs, I suddenly thought of my mother. Thinking of those days when she was alive, I would feel warm in my heart. So I come here every day to sit for a moment. In such a smell, I would feel as if my mother were waiting for her medicine in her room!"

最美的药味

那一年,我在街角的一家中药铺打工。药铺生意还不错,而且代熬中草药,药铺周围弥漫着浓浓的中药味,路人往往掩鼻而行。

不知从哪一天起,我发现有个十三四岁的少年每天都要在药铺前的台阶上坐一会儿,这让我很奇怪。

有一天,我问他:"你很喜欢中药的味道吗?"

他轻轻地说:"我就是在这种气味中长大的!"他说他妈妈常年喝中药,他小小的年纪便能给妈妈熬中药了。他每天殷勤地熬药,希望妈妈能早日好起来。

我问:"你妈妈现在全好了吧?"他摇摇头说:"妈妈3年前去世了!"我一时黯然。

他看着远方,说:"第一次经过这里时,闻到熬药的味儿,我一下子就想起了妈妈,想起了她在世时的那些日子,心里就觉得暖暖的。于是,我每天来这里坐上一会儿,在这种气味里,我就觉得妈妈正在屋子里等着喝药呢!"

For the Love of Mother

When William, a 10-year-old boy who was somewhat scruffy-looking, enrolled himself to learn the piano, the music teacher was reluctant to accept him. She preferred her students to start their music lessons at a younger age when their fingers are nimble.

"William, why do you want to learn the piano?" the teacher asked.

"I want to play for my mother."

She noticed the tears in his eyes as he answered her. She had no heart to turn him down and accepted William as her student. But at each music lesson, William appeared to be in a hurry and play badly. "My mother is waiting outside for me," he would tell the teacher. She was tempted to advise William not to waste his time as he never hit the right note. But there was something about William, which she was fascinated with-the tender look of his eyes each time he mentioned "mother."

Suddenly, William stopped coming for his lessons. At the end of the semester, the music teacher decided to organize a piano recital for her students and she sent flyers to them to participate. She was surprised to find William's application that he would like to contribute a musical piece. She again had no heart to turn him down. She would put him as the last player in case he stumbled with his notes, she would come forward to remedy the situation.

The day came and William appeared with his hair uncombed and his shirt creased. He sat quietly with his eyes closed. When it was his turn to play, William bowed before the audience and said he was thankful for the music teacher's patience with him as he may not have been the best of her pupils.

"Tonight I am dedicating my music to my mother," he said. As he sat down and put his fingers on the keyboard, the most beautiful sound of music was heard. Everyone later asked why he didn't bring his mother as she would surely be proud to hear him play.

William replied, "My mother was stone deaf and she could never hear me play during her lifetime. Yet she sacrificed her time and money to let me learn the piano. This morning mother passed away. I am sure she is now happy as she can hear my piano recital. I chose a piece from Beethoven's concerto. As you all know, Beethoven was submerged with deafness at the triumph of his career. The piece released him from darkness and so was mother." Everyone was electrified to hear what William said and tears welled over their eyes.

The music teacher proudly exclaimed, "William, not only your mother but we all are proud of you. We are deeply touched by your devotion and your love for mother," as she embraced him.

献给母亲的爱

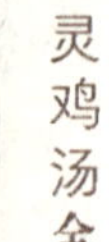

10 岁男孩威廉有点儿衣衫不整,想报名学钢琴。音乐老师勉强收下了他。她更喜欢学生年龄小时上音乐课,因为这个时候他们的手指灵活。

"威廉,你为什么想学钢琴呢?"老师问。

"我想为妈妈演奏。"

她注意到,他回答她时眼里含着泪花。她不忍心拒绝,就收下了威廉。但每次音乐课,威廉好像总是匆匆忙忙,而且弹得很糟。"妈妈在外面等着我,"他常常这样对老师说。因为威廉从来没有弹准过一个音符,所以她真想建议他别再浪费时间了。但是,威廉身上有一种东西深深地吸引着她——他每次提到"母亲"时,眼里总是带着温柔的神情。

突然,威廉不再来上课了。期末时,音乐老师决定为她的学生们筹备一场钢琴独奏会。于是,她向发出传单。她吃惊地发现了威廉想演奏一曲的申请表。她还是不忍心拒绝他,就决定让他最后演奏,万一他演奏得不顺,她可以上前救场。

这一天到了,威廉头发蓬乱,衬衣起皱,来到现场,闭着眼睛静静地坐在那里。轮到威廉演奏时,他在观众面前鞠了一躬,说他感谢音乐老师对他的耐心,因为他可能不是她最好的学生。

"今天晚上,我要把自己的音乐献给我的妈妈,"说着,他坐下来,把手指放到琴键上,顿时响起了最优美的旋律。后来,大家问他为什么不带妈妈来,因为听到他演奏,她一定会非常自豪。

威廉回答说:"我妈妈完全是个聋子,她这辈子从来都听不到我演奏。但是,她却牺牲时间和金钱让我学琴。今天早上,妈妈去世了。我敢肯定,她现在非常高兴,因为她能听到我的钢琴演奏了。我选了贝多芬的一首协奏曲。大家都知道,贝多芬是在事业成功时完全听不见,是这首曲子把他从黑暗中拯救了出来,我的妈妈也是这样。"听到威廉的话,每个人都激动万分、热泪盈眶。

音乐老师一边抱住他,一边骄傲地大声说道:"威廉,不仅是你的妈妈,而且我们所有的人都为你感到自豪。我们都为你对妈妈的奉献和爱深深感动。"

Mother Love in the Dress

"Do you like my dress?" with tears in her eyes, she asked of a passing stranger. "My mommy made it just for me."

"Well, I think it's very pretty, so tell me, why are you crying, little one?"

With a quiver in her voice the little girl answered, "After Mommy made me this dress, she had to go away."

"Well, now," said the lady, "with a little girl like you waiting for her, I'm sure she'll be right back."

"No, ma'am, you don't understand," said the child through her tears, "my daddy said that she's up in heaven with Grandpa."

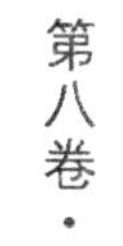

Finally, the lady realized what the child meant and why she was crying. Kneeling down she gently cradled the child in her arms.

Suddenly the little girl did something that the lady thought was a bit strange. She stopped crying, stepped back from lady and began to sing. She sang so softly that it was almost a whisper. It was the sweetest sound the woman had ever heard, just like the song of a very small bird.

After she stopped singing, the little girl explained to the lady, "My mommy used to sing that song to me before she went away, and she made me promise to sing it whenever I started crying and it would make me stop."

"See," she exclaimed, "it did, and now my eyes are dry!"

As the lady turned to go, the little girl grabbed her sleeve. "Ma'am, can you stay just a minute? I want to show you something."

"Of course," she answered, "what do you want me to see?"

Pointing to a spot on her dress, she said, "Right here is where my mommy kissed my dress, and here," pointing to another spot, "and here is another kiss, and here, and here. Mommy said that she put all those kisses on my dress, so that I would have her kisses for every booboo that made me cry."

Then the lady realized that she was not just looking at a dress. No, she was looking at a mother... who knew that she was going away and wouldn't be there to kiss away the hurts that she knew her daughter would get.

So she took all the love she had for her beautiful little girl and put them into this dress that her child now so proudly wore.

She no longer saw a little girl in a simple dress. She saw a child wrapped in her mother's love.

连衣裙里的母爱

"你喜欢我的连衣裙吗?"她眼含着泪问一个过路的陌生人。"是妈妈为我做的。"

"噢,我想它非常漂亮。小姑娘,那你告诉我,你为什么在哭?"

小女孩声音颤抖地答道:"妈妈为我做完裙子后,就不得不走开了。"

"噢,好了,"那位女士说。"有一个像你这样的小女孩在等她,我相信她会回来的。"

"不,阿姨,你不明白,"小女孩哭着说道。"爸爸说她和爷爷都在天堂里。"

最后,那位女士明白了孩子的意思,也明白了她为什么在哭。她跪下来,轻轻地把孩子搂在了怀里。

突然,小女孩又做了一件让女士有点儿奇怪的事情。她停止哭泣,从女士的怀里走出来，开始唱起了歌。她唱得非常轻柔，简直是在耳语。这是那位女士听过的最甜美的声音，就像一只小小鸟的歌声。

唱完后，小女孩向那位女士解释说："妈妈走前经常给我唱这首歌，她还让我发誓，我每次要哭时就唱这首歌，这样就能让我不哭。"

"看，"她大声叫道，"这歌真行，现在我的眼里没有泪了！"

当那位女士转身要走时，小女孩抓住她的衣袖说："阿姨，你能再待一会儿吗？我想给你看一件东西。"

"当然可以，"她答道。"你想给我看什么？"

她指着裙子上的一个地方说："这里就是妈妈吻过的地方，还是这里，"她指着另一个地方。"这里是另一个吻，还有这里和这里。妈妈说她把所有的那些吻都留在我的裙子上，这样我每次受伤要哭时，就会得到她的吻。"

这时，这位女士意识到，她看到的不仅是一件连衣裙。不，她看到的是一位母亲……她知道自己即将离去，不能守候在女儿身边吻去女儿可能受到的种种伤害。

于是，她把所有给漂亮女儿的爱，都放到了孩子现在正自豪地穿在身上的这件连衣裙里。

她看到的不再是一个穿着朴素连衣裙的小女孩，而是一个包裹在母爱里的孩子。

Mum Who Wrote Family Letters

To this day I remember my mum's letters. It all started in December 1941. Every night she sat at the big table in the kitchen and wrote to my brother Johnny, who had been drafted that summer. We hadn't heard from him since the Japanese attacked Pearl Harbor.

I didn't understand why my mum kept writing to Johnny when he never wrote back.

"Wait and see—we'll get a letter from him one day," she claimed. Mum said that there was a direct link from the brain to the written word that was just as strong as the light God has granted us. She trusted that this light would find Johnny.

I don't know if she said that to calm herself, dad or all of us down. But I do know that it helped us stick together, and one day a letter really did arrive. Johnny was alive on an island in the Pacific.

Mum signed her letters, "Cecilia Capuzzi." "Why don't you just write 'Mum'?" I asked.

I hadn't been aware that she always thought of herself as Cecilia Capuzzi. Not as Mum. I began seeing her in a new light.

She never wore make-up or jewelry except for a wedding ring. Her hair was fine, sleek and black and always put up in a knot in the neck. Her small silver-rimmed pince-nez only left her nose when she went to bed.

Whenever mum had finished a letter, she gave it to dad for him to post it.

Around next spring mum had got two more sons to write to. Every evening she wrote three different letters which she gave to dad and me afterwards so we could add our greetings.

Little by little the rumor about mum's letters spread. One day a small woman knocked at our door. Her voice trembled as she asked: "Is it true you write letters?"

"I write to my sons."

"And you can read too?" whispered the woman.

"Sure."

The woman opened her bag and pulled out a pile of airmail letters. "Read... please read them aloud to me."

The letters were from the woman's son who was a soldier in Europe, a red-haired boy who mum remembered having seen sitting with his brothers on the stairs in front of our house. Mum read the letters one by one and translated them from English to Italian. The woman's eyes welled up with tears. "Now I have to write to him," she said. But how was she going to do it?

"Make some coffee, Octavia," mum yelled to me in the living room while she took the woman with her into the kitchen and seated her at the table. She took the fountain pen, ink and airmail notepaper and began to write. When she had finished, she read the letter aloud to the woman.

"How did you know that was exactly what I wanted to say?"

"I often sit and look at my boys' letters, just like you, without a clue about what to write."

A few days later the woman returned with a friend, then another one and yet another one—they all had sons who fought in the war, and they all needed letters. Mum had become the correspondent in our part of town. Sometimes she would write letters all day long.

Mum always insisted that people signed their own letters, and the small woman with the grey hair asked mum to teach her how to do it. "I so much want to be able to write my own name so that my son can see it." Then mum held the woman's hand in hers and moved her hand over the paper again and again until she was able to do it without her help.

After that day, when mum had written a letter for the woman, she signed it herself, and her face brightened up in a smile.

One day when she came to us, all hope had disappeared from her eyes. Mum instantly knew what had happened. They stood hand in hand for a long time without saying a word. Then mum said: "We better go to church. There are certain things in life so great that we cannot comprehend them." When mum came back home, she couldn't get the red-haired boy out of her mind.

On one occasion mum admitted that she had always had a secret dream of writing a novel. "Why didn't you?" I asked.

She tried to explain why it absorbed her so. "All people in this world are here with one particular purpose," she said. "Apparently, mine is to write letters."

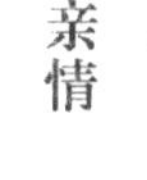

"A letter unites people. It can make them cry, it can make them laugh. There is no caress more lovely and warm than a love letter, because it makes the world seem very small, and both sender and receiver become like kings in their own kingdoms. My dear, a letter is life itself!"

Today all mum's letters are lost. But those who got them still talk about her and cherish the memory of her letters in their hearts.

爱写家书的妈妈

至今我仍记得母亲的来信。事情要从1941年12月说起。母亲每天夜里都坐在厨房的大桌边，给我哥哥约翰尼写信。那年夏天，哥哥应征入伍。自从日本袭击珍珠港以来，我们就没有听到过他的消息。

我不明白约翰尼从未回过信，母亲为什么还要一直给他写信。

“等等看——我们总有一天会收到他的回信的。”她断言说。妈妈说大脑和文字是息息相通的，就像上帝赐予我们的光一样强大。她相信这道光一定会找到约翰尼。

我不知道她这样说是不是在安慰自己、安慰爸爸或我们所有的人。但我确实知道那使我们一家人更加亲密了。而且有一天真的来了一封信。约翰尼在太平洋的一个岛上，现在还活着。

母亲总是在信上署名“塞西莉娅·卡普奇”。“为什么不直接写‘妈妈’呢？”我问。

我以前没有注意到她总是把自己当成塞西莉娅·卡普奇，而不是妈妈。我开始以一种新的眼光去看妈妈。

她从来不化妆，除了手上戴的婚戒，她从不戴珠宝。她的头发乌黑柔滑，总是盘在颈后。只有在睡觉时，她才取下小银丝眼镜。

无法什么时候妈妈写完信，她都会把信交给爸爸去邮寄。

大约第二年春天，妈妈也开始给另两个儿子写信。每天晚上，她写好三封内容不同的信后交给我和爸爸，这样我们就能加上自己的问候。

渐渐地，母亲写信的事就传开了。有一天，一个矮小的女人来敲我们家的门，用颤抖的声音问道："你真的写信了吗？"

"我是写给儿子们的。"

"那你也会读信吗？"女人小声问。

"当然会。"

那女人打开背包，掏出了一堆航空信。"念……请给我念一下。"

那些信是女人在欧洲当兵的儿子写来的，妈妈还记得那男孩的模样，他有一头红发，常和他的兄弟们坐在我们家门前的楼梯上。妈妈把信一封接一封地从英文译成意大利文读出来。那女人热泪盈眶。"现在我必须得给他写回信。"她说。可她怎么写呢？

"奥克塔维娅，去冲杯咖啡。"妈妈在客厅里向我大声说道，同时把那女人领到厨房桌边坐下。她拿出钢笔、墨水和航空信纸开始写信。写完后，她给那女人朗读了一遍。

"这正是我想说的话，你怎么知道呀？"

"我也和你一样，常坐在那里看儿子的来信，不知道该写什么。"

几天后，那女人又带来一个朋友，后来又来了一个又一个——她们都有儿子在战场上作战，都需要写信。妈妈已经成了我们镇的写信员，有时她一天到晚都在写回信。

妈妈总是坚持让那些人签上自己的名字。一位头发花白的女人要妈妈教她怎么签名。"我真想能亲手写下自己的名字，这样儿子就能看到了。于是，妈妈手把手地教她在纸上一遍一遍书写，直到她能自己签名。

那天以后，妈妈帮那个女人写好信，由她亲自签名，那女人脸上绽开了灿烂的微笑。

有一天，她来我们家时，眼里失去了所有的希望。妈妈立刻明白了是怎么回事。两人握着手，久久地站在那里，一声不吭。后来妈妈说："我们最好去教堂。生命中有些事不同寻常，我们无法理解。"妈妈回家后，怎么也无法忘记那个红发男孩。

有一次，妈妈承认她心里总有一个写小说的梦想。"你为什么不写呢？"我问。

她试图解释她为什么对写信如此着迷。她说："所有的人来到这个世界上都有一个特殊的目的。显然，我的目的就是写信。"

"一封信可以把人连在一起，能让人哭，让人笑。一封情书比任何爱抚都温暖动人，因为它让世界变得似乎很小，写信人和收信人都成为自己王国里的国王。亲爱的，信就是生命本身！"

今天，妈妈所有的信都已经丢失了。但那些收到信的人仍在谈论她，并把她写信的记忆珍藏在了心里。

A Mother's Letter to the World

Dear World,

My son starts school today. It's going to be strange and new to him for a while. And I wish you would sort of treat him gently. You see, up to now, he's been king of the roost. He's been boss of the backyard. I have always been around to repair his wounds, and to soothe his feelings. But now—things are going to be different.

This morning, he's going to walk down the front steps, wave his hand and start on his great adventure that will probably include wars and tragedy and sorrow.

To his life in the world he has to live in will require faith and love and courage.

So, World, I wish you would sort of take him by his young hand and teach him the things he will have to know. Teach him—but gently, if you can. Teach him that for every enemy there is a friend.

Teach him the wonders of books.

Give him quiet time to ponder the eternal mystery of birds in the sky, bees in the sun, and flowers on the green hill.

Teach him it is far more honorable to fail than to cheat.

Teach him to have faith in his own ideas.

Teach him to sell his brawn and brains to the highest bidder, but never to put a price on his heart and soul.

Teach him to close his ears to a howling mob... and to stand and fight if he thinks he's right.

Teach him gently, World, but don't coddle him because only the test of fire makes fine steel.

This is a big order, World, but see what you can do.

He's such a nice little fellow.

一位母亲写给世界的信

亲爱的世界：

我的儿子今天就要开始上学了。他会一时感到陌生新鲜。而我希望你能善待他一点儿。你明白，到目前为止，他都是家里的国王、后院的领袖。我总是在他身边为他疗伤，安慰他的情绪。可现在——事情将会截然不同。

今天早上，他就要走下门前台阶，向我挥手，开始伟大的事业，其间也许会有斗争、不幸和悲伤。

要在这个世界上生存度日，他需要信念、爱心和勇气。

所以，世界，我希望你能稍微握住他的小手，教给他必须知道的事情。教会他，但要尽可能温柔。教会他知道有敌人，就有朋友。

教会他书本的奇迹。

给他安静的时间去思考天空中的飞鸟、阳光里的蜜蜂和青山上的鲜花这样永恒的

奥秘。

教会他知道，失败远比欺骗光荣。

教会他对自己的想法要有信心。

教会他将自己的体力和脑力卖给最高价竞买人，但绝不能出卖自己的良心和灵魂。

教会他要对乌合之众的嚎叫闭上耳朵……并在认为正确时挺身而战。

温柔地教他，世界，但不要溺爱他，因为只有烈火的考验才能炼出好钢。

这是一个很高的要求，世界，但请尽你所能。

他是一个这样可爱的小家伙。

Mother's Final Gift

The baggy yellow shirt had long sleeves, four extra-large pockets trimmed in black thread and snaps up the front. It was faded from years of wear but still in decent shape. I found it in 1963 when I was home from university on school recess, rummaging through bags of clothes Mom intended to give away.

"You're not taking that old thing, are you?" Mom said when she saw me packing the yellow shirt. "I wore that when I was pregnant with your brother in 1954!"

"It's just the thing to wear over my clothes during art class, Mom. Thanks!" I slipped it into my suitcase before she could object.

The yellow shirt became a part of my university wardrobe. I loved it. After graduation, I wore the shirt the day I moved into my new apartment and on Saturday mornings when I cleaned.

The next year, I married. When I became pregnant, I wore the yellow shirt during big-belly days. I missed Mom and the rest of my family, since we were living far away from them. But that shirt helped. I smiled, remembering that Mother had worn it when she was pregnant, 15 years earlier.

That Christmas, mindful of the warm feelings the shirt had given me, I patched one elbow, washed and pressed the shirt, wrapped it on holiday paper and sent it to Mom.

When Mom wrote to thank me for her "real" gifts, she said the yellow shirt was lovely. She never mentioned it again.

The next year, my husband, daughter and I stopped at Mom and Dad's to pick up some furniture. Days later, when we uncrated the kitchen table, I noticed something yellow taped to its bottom. The shirt! And so the pattern was set.

On our next visit home, I secretly placed the shirt under Mom and Dad's mattress. I don't know how long it took her to find it, but almost two years passed before I discovered it under the base of our living-room floor lamp. The yellow shirt was just I needed now while refinishing furniture. The walnut stains added character.

In 1975 my husband and I divorced. With my three children, I prepared to move back to the area where I grew up. As I packed, a deep depression overtook me. I wondered if I could succeed on my own. I wondered if I would find a job. I paged through the *Bible*, looking for comfort. In *Ephesians*, I read, "So use every piece of God's armor to resist the enemy whenever he attacks, and when it is all over, you will be standing up."

I tried to picture myself wearing God's armor, but all I saw was the stained yellow shirt. Slowly, it dawned on me. Was not my mother's love a piece of God's armor? My courage was renewed.

Unpacking in our new home, I knew I had to get the shirt back to Mother. The next time I visited her, I tucked it in her bottom dresser drawer. Meanwhile, I found a good job at a radio station.

A year later I discovered the yellow shirt hidden in a ragbag in my cleaning closet. Something new had been added. Embroidered in bright green across the breast pocket were the words "I BELONG TO PAT."

Not to be outdone, I got out my own embroidery materials and added an apostrophe and seven more letters. Now the shirt proudly proclaimed, "I BELONG TO PAT'S MOTHER."

But I didn't stop there. I zigzagged all the frayed seams, then had a friend mail the shirt in a fancy box to Mom from out of town. We enclosed an official-looking letter from "The Institute for the Destitute," announcing that she was the recipient of an award for good deeds.

I would have given anything to see Mom's face when she opened the box. But, of course, she never mentioned it.

Two years later, in 1978, I remarried. The day of our wedding, Harold and I put our car in a friend's garage to avoid practical jokers. After the wedding, while my husband drove us to our honeymoon suite, I reached for a pillow in the car to rest my head. It felt lumpy. I unzipped the case and found, wrapped in wedding paper, the yellow shirt. Inside a pocket was a note: "Read *John* 14:27–29. I loved you both, Mother."

That night I paged through a *Bible* in the hotel room and found the verses: "I am leaving you with a gift: peace of mind and heart. And the peace I give isn't fragile like the peace the world gives. So don't be troubled or afraid. Remember what I told you: I am going away, but I will come back to you again. If you really love me, you will be very happy for me, for now I can go to the Father, who is greater than I am. I have told you these things before they happen so that when they do, you will believe in me."

The shirt was Mother's final gift. She had known for three months that she had terminal amyotrophic lateral sclerosis (ALS). Mother died the following year at age 57.

I was tempted to send the yellow shirt with her to her grave, but I'm glad I didn't, because it is a vivid reminder of the love-filled game she and I played for 16 years.

Besides, my older daughter is in university now, majoring in art. And every art student needs a baggy yellow shirt with big pockets.

母亲最后的礼物

那件宽松的黄衬衫有长长的袖子,4 个特大口袋周围用黑线镶边,胸前缀有按扣。由于穿了多年,已经褪色,但外观仍然得体。我是 1963 年学校放假回到家后在妈妈想送人的几袋衣服里翻找时发现的。

“你不是要留那件旧衣服吧?”妈妈看到我在叠那件黄衬衫时说。“1954 年我怀你弟弟时就穿着那件衬衫!”

“这正是我上艺术课时想穿在外面的衣服,妈妈。谢谢!”我没等她反对,就把它塞进了自己的衣箱。

这件黄衬衫就成了我大学衣柜里的一个组成部分。我非常喜欢它。大学毕业后,搬进新公寓那天和每星期六早上打扫卫生时,我都穿着这件衬衫。

第二年,我结婚成家。在怀孕挺着大肚子的那些日子,我穿着那件黄衬衫。我想念妈妈和家里其他人,因为我们住得相距很远。但那件衬衫帮了我的忙。我想起 15 年前妈妈怀孕时穿着它的样子,露出了微笑。

那年圣诞节,想起黄衬衫曾带给我的温暖感觉,我在那件衬衫的一个肘部打上补钉,洗净熨平后,用节日彩纸包好,寄给了妈妈。

妈妈写信感谢我送给她这件“真正”礼物时,说那件黄衬衫非常漂亮。她后来再也没有提起过它。

又过了一年，我和丈夫、女儿顺路去爸妈家搬了一些家具。几天后，当我们打开饭桌的包装箱时，我注意到有一件黄东西系在桌子底部。是那件黄衬衫！母亲就这样先开了头。

第二次回家时，我悄悄地把衬衫放在了爸妈的床垫下面。我不知道妈妈多长时间才发现了它，但差不多过了两年，我才在客厅的落地灯座上发现它。现在我整修家具表面时，黄衬衫正好派上用场。它上面的胡桃色印迹使它增添了特色。

1975 年，我和丈夫分道扬镳。我带着三个孩子，准备搬回从小长大的那个地方。我打点行装时，突然感到一种深深的沮丧。我不知道靠自己是不是能成功。我不知道自己会不会找到一份工作。我一页一页翻着《圣经》，想从中寻找安慰。在《以弗所书》中，我读到："因此，无论敌人何时攻击你，都要用上帝的每片盔甲来抵抗他；而当一切都结束时，你就会站立起来。"

我尽力想象着自己穿着上帝盔甲的情景，但我所看到的只有那件暗黄色的衬衫。慢慢地，我明白了。母亲的爱不就是上帝的一片盔甲吗？我重又获得了勇气。

在我们的新房里打开行李时，我知道自己得把衬衫还给妈妈。我又一次去看她时，将黄衬衫塞进了她的梳妆台最下面的抽屉里。其间，我在广播电台找到了一份好工作。

一年后，我发现那件黄衬衫藏在清扫用具储藏室的一只破布袋里。它上面增添了一些新东西，胸袋上用鲜绿色的线绣着"我属于帕特"这几个字。

我没有被难倒，拿出自己的绣花布料，又在后面添上了撇号和 7 个字母。现在，衬衫上得意地写着："我属于帕特的母亲。"

但我并没有就此打住。我用针脚弯弯曲曲将所有磨损的线缝补好，装进一个精美的盒子里，让一个朋友从城外寄给我的妈妈。我们还附上了一封"贫困协会"的公函，显示这件奖品是专门颁发她这个行善的人的。

要是能看见她打开这个盒子，我愿付出所有的一切。可是，她确实再也没有提起这件事。

两年后，1978 年，我改嫁他人。婚礼那天，我和哈罗德把我们的汽车停放在一位朋友的车库里，以防恶作剧者。婚礼过后，在丈夫开车带我去我们的蜜月套房的路上，我伸手拿了车里的一个枕头，头靠在上面。枕头凹凸不平。我拉开枕套的拉链，发现了用婚礼彩纸包着的那件黄衬衫，一个口袋里还有一张字条："看一下《约翰福音》第 14 章第 27 至 29 节。我爱你们俩。妈妈。"

那天夜里，我在旅馆套房里，翻开一本《圣经》，找到了那些章节："我要留给你一件礼物：心灵的平静。我给你的平静不像世界给你的那样脆弱。所以，不要烦恼和害怕。记住我对你说过的话：我虽然要走，但我还会回到你身边。你要真的爱我，就会为我感到非常开心，因为我现在可以去见圣父了，他比我更加伟大。在这些事发生之前，我将它们都告诉你，以便它们真的发生时，你会相信我。"

黄衬衫是母亲最后的礼物。她 3 个月前就知道自己得了晚期肌萎缩性脊髓侧索硬化症（ALS）。第二年，母亲撒手人寰，时年 57 岁。

我禁不住想把那件黄衬衫伴送进她的坟墓，但现在我很高兴自己没有那样做，因为它栩栩如生地提醒着她和我玩了16年的那个爱意浓浓的游戏。

此外,我的大女儿现在也上了大学,学的是艺术专业。艺术专业的每个学生都需要一件带有大口袋的宽松的黄衬衫。

Singing with Mom

Mom's memory went wild after my dad died. Later on, she no longer knew me, her only living child. And yet she was always delighted to see me, and believed me completely when I said, "It's your son, John, Mom."

My 87-year-old mother's recollections of an extraordinarily vibrant life were increasingly elusive. She told me a wonderful story about a cruise she and her sister, both schoolteacher, took around Cape Horn in 1925: "We were able to save money on our small salaries because we lived very simply at home with our mother. On the ship we'd walk on the deck in the morning, play badminton, talk with other young people, nap in the afternoon and then stay up late because the nights were warm and clear and there was moonlight—and starlight. I met a lovely young man, and we had a very sweet romance, standing at the railing in the evening, singing songs together."

This was a real memory, dormant for many years. But soon Mom began to talk of an imaginary second husband. She and my father had been married only briefly, she said—though actually she and Dad were married for 50 years.

She was shocked each time I reminded her that I lived in California. She was delighted by every bit of family news I gave her—and delighted all over again if I repeated the same news a moment later. Beyond that she had almost nothing to say.

Visits became painful. I wanted to spark her memory with vivid images—"I know you remember the Christmasberry tree in the back yard..." I wanted her to remember, too, new stories about my kids and my life in the West.

She remembered none of it, sensed that she was failing me and became agitated. Sometimes visits lasted only 20 minutes: I ran through all my special news, told her I loved her, and didn't know what else to say.

A few years ago, out of desperation, I began to sing to her, quietly, shyly. I brought along the copy of the old Fireside Book of Folk Songs that used to perch on Mom's baby grand piano in the 1950s.

Sitting up straight, I sang "Loch Lomond" to my mother that day, filling my lungs, enunciating, remembering her at the piano, feeling the music glow within me.

To my astonishment Mom began to sing along, reading the words above, my finger, then singing from memory.

Mom was ecstatic as we sang, and so was I. She'd clap her hands as we finished a song, and once took my hands in hers, looked into my eyes and said, "I never knew there could be such sweetness in a human relationship."

Another time, as we rested between songs, I said '90s style, "This is kinda nice." She drew herself upright, indignant at my sloppy language. "Kinda nice? This is more than kinda nice!"

During visits after that, we did nothing but make music. On my wooden recorder I conjured up more than a hundred of the songs she had originally taught me—"Red River Valley," "The Band Played On," "I'll Take You Home Again, Kathleen"—songs Mom had learned as many as 80 years ago.

Her voice floated with my recorder's melody, two frail sopranos at play. She sang without words, her voice itself an instrument.

Once, near the top of "Danny Boy," her clear voice sailed way above my high note, but exactly right, a wild perfect harmony she broke by sailing, for a timeless instant, even higher. She stopped as though she had screamed.

Shocked at herself, she looked at me to see if what she had done was okay. Yes, I said with my eyes, as I wound down through the last chorus of "Danny Boy." Mom looked back with eyes full of wonder, as she must have looked at me on the first day of my life.

与妈妈同唱

爸爸去世后，妈妈的记忆变得越发混乱了。后来，她居然连我——她唯一活着的孩子——都不认识了。然而，见到我，她总是很高兴；而且当我说："妈妈，我是你的儿子约翰"时，她总是对我深信不疑。

87岁高龄的妈妈对异常活跃的生活的回忆越发难以捉摸。以前她给我讲过一个非常精彩的故事。故事发生在1925年，当时她和妹妹——两人都是小学老师——一道乘船绕过了合恩角："我们之所以能从微薄的薪水中省下钱来，是因为我们和母亲过得非常简朴。在船上，我们早晨常常在甲板上散步、打羽毛球、聊天，下午总是睡会儿觉，然后玩到很晚。那里的夜晚温暖清爽，月光皎洁，繁星点点。在那里，我遇到了一个可爱的年轻人。我们常常站在围栏边一块唱歌，度过了一段甜蜜的浪漫时光。"

这是一段真实的回忆，隐藏了很多年。但不久，妈妈便又开始讲起了她想象中的第二个丈夫。她说，她和爸爸的婚姻只持续了很短一段时间——尽管事实上她和爸爸在一块生活了50年。

每次我提醒她我住在加州时，她都非常震惊。但只要我告诉她家里的有关情况，她就高兴得跟什么似的——过一会儿，我要再重复一遍那件事，她还会高兴一阵子。除此以外，她几乎什么也不说。

看望她成了我一块心病。我试图用生动的形象唤起她的回忆："我知道你一定记得后院的那棵圣诞浆果树……"我还想让她记起我和我的孩子在西部生活的新故事。她什么都不记得了，只知道如果没有我在她身边，她会感到忐忑不安。有时看望她的时间只持续20分钟，我只是带给她我特别的消息，告诉她我爱她，然后就不知道还能对她说些什么了。

几年前，我抱着一线希望开始给她唱歌，轻轻地、羞涩地唱给她听。我带了一本《炉边民歌集》，那是20世纪50年代经常放在妈妈的小型卧式钢琴上的一本旧书。

那天，我挺起腰板坐在那里，对妈妈唱起了《龙梦湖》。我唱时，想起了她在钢琴弹奏的情景，顿时声情并茂，感到音乐在我的内心深处熠熠闪耀。

令我惊讶的是，母亲读着我手指指着的歌词，从记忆中找到了那首歌的曲调，开始和我一道唱了起来。

我们唱歌时，妈妈心醉神迷，我也陶醉其中。我们每唱完一首歌，她就拍手鼓掌。有一次，她抓住我的手，望着我的眼睛说："我从来不知道人和人之间的关系竟然会这样甜蜜！"

又有一次，在我们唱歌的间歇，我说起了90年代的文体："这有点儿漂亮。"她坐直身体,对我的不地道的语言感到非常愤怒。“有点儿漂亮？这不仅仅是有点点儿漂亮!”

那之后,在看望妈妈期间,我们除了唱歌什么也不做。在我的木制录音机上,我收集了100多首她原来教我过的歌——《红河谷》、《乐队继续演奏》、《凯瑟琳,我要再次带你回家》——这些歌都是妈妈80年前学会唱的。

她的声音随着录音机的旋律飞扬,两个虚弱的女高音在演唱。她唱时,没唱歌词,她的声音本身就是一种乐器。

有一次,她快唱到《男孩丹尼》高潮部分时,她的声音一下子超过了我的录音机的音调,但恰到好处,仍是那样和谐完美,高亢激越。随后,她戛然而止,好像她尖叫了起来。

她对自己感到非常震惊,望着我,看她做的是否恰当。当她唱完《男孩丹尼》的最后的合唱时,我用目光说恰当。妈妈也充满好奇地望着我,就像她生下我第一天时看我那样。

A Boy with a Mission

In 1945, a 12-year-old boy saw something in a shop window that set his heart racing. But the price—five dollars—was far beyond Reuben Earle's means. Five dollars would buy almost a week's groceries for his family. Reuben couldn't ask his father for the money. Everything Mark Earle made through fishing in Bay Roberts, Newfoundland, Canada. Reuben's mother, Dora, stretched like elastic to feed and clothe their five children.

Nevertheless, he opened the shop's weathered door and went inside. Standing proud and straight in his flour-sack shirt and washed-out trousers, he told the shopkeeper what he wanted, adding, "But I don't have the money right now. Can you please hold it for me for some time?"

"I'll try," the shopkeeper smiled. "Folks around here don't usually have that kind of money to spend on things. It should keep for a while."

Reuben respectfully touched his worn cap and walked out into the sunlight with the bay rippling in a freshening wind. There was purpose in his loping stride. He would raise the five dollars and not tell anybody.

Hearing the sound of hammering from a side street, Reuben had an idea.

He ran towards the sound and stopped at a construction site. People built their own homes in Bay Roberts, using nails purchased in hessian sacks from a local factory. Sometimes the sacks were discarded in the flurry of building, and Reuben knew he could sell them back to the factory for five cents a piece.

That day he found two sacks, which he took to the rambling wooden factory and sold to the man in charge of packing nails.

The boy's hand tightly clutched the five-cent pieces as he ran the two kilometers home.

Near his house stood the ancient barn that housed the family's goats and chickens. Reuben found a rusty soda tin and dropped his coins inside. Then he climbed into the loft of the barn and hid the tin beneath a pile of sweet-smelling hay.

It was dinnertime when Reuben got home. His father sat at the big kitchen table, working on a fishing net. Dora was at the kitchen stove, ready to serve dinner as Reuben took his place at the table.

He looked at his mother and smiled. Sunlight from the window gilded her shoulder-length blonde hair. Slim and beautiful, she was the center of the home, the glue that held it together.

Her chores were never-ending. Sewing clothes for her family on the old Singer treadle machine, cooking meals and baking bread, planting and tending a vegetable garden, milking the goats and

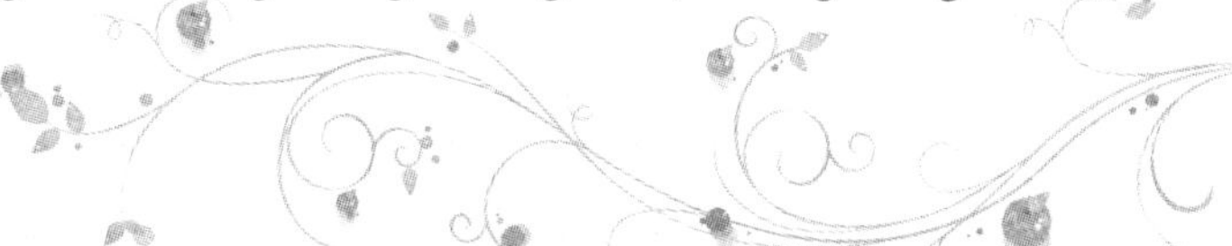

scrubbing soiled clothes on a washboard. But she was happy. Her family and their well-being were her highest priority.

Every day after chores and school, Reuben scoured the town, collecting the hessian nail bags. On the day the two-room school closed for the summer, no student was more delighted than Reuben. Now he would have more time for his mission.

All summer long, despite chores at home weeding and watering the garden, cutting wood and fetching water—Reuben kept to his secret task.

Then all too soon the garden was harvested, the vegetables canned and stored, and the school reopened. Soon the leaves fell and the winds blew cold and gusty from the bay. Reuben wandered the streets, diligently searching for his hessian treasures.

Often he was cold, tired and hungry, but the thought of the object in the shop window sustained him. Sometimes his mother would ask: "Reuben, where were you? We were waiting for you to have dinner."

"Playing, Mum. Sorry."

Dora would look at his face and shake her head. Boys.

Finally spring burst into glorious green and Reuben's spirits erupted. The time had come! He ran into the barn, climbed to the hayloft and uncovered the tin can. He poured the coins out and began to count.

Then he counted again. He needed 20 cents more. Could there be any sacks left any where in town? He had to find four and sell them before the day ended.

Reuben ran down Water Street.

The shadows were lengthening when Reuben arrived at the factory. The sack buyer was about to lock up.

"Mister! Please don't close up yet."

The man turned and saw Reuben, dirty and sweat stained.

"Come back tomorrow, boy."

"Please, Mister. I have to sell the sacks now—please." The man heard a tremor in Reuben's voice and could tell he was close to tears.

"Why do you need this money so badly?"

"It's a secret."

The man took the sacks, reached into his pocket and put four coins in Reuben's hand. Reuben murmured a thank you and ran home.

Then, clutching the tin can, he headed for the shop.

"I have the money," he solemnly told the owner.

The man went to the window and retrieved Reuben's treasure.

He wiped the dust off and gently wrapped it in brown paper. Then he placed the parcel in Reuben's hands.

Racing home, Reuben burst through the front door. His mother was scrubbing the kitchen stove. "Here, Mum! Here!" Reuben exclaimed as he ran to her side. He placed a small box in her work-roughened hand.

She unwrapped it carefully, to save the paper. A blue-velvet jewel box appeared. Dora lifted the lid, tears beginning to blur her vision.

In gold lettering on a small, almond-shaped brooch was the word Mother.

It was Mother's Day, 1946.

Dora had never received such a gift; she had no finery except her wedding ring. Speechless, she smiled radiantly and gathered her son into her arms.

男孩的使命

1945 年，一个 12 岁的男孩在一家商店橱窗里看到一样让他加快的东西。可是，价格5美元，鲁宾·厄尔根本付不起。5美元差不多够买全家一周的食品了。

鲁宾不能向父亲要钱。马克·厄尔的每分钱都是靠在加拿大纽芬兰罗伯茨湾捕鱼挣的。鲁宾的母亲多拉为了让5个孩子吃穿常常一个钱当两个钱花。

尽管如此，他还是打开商店那扇风雨剥蚀的门，走了进去。他穿着面粉袋改做的衬衫和洗得褪色的裤子，站得笔直，不卑不亢，告诉店主他想要的东西，同时补充说："可我现在没有钱。你能为我留一段时间吗？"

"我尽量吧，"店主微笑道，"这里的人通常不会花那种钱买东西的。它会留一阵的。"

鲁宾毕恭毕敬地摸了摸他的旧帽沿，走出店子。阳光下清新的微风吹得海湾泛起阵阵涟漪。鲁宾迈着大步，下定决心：他要攒够5美元，而且不告诉任何人。

听到小巷传来的铁锤声，鲁宾有了主意。

他朝响声那边跑去，在一个建筑工地停下来。人们喜欢在罗伯茨湾建房，用的钉子是从当地一家工厂买的，都装在粗麻袋里。干活时有时忙乱中会把麻袋丢在一边，鲁宾知道他可以5分钱一条把麻袋再卖给工厂。

那天，他找到了两条麻袋，拿到杂乱的木材厂，卖给负责装钉子的人。

鲁宾手里紧紧攥着两个5分硬币，跑了两公里回到了家。

他家附近有一座老谷仓，里面圈着家里的山羊和鸡。鲁宾在那里找到一个生锈的苏打罐，把两枚硬币丢了进去，然后爬上谷仓的阁楼，把铁罐藏在一堆散发着甜香味的干草下面。

晚饭时分，鲁宾回到了家里。父亲正坐在厨房大餐桌边摆弄渔网。多拉在厨灶边忙碌着，准备开饭。鲁宾在桌边坐了下来。

他望着妈妈，露出了微笑。从窗户透进的阳光将她金黄的披肩发照得金光闪闪。她身材苗条、美丽大方，是这个家的中心，是她将这个家紧紧连在了一块。

她的家务活永远也做不完。她用那台老式辛格牌踏板缝纫机为一家人缝缝补补；她要做饭、烤面包，种植、照看菜园，挤羊奶，在洗衣板上搓洗脏衣服。可是，母亲总是乐乐呵呵，全家人和他们的康乐在她心里最重要。

每天放学、做完家务事后，鲁宾就在镇上四处搜寻装钉子的粗麻袋。两间教室的学校放暑假那天，哪个学生也没有鲁宾高兴。现在他有更多时间去完成自己的使命了。

整整一个夏天，尽管在家里做家务，给菜园锄草、浇水，砍柴和打水，但鲁宾始终进行着自己的秘密任务。

转眼就到了菜园收获时，蔬菜被装罐储藏，学校也开学了。不久，树叶飘落，海湾吹来阵阵寒风。鲁宾在街头徘徊，坚持搜寻他的麻袋宝贝。

他常常饥寒交迫、疲惫不堪，但一想到商店橱窗里的那件东西，他就又坚持下去了。有时妈妈会问："鲁宾，你上哪儿了？我们都在等你吃饭呢。"

"玩去了，妈妈。对不起。"

多拉常常看着他的脸，摇摇头。男孩就是男孩。

春天终于来了，一切都郁郁葱葱；鲁宾也精神大振。到时候了！他跑进谷仓，爬到干草棚上，打开铁罐，倒出所有硬币，开始数了起来。

随后，他又数一遍，还差20分钱。镇上哪儿还会有丢弃的麻袋呢？他得在今天结束前再找4条卖掉。

鲁宾沿着沃特街向前跑。

鲁宾赶到工厂时，厂房的影子越拉越长了。收购麻袋的人正要锁门。

“先生！请先不要关门。”

那人转过身，看到了鲁宾，只见他脏兮兮、汗津津的。

“明天再来吧，孩子。”

“求您了，先生。我必须现在卖掉麻袋——行行好。”听到鲁宾的声音颤抖，那人能断定他快要哭了。

“你为什么这样急需这钱呢？”

“这是一个秘密。”

那人接过麻袋，将手伸进口袋，掏出4个硬币，放在鲁宾的手里。鲁宾轻轻说了声“谢谢”，就向家里跑去。

随后，他紧紧搂着铁罐，奔向那家商店。

“我有钱了。”他一本正经地告诉店主。

店主走到橱窗边，取出了鲁宾要的宝贝。

他拂去灰尘，用牛皮纸小心把它包好，然后把这个小包放进了鲁宾的手里。

鲁宾飞奔到家，冲过前门。妈妈正在擦洗灶台。“给，妈妈！给！”鲁宾一边跑向她，一边大叫。他把一只小盒子放在了她因辛劳而粗糙的手里。

她小心翼翼地拆开，以免损坏包装纸。一个蓝色天鹅绒首饰盒出现在了眼前。多拉掀起盒盖，泪水渐渐模糊了双眼。

在一个小小的杏仁状胸针上用金字刻着母亲。

那是1946年母亲节。

多拉从来没有收到过这样的礼物；除了婚戒，她没有一件华丽的服饰。她默默无语，容光焕发，面带微笑，一把将儿子揽进了怀里。

The Voice of Love

Many people say their most painful moments are saying good-bye to those they love. After watching Cheryl, my daughter-in-law, through the six long months her mother suffered towards death, I think the most painful moments can be in the waiting to say good-bye. Cheryl made the two-hour trip over and over to be with her mother. They spent the long afternoons praying, soothing and retelling their shared memories.

As her mother's pain intensified and more medication was needed to ease her into sedation, Cheryl sat for hours of silent vigil by her mother's bed.

Each time she kissed her mother before leaving, her mother would say tearfully, "I'm sorry you drove so far and sat for so long and I didn't even wake up to talk with you."

Cheryl would tell her not to worry, but her mother felt she had let her down and apologized at each good-bye until the day Cheryl found a way to give her mother the same reassurance her mother had given to her so many times.

"Mom, do you remember when I made the high school basketball team?" Cheryl's mother nodded. "You'd drive so far and sit for so long and I never even left the bench to play. You waited for me after every game and each time I felt bad and apologized to you for wasting your time." Cheryl gently took her mother's hand.

"Do you remember what you would say to me?"

"I would say I didn't come to see you play, but I came to see you."

"And you meant those words, didn't you?"

"Yes, I really did."

"Well, now I say the same words to you. I didn't come to see you talk, I came to see you."

Her mother understood and smiled as she floated back into sleep.

Their afternoons together passed quietly into days, weeks, and months. Their love filled the spaces between their words. To the last day they ministered to each other in the stillness, love given and received just by seeing each other.

A love so strong that, even in this deepened silence that followed their last good-bye, Cheryl can still hear her mother's love.

爱的声音

许多人说最痛苦的时刻是向自己所爱的人告别。看到儿媳妇谢丽尔经历漫长的6个月眼睁睁看着母亲经受痛苦走向死亡后,我认为最痛苦的时刻可能是等待告别。谢丽尔一次次驱车两小时来和母亲待在一起。她们常常花费漫长的下午时间祈祷、安慰和复述彼此的回忆。

当她母亲痛苦加剧、需要更多药物保持镇静时,谢丽尔会一连几个小时静静地守在她床前。

每次离开前她吻母亲时,母亲总会流着泪说:"很抱歉让你开这么远的车、坐这么久,我连清醒和你说话都不能啊。"

谢丽尔常常告诉她不要担心,但母亲还是觉得让谢丽尔失望,所以每次告别时都表示歉意。直到有一天,谢丽尔找到了让母亲放心的办法,就像母亲曾多次让她放心那样。

"妈妈,你还记得我参加中学篮球队的事吗?"谢丽尔的母亲点了点头。"你要开那么远的车过来,在我身边坐那么久,而我甚至从未离开过长椅去打球。每次比赛后你都等着我,每次我都感到糟糕,为浪费你的时间而向你道歉。"谢丽尔温柔地握住母亲的手。

"你还记得你常常对我说什么吗?"

"我常常说我不是来看你打球的,而是来看你的。"

"你说的都是真心话,对吗?"

"是,确实是。"

"那现在我也对你说同样的话。我不是来听你说话的,而是来看你的。"

她的母亲明白了,微笑着进入了梦乡。

她们一起度过的下午时光静静地流逝,一天天、一周周,然后是几个月。她们的爱填满了言语间的一个个空白。在沉静中,她们相互照顾,直到最后一天,相互凝视仅仅是我为了给予爱和接受爱。

有一种爱非常强大，即使在最后告别后最深的寂静中，谢丽尔仍能听到母爱的声音。

Love Is a Thread

Sometimes I really doubt whether there is love between my parents. Every day they are very busy trying to earn money in order to pay the high tuition for my brother and me. They don't act in the romantic ways that I read in books or I see on TV. In their opinion, "I love you" is too luxurious for them to say. Sending flowers to each other on Valentine's Day is even more out of the question. Finally my father has a bad temper. When he's very tired from the hard work, it is easy for him to lose his temper.

One day, my mother was sewing a quilt. I silently sat down beside her and looked at her. "Mom, I have a question to ask you," I said after a while. "What?" she replied, still doing her work. "Is there love between you and Dad?" I asked her in a very low voice.

My mother stopped her work and raised her head with surprise in her eyes. She didn't answer immediately. Then she bowed her head and continued to sew the quilt. I was very worried because I thought I had hurt her. I was in a great embarrassment and I didn't know what I should do. But at last I heard my mother say the following words.

"Susan," she said thoughtfully, "Look at this thread. Sometimes it appears, but most of it disappears in the quilt. The thread really makes the quilt strong and durable. If life is a quilt, then love should be a thread. It can hardly be seen anywhere or anytime, but it's really there. Love is inside."

I listened carefully but I couldn't understand her until the next spring. At that time, my father suddenly got sick seriously. My mother had to stay with him in the hospital for a month. When they returned from the hospital, they both looked very pale. It seemed both of them had had a serious illness.

After they were back, every day in the morning and dusk, my mother helped my father walk slowly on the country road. My father had never been so gentle. It seemed they were the most harmonious couple. Along the country road, there were many beautiful flowers, green grass and trees. The sun gently glistened through the leaves. All of these made up the most beautiful picture in the world.

The doctor had said my father would recover in two months. But after two months he still couldn't walk by himself. All of us were worried about him.

"Dad, how are you feeling now?" I asked him one day.

"Susan, don't worry about me," he said gently. "To tell you the truth, I just like walking with your mom. I like this kind of life." Reading his eyes, I know he loves my mother deeply.

Once I thought love meant flowers, gifts and sweet kisses. But from this experience, I understand that love is just a thread in the quilt of our life. Love is inside, making life strong and warm.

爱是一根线

有时候，我真怀疑父母之间是否有爱。他们每天忙忙碌碌拼命赚钱，为我和弟弟支付高昂的学费。他们没有像我在书里读到或在电视中看到的那样行为浪漫。他们认为，"我爱你"词藻华丽，说不出口。情人节彼此送花就更不可能了。关键是，我父亲脾气很坏。辛苦了一天后，他筋疲力尽，动不动就发脾气。

一天，母亲正在缝被子。我静静地坐在她身边看着她。“妈妈，我想问你一个问题。”过了一会儿，我说。“什么问题？”她反问道，仍在忙着手里的活儿。“你和爸爸之间有爱情吗？”我声音很低地问道。

母亲停下手里的活，抬起头，眼里露出了吃惊的神色。她没有马上回答。随后，她低下头，继续缝起了被子。我很担心，因为我想自己伤害了她。我非常尴尬，不知道该怎么办。但最后，我听到母亲说了下面这段话。

“苏珊，”她若有所思地说，“看看这根线。有时它露出来，但大多数都藏在被子里。这些线确实让被子坚固耐用。如果生活是一条被子，那么爱就应该是一根线。不可能处处时时都看到它，但它却确实在那里。爱在里面。”

我仔细听着，但直到第二年春天才明白她的话。当时，父亲突然得了重病。母亲不得不在医院里守了他了一个月。从医院回来时，他们俩都显得非常苍白，就像他们俩都得了一场重病似的。

他们回来后，每天早晨和黄昏，母亲都会搀着父亲在乡间小路上慢慢散步。父亲从来没有那样温和过。他们就像天生的一对。乡村的路边有好多漂亮的鲜花、绿草和树木。阳光闪耀，轻轻地穿过树叶。这一切成了世界上最美的画面。

医生说我父亲两个月后康复。但两个月后，他仍然无法独自行走。我们都为他担忧。“爸爸，你现在感觉怎么样？”有一天，我问他。“苏珊，别为我担心。”他温和地说。“说实话，我就喜欢和你妈妈一块散步。我喜欢这种生活。”我读懂了他的眼神，知道他深爱我的母亲。

我曾认为爱情就是鲜花、礼物和甜吻。但从这次体验，我明白爱情只是我们生活之被里的一根线。爱情在里面，使生活变得坚固温暖。

Squeeze My Hand

Remember when you were a child and you fell and hurt yourself? Do you remember what your mother did to ease the pain? My mother, Grace Rose, would pick me up, carry me to her bed, sit me down and kiss my pain. Then she'd sit on the bed beside me, take my hand in hers and say, "When it hurts, squeeze my hand and I'll tell you that I love you." Over and over I'd squeeze her hand, and each time, without fail, I heard the words, "Mary, I love you."

Sometimes, I'd find myself pretending I'd been hurt just to have that ritual with her. As I grew up, the ritual changed, but she always found a way to ease he pain and increase the joy I felt in any area of my life. On difficult days during high school, she'd offer her favorite Hershey chocolate almond bar when I returned home. During my 20s, Mom often called to suggest a spontaneous picnic lunch at Estabrook Park just to celebrate a warm, sunny day in Wisconsin. A handwritten thank-you note arrived in the mail after every single visit she and my father made to my home, reminding me of how special I was to her.

But the most memorable ritual remained her holding my hand when I was a child and saying, "When it hurts, squeeze my hand and I'll tell you that I love you."

One morning, when I was in my late 30s, following a visit by my parents the night before, my father phoned me at work. He was always commanding and clear in his directions, but I heard confusion and panic in his voice. "Mary, something's wrong with your mother and I don't know what to do. Please come over as quickly as you can."

The 10-minute drive to my parents' home filled me with dread, wondering what was happening to my mother. When I arrived, I found Dad pacing in the kitchen and Mom lying on their bed. Her eyes were closed and her hands rested on her stomach. I called to her, trying to keep my voice as calm as possible. "Mom, I'm here."

"Mary?"

"Yes, Mom."

"Mary, is that you?"

"Yes, Mom, it's me."

I was not prepared for the next question, and when I heard it, I froze, not knowing what to say.

"Mary, am I going to die?"

Tears welled up inside me as I looked at my loving mother lying there so helpless.

My thoughts raced, until this question crossed my mind: What would Mom say?

I paused for a moment that seemed like a million years, waiting for the words to come. "Mom, I don't know if you're going to die, but if you need to, it's okay. I love you."

She cried out, "Mary, I hurt so much."

Again, I wondered what to say. I sat down beside her on the bed, picked up her hand and heard myself say, "Mom, when it hurts, squeeze my hand and I'll tell you that I love you."

She squeezed my hand.

"Mom, I love you."

Many hand squeezes and "I love you" passed between my mother and me during the next two years, until she passed away from ovarian cancer. We never know when our moments of truth will come, but I do know now that when they do, whomever I'm with, I will offer my mother's sweet ritual of love every time. "When it hurts, squeeze my hand and I'll tell you that I love you."

握住我的手

还记得你小时候跌倒摔疼的情景吗？你还记得为了减轻那份疼痛妈妈是怎么做的吗？我的妈妈格雷斯·露斯总会扶我起来，把我抱到她的床上，让我坐下，吻吻我的痛处，然后在我身边坐下来，拉住我的手说："要是疼，你就握住我的手，我会告诉你我爱你。"我曾一次又一次地握住她的手，而且我每次都必定能听到这句话："玛丽，我爱你。"

有时，我发现自己假装受伤，只是为了赢得她那份礼遇。随着我渐渐长大，那份礼遇也改变了，但她总能找到减轻疼痛的办法，让我随时随地都感到生活中增添的快乐。在上中学那段艰难日子里，每次我回家，她总会拿出她最爱吃的赫尔希牌杏仁巧克力棒。在我二三十岁这段时间，妈妈常常打来电话提议到埃斯塔布鲁克公园进行一次自发的野外午餐会，仅仅是要庆祝威斯康星这阳光温暖明媚的一天。她和爸爸每次看望我的家后，邮件里总有一小封手写的感谢信，向我提醒我对她是多么亲密。

但最难忘的礼遇仍然是我小时候她握住我的手说："要是疼，你就握住我的手，我会告诉你我爱你。"

我快40岁那年，有一天晚上，父母亲来看望我。第二天，爸爸给正在上班的我打来电话。爸爸一向威风凛凛、指挥若定，但那天我却听出他的声音里有一种疑惑和惊慌。

“玛丽,你妈妈有点儿不对劲,我不知道该怎么办。请尽快过来。”

在开车前往父母亲家的10分钟的路途中,我内心充满了恐惧,不知道妈妈出了什么事。我赶到那里,发现爸爸在厨房里来回不停地踱步,妈妈躺在床上,闭着眼睛,两手放在腹部。我尽可能声音平静地向她喊道:“妈妈,我来了。”

“是玛丽吗?”

“是我,妈妈。”

“玛丽,真是你吗?”

“是的,妈妈,是我。”

我没想到妈妈接下来会问那样一个问题,听到这个问题,我僵在那里,不知道该说什么。

“玛丽,我要死了吗?”

我望着慈爱的妈妈躺在那里,是那样无助,禁不住泪如泉涌。

我浮想联翩,最后我的脑海里闪过这样一个问题:妈妈会怎么说?

我停顿了一会儿,仿佛过去了一百万年,我才说出了那些话:“妈妈,我不知道你是不是要死,但如果你需要,那就没事儿。我爱你。”

她大声哭道:“玛丽,我好疼。”

我又一次不知道该说什么。我在床上她的身边坐下来,握住她的手,脱口而出,“妈妈,要是疼,你就握住我的手,我会告诉你我爱你。”

她握住我的手。

“妈妈,我爱你。”

在接下来的两年里,我和妈妈握了一次又一次的手,我说了一次又一次的“我爱你”,直到她因卵巢癌撒手而去。虽然我们根本无法知道考验我们的时刻何时来临,但现在我确实知道,当考验的时刻来临时,无论我和谁在一起,每次我一定会献上妈妈那种甜蜜的礼节。“要是疼,你就握住我的手,我会告诉你我爱你。”

The Sunshine Zone

On a spring noon, I came home from work, seeing Mother was airing her quilts. That tempted me to air my own.

I carried my quilts out in the arms, and aired them at the ends of the clothesline. After lunch, I went to work directly.

When I came home and stepped into my house doorway, I was greeted by my quilts just there. Different from the noon, they had been moved to the sunniest place. The snow – white linings of the quilts were gently gilded by the setting sun while my mother's quilts were hanging dully and solitarily at the ends of the clothesline. On them, the dumb shadows of the house were drawing their tedious and inerratic geometric figures.

Walking in front of my quilts, I stroked them. They felt warm.

They were warm indeed, as warm as the palms of Mother.

I also gave a touch to my mother's quilts. They felt cool.

They were cool indeed, as cool as the backs of Mother's hands.

All of a sudden, a stream of past scenes floated before my eyes: the bed – sheet with the finest quality in my home, the room in the best position, the potted flower in its lovely bloom, the most delicious dishes, and even the bowl printed with the most delicate pattern... all these were mine, just as the sunshine zone where I stood.

I know that all these scenes are not happening by chance to Mother.

On the road to the short livelong life, it might be your friends who can give you happiness; it might be your lover who can make you lovely; and it might be your career that can enrich you. However, it must be your mother who makes you warm. With the backs of her hands, she shelters you from hardships as many as possible; with her palms, she keeps shining over you the warm sunlight.

Mother is the eternal sunshine zone

阳光地带

春季的一个中午，我下班回到家里，看见母亲正在晒被子，便也想把被子晒一下。

我把被子抱出来，晒在了晾衣绳的两端。吃过午饭，我便上班去了。

下班回来，我一进家门，便看见了自己的被子。与中午不同的是，它们已经被晒在了阳光最好的地带，夕阳将雪白的被里镀上了一层浅浅的金色。而母亲的被子却寂寞地待在晾衣绳的两端，房屋的阴影默默地在它们身上画着单调而规则的几何图形。

我走到自己的被子面前，用手抚摸了一下，它们是温暖的。

它们当然是温暖的，温暖得如母亲的手心。

我又抚摸了一下母亲的被子，它们是清凉的。

它们当然是清凉的，清凉如母亲的手背。

我的眼前忽然呈现出往昔的许多情节：家里质地最好的那条床单，方位最佳的那个房间，开得最漂亮的那盆鲜花，做得最好吃的那盘菜，甚至吃饭时图案最精致的那只碗……这些事物如我身处的这段阳光地带一样，都是我的。

我知道，对于母亲来说，这些情节不是偶然。

人生短暂而漫长的征途上，给你快乐的也许是你的朋友，让你美丽的也许是你的爱人，令你充实的也许是你的事业。但是，使你温暖的必定是你的母亲。她用她的手背为你阻挡着她力所能及的所有风霜，她用她的手心为你释放着绵绵不绝的温暖阳光。

母亲是永远的阳光地带。

Love in Bloom

I was nine when my father first sent me flowers. I had been taking tap-dancing lessons for six months, and the school was giving its yearly recital. As an excited member of the beginners' chorus line, I was aware of my lowly status.

So it was a surprise to have my name called out at the end of the show along with lead dancers and to find my arms full of long-stemmed red roses. I can still feel myself standing on that stage,

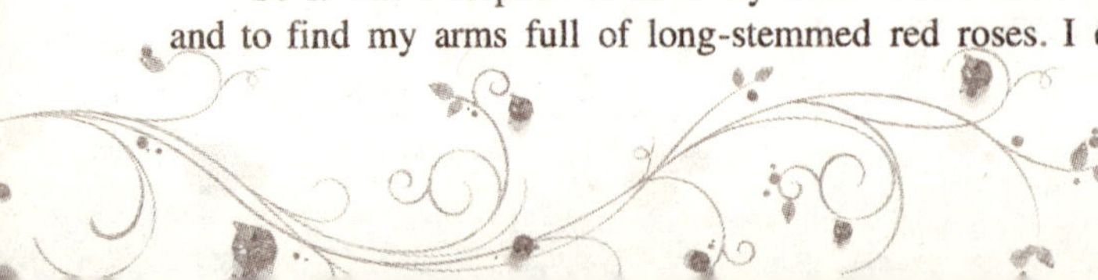

blushing furiously and gazing over the footlights to see my father's grin as he applauded loudly.

Those roses were the first in a series of large bouquets that accompanied all the milestones in my life. They brought a sense of ambivalence, of being caught between please and embarrassment. I enjoy them, but was flustered by its extravagance.

Not my father. He did everything in a big way. If you sent him to a bakery for a cake, he came back with three. Once my mother told him I needed a new party dress, he brought a dozen.

His behavior often left us without funds for other more important things. After the dress incident, there was no money for the winter coat I really needed—or the new ice skates I wanted.

Sometimes I would be angry with him, but not for long. Inevitably he would buy me something to make up with me. The gift was so apparently an offering of love he couldn't verbalize that I would throw my arms around him and kiss him-an act that undoubtedly perpetuated his behavior.

Then came my 16th birthday. It was not a happy occasion. I was fat and had no boyfriend. And my well-meaning parents furthered my misery by giving me a party. As I entered the dining room, there on the table next to my cake was a huge bouquet of flowers, bigger than any before.

I wanted to hide. Now everyone would think my father had sent flowers because I had no boyfriend to do it. Sweet 16, and I feel like crying. I probably would have, but my best friend, Phyllis, whispered, "Boy, you are lucky to have a father like that."

As the years passed, other occasions—birthdays, recitals, awards, graduations—were marked with Dad's flowers. My emotions continued to seesaw between pleasure and embarrassment.

When I graduated from the college my days of ambivalence were over. I was embarking on a new career and was engaged to be married. Dad's flowers symbolized his pride, and my triumph. They evoked only great pleasure.

Now there were bright orange mums for Thanksgiving and a huge pink poinsettia at Christmas. White lilies at Easter, and velvety red roses for birthdays. Seasonal flowers in mixed bouquets celebrated the births of my children and the move to our first house.

As my fortune grew, my father's waned, but his gifts of flowers continued until he died of a heart attack a few months before his 70th birthday. Without embarrassment, I covered his coffin with the largest, reddest roses I could find.

Often in the dozen years since, I felt an urge to go out and buy a big bouquet to fill the living room, but I never did. I knew it wouldn't be the same.

Then one birthday, the doorbell rang. I was feeling blue because I was alone. My husband was playing golf, and my two daughters were away. My 13-year-old son, Matt, had run out earlier with a "see you later", never mentioning my birthday. So I was surprised to see his large frame at the door. "Forgot my key," he said, shrugging. "Forgot your birthday too. Well, I hope you like flowers, Mom." He pulled a bunch of daisies from behind his back.

"Oh, Matt," I cried, hugging him hard. "I love flowers!"

爱在盛开

父亲第一次给我送花，是我9岁那年。我学踢踏舞才6个月，学校要举行一年一度的演出。初进合唱队，我兴致勃勃，但我明白自己的角色很不起眼。

所以，演出结束，和那些主舞演员一起被喊到了前台，我怀里抱满了长茎红玫瑰时，真让人吃惊。我现在还能感觉到自己站在那个舞台上，脸色羞红，越过舞台看到父亲一边咧嘴笑一边使劲鼓掌。

那些玫瑰是我人生里程碑中的第一束，后来每次父亲都会相应送给我一大束。而收到那些鲜花，我总是非常矛盾：既高兴又困窘。我喜爱那些鲜花，但又为这种铺张奢侈而心慌。

父亲却不这样。他做什么事都大手大脚。你让他去面包店买一块蛋糕,他会买回来3块。有一次,母亲对他说我需要一条新舞裙,他居然买回来一打。

他这样做常常让我们没有钱去买其他更重要的东西。他买回一打舞裙后,就没有钱去买我真正需要的冬装和我需要的新冰鞋。

有时我会和父亲生气,但时间都不长。他每次必定会给我买一些东西与我和好。显然,这礼物传达了他无法言表的爱。我常常搂住他亲吻他,这种举动无疑会使他再次大手大脚。

后来到了我的16岁生日。这并不是一个快乐的节日,因为我很胖,没有男朋友。好心的父母亲为我举办了生日晚会,这更让我痛苦。我走进餐室,只见餐桌上生日蛋糕旁边有一大束鲜花,比以前的任何一束都大。

我真想藏起来。现在大家都会以为我没有男朋友送花,父亲才送的。甜蜜的16岁,我却很想大哭一场。我也许当时肯定会哭,但我最好的朋友菲利斯低声说:“噢,你有这样的父亲真幸运。”

光阴荏苒,日月如梭,其他特殊时刻——生日、演出、获奖、毕业典礼——都会有爸爸的鲜花。我的情绪仍然在高兴和困窘之间摇摆。

到大学毕业时,我那种矛盾相伴的日子结束了。我踏上了新的人生轨道,订婚成家。爸爸的鲜花是他的骄傲和我的胜利的象征。它们唤起的只有极大的喜悦。

现在感恩节都会有鲜橙色的菊花,圣诞节会有一大束粉红色的一品红,复活节会有白色的百合花,生日会有天鹅绒般的红玫瑰,孩子出生和搬到我们第一座房子时会有时鲜花扎成的花束。

我好运日盛,父亲却日渐衰老,但他仍然给我送花,直到他70岁生日前几个月因心脏病而去世。我在他的灵柩上放满了我所能找到的最大、最红的玫瑰花,并不感到困窘。

在此后的12年里,我常常有一种冲动,想出去买一大束鲜花摆满客厅,但我始终没有那样做。我知道,那将不再是从前的花了。

后来有一次生日,门铃响了。那天我感到沮丧,因为只有我一个人在家。丈夫打高尔夫球去了,两个女儿到远处去了,13岁的儿子马特也早早就跑了出去,只说了声“再见”,从来没有提我的生日。所以,我看到马特宽大的身体站在门边,吃了一惊。“忘带钥匙了,”他耸了耸肩说。“也忘了你的生日。噢,我希望你喜欢鲜花,妈妈。”他从背后抽出了一束雏菊。

“噢,马特,”我紧紧抱住他,大声说道,“我爱鲜花!”

A Dance with Dad

I am dancing with my father at my parents' 50th-wedding-anniversary celebration. The band is playing an old-fashioned waltz as we move gracefully across the floor. His hand was on my waist is as guiding as it always was, and he hums the tune to himself in a steady, youthful way. Around and around we go, laughing and nodding to the other dancers.

We are the best dancers on the floor, they tell us. My father squeezes my hand and smiles at me. All the years that I refused to dance with him melt away now. And those early times come back.

I remember when I was almost three and my father came home from work, swooped me into his arms and began to dance me around the table. My mother laughed at us, told us dinner would get cold. But my father said, "She's just caught the rhythm of the dance! Our dinner can wait." Then he sang out, "Roll out the barrel, let's have a barrel of fun," and I sang back. "Let's get those blues on the run."

We danced through the years. We even won a dance contest at a Camp Fire Girls Round-Up. Then we learned to jitterbug at the USO downtown. Once my father caught on to the steps, he danced with everyone in the hall. We all laughed and clapped our hands for my father, the dancer.

One night when I was 15, lost in some painful, adolescent mood, my father put on a stack of records and teased me to dance with him. "C'mon," he said, "Let's get those blues on the run." When I turned away from him, my father put his hand on my shoulder, and I jumped out of the chair screaming, "don't touch me! I am sick and tired of dancing with you!" I saw the hurt on his face, but the words were out and I couldn't call them back. I ran to my room bursting into tears.

We didn't dance together after that night. I found other partners, and my father waited up for me after dances, sitting in his favorite chair, clad in his flannel pajamas. Sometimes he would be asleep when I came in, and I would wake him, saying, "If you were so tired, you should have gone to bed." "No, no," he'd say. "I was just waiting for you." Then we'd locked up the house and go to bed. My father waited up for me all through my high-school and college years while I danced my way out of his life.

Shortly after my first child was born, my mother called to tell me my father was ill. "A heart problem," she said. "Now, don't come. It's three hundred miles. It would upset your father."

A proper diet restored him to good health. My mother wrote that they had joined a dance club: "The doctor says it's good exercise. You remember how your father loves to dance."

Yes, I remember. My eyes filled up with remembering.

When my father retired, we mended our way back together again; hugs and kisses were common when we visited each other. He danced with the grandchildren, but he didn't ask me to dance. I knew he was waiting for an apology from me. I could never find the right words.

As my parents' 50th anniversary approached, my brothers and I met to plan the party. My older brother said: "Do you remember that night you wouldn't dance with him? Boy, was he mad. I couldn't believe he'd get so mad about a thing like that. I'll bet you haven't danced with him since." I didn't tell him he was right.

My younger brother promised to get the band. "Make sure they can play waltzes and polkas," I told him. I didn't tell him that all I wanted to do was dance once more with my father.

When the band began to play after dinner, my parents took the floor. They glided around the room, inviting the others to join them. The guests rose to their feet, applauding the golden couple. My father danced with his granddaughters, and then the band began to play the "Beer Barrel Polka."

"Roll out the barrel," I heard my father singing. Then I knew it was time. I wound my way through a few couples and tapped my daughter on the shoulder.

"Excuse me," I said, looking directly into my father's eyes and almost choking on my words, "but I believe this is my dance."

My father stood rooted to the spot. Our eyes met and traveled back to that night when I was 15. In a trembling voice, I sang, "Let's get those blues on the run."

My father bowed and said, "Oh, yes. I've been waiting for you."

Then he started to laugh, and we moved into each other's arms.

与爸爸共舞

在父母亲金婚纪念时，我和爸爸跳起了舞。乐队奏着一支老华尔兹舞曲，我们在舞厅中翩翩起舞。他像往常一样将手放在我的腰间领舞，嘴里和年轻人一样哼着这首曲子。我们跳了一圈又一圈，不时地笑着向其他跳舞的人点头致意。

那些人对我们说，我们是舞厅里跳得最好的一对。父亲握紧我的手，对我微笑。我多年来拒绝与他跳舞的隔膜现在渐渐淡去。早年的那些时光重新返回。

我记得，我差不多3岁那年，父亲下班回家，一把将我抱在怀里，开始和我围着桌子跳了起来。母亲对我们大声笑着，说晚饭都放凉了。但父亲说："她刚刚跟上舞蹈的节奏！晚饭可以等一等。"随后，他大声唱了起来："滚出桶子，让我们好好乐乐。"我也大声唱道："带走那些忧伤。"

我们跳了好多年。我们甚至还在篝火少女跳舞比赛得过奖呢。后来，我们又去市里的劳军联合会学跳吉特巴舞。父亲一跟上步调，就会和舞厅里的每一个人跳。我们都为我的舞迷父亲鼓掌大笑。

15岁那年的一天夜里，我正迷失在花季少女的痛苦之中，父亲却放了一堆唱片，强要我和他跳舞。"跳吧，"他说，"带走那些忧伤。"我转身离开时，父亲将手放在我的肩上。我从椅子上跳起来，冲他尖叫道："别碰我！我讨厌和你跳舞！"尽管我看到了他脸上的伤痛，但话已出口，无法收回。我跑到自己的房间放声大哭。

那夜之后，我们没在一块跳过。我找了其他舞伴，父亲总是穿着法兰绒睡衣裤坐在他最心爱的椅子上等我跳舞归来。有时我回来时，他会睡着，我便摇醒他说："你要是这么累，就该上床睡觉。""不，不，"他总是说。"我在等你呢。"随后，我们就锁上房门，上床睡觉。从中学到大学，我离开他外出跳舞时，他一直这样熬夜等着我。

我的第一个孩子出生后不久，母亲打电话说父亲病了。"是心脏病，"她说。"现在，不要来。有300英里呢。那会让你父亲感到不安的。"

合理的饮食调养使父亲恢复了健康。母亲写信说他们加入了一家舞蹈俱乐部："医生说这是一种很好的锻炼。你记得你父亲是多么爱跳舞。"

是的，我记得。闪现在我眼前的都是我对过去的回忆。

父亲退休时，我们再次努力想重修旧好；每次见面，我们常常拥抱和亲吻。他和外孙们跳，但他就是不找我跳。我知道他是在等我道歉。而我却怎么也找不到合适的词。

随着父母亲结婚50周年纪念日的临近，我和兄弟们聚到一起安排宴会。哥哥说："还记得你不愿和他跳舞的那个晚上吗？嗬，他跟疯了一般。我不相信会为这样一件事而那样发疯。我敢说从那以后你没和他跳过舞。"我没对他说他说的没错。

弟弟答应去请乐队。"务必要找能演奏华尔兹和波尔卡的。"我对他说。我没告诉他我所要做的就是和爸爸再跳一次。

饭后，乐队开始演奏，父母亲走进舞厅，滑着舞步绕场请其他人和他们一块跳。客人们站起来，为这一对金婚伴侣鼓掌。父亲挨个和孙女们跳着，随后乐队奏起了《啤酒桶波尔卡》。

"把桶滚出来，"我听到父亲唱道。随后，我知道是时候了。我绕过几对跳舞的客人，拍了拍女儿的肩膀。"对不起，"我直视着父亲的眼睛说，几乎把要说的话噎在了嗓子里。"但我相信这是我的舞会。"父亲像扎了根似的站在那里。我们四目相对，时光仿佛又回到了我15岁时的那个夜里。我声音颤抖地唱道："带走那些忧伤。"

父亲躬身说道："噢，是的。我一直在等着你。"

随后，他开始放声大笑，我们移动脚步，投入了对方的怀抱。

A Violin

"Wanted: Violin. Can't pay much. Call..."

Why did I notice that? I wondered, since I rarely look at the classified ads.

I laid the paper on my lap and closed my eyes, remembering what had happened many years before, when my family struggled to make a living on our farm. I, too, had wanted a violin, but we didn't have the money...

When my older twin sisters began showing an interest in music, Harriet Anne learned to play Grandma's upright piano, while Suzanne turned to Daddy's violin. Simple tunes soon became lovely melodies as the twins played more and more. Caught up in the rhythm of the music, my baby brother danced around while Daddy hummed and Mother whistled. I just listened.

When my arms grew long enough, I tried to play Suzanne's violin. I loved the mellow sound of the firm bow drawn across the strings. Oh, how I wanted one! But I knew it was out of the question.

One evening as the twins played in the school orchestra, I closed my eyes tight to capture the picture firmly in my mind. Someday, I'll sit up there, I vowed silently.

It was not a good year. At harvest the crops didn't bring as much as we had hoped. Yet even though times were hard, I couldn't wait any longer to ask: "Daddy, may I have a violin of my own?"

"Can't you use Suzanne's?"

"I'd like to be in the orchestra, too, and we can't both use the same violin at the same time."

Daddy's face looked sad. That night, and many following nights, I heard him remind God in our family devotions, "... and Lord, Mary Lou wants her own violin."

One evening we all sat around the table. The twins and I studied. Mother sewed, and Daddy wrote a letter to his friend, George Finkle, in Columbus, Ohio. Mr. Finkle, Daddy said, was a fine violinist.

As he wrote, Daddy read parts of his letter out loud to Mother. Weeks later I discovered he'd written one line he didn't read aloud: "Would you watch for a violin for my third daughter? I can't pay much, but she enjoys much, and we'd like her to have her own instrument."

When Daddy received a letter from Columbus a few weeks later, he announced, "We'll be driving to Columbus to spend the night with Aunt Alice as soon as I can find someone to care for the livestock."

At last the day arrived, and we drove to Aunt Alice's. After we arrived, I listened while Daddy made a phone call. He hung up and asked, "Mary Lou, do you want to go with me to visit Mr. Finkle?"

"Sure," I answered.

He drove into a residential area and stopped in the driveway of a fine, old house. We walked up the steps and rang the door chime. A tall man, older than Daddy, opened the door. "Come in!" he and Daddy heartily shook hands, both talking at once.

"Mary Lou, I've been hearing things about you. Your daddy has arranged a big surprise for you!" Mr. Finkle ushered us into the parlor. He picked up a case, opened it, lifted out a violin and started to play. The melody surged and spoke like waterfalls. Oh, to play like him, I thought.

Finishing the number, he turned to Daddy. "Carl, I found it in a pawnshop for seven dollars. It's a good violin. Mary Lou should be able to make beautiful music with it." Then he handed the violin to me.

I noticed the tears in Daddy's eyes as I finally comprehended. It was mine! I stoked the violin gently. The wood was a golden brown that seemed to warm in the light. "It's beautiful," I said, barely breathing.

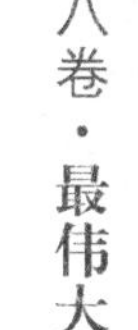

When we arrived back at Aunt Alice's, all eyes turned as we entered. I saw Daddy wink at Mother, and then I realized everyone had known but me. I knew Daddy's prayer, and mine, had been answered.

The day I carried my violin to school for my first lesson no one could imagine the bursting feeling in my heart. Over the months I practiced daily, feeling the warm wood fit under my chin like an extension of myself.

When I was ready to join the school orchestra, I trembled with excitement. I sat in the third row of violins and wore my white orchestra jacket like a royal robe.

My heart beat wildly at my first public performance, a school operetta. The auditorium filled to capacity and the audience buzzed while we softly tuned our instruments. Then the spotlight centered on us, and a hush fell as we started to play. I felt sure everyone in the audience was watching me. Daddy and Mother smiled proudly at their little girl who held her cherished violin for the whole world to admire.

The years seemed to run more swiftly then. And by the time my sisters graduated, I found myself in the first-violin chair.

Two years later, I graduated. I packed my cherished violin in its case and stepped into the grown-up world. Nurse's training, marriage, working in the hospital, rearing four daughters filled my years.

More years passed. My violin made every move with us, and I carefully stored it away when we unpacked—briefly remembering how much I still loved it and promising myself to play it soon.

None of my children cared about the violin. Later, one by one, they married and left home...

Now here I was with the newspaper want ads. I forced my thoughts to the present and read again the ad that had transported me back to childhood memories. Laying aside the paper, I murmured, "I must find my violin."

I discovered the case deep in the recesses of my closet. Opening the lid, I lifted the violin from where it nestled on the rose-velvet lining. My fingers caressed its golden wood. I tuned the strings, miraculously still intact, tightened the bow, and put rosin on the dry horsehairs.

And then my violin began to sing again those favorite tunes that had never left my memory. How long I played I'll never know. I thought of Daddy, who did all he could to fill my needs and desires when I was a little girl. I wondered if I had ever thanked him.

At last I laid the violin back in its case. I picked up the newspaper, walked to the phone and dialed the number.

Later in the day, an old car stopped in my driveway. A man in his 30s knocked on the door. "I've been praying someone would answer my ad. My daughter wants a violin so badly," he said, examining my instrument. "How much are you asking?"

Any music store, I knew, would offer me a nice sum. But now I heard my voice answer, "Seven dollars."

"Are you sure?" he asked, reminding me so much of Daddy.

"Seven dollars," repeated, and then added, "I hope your little girl will enjoy it as much as I did."

I closed the door behind him. Peeking out between the drapes, I saw his wife and children waiting in the car. A door suddenly opened and a young girl ran to him as he held out the violin case to her.

She hugged it against her, then dropped to her knees and snapped open the case. She touched the violin lightly as it caught the glow of the late-afternoon sun, then turned and threw her arms around her smiling father.

一把小提琴

"求购小提琴，出价不高。请打电话……"

我为什么偏偏注意这则广告呢？连我自己也搞不清楚。平时我很少注意这类广告。

我把报纸放在膝间，闭上双眼，往事便一幕幕浮现在了眼前：那时全家人含辛茹苦靠种地勉强度日。我也曾想要一把小提琴，但家里买不起……

我的两个孪生姐姐爱上了音乐。哈丽特·安妮学弹祖母留下的那台竖式钢琴，苏珊娜学拉父亲的那把小提琴。由于她们不断练习，因此没过多久简单的曲调就变成了悦耳动听的旋律。陶醉在音乐中的小弟弟禁不住随着音乐的节奏翩翩起舞，父亲轻轻哼唱，母亲也不由自主吹起了口哨，而我只是注意听着。

我的手臂渐渐长长了，也试着学拉苏珊娜的那把小提琴。我喜欢那绷紧的琴弓拉过琴弦时发出的柔媚圆润的声音。“噢，我多么希望能有一把琴啊！”但我明白这是不可能的。

一天傍晚，我的两个孪生姐姐在学校乐队演出时，我紧紧地闭上眼睛，以便把当时的情景深深地印在脑海里。“总有一天我也要坐在那里。”我暗暗发誓。

那年年景不好。收成不像我们盼望的那样好。尽管岁月如此艰难，但我还是迫不及待地问道：“爸爸，我可以有一把自己的小提琴吗？”

“你用苏珊娜那把不行吗？”

“我也想加入乐队，但我们俩不能同时用一把琴呀。”

父亲的表情显得非常难过。那天晚上以及随后的许多夜晚，我都听到他在全家人晚间祈祷时向上帝祷告：“……上帝啊，玛丽·露想要一把自己的小提琴。”

一天晚上，全家人都围坐在桌边，我和姐姐们复习功课，母亲做针线活，父亲给他在俄亥俄州哥伦布市的朋友乔治·芬科写信。父亲曾说，芬科先生是一名出色的小提琴家。

父亲一边写，一边把信的部分内容念给母亲听。几周后，我才发现信中的这一行字他没念：“请留神帮我三女儿寻一把小提琴好吗？我出不起高价，但她喜欢音乐，我们希望她能有自己的乐器。”

又过了几周，父亲收到哥伦布市的回信。他对大家说：“只要我能找到人帮忙照看家畜，我们就一起去哥伦布市，到爱丽斯姑姑家过一夜。”

这一天终于到来了。我们全家人驱车前往爱丽斯姑姑家。到那以后，父亲打了个电话，我在旁边听着。他挂上电话后问我：“玛丽·露，你想和我一起去看芬科先生吗？”

“当然想。”我答道。

父亲将车开进一个居民区，停靠在一座古色古香的楼房前的车道边上。我们登上台阶，按响了门铃。开门的是一个比我父亲年纪大的高个子的先生。“请进！”他和父亲亲切握手，两人马上攀谈了起来。

“玛丽·露，我早就听说过你的一些情况。你的父亲为你准备了一件礼物，一定会让你大吃一惊的。”说完，芬科先生将我们领进客厅，便开始拉了起来。乐曲时而激越高亢，时而像瀑布飞泻。“噢，要是像他那样拉该多好啊！”我心里想。

一曲终了，他转过身对我的父亲说：“卡尔，这是在一家当铺里找到的，才花了 7 美元，是一把好琴。这下玛丽·露就可以用它演奏优美的乐曲了吧。”说完，他将琴递给了我。

看到父亲眼里的泪水，我终于明白了一切。我有了自己的小提琴！我轻轻地抚摸着琴。这把琴是用金色灿烂的棕色木料制成的，在阳光的映照下显得是那样温暖。“多么漂亮啊！”我激动得透不过气来了。

当我们回到爱丽斯姑姑家时，所有人的目光都投向了我们父女俩，只见父亲正向母亲挤眼。这时，我才恍然大悟，原来只有我一个人还蒙在鼓里。我知道我和父亲的愿望已经得到了实现。

我带着那把小提琴到学校上第一堂课的那天，当时那种万分激动的心情是谁也无法想象的。随后的几个月，我天天坚持练琴，感到抵在颌下那温暖的琴木就像我身体的一部分。

加入校乐队时，我激动得浑身颤抖。我身着白色队服，俨然女王一般。我坐在小提琴组的第三排。

首次公演是学校演出的小歌剧，当时我的心狂跳不止。礼堂里座无虚席。我们乐队成员轻轻地调试音调，观众席里还在叽叽喳喳说个不停。舞台聚光灯射向我们，台下立刻鸦雀无声。我们开始了演奏。我确信观众的目光都在注视着我。我的父母亲也都在看着他们的小女儿，嘴边挂着自豪的微笑。他们的小女儿怀里抱着她那把心爱的琴，让全世界都来赞赏它。

岁月似乎过得太快了。两个姐姐双双毕业后，我便坐上了首席小提琴的席位。

两年后，我也完成了学业，将心爱的小提琴放回了琴盒，步入了成年人的世界。先是接受护士培训，然后是结婚成家。在医院工作的几年里，我先后生了4个女儿。

以后的许多年里，我们每次搬家，我都带着这把琴。每次打开行李布置居室时，我都要小心翼翼地将琴存放好，忙里偷闲时，想着我仍是多么爱它，同时对自己许愿说，用不了多久还会用这把小提琴演奏几首曲子。

我的几个孩子没有一个喜欢小提琴的。后来，她们相继结婚，离开了家。

现在我的面前摆着这张征求广告的报纸。我尽力不再去回首往事，将这则引起我对童年回忆的广告又看了一遍后，放下报纸，喃喃自语道：“一定得把我的琴找出来。”

我在壁橱深处找出了琴盒，打开盖子，将安卧在玫瑰色丝绒衬里中的小提琴拿出来。我的手指轻轻地抚摸着金色的琴木，令人惊喜的是，琴弦仍然完好无损。我调试了一下琴弦，紧了紧琴弓，又往干巴巴的马尾弓上抹了点松香。

接着，小提琴又重新奏出了那些铭记在我心中最心爱的曲子。也不知究竟拉了多长时间。我想起了父亲，在我童年时代，是他竭力满足我的一切愿望和要求，对此我不知道自己是否感谢过他。

最后，我把小提琴重新放回盒子里，拿起报纸，走到电话边，拨响了那个号码。

当天晚些时候，一辆旧轿车停靠在我家的车道旁。敲门的是个30来岁的先生。“我一直都在祈祷着会有人答复我登在报纸上的那则广告。我的女儿太希望有一把属于自己的小提琴了，”他一边说，一边查看我那把琴。“要多少钱？”

我知道，不管哪家乐器行都会出好价钱的。但此时此刻，我听到自己的声音回答说：“7美元。”

“真的吗？”他这一问，倒使我更多地想起了父亲。

“7美元，”我又说了一遍，接着补充道，“希望你的小女儿也会像我过去那样喜欢它。”

他走后，我随即关上门，从窗帘缝里看到他的妻子和孩子们正等候在车子里。车门突然打开，一个小姑娘迎着他双手托着的琴箱跑过来。

她紧紧地抱住琴盒，双膝跪倒在地，“吧嗒”一声打开盒子。她轻轻地抚摸着红彤彤的夕阳映照下的那把琴，转过身，搂住了面带微笑的父亲。

The Most Sunshiny Interpretation

On the evening she finally left, Mother sat with Daddy talking with each other overnight, but I only remember one sentence, "You go and I will explain it to Shirley."

This was what Daddy said, so I knew it was Mother who would leave.

After Mother left for several days, I kept waiting for Father's explanation every day, but he seemed to have forgotten it. As usual, he sent and met me to school, carefully filled in my preschool manual the more new words I had learned and the stories I had heard of. My father in our family always did these things, which were done by the mothers in many other classmates. But whenever Grandma said with a sigh, her mother's "heart has long gone," my father would stop her with his eyes.

One night after my mother had gone with her heart for one week, my father closed the stories book I read, tucked in me again and said, "You have heard many stories about angels. When she flies to a place, finds someone hungry, cold or in need of help, an angel will stay to be on duty; if everything is good, the angel who isn't on duty will be assured to fly away and goes on to find the one who needs help. Mom and Dad in the world are angels, who are devoted to caring for children and accompany them to grow up. In our family, Daddy can take good care of Shirley alone, so Mom is assured to leave you to me. Your mother has gone to a distant place called Australia, just like the angel who isn't on duty..."

This is the most beautiful, the best and the most sunshiny interpretation about "divorce" I have ever heard in my life the parents make in the presence of their children.

最阳光的解释

母亲最后离开的那个晚上，和爸爸整整坐了一夜，也说了一夜的话，但我只记住一句：“你走吧，由我来向雪莉解释。”

这句话是爸爸说的，所以我知道要走的是母亲。

母亲离开后的好几天里，我天天都在等着爸爸的解释，但他似乎是把这事忘了，仍一如既往地接送我上学，给我在学前班的家长手册上认真填写我又学会的新字和又听到的故事。这些在许多同学都是由母亲来做的事情，在我家里一直都是父亲来做。但每当奶奶叹气说母亲“心早就不在了”时，父亲就会用眼神制止奶奶。

等母亲的人和心一同不在了一个星期后，一天晚上，父亲合起给我读的故事书，又掖了掖我的被角，说：“你听过很多天使的故事，天使飞到一个地方，发现那里有人冷了，有人饿了，有人需要帮助了，她就会留下来当差，如果一切都很好的话，不当差的天使就会放心地飞走，继续去找需要她帮助的人。世界上的爸爸妈妈就是天使，是专门来照顾孩子，陪孩子一起长大的。咱们家里，有爸爸一个人就能照顾好雪莉，所以妈妈才放心地把雪莉留给爸爸，妈妈去了一个叫澳大利亚的很远的地方，就像不当差的天使一样……”

这是我一生中听到过的父母在孩子面前对“离婚”做出的最美、最好、最阳光的解释。

A Box of Kisses

A long time ago a man punished his 3-year-old daughter for wasting a roll of gold wrapping paper. Money was tight and he became very angry when the child tried to decorate a box to put under the Christmas tree.

However, the little girl brought the gift to her father the next morning and said, "This is for you, Daddy."

The father was upset by his earlier overreaction, but his anger flared again when he found out the box was empty. He yelled at her, "don't you know, when you give someone a present, there should be something inside?"

The little girl looked up at him with tears in her eyes and cried, "Oh, Daddy, it's not empty at all. I blew kisses into the box. They're all for you, Daddy."

The father was crushed. He put his arms around his little girl, and he begged for her forgiveness.

Only a short time later, an accident took the life of the child. Her father kept that gold box by his bed for many years and, whenever he was discouraged, he would take out an imaginary kiss and remember the love of the child who had put it there.

一盒子吻

很久以前，一位父亲因3岁的女儿浪费了一卷金包装纸而惩罚她。当时家里钱不宽余，看到女儿想把一个包装金纸的盒子放在圣诞树下，父亲勃然大怒。

然而，第二天早上，小姑娘还是把那个礼物送给父亲说：“爸爸，这是送给你的。”

那位父亲对自己先前的过激行为感到忐忑不安；可是，当发现盒子里空无一物时，他又火冒三丈，冲女儿大声嚷道：“难道你不知道送别人礼物时盒子里应该放东西吗？”

小姑娘眼噙泪水望着父亲，哭道：“噢，爸爸，盒子里一点也不空呀。我向里边飞了好多吻，它们都是送给你的，爸爸。”

那位父亲羞愧难当。他张开双臂抱住女儿，乞求她的原谅。

过了没多久，一场意外事故夺去了小女孩的生命。她的父亲好多年都把那个金纸包装的盒子存放在自己的床边。每当灰心丧气时，他就常常取出一个想象的吻，想起了女儿曾放在那里的爱。

The Most Delicious Soaked Noodle

He was a single father, raising a seven-year-old boy alone. Whenever his boy came back hurt after playing with his friend, he would feel deeply sorry for his deceased wife, the low wail surging up within him.

This occurred on the day he was on business, leaving the child alone.

In order to catch the train, he hurried out without accompanying his child to breakfast. He was worried about the child all the way and upset, not knowing if he had his meal and cried. He kept phoning his child even when he arrived at the destination. But his child always sensibly told him not to worry about him. However, because he was worried and upset, he set foot on the way home after he hastily handled the affairs.

When he got home and saw the child had slept soundly, he sighed with relief. The journey made him tired out. When he was about to sleep, he was startled to find there was an overturned bowl of soaked noodles under the quilt. "This child!" Flying into a rage, he fiercely spanked his son sleeping soundly. "Why aren't you obedient to anger daddy? You are so naughty, making the quilt dirty! Who will wash it for you?" It was the first time he punished his boy after his wife's death.

"I haven't..." the child argued as he whimpered, "I'm not naughty. This... this is the supper for daddy." It turned out that in order to coordinate the hour of daddy's return, the child soaked two bowls of noodles, one for himself, the other for daddy. But he was afraid daddy's noodle would become cool. But because he was afraid his daddy's noodle turned cold, he placed it under the quilt to keep it hot.

Hearing that, Daddy hugged his boy tightly without a word.

最美味的泡面

他是个单亲爸爸，独自抚养一个7岁的小男孩。每当孩子和朋友玩耍受伤回来，他就对过世的妻子深感歉意，心底传来阵阵悲鸣。

这是他留下孩子出差当天发生的事情。

他要赶火车，没时间陪孩子吃早餐，便匆匆离开了家门。一路上担心孩子有没有吃饭，会不会哭，心总是放不下，即使抵达了出差地点，他也不时打电话回家。可孩子总是很懂事地让他不要担心。然而，他心里牵挂不安，草草办完事，便踏上了归途。

他回到家时，孩子已经熟睡了，他这才松了口气。旅途上的疲惫让他全身无力。正准备就寝时，他突然大吃了一惊：棉被下面竟有一碗打翻了的泡面！"这孩子！"盛怒之下，他朝熟睡中的儿子的屁股一阵狠打。"为什么这么不乖，惹爸爸生气？你这样调皮，把棉被弄脏了？要谁给你洗？"这是妻子过世后他第一次体罚孩子。

"我没有……"孩子抽噎着辩解说。"我没有调皮，这……这是给爸爸吃的晚餐。"原来孩子为了配合爸爸回家的时间，特地泡了两碗泡面，一碗自己吃，另一碗给爸爸。可是，因为怕爸爸那碗面凉掉，所以就放进了棉被底下保温。

爸爸听了，一声不吭，紧紧地抱住了孩子。

Lesson From a Penguin

I've spent most of my career as a traveling salesman, and so I know that battling loneliness is an occupational hazard. But one year, my little girl Jeanne gave me the antidote for my homesickness.

It had black beady eyes, a red bow tie and orange feet—a stuffed penguin that stood about five inches tall. Attached to its left wing was a little sign bearing the hand-painted declaration "I Love My Dad!" I immediately granted the penguin a special place on my dresser.

On my next trip, I tossed the penguin in my suitcase. That night when I called home, Jeanne was upset that the penguin had disappeared. "Honey, he's here with me," I explained. "I brought him along."

From then on the penguin came with me—as essential as my briefcase or shaving kit. And we made friends along the way. In Albuquerque, I checked into a hotel, dumped out my bag and dashed to a meeting. When I returned, the maid had turned down the bed and propped the penguin on the pillow. In Boston, I found it perched in a glass on the nightstand. Once a customs agent at New York's Kennedy Airport dug the penguin out of my suitcase and, holding it up, said, "Thank God we don't charge a tax on love, or you'd owe a bundle."

One night I discovered the penguin missing, and after a frantic phone call, I learned I'd left it in my previous hotel room, where it had been rescued by a maid. I drove a hundred miles to retrieve it, and when I arrived at midnight, the penguin was waiting at the front desk. In the lobby, tired business travelers looked on at the reunion-I think with a touch of envy.

Jeanne is in college now, and I don't travel as much. The penguin sits on my dresser, a reminder that love is a wonderful traveling companion. All those years on the road, it was the one thing I never left home without.

爱心企鹅

我一生大多数时间都是做旅行推销商,所以我知道战胜孤独成了一种职业病。但有一年,我的小女儿珍宁送给了我一副想家的解药。

那是一只玩具企鹅,它乌溜溜的眼睛,打着红色蝴蝶结,长着一双橘黄色的脚,大约有5英寸高。它的左腿上粘着一个小牌子,上面手绘着一条说明:“我爱我爸!”我马上在我的梳妆台上给企鹅提供了一席之地。

在下一次旅行时,我就将企鹅放进了手提箱。当夜我给家里打电话时,珍宁忐忑不安,说企鹅不见了。“宝贝儿,它跟我在一块呢,”我解释说,“我把它带在了身边。”

从那以后,企鹅就跟我一路同行,就像我的公文包或剃须用具一样必不可少。而且我们一路上成了朋友。在阿尔伯克基市,我登记住进一家旅馆,倒出手提包,匆匆赶去参加一个会议。我回来时,女服务员已经铺过床,并将企鹅放在了枕头上。在波士顿,我发现它卧在床头几上的一只玻璃杯里。有一次,在纽约市肯尼迪机场,一位报关代理人从我的手提箱里搜出了企鹅,将它举起来,说:“谢天谢地我们对爱是不收税的,否则你就要欠一大笔钱喽。”

有天夜里,我发现企鹅不翼而飞;而在疯狂地打了电话后,我才得知我将它忘在了先前住的旅馆房间里,旅馆的一名女服务员已经把它收了起来。我驱车100英里将它取

了回来；而当我午夜赶到那里时，企鹅正在前台等着我呢。在大厅里，满脸倦容的生意人在旁边看着我们的重逢。我想，是带着一丝的嫉妒。

珍宁现已上了大学，而且我也不像以前那样经常旅行了。企鹅端坐在我的梳妆台上，它时刻提醒着我爱是妙不可言的旅伴。我出门在外在路上颠簸的那些岁月，爱是我从不离家的一件东西。

Dad's Kiss

The board meeting had come to an end. Bob started to stand up and jostled the table, spilling his coffee over his notes. "How embarrassing. I am getting so clumsy in my old age."

Everyone had a good laugh, and soon we were all telling stories of our most embarrassing moments. It came around to Frank who sat quietly listening to the others. Someone said, "Come on, Frank. Tell us your most embarrassing moment."

Frank laughed and began to tell us of his childhood. "I grew up in San River. My dad was a fisherman, and he loved the sea. He had his own boat, but it was hard making a living on the sea. He worked hard and would stay out until he caught enough to feed his family. Not just enough for our family, but also for his mom and dad and the other kids that were still at home."

He looked at us and said, "I wish you could have met my dad. He was a big man, and he was strong from pulling the nets and fighting the seas for his catch. When you got close to him, he smelled like the ocean. He would wear his old canvas, foul-weathered coat and his bibbed overalls. His rain hat would be pulled down over his brow. No matter how much my mother washed them, they would still smell of the sea and of fish."

Frank's voice dropped a bit. "When the weather was bad he would drive me to school. He had this old truck that he used in his fishing business. That truck was older than he was. It would wheeze and rattle down the road. You could hear it coming for blocks. As he would drive toward the school, I would shrink down into the seat hoping to disappear.

"Half the time, he would slam to a stop and the old truck would belch a cloud of smoke. He would pull right up in front, and it seemed like everybody would be standing around and watching. Then he would lean over and give me a big kiss on the cheek and tell me to be a good boy. It was so embarrassing for me. Here, I was twelve years old and my dad would lean over and kiss me goodbye!"

He paused and then went on, "I remember the day I decided I was too old for a goodbye kiss. When we got to the school and came to a stop, he had his usual big smile. He started to lean toward me, but I put my hand up and said, 'No, dad,'"

"It was the first time I had ever talked to him that way, and he had this surprised look on his face."

"I said, 'Dad, I'm too old for a goodbye kiss. I'm too old for any kind of kiss.'"

"My dad looked at me for the longest time, and his eyes started to well up. I had never seen him cry. He turned and looked out the windshield. 'You are right,' he said. 'You are a big boy—a man. I won't kiss you anymore.'"

Frank got a funny look on his face, and the tears began to well up in his eyes, as he spoke. "it was not long after that when my dad went to sea and never came back. It was a day when most of the fleet stayed in, but not Dad. He had a big family to feed. They found his boat adrift with its nets half in and half out. He must have gotten into a gale."

I looked at Frank and saw that tears were running down his cheeks. Frank spoke again, "Guys, you don't know what I would give to have my dad give me just one more KISS on the cheek... to feel his rough old face... to smell the ocean on him... to feel his arm around my neck. I wish I had been a man then. If I had been a man, I would never have told my dad I was too old for a goodbye kiss."

爸爸的吻

董事会议已经结束了。鲍勃站起身时，碰了一下桌子，将咖啡溅到了他的笔记上。“真尴尬！我老了，笨手笨脚的。”

每个人都大笑起来。过了一会儿，我们都讲起了自己最尴尬的时刻。弗兰克静静地听着别人的故事。有人说道：“快点儿，弗兰克，给我们说说你最尴尬的时刻。”

弗兰克笑了笑，开始给我们讲起了他的童年。“我在桑河边长大。爸爸是个渔民，他热爱大海。尽管他有自己的船，但很难在海上谋生。他拼命干活，每次出海捕到的鱼够家人吃才回来。他不仅要养活我们家，还要养活他的爸爸妈妈和家里其他的孩子们。”

他看了看我们，又说道：“我真希望你们能见一见我爸爸。他个子很高，因为捕鱼要拉网和跟大海搏斗，所以他的身体很壮。你走近他，就会闻到他有一股海的气味。他总是穿着又旧又脏的帆布外套和有围兜的罩衫。他的雨帽总是拉得很低，盖住眉毛。无论我妈妈洗多少遍，这些衣服还是有一股海水和鱼腥味。”

弗兰克的声音放低了点：“天气不好时，他就会开车送我上学。他用这辆旧卡车运送鱼。卡车比他的年龄还大，走在路上总是呼哧呼哧、嘎吱嘎吱响。隔几个街区你都能听到卡车驶来的声音。他每次送我上学时，我总是缩着身子坐在车座上，希望自己消失。

“通常，他都会砰地关上车门停下来，旧卡车总是喷出一股浓烟。他总是正好把车停在校门前，随后仿佛每个人都围站在那里目不转睛地看着。接着，他总是弯下腰，在我的脸颊上狠狠地亲一下，告诉我要做一个好孩子。这真让我难堪。嗨，我那时已经12岁了，爸爸总是弯下腰跟我吻别！”

他停了一下，又接着说道：“我现在还记得我做出年龄太大不再吻别那个决定的那天的情景。我们到达学校停下时，他像往常一样面带灿烂的笑容，开始向我弯下腰，但我举起手说：‘不，爸爸。’

“那是我第一次那样跟他说话，他脸上露出了吃惊的神情。

“我说：‘爸爸，我太大了，不要再吻别了。我太大了，什么吻都不要了。’

“爸爸久久地看着我，眼睛开始流泪。我从来没有见他哭过。他转过身，透过挡门玻璃望着外面说：‘你说得对，你是个大男孩，是个男子汉了。我不会再吻了。’”

弗兰克的脸上出现了奇异的表情，随后就泪如泉涌。“不久以后，爸爸出海，再也没有回来。那天，除了我爸爸，其他大多数渔船都没有出海。他有一大家人要养活啊。人们发现他的船漂浮在海面上，渔网一半在里一半在外，他肯定是遇到了大风。”

我望着弗兰克，发现泪水顺着他的脸颊滚滚而下。他接着又说道：“朋友们，你们不知道我多么希望爸爸能再吻一下我的脸颊……多么希望触摸他粗糙的老脸……多么希望闻他身上的大海气味……多么希望感受他抱着我脖子的手臂。我多么希望自己当时是个男子汉。如果真是一个男子汉，我就绝不会告诉爸爸：我太大了，不要再吻别了。”

My Father's Crocus

It was an autumn morning shortly after my husband and I moved into our first house. Our children were upstairs unpacking, and I was looking out the window at my father moving around mysteriously on the front lawn. My parents lived nearby, and Dad visited us several times already. "What are you doing out there?" I called him.

He looked up, smiling. "I'm making you a surprise." Knowing my father, I thought it could be just about anything. A self-employed jobber, he was always building things out of odds and ends. When we were kids, he once rigged up a jungle gym out of wheels and pulleys. For one of my Halloween parties, he created an electrical pumpkin and mounted it on a broomstick. As guests came to our door, he would light the pumpkin and have it pop out in front of them from a hiding place in the bushes.

Today, however, Dad would say no more, and, caught up in the busyness of our new life, I finally forgot about his surprise.

Until one raw day the following March when I glanced out the windows. Dismal. Overcast. Little piles of dirty snow still stubbornly littered the lawn. Would winter ever end?

Yet was it a miracle? I strained to see what I thought was something pink, miraculously peeking out of drift, and was that a dot of blue across the yard, a small note of optimism in this gloomy sky? I grabbled my coat and headed outside for a closer look.

They were crocuses, scattered oddly throughout the front lawn. Lavender, blue, yellow and my favorite pink—little faces bobbing in the bitter wind.

Dad, I smiled, remembering the bulbs he had secretly planted last autumn. He knew that the darkness and dreariness of winter always got me down. What could have been more perfectly timed, more attuned to my needs? How blessed I was, not only for the flowers but also for him.

My father's crocuses bloomed each spring for the next four or five seasons, bringing that same assurance: Hold on, keep going, light is coming soon.

Then a spring came with only half the usual blooms. The next spring there were none. I missed crocuses, but my life was busier than ever, and I had never been much of a gardener. I would ask Dad to come over and plant new bulbs, but I never did.

He died suddenly one October day. My family grieved deeply, leaning on our faith. I missed him terribly, though I knew he would always be a part of us.

Four years passed, and on a dismal spring afternoon I was running errands and found myself feeling depressed. You've got the winter blahs again, I told myself. You get them every year.

It was Dad's birthday, and I found myself thinking about him. This was not unusual—my family often talked about him, remembering how he lived his faith. But now, in the car, I couldn't help wondering, How is he now? Where is he? Is there really a heaven?

I felt guilty for having doubts, but sometimes, I thought as I turned into our driveway, faith is so hard.

Suddenly I slowed, stopped and stared at the lawn. Muddy grass and small gray mounds of melting snow. There, bravely waving in the wind, was one pink crocus. How could a flower bloom from a bulb more than 18 years old; one that hadn't blossomed in over a decade? But there was the crocus. Tears filled my eyes as I realized its significance.

Hold on, keep going, light is coming soon. The pink crocus bloomed for only a day, but it built my faith for a lifetime.

父亲的藏红花

那是我和丈夫搬进我们的第一座房子不久后的一个秋天的早晨。我们的孩子们正

在楼上打开包裹取东西。我眺望窗外，看到父亲神秘地在前草坪上走来走去。父母亲住在附近，爸爸已经来看过我们好几次了。“你在外面做什么？”我向他喊道。

他抬起头，面带微笑。“我要给你一个意外的惊喜。”我了解父亲，我想这里可能又有什么名堂。他是一名个体户，总是用零碎东西做这做那。我们小时候，他有一次曾用车轮和滑轮做了个儿童攀缘游戏立体支架。他为我的一次万圣节前夕宴会做了一只电南瓜，将它放在一把扫帚上。当客人们来到我们的门口时，他就点燃南瓜，让它从灌木丛的隐藏处蹦到他们面前噗的一声爆炸。

然而，父亲现在不再说什么了；而且，我对我们忙碌的新生活很感兴趣，所以就忘记了他说的让我惊喜的事儿。

直到第二年三月的一个阴天我向窗外望去之时。黯淡。阴沉。一小堆一小堆的脏雪仍顽固不化地堆在草坪上。冬天会结束吗？

然而，它会出现奇迹吗？我睁大眼睛看着那个我认为是粉红色的东西，正好奇地从雪堆里探出。是一丝惆怅掠过庭院，还是一个小小的欢快的音符飘过阴霾的天空？我飞快地抓起大衣，跑出门外，想靠近看个究竟。

它们是藏红花，奇异地散开在前草坪。有淡紫色、蓝色、黄色和我最喜欢的粉红色——可爱的小脸在寒风中摇来晃去。

爸爸，我微笑着，回忆起他去年秋天暗地里种的那些球茎。他知道黯淡沉闷的冬天总是让我感到沮丧。还有什么能来得这样及时、这样迎合我的需要呢？我是多么幸福，不仅是为了那些花，也是为了他。

父亲的藏红花每年春天都开放，连续四、五年都是这样。每次开放时总是给我们带来同一个信念：坚持不懈，继续努力，光明即将来临。

后来有一年春天，花只开了平常的一半。第二年春天，一朵也没开。尽管我想念藏红花，但我的生活比先前更忙，而且我压根就不是个好园丁。我常常想请爸爸过来栽新的球茎，但我从来没那样做过。

有一年10月的一天，爸爸突然去世。家人都悲痛万分，同时依靠着我们共同的信念。我非常想念他，尽管我知道他总是和我们在一起。

转眼4年过去了。后来，在一个阴沉的春天的下午，我出差在外，发现自己非常沮丧。我对自己说，你又染上冬天的单调乏味了。你每年都要染上。

那天是爸爸的生日，我发现自己又想起了他。这并非什么不同寻常的事——家人常常谈起他，回忆起他是怎样依靠信念活着。但现在，待在车里，我情不自禁地想，他现在怎么样啊？他在哪里？真的有天堂吗？

尽管我对自己有这样的怀疑感到内疚，但有时我开进我们家的车道时就想，信念是这样难啊。

突然，我放慢车速，停下来，直盯盯地望着草坪。映入眼帘的是泥泞的草地和一小堆一小堆正在融化的灰色的积雪。只见那里，有一支顽强地迎风摇曳的粉红色的藏红花。一朵花怎么能从一个球茎上开放18年多啊；而且是一支在10年多时间里没有开放的花？但正是那支藏红花。我认识到它的意义时，泪眼满眶。

坚持不懈，继续努力，光明即将来临。粉红色的藏红花只开放了一天，但它却建立了我终生的信念。

The Confession from a Father

Listen, son! I am saying this as you lie asleep, one little paw crumpled under your cheek and the blond curls stickily wet on your damp forehead. I have stolen into your room alone. Just a few minutes ago, as I sat reading my paper in the library, a hot, stifling wave of remorse swept over me. I couldn't resist it. Guiltily I came to your bedside.

These were the things I was thinking, son: I had been cross to you. I scolded you as you were dressing for school because you gave your face merely a dab with a towel. I took you to task for not cleaning your shoes. I called out angrily when I found you had thrown some of your things on the floor.

At breakfast, I found fault, too. You spilled things. You gulped down your food. You put your elbows on the table. You spread butter too thick on your bread. And as you started off to play and I made for my train, you turned and waved a little hand and called, "Good - bye, Papa!" and I frowned and said in reply, "Hold your shoulders back!"

Then it began all over again in the late afternoon. As I came up the road, I spied you, down on your knees, playing marbles. There were holes in your stocking. I humiliated you before your boy friends, by march on ahead of me, back to the house. Stockings were expensive—and if you had to buy them you would be more careful. Imagine that, son, from a father! It was such a stupid, silly logic.

But do you remember, later, when I was reading in the library, how you came in timidly, with a sort of hurt look in your eyes? When I glanced up over my paper, impatient at the interruption, you hesitated at the door.

"What is it you want?" I snapped.

You said nothing, but ran across the room, and threw your arms around my neck and kissed me, and your small arms tightened with an affection that God had set blooming in your heart and which even neglect couldn't wither. And then you were gone, puttering up the stairs.

Well, son, it was shortly afterwards that my paper slipped from my hands and a terrible fear came over me. Suddenly I saw myself as I really was, in all my horrid selfishness, and I felt sick at heart.

What had habit been doing to me? The habit of complaining, of finding fault, of reprimanding—all these were my rewards to you for being a boy. It was not that I didn't love you; it was that I expected too much of youth. I was measuring you by the yardstick of my own years.

And there is so much that was good, and fine, and true in your character. You didn't deserve my treatment of you, son. The little heart of you was as big as the dawn itself, over wide hills. All this was shown by your spontaneous impulse to rush in and kiss me goodnight. Nothing else matters, tonight, son. I have come to your bedside in the darkness, and I have knelt here, choking with emotion and so ashamed!

It is a feeble atonement. I know you wouldn't understand these things if I told them to you during your waking hours. Yet I must say what I am saying. I must burn sacrificial fires, alone, here in your own bedroom, and make free confession.

And I have prayed God to strengthen me in my new resolve. Tomorrow I will be a real daddy! I will chum with you and suffer when you suffer and laugh when you laugh. I will bite my tongue when impatient words come. I will keep saying, as if it were a ritual: "He is nothing but a boy—a little boy!"

I am afraid I have visualized you as a man. Yet as I see you now, son, crumpled and weary in your cot, I see that you are still a baby. Yesterday you were in your mother's arms, your head on her shoulder. I have asked too much, too much.

Dear boy! Dear little son! A penitent kneels at your infant shrine, here in the moonlight. I kiss the little fingers, and the damp forehead, and the golden curls, and, if it were not for waking you, I would snatch you up and crush you to my breast.

Tears came and heartache and remorse and, I think, a greater, deeper love, when you ran through the library door and wanted to kiss me!

一位父亲的忏悔

听着，儿子，我要说这事儿时，你躺在那里睡觉，一只小手弯在脸颊下面，金色的鬈发湿漉漉地粘在汗津津的前额上。我独自悄悄走进你的房间。就在几分钟前，我坐在书房看报时，一阵强烈的懊悔涌遍了我的全身，使我喘不过气来。我情不自禁，怀着内疚来到了你的床边。

儿子，我之所以在想这些事儿，是因为我以前总生你的气；你穿衣服准备上学时，我大声斥责你，因为你洗脸时只用毛巾抹一下脸；我责备你，因为你没有擦净鞋；发现你把自己的一些东西扔在地板上，我总是生气地对你大叫。

早饭时，我也找岔儿。你把东西撒到了外面。你吃东西狼吞虎咽。你把胳膊肘放在了桌子上。你在面包上抹的黄油太厚。你跑出去玩，我赶火车上班，你转过头挥挥小手，喊道："爸爸，再见！"我皱了皱眉，回答说："挺起胸！"

傍晚时也一样。我走上那条路时，看见你跪在地上打弹子，你的长袜上有几个窟窿。我当着小伙伴们的面叫你出丑，让你走在我前面回家。长袜很贵——如果你自己挣钱去买，你一定会更加小心的。儿子，想想吧，父亲居然说这样的话！这是多么愚蠢的逻辑。

可是，你记得后来我在书房里看报纸时，你羞怯地走进来，眼里流露出受伤的神情的样子？我从报纸上抬起目光，对你打断我看报而不耐烦，你犹豫地站在门口。

"你想要什么？"我厉声问。

你一声不吭，但你跑过房间，搂住我的脖子，吻我，你的小手臂用爱紧紧抱住我，这是上帝让你在心里绽开的爱，即使受到冷落，也不会凋谢。随后，你就咚咚爬上楼梯，走了。

嗨，儿子，没过多久，报纸从我的手里滑落，一种可怕的恐惧袭遍了我的全身。我突然看到了真正的自己，明白了自己所有可怕的自私自利，感到心如刀绞。

恶习把我弄成了什么样子了啊？我动不动就发牢骚、找茬儿、训斥你——所有这些都是我给予你的奖赏，你还是个孩子啊。并不是我不爱你，而是我对年轻人要求太过分。我是用自己年龄的标准来衡量你。

你的性格中有那么多优良、美好、真实的品质。儿子，你不该受到我这种对待。你幼小的心灵像照亮群山的曙光一样博大。这一切表现在你情不自禁地跑进来吻我道晚安的行动上。儿子，今晚，其他一切都无关紧要。我摸黑已经来到你的床边，跪在这里，羞愧难当，强烈的感情使我说不出话来！

这是一种无力的赎罪。我知道，在你醒着时，如果我对你说这些话，你是不会明白的。然而，我必须把要说的话说出来。我必须燃起献祭之火，独自在你的房间里真诚地忏悔。

而且，我已经祈求上帝赐给我力量，让我痛改前非。明天我会是一个真正的爸爸！我要和你成为好朋友，和你一起苦一起笑。当不耐烦的话要说出口时，我要咬住舌头。我要像举行仪式那样不断地说："他只不过是一个孩子——一个小孩子！"

我想我已经把你想象成了男子汉。可是，儿子，当我看到你现在扭弯着疲惫地躺在小床上时，我发现你还是一个娃娃。昨天，你躺在妈妈的怀里，头靠在她的肩上。我要求你太多了、太多了。

亲爱的孩子！亲爱的小儿子！一个悔罪的人跪在你的婴儿圣地边，跪在这里的月光下。我亲吻你小小的手指、潮湿的额头和金黄色的鬈发。如果不是怕惊醒你，我会一把将你抱起，紧紧地搂在怀里。

我流泪，我心痛，我悔恨。我想，你跑过书房想吻我时，你的爱更伟大、更深厚！

Penance after 50 Years

It is in a little bookshop in the city of Lichfield, England. The floor has just been swept and the shutter taken down from the one small window. The hour is early, and customers have not yet begun to drop in. Out of doors the rain is falling.

At a small table near the door, a feeble, white-haired old man is making up some packages of books. As he arranges them in a large basket, he stops now and then as though disturbed by pain. He puts his hand to his side; he coughs in a most distressing way; then he sits down and rests himself, leaning his elbows upon the table.

"Samuel!" he calls.

In the farther corner of the room there is a young man busily reading from a large book that is spread open before him. His eyesight must be poor, for, as he reads, he bends down until his face is quite near the printed page.

"Samuel!" again the old man calls.

But Samuel makes no reply. He is so deeply interested in his book that he doesn't hear. The old man rests himself a little longer and then finishes tying his packages.

He lifts the heavy basket and sets it on the table. The exertion brings on another fit of coughing; and when it is over he calls for the third time, "Samuel!"

"What is it, father?" This time the call is heard.

"You know, Samuel," he says, "that tomorrow is market day at Uttoxeter, and our stall must be attended to. Some of our friends will be there to look at the new books they expect me to bring. One of us must go down on the stage this morning and get everything in readiness. But I hardly feel able for the journey. My cough troubles me quite a little, and you see that it is raining very hard."

"Yes, father; I am sorry," answers Samuel; and his face is again bent over the book.

"Samuel, will you not go down to the market for me this time?"

The old man is putting on his great coat.

He is reaching for his hat.

The basket is on his arm.

He casts a beseeching glance at his son, hoping that he will relent at the last moment.

"Here comes the coach, Samuel," and the old man is choked by another fit of coughing.

Samuel is still reading, and he makes no sign nor motion.

The stage comes rattling down the street.

The old man with his basket of books staggers out of the door. The stage halts for a moment

while he climbs inside. Then the driver swings his whip, and all are away.

Samuel, in the shop, still bends over his book.

Out of doors the rain is falling.

Just fifty years have passed, and again it is market day at Uttoxeter.

The rain is falling in the streets. The people who have wares to sell huddle under the eaves and in the stalls and booths that have roofs above them.

A chaise from Lichfield pulls up at the entrance to the market square.

An old man alights. One would guess him to be seventy years of age. He is large and not well-shaped. His face is seamed and scarred, and he makes strange grimaces as he clambers out of the chaise. He wheezes and puffs as though afflicted with asthma. He walks with the aid of a heavy stick.

With slow but ponderous strides he enters the market place and looks around. He seems not to know that the rain is falling.

He looks at the little stalls ranged along the walls of the market place. Some have roofs over them and are the centers of noisy trade. Others have fallen into disuse and are empty.

The stranger halts before one of the latter. "Yes, this is it," he says. "I remember it well. It was here that my father, on certain market days, sold books to the clergy of the county. The good men came from every parish to see his wares and to hear him describe their contents."

He turns abruptly around. "Yes, this is the place," he repeats.

He stands quite still and upright, directly in front of the little old stall. He takes off his hat and holds it beneath his arm. His great walking stick has fallen into the gutter. He bows his head and clasps his hands. He doesn't seem to know that the rain is falling.

The clock in the tower above the market strikes eleven. The passers-by stop and gaze at the stranger. The market people peer at him from their booths and stalls. Some laugh as the rain runs in streams down his scarred old cheeks. Rain is it? Or can it be tears?

Boys hoot at him. Some of the ruder ones even hint at throwing mud; but a sense of shame withholds them from the act.

"He is a poor lunatic. Let him alone," says the more compassionate.

The rain falls upon his bare head and his broad shoulders. He is drenched and chilled. But he stands motionless and silent, looking neither to the right nor to the left.

"Who is that old fool?" asks a thoughtless young man who chances to be passing.

"Do you ask who he is?" answers a gentleman from London. "Why, he is Dr. Samuel Johnson, the most famous man in England. It was he who made the great English Dictionary, the most wonderful book of our times. He is the literary lion of England."

"Then why does he come to Uttoxeter and stand thus in the pouring rain?"

"I cannot tell you; but doubtless he has reasons for doing so," and the gentleman passes on.

At length there is a lull in the storm. The birds are chirping among the housetops.

The clock in the tower above the market strikes twelve. The renowned stranger has stood a whole hour motionless in the market place. And again the rain is falling.

Slowly now he returns his hat to his head. He finds his walking stick where it had fallen. He lifts his eyes reverently for a moment, and then, with a lordly, lumbering motion, walks down the street to meet the chaise which is ready to return to Lichfield.

We follow him through the pattering rain to his native town.

"Why, Dr. Johnson!" exclaims his hostess. "We have missed you all day. And you are so wet and chilled! Where have you been?"

"Madam," says the great man, "fifty years ago, this very day, I tacitly refused to oblige or obey my father. The thought of the pain which I must have caused him has haunted me ever since. To do away the sin of that hour, I this morning went in a chaise to Uttoxeter and did do penance publicly before the stall which my father had formerly used."

The great man bows his head upon his hands and sobs.

Out of doors the rain is falling.

50年后的忏悔

这件事发生在英国利奇菲尔德市的一家小书店里。地板刚擦过,百叶窗已从一扇小窗上取下来。时间还早,顾客还没开始进来。门外正下着雨。

在靠近门口的一张小桌子边,一个瘦弱的白发老人正在打点几包书。他在往一个大篮子里装这几包书时,不时停下来,好像因疼痛而焦虑。他将一只手放在身体一侧,非常痛苦地咳嗽着,随后双肘支在桌上,坐下来休息。

"塞缪尔!"他喊道。

在房间远处的角落里,有一个年轻人正在忙着看面前打开的一本大书。他的视力一定很差,因为他看书时弯下腰,脸离书页相当近。

"塞缪尔!"老人又喊道。

可是,塞缪尔没有回答。他正看得津津有味,所以没有听到。老人休息了一会儿,然后打好了包裹。

他提起沉重的篮子,放在桌子上。因为用力,他又咳嗽了一阵;之后,他第三次喊道:"塞缪尔!"

"父亲,什么事?"这次他听见了喊声。

"塞缪尔,你知道,"他说,"明天是尤托克西特集市日,我们的书摊必须有人照看。我们的一些朋友会到那儿去看他们希望我带去的新书。我们俩今天早晨必须有一个乘公共马车去那里,把一切准备停当。可是,我感到不能去那里了。我咳嗽得很厉害。再说,你看,雨下得很大。"

"是的,父亲,对不起,"塞缪尔答道;随后,他的脸又俯向了那本书。

"塞缪尔,你这次不愿替我到集上去吗?"

老人在穿着大衣。

他伸手去拿帽子。

篮子挎在了胳膊上。

他向儿子投去恳求的目光,希望儿子在最后一刻会发发慈悲。

"马车来了,塞缪尔。"老人又咳嗽得喘不过气来。

塞缪尔仍在看书,既没表示,又没行动。

马车沿街卡嗒卡嗒过来了。

老人挎着书篮,蹒跚着走出了门。马车停了一会儿,老人爬进了马车。随后,赶车人挥动鞭子,车子走远了。

塞缪尔待在店里,仍然俯首看书。

门外正下着雨。

整整50年过去了,又到了尤托克西特集市日。

街上正下着雨。卖东西的人纷纷挤在屋檐下,挤在有顶棚的摊子和棚子里。

从利奇菲尔德来的一辆轻便两轮马车在市场入口停了下来。

一位老人下了车。人们会以为他有70岁了。他身材高大,样子并不好看,脸上有不少疤痕。他从车里出来时愁眉苦脸,让人感到奇怪。他呼哧呼哧地喘气,好像患有哮喘病。他拄一根粗手杖走着。

他步履缓慢而沉重地走进了市场,环顾四周。他仿佛不知道正在下雨。

他看着沿市场墙边摆的一些小货摊。有些摊子有顶棚,是热闹的买卖中心。其他一些则无人使用,空荡荡的。

这个陌生人在一个空摊子前站住。"对,就是这个,"他说。"我记得很清楚。在那些集市日里,我父亲就是在这里把书卖给这个郡的牧师的。那些好人从各个教区来看他的书,听他讲书里的内容。"

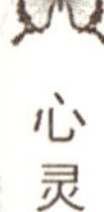

他突然转过身。"对,就是这地方。"他重复道。

他一动不动直挺挺地站在这个小小的旧摊子前。他脱下帽子,夹在腋下。他的大手杖已经掉到了路沟里。他低下头,紧握双手,似乎不知道正在下雨。

市场上方塔楼的钟敲了11下。过路的人停下来,注视着这个陌生人。集市上的人从他们的货摊里看着他。有些人看到雨水从他带有疤痕的老脸上滚滚流下,就笑出了声。是雨水?还是眼泪?

孩子们对他发出了嘲笑声。一些比较粗鲁无礼的孩子甚至示意向他扔泥块;可是,因为感到羞耻,他们就没有动手。

"他是个可怜的疯子。随他去吧。"比较有同情心的人说。

雨落在他的光头上和宽宽的肩膀上。他被雨淋透了,老冷飕飕的。可是,他站在那里一动不动,一声不吭,也不左右张望。

"那个老傻瓜是谁?"一个轻率的年轻人碰巧路过这里时问道。

"你问他是谁?"一个从伦敦来的绅士回答说,"哎呀,他是塞缪尔·约翰逊博士,英国最著名的人。我们当代最伟大的大英语词典就是他编写的。他是英国的文学巨匠。"

"那他为什么来尤托克西特,这样站在倾盆大雨中?"

"我无法告诉你;但毫无疑问,他这样做是有原因的。"说完,这位绅士就继续赶路了。

最后,暴风雨暂时停息。鸟儿在屋顶上叽叽喳喳叫个不停。

市场塔楼的钟敲了12下。这位著名的陌生人在这集市上一动不动地站了整整一个小时。雨又下了起来。

这时,他慢慢地戴上帽子,找到了掉落的手杖。他谦恭地抬了一会儿目光,然后迈着气派而迟缓的步子沿街而行,迎向那辆准备返回利奇菲尔德的马车。

我们尾随他冒着哗哗大雨回到了他的故乡。

"哎呀,约翰逊博士!"女主人大声叫道。"我们整整一天都没见到你了。你都淋成了这个样子,冻坏了吧!你到哪里去了?"

"太太,"这个伟人说。"50年前,就是这一天,我默不做声拒绝给父亲帮忙,也没有听从他的吩咐。从那时起,我就一直想着自己给他造成的痛苦,这使我心神不安。为了结束那时的罪过,我今天早上乘马车去尤托克西特,在父亲从前用过的摊子前当众忏悔。"

这个伟人低下头，双手掩面，哭了起来。

门外正下着雨。

Love Is a Two-Way Street

A father sat at his desk poring over his monthly bills when his young son rushed in and announced, "Dad, because this is your birthday and you're 55 years old, I'm going to give you 55 kisses, one for each year!" When the boy started keeping his word, the father exclaimed, "Oh, Andrew, don't do it now; I'm too busy!"

The youngster immediately fell silent as tears welled up in his big blue eyes. Apologetically, the father said, "You can finish later." The boy said nothing but quietly walked away, disappointed. That evening the father said, "Come and finish the kisses now, Andrew!" But the boy didn't respond.

Unluckily, a few days later, the boy had an accident and was drowned. His heartbroken father wrote, "If only I could tell him how much I regret my thoughtless words, and could be assured that he knows how much my heart is aching."

Love is a two-way street. Any loving act must be warmly accepted or it will be taken as rejection and can leave a scar. If we are too busy to give and receive love, our life will lose its true significance. Nothing is more important than responding with love to the cry for love from those who are near and precious to us.

爱是一条双行道

一位父亲坐在书桌边全神贯注地看每月的账单，这时他的小儿子跑进来大声说道："爸爸，因为今天是你的生日，你55岁了，我要给你55个吻，一年一个！"当男孩准备兑现诺言时，他的父亲大声说道："噢，安德鲁，现在不行，我太忙了！"

小男孩马上静了下来，蓝蓝的大眼睛涌起了泪水。父亲抱歉地说："你待会儿来吻吧。"男孩一声不吭，默默地走开了，感到非常失望。那天晚上，父亲说："来吧，安德鲁，现在来吻吧！"但小男孩没有回答。

不幸的是，几天后，小男孩发生了意外，被淹死了。他的父亲伤心地写道："如果我能告诉他，我是多么后悔自己那些有欠考虑的话，并能确信他知道我现在心里有多么痛苦，该多好啊！"

爱是一条双行道。任何爱的行为都必须热情接受，否则对方会以为你在拒绝而留下伤疤。如果我们太忙而不能给予和接受爱，那我们的生活就失去了真正的意义。对我们身边那些亲近和珍爱的人，用爱去回应他们爱的呼唤，比什么都重要。

I Hear the Love

When I was growing up, I didn't recall hearing the words "I love you" from my father. When your father never says them to you when you are a child, it gets tougher and tougher for him to say those words as he gets older. To tell the truth, I couldn't honestly remember when I had last said those words to him either. I decided to set my ego aside and make the first move. After some hesitation, in our next phone conversation, I blurted out the words, "Dad... I love you!"

There was a silence at the other end and he awkwardly replied, "Well, same back at you!"

I chuckled and said, "Dad, I know you love me, and when you are ready, I know you will say what you want to say."

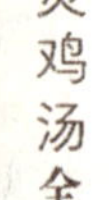

Fifteen minutes later, my mother called and nervously asked, "Paul, is everything okay?"

A few weeks later, Dad concluded our phone conversation with the words, "Paul, I love you." I was at work during this conversation and the tears were rolling down my cheeks as I finally heard the love. As we both sat there in tears we realized that this special moment had taken our father – son relationship to a new level.

A short while after this special moment, my father narrowly escaped death following heart surgery. Many times since, I have pondered the thought if I didn't take the first step and Dad didn't survive the surgery, I would have never heard the love.

我听到了爱

我渐渐长大后，想不起来曾听到过爸爸说"我爱你"这三个字。你小时候，你爸爸从来不你说"我爱你，"那随着他年纪越来越大，他会越来越难开口。说实话，我确实想不起上次我对爸爸说"我爱你"是什么时候了。我决定放下自我，主动表白。犹豫了一阵后，我在我们下一次通话时脱口说道："爸爸……我爱你！"

电话那端沉默了一会儿后，他难为情地答道："噢，对你也一样！"

我暗自笑道："爸爸，我知道你爱我，等你准备好时，我知道你会说出你想说的话的。"

15 分钟后，妈妈打来了电话，不安地问道："保罗，一切正常吧？"

几周后，爸爸在通话结束时说："保罗，我爱你。"通话时我正在上班，听到爱的声音，泪水顺着我的脸颊滑落下来。我们俩都坐在那里热泪盈眶，意识到这种特殊的时刻将我们的父子关系带到了一个新的水平。

在这个特殊时刻过后不久，爸爸做了心脏手术，勉强死里逃生。从那以后，我多次想到，如果我没有迈出第一步、爸爸的手术没有成功，那我就再也听不到爱的声音了。

Homework of Love

In a class I teach for adults, I recently did the "unpardonable." I gave the class homework! The assignment was to "go to someone you love within the next week and tell them you love them. It has to be someone you have never said those words to before or at least haven't shared those words with for a long time."

Now that doesn't sound like a very tough assignment, until you stop to realize that most of the men were over 35 and were raised in the generation of men that were taught that expressing emotions is not "macho." Showing feelings or crying was just not done. So this was a very threatening assignment for some.

At the beginning of our next class, I asked if someone wanted to share what happened when they told someone they loved them. I fully expected one of the women to volunteer, as was usually the case, but on this evening one of the men raised his hand. He appeared quite moved and a bit shaken.

As he unfolded out of his chair, he began by saying, "Dennis, I was quite angry with you last week when you gave us this assignment. I didn't feel that I had anyone to say those words to, and besides, who were you to tell me to do something that personal?

"But as I began driving home my conscience started talking to me. It was telling me that I knew exactly who I needed to say I love you to.

"You see, five years ago, my father and I had a vicious disagreement and really never resolved it since that time. We avoided seeing each other unless we absolutely had to at Christmas or other family gatherings. But even then, we hardly spoke to each other.

"So last Tuesday by the time I got home I had convinced myself I was going to tell my father I loved him.

爱的作业

我最近在教的一个成人班里做了一件“不可宽恕的事情”，给班上学生布置了课外作业！作业是“下周内走到你所爱的人面前，告诉他们你爱他们。必须是以前你从未说过，或至少很久没和他们分享过这些话的人。”

听起来这不像是一份非常费力的作业，而你要认识到这个班里大多数男生已经超过了35岁，而且他们这一代受的教育是在表达情感时缺乏“阳刚之气”。人们不会太流露感情和哭泣。因此，对有些人来说，这是一项让人生畏的作业。

第二次上课时，我首先问：当他们告诉某个人他们爱他/她时，是否有想一同分享。我满以为像平常一样，某位女士会自告奋勇，但这天晚上，一位男士举起了手。他好像很受感动，有点儿颤抖。

他从椅子上直起身来，开始这样说道：“丹尼斯，上周你给我们布置这项作业时，我非常生你的气。我认为我没有什么人需要我说那些话，再说，你是谁，凭什么让我去做这种私事？

“但我驱车回家时，我的良心开始和我对话。它告诉我说，我确实知道需要向谁说‘我爱你’。

“你明白，5年前，我和父亲发生了一场严重的争执，从那以后确实再也没有消除隔阂。除非绝对必须参加圣诞节或其他家庭聚会，我们都互相回避。但即使在那时，我们彼此几乎也不说一句话。

“因此，上周二到家时，我终于说服自己准备告诉父亲说我爱他。”

Daddy's Advice

When I was about 12, I had an enemy, a girl who liked to point out my shortcomings. Week by week her list grew: I was very thin, I was not a good student, I talked too much, I was too proud, and so on. I tried to bear all this as long as I could. At last, I became very angry. I ran to Daddy with tears in my eyes.

He listened to me quietly. Then he asked, "Are the things she says true-or not? Allen, didn't you ever wonder what you're really like? Well, you now have that girl's opinion. Go and make a list of everything she said and mark the points that are true. Pay no attention to the other things she said."

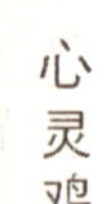

I did as he told me. To my great surprise, I discovered that about half the things were true. Some of them I couldn't change (like being very thin), but a good number I could—and suddenly I wanted to change. For the first time I got a fairly clear picture of myself.

I brought the list back to Daddy. He refused to take it. "That's just for you," he said. "You know better than anyone else the truth about yourself. But you have to learn to listen, not just closing your ears in anger and feeling hurt. When something said about you is true, you'll find it will be of help to you. Our world is full of people who think they know your duty. don't shut your ears. Listen to them all, but hear the truth and do what you know is the right thing to do."

Daddy's advice has returned to me at many important moments. In my life, I've never had a better piece of advice.

爸爸的忠告

大约 12 岁时，我有了一个对手，那是一个喜欢指出我缺点的女孩。随着一周周过去，她给我列的缺点越来越多：我很瘦，我不是好学生，我太爱说话，我太骄傲。我尽量长时间地忍受这些。最后，我变得非常生气，就眼含泪水跑去见爸爸。

爸爸静静地听我说。随后，他问道："她说的这些是不是真的？爱琳，难道你不想知道自己的真实模样吗？那么，你现在有了那个女孩的意见。去把她所说的一切都列下来，在对的上面打分。对她所说的其他事情不要在意。"

我按照爸爸说的去做了。令我大为惊讶的是，我发现大约一半都是对的。其中有些我无法改变（比如很瘦），但好多我可以改变——而且突然我想改变。我第一次对自己有了一个相当清晰的印象。

我将这个清单送给了爸爸。他没有去接。"那只是送给你的，"他说。"你比任何别的人更清楚自己真实的一面。但你必须学会去听，不要生气地闭上耳朵，感觉受到了伤害。当说到有关你的事情是对时，你会发现那会对你有帮助。我们的世界充满了自以为他们知道你的责任的人。不要闭上耳朵。要听他们所有的人的话，但要听到真话，做你知道是正确的事情。"

爸爸的建议在很多重要的时刻都回到了我的耳边。在我的一生中，我从来没有听过比这更好的建议了。

My Father's Music

That day Dad gathered my mother and me in the living room and opened the case as if it were a treasure chest. "Here it is," he said. "Once you learn to play, it'll stay with you for life."

For the next two weeks, the accordion was stored in the hall closet. Then one evening Dad announced that I would start lessons the following week. In disbelief I shot my eyes toward Mom for support. The firm set of her jaw told me I was out of luck.

Shortly after, my lessons began with Mr. Zelli at the Allegro Accordion School, tucked between an old movie theatre and a pizza parlor. On my first day, with straps straining my shoulders, I felt clumsy in every way. "How did he do?" my father asked when it was over. "Fine for the first lesson," said Mr. Zelli. Dad glowed with hope.

I was ordered to practice half an hour every day, and every day I tried to get out of it. My future seemed to be outside playing ball, not in the house mastering songs I would soon forget. But my parents hounded me to practice.

Gradually, to my surprise, I was able to string notes together and coordinate my hands to play simple songs. Often, after supper, my father would request a tune or two. As he sat in his easy chair, I would fumble through "*Lady of Spain*" and "*Beer Barrel Polka*".

"Very nice, better than last week," he'd say. Then I would segue into a medley of his favorites, "*Red River Valley*" and "*Home on the Range*", and he would drift off to sleep, the newspaper folded on his lap. I took it as a compliment that he could relax under the spell of my playing.

One July evening I was giving an almost flawless rendition of "*Come Back to Sorrento*", and my parents called me to an open window. An elderly neighbor, rarely seen outside her house, was leaning against our car humming dreamily to the tune. When I finished, she smiled broadly and called out, "I remember that song as a child in Italy. Beautiful, just beautiful."

Throughout the summer, Mr. Zelli's lessons grew more difficult. It took me a week and a half to master them now. All the while I could hear my buddies outside playing heated games of stickball.

The fall recital was impending.

"I don't want to play a solo," I said in a car one Sunday afternoon.

"You have to," replied my father.

"Why?" I shouted. "Because you didn't get to play your violin when you were a kid? Why should I have to play this stupid instrument when you never had to play yours?"

Dad pulled the car over and pointed at me.

"Because you can bring people joy. You can touch their hearts. That's a gift I won't let you throw away." he added softly, "Someday you'll have the chance I never had: you'll play beautiful music for your family. And you'll understand why you've worked so hard."

The evening of the concert Mom wore glittery earrings and more makeup than I could remember. Dad got out of work early, put on a suit and tie, and slicked down his chair. They were ready an hour early. I got the unspoken message that playing this one song was a dream come true for them.

At the theater nervousness overtook me as I realized how much I wanted to make my parents proud. Finally, it was my turn. I walked to the lone chair on stage and performed "*Are You Lonesome Tonight?*" without a mistake. The applause spilled out.

After the concert Mom and Dad came backstage. The way they walked—heads high, faces flushed—I knew they were pleased. My mother gave me a big hug. Dad slipped an arm around me and held me close. "You were just great," he said. Then he shook my hand and was slow to let it go.

As the years went by, the accordion drifted to the background of my life. Dad asked me to play at family occasions, but the lessons stopped. When I went to college, the accordion stayed behind in the hall closet next to my father's violin.

A year after my graduation, my parents moved to a house in a nearby town. Dad, at 51, finally owned his own home. On moving day, I didn't have the heart to tell him he could dispose of the

accordion, so I brought it my own home and put it in the attic.

There it remained, a dusty memory, until one afternoon several years later when my two children discovered it by accident. Scott thought it was a secret treasure; Holly thought a ghost lived inside. They were both right.

When I opened the case, they laughed and said, "Play it, play it." Reluctantly, I strapped on the accordion and played some simple songs. I was surprised my skills hadn't rusted away. Soon the kids were dancing in circles and giggling. Even my wife, Terri, was laughing and clapping to the beat. I was amazed at their unbridled glee.

My father's words came back to me: "Someday you'll have the chance I never had. Then you'll understand."

I finally knew what it meant to work hard and sacrifice for others. Dad had been right all along: the most precious gift is to touch the hearts of those you love.

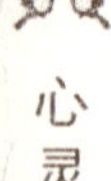

Later I phoned Dad to let him know that, at long last, I understood. Fumbling for the right words, I thanked him for the legacy it took almost 30 years to discover. "You're welcome," he said, his voice choked with emotion.

Dad never learned to coax sweet sounds from his violin. Yet he was wrong to think he would never play for his family. On that wonderful evening, as my wife and children laughed and danced, they heard my accordion. But it was my father's music.

父亲的音乐

那天父亲把我和母亲叫到了客厅，打开了那个百宝箱似的盒子。“给，”他说。“一旦你学会弹奏，它就会伴随你的一生。”

接下来的两个星期，手风琴一直放在门厅的壁橱里。后来的一天晚上，父亲宣布我下星期开始学习手风琴课程。我将信将疑地把目光投向妈妈寻求支持。她坚定的下巴告诉我，我并不走运。

不久以后，我便跟着泽利先生在位于一家旧电影院和比萨馆之间的阿里格罗手风琴学校开始了学琴。上课的第一天，带子勒得我的肩膀紧绷绷的，处处使我感到笨笨的。“他做得怎么样?”上完课时，父亲问。“第一次上课，不错。”泽利先生神采奕奕、充满希望地说。

泽利先生要求我每天得练习半小时，而每天我都想竭力从中摆脱。我的未来似乎是在外面打球，而不是待在屋子里掌握我总是很快就会忘记的歌曲。但我的父母亲硬是逼着我去练习。

渐渐地，让我吃惊的是，我已经能将音符拉到一起，协调双手弹奏出简单的歌曲了。晚饭后，父亲总是时不时地要我拉一两个曲子。他坐在安乐椅里，我总是笨拙地拉《西班牙女郎》和《啤酒桶波尔卡》。

他总是说:“非常不错，比上星期好。”随后，我会接着拉起他最喜欢的《红河谷》和《山上人家》的混合曲。之后，他总会慢慢地睡去，报纸叠放在他的膝间。我把这看成是一种赞美:他能在我拉手风琴时得以放松。

7 月的一个傍晚，我正拉着几乎无可挑剔的《回到索伦托》，父母亲把我叫到了一个敞开的窗前。一位上了年纪、很少出门的邻居正靠在我们家的汽车上合着旋律如梦般哼唱着。我拉完后，她露出了灿烂的微笑，大声说道:“我记得小时候是在意大利听的这首歌曲。真美妙,美妙极了。”

整整一个夏天,泽利先生的课变得越来越难了。我现在要花一个半星期才能掌握。与此同时,我总能听见外面我的小伙伴们在热火朝天地打棍球。

然而,秋季独奏会马上就要到了。

“我不想去演独奏曲,”一个星期天的下午,我在汽车里对父亲说。

“你必须去演奏,”父亲答道。

“为什么?”我嚷道。“就是因为你小时候没学会拉小提琴吗?你从来不必拉小提琴,我为什么必须拉这愚蠢的乐器?”

父亲停住车,指着我。

“因为你能给人们带来快乐,触动他们的心灵。那是我不愿意让你抛弃的天赋。”他轻轻地补充说,“终有一天,你会获得我从未抓住的机会:为你的家人演奏美妙的音乐。而且你会明白你曾如此努力的理由。”

独奏会那天晚上,母亲戴着亮闪闪的耳环,用的化妆品比我能记得的任何时候都多。父亲早早下班,穿上西装,打上领带,将头发梳得溜光水滑。他们提前一小时就准备停当。我感到此时无声胜有声:拉这首歌曲是实现他们的一次梦想。

一到剧院,我一想到我多想让父母亲骄傲,就感到一阵紧张。最后,终于该我上台了。我走向台上那张孤零零的椅子,分毫不差地演奏了《今晚你孤单吗?》。全场爆发出了阵阵掌声。

独奏会后,爸妈来到了后台。一瞧他们走路的姿态——昂首阔步、红光满面——我就知道他们非常高兴。母亲紧紧地拥抱了我一下。父亲伸出一只胳膊抱住我,将我紧紧地搂住。“你真了不起,”他说,随后握住我的手久久不肯松开。

随着岁月流逝,那只手风琴渐渐退到了我生活的背后。每逢家庭聚会,父亲总是要让我拉几段,但不再上手风琴课了。我上大学时,那只手风琴退到了门厅壁橱里,与父亲的小提琴放在了一起。

我毕业一年后,父母亲搬到了附近城镇的一座房子里。51岁的父亲最后终于拥有了自己的家。搬家那天,我不忍心对他说,他可以处理掉那把手风琴,所以我把它带到了我自己的家里,放在了阁楼上。

那成了一段尘封的记忆,直到几年后的一天下午,我的两个孩子无意间发现了它。斯科特认为它是一笔秘密财宝,赫利想着里面住着一个幽灵。他们俩都猜对了。

我打开箱子时,他们都大笑着说:“拉一段,拉一段。”我勉强挎上手风琴,拉了一些简单的歌曲。让我吃惊的是,我的演技并没有荒废。很快,孩子们便围成圈翩翩起舞,格格直笑。就连我的妻子泰丽也随着节拍拍手大笑。我对他们无拘无束的欢快劲儿感到惊喜。

父亲的话语又回荡在我的耳边:“终有一天,你会获得我从未抓住的机会,以后你会明白的。”

我终于懂得了为他人做出努力和牺牲意味着什么。父亲一直都是对的:最珍贵的礼物是触动你所爱的那些人的心灵。

后来,我给父亲打电话说,我终于懂了。我字斟句酌感谢他让我花了差不多30年才

发现的遗产。“别客气，”他说，他的声音因激动而哽咽。

父亲从未学会用小提琴奏出甜美的旋律。然而，他错误地认为他永远都不会为他的家人演奏曲子。在那个美妙的夜晚，当我的妻子和孩子们欢笑起舞时，她们听到了我拉的手风琴曲。不过，那是父亲的音乐。

The Unlighted Candle

A man had a little daughter—an only and much-loved child. He lived for her—she was his life. So when she became ill, he became like a man possessed, moving heaven and earth to bring about her restoration to health.

His best efforts, however, proved unavailing and the child died. The father became a bitter recluse, shutting himself away from his many friends and refusing every activity that might restore his poise and bring him back to his normal self. But one night he had a dream.

He was in Heaven, witnessing a grand pageant of all the little child angels. They were marching in a line passing by the Great White Throne. Every white-robed angelic child carried a candle. He noticed that one child's candle was not lighted. Then he saw that the child with the dark candle was his own little girl. Rushing to her, he seized her in his arms, caressed her tenderly, and then asked, "How is it, darling, that your candle alone is unlighted?" "Daddy, they often relight it, but your tears always put it out."

Just then he awoke from his dream. The lesson was crystal-clear, and its effects were immediate. From that hour on he was not a recluse, but mingled freely and cheerfully with his former friends and associates. No longer would his darling's candle be extinguished by his useless tears.

点不亮的蜡烛

一个男人有一个小女儿，那是唯一的孩子，他深深地爱着她，为她而活，她就是他的生命。所以，当女儿生病时，他像疯了一般竭尽全力想让她恢复健康。

然而，他所有的努力都无济于事，女儿还是死了。父亲变得痛苦遁世，避开了许多朋友，拒绝参加一切能使他恢复平静、回到自我的活动。但有一天夜里，他做了一个梦。

他到了天堂，看到所有的小天使正在举行盛大的游行。她们列队经过大白宝座，每一个小天使都身穿白色天使衣，手里拿着一根蜡烛。他注意到有一个小天使的蜡烛没有点亮。随后，他看到那个拿着没有点亮烛的小天使是自己的小儿。他奔过去，一把将女儿抱在怀里，亲切地爱抚着她，然后问道：“宝贝儿，为什么只有你的蜡烛没有点亮呢？”“爸爸，他们经常重新点亮蜡烛，可你的眼泪总是把它熄灭。”

就在这时，他从梦中醒来。梦给他上的一课像水晶般透明，而且立竿见影。从那个时刻起，他再也不消极遁世了，而是自由自在、兴高采烈地回到了从前的朋友和同事们中间。宝贝女儿的蜡烛再也没有被他无用的眼泪熄灭过。

有爱就有奇迹

Please Let Me Have a Little World

Please, my dear husband, be so generous as to let me have a little world of my own. If you find me scrawling on a piece of paper, please don't peep over my shoulders. It may be that I'm venting some pent-up feelings, long denied expression, or trying to compose a little poem not yet presentable for the time being, or attempting to sketch out something visualized from my childhood memories which glows in my mind like a rainbow. When I am in such a mood, please leave me alone and let me write as the pen dictates.

Don't disturb me, my dear, when I get nostalgic over some old photos or letters which bring tears to my eyes or smiles on my lips, for those were things that had happened to me before I met you, the joys and sorrows, partings and reunions that taste like green olive or glitter like scattered pearls. They are my cherished memories which, ready as I am to share with you, I would like to indulge in by myself for a while.

I hope you won't mind when I go without you for a nice chat with a close friend of mine. You are my bosom friend, but you cannot take the place of other friends any more than they can do yours. I need their care, encouragement and sobering criticism just as I do yours. A starless sky with a solitary moon would be dull and cheerless, why not let there be a moonlit night resplendent with twinkling stars?

I may occasionally want to make a tour of faraway places. Please don't hold me back when I start packing for it. You are the center of my life, but certainly not the whole of it. I yearn to see the mysteries and wonders of the world miles away beyond the mountains; so let me have a chance to explore my "Alice's Wonderland" as a "lone ranger". Some time later when I come back to you with exotic experiences and fresh insights, I'm sure you will look at me in a new light.

My dear husband, so long as you let me have such a little, little world, I'll be very much indebted to you.

请让我有一个小小的世界

亲爱的丈夫，请慷慨大方地让我有一个小小的世界。如果你发现我在纸上龙飞凤舞时，请不要在我身后窥视。那也许是我在发泄某种闷在心里、久未诉说的情感，也许是在设法构思一首暂时还拿不出手的小诗，也许是在试图勾勒某件仍在我脑海里像彩虹一般闪光的童年往事。当我处于这种心情时，请不要管我，让我诉诸笔端。

亲爱的，当我对着一些老照片或书信沉思、落泪或微笑，怀旧之情油然而生时，不要打扰我。因为那是我遇到你之前发生的一些事——那些悲欢离合就像青橄榄一样，或者像散落的珍珠闪闪发光。它们是珍藏在我心里的记忆，尽管我情愿和你共同分享，但我还是想独自在这些往事中沉湎一会儿。

当我一个人出去同一位密友神侃时，我希望你不要介意。你是我的知己，但你不能代替我的其他朋友，他们也不能代替你。我需要他们的关心、鼓励和冷静的批评，就像我需要你这样做那样。没有星星只有月亮的夜空多么乏味无趣，何不让我有一个繁星闪烁、月光如华的夜空？

我也许偶尔想去远处旅游。当我开始打点行囊时，请不要拦我。你是我生活的中心，但肯定不是我的全部。我渴望看看群山外面世界的奇妙景观，所以让我有机会作为

"独行侠"去探索自己的"爱丽丝仙境"。过一段时间,当我带着奇异的经历和新的见识回到你身边时,我相信你会对我刮目相看。

亲爱的丈夫,只要你让我有这样一个小小的世界,我就会对你感激不尽。

Love Is Understanding

As a new bride, one woman moved into the small home on her husband's ranch in the mountains. She put a shoebox on a shelf in her closet and asked her husband never to touch it.

For 50 years he left the box alone until his life partner was old and dying. One day, when he was putting their things in order, he found the box again and thought it might hold something important. Opening it, he discovered two doilies and $82,500 in cash. He took the box to her and asked about the two things.

"My mother gave me that box the day we married," she explained. "She told me to make a doily to help ease myself every time I got angry at you."

Her husband was touched, for in 50 years she'd only been angry enough to make two doilies.

"What's the $82,500 for?" he asked.

She explained, "Oh, that's the money I've made selling the doilies."

Marge Piercy beautifully said, "Everyone will get three gifts in life. Life is the first gift, love is the second and understanding is the third." But it is love that gives us life and understanding that brings about love.

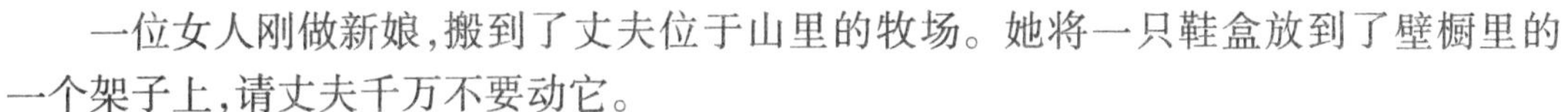

爱就是谅解

一位女人刚做新娘,搬到了丈夫位于山里的牧场。她将一只鞋盒放到了壁橱里的一个架子上,请丈夫千万不要动它。

50年来,他没有动过那只盒子,直到他的人生伴侣老态龙钟、奄奄一息。有一天,他在整理他们的东西时,又发现了那只盒子,想着那里面可能会装有一些重要东西。他打开盒子,发现有两块花边桌垫和82500美元现金。他把盒子拿到她跟前,问这些东西是怎么回事。

"那个盒子是咱们结婚那天母亲送给我的,"她解释说。"她让我每次生你的气时做一块花边桌垫来帮我消气。"她的丈夫很受感动,因为50年里她只做了两块花边桌垫。"这82500美元是做什么用的?"他又问道。她解释说:"噢,那是我卖花边桌垫赚的钱。"

玛奇·皮尔西说得好:"每个人一生都会收到三件礼物。生命是第一件礼物,爱是第二件礼物,谅解是第三件礼物。"而正是爱给了我们生命,正是谅解产生了爱。

The Love in the Telescope

There were two lovers. The man was so cowardly that he always let the girlfriend try first no matter what they would do. His girlfriend was so dissatisfied with that.

Once they went out to sea. On returning their skiff was wrecked by the hurricane. Luckily, the girlfriend held a plank to save their lives. The girlfriend asked her boyfriend, "Do you fear?" The boyfriend took out a fruit knife and said, "Yes, but if any shark comes I can cope with it with this." His girlfriend only shook her head with a wry smile.

Soon the people on a freighter spotted them. When they were wild with joy, a shoal of sharks appeared. His girlfriend screamed out, "Let's swim hard together and we'll be alright!"

But her boyfriend suddenly shoved the girl into the sea and held the plank and shouted to the freighter by himself, "Let me try first this time!"

Stunned, his girlfriend looked at her boyfriend from behind, feeling extremely desperate. The sharks were drawing near, but they were not interested in the girl and swam straight to the boy.

When he was torn and bitten fiercely by the sharks, the boyfriend wildly shouted to his girlfriend, "I love you!"

The girl was saved. All the people on the deck were standing in silent tribute. The captain sat beside the girl and said, "Miss, he is the bravest man I have ever seen. Let's pray for him!"

"No! He is a coward," said the girl coldly.

"How could you say like this? I have just been watching you through the telescope. I saw clearly he cut his wrist with the knife after shoving you away. The sharks are very sensitive to the blood. If he hadn't done this to buy time, I'm afraid you would never appear on this ship..."

望远镜里的爱

有一对情侣，男的非常懦弱，无论做什么事都让女友先试。女友对此十分不满。

有一次，两人出海。返航时，飓风摧毁了小艇。幸亏，女友抓住了一块木板才保住了两人的性命。女友问男友："你怕吗？"男友从怀中掏出一把水果刀，说："怕，但有鲨鱼来，我就用这个对付它。"女友只是摇头苦笑。

不久，一艘货轮发现了他们。正当他们欣喜若狂时，一群鲨鱼出现了。女友大叫："我们一起用力游，会没事的！"

男友却突然用力将女友推进海里，独自扒着木板，朝货轮喊道："这次我先试！"

女友惊呆了，望着男友的背影，感到非常绝望。鲨鱼正在靠近，可对女友不感兴趣，径直向男友游去。

男友被鲨鱼凶猛地撕咬着，他发疯似地冲女友喊道："我爱你！"

女友获救了。甲板上的人都在默哀。船长坐到女孩身边说："小姐，他是我见过最勇敢的人。我们为他祈祷！"

"不，他是个胆小鬼。"女孩冷冷地说。

"你怎么这样说呢？刚才我一直用望远镜观察你们，我清楚地看到他把你推开后用刀子割破了自己的手腕。鲨鱼对血腥味很敏感，如果他不这样做来争取时间，恐怕你永远不会出现在这艘船上……"

Roses for Paradise

Red roses were her favorites, her name was also Rose. And every year her husband sent them, tied with pretty bows. The year he died, the roses were delivered to her door. The card said, "Be my Valentine," like all the years before.

Each year he sent her roses, and the note would always say, "I love you even more this year, than last year on this day." "My love for you will always grow, with every passing year." She knew this was the last time that the roses would appear. She thought, he ordered roses in advance before this day. Her loving husband didn't know, that he would pass away. He always liked to do things early. Then, if he got too busy, everything would work out fine. She trimmed the stems, and placed them in a very special vase. Then, sat the vase beside the portrait of his smiling face. She would sit for hours, in her husband's favorite chair, staring at his picture with the roses sitting there.

A year went by, and it was hard to live without her mate. With loneliness and solitude, that had become her fate. Then, the very hour, as on Valentines before, the doorbell rang, and there were roses, sitting by her door. She brought the roses in, and then just looked at them in shock. Then, she went to get the telephone, to call the florist shop. The owner answered, and she asked him, if he would explain why would someone do this to her, causing her such pain.

"I know your husband passed away, more than a year ago," The owner said, "I knew you'd call, and you would want to know. The flowers you received today were paid for in advance. Your husband always planned ahead, he left nothing to chance.

"There is a standing order that I have on file down here. And he has paid, well in advance, you'll get them every year. There also is another thing that I think you should know. He wrote a special little card... he did this years ago.

"Then, should ever, I find out that he's no longer here. That's the card... that should be sent, to you the following year."

She thanked him and hung up the phone, her tears now flowing hard. Her fingers were shaking as she slowly reached to get the card. Inside the card, she saw that he had written her a note. As she stared in total silence, this was what he wrote: "Hello my love, I know it's been a year since I've been gone. I hope it hasn't been too hard for you to overcome. I know it must be lonely, and the pain is very real. For if it was the other way, I know how I would feel. The love we shared made everything so beautiful in life. I loved you more than words can say. You were the perfect wife.

"You were my friend and lover. You fulfilled my every need. I know it's only been a year, but please try not to grieve. I want you to be happy, even when you shed your tears. That is why the roses will be sent to you for years.

"When you get these roses, think of all the happiness that we had together, and how both of us were blessed. I have always loved you and I know I always will. But, my love, you must go on, you have some living still.

"Please... try to find happiness, while living out your days. I know it is not easy, but I hope you find some ways. The roses will come every year, and they will only stop when your door's not answered, when the florist stops to knock.

"He will come five times that day, in case you have gone out. But after his last visit, he will know without a doubt. To take the roses to the place where I've instructed him, and place them where we are, together once again."

天堂玫瑰

红玫瑰是她的最爱，她的名字也叫 Rose。每年她的丈夫都要送她系有漂亮蝴蝶结的红玫瑰。他去世那年，玫瑰花送到了她的门口，卡片上像往年那样写着："做我的爱人吧。"

每年他送给她红玫瑰，字条上总是这样说："今年我更爱你，比去年的今天更爱。""随着岁月的流逝，我对你的爱总是与日俱增。"她知道这是她最后一次收到玫瑰花。她想，他是提前订了玫瑰花。她的爱夫不知道，他将离去。他总喜欢提前做事。这样，如果他太忙，一切都会搞定。她整理好花茎，然后把它们插进一只非常特别的花瓶里，然后将花瓶放在了他微微含笑的相片旁边。她常常在丈夫最喜欢的椅子上坐上几个小时，望着他的相片，玫瑰花就放在那里。

一年过去了，没有他的日子很难过。孤独和寂寞成了她的生活。随后，在情人节这天那个非常时刻，门铃像以前一样响了起来，她的门边放着玫瑰花。她将玫瑰花拿进屋里，然后就那样震惊地看着它们。接下来，她走到电话边，给花店打去了电话。她问店主能否向她解释一下，为什么有人要这样做，引起她如此的痛苦。

"我知道你的丈夫一年多前就去世了，"店主说。"我就知道你会打电话，而且你想知道是怎么回事。今天你收到的那些鲜花已经提前付了钱。你的丈夫总是提前计划，从来不去碰运气。

"我的档案里有一个长期订单，他早已提前付了钱，你每年都会收到玫瑰花。还有一件事，我想你应该知道。他写了一张特别的小卡片……是他几年前就写好的。

"这样，如果我发现他已不在人世，这张卡片……这张卡片将会在下一年送给你。"

她向他表示感谢，就挂了电话，此时她泪如泉涌。她一边慢慢伸手去拿卡片，手指一边在颤抖。他在卡片里看到了他写给她的短信。她默默地看着，信是这样写的："喂，我的宝贝，我知道我离去已经一年了，我希望你度过的这段日子不是太难。我知道这段日子肯定很孤独，而且确实非常痛苦。因为如果这种事发生在我身上，我知道我会有怎样的感受。我们曾经分享的爱使生命中的每件事都是那样美好。我对你的爱难以言表，你是最完美的妻子。

"你是我的朋友和爱人，你满足我的每个需要。我知道才过了一年，请尽量不要悲伤。我想让你快乐，即使你流着泪。这就是今后的岁月每年都会给你送玫瑰的原因。

"你收到这些玫瑰花时，想一想我们一起度过的所有幸福时光，还有我们俩是何等幸福。我一直爱着你，我知道我永远爱你。可是，亲爱的，你必须继续下去，你还有一些时日。

"请……在你的生活中努力找到欢乐，我知道并不容易，但我希望你能找到一些方法。玫瑰花每年都会送来，只有花店店主停下来去敲门，你不再开门，它们才会停止。

"这天他会来5次，以防你出门。你是不是还在，他最后一次拜访就会明白。他会将那些玫瑰花送到我指定的地方，并将它们放在我们再次相聚的地方。"

The Unopened CD

There was once a kid who suffered from an incurable cancer. He was 18 years old and he could die anytime.

One day he was walking down his block when he noticed a beautiful girl about his age in a CD store and he knew it was love at first sight. He opened the door and walked in, not looking at anything else but her.

She looked up and asked, "Can I help you?"

She smiled and he thought it was the most beautiful smile he has ever seen before.

He said, "Uh... Yeah... I would like to buy a CD."

He picked one out and gave her money for it.

"Would you like me to wrap it for you?" she asked, smiling her cute smile again.

He nodded and she went to the back. She came back with the wrapped CD and gave it to him.

From then on he went to that store every day and bought a CD, and she wrapped it for him. He took the CD home and put it in his closet. He was still too shy to ask her out and he really wanted to but he couldn't.

His mother found out about this and told him to just ask her. So the next day, he took all his courage and went to the store as usual. He bought a CD like he did every day and once again she went to the back of the store and came back with it wrapped. He took it and when she was not looking, he left his phone number on the desk and ran out.

One day the phone rang, and the mother picked it up and said, "Hello?"

It was the girl! The mother started to cry and said, "You don't know? He passed away yesterday..."

The line was quiet except for the cries of the boy's mother. Later in the day, the mother was surprised to find piles and piles of unopened CDs in the boy's closet and inside the wrappers, she found a piece of paper saying, "Hi... I think you are really cute. Do you wanna go out with me? Love, Jocelyn."

没有打开的 CD

有一个少年患了无法医治的癌症。他才 18 岁，随时都可能会死去。

一天，他正顺着街区走，突然注意到一家 CD 店里有一个漂亮的同龄女孩，他知道他对她是一见钟情。他打开门，走了进去，始终望着她一个人。

女孩抬起头，问道："你想要买什么？"

她微微一笑，他认为这是他以前从未见过的最美丽的微笑。

他说："呃……是的……我想买一张 CD。"

他选了一张 CD，然后向她付了钱。

"你想让我为你包起来吗？"她又露出可爱的微笑问道。

他点点头，她走到后台。她出来时，手里拿着包装好的 CD，递给了他。

从那以后，他每天都会去那家 CD 店买一张 CD，她每次都为他包好。他把 CD 带回家，将它放进自己的壁橱。他仍然太害羞，不敢请她出来，他真的很想这样做，却又不能。

他的母亲发现了他这个秘密，告诉他去请她就行了。于是，第二天，他鼓足勇气，像

往常一样走进了那家CD店,他像每天所做的那样买了一张CD。她再一次到后台,为他包装好交给他。他接过CD,趁她不注意时,他把自己的电话号码留在柜台上,跑了出去。

一天,电话铃响了,母亲拿起电话,说:"喂?"

正是那个女孩!母亲开始哭了起来,她说:"你不知道吗?他昨天走了……"

电话线那端沉默了,只听到男孩母亲的哭声。那天晚些时候,男孩母亲吃惊地发现儿子的壁橱里有一大堆一大堆没有打开的CD,在这些包装纸里,她发现了一张纸,上面写道:"嗨……我想你确实可爱。你想和我一起出去吗?爱你的乔斯林。"

A Gift of Light

The passengers on the bus watched sympathetically as the attractive young woman with the white cane made her way carefully up the steps. She paid the driver, and using her hands to feel the location of the seats, walked down the aisle and found the seat he'd told her was empty. Then she settled in, placed her briefcase on her lap and rested her cane against her leg.

It had been a year since Susan, thirty-four, became blind. Due to a medical misdiagnosis she had been rendered sightless, and she was suddenly thrown into a world of darkness, anger, frustration and self-pity.

Once a fiercely independent woman, Susan now felt condemned by this terrible twist of fate to become a powerless, helpless burden on everyone around her. "How could this have happened to me?" But no matter how much she cried or ranted or prayed, she knew the painful truth—her sight was never going to return.

A cloud of depression hung over Susan. Just getting through each day was an exercise in frustration and exhaustion. And all she had to cling to was her husband Mark.

Mark was an Air Force officer and he loved Susan with all his heart. When she first lost her sight, he watched her sink into despair and was determined to help his wife gain the strength and confidence. Mark's military background had trained him well to deal with sensitive situations, and yet he knew this was the most difficult battle he would ever face.

Finally, Susan felt ready to return to her job, but how would she get there? She used to take the bus, but was now too frightened to get around the city by herself. Mark volunteered to drive her to work each day, even though they worked at opposite ends of the city. At first, this comforted Susan and fulfilled Mark's need to protect his sightless wife.

Soon, however, Mark realized that this arrangement was not working—it was hectic, and costly. Susan is going to have to start taking the bus again, he admitted to himself. But just the thought of mentioning it to her made him cringe. She was still so fragile. How would she react?

Just as Mark predicted, Susan was horrified at the idea of taking the bus again. "I'm blind!" she responded bitterly. "How am I supposed to know where I'm going? I feel like you're abandoning me." Mark's heart broke at these words, but he knew what had to be done. He promised Susan that each morning and evening he would ride the bus with her until she got the hang of it.

For two solid weeks, Mark accompanied Susan to and from work each day. He taught her how to rely on her other senses especially her hearing, to determine where she was and how to adapt to her new environment. He helped her befriend the bus drivers who could watch out for her and save her a seat.

He made her laugh. Each morning they made the journey together, and Mark would take a cab back to his office.

Although this routine was even more costly and exhausting than the previous one, Mark knew it was only a matter of time before Susan would be able to ride the bus on her own. He believed in her, in the Susan he used to know before she'd lost her sight, who was not afraid of any challenge and who would never, ever quit.

Finally, Susan decided that she was ready to try the trip on her own.

Monday morning arrived, and before she left, she threw her arms around Mark. Her eyes filled with tears of gratitude for his loyalty, his patience and his love. She said goodbye, and for the first time, they went their separate ways.

Monday, Tuesday, Wednesday and Thursday—each day on her own went perfectly, and Susan had never felt better. She was doing it! She was going to work all by herself!

On Friday morning, Susan took the bus as usual. As she was paying for her fare to exit the bus, the driver said, "Boy, I sure envy you."

Susan was not sure if the driver was speaking to her or not. Who would ever envy a blind woman who had struggled just to find the courage to live the past year?

Curious she asked the driver, "Why do you say that you envy me?"

The driver responded, "It must feel so good to be taken care of and protected like you are."

Susan had no idea what the driver was talking about, and asked again, "What do you mean?"

The driver answered, "You know, every morning for the past week, a fine-looking gentleman in a military uniform has been standing across the corner watching you when you get off the bus. He makes sure you cross the street safely and he watches you until you enter your office building. Then he blows you a kiss, and gives you a little salute and walks away. You are one lucky lady."

Tears of happiness poured down Susan's cheeks, for although she couldn't physically see him, she had always felt Mark's presence. She was lucky, for he had given her a gift more powerful than sight, a gift of love that can bring light where there had been darkness.

光明的礼物

一个年轻漂亮的女人拄着一根白色拐杖，小心翼翼地迈上公共汽车时，车上的乘客都同情地望着。她给司机付了钱，双手摸着找到了座位的位置，然后顺着过道走到司机说的空位上坐下来，把公文包放在腿上，将拐杖靠在了她的腿边。

苏珊今年34岁，已经失明一年了。误诊导致她失明，她被突然甩进了一个黑暗、愤怒、沮丧和自怜的世界。

苏珊曾是一个特立独行的女人。她现在感到，命运的阴差阳错使她成了一个无能为力、无依无靠的人，成了周围每个人的负担。"为什么这种事会发生在我身上?"但不管她怎样哭叫、咆哮或祈祷，她都明白一个痛苦的事实——她将无法重见光明。

沮丧之气笼罩在苏珊头上。她每天都在挫折和疲惫中度过，她唯一的依靠就是丈夫马克。

马克是一名空军军官，他一心一意爱着苏珊。苏珊刚失明时，马克看到她陷入了绝望。他决心帮助妻子获得力量和自信。马克受过军事训练，懂得如何处理各种敏感情况，但他知道这次是他最难面对的一次战役。

苏珊终于感到可以重新工作了，可她如何去上班呢？以前她是坐公共汽车上班，现在她非常害怕，不敢自己一个人在市里走动。马克主动提出每天开车送她上下班，纵使他们分别在城市两端上班。起先，这样做让苏珊很舒心，同时也了却了马克需要保护失明妻子的心愿。

然而,不久,马克认识到这样安排不行——既紧张又浪费。他承认,苏珊必须重新坐公共汽车上班。但一想到要向苏珊提这件事,马克又退缩了。她仍是那样脆弱。她会做何反应呢?

正如马克所料,听到要再次坐公共汽车上班,苏珊目瞪口呆。她痛苦地说:“我是瞎子,怎么知道我要去哪里呀?我感到你是要抛弃我。”听到这些话,马克伤心欲裂,但他知道必须这样做。他答应苏珊每天早上和傍晚都会陪她一起坐公共汽车,直到她习惯坐公共汽车。

整整两周,马克每天都陪苏珊上下班。他教苏珊如何依靠自己的其他感官(尤其是听力),去确定自己所在的位置,如何去适应新环境。他让苏珊和公共汽车司机成为朋友,因为司机可以关照她,给她留座位。

马克总是逗她笑。每天早上他们都一起坐公共汽车,然后马克乘出租车回办公室。

虽然这个程序比先前那个更贵、更累人,但马克知道苏珊能独立坐公共汽车,只是时间问题。他相信她,相信以前那个没有失明的苏珊,一个不怕任何挑战的苏珊,一个绝不放弃的苏珊。

终于,苏珊决定准备试着独自坐车上下班了。

星期一早上到了,苏珊离开前,抱住马克。她的眼里充满了感激的泪水,她对丈夫的忠诚、耐心和爱感激不尽。她道别后,他们第一次走向了不同的方向。

星期一、星期二、星期三、星期四——她独自上班的每一天都顺顺当当,苏珊从来没有感觉这么好过。她成功了!她要独自坐公共汽车上班了!

星期五早上,苏珊跟往常一样坐公共汽车,当她要付费给司机准备下车时,那位司机说:“噢,我真羡慕你。”

苏珊拿不准司机是不是跟她说话。谁会去羡慕一个过去一年都在苦苦挣扎寻找勇气的盲女人呢?

出于好奇,苏珊向司机问道:“你为什么说羡慕我呢?”

司机回答说:“像你那样得到照顾和保护感觉一定很棒。”

苏珊不明白司机在说什么,又问道:“你这话什么意思?”

司机回答说:“你知道,在过去的一周里,有一个穿军服的英俊先生一直站在街角对面,目不转睛地望着你下车。他确保你安全穿过马路,直到目送你走进办公楼,才给你一个飞吻,向你微微敬一下礼,走开。你真是一个幸运的女人。”

幸福的眼泪顺着苏珊的脸颊滚滚而下。因为尽管她无法用肉眼看见马克,但她总能感觉到他的存在。她很幸运,因为马克给了她一件比视觉更有效的礼物——一件能在黑暗处带来光明的爱的礼物。

Love Is a Telephone

Love is a telephone which always keeps silent when you are longing for a call, but rings when you are not ready for it. As a result, we often miss the sweetness from the other end.

Love is a telephone which is seldom program – controlled or directly dialed. You cannot get an immediate answer by a mere "Hello", let alone go deep into your lover's heart by one call. Usually it has to be relayed by an operator, and you have to be patient in waiting. Destiny is the operator of this phone, who is always irresponsible and fond of playing practical jokes to which she may make you a lifelong victim intentionally or unintentionally.

Love is a telephone which is always busy. When you are ready to devote yourself to or even ready to die for love, you only find, to your disappointment, the line is already occupied by someone else, and you are greeted only by a busy line. This is an eternal regret handed down from generation to generation and you are only one of those who languish for flowers.

Love is a telephone which is sometimes so sensitive that you are put through by a single dial and responded to as soon as you say "Hello". But, more often than not, you only hang it up and turn away sadly just because of its lack of challenge and effort. Once you realize your mistake, no one is available at the other end.

Love is a telephone, but it is difficult to seize the right time for dialing, and you will let slip the opportunity if your call is either too early or too late.

Love is a telephone which is not always associated with happiness. Honeyed words are transmitted by sound waves, but when the lovers are brought together, the phone serves no purpose. No wonder that many lovers observe that marriage is the doom of love.

Love is a telephone which, when you use it for the first time, makes you so nervous and excited that you either hold the receiver upside down or dial the wrong number. By the time you've calmed down, you will be at a loss to whom you should make the call.

Love is a telephone which often has crossed lines. And this usually happens to you unexpectedly. Your line will either cross or be crossed. Both cases are referred to as "triangles". Fortunately, all such occurrences are transient.

爱情是一部电话

爱情是一部电话，当你渴望它响起时，它却总是悄无声息；但你不乐意去接时，它却又丁玲玲响起。因此，我们常常错过另一端传来的甜蜜。

爱情这部电话通常不是程控或直拨。并不是仅仅说声“喂”便能马上得到回音，更不要说呼唤一声就能深深打动你的爱人的心。它通常必须由接线员转接，你得耐心等待。命运是这部电话的接线员，她总是不负责任，喜欢搞恶作剧，她也许有意无意地使你成为终生的牺牲品。

爱情是一部总是忙碌的电话。当你准备为爱献身，甚至为爱而死时，令你失望的是，你却发现有人已经占线，迎接你的只是忙音。这是一种代代相传的永恒的遗憾，你仅仅是又一个为鲜花而憔悴的人。

爱情是一部有时非常灵敏的电话，一拨即通，一喂就应。可是，你常常只是因为它缺乏挑战、不费气力而挂机，伤心地转身离去。一旦你认为到自己的错误，另一端却无人接听。

爱情是一部电话，但很难抓准拨号时机。无论拨得太早还是太晚，你都会错失良机。

爱情是一部电话，它并不总是和幸福息息相关。尽管甜言蜜语由声波传送，但当相爱的人守在一起时，电话便发挥不了作用。难怪好多相爱的人说婚姻是爱情的末日。

爱情是一部电话，你第一次使用，会让你感到紧张激动，不是拿倒了话筒，就是拨错了号码。等你平静下来时，常常不知道该给谁打电话。

爱情是一部电话，它经常串线。而且串线常常是在你意想不到时发生。不是你的电话与别人的串线，就是别人的电话与你的串线。这两种情况都被称为“三角串”。幸运的是，所有这些串线都是瞬时现象。

The Red Rose and the White Rose

My mother and father were about to celebrate their 50th anniversary. Mother called, all excited. "He got me a dozen white roses!" She sounded like a teenager who'd been asked to the prom.

This anniversary brought out a side of my parents that I never knew. For instance, that their wedding rings are each inscribed with a line of poetry: "I send you a cream-white rosebud." My father told me this in the kitchen one day. My mother said, "Oh, John," as if to stop him. My father said, "Oh, Claire."

That's the way my parents have always been about their relationship: private. There was never any mushy stuff going on that we kids could see. What we did see was buddies, a team.

"Do you remember the poem?" I asked my dad that day in the kitchen. He looked at me, took a breath and started reciting "*A White Rose*" by the Irish-American poet John Boyle O'Reilly.

"The red rose whispers of passion, /And the white rose breathes of love," he began.

My mother said, "Oh, John!"

"O, the red rose is a falcon, /And the white rose is a dove."

"Oh, John!" my mother said. Then she left the room.

"But I send you a cream-white rosebud, /With a flush on its petal tips," he went on, standing there by the sink. "For the love that is purest and sweetest, /Has a kiss of desire on the lips." My father stopped. "Isn't that beautiful?" he said, smiling. We went to find my mother, who was in the den, her head in her hands. "It's beautiful!" I said to her.

"It's embarrassing," she said.

This is a woman who in her youth had never seen a happy marriage and wondered why anyone would bother. Instead, she imagined a future as a Chaucer scholar. In university she found dating only amusing. But then she met my father.

He was the most fundamentally decent man she had ever met. It was the man, not the institution of marriage, that drew her. She went to the altar, she would tell us, feeling as if she were jumping off a cliff.

In their first year, my father went off to war. My mother was five months pregnant, and terrified. She had the baby and waited. She ate chocolate-nut sundaes to soothe her heart.

My father returned, said hello to his seven-month-old son and, with my mother, soon bought a house. Then they had a daughter, then another daughter and then me.

Even as a kid, I could tell my parents were different. Dad preferred being with Mom. And when he was not around, she didn't roll her eyes and make jokes at her husband's expense as other wives did. Instead, she'd say, "You know, he's never disappointed me."

To celebrate their 50th anniversary, my parents renewed their wedding vows in church. Some 75 friends were watching. When my father repeated his vows, he choked up and had to pause. My mother said hers with more passion. Staring into his eyes, she proclaimed, "... all the days of my life I love you... till eternity."

Then she added, "This is the happiest day of my life, better than my wedding day! Because now I know how it all works out."

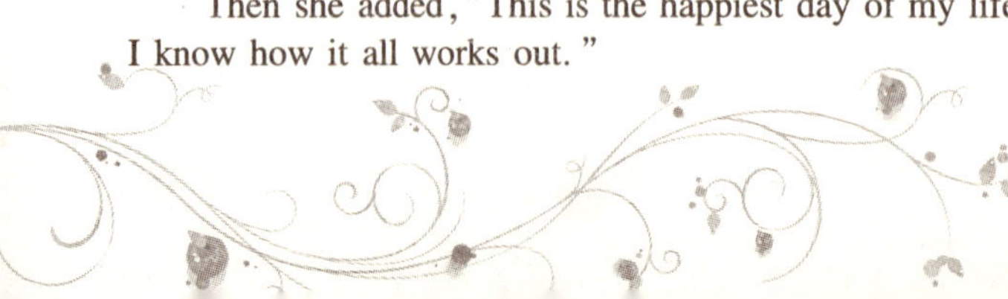

红玫瑰与白玫瑰

父母亲打算庆贺他们喜结良缘50周年。母亲打来电话时激动万分。“他给我买了一打白玫瑰!”听上去她就像一名应邀参加舞会的妙龄少女。

这次纪念将我从不知道的父母亲的一面展现了出来。比如,他们的结婚戒指上分别镌刻着一句诗行:“我送给你一朵乳白色的玫瑰花蕾。”这是有一天父亲在厨房里告诉我的。母亲说:“噢,约翰,”好像是要阻止他。父亲说:“噢,克莱尔。”

父母亲一向就是这样处理他们之间的关系:秘而不宣。我们作儿女的从未能见到他们之间多愁善感过,我们见到的就是他们的恩爱、和谐。

“你还记得那首诗吗?”那天我在厨房里问爸爸。他看了看我,吸了口气,开始背诵起爱尔兰籍美国诗人约翰·鲍埃尔·奥雷利作的那首《白玫瑰》。

“红玫瑰窃窃情语,/白玫瑰爱声息息。”他开始吟诵道。

母亲说:“噢,约翰!”

“噢,红玫瑰是猎鹰。/白玫瑰是鸽子。”

“噢,约翰!”母亲说着,便离开了厨房。

“可我送给你的是一朵乳白色玫瑰花蕾。/它的花瓣尖上含着羞红。”他站在水池边,接着吟咏道,“为了那最纯最甜的爱情,/多想在那芳唇上吻上一下。”父亲就此停住,面含微笑说:“这首诗很美吧?”随后,我们走进小屋,发现母亲正两手抱头坐在那里。我对她说:“这首诗真美!”

“真难为情。”她说。

母亲在少女时代从未见过一次幸福的婚姻,心想为什么大家要操这个心呢。于是,她便想将来当一名研究乔叟的女学者。在大学里,她发现男女约会只是为了解闷逗乐。但后来,她遇到了我的父亲。

父亲是她平生遇到的最最体面的男人。她结婚是为了这个男人,而不是什么女大当嫁的习俗。她常常告诉我们说,她走到圣坛前时,就像从悬崖上跳下来似的。

新婚第一年,父亲就离开她奔赴战场。当时,母亲已经怀孕5个月,心里非常害怕。她生下孩子后,苦苦等待,总是靠吃带巧克力豆的圣代冰淇淋安抚自己的心。

父亲归来时,向已经7个月的儿子问好,不久同母亲一道买了一座房子。随后,他们就有了一个女儿,又有了一个女儿,然后又生下了我。

甚至小时候,我就能看出父母亲不同凡响。父亲总是喜欢和母亲厮守在一块。而当他不在时,母亲从来不会像别人的妻子那样拿自己的丈夫寻开心。相反,她总是说:“你们知道,他从来都不会让我失望。”

为了庆贺金婚,父母亲在教堂里重温了他们当初的结婚誓言。当着75位朋友的面,父亲重叙他的婚誓时,声音哽咽,不得不中断;母亲说时更加富有激情,她目光炯炯地望着父亲的眼睛,郑重其事地说:“……在我生命中的每一天,我都爱你,直到永远……”

接着,她又补充道:“这是我一生中最幸福的日子,比我婚礼那天还精彩!因为现在

我知道我们终于说到做到。”

At the Small Café

Can it really be sixty-two years ago that I first saw you?

It is truly a lifetime, I know. But as I gaze into your eyes now, it seems like only yesterday that I first saw you, in that small café in Hanover Square.

From the moment I saw you smile, as you opened the door for that young mother and her newborn baby. I knew that I wanted to share the rest of my life with you.

I still think of how foolish I must have looked, as I gazed at you, that first time. I remember watching you intently, as you took off your hat and loosely shook your short dark hair with your fingers. I felt myself becoming immersed in your every detail, as you placed your hat on the table and cupped your hands around the hot cup of tea, gently blowing the steam away with your pouted lips.

From that moment, everything seemed to make perfect sense to me. The people in the café and the busy street outside all disappeared into a hazy blur. All I could see was you.

All through my life I have relived that very first day. Many, many times I have sat and thought about that the first day, and how for a few fleeting moments I am there, feeling again what is like to know true love for the very first time. It pleases me that I can still have those feelings now after all those years, and I know I will always have them to comfort me.

Not even as I shook and trembled uncontrollably in the trenches, did I forget your face. I would sit huddled into the wet mud, terrified, as the hails of bullets and mortars crashed down around me. I would clutch my rifle tightly to my heart, and think again of that very first day we met. I would cry out in fear, as the noise of war beat down around me. But, as I thought of you and saw you smiling back at me, everything around me would become silent, and I would be with you again for a few precious moments, far from the death and destruction. It wouldn't be until I opened my eyes once again, that I would see and hear the carnage of the war around me.

I cannot tell you how strong my love for you was back then, when I returned to you on leave in September, feeling battered, bruised and fragile. We held each other so tightly I thought we would melt. I asked you to marry me the very same day and I whooped with joy when you looked deep into my eyes and said, "yes" to being my bride.

I'm looking at our wedding photo now, the one on our dressing table, next to your jewelry box. I think of how young and innocent we were back then. I remember being on the church steps grinning like a Cheshire cat, when you said how dashing and handsome I looked in my uniform. The photo is old and faded now, but when I look at it, I only see the bright vibrant colors of our youth. I can still remember every detail of the pretty wedding dress your mother made for you, with its fine delicate lace and pretty pearls. If I concentrate hard enough, I can smell the sweetness of your wedding bouquet as you held it so proudly for everyone to see.

I remember being so overjoyed, when a year later, you gently held my hand to your waist and whispered in my ear that we were going to be a family.

I know both our children love you dearly; they are outside the door now, waiting.

Do you remember how I panicked like a mad man when Jonathon was born? I can still picture you laughing and smiling at me now, as I clumsily held him for the very first time in my arms. I watched as your laughter faded into tears, as I stared at him and cried my own tears of joy.

Sarah and Tom arrived this morning with little Tessie. Can you remember how we both hugged each other tightly when we saw our tiny granddaughter for the first time? I can't believe she will be eight next month. I am trying not to cry, my love, as I tell you how beautiful she looks today in her pretty dress and red shiny shoes, she reminds me so much of you that first day we met. She has her hair cut short now, just like yours was all those years ago. When I met her at the door her smile wrapped around me like a warm glove, just like yours used to do, my darling.

I know you are tired, my dear, and I must let you go. But I love you so much it hurts to do so.

As we grew old together, I would tease you that you hadn't changed since we first met. But it is true, my darling. I don't see the wrinkles and gray hair that other people see. When I look at you now, I only see your sweet tender lips and youthful sparkling eyes as we sat and had our first picnic next to that small stream, and chased each other around that big old oak tree. I remember wishing those first few days together would last forever. Do you remember how exciting and wonderful those days were?

I must go now, my darling. Our children are waiting outside. They want to say goodbye to you.

I wipe the tears away from my eyes and bend my frail old legs down to the floor, so that I can kneel beside you. I lean close to you and take hold of your hand and kiss your tender lips for the very last time.

Sleep peacefully, my dear.

I am sad that you had to leave me, but please don't worry. I am content, knowing I will be with you soon. I am too old and too empty now to live much longer without you.

I know it won't be long before we meet again in that small café in Hanover Square.

Goodbye, my darling wife.

相约小咖啡馆

我第一次看见你真的可能是62年前吗?

我知道,这是真正的一生。但此刻我凝视你的眼睛,就像我昨天在汉诺威广场小咖啡馆第一次看见你一样。

从那一时刻起,我就看见你面带微笑,为那位抱着新生儿的年轻母亲开门。我知道我想和你共度余生。

我仍想起我第一次凝视你的样子一定很傻。我记得我目不转睛地望着你摘下帽子用手指抖松短短的黑发。我感到自己对你的一举一动都心醉神迷,望着你把帽子放在桌上,双手捧起那杯热茶,噘起嘴唇轻轻地吹去热气。

从那一时刻起,一切对我似乎有了完美的意义。咖啡馆里与熙熙攘攘的街道上的人们都消失在烟雾朦胧中。我所能看到的只有你。

我这一生都在不断回味着初次相遇的那一天。我好多好多次坐在那里想着那一天,回味稍纵即逝的几个瞬间,再次感受一见钟情是什么样子。多年之后,我仍有那些感觉,我知道我永远都会拥有它们来安慰我。

即使在战壕里浑身颤抖,我也没有忘记过你的脸。我常常惊恐地蜷缩在湿泥中,周围子弹呼啸,炮声轰鸣。我将步枪紧握在胸前,又一次想起了我们第一次相遇的那一天。四周枪炮齐鸣,我常常惊恐地喊叫。但当我想起你,看到你像我微笑时,我四周的一切都会沉寂下来,而且我常常会再次与你在一起那几个宝贵的时刻,远离死亡和毁灭。直到再次睁开眼,我才会看到血流成河的战场、听到枪炮齐鸣。

9月休假,我伤痕累累,虚弱不堪,回到你身边,说不出对你的爱有多么强烈。我们相互紧紧地拥抱,我想我们会融为一体。就在那天,我请你嫁给我,你深情地望着我的眼睛说愿做我的新娘,我高兴得大声叫喊起来。

现在,我望着梳妆台上你的首饰盒边我们的结婚照。我想我们那时是多么青春天真。我还记得在教堂的台阶上笑得是那样开心,你说穿着我制服是多么勇敢英俊。照片现在已经陈旧褪色,但当我看着它时,我只看到我们青春勃发的光彩。我仍能清晰地记得当时你妈妈为你做的配着精致花边和漂亮珠宝的新婚礼服。如果我聚精会神,还能闻到你的婚礼花束的芬芳,你举着花非常自豪地让每个人都看到。

我还记得,一年后,你把我的手轻轻地放在你的腰间,在我耳旁低声说我们快有孩子了,我听到后欣喜若狂。

我知道,我们的两个孩子都深深地爱着你,他们现在就在门外等候。

你还记得乔纳森出生时我惊慌失措的样子吗?我现在还能想起你发笑我的样了,当时我笨手笨脚地第一次把他抱在怀里。我目不转睛地望着你,你的笑声渐渐变成了泪水;我望着他,也高兴得笑出了眼泪。

今天早上,莎拉和汤姆带着小泰西也赶来了。你还记得第一次看到小孙女时我们俩紧紧拥抱的情景吗?我简直无法相信,她下个月就8岁了。亲爱的,我忍着泪告诉你,她穿着漂亮的连衣裙和闪亮的红鞋今天有多美,她使我浮想联翩记起了第一次相遇时你的样子。她现在剪了短发,就像你多年前那样。亲爱的,当我在门口遇到她时,她的微笑像暖暖的手套一样裹住了我,就像你当初的样子。

亲爱的,我知道你累了,我必须放你走。但我是多么爱你,这样做是多么心痛。

当我们一起渐渐变老,我常常逗你说,自从我们第一次相遇以来你什么也没有改变。亲爱的,事实确实如此。我看不到别人所看到的你的皱纹和华发。我现在看着你,只看到你鲜嫩的香唇和青春闪亮的眼睛,当时我们坐在那条小溪边第一次野炊,绕着那棵高大的老橡树追逐。我真想让那些最初的时光永远持续下去。你还记得那些时光是多么激动和美妙吗?

亲爱的,我现在必须走了。我们的孩子们在外面等着。他们想和你道别。

我抹去眼角的泪水,弯曲弱不禁风的老腿,跪在地板上,以便我能跪在你身边。我贴向你,握住你的手,最后一次吻你的香唇。

亲爱的,安心睡吧。

我很伤心你离我而去,但请别担心。我知足了,明白自己很快会跟你在一起。没有你,我垂垂老矣、精神空虚,活不了多久。

我知道,我们不久就会又在汉诺威广场那家小咖啡馆见面。

再见,我的爱妻。

I'm Going with You

In 1959, in a small town in California, a young couple had been married a few short and disappointing months.

He had never dreamed there were so many ways to ruin friend chicken. She couldn't imagine why she ever thought his jokes were funny. Neither one said aloud what they were both thinking—the marriage was a big mistake.

One hot afternoon, they got into a terrible argument about whether they could afford to paint the living room.

Tempers flared, voices were raised, and somehow one of the wedding gift plates crashed to the floor. She burst into tears, called him heartless and a cheapskate. He shouted that he'd rather be a cheapskate than a nag, and then grabbed the car keys on his way out. His parting words, punctuated by the slam of the door, were, "That's it! I'm leaving you!"

But before he could coax their rickety car into gear, the passenger door flew open and his bride landed on the seat beside him. She stared straight ahead, her face tear-streaked but determined.

"And just where do you think you're going?" he asked in amazement.

She hesitated a moment before replying, just to be sure of the answer that would decide the direction of their lives for the next forty-three years.

"If you're leaving me," my mother said, "I'm going with you."

跟你一起走

1959年，在加州的一个小镇上，一对年轻夫妇结婚才短短几个月，就心灰意冷。

他从来没想到会有那么多方法能把炸鸡做得一塌糊涂。她难以想象她以前为什么认为他的笑话那么逗人。他们俩谁也没有大声说出来——这场婚姻是个大错。

一个炎热的午后，他们为能不能负担得起粉刷客厅的费用可怕地争吵起来。

他们火气冲天，提高嗓门，而且不知怎么的，一只婚礼礼物盘子也摔碎到了地板上。她痛哭失声，大声说他无情、小气。他大声喊着他就是做小气鬼，也不愿唠叨，随后抓起车钥匙，就出了门。他临走时说："够了！我要离开你！"随后就砰地关上了门。

但还没等他来得及发动他们那辆老爷车，乘客门就飞快地打开了，新娘坐到了他的旁边，直视前方，泪水涟涟，但意志坚定。

"你想要去哪里呀？"他惊讶地问道。

她回答前，迟疑了一会儿，只是想确定一个答案，以决定他们后来43年的生活方向。

"如果你要离开我，"我的母亲说，"我就跟你一起走。"

Salty Coffee

In the first meeting, a boy invited a girl to drink a coffee, which he was too nervous to say anything, so that she was very uncomfortable. Suddenly, he said to the waiter, "Please allow me a little salt, okay? I would like to put it in coffee."

She was surprised and asked him, "How do you have such love?"

He replied, "Every time when I drink salty coffee, I always think of my childhood, think of my hometown, I miss my hometown too much, and my parents live there, I miss them very much."

When he said these words, tears were in his eyes. She was deeply moved. Then, she began to talk about her faraway hometown, her childhood and family. This was indeed a wonderful conversation, beginning from a beautiful love story.

They continued dating. She found that, in fact, he satisfied all her requirements: he was tolerant,

good-hearted, warm and careful. Then, they got married and lived a happy life...

Making coffee for him every time, she always put some salt in it because she knew he liked it.

40 years passed, he passed away and left her a letter, which said: "My beloved, please forgive me, forgive my whole-life lie. This is my only lie to you—salty coffee."

"In my lifetime, how many times had I tried to tell you the truth, but I worried too much and I didn't do that because I swore to you that I would never lie to you. I'm dying now, no longer have any scruples, so I will tell you the truth, I don't like salty coffee, which flavor is very strange, but I have it during my whole lifetime! Since meeting you, I have never felt regretted for what I have done for you. My greatest happiness in my life is you around me. If I can have a second life, I still would like to meet you and own your life, even if I would also like to enjoy salty coffee."

Her tears soaked the letterheads.

One day, someone asked her, "How about the flavor of salty coffee?"

She replied, "Sweet."

This is just like the magic power between lovers; two people will always make sacrifices for each other. This kind of sacrifice will bring pain to the one who pays, but he or she will still feel sweet.

A sincere love is not for obtaining something from the opposite, but sincerely pay for each other. Although sometimes this devotion will bring suffering to your body, in the process of devotion, you will feel that your body is filled with tremendous sweetness and happiness. Such love is often more profound and worthy of cherishing.

咸咖啡

初次相会时,男孩邀请女孩喝咖啡。他太紧张了,说不出话来,所以她很不舒服,突然,他对服务员说:"请给我点盐,好吗?我想把它放在咖啡里。"

她吃了一惊,问他:"你怎么有这种爱好?"

他回答说:"我每次喝咸咖啡时,总会想起童年,想起家乡,我太想家乡了,我的父母亲住在那里,我非常想念他们。"

他说这些话时,热泪盈眶。她被深深地感动了。随后,她开始谈起了她遥远的故乡、她的童年和家人。这真是一场美妙的谈话,从此开始了一个美丽的爱情故事。

他们继续约会。她发现他其实符合她所有的要求:他宽容善良、热情细心。后来,他们就结为夫妻,过起了幸福生活……

她每次为他沏咖啡,总是要在咖啡里放些盐,因为她知道他喜欢。

40 年过去了,他离开了人世,留给她一封信,信上说:"我的爱人,请原谅我,原谅我一生的谎言。这是我对你唯一的谎言——咸咖啡。"

"在我有生之年,有多少次我试图告诉你真相,但我太担心,就没有那样做,因为我向你发过誓绝不对你撒谎。我现在要死了,不再有什么顾忌,所以我要告诉你真相,我不喜欢咸咖啡,那种味道很怪,但我却喝了一生的咸咖啡!自从认识了你,我就从来没有对我为你做过的事情遗憾过。有你在身边是我一生最大的幸福。假如我能有第二次生命,我还是想认识你,一生拥有你,即使我还要享用咸咖啡。"

她的泪水浸透了信纸。

有一天,有人问她:"咸咖啡的味道怎么样?"

她回答说:"甜。"

这就像情侣之间的魔力一样；两个人总会为对方做出牺牲。尽管这种牺牲会给付出的一方带来一些痛苦，但他或她仍会感觉甜蜜。

真挚的爱情不是向对方索取，而是互相真心付出，虽然有时这种付出会给身体带来痛苦，但在付出过程中，你会觉得你的身体充满无比的甜蜜和幸福。这种爱往往更深邃、更值得珍爱。

Love Wizard

An African tribal chief had three daughters. The first two daughters were clever and beautiful and married at the cost of nine cows. Locally, it was the betrothal gift of the highest standard. When it was the third daughter's turn, no one would offer nine cows to marry her, for she was not beautiful and very lazy.

Later on, a tourist from afar heard it and said to the chief, "I'm willing to exchange your daughter with nine cows."

The chief was so pleased that he really married her daughter to the non-native.

Over the years, the chief went to see his third daughter who married to the alien land. Unexpectedly, her daughter had become a refined beautiful woman and cooked the delicacies herself delicious to feast him.

Shocked, the chief asked his son-in-law privately, "Are you a wizard? How did you instruct her like that?"

His son-in-law said, "I didn't instruct her, but I only always firmly believe your daughter is worth nine cows. So she keeps acting on such a standard. It is so simple."

The effect of the psychological hint is very magic, especially in marriage. If you try to praise your sweetheart from the depth of your heart every day, not grumble or complain, then you will surely find the other side is also changing quietly and towards the direction you hope.

爱情巫师

非洲的一个部落酋长有三个女儿，前两个女儿聪明漂亮，都是被人用9头牛作聘礼娶走的。在当地，这是最高规格的聘礼了。三女儿到了出嫁时，却一直没有人肯出9头牛来娶她，原因是她不但不漂亮，而且还很懒。

后来，一个远方来的游客听说了这件事，就对酋长说："我愿意用9头牛来换你的女儿。"

酋长非常高兴，真的把女儿嫁给了外乡人。

过了几年，酋长去看自己远嫁他乡的三女儿。没想到，女儿变成了一个气质超俗的漂亮女人，而且能亲自下厨做美味佳肴来款待他。

酋长很震惊，偷偷地问女婿："难道你是巫师吗？你是怎么把她调教成这样的？"

女婿说："我没有调教她，我只是始终坚信你的女儿值9头牛，所以她就一直按照9头牛的标准来做了，就这么简单。"

心理暗示的作用非常神奇，尤其在婚姻关系中。如果你每天试着发自内心地赞美你的爱人，而不是诉苦或抱怨，那你一定会发现，对方也在悄悄改变，而且正是朝着你希望的方向。

Words from the Heart

Most people need to hear these three little words "I love you." Once in a while, they hear them just in time.

I met Connie the day she was admitted to the hospital ward, where I worked as a volunteer. Her husband, Bill, stood nervously nearby as she was transferred from the gurney to the hospital bed. Although Connie was in the final stages of her fight against cancer, she was alert and cheerful. We got her settled in. I finished marking her name on all the hospital supplies she would be using, then asked if she needed anything.

"Oh, yes," she said, "would you please show me how to use the TV? I enjoy the soaps so much and I don't want to get behind on what's happening." Connie was a romantic. She loved soap operas, romance novels and movies with a good love story. As we became acquainted, she confided how frustrating it was to be married 32 years to a man who often called her "a silly woman."

"Oh, I know Bill loves me," she said, "but he has never been one to say he loves me, or send cards to me." She sighed and looked out the window at the trees in the courtyard. "I'd give anything if he'd say 'I love you,' but it's just not in his nature."

Bill visited Connie every day. In the beginning, he sat next to the bed while she watched the soaps. Later, when she began sleeping more, he paced up and down the hallway outside her room. Soon, when she no longer watched television and had fewer waking moments, I began spending more of my volunteer time with Bill.

He talked about having worked as a carpenter and how he liked to go fishing. He and Connie had no children, but they'd been enjoying retirement by traveling, until Connie got sick. Bill couldn't express his feelings about the fact that his wife was dying.

One day, over coffee in the cafeteria, I got him on the subject of women and how we need romance in our lives; how we love to get sentimental cards and love letters.

"Do you tell Connie you love her?" I asked, knowing his answer, and he looked at me as if I was crazy.

"I don't have to," he said. "She knows I do!"

"I'm sure she knows," I said. "But she needs to hear it, Bill. She needs to hear what she has meant to you all these years. Please think about it."

We walked back to Connie's room. Bill disappeared inside, and I left to visit another patient. Later, I saw Bill sitting by the bed. He was holding Connie's hand as she slept. The date was February 12.

Two days later I walked down the hospital ward at noon. There stood Bill, leaning up against the wall in the hallway, staring at the floor. I already knew from the head nurse that Connie had died at 11 a.m.

When Bill saw me, he allowed himself to come into my arms for a long time. His face was wet with tears and he was trembling. Finally, he leaned back against the wall and took a deep breath.

"I have to say something," he said. "I have to say how good I feel about telling her. I thought a lot about what you said, and this morning I told her how much I loved her... and loved being married to her. You should have seen her smile!"

I went into the room to say my own good-bye to Connie. There, on the bedside table, was a large

Valentine card from Bill. You know, the sentimental kind that says, "To my wonderful wife... I love you."

爱,就要说出来

大多数人都需要听到"我爱你"这三个微不足道的词语。偶尔,他们听到的会非常及时。

我看到康妮那天,她刚被送到医院的病房。我在那里做志愿者。她被从装有轮子的金属担架移到病床上时,她的丈夫比尔不安地站在旁边。尽管康妮已到了与癌症对抗的最后的阶段;但她仍然活跃开心。我们把她安顿好。我在她要用的所有东西都标上她的名字后,又问她是否还需要什么东西。

"噢,是的,"她说,"请你告诉我怎么使用这电视好吗?我喜欢看肥皂剧,不想错过任何情节。"康妮是一个浪漫主义者,爱看肥皂剧、言情小说和带有精彩爱情故事的电影。随着我们渐渐熟悉,她吐露说,她真失望,竟然嫁给一个常称她"傻女人"的男人32年。

"噢,我知道比尔爱我,"她说,"但他从来没有说过他爱我,也从来没有给我寄过贺卡。"她叹了口气,望着窗外庭院里的那些树。"如果他说'我爱你',我愿意付出一切,但那恰恰不是他的本性。"

每天比尔都来看望康妮。开始,康妮看肥皂剧时,他坐在床边。后来,她睡觉的时间越来越多,他就在病房外的走廊上踱来踱去。不久,康妮不再看电视,清醒的时刻越来越少,我开始有了更多志愿时间和比尔在一起。

他说他是做木匠的,很爱钓鱼。他和康妮没有孩子,便以旅行来享受退休时光,直至康妮病倒。面对妻子病危的这个事实,比尔无法表达这种感受。

有一天,在自助餐厅喝咖啡时,我和他谈起了女人的话题,谈起了生活中我们如何需要浪漫,谈起了我们如何喜欢收到柔情的贺卡和情书。

"你告诉康妮你爱她了吗?"我明知故问。他看着我,好像我疯了一样。

"我没必要,"他说,"她知道我爱她!"

"我确信她知道,"我说,"但她需要听到,比尔。她需要听到这些年她对你意味着什么。请想一下这件事。"

我们走回康妮的病房。比尔走了进去,我离开去看另一个病人。随后,我看到比尔坐在床边,握着入睡的康妮的一只手。那天是2月12日。

两天后的中午,我顺着医院病房走廊走着,看到比尔靠墙站在那里,盯着地板。我已经从护士长那里得知,康妮上午11点已经去世。

比尔看到我,久久地扑到我的怀里。他泪流满面,浑身颤抖,最后靠回墙上,深深地吸了口气。

"我必须说点什么,"他说,"我必须说把那句话告诉她感觉真好啊。我对你说的话想了很多。今天早上我告诉她我是多么爱她,非常喜欢和她结为了夫妻。你真该看看她的微笑!"

我走进病房，和康妮告别。只见床头桌上放着比尔送的一张大大的情人节贺卡。你知道，贺卡上写着那种情意绵绵的话语："献给我的爱妻……我爱你。"

Your Name Was Carved in My Heart

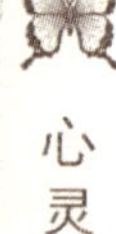

My parents loved each other at first sight and lived happily for 53 years. My father was romantic and humorous. The stories he told casually always added a lot of fun to our life. For example, my father often talked about the first scene he talked with my mother when he returned from Japan after World War II. At that time, he was driving his brother's car through the town, when he caught a glimpse of my mother entering a furniture shop. He stepped on the brake, jumped out of the car, quietly slipped into the shop and stood beside my mother.

At that time, my 26-year-old mother was making the shopkeeper show her a set of bedding she took a fancy to last week. My father, just an acquaintance strolling by, paced to her and said, "I say, Maud, we can't sleep on the two single beds!" Three months later, they married. As a result, they really had to sleep on the double single beds until they had enough money to buy the double bed.

At the age of 78, my father had an open-chest surgery. My 76-year-old mother was in the hospital to take care of him all night and accompanied him at his bed every day. When the doctors removed the ventilation duct from his throat, the first words my father said were the most romantic language I ever heard, "Maud, do you know what the doctor found when he cut my chest? He found your name was carved in my heart."

你的名字刻在我的心上

我的父母一见钟情，恩恩爱爱地生活了53年。我的父亲浪漫幽默，他信口拈来的故事总能为我们的生活添加很多乐趣。比如说，父亲常常提到二战后他从日本归来第一次与母亲交谈的情景。当时，他正驾驶着哥哥的新车穿过镇子，正好一眼瞥见母亲走进了一家家具店。他一脚踩住了刹车，跳出了汽车，不动声色地溜进了店里，站在了母亲身边。

当时，26岁的母亲正在让店主给她看她上周看中的一套卧具。我的父亲不过是一个信步路过的熟人，踱着步子走到她身边，说："我说，莫德呀，我们可不能分睡在两张单人床上啊！"3个月后，他们就喜结连理。结果，他们确实只能分睡在一双单人床上，直到他们有足够的钱买双人床。

到78岁高龄时，我的父亲做了一次开膛手术。76岁的母亲整晚在医院照顾他，每天陪伴在他的床前。当医生们把通气导管从父亲的喉咙处移开时，父亲开口说的第一句话是我听过的最浪漫的言语："莫德，你知道医生把我的胸口切开时发现了什么？他发现你的名字刻在了我的心上。"

Marriage Doesn't Need the Scorecard

As the movie came to an end the room filled with chatter. The warm fire, twinkling Christmas lights and laughter from family brought a contented smile to my face. The minute Mom said, "Who wants..." the room emptied quicker than the stands at a losing football game.

My boyfriend Todd and I were the only ones left. With a bewildered look on his face he asked me what just happened. Catching the smile on my mom's face, I said to Todd, "We're going to fill gas in my mom's car."

He quickly replied, "It's freezing out there, and it's almost 11:30 p. m."

Smiling, I said, "Then you'd better have your coat and gloves on."

After hurriedly chipping the frost off the windshield, we bundled into the car. On the way to the gas station, Todd asked me to explain why in the world we were going to get my mom gas so late at night. Chuckling, I said, "When my siblings and I come home for the holidays, we help my dad get gas for my mom. It has turned into a game with all of us. We can tell when my mom is going to ask and the last one in the room has to go."

"You have got to be kidding me!" Todd responded.

"There's no getting out of it," I said.

While pumping the gas, we rubbed our hands and jumped around to stay warm. "I still don't get it. Why doesn't your mom put the gas in the car herself?" Todd asked.

With mirth in my eyes, I said, "I know it sounds insane, but let me explain. My mom has not pumped gas in over two decades. My dad always does for her." With a confused look, Todd asked if my dad was ever annoyed with having to pump gas for his wife all the time. Shaking my head, I simply said, "No, he has never complained."

"That's crazy," Todd quickly replied.

"No, not really," I explained patiently. "When I came home for the holidays my sophomore year of college, I thought I knew everything. One evening, my mom and I were wrapping presents, and I told her that when I got married, my husband was going to help clean, do laundry, cook, the whole bit. Then I asked her if she ever got tired of doing the laundry and dishes. She calmly told me it didn't bother her. This was difficult for me to believe. I began to give her a lecture about the equality between the sexes.

"Mom listened patiently. After setting the ribbon aside, she looked me square in the eyes. 'Someday, dear, you will understand.'

"This only irritated me more. I didn't understand one bit. And so I demanded more of an explanation. Mom smiled, and began to explain:

"'In a marriage, there are some things you like to do and some things you don't. So, together, you figure out what little things you are willing to do for each other. You share the responsibilities. I really don't mind doing the laundry. Sure, it takes some time, but it is something I do for your dad. On the other hand, I don't like to pump gas. The smell of the fumes bothers me. And I don't like to stand out in the freezing cold. So, your dad always puts gas in my car. Your dad goes shopping to the grocery shops, and I cook. Your dad mows the grass, and I clean. I could go on and on.'

"'You see,' my mom continued, 'in marriage, there is no scorecard. You do little things for each other to make the other's life easier. If you think of it as helping the person you love, you don't become annoyed, because you're doing it out of love.'

"Over the years, I have often reflected on what my mom said. She has a great perspective on marriage. I like how my mom and dad take care of each other. And you know what? One day, when I'm married, I don't want to have a scorecard, either."

Todd was unusually quiet the rest of the way home. After he shut off the engine, he turned to me and took my hands in his with a warm smile. "Anytime you want," he said in a soft voice, "I'll pump gas for you."

婚姻不需要记分卡

电影结束时，房间里充满了闲聊声。温暖的炉火、闪烁的圣诞彩灯和家人的笑声，使我露出了满意的微笑。这时，妈妈说："谁想……"房间里一下就空了，比输了足球赛的看台空得还快。

房间里只剩下了我和男友托德。他一脸困惑，问我是怎么回事。看到妈妈脸上的微笑，我对托德说："我们准备去给妈妈的汽车加油。"

他马上回答说："外面冻死人了，再说都快夜里11点半了。"

我笑了笑说："那你最好穿上大衣、戴上手套。"

我们匆匆擦掉挡风玻璃上的霜，钻进车里。在去加油站的路上，托德让我解释到底为什么要这么晚给妈妈的汽车加油。我格格笑道："每次我和兄弟姐妹回来过节，我们都要帮爸爸为妈妈的汽车加油。这已经成了我们的一项游戏。我们能看出妈妈什么时候请求，最后留在房间里的人必须得去。"

"你一定是在和我开玩笑吧！"托德回答说。

"我没有和你开玩笑。"我说。

在加油时，我们搓着手，蹦来蹦去来保暖。"我还是不明白。你妈妈为什么不自己来给启齿加油？"托德问道。

我欢笑着说："我知道这听起来很疯狂，但还是让我来解释一下。我妈妈20多年都没有去加过油，总是由我爸爸来做。"托德面带困惑问，我爸爸一直为他的妻子加油，是否烦恼过。我摇了摇头，简单地说："不，他从来没有抱怨过。"

"这真是疯了。"托德马上回答说。

"不，真的不会，"我耐心地解释说。"大二回家度假时，我认为自己无所不知。一天晚上，我和妈妈包裹礼物时，我对她说，我结婚时，我的丈夫要帮我打扫卫生、洗衣服、做饭，包揽一切家务。然后，我问她对洗洗涮涮烦不烦。她平静地告诉我说这她并不烦。这让我难以相信。我开始给她讲男女平等。

"妈妈耐心地听着。她把丝带放到一边后，坚定地看着我的眼睛说：'亲爱的，总有一天你会明白的。'

"她的话只会让我更生气。我一点也不明白。于是，我要求她再解释一下。妈妈微微一笑，开始解释起来：

"'在婚姻中，有些事你喜欢做，有些事你不喜欢做。所以，你们要在一块合计一下，你愿意为对方做哪些小事，承担责任。我对洗衣服确实不介意。当然，那会花费一些时间，但这是我愿意为你爸爸做的事儿。另一方面，我不喜欢去加油，汽油味让我讨厌。再说，我不喜欢站在外面的寒风中。所以，你爸爸总是去给我的汽车加油。你爸爸去杂货店买东西，我做饭。你爸爸割草，我清理。我可以一直配合下去。'

"'你明白，'妈妈接着说，'婚姻中根本没有记分卡。你为对方做一些小事，会使他生活得更轻松。如果你把这看成是在帮助自己心爱的人，你就不会苦恼，因为你是出于

爱才这样做的。'

"这些年来,我一直在仔细考虑妈妈说的话,她对婚姻看得非常透彻。我喜欢爸爸妈妈那样相互照顾。你知道什么?有一天我结婚时,我也不要记分卡。"

在回家的路上,托德非常安静。关掉了发动机后,他转向我,面带热情的微笑,柔声说道:"无论你什么时候想加油,我都愿意。"

The Shared Love

One afternoon I toured an art museum while waiting for my husband to finish a business meeting. I was looking forward to a quiet view of the masterpieces.

A young couple viewing the paintings ahead of me chattered nonstop between themselves. I watched them a moment and decided she was doing all the talking. I admired his patience for putting up with her constant parade of words. Distracted by their noise,I moved on.

I encountered them several times as I moved through the various rooms of art. Each time I heard her constant gush of words,I moved away quickly.

I was standing at the counter of the museum gift shop making a purchase when the couple approached the exit. Before they left,the man reached into his pocket and pulled out a white object. It was a long cane. He tapped his way into the coatroom to get his wife's jacket.

"He's a brave man," the clerk at the counter said. "Most of us would give up if we were blinded at such a young age. During his recovery,he made a vow his life wouldn't change. So,as before,he and his wife come in whenever there's a new art show."

"But what does he get out of the art?" I asked. "He can't see."

"Can't see! You're wrong. He sees a lot. More than you or I do," the clerk said. "His wife describes each painting so he can see it in his head."

I learned something about patience,courage and love that day. I saw the patience of a young wife describing paintings to a person without sight and the courage of a husband who wouldn't allow blindness to alter his life.

And I saw the love shared by two people as I watched this couple walk away with their arms intertwined.

同心爱

一天下午,我的丈夫参加一个商务会议。我等他时,到一家美术馆参观,想静静地欣赏那些名画。

我前面有一对看画的年轻夫妇喋喋不休说个没完。我看了他们一会儿,断定是那个女的一直在说。我钦佩那个男人真有耐性,居然可以忍受她的滔滔不绝。他们的说话声让我心烦意乱,我就继续向前走。

我走过不同的艺术品陈列室时碰到了他们好几次。每次听到她喋喋不休,我就马上离开。

我站在美术馆礼品店的柜台前买东西,这时这对夫妇靠近了出口。他们离开前,男

人把手伸进口袋，掏出一个白色东西。那是一根长长的手杖。他轻轻叩着地板，到衣帽间去拿妻子的短上衣。

“他是个勇敢的人，”柜台店员说。“如果我们这样年轻就失明，大多数人会放弃。他在康复期间，发誓他的生活不会改变。所以，和以前一样，只要有新的美术展，他都会和妻子来。”

“可他能从美术品中获得什么呢？”我问。“他无法看见啊。”

“无法看见！你错了。他看到的东西多着呢。比你我看到的都多。”店员说。“他的妻子给他描述每一幅画，这样他就可以在脑海里就看到了。”

那天，我明白了什么是耐性、勇气和爱。我明白了年轻妻子为盲人丈夫描述一幅幅画的耐心和丈夫不让失明改变自己生活的勇气。

随后，我目送这对夫妇手挽着手离开时，明白了两人共享的那份爱。

See How Much I Love You

My grandparents were married for over half a century, and played their own special game from the time they had met each other. The goal of their game was to write the word "shmily" in a surprise place for the other to find. They took turns leaving "shmily" around the house, and as soon as one of them discovered it, it was their turn to hide it once more.

They dragged "shmily" with their fingers through the sugar and flour containers to await whoever was preparing the next meal. They smeared it in the dew on the windows. "Shmily" was written in the steam left on the mirror after a hot shower, where it would reappear bath after bath.

At one point, my grandmother even unrolled an entire roll of toilet paper to leave "shmily" on the very last sheet.

There was no end to the places "shmily" would pop up. Little notes with "shmily" scribbled hurriedly were found on dashboards and car seats, or taped to steering wheels. The notes were stuffed inside shoes and left under pillows.

"Shmily" was written in the dust upon the mantel and traced in the ashes of the fireplace. This mysterious word was as much a part of my grandparents' house as the furniture.

It took me a long time before I was able to fully appreciate my grandparents' game. Skepticism has kept me from believing in true love—one that is pure and enduring. However, I never doubted my grandparents' relationship. They had love down pat. It was more than their flirtatious little games; it was a way of life. Their relationship as based on a devotion and passionate affection which not everyone is lucky enough to experience.

Grandma and Grandpa held hands every chance they could. They stole kisses as they bumped into each other in their tiny kitchen. They finished each other's sentences and shared the daily crossword puzzle and word jumble. My grandma whispered to me about how cute my grandpa was, how handsome and old he had grown to be. She claimed that she really knew "how to pick 'em". Before every meal they bowed their heads and gave thanks, marveling at their blessings: a wonderful family, good fortune, and each other.

But there was a dark cloud in my grandparents' life: my grandmother had breast cancer. The disease had first appeared ten years earlier. As always, Grandpa was with her every step of the way. He comforted her in their yellow room, painted that way so that she could always be surrounded by sunshine, even when she was too sick to go outside.

Now the cancer was again attacking her body. With the help of a cane and my grandfather's steady hand, they went to church every morning. But my grandmother grew steadily weaker until finally she couldn't leave the house anymore. For a while Grandpa would go to church alone, praying to God to watch over his wife.

Then one day, what we all dreaded finally happened. Grandma was gone.

"Shmily." It was scrawled in yellow on the pink ribbons of my grandmother's funeral bouquet. As the crowd thinned and the last mourners turned to leave, my aunts, uncles, cousins and other family members came forward and gathered around Grandma one last time. Grandpa stepped up to my grandmother's casket and, taking a shaky breath, he began to sing to her. Through his tears and grief, the song came, a deep and throaty lullaby.

Shaking with my own sorrow, I will never forget that moment. For I knew that, although I couldn't begin to fathom the depth of their love, I had been privileged to witness its unmatched beauty.

知道我有多么爱你

我的祖父母结婚已经半个多世纪了,从他们认识以来就玩起了特殊的游戏。游戏的目的是在一个意想不到的地方写下"shmily"这个词让对方去发现。他们轮流在屋前房后留下"shmily",对方一发现,就开始新的一轮让另一方藏着写。

他们用手指在糖盒和面盆上写下"shmily",等着准备下顿饭的对方发现。他们在沾着露水的窗户上写下"shmily";一次又一次的热水澡后,总会在雾气蒙蒙的镜子上留下"shmily"。

有时,祖母甚至打开一整卷卫生纸,在最后一张纸上留下"shmily"。

没有"shmily"不可能出现的地方。匆匆写下的"shmily"的小字条会出现在汽车仪表板和车座上,或是粘贴在方向盘上。这些字条会被塞进鞋子里或留在枕头下面。

"Shmily"会写在壁炉架上的尘埃上、勾画在壁炉的炉灰上。这个神秘的词像祖父母的家具一样成了他们房子的一部分。

过了好久,我才完全明白祖父母之间游戏的意义。我疑神疑鬼不相信真爱——那种纯洁持久的爱。然而,我从未怀疑过祖父母之间的关系。他们彼此相爱。那不仅仅是轻浮的小游戏,而是一种生活方式。他们的关系是基于投入和深爱,这不是每个人都有幸体验到的。

祖父母一有机会就握着手。他们在小厨房里相遇时偷吻。他们说完彼此说了一半的句子,每天一起玩纵横拼字和字谜游戏。祖母低声对我说祖父老当益壮、好酷好帅。她宣称自己的确明白"如何选择"。每次吃饭前他们低头致谢,对自己的种种福佑大为惊奇,因为家庭幸福、好运相伴和相亲相爱。

但祖父母的生活中出现了一片乌云:祖母乳腺癌复发。第一次出现是在10年前。像往常一样,祖父总是和她走完人生的每一步。为了安慰祖母,祖父将室内涂成黄色,这样在祖母病重不能外出时,也总能感受到周围的阳光。

现在癌症再次侵袭着她的身体。在拐杖和祖父的可靠帮助下,他们每天早上去教堂。但祖母日渐消瘦,直到最后她再也不能离开家。有一阵子,祖父常常独自去教堂,向上帝祈祷照顾他的妻子。

后来有一天，我们都担心的事还是发生了。祖母撒手而去。

“Shmily”用黄色写在祖母葬花的粉色缎带上。当人群渐渐散去、最后的哀悼者转身离去时，叔伯姑婶和其他家庭成员走上前来最后一次围聚在祖母四周。祖父走向祖母的灵柩，颤抖声音开始向她歌唱。透过悲泪，这歌声低沉轻柔，犹如催眠曲。

我因悲痛而颤抖，永远无法忘记那个时刻。因为我知道，尽管我无法测量他们爱的深度，但我有幸目睹了这无与伦比的美。

The Wings of Love

No one knows where love's wings will land. At times, it turns up in the most unusual spots. There was nothing more surprising than when it descended upon a rehabilitation hospital in a Los Angeles suburb—a hospital where most of the patients can no longer move of their own accord.

When the staff heard the news, some of the nurses began to cry. The administrator was in shock, but from then on, Harry MacNarama would bless it as one of the greatest days in his entire life.

Michael strapped in his wheelchair and breathing through his ventilator, appeared at Harry's office door one morning.

"Harry, I want to get married," Michael announced.

"Married?" Harry's mouth dropped open. "To whom?"

"To Juana," Michael said. "We're in love."

Love. Love had found its way through the hospital doors, over two bodies that refused to work for their owners and penetrated their hearts—despite the fact that the two patients were unable to feed or cloth themselves, required ventilators just to breath and could never walk again. Michael had spinal muscular atrophy; Juana had multiple sclerosis.

Just how serious this marriage idea was, became quite apparent when Michael pulled out the engagement ring and beamed as he hadn't done in years. In fact, the staff had never seen a kinder, sweeter Michael, who had been one of the angriest men Harry's employees had ever worked with.

The reason for Michael's anger was understandable. For twenty-five years, he had lived his life at a medical center where his mother had placed him at age nine and visited him several times a week until she died. He was always a raspy sort of guy, who cussed out his nurses routinely, but at least he felt he had family at the hospital. The patients were his friends.

There even had been a girl once who went about in a squeaky wheelchair who he was sure had eyed him. But she hadn't stayed long at the center. And after spending more than half his life there, now Michael was not going to get to stay either.

The center was closing, and Michael was shipped to live at the rehabilitation hospital, far from his friends and worse, far from Betty.

That's when Michael turned into a recluse. He wouldn't come out from his room. His friends drove more than two hours to see him. But Michael's spirits sagged so low, no one could reach him.

And then, one day, he was lying in bed when he heard a familiar creaking sound coming down the hall.

The squeaking stopped at his door, and Juana peered in and asked him to come outdoors with her. He was intrigued and from the moment he met Juana again, it was as though she breathed life back into him.

He was staring at the clouds and blue skies again. He began to participate in the hospital's recreation programs. He spent hours talking with Juana. His room was sunny and light. And then he

asked Juana, who'd been living in a wheelchair since age twenty-four, if she would marry him.

Juana had already had a tough life. She was pulled out of school before finishing the third grade, because she collapsed and fell a lot. Her mother, thinking she was lazy, slapped her around. She lived in terror that her mother wouldn't want her anymore, so on the occasions when she was well enough, she cleaned house "like a little maid".

Before the age of twenty-four, like Michael, she had a tracheotomy just to breathe and that was when she was officially diagnosed with multiple sclerosis. By the time she was thirty, she had moved into a hospital with round-the-clock care.

"He told me he loved me, and I was so scared," she said. "I thought he was playing a game with me. But he told me it was true. He told me he loved me."

On Valentine's Day, Juana wore a wedding dress made of white satin, dotted with pearl beads and cut loose enough to drape around a wheelchair and a ventilator. Juana was rolled to the front of the room, assisted by Harry. Her face streamed with tears.

Michael wore a crisp white shirt, black jacket and a bow tie that fit neatly over his tracheotomy. He beamed with pleasure.

Nurses filled the doorways. Patients filled the room. An overflow of hospital employees spilled into the halls. Sobs echoed in every comer of the room. In the hospital's history, no two people—living their lives bound to wheelchairs—had ever married.

Janet Yamaguchi, the hospital's recreation leader, had planned everything. Employees had donated their own money to buy the red and white balloons, matching flowers, and an archway dotted with leaves. Janet had the hospital chef make a three-tiered, lemon-filled wedding cake. A marketing consultant hired a photographer.

The final touch-the kiss-couldn't be completed. Janet used a white satin rope to tie the couple's wheelchairs to symbolize the romantic moment.

After the ceremony, the minister slipped out trying to hold back her tears. "I've performed thousands of weddings, but this is the most wonderful one I've done so far," the minister said. "These people have passed the barriers and showed pure love."

That evening, Michael and Juana rolled into their own room for the first time together. They knew they had moved many people with their love, and they had been given the greatest gift of all. They had the gift of love. And it's never known where it will land.

爱的翅膀

无人知道爱的翅膀会落在哪里。有时,它会出现在最不寻常的地方。令人吃惊的是,它降临在洛杉矶郊区的一家康复医院——这里大多数病人行动无法自理。

医护人员听到这个消息时,一些护士开始哭了起来,院长哈里·麦克南拉默也大为震惊,但从那时起,哈里就把这看作是他一生中最伟大的一天。

一天早晨,迈克尔出现在哈里的办公室门口,他的身体用带子缚在轮椅上,借助呼吸器呼吸。

"哈里,我想结婚。"迈克宣布说。

"结婚?"哈里张大了嘴。"和谁?"

"胡安娜!"迈克尔说。"我们在恋爱。"

爱情,爱情穿越了医院之门,降临在两个完全瘫痪的人身上,穿透了他们的心灵——尽管两位病人衣食无法自理,需要呼吸器才能呼吸,而且再也不能行走。迈克尔得了脊髓肌肉萎缩症,胡安娜身患多发性硬化症。

结婚的念头是多么认真，当迈克尔拿出结婚戒指，露出多年不见的笑容时，越发明显了。事实上，医护人员从未见迈克尔这样善良温柔过，他一直是哈里的职员们公认的脾气最暴躁的人。

迈克尔的暴躁情有可原。他在医疗中心已经住了25年。9岁时，妈妈把他送来后，每周来看几次，直到去世。他总是大发雷霆，骂走护士，但至少他觉得医院是他的家，病人们都是他的朋友。

曾有一个女孩，坐在吱吱作响的轮椅里。迈克尔敢肯定她已经注意到了他。但她在中心并没有待多久。迈克尔在那里度过了大半生后，现在再也不想待下去了。

中心快要关门了，迈克尔被转移到了康复医院，远离了他的朋友们，而且更糟的是，远离了贝蒂。

迈克尔就是这个时候变得寂寞的，他不愿走出房间。朋友们驱车两个多小时来看他。但他还是垂头丧气，没人能影响他。

后来，有一天，他躺在床上，突然听到走廊传来一阵熟悉的嘎吱声。嘎吱声在他的门口停住了，胡安娜凝视着里面，请他和她一起出门。他一下子来了兴致。从再次见到胡安娜的那一刻起，好像她让他焕发了生机。

他又仰望起了蓝天白云，开始参加医院的娱乐节目，连续几个小时与胡安娜聊天。他的房间阳光明媚。不久，他向从24岁起就一直在轮椅上生活的胡安娜求婚，问她是否愿意嫁给他。

胡安娜曾度过一段艰苦日子。她没上完三年级就辍学了，因为她身体虚弱，经常昏倒。母亲以为她懒，总是打她。她生活在恐惧中，害怕母亲不要她。所以，她身体好些时，就会“像小女佣一样”打扫房间。

24岁前，她和迈克尔一样做过一次气管切开手术，以使呼吸畅通。也就是在那个时候，她被正式确诊患有多发性硬化症。30岁时，她被送进医院接受全天护理。

“他说爱我时，我非常害怕，”她说，“我想他是在跟我开玩笑。但他对我说是真的。他对我说他爱我。”

情人节那天，胡安娜穿着一件白色绸缎结婚礼服，上面缀满珍珠，而且宽松得足以遮住轮椅和呼吸器。哈里帮着把她推到房门前。她泪流满面。

迈克尔穿着挺括的白衬衣和黑夹克，打着蝴蝶结，刚好盖在切除的气管上。他面带幸福的微笑。

门口挤满了护士，房间里都是病人，就连大厅里也满是医护人员。房间的每个角落都传来呜咽声。有史以来，医院还没有两个在轮椅上生活的人结婚的呢。

医院的娱乐节目主持人珍妮特·山口安排好了所有的一切。医护人员用捐来的钱买了红气球和白气球，同时配上鲜花，然后在拱门上点缀上绿叶。珍妮特请医院厨师做了一个三层柠檬味的结婚蛋糕。一个营销顾问请来了摄影师。

最后一项——接吻——无法完成。珍妮特用白绸缎把这对新人的轮椅系在一起，以此来象征这浪漫的时刻。

婚礼结束后，牧师强忍眼泪，悄然而出。“我已经主持了几千次婚礼，但这次是迄今为止最棒的一次。”牧师说，“这对人已经越过了障碍，展示了真爱。”

那天晚上，迈克尔和胡安娜第一次双双进入自己的房间。他们知道他们已经用爱情打动了很多人，而且收到了最伟大的礼物。他们收到了爱的礼物，而且谁也无法知道爱会落在哪里。

100/0 Love

As a teenager I had certain ideas in my mind that constituted the idyllic life of love and marriage. In Home Economics, our teacher had us plan the perfect wedding and the perfect reception, right down to the throwing of rice and driving away in a limousine. It was just like the movies where the nice guy gets the beautiful girl and they live happily ever after. Reality was not a part of the picture.

After high school, I went to college and was determined to become a nurse. I forgot about marriage. Surprisingly, two years later I met the man I would marry.

He was from a small town in Idaho and farmed with his father. I was from a Southern town, which had a greater population than the entire state of Idaho. I had always been emphatic that I didn't know whom I would marry, but one thing was for sure—he wouldn't be a farmer or dairyman! Well, I was wrong in both cases. They were not only farmers but dairymen as well.

We were married in October just prior to the beginning of heavy snowfalls. It would snow heavily throughout the whole winter. Our only entertainment was listening to the radio or the local high school sporting events. My new husband was a lover of sports. He had been a champion boxer and also participated in most sports. I was a lover of the arts. Speech, drama and dance were my first love. The nearest town with this kind of entertainment was forty miles away and the highway was closed off and on all winter.

We had only been married seven months when I received word that my mother, who was battling cancer, wouldn't live much longer. Even though there was the dairy with 75 cows and 1,400 acres to farm, as soon as my husband read the telegram, he sadly said, "Honey, get your bags packed while I make reservations for you. Your place is with your mother and your father right now." To him there had been no other decision to make. Every week I would receive a letter telling me all about how the farm was doing and inquiring about my parents and how we were all doing. Little was said about his sadness of being alone, or of missing his new bride, except at the very end of his letters where an unmistakable "I love you" was written. Teenage dream letters would have been filled with remarks of undying love and pain of missing me, but his letters were simple words of reality.

Four months later, after the funeral, I returned to Idaho where I knew my husband would be at the airport to meet me.

The look in his eyes told me more than any dream letter could. On the 80-mile drive to our home, I talked incessantly while he quietly listened. When he finally had a chance to respond, he asked me to open the glove compartment of the car and take out an envelope with my name on it. "I wanted to give you something special to let you know how much I missed you," he said quietly.

I opened the envelope to find season tickets, for both of us, to all of the area's fine art functions. I was stunned. "I don't believe this," I cried. "You don't enjoy these things!"

He reached out, hugged me and quietly said, "No, but you do, and I will learn."

In that moment I realized marriage was not 50/50, but real love was made of 100/0 sometimes. Love means putting the other one first. His example taught his young wife a great lesson—a lesson that has made a happy marriage for 51 years.

100 比 0 也是爱

少女时代，我在脑海里对爱情和婚姻所想象的是诗情画意的生活。在家政学课上，老师让我们策划完美的婚礼、完美的婚宴，一直到撒大米、新郎新娘开着豪华轿车离去。这就像电影里帅哥赢得美人归，他们从此幸福生活在一起。现实并不是这样的景象。

中学毕业后，我上了大学，决心要成为一名护士。我把婚姻忘在了脑后。让人吃惊的是，两年后我遇到了我愿意嫁的男人。

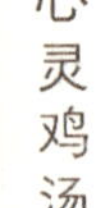

他来自爱达荷州的一个小镇，和他父亲一起经营农场。我来自南方的一个城镇，那里的人口比整个爱达荷州的人口都多。我总是强调我不知道要嫁给什么男人，但有一点是肯定的——他不会是农场主或奶牛场主！嗨，我两个都错了。我遇到的这个男人和他的父亲不仅是农场主还是奶牛场主。

我们在 10 月大雪开始前结了婚。大雪会下整整一冬天。我们唯一的娱乐就是听收音机或观看当地中学体育比赛。我的新婚丈夫是一个体育爱好者。他曾是拳击冠军，也参加过大多数的体育活动。我是一个艺术爱好者。演讲、戏剧和舞蹈是我的最爱。有这种娱乐活动的城镇距离我们最近的有 40 英里，而且整个冬天公路时开时关。

我们结婚才 7 个月时，我就得到消息说我母亲在与癌症抗争，活不了多久了。即使有 75 头奶牛和 1400 英亩地要耕种，我丈夫一看完电报就伤心地说："亲爱的，收拾好行囊，我去给你订票。你马上和你父母亲在一起。"在他看来，没有什么别的决定可作。每周我会收到他的来信，告诉我农场的所有情况，询问我父母亲，我们全家人怎样。他很少说他独处的悲伤，也很少说他思念新婚妻子，只是在每封信的结尾都明确无误地写上"我爱你"。我少女时代的梦中情书应该是写满诉说永恒的爱和思念我的痛苦，但他的信却是简单叙述现实生活的几行字。

4 个月后，举行完葬礼，我返回爱达荷州。我知道丈夫会到机场去接我。

他的眼神告诉我的要比任何梦中情书所能表达的多。在驱车 80 英里回我们家的路上，我说个没完，他静静地听着。当他最后有机会应答时，他让我打开汽车仪表板上的小柜，拿出一个上面写有我名字的信封。"我想送给你一件特别的东西，告诉你我有多么想你。"他平静地说。

我打开信封，发现有好多张参加该地区所有艺术活动的季票，是我们两个人的。我大吃了一惊。"我不相信，"我叫道。"你不喜欢这些东西！"

他伸出手臂，抱住我，平静地说："是的，但你喜欢，所以我一定要学会。"

此时此刻，我意识到婚姻不是 50 比 50，真正的爱有时是 100 比 0。爱就是把对方放在首位。他率先垂范，给他年轻的妻子上了重要的一课——这一课促成了 51 年的幸福婚姻。

The Essence of Love

At a weekend gathering, the friends talked about the true meaning of love.

One of his friends asked how he felt.

Thinking for a while, he told a story:

After work that day, he stopped on the way home to buy two blocks of glass for his bookcase. Walking to the doorway, without taking care he staggered a few steps and almost fell over himself while the glass in his hands fell to the ground with a thump shattering into pieces instantly.

His wife who was cooking in the kitchen heard the sound, hurried out to hold his hands and asked him gently, "Are your hands cut? First come in and have a rest. The meal is ready in a moment. I clean the pieces."

He said nothing, but gazed at his wife affectionately.

爱的真谛

周末聚会,朋友们谈论爱的真谛。

有朋友问他的感受。

他略一思忖,讲了一个故事:

那天下班,他顺道去为书柜配了两块玻璃。走到家门口,他没留神,一个趔趄,踉跄几步,险些摔倒,手中的玻璃"哗"地掉到地上,立时碎片四溅。

正在厨房里做饭的妻子闻声赶来,拉起他的手,柔声问道:"手划破了没有?你先进屋去休息,过一会儿饭就做好了,我来清扫一下玻璃渣。"

他什么话也没说,只是深情地看了妻子一眼。

A Letter to Sophie

Dear Sophie,

I cannot leave this place without saying a few words to you. So, my pet, you expect a good deal from me. Your happiness, your life, even depend, you say, upon my ever loving you!

Never fear, my dear Sophie, that will endure, and you shall live, and be happy. I have never committed a crime yet, and am not going to begin. I am wholly yours—you are everything to me. We will sustain each other in all the ills of life it may please fate to inflict upon us; you will soothe my troubles; I will comfort you in yours. Would that I could always see you as you have been lately! As for myself, you must confess that I am just as I was on the first day you saw me.

This is no merit of my own, but I owe it in justice to myself to tell you so. It is one effect of good qualities to be felt more vividly from day to day. Be assured of my constancy to yours, and of my appreciation of them. Never was a passion more justified by reason than mine. It is not true, my dear Sophie, that you are very amiable? Examine myself—see how worthy you are of being loved, and know that I love you very much. That is the unvarying standard of my feelings.

Good night, my dear Sophia. I am as happy as man can be in knowing that I am loved by the best of women.

Yours forever,
Dennis

写给索菲的信

亲爱的索菲:

不对你说几句话,我舍不得离开此地。你看,我的宝贝,你对我抱有多大期望。你说,你的幸福,甚至你的生命,都取决于我对你一如既往的爱!

亲爱的索菲,千万别担心,你将永远拥有我的爱,你会幸福地活下去。我从未犯过罪,也不会去犯罪。我完全属于你——你是我的一切。在人生将要经历的苦难中,我们要同甘共苦;你要除去我的烦恼,我要为你排忧解闷。但愿我能看见你永远像现在这样。至于我自己,你得承认,我就是你第一天见到我时的那个样子,没有任何改变。

这不是我的优点,但确实是我的心声,它表现出一种美好的品质,而且日复一日,你将感受更深。相信我会对你忠贞不渝,我将把你的美德铭刻在心。没有人像我这样合乎情理地对你痴迷。亲爱的索菲,难道你不亲切可人吗?看看自己吧——看你多么值得爱慕,我又是多么爱你。这就是我永恒不变的感情。

晚安,亲爱的索菲,一个男人得知自己拥有世界上最好的女人的爱,这是多么幸福啊。

你永远的
丹尼斯

The Sign Language of Love

From the very beginning, the girl's family argued against her dating this guy. They said that she would suffer for the rest of her life if she insisted on being with him.

The girl indeed was in love with the guy. She always asked him, "How much do you love me?"

A few years later, the guy graduated from college and decided to go abroad for further study. Before leaving, he proposed to the girl, "I'm not a smart mouth. All I know is that I love you. If you allow me, I will take care of you for the rest of my life. As to your family, I'll try my best. Will you marry me?" The girl said yes.

The guy kept his words and made her parents accept the fact.

They got engaged before the guy set off.

Then the girl stayed and started working while the guy focused on his study in another country. They sent their love through emails and phone calls. It was hard, but neither of them ever wanted to quit.

One day when the girl was on her way to work, a car lost control and knocked her down. Waking up and seeing her parents standing beside her bed, the girl realized that she was badly injured. Her mother kept crying. She wanted to comfort her. But all that could come out of her lips was just a sigh.

The doctor diagnosed that the girl had lost her voice due to the injury in her brain. She broke down. She wept all day, without a word.

When she got back home from hospital, she didn't feel herself deserving him anymore. So she wrote to him and told him that she hated to be kept waiting and returned the engagement ring to the guy.

He called and wrote, trying to get her back to him, but he was always refused by her parents.

Her parents decided to move away with the hope that she would forget everything and be happy. This decision really helped the girl start a new life. She began learning sign language and told herself to forget him every day.

One day her good friend dropped by and told her that he was back home and looking for her everywhere. She asked her friend not to tell him what happened to her and for his own good, to forget about her. Then, nothing new about him came.

Another year passed. Her friend came with a wedding invitation from the guy. She was shattered. Opening the invitation, she saw her name went after the "bride". Just about to ask her friend what was going on, she saw him standing in front of her.

He spoke in sign language, "I've spent a year learning sign language, just to let you know that I never wanted to break my promise. Please give me a chance. Let me speak for you. I can be your voice."

He slipped the ring back into her finger. She finally smiled.

爱的手语

女孩的家人一开始就反对她和这个男孩约会。他们说,如果她坚持要和男孩在一起,就会吃一辈子苦。

女孩确实爱这个男孩,总是问他:"你有多爱我?"

几年后,男孩大学毕业,决定出国留学。出国前,男孩向女孩求婚。"我不会花言巧语,只知道我爱你。如果你愿意,我会照顾你一辈子。至于你的家人,我会竭尽全力。你愿意嫁给我吗?"女孩答应了。

男孩说话算数,终于使女孩的家人接受了这个事实。

于是,在男孩出国前,他们就订了婚。

后来,女孩留在国内开始工作。男孩在异国他乡精心学习。他们通过电邮和电话传递爱情。尽管日子难熬,但他们俩谁也没有想过放弃。

有一天,在女孩上班的路上,一辆汽车失控,把她撞倒在地。女孩醒来后看到父母站在病床边,才明白自己受了重伤。她母亲哭个不停。女孩想安慰母亲,但嘴唇里所能发出的仅仅是一声叹息。

医生诊断说因为大脑受伤,女孩丧失了说话能力。她一下子就垮了,成天以泪洗面、一声不吭。

出院回家后,她觉得自己再也配不上他了,就写信告诉他说她不喜欢再等了,把订婚戒指也退给了男孩。

他又是打电话又是写信,想设法让她回心转意,但总是被她的父母亲拒绝。

她的父母亲决定搬家,希望女孩忘记一切、开心起来。这个决定确实帮助女孩开始了一种新的生活。她开始学习手语,每天都告诉自己要忘记他。

有一天，她的好友来访，告诉她男孩已经回国了，在四处找她。她请好友不要把她的事告诉他，为了他好，就忘了她吧。之后，就再也没有他的任何消息。

又一年过去了。女孩的好友带来了男孩的结婚请帖。她顿时心碎。打开请帖后，她看到自己的名字出现在“新娘”栏中。她正要问好友是怎么回事，只见他站在了她面前。

他用手语说：“我花了一年时间学手语，就是想告诉你，我从来没有想违背诺言。请给我一个机会。让我替你说话。我可以成为你的声音啊。”

他重新将戒指又戴回了她的手指。她终于露出了微笑。

The Supremacy of Love

When he fell in love with her, she was a 19-year-old girl, who was dreaming naively in the tower of ivory far away from the real world. He had worked for years, almost forgetting how to be romantic, so he cherished their spiritual world as possible as he could.

One day, he borrowed Sophie's Choice acted by Meryl Streep and saw it with her. After the movie was over, she couldn't understand most profound meanings of the movie, but one scene was embedded into her mind: when people opened the door and rushed into the room, they found that the two lovers had passed away, embracing each other. She wept and asked him whether it was the highest realm of love. He smiled at her, without answer. He gave her a feeling that he must know another kind of higher realm.

He waited for her for many years, and then she became his wife. Gradually, consciously or unconsciously, they got into the habit of falling asleep in each other's arms. No matter which posture they changed in their sleep or what they took no notice of each other for, she was always in his arms the next morning she woke up. She felt very happy. Later on, something happened between them and they began to suspect their feeling. He didn't say, "I love you" to her anymore; of course, she didn't say, "So do I" to him, either.

One night, they talked about separating and slept back to back.

At midnight, it thundered. When the first thunder blasted, he woke up and covered her ears with his hands subconsciously, finding that he was embracing her, not knowing when.

The second thunder followed. She might be awoken by the thunder or his hands. When she opened her eyes, the thunder rumbling in her ears, his hands were moving from her ears.

Tears welled up in her eyes at once. They closed their eyes again, pretending nothing happened, but neither fell asleep.

She thought, maybe he still loved me, fearing I was scared a little.

He thought, maybe she still loved me, or she couldn't be in tears.

The supremacy of love is the one that can stand the ordinary days. We need to savor dribs and drabs of happiness slowly.

爱的最高境界

他爱上她时，她才19岁，正在远离现实世界的象牙塔里做着纯真的梦。而他已经工作了好几年，差不多忘记了怎样浪漫，因此他尽可能小心呵护着她和他的精神世界。

有一天，他借来梅丽尔·斯特里普演的《索菲的选择》和她一起看。片子看完了，她并没有明白片子最深刻的意义，但有一个镜头从此嵌入了她的脑海：当人们打开房门冲进屋子时，发现那两个相爱的人已经相拥着告别了这个世界。她流泪了，问他这是不是爱的最高境界。他笑了笑，没有回答。他让她觉得，他一定知道还有一种更高的境界。

他等了她很多年，然后她成了他的妻子。渐渐地，不知有意无意，他们养成了相拥而眠的习惯。无论睡梦中变化了怎样的姿势，无论他们为了什么事互不理睬，第二天清晨醒来，她总是在他怀里。她觉得很幸福。再后来，他们之间发生了一些事，开始互相怀疑他们之间的感情。他不再对她说"我爱你"，当然她也不再对她说"我也是"。

一天晚上，他们谈到了分手的事，背对背睡下了。

半夜，天上打雷了。第一声雷响时，他惊醒了，下意识地猛地用双手去捂她的耳朵，才发现不知何时他又拥着她。

第二声雷紧接着炸开了，她或许是被雷声或被他的手弄醒了，睁开眼，耳里还有闷闷的雷声，他的手正从她的耳朵上拿开。

她的眼睛顿时湿润了。他们重新闭上眼，假装什么也没有发生，但谁都没有睡着。

她想，也许他还爱我，生怕我受一点点惊吓。

他想，也许她还爱我，不然她是不会流泪的。

爱的最高境界是经得起平淡的流年。我们需要慢慢地品味幸福的点点滴滴。

Written in the Stars

Ted went away to school, and we wrote letters to each other quite often at first. Then as the days passed, we wrote less and less. And that was the beginning of the end. He couldn't come home for Thanksgiving; and when he was home for Christmas, I had the measles.

We didn't get to see each other until spring vacation. But then we had been apart so long that we spent the whole week getting to know each other again. Ted was as good and sweet and wonderful as ever, but somehow he seemed different. When he went back to school, he said, "don't forget me."

"Of course not," I said, but this time I was not so sure.

As it worked out, it was Ted who met somebody else. She was a student at Tulane. Ted wrote me a letter telling about her. He said he was sorry, and he knew I would understand.

It was raining the day the letter came. I read it in the living room and then gave it to Mother to read and went upstairs to my room.

I laid on the bed and listened to the sound of the rain. I didn't hate Ted, but I couldn't believe what had happened. I didn't even hate the girl. I couldn't believe that he was now gone and he would never come back again. Never!

I was still lying there when Mother came in. Before she spoke, I knew what she was going to say.

"There are other boys," she said. "You may not believe it now, but there will be."

"I suppose so," I said, "but Ted was the one. I can never fall in love again!"

Mother was silent a moment. Then she said, "Do you have the locket I gave you?"

"The locket? Yes, of course, it's in the top drawer of the dresser."

Mother got the locket. "Put it on," she said.

I sat up and put the locket around my neck.

"You see," she said, "the locket was given to me by a special person when we were engaged."

Then I held the locket lovingly, remembering Daddy. What a happy life he and Mother had had.

"You see," she said, "he was kind, sweet, and wonderful. I was sure he was written for me in the stars." Then she added slowly, "He was killed in a train wreck three weeks after we became engaged."

"He what!" I exclaimed. "But I thought—you mean you loved somebody before Daddy—somebody you thought was The Special One?"

"Yes, that is it. If I'd married him, I'm sure that I would have been very happy. As it worked out, three years later I married your father. We loved each other, and I was happy with him."

"I don't understand," I said.

Then Mother replied, "What I'm trying to tell you, honey, is that there is no one special person who alone can make us happy. There are many fine people in the world. Ted is one of them, but he came along too soon."

I almost cried because I thought I was losing the dream of my childhood.

Then Mother said gently, "One of these days a good man will come along at the right time—he will be the one written for you in the stars."

She went out and closed the door softly and left me alone, listening to the rain.

I looked at the door Mother had just closed behind her, and I thought about the other door, the door of Hope that she had just opened.

命中吉星

特德离开家上学去了，起初我们经常写信。后来，随着一天天过去，我们写得越来越少了。而那正是结局的开始。他无法回家过感恩节；等他回家过圣诞节时，我又患上了麻疹。

我们直到第二年春假才见面。但那时我们已经分开了很久，所以我们花了整整一周来再次了解对方。特德还和以前一样善良、可爱，令人愉快，但不知何故他好像不大一样了。他返校时，说："别忘了我。"

"当然不会，"我说，但这次我却没有把握。

结果是特德遇上了另一个女孩。她是图兰学院的学生。特德在给我的信里提到了她。他说他很抱歉，并说他知道我会理解。

信来时，天正下着雨。我在客厅里看了信，又把它给妈妈看，然后就回楼上自己的房间去了。

我躺在床上，听着窗外的雨声。我不恨特德，但我无法相信发生的一切。我甚至不恨那个女孩。我无法相信，他现在飘然而去，再也不会回来了。再也不会！

妈妈进来时，我仍躺在那里。还没等她开口，我就知道她要说什么。

"男孩有的是，"她说。"现在你也许不相信，但将来会有的。"

"我想是吧，"我说。"但特德就那一个。我再也不会堕入情网了！"

妈妈沉默了一会儿，然后说道："我给你的小盒子还在吗？"

"小盒子？在，当然在，它在梳妆台最上面的抽屉里。"

妈妈拿出小盒子。"戴上吧。"她说。

我坐起身，把小盒子戴在脖子上。

“你明白，”她说。“这小盒子是一个心上人在我们订婚那天送给我的。”

于是，我爱抚着小盒子。想起了爸爸。他和妈妈曾过着多么幸福的生活啊。

“你明白，”她说。“他善良可爱、令人愉快。我确信他就是我的命中吉星。”接着，她又慢慢补充道，“我们订婚三周后，他却在一次火车失事中死去了。”

“他什么！”我惊叫道。“可我还以为——你是说你在爸爸之前还爱过别人——你原来认为另一个人是心上人？”

“是的，就是这样。如果嫁给他，我肯定自己会很幸福。结果是，3 年后我嫁给了你父亲。我们相亲相爱，我和他也很幸福。”

“我不明白。”我说。

随后，妈妈回答说：“亲爱的，我想告诉你的是，我们的幸福并不仅仅是某个心上人给我们的。世界上有许多好人。特德是其中的一个，但他来得太早了。”

我差点儿失声痛哭，因为我认为自己正在失去童年的梦想。

接下来，妈妈柔声说道：“总有一天，一个好男人会在适当时候出现——他将是你的命中吉星。”

她走了出去，轻轻地关上门，留下我独自听雨。

我看着妈妈身后刚刚关上的那扇门，随后想到了另一扇门，一扇妈妈刚刚为我打开的希望之门。

The Remembrance of Lilacs

The family had just moved to Rhode Island, and the young woman was feeling a little melancholy on that Sunday in May. After all, it was Mother's Day—and 800 miles separated her from her parents in Ohio.

She had called her mother that morning to wish her a happy Mother's Day, and her mother had mentioned how colorful the yard was now that spring had arrived. As they talked, the younger woman could almost smell the tantalizing aroma of purple lilacs hanging on the big bush outside her parents' back door.

Later, when she mentioned to her husband how she missed those lilacs, he popped up from his chair. "I know where we can find you all you want," he said. "Get the kids and c'mon."

So off they went, driving the country roads of northern Rhode Island on the kind of day only mid-May can produce: sparkling sunshine, unclouded azure skies and vibrant newness of the green growing all around. They went past small villages and burgeoning housing developments, past abandoned apple orchards, back to where trees and brush have devoured old homesteads.

Where they stopped, dense thickets of cedars and junipers and birch crowded the roadway on both sides. There was not a lilac bush in sight.

"Come with me," the man said. "Over that hill is an old cellar hole, from somebody's farm of years ago, and there are lilacs all around it. The man who owns this land said I could poke around here anytime. I'm sure he won't mind if we pick a few lilacs."

Before they got halfway up the hill, the fragrance of the lilacs drifted down to them, and the kids started running. Soon, the mother began running, too, until she reached the top.

There, far from view of passing motorists and hidden from encroaching civilization, were the

towering lilacs bushes, so laden with the huge, cone-shaped flower clusters that they almost bent double. With a smile, the young woman rushed up to the nearest bush and buried her face in the flowers, drinking in the fragrance and the memories it recalled.

While the man examined the cellar hole and tried to explain to the children what the house must have looked like, the woman drifted among the lilacs. Carefully, she chose a sprig here, another one there, and clipped them with her husband's pocketknife. She was in no hurry, relishing each blossom as a rare and delicate treasure.

Finally, though, they returned to their car for the trip home. While the kids chattered and the man drove, the woman sat smiling, surrounded by her flowers, a faraway look in her eyes.

When they were within three miles of home, she suddenly shouted to her husband, "Stop the car. Stop right here!"

The man slammed on the brakes. Before he could ask her why she wanted to stop, the woman was out of the car and hurrying up a nearby grassy slope with the lilacs still in her arms.

At the top of the hill was a nursing home and, because it was such a beautiful spring day, the patients were outdoors strolling with relatives or sitting on the porch.

The young woman went to the end of the porch, where an elderly patient was sitting in her wheelchair, alone, head bowed, her back to most of the others. Across the porch railing went the flowers, into the lap of the old woman. She lifted her head, and smiled.

For a few moments, the two women chatted, both aglow with happiness, and then the young woman turned and ran back to her family.

As the car pulled away, the woman in the wheelchair waved and clutched the lilacs.

"Mom," the kids asked, "who was that? Why did you give her our flowers? Is she somebody's mother?"

The mother said she didn't know the old woman. But it was Mother's Day, and she seemed so alone, and who wouldn't be cheered by flowers? "Besides," she added, "I have all of you, and I still have my mother, even if she is far away. That woman needed those flowers more than I did."

This satisfied the kids, but not the husband. The next day he purchased half a dozen young lilacs bushes and planted them around their yard, and several times since then he has added more.

I was that man. The young mother was, and is, my wife.

Now, every May, our own yard is redolent with lilacs. Every Mother's Day our kids gather purple bouquets. And every year I remember that smile on a lonely old woman's face, and the kindness that put the smile there.

紫丁香的回忆

5 月的那个星期天，一家人刚移居罗德岛，那个年轻女人感到有点儿忧伤。毕竟，这一天是母亲节，而她却与俄亥俄州的父母亲相距 800 英里。

她那天早上给母亲打去电话，祝母亲节日愉快。随后，她的母亲向她提到，因为春天已经来临，所以院子里的色彩是多么绚丽。在她们通话时，年轻女人几乎可以闻到悬垂在父母亲后门外大灌木丛上的紫丁香醉人的芬芳。

后来，当她向丈夫说起她是如何怀念那些丁香时，他突然从椅子上一跃而起。"我知道我们可以在哪里找到你想要的东西，"他说。"带上孩子们，走吧。"

于是，他们就出发，驱车行驶在罗德岛北部的乡村小路上，那种天气只有 5 月中旬才会有：闪闪发亮的阳光、蔚蓝色的晴空，以及生机勃勃、随处可见的鲜嫩青草。他们穿过一座座小村庄和一座座拔地而起的房屋，穿过废弃的苹果园，来到了树林和灌木丛掩映的老农场。

他们停下车。车道两边长满了茂盛的雪松、杜松和白桦树。连一棵紫丁香也没有看到。

“随我来,”那个男人说。“翻过那座小山,有个老地窖,几年前是一个人的农场,四周长满了紫丁香。这块地的主人说我可以随时到这里来闲逛。我相信,我们要是采几束紫丁香,他是不会介意的。”

还没等他们到达半山腰,紫丁香的芬芳已经向他们飘了过来。于是,孩子们开始奔跑。不久,那位母亲也开始跑了起来,直至到达山顶。

那里,远离了过往汽车司机的视野,避开了纷扰的文明世界,高耸的丁香花丛开满了硕大的圆锥形的串串花束,几乎把花茎都压弯了。那个年轻女人微笑着冲到离得最近的那处花丛,把脸埋在鲜花中,啜饮着芳香,它重新唤起了她的记忆。

在那个男人察看地窖试图向孩子们解释这个房子必定是什么样子时,那个女人不由自主地走进了丁香花丛。她小心翼翼地从这里摘一枝,在那里采一束,然后用丈夫的折刀将它们剪下来。她不慌不忙,像欣赏稀有珍宝似的欣赏着每一朵花。

然而,他们最后还是返回汽车,走在了回家的路上。孩子们叽叽喳喳说个不停,那个男人驾着车,那个女人坐在那里面带微笑,她周围放满了鲜花,眼里充满着向往。

当他们离家不足3英里时,她突然向丈夫大声喊道:“停车,就在这里停车!”

那个男人嘎地刹住车。还没等他问为什么要停,那个女人就已经下了车,匆匆走向附近的草坡,怀里仍然抱着那些丁香花。

山顶上是一家疗养院,而且因为这是一个美丽的春日,所以病人正在室外和亲友漫步或坐在门廊上。

那个年轻女人走到门廊尽头,只见那里有一个上了年纪的病人正坐在轮椅里,独自一人,低着头,背对着其他大多数人。年轻女人越过门廊栏杆,将鲜花放在了老太太的膝间。老太太抬起头,露出了笑脸。

两个女人聊了一会儿,都兴高采烈的。随后,那个年轻女人转身跑回家人的身边。

汽车开动时,坐在轮椅里的那个女人挥动着手,手里紧握着那束丁香。

“妈妈,”孩子们问。“那人是谁?你为什么把我们的花送给她?她是谁的母亲?”

他们的母亲说,她不认识那个老太太,但今天是母亲节,她看起来是那么孤独,谁不情愿用鲜花为自己喝彩呢?“再说,”她补充道。“我拥有你们所有的人,而且我还有自己的母亲,即使她离我很远。那个女人比我更需要那些鲜花。”

她这一席话使孩子们都很满意,但她的丈夫却不是这样。第二天,他买了半打丁香幼苗,栽到了院子四周;而且,从那以后,每隔一段时间,他就会增加一些。

我就是那个男人,那个年轻母亲是我的妻子。

如今,每年5月,我们自家的院子都会散发出紫丁香的浓郁芬芳。每逢母亲节,我们的孩子都要采撷紫丁香花束。而且,每年我都会记起一位孤独的老太太脸上露出的那种笑容,以及笑容里呈现出的那种慈祥。

The Envelope on Christmas Morning

It's just a small, white envelope stuck among the branches of our Christmas tree. No name, no identification, no inscription. It has peeked through the branches of our tree for the past 10 years or so.

It all began because my husband Mike hated Christmas—oh, not the true meaning of Christmas, but the commercial aspects of it—overspending... the frantic running around at the last minute to get a tie for Uncle Harry and the dusting powder for Grandma—the gifts given in desperation because you couldn't think of anything else.

Knowing he felt this way, I decided one year to bypass the usual shirts, sweaters, ties and so forth.

Our son Kevin, who was 12 that year, was wrestling at the junior level at the school he attended; and shortly before Christmas, there was a non-league match against a team sponsored by an inner-city church. These youngsters dressed in sneakers so ragged that shoestrings seemed to be the only thing holding them together, presented a sharp contrast to our boys in their spiffy blue and gold uniforms and sparkling new wrestling shoes.

As the match began, I was alarmed to see that the other team was wrestling without headgear, a kind of light helmet designed to protect a wrestler's ears. It was a luxury the ragtag team obviously couldn't afford. Well, we ended up walloping them. We took every weight class. And as each of their boys got up from the mat, he swaggered around in his tatters with false bravado, a kind of street pride that couldn't acknowledge defeat.

Mike, seated beside me, shook his head sadly. "I wish just one of them could have won," he said. "They have a lot of potential, but losing like this could take the heart right out of them."

Mike loved kids—all kids—and he knew them, having coached little league football, baseball and lacrosse. That's when the idea for his present came. That afternoon, I went to a local sporting goods store and bought an assortment of wrestling headgear and shoes and sent the anonymously to the inner-city church.

On Christmas Eve, I placed the envelope on the tree, the note inside telling Mike what I had done and that this was his gift from me. His smile was the brightest thing about Christmas that year and in succeeding years.

For each Christmas, I followed the tradition—one year sending a group of mentally handicapped youngsters to a hockey game, another year a check to a pair of elderly brothers whose home had burned to the ground the week before Christmas...

The envelope became the highlight of our Christmas. It was always the last thing opened on Christmas morning and our children, ignoring their new toys, would stand with wide-eyed anticipation as their dad lifted the envelope from the tree to reveal its contents.

As the children grew, the toys gave way to more practical presents, but the envelope never lost its allure. The story doesn't end there. You see, we lost Mike last year due to dreaded cancer. When Christmas rolled around, I was still so wrapped in grief that I barely got the tree up. But Christmas Eve found me placing an envelope on the tree, and in the morning, it was joined by three more.

Each of our children, unbeknownst to the others, had placed an envelope on the tree for their dad. The tradition has grown and someday will expand even further with our grandchildren standing around the tree with wide-eyed anticipation watching as their fathers take down the envelope. Mike's spirit, like the Christmas spirit, will always be with us.

圣诞节早晨的信封

卡在我们的圣诞树枝上的仅仅是一个小小的白色信封。没有姓名，没有身份证明，

也没有题字。放在我们树枝上的这封信已有10年左右了。

开始都是因为丈夫迈克不喜欢圣诞节——噢,并不是真的指圣诞节,而是指它的商业方面——花费超支……为了给哈利叔叔买领带,给奶奶买爽身粉,他拼命地跑前跑后,只能送这些礼物,因为你想不出别的东西。

有一年,我知道他也这样想,就决定不再像以往那样买衬衫、毛线衫、领带等东西。

我们的儿子凯文那年12岁,正在学校练习初级摔跤。圣诞节前不久,他们要举行一项不结盟比赛,他们的对手由市里一家教堂赞助。这些少年穿的运动鞋破旧,似乎脚上就剩鞋带了。我们这边的孩子身穿漂亮的金蓝色制服和新灿灿的摔跤鞋,和他们形成了鲜明的对比。

比赛开始,我看到对方没有戴那种保护摔跤选手耳朵的浅色护头。对他们这样的乌合之众来说是一种奢侈,显然他们买不起。那么,最终我们以击败他们而告终,而且打败了每一个举重班。那些男孩从垫子上站起来时,穿着破旧的衣服,虚张声势地走来走去,带着一种不承认失败的街头傲气。

迈克坐在我旁边,伤心地摇着头,说:“我真希望他们能有人赢,他们很有潜力,但这样输了,可能会使他们失去信心。”

迈克喜欢小孩——喜欢所有的小孩——他了解他们,他曾担任过小足球队、垒球队和长曲棍球队的教练。那天下午,我去附近的一家体育用品店买了一套摔跤护头和鞋子,匿名把东西送给了市里的教堂。

圣诞节前夕,我把信封放在了圣诞树上,信的内容是告诉迈克我所做的事儿,这就是我送给他的礼物。那年和接下来几年的圣诞节,他的笑容是最灿烂。

每年圣诞节,我都遵循这个传统——有一年是送一些残障少年参加一场曲棍球比赛,还有一年是看望了两位上年纪的兄弟,他们的房屋在圣诞节前烧成了平地……

信封渐渐成为我们圣诞节时最重要的部分。圣诞节早上,信封总是最后一个拆开。我们的孩子们对他们的新玩具熟视无睹,而的常常瞪大眼睛,站在那里,期待着爸爸把信封从圣诞树上摘下来,披露其中的内容。

随着孩子们渐渐长大,他们都要更实用的礼物,但信封从来没有失去吸引力。故事并没未到此结束。你明白,去年迈克因可怕的癌症离开了我们。圣诞节来临时,我还处在悲伤中,几乎没有装饰圣诞树。但在圣诞节前夕,我在树上放了一封信,到了第二天早上,又多了三封。

趁大家不注意时,我们的每个孩子都在圣诞树上放了一封写给爸爸的信。这个传统一直延续着,有一天我们的孙子也会站在圣诞树边,瞪大眼睛盼望着他们的父亲取下信封。迈克的灵魂,就像圣诞精神一样,永远和我们同在。

The Heart-Shaped Pillow

Valentine's Day had arrived and like every other day of the year, I was very busy.

My romantic husband, Roy, planned a date like we had never had before. A reservation at an expensive restaurant was made. A beautifully wrapped present had been sitting on my dresser for a few days prior to the heart-filled holiday.

After a hard day at work, I hurried home, ran into the bathroom and jumped into the shower. When my sweetheart arrived, I was dressed in my finest outfit and ready to go. He hugged me, just as the sitter arrived. We were both excited.

Unfortunately, the littlest member in our household was not so happy.

"Daddy, you were going to take me to buy Mamma a present," Becky, my eight-year-old daughter said, as she sadly walked over to the couch and sat down beside the babysitter.

Roy looked at his watch and realized that if we were to make our reservations, we had to leave right away. He didn't even have a few minutes to take her to the corner drugstore, to buy a heart-shaped box of chocolate candy.

"I'm sorry, I was late getting home, honey," he said.

"That's OK," Becky replied. "I understand."

The entire evening was bittersweet. I couldn't help being concerned about the disappointment in Becky's eyes. I remembered how the joyful Valentine's Day glow had left her face, just before the door closed behind us. She wanted me to know how much she loved me. She didn't realize it, but I already knew it very well.

Today, I can't remember what was wrapped in that beautiful box, which I swooned1 over for several days, but I'll never forget the special gift, which I received when we arrived, back home.

Becky was asleep on the couch, clutching a box, which was sitting on her lap. When I kissed her cheek, she awoke. "I've got something for you, Mamma," she said, as a giant smile covered her tiny face.

The little box was wrapped in newspaper. As I tore the paper off and opened the box, I found the sweetest Valentine gift that I have ever received.

After Roy and I left for our date, Becky got busy. She raided my fabric and cross-stitch box. She stitched the words "I Love Ya" on a piece of red fabric, cut the fabric in the shape of a heart, stitched the two pieces together, adorned it with lace and stuffed it with cotton. It was a heart-shaped pillow, filled with love, which I'll cherish forever.

My wonderful Valentine gift has a special place in my bedroom today, some thirteen years later. As she was growing up into a young woman, many times I held that pillow close to my heart. I don't know if a pillow can hold magic, but this pillow has surely held a great deal of joy for me over the years. It has helped me through several sleepless nights since she left home for college. I not only cherish the gift, but the memory, as well.

I know that I am a very lucky mother, indeed, to have such a wonderful little girl, who wanted so desperately to share her heart with me. As long as I live, there will never be another Valentine's Day, which will be any more special to me.

心形枕头

情人节已经到了，和一年中的其他每天一样，我都很忙。

我的丈夫罗伊非常浪漫，他安排了一个我们以前从未有过的约会，在一家豪华饭店预定了座位。在充满爱心的日子到来的前几天，一件包装精美的礼物一直放在我的梳妆台上。

一天辛劳后，我匆匆赶回家，跑进浴室，进行淋浴。等爱人回来时，我穿好了最漂亮的衣服，准备出发。他紧紧地抱住我，临时保姆也刚好赶到。我们俩都非常高兴。

不巧的是，我们家里最小的成员却不高兴。

“爸爸,你说过要带我去给妈妈买礼物,”说着,8 岁的女儿贝基伤心地走到了沙发边,在临时保姆身边坐下来。

罗伊看了一下手表,意识到如果我们要按时到达预订的饭店,不得不立刻动身。他甚至抽不出几分钟时间带女儿到街角小店买一盒鸡心形巧克力糖。

“对不起,我今天回家晚了,宝贝儿。”他说。

“没关系,”贝基回答说。“我明白。”

整个夜晚苦甜参半。我总会情不自禁地想起贝基失望的眼神。我想起了房门在我们身后关闭之前,贝基因情人节而兴奋的光芒从脸上已经消失了。她想让我知道她是多么爱我。尽管她没有意识到,但我心里已经非常清楚。

如今,那个漂亮盒子里装了什么礼物我无法记得了。虽然我因它兴奋了好几天,但那晚回到家时收到的另一件特殊礼物,我却永远难忘。

贝基在长沙发上睡着了,手里还紧紧地抱着一个盒子,盒子放在她的膝间。当我吻她的脸颊时,她醒了。“妈妈,我要送给您一件东西。”她说着,灿烂的笑容绽开在了她的小脸上。

小盒子用报纸包裹着。我撕开报纸,打开盒子,发现了我曾收到过的最甜美的情人节礼物。

在我和罗伊离开家去约会后,贝基就忙了起来。她把我的织品和十字绣盒都翻出来。她在一块红织品上绣上了“我爱你”,把布料剪成心形,将两块布缝到了一起,缀上了花边,并在里面塞满了棉花。这是一个充满爱的心形枕头,我会永远珍惜它。

大约 13 年后,那件奇妙的情人节礼物在我的卧室里仍占一席之地。女儿渐渐长大成人,这期间我多次将枕头紧紧地贴在心口。我不知道这个枕头是否藏有魔力,但我确信,这么多年来它曾给我带来了很多快乐。女儿离开家去上大学时,它帮助我度过了好几个不眠之夜。我不仅珍爱这件礼物,而且珍爱这份记忆。

我知道我确实是一位非常幸运的母亲,能有这样一个了不起的可爱女儿,她是那样渴望与我分享她的心。在我看来,只要我活着,绝不会再有比这更特殊的情人节了。

The Seed of Love

I saw my six-year-old son wrestling with a limb of my azalea bush. By the time I got out side he'd broken it. “Can I take this to school today?” he asked.

With a wave of my hand, I sent him off. I turned my back so he wouldn't see the tears gathering in my eyes. I loved that azalea bush. I touched the broken limb as if to say silently, “I m sorry.”

I wished I could have said that to my husband earlier, but I'd been angry. The washing machine had leaked on my brand-new linoleum. If he'd just taken the time to fix it the night before when I asked him instead of playing checkers with Jonathan. What are his priorities anyway? I wondered. I was still mopping up the mess when Jonathan walked into the kitchen. “What's for breakfast, Mom?” I opened the empty refrigerator. “Not cereal,” I said, watching the sides of his mouth drop. “How about toast and jelly?” I smeared the toast with jelly and set it in front of him. Why was I so angry? I tossed my husband's dishes into the sudsy water.

It was days like this that made me want to quit. I just wanted to drive up to the mountains, hide in a cave, and never come out.

Somehow I managed to lug the wet clothes to the laundromat. I spent most of the day washing and drying clothes and thinking how love had disappeared from my life. As I finished hanging up the last of my husband's shirts, I looked at the clock. 2:30. I was late. Jonathan's class let out at 2:15. I dumped the clothes in the back seat and hurriedly drove to the school.

I was out of breath by the time I knocked on the teacher's door and peered through the glass. With one finger, she motioned for me to wait. She said something to Jonathan and handed him and two other children crayons and a sheet of paper. What now? I thought, as she rustled through the door and took me aside. "I want to talk to you about Jonathan," she said.

I prepared myself for the worst. Nothing would have surprised me.

"Did you know Jonathan brought flowers to school today?" she asked. I nodded, thinking about my favorite bush and trying to hide the hurt in my eyes. I glanced at my son busily coloring a picture. His wavy hair was too long and flopped just beneath his brow. He brushed it away with the back of his hand. His eyes burst with blue as he admired his handiwork.

"Let me tell you about yesterday," the teacher insisted. "See that little girl?"

I watched the bright-eyed child laugh and point to a colorful picture taped to the wall. I nodded.

"Well, yesterday she was almost hysterical. Her mother and father are going through a nasty divorce. She told me she didn't want to live, and she wished she could die. I watched that little girl bury her face in her hands and say loud enough for the class to hear, 'Nobody loves me.' I did all I could to console her, but it only seemed to make matters worse."

"I thought you wanted to talk to me about Jonathan," I said. "I do," she said, touching the sleeve of my blouse. "Today your son walked straight over to that child. I watched him hand her some pretty pink flowers and whisper, I love you."

I felt my heart swell with pride for what my son had done. I smiled at the teacher. "Thank you," I said, reaching for Jonathan's hand, "you've made my day."

Later that evening, I began pulling weeds from around my lopsided azalea bush. As my mind wandered back to the love Jonathan showed the little girl, a biblical verse came to me: "... these three remain: faith, hope and love. But the greatest of these is love." While my son had put love into practice, I had only felt anger.

I heard the familiar squeak of my husband's brakes as he pulled into the drive. I snapped a small limb bristling with hot pink azaleas off the bush. I felt the seed of love that God planted in my family beginning to bloom once again in me. My husband's eyes widened in surprise as I handed him the flowers. "I love you," I said.

爱的种子

我看见6岁的儿子在使劲攀折我的一大枝杜鹃花丛。等我走到外面时,他已经把它折断了。"我今天能把这个带去学校吗?"他问。

我挥了挥手,让他上学去。我转过身,这样他就看不见我眼里涌起的泪水了。我爱那个杜鹃花丛。我抚摸那被折断的枝条,好像默默地说:"对不起。"

我真希望能早一点对丈夫这样说,但当时我很生气。洗衣机里的水漏在了我崭新的油毯上。如果他前一天晚上听我的话,不和乔纳森下跳棋,而是花点时间把它修好,就不会发生这种事了。我不知道,对他来说什么事更重要。当乔纳森走进厨房时,我仍在拖地上的水。"早饭吃什么,妈妈?"我打开空空的冰箱。"没有麦片粥了,"我话音刚落,就看见他的嘴耷拉了下来。“吐司面包和果酱怎么样?”我把果酱涂在吐司面包上,放在他面前。我为什么这样生气?我把丈夫的碟子扔进冒着泡沫的水里。

这样的日子常使我想离开。我只想驱车上山,躲在一个洞穴,再也不出来。

不管怎么说,我还是设法把那些湿衣服费力弄到了自助洗衣店。我花了大半天时间在那里把那堆衣服洗净烘干,一边洗一边想着爱是怎样从我的生活中消失的。我把丈夫的最后一件衬衫收好时,看了看时钟。2点30分。我迟到了。乔纳森2点15分放学。我把衣服丢在后座上,慌忙开车向学校驶去。

待赶到教室门敲门,透过玻璃向里张望时,我已是气喘吁吁。老师用一根手指示意我等一会儿。她对乔纳森说了些什么,然后递给他和另两个孩子每人一些蜡笔和一张纸。我心里想,现在怎么了?她快步走出教室,把我拉到了一边,说:“我想跟你谈谈乔纳森。”

我做好了最坏的准备。什么都不会让我吃惊。

“你知道乔纳森今天带花到学校里来了吗?”她问。我点了点头,同时想到了我心爱的杜鹃花丛,竭力隐藏起眼里的受伤神情。我瞥了一眼正在忙着给一幅图画上色的儿子。他的鬈发太长了,耷拉到了眉毛下。他用手背把它拂到了一边。他欣赏自己的作品时,眼睛里突然流露出了沮丧的神色。

“让我告诉你昨天的事吧,”老师强调说。“看见那个小女孩了吗?”

我发现那个眼睛明亮的孩子笑出了声,指着贴在墙上的一幅鲜艳的图画。我点了点头。

“噢,昨天她差不多歇斯底里了。她的父母正在闹离婚。她告诉我她不想活了,她希望一死了之。我看着那个小女孩把脸埋进小手里,大声说:‘没有人爱我。’她的声音大得足以让全班同学听见。我竭力安慰她,但那似乎只能让事情变得更糟。”

“我以为你想跟我谈有关乔纳森的事。”我说。“是的,”她抚摸着我的衬衫袖说。“今天,你的儿子径直走到那个女孩身边。我看着他把一些漂亮的粉红色杜鹃花递给她,低声说,我爱你。”

我感到心里涌起一种自豪感,为儿子所做的事感到骄傲。我对老师笑了笑。“谢谢你,”说着,我伸手去拉乔纳森的手。“你让我今天很开心。”

那天晚上晚些时候,我开始为倒向一边的杜鹃花拔去了杂草。当我回想起乔纳森向那个小女孩展示爱时,我的脑海里浮现起了《圣经》里的一句诗:“……这三点保持不变:信任,希望和爱。但其中最重要的是爱。”当我的儿子把爱付诸实践时,我却只感到生气。

我听到外面车道上传来了丈夫开进车道时的汽车刹车声。我从花丛中折下了一小枝开着火红色的杜鹃花。我感到上帝种在我家里的爱的种子又开始在我的心里盛开了。当我把花递给丈夫时,他惊讶得睁大了眼睛。“我爱你。”我说。

Dial the Phone Again

Once when I sat in my classmate's home, I found he dialed the phone number twice as he called his parents. After he dialed for the first time, he hung up when it rang three times; then he dialed the second time and talked on the phone.

"Was the line busy for the first time?" I asked casually.

"No."

"Didn't you think out what to say?"

"No."

"Why did you dial twice?"

He smiled. "You don't know my parents both answer the phone eagerly. Whenever they hear the phone ring, they will run to answer. Once, in order to answer the phone, my mother tripped her little toe against the table foot and made it swollen for a long time. Since then, I have agreed with them: don't run to answer the phone; I first dial once to give them the time to prepare."

My heart suddenly felt very moist. We often say how we care for our parents, but isn't the tiny detail the most vivid love for parents?

再拨一次电话

有一次，我在一位同学家入座，发现他给父母打电话时拨两遍号码。拨过第一遍后，铃响三声就挂断了；再拨第二遍，然后才通话。

"第一遍占线吗？"我随意地问。

"没有。"

"是没想好说什么？"

"不是。"

"那为什么拨两遍号码？"

他笑了笑："你不知道，我父母亲都是接电话非常急的人。只要听见铃响，就会跑着去接。有一次，我母亲为了接电话还让桌脚把小脚趾绊了一下，肿了很长时间。从那时起，我就和他们约定：接电话不准跑，我先拨一遍，给他们预备的时间。"

我的心突然觉得十分湿润。平日都常说如何如何孝敬父母，这个小小的细节，不是对父母最生动的疼惜吗？

Tomorrow Shining Ahead

Jennifer Paige was halfway down the stairs, her hand trailing lightly along the banister, when she turned and went back to the door of her room. Though she knew it all by heart, she wanted to take one last look. Good-bye, room... She lingered over the soft and faded quilt that lay folded at the foot of bed... the window curtains tied back, framing a view of the elm top... Oh, the wide-awake dreams that had often drifted through her head as she gazed out that window.

Not that she was sentimental about such things. Not now. She couldn't afford to be. Certainly there was no reluctance in her farewell. It was like the brief pause at the ending of a chapter in a good book, and she was eager to turn the page. All spring she had waited for this day. Longer than that, really. Finishing high school and going away to school was so much more than just going away to school...

Jennifer went down the stairs again to where her mother and father, strangely quiet, were waiting. Mother was sitting on the little chair that no one ever sat on, her head tilted to one side, and Dad just standing there with his hands thrust into his trouser pockets. The best parents in the world—she knew it—if you didn't consider the few occasions when they were completely unreasonable about some small matter. Sometimes she wondered if they loved her too much. A twinge of guilt stirred deep within her when she admitted to herself how longingly she had looked forward to getting "out from under."

"It seems like only yesterday you were starting to kindergarten," her mother said.

Jennifer had heard those words at least a half dozen times a day in the last week. "Mother, do you realize how many times you've said that lately?" she asked.

"I may say it again before you're on the train," her mother said. "I can't promise that I won't, dear."

"Be patient with your mother," Dad said, winking. "It isn't every day she loses a daughter to higher education and a career."

Jennifer smiled in acknowledgment and then paused. In front of the hall mirror for a quick glance. The dark cotton dress looked just appropriate for a warm day, serious enough for someone who was going to be a nurse.

Her raincoat lay across the luggage stacked beside the front door. "I keep asking myself if we've forgotten anything," her mother said. "I know, the camera! I want a snapshot of you getting on the train."

"I thought of that," her father announced proudly. "I put it in the car last night. Just to be sure."

As they were going out the front door, her mother said, "Around the world would only be a trip... This is a milestone, Jenny."

Dad put the suitcases in the back. Of the car, and then came forward to hold the front door open. "Sit in the middle, dear," her mother suggested, touching Jennifer's arm gently, and Jennifer noticed her mother was wearing one of those sad-looking smiles. Her mother had enjoyed talking about all of it—the school catalogue, how lucky Jennifer was to have only one roommate in the dormitory, which clothes to take along. But in the last few days, as the time drew nearer, she had reflected less and less of her early enthusiasm. In fact, Jennifer was afraid her mother might even get weepy at the station.

Her father pulled out of their driveway and Jennifer turned for one last look at the house.

Her father pulled out of their driveway and Jennifer turned for one last at the house.

"Do you know what just came to my mind?" Her mother said. "The hanky. Do you remember when you were in kindergarten all the children were supposed to wear a handkerchief pinned to their clothes?"

"Oh, Mother!" Then she caught her mother's teasing glance and she had to laugh. She kissed her mother on the cheek and then leaned head back against the seat. "You know something?" she said. "I love you both very much."

They pulled up at the station then, and suddenly there was no more time. They walked across the gravel to the platform. Dad checked the luggage and placed the ticket in Jennifer's hand. The train was coming. There were last-minute reminders and questions... last-minute words of advice... and then last-minute embraces.

"Well, I'm on my way," Jennifer said brightly.

When her father snapped the picture, she noticed her mother was not weepy at all-the smile on her face was not even sad-looking.

Through the window, Jennifer held them with her eyes as the train moved slowly from the

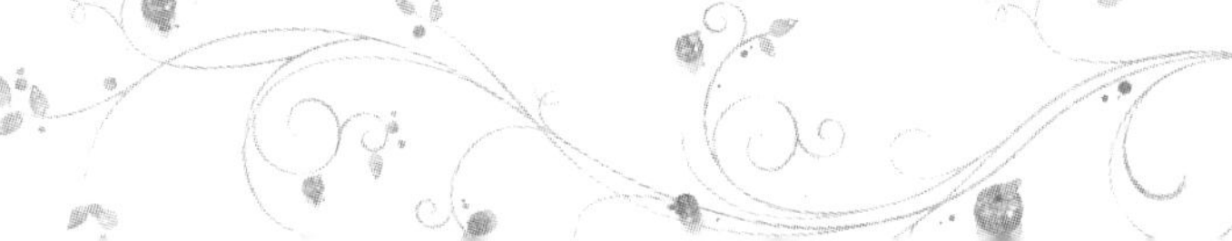

station. They were standing close together, and somehow it brought back the memory of that day when she was seven... maybe eight—when she had persuaded them to let her ride the big county-fair Ferris wheel "all by myself." They had stood the same way then, close together, waiting... and she had sat rigidly still in the exact middle of the seat, but certain that even if she fell, even if the Ferris wheel itself tumbled, even if... she had known they would catch her.

And now they began to blur before they were out of sight. "Jennifer Paige, don't you know you'd bawl," she whispered, fumbling for a tissue. She wiped her eyes and thought: isn't this the weirdest thing? The beginning of something bright and wonderful and she was crying. Tomorrow was shining ahead of her. She wiped her eyes one last time and when she looked again, her parents were out of sight.

明天就在眼前

詹妮弗·佩奇轻轻地扶着楼梯扶手下楼，走到半道，又转身返回了房门口。尽管她悉数在心，但她还想最后再看一眼。再见了，房间……她的目光慢慢扫过床头叠好的柔软褪色的被子……束起来的窗帘，显出窗外风景的榆树梢……噢，还有她凝望窗外时常浮现在脑海里的漫无边际的梦想。

并不是因为她正在为这些东西感伤，现在不行，她没有时间。当然，她的告别没有勉强的成分。这就像一本好书中某一章结尾时的短暂停顿一样，她急于想翻到下一页。整个春季，她都在等待着这一天。真的，时间比那还要长。中学毕业离家上学比平时上学大不一样……

詹妮弗又下了楼梯，来到了父母亲那里。他们正在等着她，出奇的安静。妈妈坐在一把从来没人坐过的小椅子上，头歪向一边；爸爸站在那里，两手插在裤袋里。她知道，如果不计较他们偶尔在一些小事上完全不讲道理的话，他们是世界上最好的父母亲。有时她想知道他们是否爱她爱得过分。当她自己承认她曾多么渴望从父母亲的“羽翼下钻出来”时，她内心深感内疚。

“就像昨天你才开始上幼儿园似的。”她妈妈说。

上周，詹妮弗每天至少听妈妈这样说过五、六次。“妈妈，你知道这话你最近说了多少遍吗？”她问。

“在你上火车前我可能还会说，”妈妈说。“我不能保证我不说，亲爱的。”

“对你妈妈要有耐心，”爸爸眨了眨眼说。“并不是每天都有高等教育和事业来让她失去女儿的。”

詹妮弗默然一笑，然后在大厅镜子前暂时停住脚步，飞快地瞥了一眼。黑棉布裙看上去正合适——适合暖和天穿，而且对一个即将当护士的人来说，这套衣服也足够庄重。

她的雨衣搭在堆在前门旁边的行李上。“我一直在问自己是否我们忘记了什么，”妈妈说。“我知道了，照相机！我要抓拍一张你上火车的照片。”

“我早就想到了，”爸爸得意地说，“昨晚我就把它放在汽车里了，一定不会忘的。”

他们一边走出前门，她妈妈一边说：“周游世界只是一次旅行……这是一个里程碑，詹妮。”

爸爸把皮箱放进车后面，然后走过来，打开车前门。“亲爱的，坐在中间，”妈妈建议道，轻轻地抚摸着詹妮弗的胳膊。詹妮弗注意到妈妈脸上带着伤心的微笑。妈妈曾热衷于谈论大学简要说明中所有的内容，詹妮弗多么走运，宿舍里只有一个室友，要带哪些衣服。但最近几天，随着日期越来越近，她早些日子的那种热情变得越来越少。真的，詹妮弗真怕妈妈甚至会在车站流泪。

爸爸将车驶出车道，詹妮弗转身最后看了一眼房子。

"你知道我突然想起了什么吗？"妈妈说。"手帕。你还记得当初你在幼儿园时，所有的孩子都应该在衣服上别上一块手帕吗？"

"噢，妈妈！"这时，她看到妈妈取笑的眼神，便忍不住笑了起来。她亲了亲妈妈的脸颊，然后仰头靠在座位上，说："你们知道吗？我非常爱你们俩。"

他们驱车来到了车站。这时，他们突然发现时间已经不多了。他们走过碎石路，来到站台，爸爸托运了行李，将车票放到詹妮弗手里。火车来了。于是，他们再作临别的提醒和询问……临别的嘱咐……然后是临别的拥抱。

"好了，我走了。"詹妮弗兴高采烈地说。

当爸爸按动快门时，詹妮弗看到妈妈一点没有流泪——她带着笑容的脸上甚至看不出伤感。

火车慢慢地驶离了车站。詹妮弗透过车窗目送着父母亲，只见他们紧紧地站在一起。不知怎么的，这使詹妮弗想起她七、八岁时的一天，那时她说服父母同意让她"独自一人"去坐当地博览会上的空中大转轮，他们那时就是这样站着，紧紧地靠在一起，等待着……她当时坐在座位的正中央一动都不敢动，但心里确信：即使她摔下去，即使转轮翻倒，即使……她知道父亲一定会上来接住她。

此时，詹妮弗泪眼模糊地望着父亲，他们依然站在那里。"詹妮弗·佩奇，你不知道会哭出声来吧，"她低声说着，摸出一张纸巾，擦了擦眼睛，心里想：这是不是世界上最不可思议的事儿？辉煌而精彩的事情有了开端，她却在哭泣。明天在她面前是那样灿烂。她最后一次擦去眼中的泪水，又去看父母亲时，他们已经不见了踪影。

The Happy Small Paper Boat

A mother took her daughter to the hospital for an examination. The doctor told her that her daughter was suffering from an incurable disease. She didn't tell her daughter about the illness but stood such anguish alone.

Her daughter was only 10 years old and her blossom of life had just bloomed but would wither and fall. In the quiet of night, her mother always shed tears.

One day, the daughter kept asking her mother to launch the paper boat. The paper boat was slowly floating on the crystal-clear stream while the stream slowly splashed the paper boat, so the paper boat sank little by little and was finally drowned by the water.

The mother looked at the sunken small paper boat, thinking of her daughter's illness, as her tears couldn't help coursing down. "Mom, you shed tears again. If you saw the paper boat sink?" her daughter asked softly.

Her daughter folded another small paper boat, put it in the stream and let it slowly float. "Mom,

this small paper boat is really happy. Look, below the paper boat is the clear stream, above it is the warm sunshine and along the way are flowers, butterflies and the singing stream. Mom, last time in the hospital, I heard the conversation between you and the doctor... Mom, in fact, I'm also a happy small paper boat. In this clear world, with your warm embrace, the schoolmates' friendship and the comfort and encouragement from the teachers and relatives, I'm already happy enough. Mom, do you know what the small paper boat likes best to say from her heart?"

Nestling in her mother's arms, the daughter looked up into her mother's face, "Mom, the small paper boat will surely say, 'I have come to this world, so I'm very happy!'"

The mother held her daughter tightly, a ray of bright sunshine penetrating the mother's tears.

幸福的小纸船

妈妈带女儿去医院检查。医生告诉她，她女儿患了绝症。她没有把病情告诉女儿，独自承受着这份巨大的痛苦。

女儿才10岁，生命的花朵刚刚绽放就要凋谢。夜深人静时，妈妈总是以泪洗面。

一天，女儿缠着妈妈去放纸船。纸船在清亮的溪水上缓缓地漂着，溪水慢慢地打湿了纸船，纸船渐渐往下沉，最后被溪水淹没了。

妈妈看着沉没的小纸船，想起女儿的病情，泪水不由得又掉了下来。"妈妈，你又掉泪了。是不是见纸船沉了？"女儿轻声问道。

女儿又折了一条小纸船，把它放进溪水里，让它缓缓地漂。"妈妈，这小纸船其实很幸福。你看，纸船下是清亮的溪水，上面是温暖的阳光，沿路还有鲜花、彩蝶和溪水的歌唱。妈妈，上次在医院，你和医生的谈话，我都听见了……妈妈，其实，我也是一条幸福的小纸船，在这个清亮的世界里，有你温暖的怀抱，有同学们的友谊，还有老师和亲人的安慰与鼓励，我已经足够幸福的了。妈妈，你知道小纸船心里最想说的一句话是什么吗？"

女儿依在妈妈的怀里，仰起头，看着妈妈的脸："妈妈，小纸船一定会这样说：'我来过，我很快乐！'"

妈妈紧紧地抱着女儿，泪水里第一次透进了明亮的阳光。

The Weight of Love

A Hindu walked to the sacred shrine in the Himalayas for pilgrimage. The journey was long and the mountain road was hard to walk. So though he carried little baggage, he still walked along hard. Just ahead of him, he saw a little girl, less than 10 years old, carrying a chubby boy on her back and also moving on slowly. She panted heavily and kept sweating, but her hands still firmly protected the boy on her back.

When passing by the little girl, the Hindu said to her sympathetically, "My girl, you must be very tired because what you carry is so heavy!"

Hearing this, the little girl said unhappily, "What you carry is a weight, but what I carry is not a weight, he is my little brother."

It is true, on the scale, whether it is a brother or a burden, there is no difference, for it will show the actual weight, but for a heart, what the little girl said is right: what she carried was her little brother, not a weight, for the burden was the weight. She loved her little brother from the heart.

Love has no weight, so love is not a burden but the happy solicitude and selfless devotion.

爱的重量

一位印度教徒步行到喜马拉雅山的圣庙去朝圣。路途遥远，山路难行，他虽然携带很少的行李，但沿途走来，还是举步维艰。就在他前方，他看到一个小女孩，年纪不会超过 10 岁，背着一个胖嘟嘟的小孩，也正缓慢地向前移动。她气喘得很厉害，也一直在流汗，可她的双手还是紧紧地呵护着背上的小孩。

印度教徒经过小女孩身边，很同情地对她说："我的孩子，你一定很疲倦，你背得那么重！"小女孩听了很不高兴地说："你背的是一个重量，但我背的不是一个重量，他是我的弟弟。"

没错，在磅秤上，无论是弟弟还是包袱，都没有差别，都会显示出实际的重量，但就心而言，那小女孩说的一点没错，她背的是弟弟，不是一个重量，包袱才是一个重量。她对弟弟是发自内心的爱。

爱没有重量，爱不是负担，而是一种喜悦的关怀与无私的付出。

Christmas Present

Paul received an automobile from his brother as a Christmas present. On Christmas Eve when Paul came out of his office, a street boy was walking around the shiny new car, admiring it. "Is this your car, Mister?" he asked.

Paul nodded. "My brother gave it to me for Christmas." The boy was shocked. "You mean your brother gave it to you and it didn't cost you anything? Boy, I wish..." He hesitated.

Of course Paul knew what he was going to wish for. He was going to wish he had a brother like that. But what the lad said shocked Paul all the way down to his heels.

"I wish," the boy went on, "that I could be a brother like that."

Paul looked at the boy in surprise, then impulsively he added, "Would you like to take a ride in my automobile?"

"Oh yes, I'd love that."

After a short ride, the boy turned and with his eyes aglow, said, "Mister, would you mind driving in front of my house?"

Paul smiled a little. He thought he knew what the lad wanted. He wanted to show his neighbors that he could ride home in a big automobile. But Paul was wrong again.

"Will you stop where those two steps are?" the boy asked.

He ran up the steps. Then in a little while Paul heard him coming back, but he was not coming fast. He was carrying his little crippled brother. He sat him down on the bottom step, then sort of squeezed up against him and pointed to the car. "There she is, Buddy, just like I told you upstairs. His

brother gave it to him for Christmas and it didn't cost him a cent. And some day I'm gonna give you one just like it, then you can see for yourself all the pretty things in the Christmas windows that I've been trying to tell you about."

Paul got out and lifted the lad to the front seat of his car. The shining-eyed older brother climbed in beside him and the three of them began a memorable holiday ride.

On that Christmas Eve, Paul learned what it means by "It is more blessed to give..."

My wish for the world is that we all could be brothers like that.

圣诞礼物

保罗从哥哥那里得到一辆新车,作为圣诞礼物。圣诞节前夜,保罗离开办公室的时候。街道上的一个小男孩绕着那辆闪闪发亮的新车,羡慕地问道:"先生,这是你的车吗?"

保罗点点头说:"这是我哥哥送给我的圣诞礼物。"男孩满脸惊讶:"你是说这是你哥哥送的礼物,你没有花一分钱?嗨,真希望……"他欲言又止。

保罗当然知道他希望什么:他是希望也能有个那样的哥哥送给他一辆车。但男孩的话却让保罗非常震惊。

"我希望自己也能成为那样的哥哥,送一辆车给弟弟。"男孩继续说。

保罗惊讶地看着男孩,然后脱口而出:"愿意坐我的车兜风吗?"

"噢愿意,我非常乐意。"

车子开了一小段路后,小男孩转过身,两眼熠熠生辉:"先生,你能把车子开到我的家门前吗?"

保罗微微一笑,新想自己知道小家伙有什么打算:他是想向邻居们炫耀一番,他能坐一辆大汽车回家。但保罗又错了。

"你能把车子停在那两级台阶前面吗?"男孩问道。

男孩跑上台阶。过了一会儿,保罗听到他返回的脚步声,但动作有些缓慢。他搂着跛脚的弟弟,把他安顿在最底下一级台阶上坐下,然后紧贴着他,指着那辆新车说:"看见了吧,弟弟,刚才我在楼上全告诉你了。这是保罗的哥哥送给他的圣诞礼物!没有花他一分钱。将来有一天,我也要送给你一辆这样的车子。到时候,你就能亲眼去看那些我总是对你说起的挂在橱窗里的漂亮东西了。"

保罗走下车,将跛脚的弟弟抱到了车子的前座。满眼发亮的哥哥也爬上车子,坐在弟弟的身边。三个人开始了一次令人难忘的节日之旅。

那个圣诞节前夜,保罗才真正体会到"施与比接受更有福"这句话的含义。

但愿世界上的人都能成为那样的哥哥。

The Philosophy of Holding the Sand in Both Hands

One girl who was about to get married asked her mother a question,"Mom,how will I keep my love after marriage?" Hearing the girl's question, her mother smiled tenderly, slowly squatted and cupped a handful of sand from the ground.

The girl found the sand in her mother's hands was round,without running off or sifting. Then,her mother tried to hold her hands tightly. The sand immediately ran out from her fingers. When her mother opened her hands again,the former sand had left little and the round shape had also been pressed flat,with no sense of beauty at all.

In fact,the mother wanted to tell her daughter:There's no need to keep your love deliberately because more tightly you seize your love,more easily you will lose. Just as holding a handful of sand in both hands,the more tightly you hold,the less you leave in your hands;and those leaving out from the fingers is all you try to hold hard, treasure too much and long to maintain. As love can't be clutched,many things in life are the same—going too far is as bad as not going far enough. If you exceed that limit,you will be hard to have the sense of beauty but frustrated and helpless to face the sand left in your hands.

握沙的哲学

一位即将出嫁的女孩向母亲提了一个问题:“妈妈,婚后我该怎么把握爱情呢?”母亲听了女孩的问话,温情地笑了笑,然后慢慢地蹲下,从地上捧起一捧沙子。

女孩发现那捧沙子在母亲的手里,圆圆满满的,没有流失,没有洒落。接着,母亲用力将双手握紧,沙子立刻从母亲的指缝间泻落下来。待母亲再把手张开时,原来那捧沙子已经所剩无几,其圆圆满满的形状也早已被压得扁扁的,毫无美感可言。

其实,那位母亲是要告诉她的女儿:爱情无需刻意去把握,越是想抓牢自己的爱情,反而越容易失去。正如掬一把沙子,握得越紧,反而手中所剩越少,而那些从指缝中间漏掉的,全是自己太用力,太珍惜,太想留住的。像爱情不能抓紧一样,人生中许多事情都一样,过犹不及,超过了那个度,就难有美感可言,只能面对手中的余沙惆怅与无奈了。

Don't Wait Till the Flowers Wilt

Each spring brings a new blossom of wildflowers in the ditches along the highway I travel daily to work.

There is one particular blue flower that has always caught my eye. I've noticed that it blooms only in the morning hours,for the afternoon sun is too warm for it. Every day for approximately two weeks,I see those beautiful flowers.

This spring, I started a wildflower garden in our yard. I can look out of the kitchen window while doing the dishes and see the flowers. I've often thought that those lovely blue flowers from the ditch would look great in that bed alongside other wildflowers.

Every day I drove past the flowers thinking, "I'll stop on my way home and dig them." "Gee, I don't want to get my good clothes dirty..." Whatever the reason, I never stopped to dig them. My husband even gave me a folding shovel one year for my trunk to be used for that expressed purpose.

One day on my way home from work, I was saddened to see that the highway department had mowed the ditches and the pretty blue flowers were gone. I thought to myself, "Way to go, you waited too long. You should have done it when you first saw them blooming this spring."

A week ago we were shocked and saddened to learn that my oldest sister – in – law has a terminal brain tumor. She is 20 years older than my husband and unfortunately, because of age and distance, we haven't been as close as we all would have liked.

I couldn't help but see the connection between the pretty blue flowers and the relationship between my husband's sister and us. I do believe that God has given us some time left to plant some wonderful memories that will bloom every year for us.

And yes, if I see the blue flowers again, you can bet I'll stop and transplant them to my wildflower garden.

莫等到花儿都谢了

在我每天上班沿途公路的那些沟渠里，每年春天都会绽放野花。

有一种独特的蓝花总是吸引我的注意。我注意到，它只在早晨开放，午后阳光对它太热了。大约两周时间，我每天都看到那些美丽的花朵。

今年春天，我在我们的院子里着手建了一个野花园。我在做菜时，通过厨房窗口可以看到那些鲜花。我常常想，沟渠里那些可爱的蓝花在沟底其他野花的衬托下看上去一定会很棒。

每天我开车经过那些花朵就会想：“我要在回家的路上停下来，把它们挖走。”“哎呀，我不想把好衣服弄脏……”无论什么原因，我从来没有停下来挖那些花。有一年，丈夫甚至曾特地为我的汽车尾部行李箱配了一把折叠铲。

有一天，下班回家途中，我非常伤心地看到，公路部门已经填平了那些沟渠，漂亮的蓝花不见了踪影。我想：“你等得太久了，你应该在刚看到它们开花的这个春天就挖的。”

一周前，我们既震惊又悲痛地获悉，年龄最大的姐姐得了脑瘤晚期。她比我的丈夫大20岁。不幸的是，由于年龄和距离远，我们都没有像以前那样密切联系了。

我不禁明白了那些漂亮蓝花的联系以及丈夫的姐姐和我们的关系。我确实相信，上帝已经给了我们一些时间来种植一些美好的回忆，这些回忆每年都会为我们开放。

是的，如果我再次看到那些蓝花，你可以断定，我会停下来，把它们移栽到我的野花园里。

The 100th Guest

At noon the rush hour had passed. In the initially crowded noshery, the guests had melted away. When the boss was about to take a break to read a newspaper, in came an old lady and a little boy.

"How much money is a bowl of beef soup?" the grandma sat down, fumbled out her purse, counted the money and ordered a bowl of steaming beef soup. The grandma pushed the bowl towards the little boy, who swallowed his saliva, looking at his grandma and saying, "Grandma, did you really have lunch?" "Of course," his grandma chewed a piece of pickled radish slowly. In a flash, the little boy ate up the meal.

Seeing this sight, the boss went over to them and said, "Old lady, congratulation, you're lucky to be free of charge, for you're our 100th guest."

Afterwards, over a month or more, one day, the small boy squatted across the noshery, where he seemed to be counting something, which shocked the boss when he happened to look out of the window.

It turned out that when he saw a guest walk into the noshery, the small boy would put a small stone into the circle he drew, but the lunch time had almost elapsed, the small stones he put into the circle were hardly 50.

The extremely anxious boss called up all the old customers. The customers started coming one after another.

"81, 82, 83..." the small boy counted faster and faster. At last, when the 99th small stone was put into the circle, the little boy hurried to pull his grandma's hand and went into the snack bar.

"Grandma, this time it's on me," the little boy said kind of proudly. The grandma who had become the real 100th guest was entertained a bowl of steaming beef soup by her grandson. As his grandma as before, the small boy chewed a piece of pickled radish in his mouth.

第100个客人

中午高峰时间过去了,原本拥挤的小吃店,客人都已散去了。老板正要喘口气翻阅报纸时,走进了一位老奶奶和一个小男孩。

"牛肉汤饭一碗要多少钱?"奶奶坐下来拿出钱袋数了数钱,要了一碗热气腾腾的汤饭。奶奶将碗推到了孙子面前,小男孩吞了吞口水望着奶奶说:"奶奶,您真的吃过午饭了吗?""当然啦。"奶奶含着一块萝卜泡菜慢慢咀嚼。一眨眼工夫,小男孩就把一碗饭吃了个精光。

老板看到这幅景象,走到两个人面前说:"老太太,恭喜您,您今天运气真好,是我们的第100个客人,所以免费。"

之后,过了一个多月的某一天,小男孩蹲在小吃店对面像在数着什么东西,使无意间望向窗外的老板吓了一大跳。

原来小男孩每看到一个客人走进店里,就把小石子放进他画的圆圈里,但午餐时间都快过去了,小石子却连50个都不到。

心急如焚的老板打电话给所有的老顾客。客人开始一个接一个到来。

"81、82、83……"小男孩数得越来越快了。终于,当第99个小石子被放进圆圈时,小男孩匆忙拉着奶奶的手走进了小吃店。

“奶奶，这次换我请客了。”小男孩有些得意地说。真正成为第100个客人的奶奶，让孙子招待了一碗热腾腾的牛肉汤饭。而小男孩就像之前奶奶一样，含了一块萝卜泡菜在嘴里咀嚼着。

The Miracle of Love

An 8-year-old girl heard her parents talking about her little brother. She only knew he was extremely ill, but her parents didn't have the money for his medical treatment. They were planning to move to a smaller house to live in because after the payment of medical expenses, they couldn't afford the present house rent. Now, only an expensive operation could save her little brother's life. But they failed to borrow money.

When she heard her father whispered to her tearful mother despairingly, "Now, only a miracle can save him." The little girl returned to her bedroom, took out her piggy bank hidden in the closet, emptied all the changes on the floor, carefully counted, held this valuable bank tightly in his arms and slipped from the back door. After crossing six blocks, she went into a local drugstore, where she fumbled out a 25-cent coin from her bank and put it on the glass counter.

"What can I do for you?" the pharmacists asked.

"I come to buy medicine for my little brother," the little girl replied. "He's got very ill, so I want to buy him a miracle."

"What did you say?" the pharmacists asked.

"His name is Andrew, with something in his brain. My father said only a miracle can save him. How much money does a miracle need?"

"I'm sorry we don't sell miracles here, little girl," the pharmacists said to the little girl sadly.

"Listen, I have the money to buy it. If not enough, I can try my best to get more money. So long as you tell me how much money it takes."

At this moment, a well-dressed customer in the pharmacy leaned down to ask the little girl, "What kind of miracle does your brother need?"

"I don't know," she lifted her tear-blurred eyes at him, "he's got extremely ill. Mummy said he needs surgery. But my father can't afford the charge for surgery, so I bring all the money I've saved up to buy a miracle."

"How much money do you have?" the man asked.

"One dollar eleven cents, but I can also try my best to get more money," her voice was inaudibly light.

"Oh, what a coincidence," the man said with a smile, "one dollar eleven cents-just right the money to buy the miracle for your little brother."

He received her money with one hand and the other hand pulled her little hands. He said, "Bring me to your home. I want to see your little brother and your parents. Let's see if I have the miracle you need."

The well-dressed gentleman was no other than Carleton Armstrong, the surgeon specializing in neurosurgery. The surgery was completely free of charge. Shortly after the surgery, Andrew went back home and soon recovered.

"That surgery," her mother said softly, "was really a miracle. I want to know how much it cost on earth."

The little girl smiled. She knew the exact price of the miracle: One dollar eleven cents, plus a child's firm faith.

The firm faith can create a miracle of love.

爱的奇迹

一个8岁的女孩听到她的父母亲正在谈论她的小弟弟。她只知道他病得非常厉害，但父母亲没有钱为他医治。他们正准备搬到一所小一点的房子里去住，因为支付了医药费后，他们付不起现在这所房子的房租。现在，只有一个费用昂贵的手术才能救她小弟弟的命了。但他们借不到钱。

当听到爸爸绝望地低声对眼中含泪的妈妈说"现在，只有奇迹才能救他"时，小女孩回到她的卧室，拿出藏在壁橱里的扑满，将里面的零用钱全部倒在地板上，仔细数了数，把这个宝贵的储蓄罐紧紧地抱在怀里，然后从后门溜出去。走过6个街区，她来到当地的一家药店里，从储蓄罐里拿出一个25美分的硬币，放在玻璃柜台上。

"你想要什么？"药剂师问。

"我是来为我的小弟弟买药的。"小女孩回答道。"他病得很厉害，我想为他买一个奇迹。"

"你说什么？"药剂师问。

"他叫安德鲁，脑里长了一个东西，我爸爸说只有奇迹才能救他。一个奇迹需要多少钱？"

"孩子，很抱歉，我们这里不卖奇迹。"药剂师伤心地对小女孩笑了笑说。

"听着，我有钱买它。如果这些不够，我可以想办法再多弄些钱。只要你告诉我它需要多少钱。"

此时，药店里一位衣着考究的顾客俯下身，问这个小女孩："你的弟弟需要什么样的奇迹？"

"我不知道，"她抬起泪水模糊的眼睛看着他。"他病得很重，妈咪说他需要做手术。可我爸爸付不起手术费，所以我就把攒起来的钱全都拿来买奇迹了。"

"你有多少钱？"那人问。

"1美元11美分，不过我还可以想办法多弄到一些钱。"她的声音轻得几乎听不见。

"噢，真是巧极了，"那人微笑着说。"1美元11美分，这正好是为你的小弟弟购买奇迹的钱。"

他一只手接过她的钱，另一只手牵起她的小手，说："带我到你家里去。我想看看你的小弟弟，见见你的父母。让我们看看我是不是有你需要的那个奇迹。"

那位衣着考究的绅士就是专攻神经外科的外科医生卡尔顿·阿姆斯特朗。手术完全是免费的。手术后没多久，安德鲁就回家了，很快恢复了健康。

"那个手术，"她的妈妈轻声说。"真是一个奇迹。我想知道它到底能值多少钱。"

小女孩微笑了。她知道这个奇迹的确切价格：1美元11美分，加上一个小孩子的坚定信念。

坚定的信念能够创造爱的奇迹。

I Love the Blue Flowers

I ran into a stranger as he passed by. "Oh, excuse me, please," was my reply.

He said, "Please excuse me, too; I just was not watching for you."

We were very polite, this stranger and I.

We said good-bye and went on our way.

But at home, a different story is told: how we treat our loved ones.

That day, when I was cooking the supper, my son stood beside me, very still.

When I turned, I nearly knocked him down.

"Move out of the way," I said with a frown.

He walked away, his little heart broken.

I didn't realize how harshly I'd spoken.

While I lay awake in bed, God's small voice came to me and said, "While dealing with a stranger, you're very polite, but the family you love, you seem to abuse. Go and look on the kitchen floor; you'll find some flowers there by the door. Those are the flowers he brought for you. He picked them himself: pink, yellow and blue. He stood very quietly not to spoil the surprise; you never saw the tears that filled his eyes."

By this time I felt very small. And now my tears began to fall.

I quietly went and knelt by his bed. "Wake up, little one, wake up," I said. "Are these the flowers you picked for me?"

He smiled. "I found them, out by the tree. I picked them because they're pretty like you. I know you'd like them, especially the blue."

I said, "Son, I'm sorry for the way I acted today; I shouldn't have yelled at you that way."

He said, "Mom, that's okay. I love you, anyway."

I said, "Son, I love you, too. And I do like the flowers, especially the blue."

我爱蓝花

我和一个过路的陌生人撞在一起。"噢,请原谅。"我回答说。

他说:"也请原谅;我确实没有注意到你。"

我和这个陌生人都彬彬有礼。

我们彼此道别,继续前行。

但在家里,我们对待我们所爱的人,情况却不一样。

那天,我正在做晚饭时,儿子站在我身边,一动不动。

我转身时,差点儿把他撞倒。

"一边去,别碍事。"我皱着眉头说。

他走开了,幼小的心灵受到了伤害。

我没有注意到我说的话是多么严厉。

我睁眼躺在床上,上帝小声对我说:"对待一个陌生人,你彬彬有礼,但对你所爱的家人,你似乎出言不逊啊。去看看厨房的地板,你会发现门边有一些花朵。那是他为你采的花儿。是他亲自去采的,有粉红的、黄的和蓝的。他静静地站着,不想破坏了那份惊喜。你压根就没有看到他眼里含的泪花。”

此时,我感到自己非常渺小,泪水开始流了下来。

我悄悄地来到他的床边跪下来,说:“醒一醒,小宝贝,醒一醒。这些花是你为我采的吗?”

他微笑着说:“我在外面的树边发现了它们。我摘它们,是因为它们像你一样漂亮。我知道你会喜欢它们,特别是那些蓝花。”

我说:“儿子,我对自己今天的所作所为感到抱歉。我不该对你那样大喊大叫。”

他说:“妈妈,没事儿。不管怎样,我都爱你。”

我说:“儿子,我也爱你。我真喜欢那些花,特别是那些蓝花。”

Grandma's Love Letters

I was only seventeen when Grandma Elsie died. She was my last living grandparent and I was her only grandchild. It was until the lawyer read her will that I never fully appreciated the depth of the old lady's love. It was a moment I will never forget—a day that made me the richest kid in town.

Mom, Dad, Aunt Sophie, Uncle Bill and I sat around a small conference table in her attorney's office. She wanted her daughters and their husbands to share what little monetary wealth she left-the proceeds of her small insurance policy, an antique cameo, a few bracelets, some costume jewelry and her wedding band. She also bequeathed them the deed to her house, her bank account, a few shares of stock in the local Gas and Electric Company, as well as the American flag she was presented with at Grandpa Edwin's military funeral.

As we rose to leave, the attorney said, "There are three more things." He reached into his briefcase and brought out a small jewelry box, a letter, and a stack of envelopes neatly wrapped in tissue paper and tied with a fading pink ribbon. "Jeffrey, your grandmother left you her diamond engagement ring, hoping you'll make good use of it soon." Everyone smiled.

"These are also for you, Jeffrey," he said. "It may be the most precious legacy of all—a letter and this stack of love notes."

Grandma's letter began, "Dear Jeffrey, I am leaving you one of my most precious treasures—my memories. These memories are the letters your grandfather Edwin wrote when he was away from me. Please read them. They are both priceless and valuable—a guidebook that will teach you how to love a woman, how to understand people, and how to respect and maintain your integrity.

"When you read them, you will share the longing and passion a good man feels for a good woman, and you will also discover the empowering enchantment they will give you. You will also understand the fears and tears of war. And you will realize the differences between right and wrong. You will learn to trust the people you love and keep you distance from those you mistrust. You will learn about mature friendship and how true love can become the core of your life.

"I have been fortunate, Jeffrey. I loved a wonderful man. And he loved me. While his love is now a memory, it is also a real dream that never ends. Love is like a beautiful photograph you treasure in an album. You can enjoy its beauty each time you stare at its wonderment. It stops time. And, it makes you young again—forever! Grandpa Edwin was a professional Army officer who chased Pancho Villa back to Mexico with John J. Pershing. He also served under General Pershing in the trenches in France during World War II. To understand your grandfather's soul, read his loving letters to me. You'll learn how romantic and beautiful a real man can be. To truly understand Grandpa's character, read the personal note Jack Pershing wrote me when he heard that Edwin was killed in action.

"Jeffrey, I said this packet of notes was priceless and valuable. I've just shown you how priceless his love notes are. Please learn from them. Then find the right girl to love and love her ardently. This love will enrich both your lives and make you both happier.

"As for being valuable, save the envelopes. An appraiser at Sotheby's said the old stamps are worth far more than the rest of my estate. And, the personal handwritten note from General Pershing is even more valuable than the stamps. Have a loving, bountiful life. God bless you.

"I love you, Grandma Elsie."

外婆的情书

外婆埃尔希去世时，我才17岁。她是我最后一位在世的祖辈，我是她唯一的外孙。直到律师宣读她的遗嘱，我才完全意识到外婆对我的爱有多深。那是一个我永远难忘的时刻，因为那天我成了城里最富有的男孩。

我和爸爸、妈妈、索菲姨妈、比尔姨父坐在外婆的律师办公室的一张小会议桌边。她想让她的女儿们、她们的丈夫分享她留下的一点财富：一小笔保险单收益、一块刻有浮雕的古宝石、几只镯子、一些人造宝石和她的结婚戒指。她还把房契、银行存款、在当地天然气和电力公司的几个股份，以及外公埃德温军事葬礼时获赠的美国国旗留给了他们。

我们起身离开时，律师说："还有三件东西。"他从公文包里拿出一个小珠宝盒、一封信和一叠用棉纸整洁包着、用褪色的粉红缎带扎着的信封。"杰弗里，你外婆把她的订婚钻戒留给了你，希望你不久好好利用它。"大家都露出了微笑。

"杰弗里，这些也是给你的，"他说。"也许是所有遗物中最珍贵的——一封信和一叠情书。"

外婆的信这样写道："亲爱的杰弗里：我要把最珍贵的财富——我的回忆留给你。这些回忆是你外公不在我身边时写给我的信。请你读一下这些信，它们是无价之宝，是一本教会你如何去爱一个女人、如何去理解他人以及如何自尊和保持气节的人生指南。

"看完后，你会分享到一个好男人对一个好女人的思念和深情，你也会发现它们将给你无穷的魅力。你还会明白战争带来的恐惧和眼泪。然后，你会明辨是非。你会学会去信赖所爱的人，远离不信任的人。你还会得知什么是成熟的友谊，真爱怎样才能成为你生命的核心。

"我很幸运，杰弗里。我爱上了一个了不起的男人。他也爱我。尽管他的爱现在成了一种回忆，但它也是一个永无止境的真实的梦。爱就像你珍藏在相册里的一张美丽的照片。每次凝视它，你都能欣赏到它的精彩和美丽。它让时光停住，并会让你青春焕发，永远年轻！埃德温外公是一名职业陆军军官。他和约翰·J.珀欣把潘乔·维亚追赶回了墨西哥。二战期间，他又在珀欣将军领导下转战法国。如果想了解你外公的为人，就看一下他写给我的情书。你会明白一个真正的男人可以多么浪漫和温文尔雅。如果想真正了解他的性格，就看一下杰克·珀欣得知你外公阵亡后写给我的私人信件。

"杰弗里，我说过这包信是无价之宝。我刚才给你看了他的情书是多么珍贵。请向它们学习，然后找一个合适的姑娘，好好爱她。这种爱将会丰富你们彼此的人生，也会让双方更加幸福。

“信件非常珍贵，要保存好那些信封。索思比的一位鉴定师说，这些旧邮票比我剩余的财产要值钱得多。而且，珀欣将军的亲笔信比那些邮票还要珍贵。度过一场相亲相爱、丰富多彩的人生。上帝保佑你！

“我爱你，埃尔希外婆。”

The Sweet Memory

It had been a long year for me, and the drive past the maturing vineyard, brought back memories of the many previous seasons that we had worked, to harvest the ripe Concord grapes. The memory of the taste itself brought back thoughts of my childhood, on a cool, fall afternoon, when I had first picked grapes.

As my grandma and I stepped out of the old, rusty, green pickup, we reached for the baskets that showed the age of many harvests. Soft, woven wood, stained in black – purple, from the many bunches of Concord grapes they had held in previous years. Now that the baskets were ready, we headed towards the seemingly endless rows of grapes.

With every visit to the vineyard, I was always over – awed by the way the grapevines grew and trailed off into the horizon. In every direction around me, there were rows upon rows of grapes, twinkling, as the morning sun glimmered its glow off the dew, still balancing on each tiny, round grape. It was as if the bunches of grapes were diamonds sparkling in the light.

As we continued to walk, further into the vineyard, I could hear the birds chirping their soft sounds, as they warned each other that we were approaching. I paused for a moment as my grandma continued ahead of me by a few feet. I watched her as she reached out to touch the ripening grapes, as if the coolness from the shimmering dew would let her know that this is where we were to begin.

We knelt on the ground and laid our baskets down at our sides as the birds began a different message in a much louder pitch, quite different from their first sounds. It was as if they were now accepting us and allowing us into their area. You could hear the rustling of the leaves, as the cool morning breeze swept past our faces and brought the fresh smell of the ripening grapes. The sweetly delicious smell would penetrate your senses.

I reached out delicately and removed one single grape from its bunch of many. Looking at this grape as if it were a perfect piece of art, I turned it around in my fingers, from side to side. The skin was cool and soft, more blue in color than black. I could smell and feel the juice dripping from the opened top, from where it had been attached to the bunch.

Slowly I brought the single grape closer to my mouth. I could feel my mouth filling with moisture. I brought the grape to the edge of my mouth and quickly squeezed it, so that the juicy, middle portion popped out of the smooth skin and into my mouth. The grape was even sweeter than I had hoped for and I enjoyed the texture of the smooth, meaty wetness inside my mouth. As my mouth enjoyed the motion of chewing this fruit, slowly swallowing it down my throat, I took the remaining skin of the grape, still positioned in my fingers.

Afterwards, I began to fill my basket with the wonders of nature. The bunches of grapes were plump and heavy to the touch, yet as delicate as small vulnerable creatures in your trusting care. I carefully piled them one on top of another, taking a moment, here and there, to taste another of these perfect fruits.

I knew that the taste would soon be another memory and I hoped that I would be available for the next harvest season.

甜蜜的回忆

这对我来说是漫长的一年，驱车驶过成熟的葡萄园，多年前在康科德葡萄园一季季采摘熟葡萄的情景又浮现在眼前。葡萄的美味使我的思绪回到了童年，那个凉爽的秋日午后是我第一次摘葡萄。

我和祖母从一辆又旧又锈的绿色敞篷小货车上下来，去取放葡萄的篮子，可以看出，那些篮子已经历了很多收获季节，软软的，木条编制，已被康科德前些年的葡萄染成了紫黑色。篮子准备好后，我们走向那仿佛一望无际的葡萄园。

每次来到葡萄园，面对这茁壮成长直至天际的葡萄藤，我总是诚惶诚恐。我身边四周各个方向都有一排排葡萄。在晨光照耀下，每颗小圆葡萄上都有露珠闪耀，一串串的葡萄像灯光中的钻石一样波光闪闪。

我们继续向前走，听到小鸟轻柔的啁啾声，它们是相互提醒同伴我们正在走近。祖母向前继续走了几英尺，我暂停了一会儿，看到她伸手去摸成熟的葡萄，葡萄上闪耀凉爽的露水似乎告诉她我们该从这里开始。

我们跪在地上，把篮子放在身边，鸟儿们开始以响亮得多的音高发出不同的消息。好像现在它们正在接待我们并允许我们进入它们的区域。清晨的凉风拂面，树叶沙沙作响，葡萄成熟的清香随风飘来。甜美的气息会渗透你的各个感官。

我小心翼翼地伸出手，摘下其中一颗葡萄。我看着这只葡萄，在手指间翻来覆去把玩着，就像它是一件完美的艺术品似的。葡萄的外皮清凉柔软，蓝色比黑色多。我可以闻到并感觉到连接着葡萄串的开口处滴下的汁液。

我慢慢地把那颗葡萄送近嘴边，可以感受到嘴里充满了润泽。我把葡萄放在嘴边，飞快地一挤，于是汁液和果肉脱离光润的果皮滑进了我的嘴里。葡萄比我希望的还要香甜。我享受着嘴里咀嚼的鲜润和果肉，慢慢咽下喉咙，然后开始吮吸留在手里的葡萄皮。

品尝过后，我开始向篮子里装这一个个自然的奇迹。一串串葡萄摸起来圆润厚实，而又小巧易碎，需要细心呵护。我小心翼翼地摞起一串串葡萄，不时地抽空品尝一下这完美的果实。

我知道这滋味很快会成为另一次回忆，我希望不会错过下一个丰收的季节。

A Letter to Grandpa

Dear Grandpa,

I cannot help but think about you, who have so much to give and share with me happily.

Even when I was young, you were a constant figure. You were there to see me grow up. I cried, I laughed, I learned, and you were there to guide me. With your gray hair and chunky glasses, I would watch you think and brood, and your sudden smile would light up your face as quickly as it came.

That is the very thing I love about you—your smile!

I think about the times I missed being with you. So many years have passed since I saw you again, and for a brief moment, I imagined you not being in my life. I wanted to cry. But I knew you would be there, as you always were. The gray hair has turned to white, and with that came a wiry frame that was fragile. Still the eyes were as vibrant as ever, and a mind that was well - running.

You taught me to be strong and live for my dreams. With your voracious hunger for knowledge you taught me to love learning; always telling me that knowledge is a constant thing. You were so strong, so wise and your presence was always a comfort. I always loved being by your side. You always gave me a hug when I fell down. I never loved crowds, and you always seemed to understand that, not pressuring me to join the others or to pretend to have a good time.

I got lost in the books you taught me to read. Those books which you gave me to learn more about the world, to never give up on things, to help me know myself and more. I read them constantly, ever so often reminded of the things you taught me.

I remember you with a teary face and a wistful smile. My pain is more insistent as I try to hold on to the hope that you will pull through this, like the strong person that you are.

I love you, Grandpa!

Your loving granddaughter
Sylvia

写给爷爷的信

亲爱的爷爷：

我无时无刻不在想着您，想着您对我的好，想着我们在一起分享快乐的时光。

我小时候，您就一直守在我身边，您一直关注着我的成长，无论是我在哭泣，在欢笑，还是在学习，您都在身边引导我。我常常想起您戴着一副厚眼镜的样子，您满头灰白的头发，常常情不自禁地陷入沉思，但突然的一个微笑能让您一下子容光焕发。

那正是我最喜欢您的东西——您的微笑！

我想起那些我们无法在一起的时光，我们再次见面竟然间隔了好几年时间。如果我的生命里没有您，我真的会放声大哭，但我知道您会一直陪着我。灰白的头发被岁月染成了银白，让我们明白了时间的无情和生命的脆弱。尽管如此，您的眼睛仍然那样明亮，思维仍然那样清晰。

您教我要坚强，要追求自己的梦想。您自己是那样孜孜不倦地学习，您也常常鼓励我要爱学习，因为知识是无价之宝。您是那样坚强，那样充满智慧。有您在身边总能让我感到安慰。我一直都喜欢待在您的身边。当我跌倒的时候，您会给我一个拥抱。我从来都不喜欢到热闹的人群中去，而您给了我很大程度的理解和尊重，从不勉强我去参加一些聚会或假装自己很快乐。

我深深地迷上了那些您推荐给我的书，那些书让我更多地了解了这个世界，让我知道不能轻易放弃对理想的追求，也让我更多地了解了自己。我常常捧着那些书看，也常常想起您教我的那些事情。

您的话从来就不多，但每次我们见面，我都知道您非常开心，就像我见到您时非常开心一样。

我含着泪面带微笑地想起您。虽然我还是那样痛苦难受，但我还是期待着您能挺过这一关，因为您从来就是那样坚强。

我爱您，爷爷！

您心爱的孙女
西尔维亚

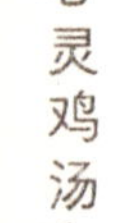

Tommy's Essay

A gray sweater hung limply on Tommy's empty desk, a reminder of the dejected boy who had just followed his classmates from our third-grade room. Soon Tommy's parents, who had recently separated, would arrive for a conference on his failing schoolwork and disruptive behavior. Neither parent knew that I had summoned the other.

Tommy, an only child, had always been happy, cooperative and an excellent student. How could I convince his father and mother that his recent failing grades represented a broken-hearted child's reaction to his adored parents' separation and pending divorce?

Tommy's mother entered and took one of the chairs I had placed near my desk. Soon the father arrived. Good! At least they were concerned enough to be prompt. A look of surprise and irritation passed between them, and then they pointedly ignored each other.

As I gave a detailed account of Tommy's behavior and schoolwork, I prayed for the right words to bring these two together, to help them see what they were doing to their son. But somehow the words wouldn't come. Perhaps if they saw one of his smudged, carelessly done papers.

I found a crumpled tear-stained sheet stuffed in the back of his desk, an English paper. Writing covered both sides—not the assignment, but a single sentence scribbled over and over. Silently I smoothed it out and gave it to Tommy's mother. She read it and then without a word handed it to her husband. He frowned. Then his face softened. He studied the scrawled words for what seemed an eternity.

At last he folded the paper carefully, placed it in his pocket, and reached for his wife's outstretched hand. She wiped the tears from her eyes and smiled up at him. My own eyes were brimming, but neither seemed to notice. He helped her with her coat and they left together.

In his own way God had given me the words to reunite that family. He had guided me to the sheet of yellow copy paper covered with the anguished outpouring of a small boy's troubled heart.

The words were, "Dear Mom... Dear Daddy... I love you... I love you... I love you."

汤米的随笔

一件灰色羊毛衫无力地挂在汤米空荡荡的书桌上，这使人想起了刚刚跟随同学们走出我们三年级教室的那个垂头丧气的男孩。很快，最近分居的汤米的父母亲就会来到这里，讨论他错误百出的作业和扰乱课堂的行为。汤米的父母亲都不知道我也叫了对方。

汤米是独生子，过去一向是快乐合作、非常优秀的学生。我怎样才使他的父母亲相信，他最近考试屡屡不及格，是一个伤心的孩子对他心爱的父母亲分居、即将离婚做出的反应呢？

汤米的妈妈走进来，在我桌边的一张椅子上坐下。很快，他的父亲也来了。好！他们都很准时，说明都很关心。他们俩的表情既惊讶又愤怒，之后显然就不理睬对方了。

我一边详细讲述汤米的行为和作业，一边祈求上帝赐给我合适的词语使这两个人重归于好，帮助他们明白他们正在给孩子造成怎样的影响。但是，不知何故，我没有想出合适的词语。也许他们看到他污迹斑斑、马马虎虎的作业会起作用吧。

我在他的书桌后部找到了一张皱皱巴巴、泪迹斑斑的纸，是英语作业纸。正反两面写的都是字，不是作业，而是反反复复、潦潦草草的一句话。我默默地捋平作业纸，把它递给汤米的妈妈。她看过后，什么也没说，递给了丈夫。他皱了皱眉，然后表情柔和了下来。他端详着那些潦草的字，看了好长时间。

最后，他仔细叠起了那张纸，放进了口袋里，然后去拉妻子伸出的手。她擦掉了眼上的泪水，抬头向他微笑。我也流出了眼泪，但他们好像谁也没注意到。他帮她穿上了大衣，他们一起走了。

上帝以自己的方式赐给我话语，使那个家庭破镜重圆。他指引我去拿那张流露出一个伤心小男孩痛苦情绪的黄色作业纸。

那上面的话是："亲爱的爸爸……亲爱的妈妈……我爱你们……我爱你们……我爱你们。"

The Love of a Full Moon

My daughter Kate turns the page of the kitchen calendar to a new month and motions to her sister, Kenna. Together they find "Full Moon Night" and mark it with a bright sticker. At our house, full moons signal the time for magical after - dark forays.

My inspiration for this tradition was an October canoe outing with friends years ago. I had loved the way the full moon transformed the night, making the familiar landscape serene and mysterious. By the time my daughters were both three, I was sure they would enjoy such an evening.

Our first full - moon outing as a family fell on a frosty Wisconsin evening. The birch trees in our front yard cast an intricate pattern of shadows as we stepped into our cross - country skis. Although the air was cold, our physical activity and sheer exhilaration kept us warm.

We were surprised at how bright the moonlight was as it reflected off the untracked snow. "The Indians in this region had different names for each full moon," I told the girls. This one was called Shaking Hands Moon.

Kate led the way, with Kenna close behind; my husband, Tom, and I brought up the rear. Soon we were gliding across a frozen lake, our shadows gliding beside us. Finally, we meandered back along the shoreline, toward the glow of our windows.

Inside, we celebrated our trek with hot cider and popcorn. The girls' rosy cheeks and smiles assured me we'd have more moonlit adventures.

We did, under February's Sturgeon Moon; then under full moons called Crusted Snow, Maple Sugar and Budding for March, April and May, respectively. A warm June evening proved just right for skinny - dipping under a girls—only Strawberry Moon. Father - daughter night yielded a bucketful of freshly caught lake perch, as July's Half - Summer Moon lit the sky.

Another year, on a star - filled August night, with a Blueberry Moon on the rise, we spread a blanket in the back yard. The northern lights were dancing, and questions came quickly: "What makes all the colors, Daddy?" "Where will that star land, Mommy?" The girls returned to the house bubbling with enthusiasm. Out came books on the moon, stars, planets and space exploration.

I shouldn't have been surprised when, a few weeks later, Kate looked up at a quarter moon and observed: "That's a waning moon—it's getting smaller. If it were getting bigger, it would be a waxing moon."

As the holidays neared, one of the girls asked, "Could we cut down our Christmas tree on Full Moon Night?" Why not? I thought. And it was not long before Kate and Kenna were running ahead in the woods behind our house, searching for the perfect specimen, their pink snowsuits made softer in the moonglow. "Here it is," shouted Kenna. "It's perfect," said Kate, pointing to a different tree. We finally found the right one for all of us, and with December's Night Moon smiling down, the girls made snow angels around the tree in celebration.

Another of our favorite nights of full - moon magic was spent exploring a ghost town on the Upper Peninsula of Michigan. Walking down a dusty road through a long - forgotten town can be daunting enough in daylight. At night we tiptoed around the abandoned buildings, holding hands. Ordinary sounds became extraordinary in the silent emptiness. Wispy clouds temporarily masked our moonlight. Then the hoot of an owl made us all jump—and we broke into laughter.

We have yet to run out of ideas for our adventures. The girls want to try a moonlight treasure hunt, and Kenna suggested building a snowman in her grandmother's yard. "She'd wake up and wonder how he got there."

On our most recent adventure, we packed an evening picnic and headed for an observation tower in a nearby state park. We climbed the steps until we thought we must be on top of the world: we could see the twinkling lights of towns up and down the shore and hear the lapping of waves below us. In the distance, a lighthouse cast its beam across the water.

We had gazed at the view countless times before, but this was different. The four of us were seeing it in a gloriously new light.

满月情

我的女儿凯特将厨房里的日历翻到了新的一月，然后向她的妹妹凯娜打了个手势。她们一起找出了“满月之夜”，用一个背面有粘胶的鲜艳标签做了个记号。在我们家，满月标志着黑暗过后神奇的短暂出游。

几年前，我与朋友们在10月一起乘着独木舟外出郊游，使我对这个传统获得了灵感。我喜欢满月改变了夜空，使熟悉的景色变得宁静而神秘。到两个女儿都3岁时，我确信她们会喜欢这样一个夜晚的。

我们第一次的满月郊游是一家人到威斯康辛州度过的一个寒夜。我们跨入横穿村庄的雪橇时，我们前院的白桦树已经投下了一片斑驳的阴影。虽然空气寒冷，但身体的活动和极度的兴奋使我们都感到暖融融的。

月光反射着无人走过的雪地，明亮得使我们吃惊。我对姑娘们说：“本地区的印第安人给每个满月都取有不同的名字。”本月的满月被称为“握手月”。

凯特领路，凯娜紧随其后；我和丈夫汤姆殿后。不久，我们滑行在一个冰冻的湖上。我们的身影也不离左右地滑动着。最后，我们沿着湖岸线恋恋不舍地朝我们家窗户的灯光返回。

到了家里,我们用热果汁和爆米花庆祝这次旅行。姑娘们红润的脸颊和微笑使我确信,我们还会有更多的月光冒险之行。

我们的确在 2 月的鲟月下,然后在 3 月、4 月和 5 月分别被称为硬壳雪、槭糖和萌芽的满月下进行了冒险旅行。温暖的 6 月之夜正是姑娘们在草莓月下单独裸泳的好时光。当 7 月的仲夏月照亮天空时,父女们则在夜里呈上来满满一桶刚捉到的湖鲈。

还有一年,在星星满天的一个 8 月之夜,一轮蓝莓月冉冉升起。我们在后院里铺开一张毛毯。北极光在熠熠闪动。很快,姑娘们产生了疑问:"爸爸,所有那些颜色是怎么来的?""妈妈,那颗星星会落到哪里?"姑娘们兴致勃勃地回到了房子里。翻翻有关月亮、恒星、行星和太空探索的书,问题就迎刃而解了。

几周后,凯特仰望一弯弦月说:"那是一个亏月,它正变得越来越小。如果它变得越来越大,它就是一个盈月。"对此,我一点没有感到意外。

每当节日临近时,其中一个女儿就问:"我们可以在满月之夜砍下我们的圣诞树吗?"为什么不可以呢?我想。不久,凯特和凯娜就一头钻进我们家屋后的树林里,寻找起完美的样板树。她们粉红色的风雪衣在月光下变得越发柔和。"这棵树!"凯娜大声说。"这棵完美。"凯特指着另一棵不同的树说。最后,我们找到了每个人都满意的一棵树。随后,在 12 月的夜月面带微笑的俯视下,姑娘们在那棵树四周堆起了几个白雪天使,以示庆祝。

我们度过的另一个最让人喜欢的神奇的满月之夜,是去密歇根州北方半岛上的一座鬼城探险。大白天沿着一条土路越过一座久被遗忘的城镇就足以让人感到胆怯了。夜里,我们蹑手蹑脚地手拉手绕着那些荒凉的建筑行走。寂静的空旷中,平常声音也变得异常起来。几缕云彩暂时遮住了我们的月光。接着,一只猫头鹰的鸮叫吓得我们都一下子跳了起来。随后,我们爆发出了朗朗的笑声。

然而,我们不得不绞尽脑汁考虑着我们的冒险旅行。姑娘们想尝试月光探宝旅行,而凯娜则建议在她外婆的院子里堆一个雪人。"外婆醒来后会纳闷雪人是怎么到那里的。"

在最近的一次冒险中,我们打点好一顿晚餐,前往附近的一家州立公园的观测塔。我们爬上台阶,直至我们认为一定站在了世界之巅:我们可以看到沿岸上下灯光闪烁,听到我们下面浪花拍岸。远处,一座灯塔的光线掠过水面。

我们曾观赏过无数次这样的情景,但这次不同。我们 4 人是在新的一轮灿烂月光中看的。

Love Notes

It's been over eleven years now. It was a wintry afternoon, the snow swirling around the cedar trees outside, forcing little icicles to form the tips of the deep green foliage clinging to the branches.

My older son, Stephen, was at school, and Reed, my husband, at work. My three little ones were clustered around the kitchen counter, the tabletop piled high with crayon and markers. Tom was

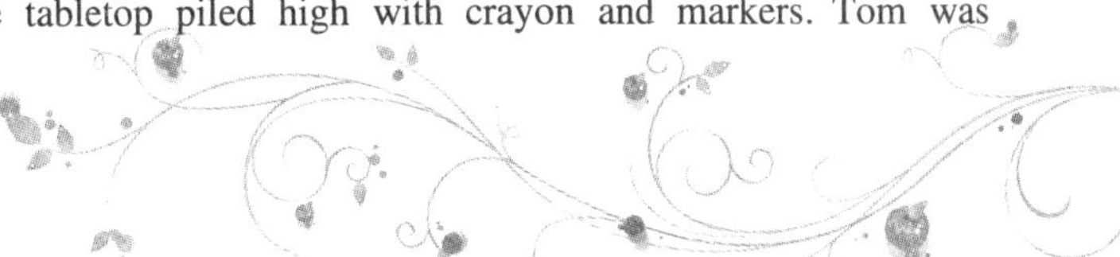

perfecting a paper airplane, creating his own insignia with stars and stripes, while Sam worked on a self-portrait, his chubby hands drawing first a head, then legs and arms sticking out where the body should had been. The children most concentrated on their work, Tom occasionally tutoring his younger brother on exactly how to make a plane that would fly the entire length of the room.

But Laura, our only daughter, sat quietly, engrossed in her project. Every once in a while she would ask how to spell the name of someone in our family, then painstakingly form the letters one by one. Next, she would add flowers with small green stems, complete with grass lining the bottom of the page. She finished off each with a sun in the upper right-hand corner, surrounded by an inch or two of blue sky. Holding them at eye level, she let out a long sigh of satisfaction.

"What are you making, Honey?" I asked.

She glanced at her brothers before looking back at me.

"It's a surprise," she said, covering up her work with her hands.

Next, she taped the top two edges of each other of paper together, trying her best to create a cylinder. When she had finished, she disappeared up the stairs with her treasure.

It was not until later that evening that I noticed a "mailbox" taped onto the doors to each of our bedrooms. There was one for Steve. There was one for Tom. She hadn't forgotten Sam or baby Paul.

For the next few weeks, we received mail on a regular basis. There were little notes expressing her love for each of us. There were short letters full of tiny compliments that only a seven-year-old would notice. I was in charge of retrieving baby Paul's letter, page after page of colored scenes including flowers with happy faces.

"He can't read yet," she whispered. "But he can look at the pictures."

Each time I received one of my little girl's gifts, it brightened my heart.

I was touched at how carefully she observed our moods. When Stephen lost a baseball game, there was a letter telling him she thought he was the best ballplayer in the whole world. After I had a particularly hard day, there was a message thanking me for my efforts, complete with a smiley face tucked near the bottom corner of the page.

This same little girl is grown now, driving off every day to the community college. But some things about her have never changed. One afternoon only a week or so ago, I found a love note next to my bedside.

"Thanks for always being there for me, Mom," it read. "I'm glad that we're the best friends."

I couldn't help but remember the precious child whose smile has brought me countless hours of joy throughout the years. There are angels among us. I know, I live with one.

爱的纸条

那已是11年前的事了。一个冬天的下午，雪在门外的雪松四周飞舞，使树枝上深绿色的叶尖挂上了小小的冰柱。

大儿子史蒂芬上学去了，丈夫里德上班去了。三个小家伙挤在厨柜边，桌面上高高地堆着蜡笔和记号笔，汤姆正用星星和条纹画徽章，让纸飞机尽善尽美。山姆正在忙着自画像。他胖胖的小手先画了一个脑袋，然后在本该是身体的位置画出了腿和胳膊。孩子们大都聚精会神忙自己的事儿。汤姆不时地教弟弟怎样正确制作一架能飞过整个房间的飞机。

我们唯一的女儿劳拉却安静地坐在那里，全神贯注地忙她的事儿。偶尔她也会询问怎样拼写我们家某个人的名字，然后一个字母、一个字母用心地拼写出来，接着又画了一些带细小绿茎的花朵，纸张底部还有一些草边。她每画完一页，都会在右上角画上太阳，周围是一两寸的蓝天。她把它们举到和眼水平的位置，然后满意地长出了口气。

“宝贝，你在做什么?”我问。

她在看我之前，瞥了一眼她的兄弟们。

“这是一个意外的惊喜。”她双手捂住自己的作品说。

接下来，她粘住每张纸的上面两边，尽力做成一个圆筒。做好后，她带着那些宝贝消失在楼梯上。

直到那天晚上晚些时候，我才注意到每个人的卧室门上都贴着一个“邮箱”。史蒂夫有一个，汤姆有一个，她也没有忘记萨姆和小保罗。

随后的几周里，我们都定期收到信件。小小的纸条表达了她对我们每个人的爱。有些短信里充满了一个只有7岁孩子才会注意到的小小问候。我负责取小保罗的信件，那是一页又一页的彩色图画，其中包括花朵和笑脸。

“他还不会念字，”她低声说道。“但他可以看这些图画。”

每次收到小女儿的礼物，我就心情愉悦。

她对我们心情的细微观察让我感动。史蒂芬输了棒球赛时，便有一封信告诉他，她认为他是全世界最好的棒球手。我哪天特别辛苦时，便会有一封信感谢我的努力，并在信封上画有一张笑脸。

如今，这个小女孩已经长大，每天开车上社区学院。但她身上的有些事从未改变。大约仅仅在一周前的一天下午，我在枕边发现了一张爱的纸条。

“妈妈，感谢您一直以来都支持我。”上面写道。“我很高兴我们是最好的朋友。”

我情不自禁想起，这些年来这个心爱的孩子的笑容带给了我无数欢乐时刻。我们中间有天使。我知道，我正和其中一位生活在一起。

The Warmth at This Moment

At an end of an old yellow bamboo pole was a blind man and at the other end was also a blind woman: the blind couple in rags were going to cross the road.

The bamboo pole was eagerly tapping the road. They didn't know it was the busiest crossroad of the city, not knowing precisely it was the red light at this moment.

With an exclamation, a saloon car stopped short, only a few centimeters away from them! Also a truck stopped, one after another... no one sounded the horn. In a split second, when the blind couple were walking on the road, the red light turned green: the whole bustling street became quiet instantly.

The blind couple were walking peacefully, not knowing the whole world was quietly watching them crossing the busiest crossroad of the city.

On that afternoon of autumn, the whole world made a bright way for a blind couple.

温情此刻

一根又黄又旧的竹竿，一头是个盲人，另一头也是个盲人：一对衣着褴褛的盲人夫

妻要过马路了。

竹竿在急切地敲打着路面，他们不知道这里是城市最繁忙的十字路口，更不知道此刻正是红灯。

一声惊呼，一辆轿车猛地刹住了，仅仅相差了几公分！又一辆卡车刹住了，一辆、又一辆……没有谁按一声喇叭。霎时间，盲人夫妻正走着的那条路红灯变成了绿灯，整条喧哗的大街霎时静寂了。

那对盲人夫妻在安然地走着，不知道整个世界都在默默地注视着他们走过这个城市最繁忙的十字路口。

那个秋日的下午，整个世界为一对盲人夫妻让了一次光明大道。

Love Is Not a Single Act

It was an autumn night in my native Nova Scotia. A light rain was falling, pattering on the porch roof, and it was cool enough for a fire on the Franklin stove. My father went over to the piano and began picking out a tune with one finger. My mother smiled as though recognizing a signal, put down her sewing and joined him on the bench.

In a moment they were singing—he in his sweet high tenor, Mother in her crystal clear soprano. My brother, coming in at that moment, drifted to the piano and joined in. Finally, I, the non - singer of the family, added my voice, and for once I held a makeshift alto for a line or two. My father gave me a hug. "See, you can," he said. "That was good."

I have often remembered how warm and happy—and loved—I have felt at that moment. It took me years, though, to learn that the love surrounding our family didn't just happen. We had to learn about love from one another. In fact, love never just happen—not even to people who seem as naturally loving as my mother and father. But there is, I think, a climate that is best for love—a way of living that hastens the maturity of this matchless gift.

First, love needs time. Perhaps people can fall in love in a moment, but mature love is like a tree, moving slowly from the seed in the ground to the sheltering splendor of its prime. People need time to deepen their affection, to appreciate one another's differences, to share one another's joys and grievances. So it is sad when divorces come with small provocations, when parents and children give up on one another, when friendships falter at the first injury; for thus we forfeit a great work of art—the long love.

When we accept the differences of loved ones, we find that those very differences provide the mystery and wonder of human relationships. It's foolish to expect perfection, for it doesn't exist. The key is to recognize and enjoy our differences.

To grow, love needs another, more elusive quality—the ability to let go.

Finally, love needs words to make it real. Without words, quarrels can't be resolved, resentment can't come to the surface, we lose the power to share the meaning of our lives. There are many ways of communication. The important thing is to acknowledge and express our feelings. If we don't, we deprive others of the knowledge of our love and ourselves of the joy that comes from expressing it.

Love is not a single act, but a climate in which we live, a lifetime venture in which we are always learning, discovering, growing. It is not destroyed by a single failure, or won by a single caress.

Love is a climate—a climate of the heart.

爱不是一场独角戏

那是在我的家乡新斯科舍省的一个秋夜。细雨蒙蒙，雨水滴滴答答地打在门廊顶上。天已经很凉了，我们在富兰克林壁炉式取暖炉里生起了火。父亲走到钢琴前，用一根手指一个音节、一个音节地弹奏着一首曲调。母亲面带微笑，好像听出了约定的信号，她放下手中的针线活，挨着父亲坐到琴凳上。

他们立马唱了起来，爸爸用的是甜美的男高音，妈妈用的是清亮的女高音。此时，哥哥走进来，飘然来到钢琴边和他们一起唱。最后，就连我这个家中不会唱歌的人也加入了他们的行列，我用女低音不时地插上一两句。父亲拥抱着我说："瞧，你会唱，唱得不错。"

我时常回忆起当时的那份温暖、幸福和受到关爱的感觉。然而，我多年以后才明白我们家中那种爱的氛围不是偶然形成的。我们必须得了解彼此的爱。实际上，爱从来就不会偶然产生，即使像父母亲这样的人也是如此，尽管他们看上去是天生相爱的一对。但我想有一种氛围对爱的生长是再好不过的，那就是一种可以促进这种无与伦比的天赋成熟的生活方式。

首先，爱需要时间。也许人们可能会一见钟情，但成熟的爱情就像一棵树，由土壤里的一粒种子慢慢长成参天大树。人们需要时间加深彼此的感情，理解双方的差异，分享相互的苦乐。因此，为鸡毛蒜皮的一点小事便分道扬镳，父母和子女各自心灰意冷，以及彼此的友谊因一次伤害而发生动摇，这些都是令人伤心的事情，因为我们会因而失去一件伟大的艺术品——持久的爱。

当接受与所爱的人之间的差异时，我们发现正是那些差异造就了人际关系中的奥妙和神奇。期望尽善尽美是非常愚蠢的，因为它并不存在。关键是要认识并分享彼此的差异。

为了使爱得到升华，还需要具有另一种独有的品质——放手的能力。

最后，爱需要通过语言使它成为现实。没有语言，分歧就无法解决，怨恨也无法显露出来，我们也就失去了分享生活意义的权利。交流的方式有许多。重要的是了解并能表达我们的情感。如果不进行情感交流，我们就会剥夺别人了解我们之间爱的权利，同时也剥夺了我们自己表达爱情时的那种快乐。

爱不是一场独角戏，而是一种生活氛围，也是我们毕生所追求的，在这一过程中我们要不断学习，不断发现并逐渐成熟起来。爱不会因为一次小小的挫折而毁灭，也不会因为一次的爱抚而赢得。

爱是一种氛围，一种心灵的氛围。

Greet This Day with Love

I will greet this day with love in my heart. For this is the greatest secret of success in all ventures. Muscle can split a shield and even destroy life but only the unseen power of love can open the hearts of men. I will make love my greatest weapon and none can defend against its force.

And how will I do this? Henceforth will I look on all things with love and I will be born again. I will love the sun, for it warms my bones; yet I will love the rain, for it cleanses my spirit. I will love the light, for it shows me the way; yet I will love the darkness, for it shows me the stars. I will welcome happiness, for it enlarges my heart; yet I will endure sadness, for it opens my soul. I will acknowledge rewards, for they are my due; yet I will welcome obstacles, for they are my challenge.

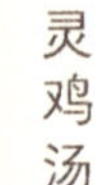

And how will I speak? I will laud my enemies and they will become friends; I will encourage my friends and they will become brothers. Always will I dig for reasons to applaud; never will I scratch for excuses to gossip. When I am tempted to criticize I will bite on my tongue; when I am moved to praise I will shout from the roofs.

Is it not so that birds, the wind, the sea and all nature speaks with the music of praise for their creator? Cannot I speak with the same music to his children? Henceforth will I remember this secret and it will change my life.

And how will I act? I will love all manner of men, for each has qualities to be admired even though they are hidden. With love I will tear down the wall of suspicion and hate which they have built round their hearts and in its place will I build bridges so that my love may enter their souls.

I will love the ambitious, for they can inspire me! I will love the failures, for they can teach me. I will love the kings, for they are but humans; I will love the meek, for they are divine. I will love the rich, for they yet lonely.

I will love the poor, for they are so many. I will love the young, for the faith they hold; I will love the old, for the wisdom they share. I will love the beautiful, for their eyes of sadness; I will love the ugly, for their souls of peace.

But how will I react to the actions of others? With love. For just as love is my weapon to open the hearts of men, love is also my shield to repulse the arrows of hate and the spears of anger. Adversity and discouragement will beat against my new shield and become as the softest of rains.

And how I confront each whom I meet? In only one way. In silence and to myself I will address him and say, "I Love You." Though spoken in silence these words will shine in my eyes, unwrinkle my brow, bring a smile to my lips, and echo in my voice; and his heart will be opened.

用爱迎接今天

我要用心中的爱迎接今天，因为这是所有冒险中最大的成功秘诀。臂力能劈开盾牌，甚至毁灭生命，但只有无形的爱的力量才能打开人们的心灵。我要让爱成为无人抵御的最强大武器。

我将做什么呢？从此，我将充满爱心地看待一切，使自己重获新生。我爱太阳，因为它能温暖我的身体。我爱雨水，因为它能净化我的心灵。我爱光明，因为它能照亮我的道路。我爱黑夜，因为它使我看到满天繁星。我将迎接快乐，因为它使我心胸开阔；我将忍受悲伤，因为它将打开我的灵魂。我将接受报酬，因为它们是我应该得到的。我将迎接困难，因为我愿迎接挑战。

我将说什么呢？我赞美敌人，他们会成为我的朋友；我鼓励朋友，他们将成为我的兄弟。我总要找理由赞美别人，而绝不挖空心思找借口说三道四。当我忍不住要批评人时，就咬住舌头；当我感动得赞美别人时，就大声说出口。

小鸟、风、海浪和世间万物，不都在用美妙悦耳的歌声赞美造物主吗？难道我不能同样的歌声去赞美它的儿女们吗？从此，我要记住这个秘诀，它将改变我的生活。

我将如何行动呢？我爱所有的人，因为每个人都有值得敬佩的优秀品质，即使他们秘而不宣。我要用爱摧垮阻碍人们心灵自由沟通的怀疑和仇恨之墙，同时我要用爱在人们之间搭建一座桥梁，使我的爱能进入他们的灵魂。

我爱有抱负的人，因为他们能激励我！我爱失败者，因为他们能教育我。我爱国王，因为他们不过是凡人。我爱谦恭者，因为他们是天才。我爱富人，他们更孤独。

我爱穷人，因为他们有很多人。我爱年轻人，因为他们坚定的信念。我爱长者，因为他们睿智。我爱美人，因为他们的眼神忧郁。我爱丑人，因为他们有平和的心灵。

但我对他们的行动怎样做出反应呢？用爱。因为爱不仅是打开人们心灵的钥匙，也是反击仇恨之箭和愤怒之矛的盾牌。逆境和挫折在我的新盾面前也会变得像细雨一样柔软。

我该怎样面对和我相遇的每个人呢？只有一种办法。我将默默地一心一意地对待他，并说“我爱你”。尽管无声，但这些话语将会闪现在我的眼神中，舒展我的眉头，让我的嘴唇露出微笑，引起我的共鸣，随后将会打开他的心灵。

The Old Man with Flowers

We were a very motley crowd of people who took the bus every day that summer 3 years ago. During the early morning ride from the suburb, we sat drowsily with our collars up to our ears, a cheerless and taciturn bunch.

One of the passengers was a small gray man who took the bus to the center for senior citizens every morning. He walked with a stoop and a sad look on his face when he, with some difficulty, boarded the bus and sat down alone behind the driver. No one ever paid very much attention to him.

Then one July morning he said good morning to the driver and smiled down through the bus before he sat down. The driver nodded guardedly. The rest of us were silent.

The next day, the old man boarded the bus energetically, smiled and said in a loud voice, "And a very good morning to you all!" Some of us looked up, amazed, and murmured "Good morning" in reply.

The following weeks we were more alert. Our friend was now dressed in a nice old suit and a wide out-of-date tie. The thin hair had been carefully combed. He said good morning to us every day and we gradually began to nod and talk to each other.

One morning he had a bunch of wild flowers in his hand. They were already dangling a little because of the heat. The driver turned around smilingly and asked: "Have you got yourself a girlfriend, Charlie?" We never got to know if his name really was "Charlie", but he nodded shyly and said yes.

The other passengers whistled and clapped at him. Charlie bowed and waved the flowers before he sat down on his seat.

Every morning after that Charlie always brought a flower. Some of the regular passengers began bringing him flowers for his bouquet, gently nudged him and said shyly: "Here." Everyone smiled. The men started to jest about it, talk to each other, and share the newspaper.

The summer went by, and autumn was closing in, when one morning Charlie was not waiting at his usual stop. When he was not there the next day and the day after that, we started wondering if he was sick or on holiday somewhere.

When we came nearer to the center for senior citizens, one of the passengers asked the driver to wait. We all held our breaths when she went to the door. Yes, the staff said, they knew who we were talking about. The elderly gentleman was fine, but he hadn't been coming to the center that week. One of his very close friends had died at the weekend. They expected him back on Monday. How silent we were the rest of the way to work.

The next Monday Charlie was waiting at the stop, stooping a bit more, a little bit more gray, and without a tie. He seemed to have shrunk again. Inside the bus was a silence akin to that in a church. Even though no one had talked about it, all those of us, who he had made such an impression on that summer, sat with our eyes filled with tears and a bunch of wild flowers in our hands.

手持鲜花的老人

3年前的夏天，我们这些芸芸众生每天乘坐同一辆公共汽车。在郊区开往市里的早班车上，我们竖起衣领盖住耳朵，坐在那里昏昏欲睡，沉默寡言，了无情趣。

其中一名乘客是一个头发花白的小个子，他每天早上乘车去老年活动中心。他走起路来弓着腰、神情忧郁，每次有些吃力地上车后，就独自坐到司机后面。没有人过多地注意过他。

后来，7月的一个早晨，他向司机说了声早安，然后向车厢里的人微微笑了一下，才坐下来。司机谨慎地点了点头，我们其他人都一声不吭。

第二天，这位老人精神饱满地上了车，微微一笑，朗声说道："大家早上好！"我们中一些人抬起头，吃了一惊，低声回答说："早上好。"

接下来的几个星期，我们更加注意起了他。我们这位朋友穿着一件漂亮的旧西装，打着一条过时的宽领带，稀疏的头发梳得一丝不苟。每天他都向我们问早安。我们渐渐开始点头，相互交谈。

一天早上，他手里拿着一束野花。因为天气炎热，它们已经有点儿耷拉了。司机微笑着转过头，问道："你自己找女朋友了吧，查理？"我们根本不知道他是不是叫"查理"，但他不好意思地点头称是。

其他的乘客对他又是吹口哨，又是鼓掌。查理鞠了一躬，挥了挥手里的鲜花，然后在座位上坐了下来。

从那以后，查理每天早上都会带一朵花，有些老乘客也开始给他带鲜花，轻轻地用胳膊肘推他一下，不好意思地说："给。"每个人都面带微笑。大家开始开玩笑，聊天，一起看报纸。

夏去秋来。一天早上，查理没在以往那个站等车。以后的两天，他都没来，我们开始纳闷他是不是病了，或者是到什么地方度假去了。

当我们的车靠近老年活动中心时，一个乘客让司机停车。当她走到门口时，我们都屏住呼吸。那个职员说：是的，他们都知道我们说的是谁。那位老先生身体很好，但他那个星期没来活动中心。上周末，他非常亲近的一个朋友去世了，他们盼望他星期一能回来。剩下的路程，我们都沉默不语。

接下来的那个星期一，查理在那个站等车，他的背更弯了，头发更白了，也没打领带。他好像又缩回了从前。车里像教堂一样寂静。即使谁都没说话，我们所有的人也都眼噙热泪、手持一束野花，因为那个夏天，是他给我们留下了那样深刻的印象。

The Chain of Love

He was driving home one evening, on a two-lane country road. Work, in this small mid-western community, was almost as slow as his beat-up Pontiac was.

But he never quit looking. Ever since the factory closed, he'd been unemployed. And with winter raging on, the chill had finally hit home. It was a lonely road. Not very many people had a reason to be on it, unless they were leaving. Most of his friends had already left. They had families to feed and dreams to fulfill. But he stayed on. After all, this was where he buried his mother and father. He was born here and he knew the country. He could go down this road blind, and tell you what was on either side, and with his headlights not working, that came in handy.

It was starting to get dark and light snow flurries were coming down. He'd better get a move on. He almost didn't see the old lady, stranded on the side of the road. But even in the dim light of day, he could see she needed help.

So he pulled up in front of her Mercedes and got out. His Pontiac was still sputtering when he approached her. Even with the smile on his face, she was worried. No one had stopped to help for the last hour or so. Was he going to hurt her? He didn't look safe; he looked poor and hungry.

He could see that she was frightened, standing out there in the cold. He knew how she felt. It was that chill which only fear can put in you. He said, "I'm here to help you, Madam. Why don't you wait in the car where it's warm? By the way, my name is Joe." Well, all she had was a flat tire, but for an old lady, that was bad enough. Joe crawled under the car looking for a place to put the jack, skinning his knuckles a time or two. Soon he was able to change the tire. But he had to get dirty and his hands hurt.

As he was tightening up the lug nuts, she rolled down the window and began to talk to him. She told him that she was from St. Louis and was only just passing through. She couldn't thank him enough for coming to her aid. Joe just smiled as he closed her trunk.

She asked him how much she owed him. Any amount would have been all right with her. She had already imagined all the awful things that could have happened had he not stopped. Joe never thought twice about the money. This was not a job to him. This was helping someone in need, and God knows there were plenty who had given him a hand in the past.

He had lived his whole life that way, and it never occurred to him to act any other way. He told her that if she really wanted to pay him back, the next time she saw someone who needed help, she could give that person the assistance that they needed, and Joe added "... and think of me."

He waited until she started her car and drove off. It had been a cold and depressing day, but he felt good as he headed for home, disappearing into the twilight.

A few miles down the road the lady saw a small café. She went in to grab a bite to eat, and take the chill off before she made the last leg of her trip home. It was a dingy-looking restaurant. Outside were two old gas pumps. The whole scene was unfamiliar to her. The cash register was like the telephone of an out-of-work actor—it didn't ring much. Her waitress came over and brought a clean towel to wipe her wet hair.

She had a sweet smile, one that even being on her feet for the whole day couldn't erase. The lady noticed that the waitress was nearly eight months pregnant, but she never let the strain and aches change her attitude.

The old lady wondered how someone who had so little could be so giving to a stranger. Then she remembered Joe. After the lady finished her meal, and the waitress went to get change for her hundred-dollar bill, the lady slipped right out the door. She was gone by the time the waitress came back. She wondered where the lady could be, and then she noticed something written on the napkin.

There were tears in her eyes when she read what the lady wrote. It said, "You don't owe me anything, I have been there too. Someone once helped me out, the way I'm helping you. If you really want to pay me back, here is what you do: don't let the chain of love end with you."

Well, there were tables to clean, sugar bowls to fill, and people to serve, but the waitress made it through another day. That night when she got home from work and climbed into bed, she was thinking about the money and what the lady had written.

How could the lady have known how much she and her husband needed it? With the baby due next month, it was going to be hard. She knew how worried her husband was, and as he lay sleeping next to her, she gave him a soft kiss and whispered, "Everything's gonna be all right; I love you, Joe."

爱的链条

一天晚上，他开车回家，行驶在一条双行道的乡村公路上。在这个中西部小镇找工作几乎就像他那辆庞帝亚克老爷车一样慢。

但他从不放弃寻找。自从工厂关门后，他就失业了。而随着冬天不断肆虐，严寒终于长驱直入。这是一条偏僻公路，除非有人正要离开，否则不会有多少人有理由出现在这里。他的大部分朋友都已经离去。他们要养家糊口，要实现梦想。但他留了下来。毕竟，这里是他安葬父母的地方。他出生在这里。他熟悉这里。这条路他可以闭着眼走下去，并告诉你道路的两边都是什么。他那辆车的前灯坏了，所以这派上了用场。

天色渐渐暗了下来，小雪正纷纷飘落。他最好赶路。他几乎没有看到困在路边的那位老太太。但即使在昏暗的暮色里，他还是能看清她需要帮助。

于是，他在她那辆奔驰车前停下来，下了车。当他走近这位老太太时，他那辆庞帝亚克老爷车还在喷气。虽然看到他脸上的笑容，老太太还是担心。在过去的一小时左右，没有人停下来帮她。他会伤害她吗？他看上去不可靠，而是又穷又饿。

他可以看到站在寒风中的她非常害怕。他明白她的感受。这种寒冷只会让你感觉恐惧。他说："我是来帮你的，太太。你何不待在车里，车里暖和？顺便说一下，我叫乔。"呃，她的车轮胎漏气了，但对一位老太太来说，这够糟了。乔爬到车底下，寻找支千斤顶的地方，他的指关节磨破一两处。很快他就能换车胎了。可是，他不得不把身上弄脏，手也受了伤。

当他在上紧接线片螺丝时，她摇下车窗开始和他聊了起来。她对他说她来自圣路易斯，只不过是路过这里。对他能赶来相助，她感激不尽。乔只是微微一笑，合上了她的汽车尾部的行李箱。

她问付给他多少钱，多少钱她都没事儿。她已经想象到了，如果他不停下来，可能会发生的种种可怕的事情。乔从来没想到过要钱。这对他来说不是工作，而是救人所急，而且上帝知道，过去曾有好多人帮助过他。

他的一生都是这样度过的，他从未想过采取其他方式。他告诉她说，如果她真的想报答他，下次看到有人需要帮助，她就可以提供那人所需的帮助。随后，乔补充说："……然后想起我。"

他一直等到她发动车子离去。这天寒冷阴沉，但他朝家驶去，消失在暮色中时，感觉良好。

沿路行驶了几英里后，老太太看到了一家小咖啡馆。她进去想吃点东西，暖暖身子，然后走完回家的最后一程。这是一家看上去寒酸的咖啡馆。外面是两台旧加油泵。她对整个场景都不熟悉，收银台像是一部失业演员的电话——总也不响。女招待向她走来，拿来了一条干净毛巾，让她擦干了湿发。

她带着甜甜的笑容，甚至跑了一整天的腿都无法抹去那笑容。老太太注意到女招待差不多已有八个月的身孕，但她却从不让疲劳和持续疼痛来改变自己的态度。

老太太纳闷，为什么一个这样穷的人却能对一个路人这样慷慨相助。接着，她想起了乔。在老太太用完餐，女招待去拿一百美元钞票找零钱时，老太太溜出了门外。等到女招待回来，老太太已经不见了。她纳闷老太太会可能去哪里呢，随后她注意到了餐巾上写着什么东西。

她念着老太太的留言，热泪盈眶。上面写道："你什么也不欠我，我也曾有过你的处境，有人帮我摆脱了困境，正如我现在帮你一样。如果你真想报答我，就这样做：别让爱的链条在你那里终止。"

噢，还有桌子需要收拾，糖碗需要加满，顾客需要招待，但女招待又坚持挺过了一天。当晚，她下班回到家里钻进被窝时，她还在想着那笔钱和老太太写下的那段话。

老太太怎么可能会知道她和丈夫多么需要钱呢？婴儿下个月就要降生了，日子会非常艰难。她知道丈夫多么为难。当他挨着她躺下睡觉时，她温柔地吻了他一下，低声说道："一切都会好起来的；我爱你，乔。"

Saving Happiness

The small, well - poised and alert 92 - year - old lady, who is up and dressed each morning by eight o'clock with her hair nicely combed even though she is blind, moved to a nursing home today.

Her husband of 70 years recently died, making the move necessary. After an hour of waiting patiently in the lobby of the nursing home, she smiled when I told her that her room was ready.

As she maneuvered her walker to the elevator, I described her tiny room, including the eyelet curtains that had been hung on her window.

"I love it!" she said.

"Mrs. Jones, you haven't even seen the room... just wait."

"That doesn't have anything to do with it," she replied. "Happiness is something you decide on ahead of time. Whether I like my room doesn't depend on how the furniture is arranged; it's how I arrange my mind. I already decided to love it. It's a decision I make every morning when I wake up. I have two choices: I can spend the day in bed recounting the difficulties I have with the parts of my body that no longer work, or get out of bed and be thankful for the ones that do. Each day is a gift, and as long as my eyes open I'll focus on the new day and all the happy memories I've stored away just for this time in my life. Old age is like a bank account: you withdraw from what you've put in. Thank you for your part in filling my Memory Bank. I am still making deposits."

Please remember the five simple rules to being happy:

Free your heart from hatred.

Free your mind from worries.

Live simply.

Give more.

Expect less.

Your happiness will increase every day.

储存幸福

这位小巧、安详而机警的92岁的老太太每天早上8点起床，头发梳得一丝不乱，即使她已经失明，今天要搬到一家疗养院。

她70岁的丈夫刚刚去世，所以她必须搬过来。在疗养院的休息室耐心等待了一小时后，我告诉她房间已经准备好，这时她露出了微笑。

她一边将助步架移上电梯，我一边向她描述她的小房间，其中包括挂在她窗户上的金属挂环窗帘。

"我非常喜欢！"她说。

"琼斯太太，您还没有看到房间，请等一下。"

"那没关系，"她回答说。"幸福是你提前决定的东西。我是不是喜欢自己的房间并不取决于家具如何安排，而是取决于我如何调整心态。我已经决定喜欢它。每天早上一醒来，我都做这样的决定。我有两个选择：我是一天躺在床上数说自己因身体的一部分器官不能再工作而遇到的那些困难，还是起床对那部分能工作的器官心怀感激。每天都是一件礼物。只要我睁开眼睛，就要关注这新的一天以及我在生活中这一刻存储的所有幸福记忆。老年就像银行账户：你总是提取你存储的东西。谢谢你为我的记忆库存储的部分。我也在存储着。"

请记住幸福的五个简单原则：

让心远离仇恨。

让心远离烦恼。

简单生活。

多给予。

少期盼。

你每天的幸福就会越来越多。

Walk for Love

A boy living on a remote Hawaiian island listened carefully to the teacher to explain why people should exchange gifts at Christmas.

The teacher said,"The gifts express our love and our joy for Jesus, who is the greatest gift."

At Christmas, the boy brought his teacher a gift—a shiny shell, which was the treasure among the shells washed ashore.

The teacher asked,"Where did you discover such an unusual shell?"

The boy told his teacher, as far as he knew, there was only one place such an unusual shell could be found: on some beach more than 20 miles away from here such shells would be washed ashore sometimes.

The teacher said,"Oh, it is really so beautiful that I will treasure it all my life, but you shouldn't go so far to bring me back the gift."

Still remembering the lesson of giving gifts, the boy flashed his eyes and said,"Walking is part of the gift."

为爱而走

一个住在夏威夷偏远小岛上的男孩,仔细聆听老师解释为什么人们在圣诞节时要互赠礼物。

老师说:"礼物表示我们的爱意与我们对耶稣降临的欢喜,耶稣是最伟大的礼物。"

圣诞节到了,男孩为老师带来一份礼物——一个闪闪发亮的贝壳,是海水冲上岸的贝壳中的珍品。

老师问:"你是在哪里发现这样一个不同寻常的贝壳?"

男孩告诉老师,据他所知,只有一个地方能找到这种非同寻常的贝壳:20 多英里外某个神秘的海滩有时会有这种贝壳冲上岸。

老师说:"噢,它真是太美了,我会一辈子珍惜它的,但你不应该走那么远的路为我带回礼物。"

男孩仍然记着关于赠送礼物的那一课,他闪着眼睛说:"走路是礼物的一部分。"

As Long As You Have Love in Your Heart

It was a winter morning without the sun, the freezing cold quietly nipping to the bone of the people waiting for the bus. They were all black, sometimes raising their heads to look afar or looking up at the sullen sky.

Suddenly, the crowd stirred up. Yes, here came a bus, a minibus rolled along in no hurry. Curiously, the people still stood where they were, still raising their head and looking at the place farther away; they didn't seem to be anxious to get on the bus, still expecting something. Who were they waiting for? Did they have a partner not to come?

Sure enough, after a figure appeared from afar, the crowd stirred up once again. The figure walked hurriedly, sometimes trotted and finally drew near. It was a woman, a white woman. At this time, the crowd was on the point of cheering. Undoubtedly, she was the partner who the black people were waiting for together.

Why? You know, in this country, the white and the black were always hostile to each other. What force made them so close?

Formerly, it was a remote way station, the bus moved to and fro every two hours, and the bus drivers had a privity: the bus stopped in the presence of white people, but the people who lived nearby were almost black. It was said that the white woman was a writer who lived in a place three miles ahead, where there was also a station. But in order to make the black people ride the bus favorably, she insisted walking here for three miles to board the bus, rain or shine.

The black people almost embraced the writer to send her on to the bus.

"Hi, Susan." Before the female writer kept her legs, she heard someone call her name. Looking up, she saw her friend Jay.

"Why do you get on the bus here?" asked Jay in confusion.

"Because," the writer said, pointing to the station, "the bus doesn't stop without white people, so I come here." With that, the writer tidied up the goods in her arms.

Surprised, Jay stared at the writer and said, "Just for these black people?"

The writer also widened her eyes, "Why, is it very important?"

We were also surprised and then came to understand: as long as you have love in your heart, everything will be as pure as nature.

只要心中有爱

这是一个没有太阳的冬天的早晨，刺骨的寒气悄悄地渗进候车人的骨髓。他们都是黑人，时而翘首远方，时而抬头望着阴沉的天空。

突然，人群骚动起来，是的，车来了，一辆中巴正不紧不慢地开了过来。奇怪的是，人们仍站在原地，仍在翘首更远的地方，他们似乎并不急于上车，似乎还在企盼着什么。他们在等谁？难道他们还有一个伙伴没来？

果然，远方隐隐约约出现了一个身影后，人群又一次骚动起来。身影走得很急，有时还小跑一阵，终于走近了，是一个女人，白种女人。这时，人群几乎要欢呼了。无疑，她就是黑人们共同等候的伙伴。

怎么回事？要知道，在这个国家，白人与黑人一向互相敌视。是什么力量让他们如此亲近？

原来，这是一个偏僻小站，公交车每两小时才来一趟，而且这些公交车司机们都有一种默契：有白人才停车，而偏偏这附近住的几乎都是黑人。据说，这个白种女人是个作家，她住在前面 3 英里处，那里也有一个车站。可为了让这里的黑人顺利地坐上公交车，她每天坚持走 3 英里来这里上车，风雨无阻。

黑人们几乎是拥抱着将女作家送上了车。

"苏珊，你好。"女作家脚还没站稳，就听见有人叫自己的名字。抬头一看，是朋友杰伊。

"你怎么在这里上车？"杰伊疑惑地问。

"这个站,"女作家指了指上车的地方。"没有白人就不停车,所以我就赶到这里来了。"说着,女作家理了理怀里的物品。

杰伊惊讶地瞪着女作家,说:"就因为这些黑人?"

女作家也瞪大了眼睛:"怎么,这很重要吗?"

我们也惊讶了,继而又明白了:只要心中有爱,一切都会纯如天然。

Make the Love Grow in the Heart

Maybe God wants us to meet a few wrong people before meeting the right one so that when we finally meet the right person, we will know how to be grateful for that gift.

When the door of happiness closes, another opens, but oftentimes we look so long at the closed door that we don't see the one, which has been opened for us.

The best kind of friend is the kind you can sit on a porch and swing with, never say a word, and then walk away feeling like it was the best conversation you've ever had.

It's true that we don't know what we've got until we lose it, but it's also true that we don't know what we've been missing until it arrives.

Giving someone all your love is never an assurance that they'll love you back! don't expect love in return; just wait for it to grow in their heart but if it doesn't, be content it grew in yours. It takes only a minute to get a crush on someone, an hour to like someone, and a day to love someone, but it takes a lifetime to forget someone.

don't go for looks; they can deceive. don't go for wealth; even that fades away. Go for someone who makes you smile because it takes only a smile to make a dark day seem bright. Find the one that makes your heart smile.

让爱在心中成长

也许是上帝让我们在最终找到知音之前总要遇到几个不尽如意的人,这样我们才能对知音这份礼物充满感激之情。

一道幸福之门关闭时,另一扇就会打开,但我们常常久久地看着关闭的门,而看不见已经对我们开启的门。

最好的朋友就是你坐在门廊和秋千上,一句话没说,然后走开时却感到好像你曾有过最好的交谈。

的确,我们失去自己拥有的东西时,才会知道。同样,一件东西得来时,我们才知道自己一直缺少。

付出全部的爱,并不能确保你一定会得到回报!别指望爱有什么回报;耐心等待让它在他们心中成长。但如果不能成长,也要满足爱已在你的心中成长。迷恋一个人只需要一分钟,喜欢一个人需要一个小时,爱上一个人需要一天,但忘记一个人则需要一辈子。

不要追求外表,外表常会骗人。不要追求财富,财富也会散尽。追求能使你微笑的人,因为只有微笑才能使黑暗的日子变得光明。找到那个能使你的心灵微笑的人吧。

The Petals of Love

One summer evening, I dated my girlfriend in the park.

Across the bench sat a blind old woman, holding a large bunch of flowers. I wanted to buy a bouquet for my girlfriend, so I went up to her.

"These flowers are not sold but sent."

"Sent? To whom?" I asked in surprise.

"The good people."

It turned out that the old woman's home was far from the park, but she would like to come to sit in the park only for breathing the pure and fresh air and the fragrant flowers while she could still hear the children's frolic laughter.

She would meet many kind-hearted people on the road every day. They would help her one after another journey. By and by, the old woman felt warm and sorry: what she felt warm was the kind hands, but what she regretted was that she couldn't see their faces. So she planted many flowers in her courtyard. When the flowers were all in bloom, she carried them and gave them to the kind-hearted people. This was her long-cherished desire of heart.

The old woman brought out a bouquet of fiery-red roses and handed them to me, "I wish you happiness."

I'm grateful for this bouquet of roses, for the old woman with good wishes and for every good man on earth, because it is they who weave the caring wings with the petals in their hands and carry us to fly to the blest heaven.

I think as long as we hold the petals of love in our hands, the spring will always stay in our heart.

爱的花瓣

夏天的一个黄昏,我和女友在公园里约会。

对面长椅上坐着一位盲人老太太,手里捧着一大堆鲜花。我想买一束送给女友,便走到她跟前。

"这花不是卖的,是送人的。"

"送人,送给谁?"我诧异地问。

"送给好人。"

原来,老人的家离这个公园很远,可她每天都喜欢来这个公园坐坐,只为呼吸到公园里清新的空气和花草的芳香,还能听到孩子们嬉闹的笑声。

每天在路上她都会碰见许多好心人,他们扶着老人走上一程又一程。天长日久,老人觉得既温暖又遗憾,温暖的是那一双双善良的手,遗憾的是自己无法看见他们的脸。她就在自己的院子里种了很多很多的鲜花,等到有一天,花全都开了,她就带上它们,送给路上的一个个好心人,这是她长久以来的心愿。

老人凭感觉从那堆鲜花里取出一束火红火红的玫瑰递给我说:"祝你们幸福。"

我感激这束玫瑰,感激这个怀揣美好心愿的老人,感激这个尘世的每个好人,是他们用手中的花瓣编织出爱心的翅膀,带着我们飞抵幸福的天堂。

我想,只要手握爱的花瓣,春天就会永远停驻在我们心间。

Bobby's Gift

Bobby was getting cold standing in his backyard in the snow. Bobby didn't wear boots;he didn't like them and anyway he didn't own any. The thin sneakers he wore had a few holes in them and they did a poor job of keeping out the cold.

Bobby had been in his backyard for about an hour already. And, try as he might, he couldn't come up with an idea for his mother's Christmas gift. He shook his head as he thought, "This is useless, even if I do come up with an idea, I don't have any money to spend."

Ever since his father had passed away three years ago, the family of five had struggled. It was not because his mother didn't care or try, there just never seemed to be enough. She worked nights at the hospital, but the small wage that she was earning could only be stretched so far.

While the family lacked in money and material things, they more than made up for in love and family unity. Bobby had two older and one younger sisters, who ran the household in their mother's absence.

All three of his sisters had already made beautiful gifts for their mother. Here it was Christmas Eve already, and he had nothing. Wiping a tear from his eye, Bobby kicked the snow and started to walk down to the street where the shops and stores were.

Bobby walked down from shop to shop, looking into each decorated window. Everything seemed so beautiful and so out of reach. It was starting to get dark and Bobby reluctantly turned to walk home when suddenly his eyes caught the glimmer of the setting sun's rays reflecting off of something along the curb. He reached down and discovered a shiny dime.

As he held his new found treasure, a warmth spread throughout his entire body and he walked into the first store he saw. His excitement quickly turned cold when salesperson after salesperson told him that he couldn't buy anything with only a dime.

He went into a flower shop and waited in line. When the shop owner asked if he could help him, Bobby presented the dime and asked if he could buy one flower for his mother's Christmas gift. The shop owner looked at Bobby and his dime. Then he put his hand on Bobby's shoulder and said, "You just wait here and I'll see what I can do for you."

As Bobby waited, he looked at the beautiful flowers and even though he was a boy, he could see why mothers and girls liked flowers.

The sound of the door closing as the last customer left jolted Bobby back to reality. All alone in the shop, Bobby began to feel alone and afraid. Suddenly the shop owner came out and moved to the counter. There, before Bobby's eyes, lay twelve long-stemmed, red roses, all tied together with a big silver bow. Bobby's heart sank as the owner picked them up and placed them gently into a long white box.

"That will be ten cents, young man," the shop owner said reaching out his hand for the dime. Slowly, Bobby moved his hand to give the man his dime. Could this be true? No one else would give him a thing for his dime? Sensing the boy's reluctance, the shop owner added, "I just happened to have some roses on sale for ten cents a dozen. Would you like them?"

This time Bobby didn't hesitate, and when the man placed the long box into his hands, he knew it was true. Walking out the door that the owner was holding for Bobby, he heard the shop keeper say, "Merry Christmas, son."

As he returned inside, the shopkeeper's wife walked out. "Who were you talking to back there and where are the roses you were fixing?" Staring out the window, he replied, "A strange thing happened to me this morning. While I was setting up things to open the shop, I thought I heard a voice telling me to set aside a dozen of my best roses for a special gift. I was not sure at the time whether I had lost my mind or what, but I set them aside anyway. Then just a few minutes ago, a little boy came into the shop and wanted to buy a flower for his mother with one small dime. When I looked at him, I saw myself many years ago. I too was a poor boy with nothing to buy my mother a Christmas gift.

A bearded man, whom I never knew, stopped me on the street and told me that he wanted to give me ten dollars. When I saw that little boy tonight, I knew whose voice it was, and I put together a dozen of my very best roses.

The shop owner and his wife hugged each other tightly, and as they stepped out into the bitter cold, they somehow didn't feel cold at all.

博比的礼物

博比站在后院的雪地里,感觉越来越冷。他没有穿靴子;他不喜欢穿,也穿不起。他穿的薄运动鞋有几个窟窿,无法抵挡严寒。

博比已经在后院待了大约一小时。尽管他左思右想,但他拿不定主意给母亲买什么圣诞礼物。他一边想一边摇头:"这没用,即使我想起来送什么,我也没钱买呀。"

自从3年前他的父亲去世以来,一家5口人就苦苦挣扎着。不是因为他的母亲不关心,也不是因为没有尽力,只是她的工资好像总不够用。她在医院上夜班,她赚的那点微薄工资仅仅能维持到现在。

尽管家里缺钱少物,但他们相亲相爱、团结和睦。博比有两个姐姐和一个妹妹,母亲不在家时,她们就管理家务。

姐妹们都已经为母亲准备好了漂亮的礼物。现在已是平安夜了,他还是两手空空。博比擦去眼角的一滴泪水,踢着地上的雪,向街上的一排排商店走去。

博比走过了一家家商店,从每个装饰的窗户往里看,里面的东西好像是那样漂亮、那样遥不可及。天渐渐黑了,博比勉为其难地转身往回走。突然,他看到了路边的一个东西在夕阳映照下闪闪发光。他伸手拿起来,发现那是一枚亮晶晶的一角硬币。

他手握新发现的宝贝,一股暖流涌遍了全身。他走进自己看到的第一家商店。当一个个店员都告诉他一角钱什么也买不到时,他的兴奋感顿时冷了下来。

他走进一家鲜花店,排队等候买花。店主问他买什么,博比拿出那枚硬币,问店主他能不能买一枝鲜花,送给他母亲作为圣诞节礼物。店主看了看博比和他那枚硬币,然后拍了拍他的肩膀说:"你就在这里等一会儿,我看看能不能帮上你的忙。"

博比一边等,一边看着商店那些美丽的鲜花,即使他是个男孩,也能明白母亲们和女孩们为什么喜欢鲜花。

最后一位顾客离开时,商店关门的声音使博比醒过神来。店里只剩下博比一个人了,他开始感到孤独和害怕。突然,店主出来,走到了柜台前。博比眼前出现了12朵长茎红玫瑰。所有这些花都用一只银色大蝴蝶结束在一起。店主将这束花轻轻地放进一个白色长盒里时,博比的心沉了下来。

"小伙子,这束花10美分,"店主一边说,一边伸手去拿那一角硬币。博比慢慢地把钱递给了那个人。这会是真的吗?没有人愿意用一件东西换一角硬币呀?店主感觉到博比勉为其难的样子,便补充说:"我刚好有一角钱一打的玫瑰要卖。你想买吗?"

这次,博比不再犹豫了。当店主把长盒放到他手里时,他才明白这是真的。博比向门外走去,店主为他打开了门。他听到店主说:"圣诞快乐,孩子。"

店主返回店里时，他的妻子走了出来。“你刚才和谁在说话？你扎好的那束玫瑰在哪里？”店主望着窗外，回答说：“今天早上我遇到了一件怪事。我收拾好东西要开门时，我想我听到有个声音在对我说，扎 12 朵最好的玫瑰作为一件特殊的礼物。当时我拿不准我是不是精神错乱什么的，但我还是这样做了。后来，也就是几分钟前，一个小男孩走进店里，要拿微不足道的一角钱给他母亲买一朵花。我看着他，就看到了多年前的自己。当时，我是个穷孩子，没有钱给母亲买一件圣诞礼物。我根本不认识的一个留有胡子的男子在街上拦住我，告诉我他要给我 10 美元。我今晚看到那个小男孩时，明白了早上那是谁的声音了。于是，我就扎了 12 朵最好的玫瑰。”

店主和妻子紧紧地拥抱在一起。他们走出店子、进入凛冽的寒风中时，不知何故，一点也不感觉到冷。

The Strength of Kindness

A couple luckily booked two train tickets. Getting on the train, they found a lady sitting on their seat. The husband motioned his wife to take the seat next to the lady but didn't ask her to move away.

After seating herself well, the wife examined the lady and noticed the lady's right foot was a bit inconvenient. Then the wife understood why her husband did so. And he just stood there all the way from Jiayi to Taipei.

Getting off the train, the wife said lovingly, "Offering a seat is benevolence, but for such a long distance from Jiayi to Taipei, you can ask her to give back your seat to have a rest midway."

The husband said, "She is inconvenient all her life while we are just for these three hours."

Hearing that, the wife was so moved that she felt the world gentler and softer in a moment.

善良的力量

一对夫妻很幸运地订到火车票，上车后，却发现有一位女士坐在他们的位子上。先生示意太太去坐那个女士旁边的位子，却没有请她让出座位。

太太坐定后仔细一看，发现那位女士的右脚有点不方便，这才明白先生为何不请她起来。他就这样从嘉义一直站到了台北。

下车后，心疼先生的太太就说：“让座是善行，但从嘉义到台北这么久，中途可以请她把位子还给你，换你坐一下。”

先生说：“人家不方便一辈子，我们不方便只是这 3 个小时而已。”

太太听了相当感动，觉得世界都变得温柔了许多。

What Is Love?

A few nights ago, my friend Lisa asked me what I thought love was. At the time I thought that there were so many different types of love that I really struggled to answer her. The love of a child, the love of a parent, the love of a friend, the love of a partner. What I did say was that I thought you had to first be truthful and show love to yourself before you could show love to another. I still believe this is true and now I have learned that there is only one type of love.

Both Lisa and I have been hurt by men who lied to us. She felt that if these men had lied to us, then they were not worthy of our love. I am now able to move on. I found my answer for her about what I think love is. So here is my letter to my friend Lisa.

Lisa,

I think I have finally found my answer to your question, "What is love?"

Real love truly is unconditional.

I have been looking back to the times I spent with my grandma. As you know, I grew up with her. I was not very nice to her at times, like most teenagers. As I was growing up, I really did some nasty things to hurt her.

You know, Lisa, she was always there to forgive me, once I realized my mistakes.

She did this openly and honestly and with her arms wide open. Her love never judged me. Her love never condemned me. Her love never knew spiteful words. She would tell me that my actions had hurt her, but she never did say mean things or even punish me. Ever.

She held me up, she let me become myself and then she let me go.

To me, if you can't love without judging, then you don't love. If you can't love without expectation, then you don't love. If you can't love just because you can, then why would you do it? Does someone have to show you love in return for you to feel it? My grandma never did. She just loved all of me, no matter what my actions were.

I believe that to love, you have to be patient. To love, you have to be kind. To love, you have to forgive. I'm not saying that you should put your life on hold, but all the same, I don't believe that you should turn your back just because that person hasn't yet found the strength to know who they are.

Sometimes people just make mistakes. This is their walk, not ours. Their life lessons, not ours. Who are we to judge? And if you truly did love in the first place, then you will be there to forgive. To me, this is real love.

爱是什么?

前几天夜里,我的朋友丽莎问我:爱是什么? 当时我认为,爱的种类太多,各不相同,我确实得绞尽脑汁才能回答她。孩子的爱,父母的爱,朋友的爱,伴侣的爱。我对她说的是,在你对另一个人示爱之前,你得先诚实,对自己示爱。我仍然相信这话不错,现在我已经明白只有一种爱。

我和丽莎都曾被向我们撒谎的男人伤害过。她感到,如果这些男人对我们撒谎,那他们就不值得我们去爱。我现在能继续向前。我找到了她那个爱是什么的问题的答案。这是我写给朋友丽莎的一封信。

丽莎:

我想我终于找到了你问我的"爱是什么?"这个问题的答案。

真爱的确是无条件的。

我一直在回想和奶奶一起度过的那些岁月。你知道,是她看着我长大的。就像大多数青少年一样,有时我对她不是很好。我在成长过程中的确做过一些伤害她的坏事。

丽莎,你知道,一旦我认识到自己的错误,她总是原谅我。

她原谅我时坦率真诚,张开怀抱。她对我的爱从不评判,她对我的爱从不责难,她对我的爱从不恶言恶语。她常常告诉我说我的行动已经伤害了她,但从不说刻薄话,也不惩罚我。从来都不会。

她支撑着我,让我做自己的主人,然后才放我走。

对我来说,如果你无法不加评判地去爱,那你就不要爱。如果你无法不带期望地去爱,那你就不要爱。如果你不能仅仅因为爱而去爱,那你为什么还要这样做呢?难道必须有人给你回报你才能感觉到爱吗?我奶奶从不这样做。她只爱我的一切,无论我曾做过什么。

我相信,要爱,你就必须有耐心。要爱,你就必须善良。要爱,你就必须原谅。我并不是说你应该一辈子都悬在那里,但我也同样相信,不能仅仅因为你爱的人还没有找到了解自己的力量,你就应该转身离去。

有时,人总会犯错误。这是他们的道路,不是我们的。这是他们的人生教训,不是我们的。我们要去评判谁呢?如果你首先确实心中有爱,那你一定会去原谅。对我来说,这才是真爱。

The Wallet of Love

As I walked home one freezing day, I stumbled on a wallet someone had lost in the street. I picked it up and looked inside to find some identification so I could call the owner. But the wallet contained only three dollars and a crumpled letter.

The envelope was worn and the only thing that was legible on it was the return address. I started to open the letter, hoping to find some clue. The letter had been written almost sixty years ago. It was written in a beautiful feminine handwriting on powder blue stationery with a little flower in the left-hand corner. It was a "Dear John" letter that told the recipient, whose name appeared to be Michael, that the writer couldn't see him any more because her mother forbade it. Even so, she wrote that she would always love him. It was signed, Hannah. It was a beautiful letter, but there was no way except for the name Michael, that the owner could be identified. Maybe if I called information, the operator could find a phone listing for the address on the envelope.

"Operator," I began, "this is an unusual request. I'm trying to find the owner of a wallet that I found. Is there anyway you can tell me if there is a phone number for an address that was on an envelope in the wallet?"

She suggested I speak with her supervisor, who hesitated for a moment, then said, "There is a phone listing at that address, but I can't give you the number." She said, as a courtesy, she would call that number, explain my story and would ask them if they wanted her to connect me. I waited a few minutes and then she was back on the line, "I have a party who will speak with you."

I asked the woman on the other end of the line if she knew anyone by the name of Hannah. She gasped, "Oh! We bought this house from a family who had a daughter named Hannah. But that was 30

years ago!" "Would you know where that family could be located now?" I asked.

"I remember that Hannah had to place her mother in a nursing home some years ago," the woman said. "Maybe if you got in touch with them they might be able to track down the daughter." She gave me the name of the nursing home and I called the number.

They told me the old lady had passed away some years ago but they did have a phone number for where they thought the daughter might be living. I thanked them and phoned. The woman who answered explained that Hannah herself was now living in a nursing home.

I called the nursing home in which Hannah was living and the man who answered the phone told me, "Yes, Hannah is staying with us."

I thanked him and drove over to the nursing home. The night nurse and a guard greeted me at the door. We went up to the third floor of the large building. In the day-room, the nurse introduced me to Hannah. She was a sweet, silver-haired old timer with a warm smile and a twinkle in her eye. I told her about finding the wallet and showed her the letter.

The second she saw the powder blue envelope with that little flower on the left, she took a deep breath and said, "Young man, this letter was the last contact I ever had with Michael." She looked away for a moment deep in thought and then said softly, "I loved him very much. But I was only 16 at the time and my mother felt I was too young. Oh, he was so handsome."

"Yes," she continued. "Michael Goldstein was a wonderful person. If you should find him, tell him I think of him often. And," she hesitated for a moment, almost biting her lip, "tell him I still love him. You know," she said smiling as tears began to well up in her eyes, "I never did marry. I guess no one ever matched up to Michael..."

I thanked Hannah and said goodbye. I took the elevator to the first floor and as I stood by the door, the guard there asked, "Was the old lady able to help you?" I told him she had given me a lead. "At least I have a last name."

I had taken out the wallet. When he saw it, the guard said, "Hey, wait a minute! That's Mr. Goldstein's wallet. He's always losing that wallet. I must have found it in the halls at least three times."

"Who's Mr. Goldstein?" I asked as my hand began to shake.

"He's one of the old timers on the 8th floor. That's Mike Goldstein's wallet for sure."

On the eighth floor, the floor nurse said, "I think he's still in the day room. He likes to read at night. He's a darling old man."

We went to the only room that had any lights on and there was a man reading a book. The nurse went over to him and asked if he had lost his wallet. Mr. Goldstein looked up with surprise, put his hand in his back pocket and said, "Oh, it is missing!"

"This kind gentleman found a wallet and we wondered if it could be yours?" I handed Mr. Goldstein the wallet and the second he saw it, he smiled with relief and said, "Yes, that's it! It must have dropped out of my pocket this afternoon. I want to give you a reward."

"No, thank you," I said. "But I have to tell you something. I read the letter in the hope of finding out who owned the wallet." The smile on his face suddenly disappeared. "You read that letter?"

"Not only did I read it, I think I know where Hannah is." He suddenly grew pale. "Hannah? You know where she is? How is she? Is she still as pretty as she was? Please, please tell me," he begged.

"She's fine... just as pretty as when you knew her." I said softly. The old man smiled with anticipation and asked, "Could you tell me where she is? I want to call her tomorrow." He grabbed my hand and said, "You know something, mister, I was so in love with that girl that when that letter came, my life literally ended. I never married. I guess I've always loved her."

"Mr. Goldstein," I said, "Come with me." We took the elevator down to the third floor. The hallways were darkened and only one or two little night-lights lit our way to the day-room where Hannah was sitting alone watching the television. The nurse walked over to her.

"Hannah," she said softly, pointing to Michael, who was waiting with me in the doorway. "Do you know this man?" She adjusted her glasses, looked for a moment, but didn't say a word. Michael said softly, almost in a whisper, "Hannah, it's Michael. Do you remember me?"

She gasped, "Michael! I don't believe it! Michael! It's you! My Michael!" He walked slowly towards her and they embraced.

About three weeks later I got a call at my office from the nursing home. "Can you break away on Sunday to attend a wedding? Michael and Hannah are going to tie the knot!"

It was a beautiful wedding with all the people at the nursing home dressed up to join in the celebration. Hannah wore a light beige dress and looked beautiful. Michael wore a dark blue suit and stood tall. They made me their best man. The nursing home gave them their own room and if you ever wanted to see a 76-year-old bride and a 79-year-old groom acting like two teenagers, you had to see this couple. A perfect ending for a love affair that had lasted nearly 60 years.

爱的钱包

一个严寒的日子，我正往家走时，有人遗失在大街的钱包绊了我一下。我捡起钱包，打开看了看里面，看有没有一些身份证明，这样我就能给失主打电话，但钱包里只有3美元和一封皱巴巴的信。

信封破旧，上面唯一能看清的就是回信地址。我打开信，希望找到一些线索。信是差不多60年前写的。粉蓝色的信纸左侧一角有朵小花，上面是娟秀的字体。这是一封绝交信，写信人想告诉收信人，因为她母亲反对，她不能再见他了。上面显示收信人是迈克尔。虽然这样，她还是写着她会永远爱他。署名是汉娜。信写得很美，但信里除了"迈克尔"这个名字，没有任何能证明失主身份的途径。也许给信息台打电话，接线员能找到信封上所写地址的电话。

"接线员，"我开口说道，"这是一个不同寻常的请求。我正在设法寻找我拾到的一个钱包的主人。钱包里有封信，上面有一个地址，你能告诉我有什么办法找到这个地址的电话号码吗？"

她建议我跟她的主管谈谈。她的主管犹豫了片刻，然后说："那个地址列有一个电话号码，但我不能给你。"出于礼貌，她说她会打那个号码，向对方说明我的情况，询问他们是不是想让她跟我联系。我等了几分钟，随后她回电话说："我有一个当事人愿意跟你说话。"

我问电话那端那个女的，她是否认识一个叫汉娜的人。她喘着气说："噢！我们买的这个房子先前的房主的女儿叫汉娜。但那是30年前的事了！""那你知道那户人家现在可能住的地方吗？"我问。

"我记得几年前汉娜不得不把她母亲安置在一家疗养院。"那个女的说。"也许你跟他们联系，他们说不定能查到她女儿的下落。"她把那家疗养院的名字给了我，我就按那个号码拨了过去。

对方告诉我说老太太几年前就去世了，但他们确实有他们认为是那个女儿可能住的地方的电话号码。我谢过他们，把电话打了过去。接电话的妇女解释说，汉娜本人现在住在一家疗养院。

我给汉娜住的那家疗养所去了电话。接电话的男子告诉我："是的，汉娜和我们住在一起。"

我谢过他，便开车前往那家疗养院。夜班护士和一名保安在门口迎接我。我们上到那座大楼的三楼。在休息室，那名护士把我引见给汉娜。她是一位和蔼可亲、满头银发的老太太。她面带亲切的微笑，眼睛炯炯有神。我对她说了我拾到那个钱包的情况，并让她看了那封信。

她一看到那个左侧有朵小花的粉蓝色信封，深吸了口气说："年轻人，这封信是我和迈克尔的最后一次联系。"她把目光移开，沉思了片刻，接着又轻轻地说，"我非常爱他。但我当时只有16岁，妈妈觉得我太小。噢，他是那么帅。"

"是的，"她继续说道。"迈克尔·戈尔茨坦的确很帅。如果你找到他，就告诉他我时常想起他。还有，"她犹豫了一下，几乎是咬着嘴唇，"告诉他我依然爱他。你知道，"她微笑着说，眼里涌起了泪水，"我始终没有结婚。我想没有人配得上迈克尔……"

我谢过汉娜，向她道别，乘电梯来到一楼。当我来到门口时，那名保安问："那个老太太能帮上忙吗？"我告诉他，她给了一个线索。"至少，我有了这个人的姓。"

我拿出那个钱包。保安一看，便叫道，"嘿，等一下！那是戈尔茨坦先生的钱包。他总是丢那个钱包。我在大厅里肯定拾到过至少三次。"

"戈尔茨坦先生是谁？"我一边问，手一边开始颤抖。

"他是8楼的一位老先生。那肯定是迈克尔·戈尔茨坦的钱包。"

我来到8楼，楼层值班护士说："我想他还在休息室。他喜欢晚上看书。他是个可爱的老头。"

我们走向那个唯一亮着灯的房间。那里有一个男的正在看书。护士走到他身边，问他是不是丢了钱包。戈尔茨坦先生吃惊地抬起头，把一只手伸进后面的口袋说："噢，就是不见了！"

"这位好心先生拾到了一个钱包，我们不知道是不是你的？"我把那个钱包递给戈尔茨坦先生。一看到钱包，他就松了口气，笑道："是的，就是它！一定是今天下午从我的口袋里掉出来了。我要酬谢你。"

"不，谢谢。"我说。"但我必须告诉你一件事。我看了那封信，希望找到钱包的主人。"他脸上的微笑突然消失了。"你看了那封信？"

"我不仅看了信，我想我还知道汉娜在哪里。"他突然脸色煞白。"汉娜？你知道她在哪里？她怎么样？她还像过去那样漂亮吗？请、请告诉我。"他恳求道。

"她很好……就像你认识她时一样漂亮。"我轻声说道。老人满怀期望地露出微笑，问道，"你能告诉我她在哪里吗？我明天要给她打电话。"他一把抓住我的手说，"先生，你知道，我有多爱那个姑娘，收到那封信时，我觉得一生简直完了。我始终未娶。我想我会永远爱她。"

"戈尔茨坦先生，"我说，"随我来。"我们乘电梯下到3楼。走廊里昏暗。只有一两盏小夜灯为我们照亮前往汉娜正独自坐在里面看电视的那个休息室。护士向她走了过去。

"汉娜，"她指着迈克尔轻声说，迈克尔和我等在门口，"你认识这个人吗？"她调整了一下眼镜，打量了片刻，但一句话也没说。迈克轻轻地说，几乎是耳语："汉娜，我是迈克尔。你记得我吗？"

她喘着气说："迈克尔！我不相信！迈克尔！真是你！我的迈克尔！"他慢慢地走向

她，他们拥抱在一起。

大约3周后，我在办公室接到了那家疗养院打来的电话。“星期天你能抽空参加一个婚礼吗？迈克尔和汉娜要喜结良缘！”

那是一场美丽的婚礼，疗养所所有的人都衣着盛装前来庆祝。汉娜身穿淡米黄色婚纱，非常漂亮。迈克身穿深蓝色西装，身材高大。他们让我做伴郎。疗养院给了他们一个房间。如果你想看76岁的新娘和79岁的新郎如何像青年男女那样扮相，那就来看这对伴侣。持续了将近60年的恋情终于有了一个完美的结局。

Rudy's Angel

I walked into the grocery store not particularly interested in buying groceries. I was not hungry. The pain of losing my husband of 37 years was still too raw. And this grocery store held so many sweet memories.

Rudy often came with me and almost every time he'd pretend to go off and look for something special. I knew what he was up to. I'd always spot him walking down the aisle with the three yellow roses in his hands. Rudy knew I loved yellow roses.

With a heart filled with grief, I only wanted to buy my few items and leave, but even grocery shopping was different since Rudy had passed on.

Standing by the meat, I searched for the perfect small steak and remembered how Rudy had loved his steak.

Suddenly a woman came beside me. She was blond, slim and lovely in a soft green pantsuit. I watched as she picked up a large pack of T-bones, dropped them in her basket, hesitated, and then put them back. She turned to go and once again reached for the pack of steaks. She saw me watching her and she smiled. "My husband loves T-bones, but honestly, at these prices, I don't know."

I swallowed the emotion down and met her pale blue eyes. "My husband passed away eight days ago," I told her. Glancing at the package in her hands, I fought to control the tremble in my voice. "Buy him the steaks. And cherish every moment you have together."

She nodded her head and I saw the emotion in her eyes as she placed the package in her basket and wheeled away.

I turned and pushed my cart across the length of the store to the dairy products. There I stood, trying to decide which size milk I should buy. A quart, I finally decided and moved on to the ice cream section near the front of the store. I placed the ice cream in my cart and looked down the aisle toward the front. I saw first the green suit, then recognized the pretty lady coming toward me. In her arms she carried a package. On her face was the brightest smile I had ever seen. I would swear a soft halo encircled her blond hair as she kept walking toward me. As she came closer, I saw what she held and tears began misting in my eyes.

"These are for you," she said and placed three beautiful long-stemmed yellow roses in my arms. "These are paid for." She leaned over and placed a gentle kiss on my cheek, then smiled again.

I wanted to tell her what she'd done meant to me, but still unable to speak. I watched as she walked away, tears clouding my vision. I looked down at the beautiful roses nestled in the green tissue wrapping and found it almost unreal. How did she know?

Suddenly, the answer seemed so clear. I was not alone. "Oh, Rudy, you haven't forgotten me, have you?" I whispered, with tears in my eyes. He was still with me, and she was his angel.

We should be thankful for what you have every day and love can grow in our heart.

鲁迪的天使

我走进了一家食品杂货店，但对买食物并不是特别感兴趣。我不饿。失去和我共同生活了37年的丈夫仍然非常痛心。而这个食品杂货店留下了很多很多甜蜜的回忆。

鲁迪经常常陪我一起来这里，几乎每次他都要假装离开一会儿，去找一些特别的东西。我知道他要做什么。我总是看到他手里拿着三枝黄玫瑰沿着过道走来。鲁迪知道我喜欢黄玫瑰。

我心里充满悲伤，只想买一些东西就离开，但自从鲁迪去世以来，就连到这里买东西也不一样了。

我站在肉食柜台边，寻找那种最好的小牛排，想起了鲁迪是多么喜欢吃牛排。

突然，一个女人来到了我身边。她金发碧眼，身材苗条，身穿淡绿色套装。我看到她拿起一大包丁字牛排，把它们放进购物车，犹豫了一下，然后又放了回去。她转身要离开时，又拿起那包牛排。看到我在看她，她露出了微笑。“我丈夫喜欢丁字牛排，但说实话，我不知道是这种价钱。”

我抑制住自己的情绪，望着她淡蓝色的眼睛，告诉她说：“我丈夫8天前去世了。”看着她手里那包牛排，我拼命抑制自己颤抖的声音。“给他买牛排吧。珍惜你们一起相处的时光。”

她点了点头，把牛排放回购物车推走时，我看到了她眼里激动的神情。

我转过身，推着购物车，走到商店的乳制品区。我站在那里，想着自己应该买多大量的牛奶。我最后决定买一夸脱，随后又来到了商店门前的冰淇淋区。我把一支冰淇淋放进购物车里，然后顺着过道向前面望了一眼。我第一眼就看到了那个淡绿色套装，随即认出了是那个漂亮的女士正朝我走来。她怀里抱着一包东西，面带我所见过的最灿烂的微笑。我发誓，她向我走来时，一圈柔光环绕在她的金发四周。她越走越近了，我看到了她怀里抱的东西，泪水开始模糊了我的双眼。

“这是送给你的，”说着，她把三枝漂亮的长茎黄玫瑰放在了我的怀里。“这付过账了。”她侧过身，轻轻地吻了吻我的脸颊，然后又微微一笑。

我想告诉她，她做的一切对我来说意味着什么，却说不出话来。我望着她离开时，泪水模糊了我的视线。我低头看着这束用绿色薄包装纸包好的漂亮玫瑰，简直不敢相信是真的。她怎么会知道呢？

突然，答案好像清楚了。我并不孤单。“噢，鲁迪，你没有忘记我，对吗？”我眼含泪水低声说。他仍和我在一起，她就是鲁迪的天使。

我们应该为我们拥有的一切怀着感恩之心，爱才会在我们的心中成长。